INTERNATIONAL CRIMINAL LAW
A CRITICAL INTRODUCTION

INTERNATIONAL CRIMINAL LAW

A CRITICAL INTRODUCTION

ALEXANDER ZAHAR

*United Nations International Criminal Tribunal
for the Former Yugoslavia*

GÖRAN SLUITER

University of Amsterdam

OXFORD
UNIVERSITY PRESS

OXFORD
UNIVERSITY PRESS

Great Clarendon Street, Oxford OX2 6DP
United Kingdom

Oxford University Press is a department of the University of Oxford.
It furthers the University's objective of excellence in research, scholarship,
and education by publishing worldwide. Oxford is a registered trade mark of
Oxford University Press in the UK and in certain other countries

© Oxford University Press, 2008

The moral rights of the author have been asserted

First published 2008
Reprinted 2012

Crown copyright material is reproduced under Class Licence
Number C01P0000148 with the permission of OPSI
and the Queen's Printer for Scotland

British Library Cataloguing in Publication Data
Data available

Library of Congress Cataloging in Publication Data
Data available

ISBN 978-0-406-95904-1

Printed and bound by CPI Group (UK) Ltd, Croydon, CR0 4YY

To
Anna-Sophia Rahel Zahar
Charlotte Yi Yan and Anna Yi Jin Sluiter

PREFACE

International criminal law is the criminal law of the international community. Although it has undergone spectacular developments over the past decade, compared with domestic criminal justice systems it is still a very imperfect legal system. In this regard it is undeniably a branch of *international* law.

We make no attempt to shield our readers from the evident shortcomings of the system of international criminal justice. By the end of 2006 a total of 96 defendants had been tried and 86 convicted at the ad hoc international tribunals in The Hague and Arusha. Would these cases have gone untried had there been no such tribunals? Perhaps — or perhaps not. Rwanda and the states of the former Yugoslavia have been conducting their own war-crimes and genocide trials, as have several European states pursuant to the doctrine of universal jurisdiction. The international tribunals claim to be in the service of 'reconciliation' as well as justice. But the field has no operative definition of success. Thus no one is in a position to tell whether the enormous sums[1] and effort that have been invested in the operations of international criminal tribunals since the mid-1990s are justifiable in themselves or in relation to alternative approaches to criminal justice. This is quite apart from the nagging question of the legality of such tribunals (further discussed in this book). The consensus, so necessary for justice, which characterizes municipal systems of criminal law is not to be found to anything like the same degree in their international counterpart. The rift over the International Criminal Court caused by the United States, among other nations, is notorious, but the discourse is divergent in every area of the field one cares to examine. The year 2006 ended in acrimony at the ICTY, with the Appeals Chamber of that institution locked in a struggle with the Trial Chamber hearing the case of Vojislav Šešelj, an ultranationalist former paramilitary leader and current leader of one of Serbia's largest political parties. Šešelj insisted on his 'absolute right' to defend himself as his own counsel before the Trial Chamber. He went on 'hunger strike' when the trial judges appointed standby counsel to shadow the trial and be prepared to take over the defence should Šešelj be unable to continue. The Appeals Chamber capitulated to Šešelj's blackmail and fired the standby counsel.[2] Dismay was expressed inside and outside the institution, but no one was greatly surprised. By this time political pressure and compromise were not exceptional at the international tribunals. The Appeals Chamber's approach to Šešelj's hunger strike is reminiscent of the second *Barayagwiza* decision.[3] There, in a reversal of a decision of its own, the ICTR Appeals Chamber distorted the law in order to breathe new life into legal proceedings which had been terminated, by its first decision, for no reason other than to

---

[1] The final cost of the ICTR alone will be well in excess of one billion dollars; see 'Cost of the ICTR to Reach One Billion USD by the End of 2007,' Hirondelle News Agency Report, 11 May 2006.

[2] See *Prosecutor* v. *Vojislav Šešelj*, Decision on Appeal Against the Trial Chamber's Decision (No. 2) on Assignment of Counsel, 8 December 2006.

[3] *Prosecutor* v. *Barayagwiza*, Decision (Prosecutor's Request for Review or Reconsideration), 31 March 2000.

appease the Rwandese government which was furious about the release of a prominent defendant over what the government saw as a trivial human rights violation.

In addition to the unseemly quarrel in Šešelj's case, the end of 2006 saw an extraordinary jurisprudential obfuscation in the *Galić* judgment of the ICTY Appeals Chamber. The fundamental conflict between two schools of thought concerning the sources and subject-matter jurisdiction of the ICTY (discussed in Chapter 3 of this book) was not tackled head-on, as was expected, but was brushed aside.[4]

There is an important difference, which we need not articulate, between a polemic and a systematic critique. This book is not a polemic. Both authors have worked in the field for years and recognize the urgent need for an efficient and effective criminal justice system aimed at persons who have committed crimes against humanity and who are likely to go unpunished due to the collapse or incapacity of local structures. We also realize that in international relations, which are still very much dominated by the self-interest of sovereign states, reaching an agreement, however marginal, concerning the advancement of international criminal law is no mean achievement. Indeed, the current system of international criminal justice — which now exists in the form of the ICC, a variety of ad hoc international or internationalized tribunals, state courts in neutral countries exercising universal jurisdiction, and special courts in latterly stabilized countries which have begun to repatriate lesser cases which had been pending before the international tribunals or are trying cases based on their own investigations — is a major advance over the situation a decade ago. This emergent mix of fora where international criminal law is practised is likely to persist indefinitely. No polemic will displace it. A systematic critique can only improve it. Its claim to maturity invites every concerned person to put it to the test.

There is also the danger that international criminal law, which is being developed within a relatively small group of practitioners, will become overly self-referential. Already the decisions of the ICTY, ICTR, etc., are primarily — and often exclusively — citing their own case law in support. This bootstrapping tendency is another reason to maintain a critical watch.

The critical approach is also vital to the pedagogical aim of this book. Several works are already in print which ably describe important elements of international criminal law, for example by detailing the elements of crimes in the international jurisdiction. It is not our purpose to compete with this body of descriptive work. Rather, we have sought to engage the student of international criminal law by exposing him or her to the assumptions underlying the surface rhetoric. Even the most idealistic student new to this field knows, of course, that the field is affected by serious political and operational issues. He or she will know, for instance, that while many states decided to establish the ICC, many others decided to oppose it or to qualify their support for it. Hence the ICC has so far spent its days out of sight and out of mind in a suburb of The Hague

---

[4] See *Prosecutor* v. *Stanislav Galić*, Judgment on Appeal, 30 November 2006, para. 83. Chapter 3 was completed prior to the publication of this judgment, and thus the significance of the latter is not further discussed in this book. However, it will be evident to the reader, having examined Chapter 3, why para. 83 of the *Galić* appeal judgment amounts to an obfuscation.

and has not yet lived up to expectations. Across town, the ICTY, after having experienced a similar slow start, is a hive of activity, now positively rushing through its remaining cases[5] (and sending a fair number of them back to the states of the former Yugoslavia) in order to close its doors by around 2012. The ICTY holds a pivotal position and currently dominates international criminal law, both in doctrine and in practice. This, too, a newcomer to the subject will be aware of. What is less obvious, is that the ICTY is not held in pious regard by all. On the up side, the European Union has a policy of blocking states from negotiations on entry to the EU if they fail to cooperate in good faith with the ICTY. The Russian Federation, by contrast, to say nothing of the Republic of Serbia, despises the ICTY for what it sees as its focus on the followers of the Serbian Orthodox Church, and would cut off its funding because of this. This does not make the Russians right — in fact, they are wrong. It is the ICTY's legality and the quality of its jurisprudence which are questionable on a number of points, its procedures which are often wasteful, and the selection mechanism for its judges which is wanting — but the ICTY has no axe to grind with the Serbs. Ironically, the one international court which does live up to the Russians' fears of ethnic discrimination is the ICTR. Here, the Russians, oblivious to factual considerations, have held up the ICTR as a model for the ICTY. At the ICTR, though, only the vanquished are on trial. The victors of Rwanda's civil war, those very persons who probably assassinated the presidents of Rwanda and Burundi in April 1994 and triggered the conflagration, are comfortably in power in the country, dictating the constraints within which the ICTR operates. At the time of writing, a French magistrate — not the ICTR! — had issued arrest warrants against Rwanda's leaders.[6]

While it is our hope that the student as well as the practitioner of international criminal law will be stimulated by the critical approach developed in this book, we of course do not expect agreement on every point. And while we have identified many themes which we consider important and interesting, we have not discussed all of them in the same degree of detail. Space constraints played a role in this decision, but also our hope that the student will adopt the critical approach of this book to investigate those matters further. Some themes — for example, the tribunals' overwhelming reliance on eyewitness testimony and, to a lesser extent, on documents (other 'real' evidence, such as DNA testing, has played no role at all at the ICTR, for example), the question of tribunals and reconciliation, alternative criminal justice models, the appointment of judges, judicial independence, sentencing principles, consistency in penalties, the role of the appeals chamber, the pressure on judges to write history (and *for* history) — are not pursued in this book at all, or are barely touched upon. No diminution of these subjects is intended. Indeed, the importance, for example, of a proper mechanism for judicial appointments cannot be exaggerated. The current mechanism has brought several good minds and competent judges to the international bench, but it has also led to

---

[5] The judgment in the ICTY's highly complex *Krajišnik* case came less than four weeks after closing arguments were heard — an all-time record.

[6] See BBC article, 'Rwanda recalls its envoy to Paris after a French judge signs arrest warrants for nine senior Rwandans', 24 November 2006, http://news.bbc.co.uk/go/em/fr/-/2/hi/africa/6179436.stm.

the appointment of persons who lack relevant knowledge and experience. The mechanism in place is, in other words, unreliable and damaging. And it is directly related to the question of judicial independence.

The reader will notice our focus on the operations of the ICTY and the ICTR. This is because the output of other fora where international criminal law is practised is still of little significance by comparison. The ICTY and the ICTR are the main precedent-setting tribunals in international criminal law, which means that their jurisprudence will dominate the field long after the closure of the institutions themselves. Nevertheless, we have not neglected to include in our discussion, as much as possible, the other components of the present system of international criminal justice.

The structure of this book takes account of the nature of international criminal law as a system of both *criminal* and *public international* law. While Parts II and III echo the traditional dichotomy between substantive and procedural criminal law, there are slight deviations, in that, for example, the matter of defences is explored from a perspective of procedure, that is, defence practice and strategy, even if it includes questions of substantive international criminal law. The international law aspects are predominant in Parts I and IV. Part I offers an introduction to international criminal law, including an introduction to the sources of international criminal law and an overview of international criminal tribunals as new participants in the international institutional legal order. Part IV concentrates on matters of coordination and impact between the international and national legal spheres in the application of international criminal law.

Below we offer a short overview of the 13 chapters of this book.

In Chapter 1 we introduce past and current international and internationalized criminal tribunals as new members of the international institutional legal order. The fact that these criminal tribunals are (organs of) international organizations influences their operations more than a nationally oriented criminal lawyer might imagine. Compared with domestic criminal courts, international criminal tribunals must come to terms with challenges to their legality and the consequences of international legal personality. The latter subject raises such questions as applicable sources of international law, implied and inherent powers available to international organizations, privileges and immunities, and the relationship to other subjects of international law, all of which generally fall outside the purview of national courts.

Chapter 2 builds upon the previous chapter. It explores the position and roles of the main actors in the context of international criminal procedure with the aim of understanding the rules and principles underlying international criminal proceedings. The role and position of the prosecution, judicial branch, defence, registry, and victims are all explored. While an inquiry into the fundamental notions of criminal proceedings raises traditional questions of criminal procedure, such as control over the proceedings (*dominus litis*), the operational environment is highly determinative in answering these questions. We are dealing with a self-contained regime, called a court or tribunal, in which all actors have their place and where each is highly dependent upon other actors both inside and outside that regime.

In Chapter 3 we identify the tensions that have arisen from the use of sources in international criminal law. The war-crimes trials that followed the Second World War are a problematic source for today's tribunals, as they were conducted for the most part by state military commissions and at a time when due-process rights were elementary. Yet the great debate over sources at today's tribunals does not concern the Second World War cases, which tribunal judges have drawn upon liberally, but the use of customary as opposed to conventional rules of international humanitarian law. Two schools of thought have emerged at the ICTY (the ICTR has not figured in this debate), with one side insisting that only those rules which have achieved customary-law status may be relied upon by the ad hoc tribunals, while the other side holds that conventional rules of humanitarian conduct which are binding upon parties to a conflict under treaty law are sufficient for the adjudication of criminal offences. More importantly, Chapter 3 demonstrates that no single or consistent methodology for the identification of rules of customary international law has been articulated at the international tribunals, making the rhetoric surrounding customary international law sound rather hollow.

War-crimes law has been elaborated for the most part at the ICTY. Chapter 4 shows that the main focus of the Hague tribunal (and of its prosecutor) has been Common Article 3 of the 1949 Geneva Conventions, namely the protection of civilians and non-combatants in armed conflict, whether international or non-international in character. Common Article 3 is laconic and vague as a criminal statute. The ICTY's judges have displayed great creativity in making good of this shortcoming. Also, the conflicts handled by the ICTY and other international tribunals have been, for the most part, civil wars. As a result, the textbook regime of the 'grave breaches' law has receded into relative insignificance, and the distinction between international and non-international armed conflict has all but disappeared from the discourse of the tribunals as a relevant category in determining criminal conduct.

Genocide law, by contrast, has been the domain of the ICTR. Chapter 5 argues that the ICTR's first trial judgment, *Akayesu*, dealt a heavy blow not only to the early credibility of that tribunal but to the understanding and development of the law of genocide. Sentimentalism and high-handedness in *Akayesu* prevailed over reason and analysis, with lamentable long-term consequences, visible in a series of decisions culminating in the wholly flawed *Nahimana* judgment of December 2003.

The case law of crimes against humanity is another important growth area at the tribunals. In contrast with genocide and war-crimes law, which have been based on quasi-statutory conventions, the entire law of crimes against humanity is judge-made. While there has been very little state practice since Nuremberg and the lesser Second World War trials, the *Tadić* Appeals Chamber has contended that the law of crimes against humanity had, by 1995, been elevated to customary law. This contention, among others, is examined in Chapter 6.

There are many interesting facets of personal-liability law for the student of the subject to explore. Chapter 7 critically examines two key topics in this area, which help contrast international criminal responsibility with domestic criminal responsibility. First, there is the doctrine of joint criminal enterprise, which is now the dominant personal-liability doctrine at the ICTY. Its use has spread to the ICTR and farther afield. Chapter 7 discusses the problem-ridden growth of JCE up to the point of its relative stabilization in late 2006 in the ICTY's *Krajišnik* judgment. Secondly, Chapter 7 probes the doctrine of command responsibility. Despite the extensive use that this doctrine has received at the tribunals, command responsibility law has never been correctly analysed in tribunal jurisprudence. In particular, the core element of this form of omission liability — the duty to act — has been utterly neglected, with the result that the original constraints upon the application of the doctrine have disappeared and a shapeless construct has taken its place.

Chapter 8 addresses the protection of human rights in international criminal proceedings. It offers a critical analysis of most fair-trial rights, habeas corpus rights, and rights governing the treatment of prisoners. The central question running through this chapter is whether international criminal tribunals, as models of criminal justice, live up to their obligations and expectations in this respect. While recognizing that the corpus juris of human rights was very much developed for application by states, we take issue with the unprincipled — and often also unnecessary — approach according to which the judges seek to justify a more liberal or restrictive application of human rights on the basis of the 'unique' mandate of international criminal tribunals and the 'difficult' circumstances under which they have had to operate.

Much interesting litigation occurs before the first witness in a case is heard. Chapter 9 provides an introduction to this area. It is here that challenges to the legality and jurisdiction of the tribunals are concentrated. Two important trends in the practice of international criminal law, also treated in this chapter, are the greater use of provisional release or bail (although not at the ICTR) and the movement away from oral testimony. (The above topics are also dealt with, from different angles, in Chapters 1, 8, and 10.)

Chapter 10 is a pivotal chapter in understanding international criminal procedure. It analyses the law and practice of evidence in international criminal proceedings, setting out the central questions regarding the evidentiary process. The law of evidence is shown to be one of the most vulnerable aspects of the law of international criminal procedure. The essential reason for this lies in the unsound aspiration of inserting into a predominantly adversarial criminal procedure an inquisitorial type of law of evidence.

The student of international criminal justice is well advised to study actual defence practice. This cannot be abstracted from tribunal decisions, because tribunal judges often ignore or underestimate or misrepresent defence arguments. There are, on the one hand, theoretically available textbook defences, which are hardly ever used, and, on the other hand, the actual methods found at the coalface of defence practice. For the latter, the student must go to the original sources. Chapter 11 provides a new classification of defence practice and looks at how some of the lesser known defences have fared. As mentioned above, the approach draws on both substantive-law and procedural-law considerations.

Chapter 12 is the first chapter in Part IV, 'Tribunal-State Interactions: Coordination and Impact'. It addresses the relations with national jurisdictions from three perspectives. First, there is the matter of coordination of jurisdictional conflicts. Where may a case best be prosecuted? Secondly, when a case is found to belong to the competence of an international criminal tribunal, the question arises to what extent it can count on legal assistance from states for investigation and prosecution of the case. Thirdly, after a 'final' conviction or acquittal for international crimes, either by a national or international court, the question of mutual recognition arises. To what extent does the supposedly final verdict constitute a bar to subsequent prosecution?

Chapter 13 explores the relationship between international and national criminal courts from the perspective of substantive criminal law. It deals with the application of international criminal law by domestic courts. There is a close connection with the first section of the previous chapter, in that the active national application of international criminal law is a presumed necessity underlying the division of the caseload between the international and the national levels. The chapter offers an overview of, and introduction to, national application, with a special focus on a number of key principles of international criminal law. A vital question dealt with in the chapter concerns the extent to which national courts should be regarded in the application of international criminal law as outposts of the international community or as autonomous courts strongly embedded in the national law and structures of sovereign states.

We wish to express our gratitude to a number of people and institutions. We are very much indebted to Sergey Vasiliev for his assistance in carefully reviewing the drafts of this book. Oxford University Press, Philippa Groom, Susan Faircloth, and Matthew Baldwin have been extremely patient with us and have helped us bring this work to conclusion. Göran Sluiter's research and writing have been conducted within the framework of the research programme 'International Criminal Procedure: In Search of General Rules and Principles', financed by the Netherlands Organization of Scientific Research (NWO). He is also much indebted to the Amsterdam Centre of International Law and the Law Faculty of the University of Amsterdam for their support. Alexander Zahar wishes to thank his colleagues at the ICTR and ICTY, including judges, prosecutors, and defence counsel, for their help over the years with dissecting many of the issues discussed in this book (no agreement implied!).

The views expressed in these pages represent solely our own views and not those of the organizations we work for.[7] The typescript was finalized on 20 November 2006. We remain responsible for all errors found in this book.

20 December 2006

Alexander Zahar, The Hague
Göran Sluiter, Amsterdam

---

[7] Due to the employment position of one of the authors (A.Z.), the ICTY Registrar obliged the authors to submit the proofs of this book to an internal review conducted by representatives of the Registrar and the ICTY President. Some material critical of the tribunals, the UN, or its member states was removed in the course of the review. A.Z. was also obliged by the Registry to insert the following official disclaimer: "The opinions expressed in this book are those of the author and do not necessarily reflect those of the International Tribunal or the United Nations."

CONTENTS

PART I INTRODUCTION TO THE TRIBUNALS AND INTERNATIONAL CRIMINAL LAW

PART II CRITICAL REVIEW OF THE SUBSTANTIVE LAW

PART III PROCEDURE, EVIDENCE, AND DEFENCES

PART IV TRIBUNAL–STATE INTERACTIONS: COORDINATION AND IMPACT

TABLE OF INTERNATIONAL CASES

UNITED NATIONS HUMAN RIGHTS COMMITTEE

TABLE OF DOMESTIC CASES

ABBREVIATIONS

Leading tribunal judgments and decisions

Tribunal judgments and decisions shown here are available from the ICTY and ICTR Internet sites.

Akayesu	Trial judgment: *Prosecutor* v. *Jean-Paul Akayesu*, Judgment, 2 September 1998
	Appeal judgment: *Prosecutor* v. *Jean-Paul Akayesu*, Judgment (on appeal), 1 June 2001
Aleksovski	Trial judgment: *Prosecutor* v. *Zlatko Aleksovski*, Judgment, 25 June 1999
	Appeal judgment: *Prosecutor* v. *Zlatko Aleksovski*, Judgment (on appeal), 24 March 2000
Babić	Sentencing judgment: *Prosecutor* v. *Milan Babić*, Sentencing judgment, 29 June 2004
Bagilishema	Trial judgment: *Prosecutor* v. *Ignace Bagilishema*, Judgment, 7 June 2001
	Appeal judgment: *Prosecutor* v. *Ignace Bagilishema*, Judgment (Reasons) (on appeal), 3 July 2002
Banović	Sentencing judgment: *Prosecutor* v. *Predrag Banović*, Sentencing judgment, 28 October 2003
Barayagwiza (see also *Nahimana et al.*)	I Appeal decision: *Prosecutor* v. *Jean-Bosco Barayagwiza* Decision, 3 November 1999
	II Appeal decision: *Prosecutor* v. *Jean-Bosco Barayagwiza*, Decision (Prosecutor's Request for Review or Reconsideration), 31 March 2000
Blagojević and Jokić	Trial judgment: *Prosecutor* v. *Vidoje Blagojević and Dragan Jokić*, judgment 15 January 2005
Blaškić	Subpoena trial decision: *Prosecutor* v. *Tihomir Blaškić*, Decision on the Objection of the Republic of Croatia to the Issuance of Subpoena Duces Tecum, 18 July 1997
	Subpoena appeal decision: *Prosecutor* v. *Tihomir Blaškić*, Judgment on the Request of the Republic of Croatia for Review of the Decision of Trial Chamber II of 18 July 1997, 29 October 1997
	Trial judgment: *Prosecutor* v. *Tihomir Blaškić*, Judgment, 3 March 2000

	Appeal judgment: *Prosecutor* v. *Tihomir Blaškić*, Judgment (on appeal), 29 July 2004
Brđanin	Trial judgment: *Prosecutor* v. *Radoslav Brđanin*, Judgment, 1 September 2004
Delalić et al. (Čelebići)	Trial judgment: *Prosecutor* v. *Zejnil Delalić, Zdravko Mucić, Hazim Delić, Esad Landžo*, Judgment, 16 November 1998
	Appeal judgment: *Prosecutor* v. *Zejnil Delalić, Zdravko Mucić, Hazim Delić, Esad Landžo*, Judgment (on appeal), 20 February 2001
Deronjić	Sentencing judgment: *Prosecutor* v. *Miroslav Deronjić*, Sentencing judgment, 30 March 2004
Erdemović	Sentencing judgment (no. 1): *Prosecutor* v. *Dražen Erdemović*, Sentencing judgment, 29 November 1996
	Appeal judgment: *Prosecutor* v. *Dražen Erdemović*, Judgment (on appeal), 7 October 1997
	Sentencing judgment (no. 2): *Prosecutor* v. *Dražen Erdemović*, Sentencing judgment, 5 March 1998
Furundžija	Trial judgment: *Prosecutor* v. *Anto Furundžija*, Judgment, 10 December 1998
	Appeal judgment: *Prosecutor* v. *Anto Furundžija*, Judgment (on appeal), 21 July 2000
Gacumbitsi	Appeal judgment: *Prosecutor* v. *Sylvestre Gacumbitsi*, Judgment (on appeal), 7 July 2006
Galić	Trial judgment: *Prosecutor* v. *Stanislav Galić*, Judgment and Opinion, 5 December 2003
Halilović	Trial judgment: *Prosecutor* v. *Sefer Halilović*, Judgment, 16 November 2005
Jelisić	Trial judgment: *Prosecutor* v. *Goran Jelisić*, Judgment, 14 December 1999
	Appeal judgment: *Prosecutor* v. *Goran Jelisić*, Judgment (on appeal), 5 July 2001
Kajelijeli	Trial judgment: *Prosecutor* v. *Juvénal Kajelijeli*, Judgment and Sentence, 1 December 2003
	Appeal judgment: *Prosecutor* v. *Juvénal Kajelijeli*, Judgment (on appeal), 23 May 2005
Kambanda	Sentencing judgment: *Prosecutor* v. *Jean Kambanda*, Judgment and Sentence, 4 September 1998

Limaj et al.	Trial judgment: *Prosecutor* v. *Fatmir Limaj, Haradin Bala, Isak Musliu*, Judgment, 30 November 2005
Mpambara	Trial judgment: *Prosecutor* v. *Jean Mpambara*, Judgment, 11 September 2006
Mucić et al.	Sentencing judgment (no. 2): *Prosecutor* v. *Zdravko Mucić, Hazim Delić, Esad Landžo*, Sentencing Judgment, 9 October 2001 (continuation of the *Delalić et al.* case)
Musema	Trial judgment: *Prosecutor* v. *Alfred Musema*, Judgment and Sentence, 27 January 2000
	Appeal judgment: *Prosecutor* v. *Alfred Musema*, Judgment (on appeal), 16 November 2001
Muvunyi	Trial judgment: *Prosecutor* v. *Tharcisse Muvunyi*, Judgment, 12 September 2006
Nahimana et al.	Trial judgment: *Prosecutor* v. *Ferdinand Nahimana, Jean-Bosco Barayagwiza, Hassan Ngeze*, Judgment and Sentence, 3 December 2003
Naletilić and Martinović	Trial judgment: *Prosecutor* v. *Mladen Naletilić and Vinko Martinović*, Judgment, 31 March 2003
	Appeal judgment: *Prosecutor* v. *Mladen Naletilić and Vinko Martinović*, Judgment (on appeal), 3 May 2006
D. Nikolić	Jurisdiction trial decision: *Prosecutor* v. *Dragan Nikolić*, Decision on Defence Motion Challenging the Exercise of Jurisdiction by the Tribunal, 9 October 2002
	Jurisdiction appeal decision: *Prosecutor* v. *Dragan Nikolić*, Decision on Interlocutory Appeal Concerning Legality of Arrest, 5 June 2003
M. Nikolić	Sentencing judgment: *Prosecutor* v. *Momir Nikolić*, Sentencing judgment, 2 December 2003
Ntagerura et al.	Trial judgment: *Prosecutor* v. *André Ntagerura, Emmanuel Bagambiki, Samuel Imanishimwe*, Judgment and Sentence, 25 February 2004
Ntakirutimana	Trial judgment: *Prosecutor* v. *Elizaphan Ntakirutimana and Gérard Ntakirutimana*, Judgment and Sentence, 21 February 2003
	Appeal judgment: *Prosecutor* v. *Elizaphan Ntakirutimana and Gérard Ntakirutimana*, Judgment (on appeal), 13 December 2004
Niyitegeka	Trial judgment: *Prosecutor* v. *Eliézer Niyitegeka*, Judgment and Sentence, 16 May 2003
	Appeal judgment: *Prosecutor* v. *Eliézer Niyitegeka*, Judgment (on appeal), 9 July 2004

Obrenović	Sentencing judgment: *Prosecutor* v. *Dragan Obrenović*, Sentencing judgment, 10 December 2003
Orić	Trial judgment: *Prosecutor* v. *Naser Orić*, Judgment, 30 June 2006
Plavšić	Sentencing judgment: *Prosecutor* v. *Biljana Plavšić*, Sentencing judgment, 27 February 2003
Rutaganda	Trial judgment: *Prosecutor* v. *Georges Rutaganda*, Judgment and Sentence, 6 December 1999
	Appeal judgment: *Prosecutor* v. *Georges Rutaganda*, Judgment (on appeal), 26 May 2003
Rutaganira	Sentencing judgment: *Prosecutor* v. *Vincent Rutaganira*, Sentencing judgment, 14 March 2005
Rwamakuba	Trial judgment: *Prosecutor* v. *André Rwamakuba*, Judgment, 20 September 2006
Semanza	Trial judgment: *Prosecutor* v. *Laurent Semanza*, Judgment and Sentence, 15 May 2003
	Appeal judgment: *Prosecutor* v. *Laurent Semanza*, Judgment (on appeal), 20 May 2005
Serushago	Sentencing judgment: *Prosecutor* v. *Omar Serushago*, Sentence, 5 February 1999
Sikirica et al.	No-case-to-answer decision: *Prosecutor* v. *Duško Sikirica, Damir Došen, Dragan Kolundžija*, Judgment on Defence Motions to Acquit, 3 September 2001
Simba	Trial judgment: *Prosecutor* v. *Aloys Simba*, Judgment, 13 December 2005
Simić et al.	Trial judgment: *Prosecutor* v. *Blagoje Simić, Miroslav Tadić, Simo Zarić*, Judgment, 17 October 2003
Stakić	No-case-to-answer decision: *Prosecutor* v. *Milomir Stakić*, Decision on Rule 92 *bis* Motion for Judgment of Acquittal, 31 October 2002
	Trial judgment: *Prosecutor* v. *Milomir Stakić*, Judgment, 31 July 2003
	Appeal judgment: *Prosecutor* v. *Milomir Stakić*, Judgment (on appeal), 22 March 2006
Strugar	Trial judgment: *Prosecutor* v. *Pavle Strugar*, Judgment, 31 January 2005
Tadić	Protective measures decision: *Prosecutor* v. *Duško Tadić*, Decision on the Prosecutor's Motion Requesting Protective Measures for Victims and Witnesses, 10 August 1995

Jurisdiction trial decision: *Prosecutor* v. *Duško Tadić*, Decision on the Defence Motion on Jurisdiction, 10 August 1995

Jurisdiction appeal decision: *Prosecutor* v. *Duško Tadić*, Decision on the Defence Motion for Interlocutory Appeal on Jurisdiction, 2 October 1995

Trial judgment: *Prosecutor* v. *Duško Tadić*, Opinion and Judgment, 7 May 1997

Sentencing judgment (no. 1): *Prosecutor* v. *Duško Tadić*, Sentencing judgment, 14 July 1997

Appeal judgment: *Prosecutor* v. *Duško Tadić*, Judgment (on appeal), 15 July 1999

Sentencing judgment (no. 2): *Prosecutor* v. *Duško Tadić*, Sentencing judgment, 11 November 1999

Sentencing judgment (no. 3): *Prosecutor* v. *Duško Tadić*, Judgment in Sentencing Appeals, 26 January 2000

Todorović Sentencing judgment: *Prosecutor* v. *Stevan Todorović*, Sentencing judgment, 31 July 2001

Vasiljević Trial judgment: *Prosecutor* v. *Mitar Vasiljević*, Judgment, 29 November 2002

Appeal judgment: *Prosecutor* v. *Mitar Vasiljević*, Judgment (on appeal), 25 February 2004

Other frequently cited sources

ACHR American Convention on Human Rights, signed in San José, 22 November 1969, *OAS Treaty Series* No. 36, 1144 *UNTS* 123, entered into force 18 July 1978, reprinted in *Basic Documents Pertaining to Human Rights in the Inter-American System*, OEA/Ser.L.V/II.82 doc.6 rev.1 at 25 (1992)

Additional Protocol I Protocol Additional to the Geneva Conventions of 12 August 1949, and relating to the Protection of Victims of International Armed Conflicts (Protocol I), 8 June 1977, 1125 *UNTS* 3, entered into force 7 December 1978

Additional Protocol II Protocol Additional to the Geneva Conventions of 12 August 1949, and relating to the Protection of Victims of Non-International Armed Conflicts (Protocol II), 8 June 1977, 1125 *UNTS* 609, entered into force 7 December 1978

Apartheid Convention International Convention on the Suppression and Punishment of the Crime of Apartheid, adopted and opened for signature and ratification by General Assembly resolution 3068 (XXVIII) of 30 November 1973, 1015 *UNTS* 243, entered into force 18 July 1976

Ashworth, *Principles*	Andrew Ashworth, *Principles of Criminal Law*, 3rd edn, Clarendon Press, 1999
Bassiouni and Manikas, *Law of the ICTY*	M. Cherif Bassiouni and P. Manikas, *The Law of the International Criminal Tribunal for the Former Yugoslavia*, Transnational, 1996
Cassese, *International Criminal Law*	Antonio Cassese, *International Criminal Law*, Oxford University Press, 2003
Cassese et al., *Rome Statute Commentary, vol. I or II*	Antonio Cassese, Paola Gaeta, and John R. W. D. Jones (eds), *The Rome Statute of the International Criminal Court — A Commentary*, 2 vols, Oxford University Press, 2002
Dixon and Khan, *Archbold*	Rodney Dixon and Karim Khan, *Archbold International Criminal Courts: Practice, Procedure and Evidence*, Sweet & Maxwell, 2003
ETSP Statute	Statute of the East Timor Special Panels, UN Doc. UNTAET/REG/2000/15, 6 June 2000
European Convention on Human Rights	Convention for the Protection of Human Rights and Fundamental Freedoms, 4 November 1950
Fleck, *Handbook of Humanitarian Law*	Dieter Fleck (ed.), *The Handbook of Humanitarian Law in Armed Conflicts*, Oxford University Press, 1995
Geneva Convention I	Convention (I) for the Amelioration of the Condition of the Wounded and Sick in Armed Forces in the Field, 12 August 1949, 75 *UNTS* 31, entered into force 21 October 1950
Geneva Convention II	Convention (II) for the Amelioration of the Condition of Wounded, Sick and Shipwrecked Members of Armed Forces at Sea, 12 August 1949, 75 *UNTS* 85, entered into force 21 October 1950
Geneva Convention III	Convention (III) Relative to the Treatment of Prisoners of War, 12 August 1949, 75 *UNTS* 135, entered into force 21 October 1950
Geneva Convention IV	Convention (IV) Relative to the Protection of Civilian Persons in Time of War, 12 August 1949, 75 *UNTS* 287, entered into force 21 October 1950
Genocide Convention	Convention on the Prevention and Punishment of the Crime of Genocide; approved and proposed for signature and ratification or accession by General Assembly resolution 260A (III) of 9 December 1948, 78 *UNTS* 278, entered into force 12 January 1951

Green, *Contemporary Law of Armed Conflict*	Leslie C. Green, *The Contemporary Law of Armed Conflict*, 2nd edn., Manchester University Press, 2000
Green, *Essays*	Leslie C. Green, *Essays on the Modern Law of War*, 2nd edn, Transnational, 1999
Hague Regulations 1907	Laws of War: Laws and Customs of War on Land (Hague IV), 18 October 1907, entered into force 26 January 1910
ICC Statute	Statute of the International Criminal Court (Rome Statute), UN Doc. A/CONF.183/9, 17 July 1998
ICCPR	International Covenant on Civil and Political Rights, adopted and opened for signature, ratification, and accession by General Assembly resolution 2200A (XXI) of 16 December 1966, 21 UNGAOR Supp. (No. 16) at 52, UN Doc. A/6316 (1966), 999 *UNTS* 171, entered into force 23 March 1976
ICTR Statute	Statute of the International Criminal Tribunal for Rwanda, 8 November 1994, UN Security Council Resolution 955
ICTY Statute	Statute of the International Criminal Tribunal for the Former Yugoslavia, 25 May 1993, UN Security Council Resolution 827 (amended by Resolutions 1166, 1329, 1411, 1431, 1481)
ILC Draft Code of Crimes	International Law Commission, Draft Code of Crimes Against the Peace and Security of Mankind, *Report of the International Law Commission to the General Assembly*, 51 UN GAOR Supp. (No. 10) at 88, UN Doc. A/51/10 (1996)
IMT Charter	Agreement for the Prosecution and Punishment of Major War Criminals of the European Axis, 8 August 1945, 82 *UNTS* 279
IMT Indictment	International Military Tribunal, Indictment Number 1, *Nazi Conspiracy and Aggression*, vol. 1, ch. 3, at 13–82, US Government Printing Office, 1946
IMT Judgment	*Trial of Major War Criminals Before the International Military Tribunal, Nuremberg, 14 November 1945–1 October 1946*, William S. Hein & Co., 1995, 41 volumes
Jones and Powles, *International Criminal Practice*	John R. W. D. Jones and Stephen Powles (eds), *International Criminal Practice*, Transnational, 2003
Klip and Sluiter, *Annotated Leading Cases, vol. I*	André Klip and Göran Sluiter (eds), *Annotated Leading Cases of International Criminal Tribunals. Vol. I: The International Criminal Tribunal for the former Yugoslavia 1993–1998*, Intersentia, 1999

Klip and Sluiter, *Annotated Leading Cases, vol. II*	*Idem, Annotated Leading Cases of International Criminal Tribunals. Vol. II: The International Criminal Tribunal for Rwanda 1994–1999*, Intersentia, 2001
Klip and Sluiter, *Annotated Leading Cases, vol. III*	*Idem, Annotated Leading Cases of International Criminal Tribunals. Vol. III: The International Criminal Tribunal for the former Yugoslavia 1997–1999*, Intersentia, 2001
Klip and Sluiter, *Annotated Leading Cases, vol. IV*	*Idem, Annotated Leading Cases of International Criminal Tribunals. Vol. IV: The International Criminal Tribunal for the former Yugoslavia 1999–2000*, Intersentia, 2002
Klip and Sluiter, *Annotated Leading Cases, vol. V*	*Idem, Annotated Leading Cases of International Criminal Tribunals. Vol. V: The International Criminal Tribunal for the former Yugoslavia 2000–2001*, Intersentia, 2003
Klip and Sluiter, *Annotated Leading Cases, vol. VI*	*Idem, Annotated Leading Cases of International Criminal Tribunals. Vol. VI: The International Criminal Tribunal for Rwanda 2000–2001*, Intersentia, 2003
Klip and Sluiter, *Annotated Leading Cases, vol. VII*	*Idem, Annotated Leading Cases of International Criminal Tribunals. Vol. VII: The International Criminal Tribunal for the former Yugoslavia 2001*, Intersentia, 2005
Klip and Sluiter, *Annotated Leading Cases, vol. VIII*	*Idem, Annotated Leading Cases of International Criminal Tribunals. Vol. VIII: The International Criminal Tribunal for the former Yugoslavia 2001–2002*, Intersentia, 2005
Klip and Sluiter, *Annotated Leading Cases, vol. IX*	*Idem, Annotated Leading Cases of International Criminal Tribunals. Vol. IX: The Special Court for Sierra Leone 2003–2004*, Intersentia, 2006
Klip and Sluiter, *Annotated Leading Cases, vol. X*	*Idem, Annotated Leading Cases of International Criminal Tribunals. Vol. X: The International Criminal Tribunal for Rwanda 2001–2002*, Intersentia, 2006
Lee, *Making of the Rome Statute*	Roy S. Lee (ed.), *The International Criminal Court — The Making of the Rome Statute: Issues, Negotiations, Results*, Kluwer, 1999
LRTWC	*Law Reports of Trials of War Criminals*, United Nations War Crimes Commission, London: HMSO, 1948
May et al., *Essays on ICTY Procedure and Evidence*	Richard May et al. (eds), *Essays on ICTY Procedure and Evidence — In honour of Gabrielle Kirk McDonald*, Kluwer, 2001
May and Wierda, *International Criminal Evidence*	Richard May and Marieke Wierda, *International Criminal Evidence*, Transnational, 2002
Mettraux, *International Crimes*	Guénaël Mettraux, *International Crimes and the Ad Hoc Tribunals*, Oxford University Press, 2005

Morris and Scharf, *Insider's Guide*	Virginia Morris and Michael P. Scharf, *An Insider's Guide to the International Criminal Tribunal for the Former Yugoslavia*, Transnational, 1995
Morris and Scharf, *International Criminal Tribunal for Rwanda*	Virginia Morris and Michael P. Scharf, *The International Criminal Tribunal for Rwanda*, 2 vols, Transnational, 1998
Official Records	*Official Records of the Diplomatic Conference on the Reaffirmation and Development of International Humanitarian Law Applicable in Armed Conflicts*, 17 vols, ICRC, 1974–1977
Report of the Secretary-General on ICTY	*Report of the UN Secretary-General Pursuant to Paragraph 2 of Security Council Resolution 808 (1993)*, 3 May 1993, UN Doc. S/25704
Robinson, *Genocide Convention*	Nehemiah Robinson, *The Genocide Convention: A Commentary*, New York, 1960
Schabas, *Genocide*	William A. Schabas, *Genocide in International Law*, Cambridge University Press, 2000
SCSL Rules	Rules of Procedure and Evidence, Special Court for Sierra Leone
SCSL Statute	Statute of the Special Court for Sierra Leone, 16 January 2002
Torture Convention	Convention Against Torture and Other Cruel, Inhuman or Degrading Treatment or Punishment, adopted and opened for signature, ratification, and accession by General Assembly Resolution 39/46 of 10 December 1984, entered into force 26 June 1987
Trechsel, *Human Rights in Criminal Proceedings*	Stefan Trechsel, *Human Rights in Criminal Proceedings*, Oxford University Press, 2005
Triffterer, *Commentary on the Rome Statute*	Otto Triffterer (ed.), *Commentary on the Rome Statute of the International Criminal Court: Observers' Notes, Article by Article*, Baden-Baden, 1999
TWC	*Trials of War Criminals Before the Nuernberg Military Tribunals under Control Council Law No. 10*, Hein & Co., 1997
UN/Cambodia Agreement	Agreement Between the United Nations and The Royal Government of Cambodia Concerning the Prosecution Under Cambodian Law of Crimes Committed During the Period of Democratic Kampuchea, 6 June 2003, annex to A/RES/57/228B, 13 May 2003, entered into force 29 April 2005
UN/Sierra Leone Agreement	Agreement Between the United Nations and the Government of Sierra Leone on the Establishment of a Special Court for Sierra Leone, 16 January 2002, 2178 *UNTS* 138

Vienna Convention on the Law of Treaties	Vienna Convention on the Law of Treaties, 22 May 1969, 1155 *UNTS* 331, entered into force 27 January 1980
Zappalà, *Human Rights in International Criminal Proceedings*	Salvatore Zappalà, *Human Rights in International Criminal Proceedings*, Oxford University Press, 2003

Acronyms and initialisms

ACHR	American Convention on Human Rights
A. Ch.	Appeals Chamber
ADC	Association of Defence Counsel
AJIL	American Journal of International Law
APIC	Agreement on Privileges and Immunities of the International Criminal Court
ASP	Assembly of State Parties to the ICC
BIA	bilateral immunity agreement
CAT	Convention Against Torture
CLF	Criminal Law Forum
ECHR	Convention for the Protection of Human Rights and Fundamental Freedoms (European Convention on Human Rights)
ECtHR	European Court of Human Rights
ECR	European Court Reports
EEC	European Economic Community
FRY	Federal Republic of Yugoslavia
GA Res.	Resolution of the General Assembly of the United Nations
ICB	International Criminal Bar
ICC	International Criminal Court
ICCPR	International Covenant on Civil and Political Rights
ICESCR	International Covenant on Economic, Social, and Cultural Rights
ICJ	International Court of Justice
ICLR	International Criminal Law Review
ICTR	International Criminal Tribunal for Rwanda
ICTY	International Criminal Tribunal for the Former Yugoslavia
ILC	United Nations International Law Commission
ILM	International Law Materials
ILR	International Law Reports
IMT	International Military Tribunal

IMTFE	International Military Tribunal for the Far East ('Tokyo Tribunal')
JCE	joint criminal enterprise
JICJ	Journal of International Criminal Justice
JNA	Jugoslovenska Narodna Armija (Yugoslav People's Army)
LJIL	Leiden Journal of International Law
LRTWC	Law Reports of Trials of War Criminals
MOU	Memorandum of Understanding
NGO	non-governmental organization
OTP	Office of the Prosecutor
PTC	Pre-Trial Chamber of the International Criminal Court
RPE	Rules of Procedure and Evidence
RPF	Rwanda Patriotic Front
SCSL	Special Court for Sierra Leone
SRK	Sarajevo-Romanija Korpus (Sarajevo-Romanija Corps of the VRS)
T. Ch.	Trial Chamber
TIAS	Treaties and other International Acts Series
TRC	Truth and Reconciliation Commission
UDHR	Universal Declaration of Human Rights
UN	United Nations
UNMIK	United Nations Interim Administration Mission in Kosovo
UNSC	United Nations Security Council
UNSCR	United Nations Security Council Resolution
UNTAET	United Nations Transitional Administration in East Timor
UNTS	United Nations Treaty Series
UNWCC	United Nations War Crimes Commission
VCLT	Vienna Convention on the Law of Treaties
VRS	Vojska Republike Srpske (army of the Bosnian-Serb Republic)

PART I

INTRODUCTION TO THE TRIBUNALS AND INTERNATIONAL CRIMINAL LAW

1

INTERNATIONAL CRIMINAL TRIBUNALS: NEW FACES IN THE INTERNATIONAL LEGAL ORDER

SUMMARY

1.1 INTRODUCTION

International criminal tribunals play an increasingly prominent role in the enforcement of substantive norms of international criminal law. These institutions serve a dual objective. By conducting trials, they give direct effect to international law establishing criminal responsibility of individuals. In addition, these trials give impetus to national criminal proceedings regarding international crimes. International criminal proceedings highlight the importance of respect for substantive international criminal law and remind states of their primary responsibility for its enforcement.

While a system of international criminal law could in theory function through national courts only, the establishment of international criminal tribunals, whose exclusive purpose is to try persons for international crimes, has resulted in a truly *international* criminal justice system: individuals violating substantive norms of *international* law can be tried by institutions established pursuant to *international* law. It is the combination of substantive international criminal law and enforcement by means of international institutions which makes it possible to distinguish an international criminal justice system, as imperfect as it may be, from domestic criminal justice systems.

As key elements of the international criminal justice systems, international criminal tribunals are important objects of study. Before we concentrate on their role in and contribution to international criminal law, we should determine their place as new participants in the international legal order. As they are creations of international law, their functioning and operation are governed by that body of law, which is not confined to the statutes, rules and substantive norms of international criminal law, but also includes, for example, relevant general rules of the law of international organizations.

The purpose of this chapter is to introduce to the reader the different international criminal tribunals as new subjects of international law, their position in the system of international institutions, and their competence. This will be done by analysing their method of establishment, legal personality, powers, privileges and immunities, and relationship to other subjects of international law.

A comprehensive study is beyond the purpose of this book. A certain degree of selectivity and simplification is therefore inevitable.

1.2 ESTABLISHMENT OF INTERNATIONAL CRIMINAL TRIBUNALS

1.2.1 International Military Tribunal at Nuremberg and International Military Tribunal for the Far East

The International Military Tribunal at Nuremberg ('Nuremberg Tribunal') was established pursuant to a multilateral treaty concluded between the United Kingdom, the

United States, the Soviet Union, and France.[1] Defining the legal character of the tribunal was in this early phase of international criminal law certainly problematic. Should it be considered a new international institution or rather an 'occupation tribunal', operated by the occupying powers jointly? The establishment by treaty has been advanced as proof of the tribunal's international character, and thus also as proof of its separate legal personality.[2] There was, however, criticism that the state of nationality of the accused persons, Germany, was not a party to the agreement and that, moreover, the international community as a whole did not participate in or support the trial.[3] This may have affected the perceived legitimacy of the tribunal, but does it also determine its international character? The genuinely international character of the tribunal and the fact of its legal personality being separate from that of the founding states are undisputed, as far as the four signatory states are concerned.[4] In respect of other states, the question of recognition of the Tribunal arises. Nineteen states subscribed to the London Agreement,[5] and the United Nations affirmed the 'Nuremberg principles', thereby expressing its endorsement of the trial.[6]

Although international legal personality vis-à-vis states other than the four signatory states may thus be assumed, this issue is of little practical relevance. Important elements of international legal personality are the treaty-making capacity and the right to bring and receive claims.[7] In the operation of the Nuremberg Tribunal there was no need to resort to those elements of international legal personality.

This also applies to the International Military Tribunal for the Far East ('Tokyo Tribunal'), making an inquiry into its legal character an essentially theoretical exercise. Yet the difference in establishment, compared to the Nuremberg Tribunal, is noteworthy. According to Article 1 of the Tokyo Tribunal's Charter, the establishment of an *international* tribunal was clearly envisaged.[8] Unlike the Nuremberg Tribunal, the Tokyo Tribunal was not established by a (multilateral) treaty, but by an executive decree of General Douglas MacArthur, Supreme Commander for the Allied Powers in Japan, acting under orders from the United States Joint Chiefs of Staff.[9] Although this exercise of power can be traced back to the peace agreement (Instrument of Surrender) between

---

[1] Agreement for the Prosecution and Punishment of Major War Criminals of the European Axis, and Establishing the Charter of the International Military Tribunal (IMT), 8 August 1945, 82 *UNTS* (1951) 279.

[2] In this sense G. Dahm, *Zur Problematik des Völkerstrafrechts* (Stuttgart: Kohlhammer, 1956), at 17, and R. K. Woetzel, *The Nuremberg Trials in International Law* (London: Stevens and Sons Ltd, 1960), at 41.

[3] H. Ehard, 'Der Nürnberger Prozess gegen die Hauptkriegsverbrecher und das Völkerrecht' (1948) 353 *Süddeutsche Juristenzeitung*, and R. K. Woetzel, *The Nuremberg Trials in International Law*, at 43.

[4] This can be inferred from their wish to establish an *international* tribunal.

[5] The additional ratifying states were Austria, Belgium, Czechoslovakia, Denmark, Ethiopia, Greece, Haiti, Honduras, India, Luxembourg, the Netherlands, New Zealand, Norway, Panama, Paraguay, Poland, Republic of Servia, Uruguay, and Venezuela.

[6] Affirmation of the Principles of International Law Recognized by the Charter of the Nürnberg Tribunal, GA Res. 95(I), UN GAOR, 1st Sess., pt. 2, at 1144, UN Doc. A/236 (1946).

[7] Jan Klabbers in this respect speaks of 'indicators of "subjectivity"'. See J. Klabbers, *An Introduction to International Institutional Law* (Cambridge: Cambridge University Press, 2002), at 43–8.

[8] International Military Tribunal for the Far East, Special Proclamation by the Supreme Commander for the Allied Powers at Tokyo, 19 January 1946; Charter dated 19 January 1946, 1589 *TIAS* 3, reprinted in C. I. Bevans (ed.), *Treaties and Other International Agreements, vol. 4*, 1970, at 20; Amended Charter dated 26 April 1946, ibid., at 27.

[9] Special Proclamation on the Establishment of an International Military Tribunal for the Far East, at 3; see also R. H. Minear, *Victor's Justice — The Tokyo War Crimes Trial* (Princeton: Princeton University Press, 1971), at 20.

the USA and Japan,[10] the establishment of the Tokyo Tribunal certainly does not have a direct basis in international law. Its international character rather follows from its composition and the applicable law.[11] While not being a new international institution, the Tokyo Tribunal can also not be characterized as a US court, as the US Supreme Court confirmed in the *Hirota* case.[12] Established neither pursuant to international law, nor as part of a domestic court structure, the Tokyo Tribunal may very well be the first 'internationalized' criminal tribunal, namely a 'hybrid' legal edifice possessing elements of both national and international courts. This species will be examined below in section 1.2.4.

1.2.2 International Criminal Tribunal for the Former Yugoslavia and International Criminal Tribunal for Rwanda

Challenges to legality of establishment

A combination of factors prompted the United Nations Security Council to establish ad hoc criminal tribunals for the former Yugoslavia and for Rwanda.[13] This was by no means an uncontroversial exercise of powers by the Council, since prior to the ICTY's creation the Council had never set up a criminal court to assist it in its task of maintaining international peace and security. The UN Secretary-General acknowledged in his report on the ICTY Statute that 'in the normal course of events' an international tribunal would be established by treaty.[14] But is deviating from this 'normal course' lawful?

The Security Council resolutions establishing the tribunals — 808, 827 (1993), and 955 (1994) — do not indicate which articles of Chapter VII of the UN Charter constitute the legal basis for their creation. While that chapter confers upon the Council discretionary powers with a view to maintaining international peace and security, the question arose whether they had been properly exercised in the given instance.

[10] Signed on 2 September 1945 aboard the USS *Missouri* at Tokyo Bay, Japan. *Surrender of Italy, Germany and Japan, World War II. Instruments of Surrender. Public Papers and Addresses of the President and of the Supreme Commanders*, presented by Senator Barkley on 4 October 1945, 79th Congress, Doc. No. 93, DOC Y1.1/2 10949, available at www.ibiblio.org/pha/war.term/093_00.html (last visited 31 October 2006).

[11] According to Article 2 of the Tokyo Tribunal's Charter, the Tribunal shall consist of members appointed by the Supreme Commander from the names submitted by the Signatories to the Instrument of Surrender, India, and the Commonwealth of the Philippines. From the Tribunal's subject-matter jurisdiction (Article 5 of the Charter) it follows that international law is applied exclusively.

[12] *Hirota* v. *MacArthur*, 338 US 197, argued 16–17 December 1948, decided 20 December 1948, Concurring Opinion Announced 27 June 1949. In this case a few convicted Japanese war criminals lodged a writ of habeas corpus with the US Supreme Court, thereby 'appealing' the decision of the Tokyo Tribunal. The latter dismissed the application on the ground that the IMTFE 'is not a Tribunal of the United States' and, as a result, US courts had no authority to review its decisions.

[13] It is beyond the scope of this book to go into those factors. The following should be mentioned: large-scale atrocities in both cases; widespread and penetrating media coverage; favourable political climate (the end of the cold war); tentative start of work on the ICC; and Rwanda in its capacity as a temporary member of the UN Security Council asking for establishment of the tribunal. For an analysis of the events leading to the establishment of the ICTY and ICTR, see Morris and Scharf, *Insider's Guide*, at 17–36.

[14] Report of the Secretary-General on ICTY, para. 19.

In the first case before the ICTY the accused, Duško Tadić, submitted a preliminary motion challenging the Tribunal's jurisdiction pursuant to Rule 72. One of his arguments was that the Tribunal was established in violation of the UN Charter and should therefore decline to exercise jurisdiction. The ICTY Trial Chamber refused to deal with the substance of the argument, because this involved scrutiny of the powers of the Security Council and was therefore not a matter of jurisdiction open to determination by the Tribunal.[15] Yet, although it declined to judge the reasonableness of the Security Council's acts, the Chamber nevertheless dealt with arguments raised by the defence in *obiter dicta* covering no fewer than 33 paragraphs.[16] The Chamber's findings do not differ markedly from those reached on appeal, which will be examined next.

With Judge Li dissenting on this point, the Appeals Chamber did not consider the legality question to be beyond the scope of the Tribunal's jurisdiction and resorted to a full review of the method of establishment.[17] The Appeals Chamber held Article 41 of the UN Charter, because of its open-ended character, to be an appropriate legal basis for the establishment of the ICTY.[18] The Chamber further acknowledged that the Security Council was not endowed with judicial powers, but that this did not preclude the establishment of a subsidiary organ with such powers.[19] The Appeals Chamber held that the Security Council resorted to the establishment of a judicial organ in the form of an international criminal tribunal as an instrument for the exercise of its own principal function of maintenance of peace and security.[20] It did not consider the establishment of an international criminal tribunal to exceed the powers of the Security Council, nor did it find that by establishing the Tribunal the Council violated rules of international law or encroached upon the powers of other UN organs.[21] An important argument upholding the legality of the creation of the ICTY was that the establishment of a subsidiary judicial body by a parent body of an exclusively political nature was not unprecedented within the United Nations framework. The Appeals Chamber referred to the establishment of the UN Administrative Tribunal by the General Assembly,[22] the legality of which was clearly sanctioned by the ICJ in the *Effect of Awards* case.[23]

---

[15] *Tadić* jurisdiction trial decision, para. 4. Notably, even the principal judicial organ of the United Nations, the International Court of Justice, has never assumed full review power over decisions of other UN organs; see, e.g., Questions of Interpretation and Application of the 1971 Montreal Convention arising from the Aerial Incident at Lockerbie (*Libyan Arab Jamahiriya* v. *United Kingdom and United States*), Provisional Measures, Order of 14 April 1992, *ICJ Reports* 1992, at 3 and 114.   [16] *Tadić* jurisdiction trial decision, paras 7–40.

[17] *Tadić* jurisdiction appeal decision, paras 13–25. The Appeals Chamber based the Tribunal's review power not on a specific provision in the Statute, but found that the power to review one's own jurisdiction is inherent or incidental to the nature of a court of law. In section 1.4.3 below we will examine further the notions of implied and inherent powers.

[18] *Tadić* jurisdiction appeal decision, paras 33–6, providing analysis in this respect; note the conclusion: 'In sum, the establishment of the International Tribunal falls squarely within the powers of the Security Council under Article 41 [of the UN Charter]'.   [19] Ibid., paras 37 and 38.

[20] Ibid., para. 38.

[21] Ibid., para. 28, where the Appeals Chamber clearly recognizes the existence of limits to the powers of the Council.   [22] Ibid., para. 38.

[23] *Effect of Awards of Compensation Made by the UN Administrative Tribunal*, Advisory Opinion of 13 July 1954, *ICJ Reports* 1954, at 47 and 61.

After *Tadić*, a few other accused have tried to challenge the legality of the establishment of the ICTY and the ICTR, again through jurisdictional motions. Both tribunals generally respond by referring to the findings of the Appeals Chamber on this point in the *Tadić* case.[24] Only in *Karemera* does an ICTR Trial Chamber endorse the views of Li and the *Tadić* Trial Chamber that review of the establishment exceeds the Tribunal's jurisdiction.[25]

In *Milošević* the ICTY was again confronted with the 'legality issue', a matter it thought had then long been put to rest. In the decision the Trial Chamber did little more than merely refer to the *Tadić* jurisdiction appeal decision.[26]

Relying exclusively on *Tadić* raises the suspicion of *iudex in sua causa*. The proposition by the amici in *Milošević* to have a third party look at the legality question seems thus not totally without merit.[27] One may also try to seek support for the legality of the Security Council establishment elsewhere than in the *Tadić* case. In this respect one can mention the decision of The Hague District Court, dealing with Milošević's claim that the Netherlands is hosting an 'illegal organization'. The District Court explicitly affirmed the analysis provided by the Appeals Chamber in the *Tadić* case, in particular that the establishment of the ICTY can be considered a lawful exercise of the powers vested in the Council by Article 41 of the UN Charter.[28]

More important than this national court's decision is the subsequent practice in the application of the statutes following the establishment of the ad hoc tribunals. The question whether the UN Security Council may establish subsidiary organs of a judicial nature is in fact a question of the interpretation of the UN Charter. According to the law of treaties, subsequent practice in the application of a treaty may be taken into account when interpreting a treaty.[29] In this regard, it is worth mentioning that the overwhelming majority of states have in a variety of ways recognized or expressed their support for the ad hoc tribunals. In particular mention should be made of the General Assembly resolutions in which UN members have 'welcomed' the establishment of

---

[24] See Decision on the Defence Motion on Jurisdiction, *Prosecutor* v. *Kanyabashi*, Case No. ICTR-96-15-T, ICTR, T. Ch. II, 18 June 1997. For a commentary, see V. Morris (1998) 92 *AJIL*, at 66–70. See also Decision on Motion Challenging Jurisdiction — With Reasons, *Prosecutor* v. *Krajišnik*, Case No. IT-00-39 & 40, ICTY, T. Ch. III, 22 September 2000.

[25] Surprisingly, it ruled that 'the Chamber considers that it does not have the authority to review or assess the legality of Security Council decisions and, in particular, that of Security Council Resolution 955' (Decision on the Defence Motion, pursuant to Rule 72 of Rules of Procedure and Evidence, pertaining to, inter alia, Lack of Jurisdiction and Defects in the Form of the Indictment, *Prosecutor* v. *Karemera*, Case No. ICTR-98-44-T, ICTR, T. Ch. II, 25 April 2001, para. 25). One can but speculate why the ICTR Trial Chamber did not follow and not even refer to, the decision on appeal on jurisdiction in the *Tadić* case.

[26] Decision on Preliminary Motions, *Prosecutor* v. *Milošević*, Case No. IT-99-37-PT, ICTY, T. Ch. III, 8 November 2001, paras 6 and 7.

[27] See the amici curiae brief in the *Milošević* case suggesting resolution of the matter by an impartial 'third party', this being the International Court of Justice (Amici Curiae Brief on Jurisdiction, *Prosecutor* v. *Milošević*, Case No. IT-99-37-PT, T. Ch. III, 19 October 2001, para. 20).

[28] *Slobodan Milošević tegen de Staat der Nederlanden*, Arrondissementsrechtbank 's-Gravenhage, Sector Civiel Recht — President, Vonnis in kort geding van 31 augustus 2001 (rolnummer KG 01/975) (*Slobodan Milošević* v. *Netherlands*, Case No. KG 01/795, District Court of The Hague, 31 August 2001), para. 2 and para. 3.3.

[29] See Article 31(3)(b) of the Vienna Convention on the Law of Treaties.

both ad hoc tribunals.[30] The practice of states of recognizing and expressing support for the tribunals is an important tool for interpreting the provisions of the UN Charter that attribute certain powers to the Security Council. This subsequent practice may confirm that the establishment of the ad hoc tribunals is a lawful exercise of the powers attributed to the UN Security Council by the UN Charter.

ICTY and ICTR as subsidiary UN organs

The Security Council, acting under Chapter VII, set up the ad hoc tribunals as subsidiary organs in the sense of Article 7(2) and Article 29 of the UN Charter. The Security Council resolutions creating the ad hoc tribunals make, however, no explicit reference of Articles 7(2) and 29 of the UN Charter.[31]

The concept of subsidiary organ appears to place the ad hoc tribunals in a position of inferiority and dependency vis-à-vis the parent organ. This view seems to be confirmed by the definition of subsidiary organ in the *Repertory of Practice of United Nations Organs*, which attributes the following features to a UN subsidiary organ:

(a) A subsidiary organ is created by, or under the authority of, a principal organ of the United Nations;

(b) The membership, structure and terms of reference of a subsidiary organ are determined, and may be modified by, or under the authority of, a principal organ;

(c) A subsidiary organ may be terminated by, or under the authority of, a principal organ.[32]

However, the tribunals have more than once underlined that they are not just a subsidiary organ of the UN, but 'a special kind of "subsidiary organ": a tribunal'.[33] Furthermore, in the *Blaškić* subpoena trial decision, the ICTY Trial Chamber held that the concept of a subsidiary organ is flexible and amorphous.[34] It underscored that each subsidiary organ established within the UN system requires evaluation in its own

---

[30] See, regarding the ICTY, Resolution 48/88 (1993) on the situation in Bosnia and Herzegovina, operative paragraph 24, and Resolution 49/10 (1994) on the situation in Bosnia and Herzegovina, preamble; regarding the ICTR, see Resolution 49/206 (1994) on the situation of human rights in Rwanda, operative paragraph 5, and Resolution 50/2000 (1995) on the situation of human rights in Rwanda, preamble. Other examples of 'subsequent practice' in support of the lawful establishment of the ad hoc tribunals are the following. The states most concerned with the ICTY have concluded the Dayton Peace Agreement, of which support to the ICTY forms an important element (see below, Chapter 12, section 12.3.4). More than twenty states have adopted legislation with a view to assisting the tribunals in their work. Virtually the entire international community has participated in the election of judges within the General Assembly of the United Nations (with the exception of Mexico, which believed that in establishing the tribunals the Security Council had gone beyond its powers). Moreover, a great number of states have put forward candidates for these elections.

[31] It has been argued that the legal basis for the creation of the ICTY and ICTR as subsidiary organs is not Article 29 but Article 7 of the UN Charter. Since the tribunals are endowed with (judicial) powers that the Council itself does not possess, Article 29, which refers to the functions of the Council, could not be applicable. See D. Sarooshi, *The United Nations and the Development of Collective Security — The Delegation by the UN Security Council of its Chapter VII Powers* (Oxford: Clarendon Press, 1999), at 92 *et seq.*). However, the Report of the UN Secretary-General, approved by the UN Security Council in Resolution 827, explicitly mentions Article 29 of the UN Charter as the applicable provision (Report of the Secretary-General on ICTY, para. 28).

[32] Repertory of Practice of United Nations organs, vol. I, at 228.

[33] *Tadić* jurisdiction appeal decision, para. 15. [34] *Blaškić* subpoena trial decision, para. 19.

particular context.[35] With respect to a subsidiary organ of a judicial nature, it stated that it cannot be overemphasized that a fundamental prerequisite for its fair and effective functioning is its capacity to act autonomously.[36]

The manner in which the Trial Chamber in *Blaškić* seems to 'define' its own status as a subsidiary organ undeniably has consequences for its relationship vis-à-vis the parent organ. The notions of flexibility, of one's own particular context, and of autonomy from the parent body seem to be crucial for the Trial Chamber.[37] It would be a violation of the independence and autonomy of the judiciary and even more so of an accused's right to an impartial and independent tribunal, if the ICTY or ICTR were to receive instructions in the exercise of their powers from their parent organ, which is clearly a political organ.[38] The rare case in which it was claimed that the Security Council had interfered with the operation of the ICTY or ICTR risks affecting the autonomy and credibility of these bodies and should be looked upon in a highly critical way. In Resolution 1160 (1998) the Security Council' *urged* the Office of the Prosecutor of the International Tribunal established pursuant to resolution 827 (1993) of 25 May 1993 to begin gathering information related to the violence in Kosovo that may fall within its jurisdiction'.[39] The Security Council should be aware that, when establishing *judicial* subsidiary organs, it has no control over the exercise of *judicial* powers by these organs, in the sense that the Council may not interfere with the administration of justice. However, this does not alter the power of the Security Council to put an end to the tribunals when it believes their work is no longer required to maintain or restore international peace or security.[40]

---

[35] Ibid., para. 20.   [36] Ibid., para. 23.

[37] In this sense, see also the Report of the Secretary-General on ICTY, para. 28: 'This organ would, of course, have to perform its functions independently of political considerations; it would not be subject to the authority or control of the Security Council with regard to the performance of its judicial functions'. It is important to note that the Council has approved the report in Resolution 827 (1993) establishing the ICTY, operative paragraph 1.

[38] In this respect it may be noted that the drafting history of the ICC demonstrates that the role played by the Security Council with respect to the ICC is quite controversial. In particular, the fact that the Security Council, as a political organ, may bar prosecution, at least for a period of 12 months, raised concerns about the independence of the Court with a number of delegations. See M. Bergsmo and J. Pejic, 'Article 15', in Triffterer, *Commentary on the Rome Statute*, at 373–82, and F. Berman, 'The Relationship between the International Criminal Court and the Security Council', in H. A. M. von Hebel et al. (eds), *Reflections on the International Criminal Court. Essays in Honour of Adriaan Bos* (The Hague: TMC. Asser Press, 1999), at 173–80. However, the interference of the Security Council with respect to the ICC does not go beyond the exercise of jurisdiction; instructions to the Court or Prosecutor regarding their judicial activities would be clearly improper.

[39] Security Council Resolution 1160 (1998), operative paragraph 17. See also G. Sluiter's commentary to the *Milošević* indictment and confirmation decision, in Klip and Sluiter, *Annotated Leading Cases, vol. III*, at 43–9. Such an 'instruction' is improper and casts doubt on the impartiality and independence of the Tribunal. The ICTY Prosecutor should of course be distinguished from the judicial branch, but this organ is also under an obligation to act impartially and independently. According to Article 16(2) of the ICTY Statute, the Prosecutor shall not seek or receive instructions from any government or from any other source. However, the Trial Chamber in the *Milošević* case did not consider the above-mentioned Security Council resolution to 'vitiate the independence of the Prosecutor'. The Trial Chamber ruled in this respect that '[w]hat would impugn her independence is not the initiation on the basis of information from a particular source, such as the Security Council, but whether, in assessing that information and making her decision as to the indictment of a particular person, she acts on the instructions of any government, any institution or person'. See Decision on Preliminary Motions, *Prosecutor* v. *Milošević*, Case No. IT-99-37-PT, ICTY, T. Ch. III, 8 November 2001, para. 15.

[40] For an analysis of the relationship between the ad hoc tribunals and the UN Security Council from the perspective of the right to an independent tribunal see Chapter 8, section 8.5.2.

The question arises whether the Security Council can delegate to the tribunals, as subsidiary organs, a power of taking binding decisions, or whether it can only itself impose binding obligations on states. It is generally accepted that subsidiary organs may be empowered to perform the functions of the Security Council even to the extent that this may have external consequences.[41] Article 25 of the UN Charter obliges member states to accept and execute the decisions of the Security Council. These include the decisions of subsidiary organs to the extent that they confine themselves to the scope of the functions and powers transferred by the Security Council.[42] However, it should be noted that the bulk of the subsidiary organs established by the Security Council have not been endowed with far-reaching powers similar to those of the ad hoc tribunals.[43]

1.2.3 International Criminal Court

The ICC can to some extent be considered an international organization in the 'classic sense', established by a treaty, albeit one of a special, namely judicial, character. The complicating aspect of the ICC is that the Treaty of Rome not only creates a Court, composed of various organs,[44] but also sets up an Assembly of States Parties,[45] which has been vested with several powers, inter alia to supervise the enforcement of the decisions of the Court. In fact, the Treaty of Rome established two different organizations. According to Article 1 of the ICC Statute, the ICC is established, and pursuant to Article 112(1) of the ICC Statute, an Assembly of States Parties is set up. Their separate character is confirmed by Article 34 of the Statute, which does not include the Assembly of States Parties as an organ of the Court. As a result, when one speaks of 'the Court', one should distinguish between (1) the Court as a broader edifice including the 'legal apparatus', established by Article 1 of the ICC Statute, and the Assembly of States Parties, envisaged in Article 112(1) of the ICC Statute, and (2) the Court exclusively in the sense of Article 1, consisting of the judicial branch, the Prosecutor, and the Registrar.

1.2.4 Recent additions: 'internationalized' criminal tribunals

Criminal courts as part of temporary UN administrations: East Timor and Kosovo

In East Timor and in Kosovo the UN has been acting as a transitional administrator, including the administration of justice.[46] Given the large-scale atrocities that took place in those regions prior to the UN administration, it is not surprising that the temporary court structure set in place by the UN is also involved in the prosecution of international crimes;

---

[41] M. Hilf, 'Article 29', in B. Simma et al. (eds), *The Charter of the United Nations: A Commentary* (New York: Oxford University Press, 1994), at 486.   [42] Ibid.

[43] For an overview of subsidiary organs of the UN Security Council, see E. Decaux, 'Article 29', in J.-P. Cot and A. Pellet (eds), *La Charte des Nations Unies. Commentaire article par article* (2nd edn, Paris/Brussels: Economica, 1991), at 528–41.

[44] According to Article 34 of the ICC Statute, the Court is composed of the Presidency, an Appeals Division, a Trial Division and a Pre-Trial Division, the Office of the Prosecutor, and the Registry.

[45] See Part 11 of the ICC Statute, containing a single provision, Article 112.

[46] UN Security Council Resolutions 1244 (1999) and 1272 (1999).

in the case of East Timor special panels have been put in place to that end.[47] In respect of Kosovo a different solution was adopted. Pursuant to UNMIK Regulation 2000/64, the prosecutor, the accused, or the defence counsel in 'serious crimes' cases have the right to ask UNMIK to assign international judges and prosecutors or to change the venue of proceedings. These officials function, however, within the regular court structure.[48]

The question arises of the legal characterization of these prosecutions. Where should these temporary 'UN courts' (in particular the East Timor special panels) be positioned in the international legal order? If one regards the method of establishment as indicative of their legal character,[49] it can be argued that they are part of the international rather than the domestic legal order, since they are operated by the UN. It should also be noted that the Kosovo courts are part of the 'civil presence', set up by the UN Secretary-General, as authorized by UN Security Council Resolution 1244. Furthermore, it has been pointed out above that the 'international judges programme' operates within the domestic court structure. The East Timor special panels are part of the UN Transitional Administration in East Timor directly established by the UN Security Council. They can thus be considered elements of the UN structure, which affirms their international character and has consequences for the applicable law, as will be examined below. However, they fall short of the status of a subsidiary UN organ, since the courts are only part of administrations and were not directly established by a principal UN organ, as were the ICTY and ICTR. Therefore, no legal personality distinct from that of the UN administration concerned can be attributed to them.

Bilateral agreement between the United Nations and a state: Sierra Leone and Cambodia

The United Nations is also involved in the prosecution of international crimes by supporting domestic efforts in that respect. The United Nations has concluded agreements with Cambodia and Sierra Leone.[50] The role of the international community, acting through the UN, is unique. The bilateral agreements should of course be

---

[47] See UNTAET Regulation 2000/15 of 6 June 2000 on the Establishment of Panels with Exclusive Jurisdiction over Serious Criminal Offences.

[48] UNMIK Regulation 2000/64 of 15 December 2000 on Assignment of International Judges/Prosecutors and Change of Venue. For a more detailed analysis, see J.-C. Cady and N. Booth, 'Internationalized Courts in Kosovo: An UNMIK Perspective', in C. P. Romano et al. (eds), *Internationalized Criminal Courts — Sierra Leone, East Timor, Kosovo and Cambodia* (Oxford: Oxford University Press, 2004), at 59–78.

[49] Although composition and applicable law have been advanced as determining characterization of a court as factors in the 'internationalized' or 'hybrid', only the method of establishment, the source of the court's authority, is in our view decisive as to the institution's position as part of the international or the national legal order. As will be demonstrated below, the Sierra Leone Court also applies national law and is partly composed of Sierra Leonean nationals, but can nevertheless be characterized as a subject of international law.

[50] The negotiations between Cambodia and the United Nations on the establishment of extraordinary chambers were unsuccessful for a considerable period of time. On 8 February 2002, the United Nations announced its withdrawal from the negotiations. However, late in 2002 the UN General Assembly requested the UN Secretary-General 'to resume negotiations, without delay, to conclude an agreement with the Government of Cambodia, based on previous negotiations' (Resolution 57/228 (2002) on Khmer Rouge trials (UN Doc. A/RES/57/228, 18 December 2002)). A Draft Agreement between the United Nations and the Royal Government of Cambodia concerning the Prosecution under Cambodian Law of Crimes Committed during the Period of Democratic Kampuchea was then recommended to the General Assembly for adoption by the Third Committee on

distinguished from the multilateral treaty establishing the ICC, but the UN being one of the parties implies the support of the international community as a whole.[51] It is therefore difficult to imagine that any UN member will not recognize the results of these bilateral agreements.[52]

There is a crucial distinction between the Cambodia Extraordinary Chambers and the Special Court for Sierra Leone with respect to their legal character. The UN/Cambodia Agreement is intended to regulate cooperation between the UN and Cambodia in respect of the prosecution of international crimes by the Cambodian courts.[53] The Extraordinary Chambers remain part of the Cambodian court structure.[54] Thus, no new participant in the international legal order has been created. The Special Court for Sierra Leone, however, is set up as a new institution to prosecute international crimes and serious crimes under Sierra Leonean law.[55] In his report on the Court's establishment, the UN Secretary-General refers to it as 'a treaty based organ . . . not anchored in any existing system (i.e. United Nations administrative law or the national law of the State of the seat)'.[56] This positions the Court firmly within the international legal order as a treaty-based institution. Not only the role of the UN as contracting party, but also the approach of the UN Security Council to the Sierra Leone Court contributes to the latter's unique place in the international legal order. It was in fact the Security Council which requested the UN Secretary-General to negotiate an agreement with the government of Sierra Leone to create an independent special court.[57] In later resolutions the Council welcomed the Court's creation, urged states and called upon them to cooperate with the Court.[58] Furthermore, the initial case law of the Special Court consistently emphasized its international character, in light of the initiating role of the Security Council and the position of the UN as a contracting party.[59]

6 May 2003 (Report of the Third Committee, UN Doc. A/57/806, 6 May 2003). The General Assembly approved the draft agreement by consensus on 13 May 2003 (Press Release GA/10135).

The Special Court for Sierra Leone was established pursuant to the Agreement between the United Nations and the Government of Sierra Leone on the Establishment of a Special Court for Sierra Leone, 2178 *UNTS* 138.

[51] In this sense, see the SCSL Appeals Chamber statement in *Taylor*: 'The Agreement between the United Nations and Sierra Leone is thus an agreement between all members of the United Nations and Sierra Leone. This fact makes the agreement an expression of the will of the international community. The Special Court established in such circumstances is truly international' (Decision on Immunity from Jurisdiction, *Prosecutor* v. *Taylor*, Case No. SCSL-2003-01-I, SCSL, A. Ch., 31 May 2004, para. 38).

[52] Note that the attacks on the legality of the UN/Sierra Leone Agreement were based on the claim that the Security Council had unlawfully delegated powers to the Secretary-General. However, the challenges, which were reminiscent of those advanced in the *Tadić* case, were without much difficulty dismissed by the Appeals Chamber: Decision on Preliminary Motion on Lack of Jurisdiction: Illegal Delegation of Powers by the United Nations, *Prosecutor* v. *Fofana et al.*, Case No. SCSL-2004-14-AR72(E), SCSL, A. Ch., 25 May 2004.

[53] Cf. Article 1 of the UN/Cambodia Agreement.

[54] Article 2 of the Cambodian Law on the Extraordinary Chambers.

[55] Cf. Article 1(1) of the UN/Sierra Leone Agreement: 'There is hereby established a Special Court for Sierra Leone'.

[56] Report of the Secretary-General on the establishment of a Special Court for Sierra Leone, UN Doc. S/2000/915, 4 October 2000, para. 9.

[57] Cf. UN Security Council Resolution 1315 (2000), 14 August 2000.

[58] In Resolution 1470 (2003) the Security Council 'urges all States to cooperate fully with the Court'. Furthermore, in the preamble of Resolution 1478 (2003) the Council calls 'on all States, in particular the Government of Liberia, to cooperate fully with the Special Court'.

[59] Cf. Decision on Immunity from Jurisdiction, *Prosecutor* v. *Taylor*, Case No. SCSL-2003-01-I, SCSL, A. Ch., 31 May 2004; Decision on Preliminary Motion on Lack of Jurisdiction: Illegal Delegation of Powers by the

I.3 INTERNATIONAL LEGAL PERSONALITY

1.3.1 Incidence

For an international organization — including international criminal tribunals — possessing international legal personality means possessing rights and duties, powers, and liabilities as an entity distinct from its members or its creators in the international sphere and in international law.[60] Having regard to the purposes and functions of international criminal tribunals, one may mention as important consequences of legal personality the capacity and right to conclude treaties (or memoranda of understanding), the capacity to claim fulfilment of cooperation obligations by states, and the duty to comply with applicable sources of international law. The question of applicable law will be examined in the next subsection.

An international organization's possession of legal personality is seldom apparent on the basis of its constitutive document and therefore, as follows from the ICJ's ruling in the *Reparations for Injuries* case,[61] regard should be had to the 'intention' of the drafters of the constitution.[62] For example, if nothing is specified in the constitutive document, the deciding factor is whether the drafters intended a particular international criminal tribunal to have the capacity to conclude treaties.

The question of the international legal personality of various international criminal tribunals is addressed below. Obviously, our inquiry is confined to those criminal tribunals that can be considered to operate in the international sphere, separately from any other subject of international law.[63]

The legal personality of the ICC is explicitly provided for in the Statute. Article 4(1) of the ICC Statute provides simply that the Court shall have international legal personality. This is further evidenced by the Court's power to conclude agreements (Article 87(5) of the ICC Statute) and the recognition of duties under general international law (see Applicable sources provision, Article 21 of the ICC Statute). The Assembly of States Parties, as a separate entity, does not have explicit legal personality and it is doubtful whether it was the drafters' intention that it should have. Testament to the 'fully fledged' international legal personality of the ICC vis-à-vis non-party states is that the threshold of sixty ratifications was reached in 2002. This substantial level of

United Nations, *Prosecutor* v. *Fofana*, Case No. SCSL-2004-14-AR72(E), SCSL, A. Ch., 25 May 2004; Decision on Challenge to Jurisdiction: Lomé Accord Amnesty, *Prosecutor* v. *Kallon and Kamara*, Cases No. SCSL-2004-15-AR72(E) and SCSL-2004-16-AR72(E), SCSL, A. Ch., 13 March 2004.

[60] C. F. Amerasinghe, *Principles of the Institutional Law of International Organizations* (Cambridge: Cambridge University Press, 1996), at 78.

[61] *Reparation for Injuries suffered in the Service of the United Nations*, Advisory Opinion, *ICJ Reports* 1949, at 174.

[62] This is an extreme simplification of the difficult theoretical debate underlying the possession of international legal personality by international organizations. For analyses that do justice to the matter's complexity, refer to C. F. Amerasinghe, *Principles of the Institutional Law of International Organizations*, at 77–90 and J. Klabbers, *An Introduction to International Institutional Law*, at 52–7.

[63] Thus, the legal personality of Kosovo courts, the East Timor special panels, and the Cambodia extraordinary chambers will not be examined.

support makes the issue of recognition by the international community a less immi-nent problem.

The attribution of legal personality to the Sierra Leonean Special Court is certainly more circumscribed and functional. Article 10 of the UN/Sierra Leone Agreement attributes the 'juridical capacity necessary to (a) contract; (b) acquire and dispose of movable and immovable property; (c) institute legal proceedings; (d) enter into agree-ments with States as may be necessary for the exercise of its functions and for the oper-ation of the Court'. Given the clear language of this provision, expressing the intention of the contracting parties, a more comprehensive degree of legal personality is difficult to imagine. A limited degree of legal personality, mainly having effect within the Sierra Leonean legal order, is understandable, bearing in mind that no states other than Sierra Leone are direct parties to the treaty establishing the Court.

As subsidiary organs of the Security Council, the ICTY and ICTR are integral parts of the UN and as such have in principle no international legal personality distinct from that of the UN.[64] In the operation of the tribunals this is evidenced by the conclusion of headquarters agreements and treaties pertaining to the enforcement of sentences between the UN and states, and not between the ad hoc tribunals and states. Yet the tri-bunals have autonomously concluded two agreements with the United States regulating the surrender of indicted persons.[65] This supposes the possession of a certain degree of international legal personality separate from the UN, unless the conclusion of the agree-ments is an ultra vires act.[66] Other UN subsidiary organs, such as UNICEF, they have also concluded agreements and may thus be considered to possess legal personality dis-tinct from the United Nations and legal capacities necessary to fulfil their functions.

Finally, the agreement establishing the Nuremberg Tribunal and its charter are silent on the matter of legal personality. Given the limited mandate of the tribunal and bear-ing in mind the intention of the drafters, no substantive interaction with other subjects of international law was envisaged (for example, no cooperation relationships with states). Yet, since an *international* tribunal was created it can be said to incur duties directly under international law. Legal personality should thus focus on the position of the tribunal as bearer of duties.[67]

1.3.2 Consequences: applicable law

Operating in the international sphere and possessing (a certain degree of) international legal personality, international criminal tribunals are bound by relevant sources of

---

[64] D. Sarooshi, *The United Nations and the Development of Collective Security — The Delegation by the UN Security Council of its Chapter VII Powers*, at 161.

[65] US/ICTY Surrender Agreement of 5 October 1994, and US/ICTR Surrender Agreement of 24 January 1995.

[66] In this vein, see J. Dutheil de la Rochère, 'Article 7', in J.-P. Cot and A. Pellet (eds), *La Charte des Nations Unies. Commentaire article par article*, at 219: 'On peut affirmer ... que l'organe subsidiaire créé par une manifest-ation de volonté de l'Organization et non pas par un accord intergouvernemental ne saurait prétendre à la plénitude de la personnalité juridique internationale. Toutefois l'organe subsidiaire chargé de missions opérationnelles, entrant en contact direct avec les Etats souverains peut se voir reconnaître un certain degré de personnalisation internationale ou certains aspects de cette personnalité.'

[67] However, one may question whether this was the intention of the drafters of the agreement and charter.

international law, in addition to their legal frameworks.[68] It has been recognized that international organizations, including their subsidiary organs, are creations of international law and are, as such, subject to international law.[69] A practical application of this view can be found in the case law of the European Court of Justice, according to which 'the European Community must respect international law in the exercise of its powers'.[70]

In the initial case law of the ICTY the Tribunal was quite reluctant to consider itself bound by rules other than those set out in its Statute and the RPE. In the *Tadić* decision on protective measures the Trial Chamber was clearly struggling with the question of the applicability of sources of law outside the Statute and the RPE.[71] The gist of the reasoning of the majority in this decision seems to be that the unique character of the Tribunal may justify derogation from relevant internationally recognized standards.[72] In his separate opinion Judge Stephen seems to have adopted a different approach, in interpreting the Statute and Rules in the wider context of 'internationally recognized standards'.[73] In fact, Judge Stephen's approach has been receiving growing support in later decisions of the ICTY, where the Statute and the RPE seem to be interpreted more in light of relevant international law than in light of the Tribunal's 'unique character'. Thus, after initial reservations, the ICTY gradually took international law into account without, however, implicitly expressing the view that it considered itself bound by international law outside the Statutes and Rules.[74]

In the *Erdemović* appeal judgment, focusing on the legality of the accused's guilty plea and on duress as a defence under international law, Judges MacDonald and Vohrah considered in a separate opinion the sources set out in Article 38(1) of the ICJ Statute as applicable and examined whether, with a view to determining the issue at hand, relevant rules of customary international law and general principles of law could be found.[75]

---

[68] The 'legal frameworks' of international criminal tribunals consist of the statutes, rules of procedure and evidence, and other 'secondary' regulations, directions, or directives.

[69] See the ruling of the ICJ in *Interpretation of the Agreement of 25 March 1951 between the WHO and Egypt*, Advisory Opinion, *ICJ Reports* 1980, at 73, 89–90: 'international organizations are subjects of international law and, as such, are bound by any obligations incumbent upon them under general rules of international law'. For compelling arguments as to why international organizations should be considered to be bound by international law, even without their consent, see H. Schermers and N. Blokker, *International Institutional Law — Unity within Diversity* (The Hague: Martinus Nijhoff, 1995), at 983–4.

[70] Case C–286/90, *Anklagemyndigheden* v. *Poulsen and Diva Navigation Corp.* [1992] ECR I-6019, para. 9; and Case C–162/96, *Racke* v. *Hauptzollamt Mainz* [1998] ECR I-3655, para. 45. The latter case related to the suspension of the operation of a cooperation agreement between the Socialist Federal Republic of Yugoslavia and the EEC. In that respect, the Court held that the 'rules of customary international law concerning the termination and suspension of treaty relations by reason of a fundamental change of circumstances are binding upon the Community institutions and form part of the Community legal order' (ibid.).

[71] *Tadić* protective measures decision, paras 17–30. See also N. Affolder, 'Tadic, the Anonymous Witness and the Sources of International Procedural Law' (1998) 19 *Michigan J. of International Law*, at 448, where she argues that the decision 'uncovers a deep uncertainty about the sources of international procedural law and the relevance of international standards in making procedural decisions'. [72] Affolder, at 477.

[73] Ibid., at 494.

[74] See, e.g., Decision on Zdravko Mucić's Motion for the Exclusion of Evidence, *Prosecutor* v. *Delalić et al.*, Case No. IT-96-21-T, ICTY, T. Ch., 2 September 1997, where the Trial Chamber proceeded to an elaborate analysis of human rights case law with respect to the right to counsel.

[75] Judges MacDonald and Vohrah expressed the view that in order to establish a general principle of law a comprehensive survey of all the legal systems in the world is not necessary, but the examination may be confined to those

In the *Blaškić* subpoena decision the Appeals Chamber considered the Tribunal bound by customary international law, because rules of customary international law 'must also be taken into account, and indeed [they] have always been respected, by international organizations as well as international courts'.[76] It further ruled that 'although it is true that the rules of customary international law may become relevant where the Statute is silent on a particular point . . . there is no need to resort to these rules where the Statute contains an explicit provision on the matter'.[77] In another case, it was confirmed that the tribunals are bound by customary international law.[78] This case also gave a strong indication of how customary international law may affect the tribunals. It was held that 'there may be instances where the discretionary power to admit any relevant evidence with probative value may not be exercised where the admission of such evidence is prohibited by a rule of customary international law'.[79] Finally, in the second decision of the Appeals Chamber in *Barayagwiza* it was ruled that '[t]he International Tribunal is a unique institution, governed by its own Statute and by the provisions of customary international law, where these can be discerned'.[80]

The gist of the above rulings is that customary law is applicable and binding when the Statute and Rules are silent on a particular point. In the hierarchy of sources applicable to the tribunals, customary international law has a gap-filling function and is inferior to the Statutes and RPE. However, it goes without saying that peremptory norms of international law, *jus cogens*, occupy the highest place in any hierarchy, above the Statutes and RPE.

In addition to the rules of general international law, the ICTY and ICTR, as part of the UN structure, are also bound by the law of the UN Charter. In this respect, special account should be taken of Article 24 of the UN Charter. Article 24(2) of the Charter obliges the Security Council to 'act in accordance with the Purposes and Principles of the United Nations'. Thus, the activities of the tribunals are also governed by these 'Purposes and Principles'. It is uncertain what this means in practice, given that the United Nations serves many different purposes and is based on different principles.

As an international organization, a creation of international law, the ICC is bound by general international law in the exercise of its powers, as are ad hoc tribunals. Unlike the statutes of the ad hoc tribunals, the ICC Statute contains a specific provision, Article 21, which not only lists the applicable sources of law, but also sets out a hierarchy among them. It is self-evident that the primary sources to be applied by the Court are its Statute, the elements of crimes, and the RPE. As secondary sources the Court shall apply 'applicable treaties and the principles and rules of international law'.

---

jurisdictions accessible to the judges. See *Erdemović* appeal judgment, Joint separate opinion of Judge McDonald and Judge Vohrah, paras 56–8. With regard to the question whether or not a rule of customary international law can be discerned, the judges analysed the requirements of state practice and *opinio juris*. Ibid., paras 49–51.

[76] *Blaskić* subpoena appeal decision, para. 41.

[77] Ibid., para. 64. The question as to whether the Statute is silent on a certain point is, of course, a matter of interpretation.

[78] Decision on the Prosecution Motion under Rule 73 for a Ruling concerning the Testimony of a Witness, *Prosecutor* v. *Simić et al.*, Case No. IT-95-9-PT, ICTY, T. Ch. II, 27 July 1999, para. 42: 'It is trite that the International Tribunal is bound by customary international law.'   [79] Ibid.

[80] *Barayagwiza* II appeal decision, para. V.A.3.b.

The lowest rank in the hierarchy of applicable sources of law, as set out in Article 21 of the ICC Statute, is occupied by general principles of law derived by the Court from national laws.

The above hierarchy is not complete. According to Article 21(3) of the ICC Statute, the application and interpretation of the sources of law mentioned above must be consistent with internationally recognized human rights. As a result, internationally recognized human rights occupy the highest place in the hierarchy of norms, even above the Statute. In the case of a conflict between a provision in the Statute or the RPE with an internationally recognized human right, the latter will prevail.[81]

Compared to the statutes of the ad hoc tribunals, Article 21 of the ICC Statute provides for a desirable clarity in the applicable sources and their hierarchy *inter se*. However, even though the hierarchy of applicable sources of law is not explicitly set out within the statutes of the ad hoc tribunals, one reaches in this respect basically the same result as that warranted by Article 21 of the ICC Statute.

The Statute and Rules of the Special Court for Sierra Leone do not contain a provision on applicable law. As a result, the analysis above in respect of the ad hoc tribunals is equally applicable to the Special Court. Like the case law of the ad hoc tribunals, the initial jurisprudence of the Special Court displays reluctance to apply sources of law other than the Statute and the Rules. For example, whereas Article 20(3) of the SCSL Statute provides that judges of the SCSL shall be guided by decisions taken by the ICTY and ICTR, SCSL judges have emphasized that it is confined to mere guidance.[82] Furthermore, remarkable observations have been made by Judge Boutet, who considers that the right to a fair trial is not part of customary international law, and that, even if it were, the SCSL could deviate from it as it is not *jus cogens*.[83]

I.4 STRUCTURE AND POWERS

1.4.1 Internal organization

The structure of international criminal tribunals is such that they are not international organizations in the classical sense and that they also cannot be considered tribunals in the 'ordinary' (domestic) meaning of the word.

International organizations are usually composed of members that participate in the decision-making process. International criminal tribunals may be set up, either directly

---

[81] Such a conflict is a highly theoretical possibility. It is more likely that the *exercise* of discretionary powers attributed by the Statute could potentially conflict with human rights norms.

[82] Cf. Decision on the Prosecutor's Motion for Immediate Protective Measures for Witnesses and Victims and for Non-Public Disclosure, *Prosecutor* v. *Kallon*, Case No. SCSL-2003-07-PT, SCSL, T. Ch., 23 May 2003, para. 12, and Decision on the Prosecution Motion for Immediate Protective Measures for Witnesses and Victims and for Non-Public Disclosure, *Prosecutor* v. *Gbao*, Case No. SCSL-2003-09-PT, SCSL, T. Ch., 10 October 2003, para. 31.

[83] Decision on the Prosecution Motion for Immediate Protective Measures for Witnesses and Victims and for Non-Public Disclosure, *Prosecutor* v. *Gbao*, Case No. SCSL-2003-09-PT, SCSL, T. Ch., 10 October 2003, paras 39–42.

or indirectly, by states, but the latter for obvious reasons cannot influence the judicial process. This also applies to the ICC Assembly of States Parties. Although this body is composed of ICC states parties, which take decisions by a simple or two-thirds majority, the body must remain aloof from the legal process.

The structure of the various international criminal tribunals is such that the term 'tribunal' is in fact misleading. It is self-evident that a domestic tribunal concerns only the judicial branch or activity of the state, which tends to be separated from the prosecutorial function. Montesquieu's division of powers may seem blurred in the structure of international criminal tribunals, which include the prosecutorial service as an organ of the tribunal or court. In order to avoid this impression, it would be more appropriate to refer to the ICC, the ICTY, and the ICTR as a 'judicial apparatus', consisting of a *separate* prosecutorial service and a judicial branch. That the two branches are separate follows from the internal organization and the division of powers and functions between the organs.

All the recent *international* criminal tribunals — the ICTY and the ICTR, the ICC, and the Special Court for Sierra Leone — consist of three main organs: the judicial branch, the Office of the Prosecutor, and the Registrar.[84] The judicial branch consists of different judicial organs: Trial Chambers and an Appeals Chamber, for all tribunals mentioned above; and a Pre-Trial Chamber and a Presidency for the ICC.[85] The Registrar of international criminal tribunals cannot be compared with his or her counterpart in domestic jurisdictions. The Registrar, as a separate organ, is responsible for the administration and servicing of the entire tribunal or court, and is thus not confined to supporting the judicial branch.

One may note that in none of the statutes has the defence been integrated in the organization. Thus, there is no 'defence unit' as an organ of the tribunals or courts. In their commentary on Article 11 of the ICTY Statute, Bassiouni and Manikas regret the omission of a reference to the defence function.[86] They found that had the Security Council specifically included a defence organ in the Statute, it would have emphasized the importance of this function in ensuring that the rights of the accused are observed.[87] The same argument can apply to the ICC and to the Sierra Leone Court. In respect of the ICC Statute it cannot convincingly be argued that this is anything other than a deliberate omission; the ICC Statute is an elaborate document and it seems improbable that discussions of the organization of the Court would not have considered the position of the defence.[88] What is more, the ICC Statute does provide for organs of the Court other than those mentioned in Article 34 of the ICC Statute.

---

[84] Article 11 of the ICTY Statute, Article 10 of the ICTR Statute, Article 34 of the ICC Statute, and Article 11 of the SCSL Statute.

[85] Presidency and pre-trial judges also are part of the organic structure of the ICTY and the ICTR. Not on the basis of the statutes, but on the basis of the rules, they have a special position and tasks. See Rule 19 of the ICTY and ICTR RPE, and Rule 65 *ter* of the ICTY RPE.

[86] Bassiouni and Manikas, *Law of the ICTY*, at 798.   [87] Ibid., at 798–9.

[88] See R. Lee (ed.), *The International Criminal Court: Elements of Crimes and Rules of Procedure and Evidence* (Ardsley, NY: Transnational Publishers, Inc., 2001), at 277–8: 'At the Rome Conference, the issue of explicit provisions establishing an "Office of the Defence" was discussed informally but no formal proposal to that effect was put forward.'

Article 43(6) of the ICC Statute provides for the establishment of a Victims and Witness Unit by the Registrar.

It should be mentioned that the defence's place in the structures of functioning tribunals is currently under the umbrella and the authority of the Registrar. This will be examined from the perspective of the law of criminal procedure in Chapter 2, section 2.5. From the viewpoint of institutional international law, this approach has the following consequences. The defence is not attributed powers, it may not invoke implied powers, and its activities are not governed by general international law, with the exception of specifically designed instruments, such as the Code of Conduct for Defence Counsel.[89]

1.4.2 Attributed powers

Like other organizations, the tribunals and courts act through their organs. This raises the question of the powers these organs may exercise under international law.

The starting point of any discussion of such matters is that an organ of an international organization possesses those powers that are attributed to it by the organization's constitutive document.[90] This also applies to the international criminal tribunals, albeit that their constitutive documents and their functioning contain a number of particularities worth mentioning.

First, the statutes of the ICTY, the ICTR, and the SCSL attribute to the judges a rule-making power, in that they may adopt rules of procedure and evidence to regulate procedural and other appropriate matters.[91] This gives the judges a certain amount of leeway in determining the scope of their own activities and powers, as well as those of the other organs, the prosecutor, and the Registrar. Although this is not explicitly stated, the rules may not go against the statute.[92] One need only consider the size of the RPE of the ICTY and ICTR and the number of amendments that have been made to conclude that the judges have made extensive use of this delegated power. This can be explained by the rudimentary character of the statutes, which leave many issues

---

[89]   Code of Professional Conduct for Counsel Appearing before the International Tribunal, ICTY, IT/125 REV. 2, last amended 29 June 2006; Code of Professional Conduct for Defence Counsel, ICTR, 8 June 1998; Code of Professional Conduct for Counsel, ICC-ASP/4/3/Res.1, 2 December 2005.

[90]   This is also known as the principle of speciality or the principle of attribution; for a more detailed analysis, see J. Klabbers, *An Introduction to International Institutional Law*, at 63–7.

[91]   Article 15 of the ICTY Statute and Article 14 of the ICTR Statute. The latter article provides that the ICTR judges shall adopt the RPE of the ICTY 'with such changes as they deem necessary'. Article 14(1) of the SCSL Statute stipulates that the ICTR Rules 'shall be applicable *mutatis mutandis* to the conduct of the legal proceedings before the Special Court'. Article 14(2) allows for amendment or adoption of additional rules where the ICTR Rules do not adequately provide for a specific situation. The SCSL judges have used this power for effecting significant changes, such as a very simplified Rule 92 *bis* (see Chapter 10, section 10.7.5) and the abolition of appeals for preliminary motions (see Chapter 8, section 8.5.9).

[92]   Morris and Scharf, *International Criminal Tribunal for Rwanda, vol. I*, at 419; Morris and Scharf, *Insider's Guide*, at 178. The relationship between the ICTY and ICTR statutes and the rules may be difficult to establish. Hafner made an analogy with the system of European law: 'Leaving aside the Charter, the Statute could . . . be seen as the primary law, the RPE and other instruments drawn up within the Tribunal as secondary law' (G. Hafner, 'Limits to the Procedural Powers of the International Tribunal for the Former Yugoslavia', in K. Wellens (ed.), *International Law: Theory and Practice — Essays in honour of Eric Suy* (The Hague: Nijhoff, 1998), at 655).

unaddressed. The far more detailed ICC Statute contains no similar delegated power to the judges. The ICC's RPE need to be established by the states parties to the Rome Statute.[93]

The rudimentary and sometimes clearly ambiguous character of the ICTY and ICTR statutes, as well as of the Statute for the Special Court for Sierra Leone, brings us to the second point. The jurisprudence of the ad hoc tribunals is frequently based on an interpretation of the statutes that extends the attributed powers to the maximum, in light of their objects and purposes. In the *Tadić* case the Trial Chamber described the object and purpose of the ICTY as follows: to do justice, to deter further crimes, and to contribute to the restoration and maintenance of peace.[94] In the *Tadić* jurisdiction decision the Appeals Chamber, examining the question of the interpretation of Articles 2, 3, and 5 of the ICTY Statute, considered the object and purpose of the enactment of the Statute.[95] It resorted to a teleological and logical, and rather broad interpretation of these provisions.[96]

While the ICTY and the ICTR, and to a certain degree also the Special Court for Sierra Leone, can argue that the maintenance of international peace and security, plus the rudimentary nature of their statutes, justify an interpretation of attributed powers that is quite broad, this is more difficult for the ICC. The latter's Statute and Rules being both the result of protracted negotiations, and far more detailed, appear to limit any resort to a broad interpretation.

1.4.3 Implied and inherent powers

Since there are limits to a broad interpretation of explicitly attributed powers, it may be asked whether international criminal tribunals, in addition to the powers explicitly attributed to them by the statutes, may claim powers necessary for their functioning. In other words, can they invoke so-called implied or inherent powers?

Implied powers are generally considered to be those powers that, although not expressly conferred upon an organ by its constitutive document, arise by necessary implication as being essential to the performance of the organ's duties and which can be derived from the express powers of an organization or its functions.[97] Inherent powers,

---

[93] Article 51 of the ICC Statute.

[94] *Tadić* protective measures decision, para. 18, referring to the First Annual Report of the ICTY (Report of the International Tribunal for the Prosecution of Persons Responsible for Serious Violations of International Humanitarian Law committed in the Territory of the former Yugoslavia since 1991 (UN Doc. A/49/342, S/1994/1007, 29 August 1994)), para. 11.   [95] *Tadić* jurisdiction appeal decision, para. 71.

[96] For example, the Appeals Chamber interpreted Article 3 of the ICTY Statute as a general clause covering all violations of humanitarian law not falling under Article 2 or covered by Articles 4 or 5 of the ICTY Statute. It came to this interpretation, inter alia, by viewing Article 3 in a general perspective and appraising it in a historical context. Ibid., paras 87–93. See also W. Fenrick, 'International Humanitarian Law and Criminal Trials' (1997) 7 *Transnational Law & Contemporary Problems*, at 35: 'the Appeals Chamber ... adopted an extremely progressive and creative approach concerning Article 3 of the Statute'.

[97] See K. Skubiszewski, 'Implied Powers of International Organizations', in Y. Dinstein and M. Tabory (eds), *International Law at a Time of Perplexity: Essays in Honour of Shabtai Rosenne* (Dordrecht: Martinus Nijhoff, 1989), at 856–7; N. White, *The Law of International Organisations* (Manchester: Manchester University Press, 1996), at 129; H. Schermers and N. Blokker, *International Institutional Law*, at 158–63.

on the other hand, can be described as those powers which are derived from the very existence of the organization.[98]

Bearing in mind this distinction, the tribunals have asserted both inherent *and* implied powers. In the *Tadić* case the Appeals Chamber considered that the Tribunal, as a subsidiary organ of a judicial nature, possessed the inherent power to determine its own jurisdiction.[99] In the *Blaškić* subpoena decision the Trial Chamber claimed that the power to issue a subpoena to a state could be *implied* if such a power were necessary for the tribunal to fulfil its functions.[100]

It is beyond the scope of this book to focus on the implied or inherent powers doctrines in general. Suffice it to say that the ICJ has confirmed the legality of the use of implied powers by international organizations.[101]

The central question with respect to the international criminal tribunals is whether in asserting implied or inherent powers they have respected the confines of these respective doctrines.

The statutes of the ad hoc tribunals are clearly intended as the rudimentary frameworks within which the tribunals should operate. The assertion of additional powers was, given the delegation of the establishment of RPE, clearly envisaged. Since the statutes have endowed the (major) organs of the tribunals with sweeping powers, it will not be difficult to tie any asserted implied power to an express power.[102] Nor will it be difficult for the tribunals to prove that certain additional powers are essential for their effective operation. In this way, they respect the conditions attached to invoking implied powers.

An overview of the tribunals' practice with regard to inherent and implied powers demonstrates they have been cautious in claiming such powers. It can be safely concluded that the implied and inherent powers claimed by the tribunals can be tied to express powers attributed by the statutes and are within the clear purview of the statutes. In the *Blaškić* case the Trial Chamber found that the ICTY has the inherent

---

[98] See the case law of the ICJ, which has asserted inherent powers, for example in the *Nuclear tests* case (*Nuclear Tests (Australia v. France)*, Judgment of 20 December 1974, *ICJ Reports* 1974, at 253, 259), para. 23: 'By virtue of an inherent jurisdiction which the Court possesses qua judicial organ, it has first to examine a question which it finds to be essentially preliminary, namely the existence of a dispute for, whether or not the Court has jurisdiction in the present case, the resolution of that question could exert a decisive influence on the continuation of the proceedings.' For further analysis of the concept of inherent powers see K. Skubiszewski, 'Implied Powers of International Organizations', at 862–3.

[99] *Tadić* jurisdiction appeal decision, para. 18 (Judge Li dissenting on this point).

[100] *Blaškić* subpoena trial decision, para. 30 (this point was overruled on appeal).

[101] N. White, *The Law of International Organisations*, at 129. A series of decisions by international judicial organs has accepted the implied powers doctrine. See *Competence of the International Labour Organization to Regulate, Incidentally, the Personal Work of the Employer* (Advisory Opinion of 23 July 1926, *PCIJ Reports Series B*, no. 13, at 18); *Jurisdiction of the European Commission of the Danube between Galatz and Braila* (Advisory Opinion of 8 December 1927, *PCIJ Reports Series B*, no. 14, at 25–37); *Reparation for Injuries suffered in the Service of the United Nations*, Advisory Opinion, *ICJ Reports* 1949, at 174, 182–3; *International Status of South-West Africa*, Advisory Opinion, *ICJ Reports* 1950, at 128, 136; *Effect of Awards of Compensation made by the UN Administrative Tribunal*, Advisory Opinion of 13 July 1954, *ICJ Reports* 1954, at 47, 56–8; *Certain Expenses of the United Nations (Article 17, paragraph 2, of the Charter)*, Advisory Opinion of 20 July 1962, *ICJ Reports* 1962, at 151, 167–8; *Legal Consequences for States of the Continued Presence of South Africa in Namibia (South-West Africa) notwithstanding Security Council Resolution 276 (1970)*, Advisory Opinion, *ICJ Reports* 1971, at 16, 47–9, and 52.

[102] See N. White, *The Law of International Organisations*, at 129.

power to compel the production of documents by states necessary for a proper execution of its judicial function.[103] It also concluded that the Tribunal has the inherent power and express power to issue a subpoena to a state.[104] Finally, the Trial Chamber claimed an inherent power to hold individuals in contempt of court.[105] The Appeals Chamber reversed the decision of the Trial Chamber as far as the inherent power to subpoena a state and a state official is concerned.[106] It confirmed, however, the 'inherent' contempt power asserted by the Trial Chamber.[107] Moreover, it attributed to the Tribunal the inherent power to make a judicial finding of non-compliance if a state fails to fulfil its obligations under the Statute.[108] Finally, the Appeals Chamber found that the Tribunal possesses an 'inherent' power to enter into direct contact with individuals when this is required for evidence-gathering purposes.[109]

The above powers claimed by the ICTY, although not explicitly set out in the constitutive documents, also stand the test of legality, and do not exceed what is acceptable from an institutional law perspective. They can easily be connected to the (extensive) powers attributed to the tribunals and are furthermore of vital importance for their effective functioning.

Since the Special Court for Sierra Leone has much the same legal framework as the ICTY and the ICTR, evidenced by the fact that the ICTR Rules are applicable to it,[110] this Court also has open to it the use of implied and inherent powers comparable to those used by the ICTY and the ICTR. However, one important difference may stand in the way of this. Unlike the ICTY and the ICTR, the Sierra Leone Court is not directly established by a Security Council resolution and, although it is supported by the Council, it may not involve the maintenance of international peace and security as justification for implied powers.[111]

Regarding the ICC, the question also arises whether and to what extent the Court may invoke powers inherent in its judicial function, or implied in its constitutive document, that exceed, and are in addition to, the powers already attributed to it by the Statute. The Court is an international organization and the law of international organizations with respect to inherent and implied powers is thus applicable here. Consequently, the Court, in particular the judicial branch, may claim certain inherent or implied powers.

However, unlike the legal frameworks of the ad hoc tribunals, the ICC Statute and RPE seek to regulate in much more detail all the matters that are important for the effective functioning of the Court. Both instruments appear to almost specify

---

[103] *Blaškić* subpoena trial decision, para. 41.   [104] Ibid., para. 64.   [105] Ibid., para. 62.

[106] *Blaškić* subpoena appeal decision, para. 25.   [107] Ibid., para. 59.   [108] Ibid., para. 33.

[109] Ibid., para. 55.

[110] Article 14(1) of the SCSL Statute: 'The Rules of Procedure and Evidence of the International Criminal Tribunal for Rwanda obtaining at the time of the establishment of the Special Court shall be applicable *mutatis mutandis* to the conduct of the legal proceedings before the Special Court.'

[111] Nevertheless, this conclusion might be questioned in view of the explicit language of the very resolution (UNSCR 1315 (2001)) that requested the Secretary-General to negotiate an agreement on the establishment of the SCSL with the Government of Sierra Leone. It seems quite clear that the Court is a child of the peace-maintaining initiative of the Council in Sierra Leone, which was furthermore mandated by the Council to further and promote peace and security in the country and region. This might be invoked as a justification for implied powers.

exhaustively and to limit the powers attributed to the Court. One may argue that the objective of the framers would appear to have been to limit the powers of the Court to those set out in the Statute.[112] The assertion of broad implied or inherent powers is difficult to reconcile with this objective.[113] A limited use of implied or inherent powers appears inevitable, to ensure the effective operation of the Court. In spite of the protracted nature of the negotiations and the detailed character of the Statute and Rules, the drafters may still have overlooked certain matters. In this respect, one may mention the establishment of a defence unit as a subsidiary organ of the registry, with the aim of a better organization of the defence.[114] If there is a clear omission one would expect that a claim for an implied power to 'fill the gap' would satisfy the test of legality and would not encounter much opposition from the states parties. On the other hand, if the attribution of a power was discussed during the negotiations but has deliberately been left out of the Statute and Rules or has been regulated in a certain manner, assertion of the power on the basis of the implied powers doctrine should be considered ultra vires.

A complicating factor with respect to a claim of implied powers by the Court is the rule-amendment procedure contained in Article 51(2) of the ICC Statute. Pursuant to Article 51(2), any state party, the judges, or the prosecutor may propose amendments to the Rules and an amendment enters into force upon its adoption by a two-thirds majority of the members of the Assembly of States Parties. One may argue that Article 51(2) provides an opportunity for granting through the Rules, to (organs of) the Court, those additional powers that are necessary for its effective functioning. In the case of the ad hoc tribunals, claims of inherent and implied powers have in most instances been codified in their Rules. Since this path is available, one may be tempted to argue that the Court must use it for any assertion of implied powers. Yet, there are two reasons why the Court may continue to invoke implied powers while also having available to it the possibility of proposing amendments to the Rules. In the first place, there may not be time to amend the Rules, particularly when the claim of an implied power is required to address effectively a question that has come up in the course of a trial. Urgency may, however, be more difficult to prove with respect to institutional changes, such as the establishment of a defence unit. Secondly, under Article 51(2) of the ICC Statute, the Registrar cannot propose amendments to the Rules and thus has no option other than to claim implied powers if this is in his or her opinion necessary for the effective functioning of the Court.

---

[112] B. Swart and G. Sluiter, 'The International Criminal Court and International Criminal Co-operation', in H. A. M. von Hebel et al. (eds), *Reflections on the International Criminal Court — Essays in honour of Adriaan Bos*, at 102–3.

[113] As an example, one may think of the power to compel the attendance of witnesses. It could be argued that this is a power inherent in a criminal court, and necessary for its effective functioning (i.e. an implied power). However, Articles 93(1)(e) and 93(7) of the Statute make the appearance of a witness dependent on his or her consent. Claiming an inherent or implied power compelling the attendance of witnesses would be ultra vires the Statute. On compelling the appearance of witnesses, see Chapter 10, section 10.5.3.

[114] On the defence unit, see Chapter 2, section 2.5.

1.5 PRIVILEGES AND IMMUNITIES

In order to function effectively, international organizations have privileges and immunities.[115] Like state and diplomatic immunities, these privileges and immunities are not confined to legal persons, but extend to persons working for international organizations. The privileges and immunities of international organizations are not rooted in sovereignty, but in considerations of 'functional necessity', meaning that such immunities are necessary to ensure the effective functioning of the organization.[116] Furthermore, whereas the content and scope of immunities and privileges are virtually identical for all states, those for international organizations differ according to the intention of the founding states, as evidenced by the organizations' constitutive documents.

The international criminal tribunals which have been created to operate independently in the international sphere — the ICTY, the ICTR, the ICC, and the Special Court for Sierra Leone — have all been endowed with certain privileges and immunities.

1.5.1 Applicable law

In order to determine the scope and content of privileges and immunities of international criminal tribunals, a rudimentary distinction should be made between different states: the host state, states parties to the constitutive treaty, and states that are not parties to that instrument.

The privileges and immunities of international criminal tribunals in the host state are governed by specific headquarters agreements. The Netherlands has concluded such an agreement with the United Nations in respect of the ICTY and the part of the ICTR functioning in The Hague.[117] A similar agreement with the ICC is still to be finalized.[118] Tanzania has concluded a headquarters agreement with the United Nations in respect of the ICTR.[119] The SCSL has concluded a headquarters agreement with

---

[115] See Advisory Opinions of the ICJ on the privileges and immunities of UN personnel: *Reparation for Injuries suffered in the Service of the United Nations*, Advisory Opinion, *ICJ Reports* 1949, and, *Difference Relating to Immunity from Legal Process of a Special Rapporteur of the Commission on Human Rights*, Advisory Opinion, 29 April 1999, *ICJ Reports* 1999.

[116] J. Klabbers, *Introduction to International Institutional Law*, at 147–53. In respect of the rationale of 'functional necessity' it is important to bear in mind that international organizations have no territory over which they exercise sovereign rights. As a result, their personnel are always operating on a state's territory, necessitating a high level of protection.

[117] Agreement between the United Nations and The Kingdom of the Netherlands Concerning the Headquarters of the International Tribunal for the Prosecution of Persons Responsible for Serious Violations of International Humanitarian Law Committed in the Territory of the Former Yugoslavia Since 1991, signed at New York on 29 July 1994, S/1994/848, 1792 *UNTS* 351, Corr. 20 July 2001, 2163 *UNTS* 255.

[118] Until the conclusion of its headquarters agreement, relations between the ICC and the host state are governed, *mutatis mutandis*, by the headquarters agreement with the ICTY.

[119] Agreement between the United Nations and the United Republic of Tanzania concerning the headquarters of the International Criminal Tribunal for Rwanda, signed at New York on 31 August 1995, A/51/399-S/1996/778, appendix, 1887 *UNTS* 63.

Sierra Leone.[120] The purpose of those agreements is to 'regulate matters relating to or arising out of the establishment and the proper functioning of the Tribunal' in the host state.[121] Privileges and immunities are only part of the agreement.

UN member states (with respect to the ICTY and ICTR) and states parties to the ICC Treaty (in relation to the ICC) are bound by the provisions in the institutions' statutes concerning privileges and immunities. Article 30 of the ICTY Statute and Article 29 of the ICTR Statute do not contain the substance of privileges and immunities, but declare that the Convention on the Privileges and Immunities of the United Nations of 13 February 1946 applies to the tribunals' personnel, while international law applies to diplomatic envoys.[122] Article 48 of the ICC Statute makes a similar reference, but here to immunities and privileges attributed under international law to heads of diplomatic missions and to the Agreement on the Privileges and Immunities of the Court.[123]

The position of non-party states is especially relevant for the ICC and the SCSL. Respect for the ICTY and ICTR immunities is ensured by practically universal adherence to the UN.[124] The ICC cannot (yet) count on a similar degree of adherence. Therefore, non-party states may choose not to respect any claim of immunities and privileges of the Court, unless they have ratified the special agreement on privileges and immunities of the Court.[125] In the case of the SCSL, the position of non-party states, that is, every state except Sierra Leone, is less complicated. The privileges and immunities, as accorded by the headquarters agreement, have intended effect only for Sierra Leone. However, the Agreement establishing the Court also contains provisions on privileges and immunities.[126] This binds both parties, Sierra Leone and the United Nations. In respect of the latter, it may be argued that the United Nations as a legal person has to respect these obligations, and member states have to assist the organization in that endeavour.

---

[120] Headquarters Agreement between the Republic of Sierra Leone and the Special Court for Sierra Leone, 21 October 2003. The issue of privileges and immunities of the SCSL in other countries emerged in connection with the trial of Charles Taylor in The Hague. A special memorandum of understanding was concluded between the ICC and the SCSL, regulating administrative arrangements (Doc. ICC/Pres-03-01-06). UN Security Council resolution 1688 (2006), endorsing the transfer of the trial to the Netherlands, is the basis for subsequent arrangements between the Netherlands and the SCSL.

[121] Article II of the headquarters agreements between the UN, on the one side, and the Netherlands and Tanzania, on the other.

[122] Given the status of the ICTY and the ICTR as subsidiary UN organs, their privileges and immunities are effective in the territory of any UN member state that has ratified the Convention on the Privileges and Immunities of the United Nations (1 *UNTS* 15, 13 February 1946). These tribunals' privileges and immunities are thus of considerably wider territorial scope than those under other arrangements, such as those of the SCSL (bilateral) and the ICC's APIC (multilateral).

[123] Agreement on the Privileges and Immunities of the Court, 9 September 2002, ICC-ASP/1/3, entered into force 22 July 2004.

[124] Even in respect to non-members of the UN a claim of privileges and immunities may be sustained on the basis of the ICJ's Advisory Opinion in *Reparation for Injuries*.

[125] Such a possibility is allowed for by Article 34 of the ICC APIC.

[126] See Articles 8, 9, and 12–15 of the UN/Sierra Leone Agreement.

1.5.2 Content and scope

In order to determine the content of accorded privileges and immunities, a distinction should be made between (1) the tribunal or court as a legal person; (2) assets, property, and premises of the tribunal or court; (3) persons employed by the tribunal or court; and (4) persons whose presence at, or participation in, the criminal proceedings is indispensable for the effective functioning of the tribunal or court concerned.

What matters most for the effective functioning of international criminal tribunals are points (3) and (4). For example, it is a fundamental requirements that a prosecutor's investigator must be free to conduct on-site investigations without the risk of being arrested by national authorities.[127] Generally, the staff of international criminal tribunals are entitled to a level of immunity protection sufficient to enable them to exercise their functions effectively, although in the case of the ICC immunities are granted only by states parties to the APIC. However, defence counsel or defence investigators do not have similar protection. As far as the ad hoc tribunals are concerned, defence counsel only enjoy immunities in the respective host states.[128] In other states, the defence are at the mercy of national authorities. This has led them in at least two cases — *Tadić* and *Musema* — to apply for safe conduct letters, which were issued by the then ICTY president and the ICTR registrar.[129] This unfortunate situation, of insufficient protection for the defence and inequality between defence and prosecutor, was rectified for the ICC. Article 48(4) of the ICC Statute provides that counsel shall be accorded 'such treatment as is necessary for the proper functioning of the Court, in accordance with the agreement on the privileges and immunities of the Court'. Article 16 of the APIC gives effect to this intention; under this provision, any 'privileged treatment' of defence counsel depends on their appointment being in accordance with the ICC Statute. As a result, counsel or assistants who have not been so appointed but who nevertheless conduct on-site investigations for the defence do not enjoy any 'privileged treatment' under the ICC legal framework.

The scope of immunity for counsel raises interesting questions in respect of conflicting professional and ethical standards. At present, it is the practice at the ICTY, the ICTR, and the SCSL that counsel may be called on to represent clients against their wishes.[130] While not in conflict with the rules prevailing in the context of

---

[127] For more detail on the scope of immunities in respect of on-site investigations, see G. Sluiter, *International Criminal Adjudication and the Collection of Evidence: Obligations of States* (Antwerp: Intersentia, 2002), at 334–7.

[128] Cf. Article XIX of the headquarters agreements concluded with Tanzania and the Netherlands:

   1. The counsel of a suspect or an accused who has been admitted as such by the Tribunal shall not be subjected by the host country to any measure which may affect the free and independent exercise of his or her functions under the Statute.
   2. In particular, the counsel shall, when holding a certificate that he or she has been admitted as a counsel by the Tribunal, be accorded:
      ... immunity from criminal and civil jurisdiction in respect of words spoken or written and acts performed by them in their official capacity as counsel. Such immunity shall continue to be accorded to them after termination of their functions as a counsel of a suspect or accused.

[129] See S. Kay and B. Swart, 'The Role of the Defence' in Cassese et al., *Rome Statute Commentary*, at 1401.

[130] For example, a client who wishes to conduct his own defence (such as Milošević, Šešelj (ICTY), and Norman (SCSL)), or an accused who does not want to be defended (Barayagwiza (ICTR) and Gbao (SCSL)). On the matter of self-representation, see Chapter 2, section 2.5 and Chapter 8, section 8.5.7.

these proceedings, given that trial chambers have actually prohibited counsel from withdrawing,[131] it could be asked whether representing an unwilling client might violate domestic codes of ethics.[132] The preliminary question is, however, one of immunity. From a functional perspective it appears undesirable that national law may influence the conduct of defence counsel before international criminal tribunals. Yet, Article XIX(3) of the ICTY and ICTR headquarters agreements explicitly mentions that the attribution of immunities to counsel pursuant to Article XIX shall be without prejudice to such disciplinary rules as may be applicable to the counsel. This has resulted in three disciplinary proceedings of Dutch counsel in the Netherlands where their performance was substantially reviewed by the Disciplinary Board.[133] This is not a situation conducive to an effective defence, and furthermore is unnecessary as one need no longer fall back on domestic disciplinary proceedings if they are available at the international level.

The law of immunities of the ICC may reassure counsel performing before them. Article 18 of the APIC does not make a reservation for domestic disciplinary proceedings in respect of immunities attributed to defence counsel. As a result, domestic disciplinary proceedings of the aforementioned kind appear to violate Article 18(1)(b) APIC:

Immunity from legal process of every kind in respect of words spoken or written and all acts performed by him or her in official capacity, which immunity shall continue to be accorded even after he or she has ceased to exercise his or her functions.

I.6 RELATIONSHIP TO OTHER SUBJECTS OF INTERNATIONAL LAW

In order to gain a better understanding of the position of international criminal tribunals in the international legal order, we must explore their relationship to other subjects of international law. Here, only general introductory remarks will be made. The relationship with states will be explored in more detail in Chapter 12.

1.6.1 States

From the perspective of the operation of international criminal tribunals there are four important dimensions to the relationship with states.

---

[131] Cf. Decision on Defence Counsel Motion to Withdraw, *Prosecutor* v. *Baryagwiza*, Case No. ICTR-97-19-T, ICTR, T. Ch. I, 2 November 2000.

[132] See ibid., para. 19 on counsel's submission to the chamber that they are prevented from acting against their client's instruction according to the codes of ethics of Canada and the USA (State of Washington).

[133] For instance, see Disciplinary Court, 12 March 2004, no. 3884, dealing with a complaint by Milošević concerning the performance of M. Wladimiroff as amicus curiae. (See also Disciplinary Board 13 July 2005, no. R.2536/05.93, dealing with the performance of Van der Spoel as standby counsel in *Šešelj*; finally, mention must be made of Disciplinary Board 22 September 2003, no. 02-254A, concerning the position of another Dutch counsel in one of the ICTR cases. Remarkably, in this case the Board found in favour of the plaintiff and issued a warning to counsel.)

First, there is the delineation of state jurisdiction and the jurisdiction of international criminal tribunals and the consequences for the division of cases. The ICTY, the ICTR, the ICC, and the SCSL all function on the basis of concurrent jurisdiction, although priority in the exercise of this jurisdiction has been attributed to either the international court (ICTY, ICTR, and SCSL) or the national court (ICC).

The ICTY and ICTR statutes explicitly acknowledge concurrent jurisdiction with every national court over the crimes set out therein.[134] The SCSL Statute does so only in relation to the national courts of Sierra Leone.[135] This is not to say that other states cannot exercise jurisdiction over the crimes set out in the SCSL Statute, but rather that only in relation to Sierra Leonean courts can the Special Court claim primacy.

The ICC Statute assumes (universal) jurisdiction for every state over the crimes falling within the Court's jurisdiction. This follows from the principle of complementarity according to which the crimes set out in the Statute should preferably be tried at the national level.[136]

Positive jurisdiction conflicts are to be settled in accordance with the relevant provisions in the statutes. The statutes of the ICTY and ICTR provide for primacy over national courts.[137] At any stage of the national proceedings, the ICTY or the ICTR may intervene and order a national court to defer to its jurisdiction. The Rules of these Tribunals do not accord them carte blanche as to the exercise of their 'primacy right'.[138] But, the Prosecutor has considerable leeway in this respect and judicial review appears only marginal.[139]

The complementarity principle attributes to the ICC a subsidiary role in the prosecution of international crimes. A positive jurisdiction conflict is solved by declaring inadmissible a case that has been duly investigated and prosecuted at the national level.[140] The 'admissibility mechanism' is applicable to all national investigations and prosecutions, including those of non-party states.

The second dimension of the relationship with states concerns the mutual effect of judicial decisions. This especially relates to final judgments and the ensuing question of *ne bis in idem*.[141] In other words, may an international criminal tribunal prosecute and

---

[134] Article 8(1) of the ICTR Statute and Article 9(1) of the ICTY Statute.

[135] Article 8(1) of the SCSL Statute.

[136] For more details, see J. T. Holmes, 'The Principle of Complementarity', in Lee, *Making of the Rome Statute*, at 41–78.

[137] Article 8(2) of the ICTR Statute and Article 9(2) of the ICTY Statute.

[138] See the conditions set out in Rule 9 of the ICTY and ICTR Rules:
  (i) the act being investigated or which is the subject of those proceedings is characterized as an ordinary crime;
  (ii) there is a lack of impartiality or independence, or the investigations or proceedings are designed to shield the accused from international criminal responsibility, or the case is not diligently prosecuted; or
  (iii) what is in issue is closely related to, or otherwise involves, significant factual or legal questions which may have implications for investigations or prosecutions before the Tribunal.
  This Rule is also applicable to the SCSL.

[139] See the decision related to the exercise of the 'primacy right' in *Tadić*: Decision on the Defence Motion on the Principle of *Non-Bis-In-Idem*, *Prosecutor* v. *Tadić*, Case No. IT-94-1-T, ICTY, T. Ch., 14 November 1995.

[140] Article 17(1) of the ICC Statute.

[141] The effect of other decisions relates mainly to cooperation issues. Thus, a subpoena issued by the ICTY or the ICTR needs to be implemented by national courts. The cooperation relationship between states and

try an individual accused of the same facts for which he or she has been tried by a national court, and vice versa?

The Statutes of the ICTY, the ICTR, the ICC, and the SCSL all contain provisions on *ne bis in idem*.[142] The content and scope of these provisions on the one hand are inspired by the protection of the rights of convicted persons,[143] but on the other hand take into account the problem of sham trials at the national level and the distinction between 'ordinary' crimes and international crimes. Thus, the international criminal tribunals must respect the outcome of 'serious' trials at the national level for war crimes, crimes against humanity, or genocide, but may nevertheless try an individual for the same facts if these facts have been charged as ordinary crimes, for example murder, and not as international crimes and when the case has not been 'diligently' prosecuted by the national authorities. Similarly, national courts must always respect the outcome of international trials and cannot try the acquitted or convicted individual for the same facts.[144]

The scope of application of the *ne bis in idem* provisions varies. In respect of the ICTY and the ICTR, reference is made simply to a national court, the implication being that every national court needs to respect final judgments from those tribunals. Whereas in the case of the ICTY and the ICTR this will not in practice raise questions about the position of non-party states, the same cannot be said for the ICC, which does not (yet) enjoy universal adherence. According to Article 20(2) of the ICC Statute, no person may be tried by *another court* for a crime for which that person has already been convicted or acquitted by the ICC. To the extent that it is envisaged that obligations follow from this provision for courts of non-party states, the latter could argue that treaties may not impose obligations on non-party states.[145]

The SCSL Statute is far more modest in its aspirations: only the national courts of Sierra Leone are under a duty to respect the final judgments of the Special Court.[146]

---

international criminal tribunals will be addressed later on in this section and in more detail in Chapter 12, section 12.3. It is beyond the scope of this book to deal in detail with other types of decisions and their effect in the 'other', either national or international, legal order. E.g., decisions related to property rights. From Article 109(1) of the ICC Statute it follows that state parties, in the enforcement of fines and forfeiture orders imposed by the Court, have to respect the rights of bona fide third parties. It may therefore be assumed that the ICC follows national court decisions determining those rights.

[142] Article 9 of the ICTR Statute, Article 10 of the ICTY Statute, Article 20 of the ICC Statute, and Article 9 of the SCSL Statute.

[143] Article 14(7) of the ICCPR; Article 4 of Protocol 7 to the ECHR.

[144] For a commentary, see I. Tallgren, 'Article 20', in Triffterer, *Commentary on the Rome Statute*, at 419–34. What is permissible, for example, is that, after an acquittal for crimes against humanity because of lack of wide-spread or systematic attack, the individual concerned can be convicted for murder at the national level. In this case we are then not dealing with the same conduct.

[145] This is a general rule of international law embodied in Article 34 of the Vienna Convention on the Law of Treaties, also known as *pacta tertiis nec nocent nec prosunt*. Whether or not this rule is violated by reading an obligation in Article 20(2) of the ICC Statute as applicable before any national court depends on whether this provision merely codifies an existing obligation of all states under customary international law to refrain from retrying a person previously convicted or acquitted for the same conduct by another court, or whether it imposes a new obligation. The latter is in our view the case, since a rule of *ne bis in idem* with a transjurisdictional scope of application is not (yet) part of customary international law.　　　[146] Article 9(1) of the SCSL Statute.

Although the courts of other states may not be barred under international law from a new trial for the same facts, it is unlikely that any other state will be interested in it, and if it is, it should be persuaded not to conduct that trial.

The first interlocutory decision in the *Tadić* case dealt with the scope of application of *ne bis in idem* protection.[147] It is confined to the situation where an individual has been tried, in the sense of the trial being finalized.[148] Thus, unlike in certain national jurisdictions, 'jeopardy' is not considered to attach in an earlier part of the proceedings.

The third dimension concerns cooperation between states and international criminal tribunals. Given the importance of this matter for the effective functioning of any international criminal tribunal, the matter will be dealt with separately in Chapter 12. It suffices to say in this chapter that there are far-reaching duties for states to provide the international criminal tribunals with various forms of assistance.[149]

The fourth and final dimension relates to the position of member states in the operation of international criminal tribunals. In addition to legal assistance, member states are also expected to support international criminal tribunals in a broader sense, by contributing to the budget, electing judges and prosecutors, submitting candidates for elections, and so on. Such broader participation in the functioning of the tribunals may not be very spectacular from a legal perspective, but its importance for their operation is unquestionable.

For the ICTY and the ICTR, existing UN structures, namely the General Assembly and the Security Council, are used to establish the budget and to elect the judges and prosecutors.[150] The ICC lacks any such pre-existing 'administrative framework'. For this reason not only a court system was set up, but also an Assembly of States Parties. The latter body supervises the effective operation of the Court in various ways. It is a platform not only to vote on the budget, elect judges, prosecutor, and registrar, but also to enforce the duty to cooperate and to adopt and amend the applicable law.[151]

The SCSL is closer to the UN structure, being established by a multilateral treaty to which the UN is a party. However, UN members have no direct role in the functioning of the Court. For example, the 'international' judges are appointed by the UN Secretary-General and not elected. The expenses of the Special Court are met from voluntary contributions by the international community and are not part of the UN budget.[152]

---

[147] Decision on the Defence Motion on the Principle of *Non-Bis-In-Idem*, *Prosecutor* v. *Tadić*, Case No. IT-94-1-T, ICTY, T. Ch. II, 14 November 1995.   [148] Ibid., para. 10.

[149] By 'states concerned' we refer to UN members (in the case of the ICTY and the ICTR), state parties to the ICC Treaty, and Sierra Leone, the only state party to the treaty establishing the SCSL.

[150] As of 15 September 2003, the ICTY and ICTR have a separate prosecutor.

[151] Respectively, Articles 112, 51, and 87(7) of the ICC Statute.

[152] See Article 6 of the UN/Sierra Leone Agreement. Also of interest for the management of the Court is Article 7 of this agreement: 'It is the understanding of the Parties that interested States will establish a management committee to assist the Secretary-General in obtaining adequate funding, and provide advice and policy direction on all non-judicial aspects of the operation of the Court, including questions of efficiency, and to perform other functions as agreed by interested States. The management committee shall consist of important contributors to the Special Court. The Government of Sierra Leone and the Secretary-General will also participate in the management committee.'

1.6.2 United Nations and other international organizations

The relationship between international criminal tribunals and other international organizations is of interest from two perspectives. First, there is the question of the extent to which the support and assistance of other international organizations is required for the tribunals to function effectively. Secondly, it is a matter for discussion whether the mandates of international criminal tribunals overlap with those of other international organizations and, if so, how they should be harmonized in order to avoid conflict.

As to the first question, the starting point of all statutes of international criminal tribunals is a cooperation relationship with states. The cooperation provisions of the ICTR and ICTY statutes do not mention any other subjects of international law besides states. In its jurisprudence the ICTY has, however, extended the duty to cooperate to international organizations or, more specifically, to certain of their organs. While in *Kovačević* the ICTY Trial Chamber held that the ICTY could not solicit the cooperation of an international organization, in this case the OSCE,[153] in *Simić* and in *Kordić* cooperation orders were issued to the European Community Monitoring Mission (ECMM) and SFOR directly.[154] The underlying argument for this direct order was that those organizations were composed of UN members which have a duty, both individually and collectively, to cooperate with the ad hoc tribunals.

Whether the ICC will adopt a similar approach in respect of the cooperation relationship with international organizations remains to be seen. Unlike the ad hoc tribunals, there is no universal adherence to the ICC and it does not benefit from the legal framework prevailing over any other international obligations which is characteristic of the UN position by virtue of Article 103 of the UN Charter. As a result, the ICC Statute provides for the solicitation of cooperation from international organizations as agreed upon by them and in accordance with their competences and mandates.[155]

The Sierra Leone Court focuses exclusively on the cooperation relationship with Sierra Leone and there is therefore no mention of a cooperation relationship with international organizations in either the Statute or the UN/Sierra Leone Agreement. Yet the Court possesses legal personality, including a treaty-making capacity that may be used to enter into ad hoc cooperation agreements with any subject of international law.[156]

The issue of overlapping and possible conflicting mandates arises especially in relation to the ICC and the United Nations Security Council. Since the ad hoc tribunals were established by the UN Security Council directly and since the Special Court for Sierra Leone was set up at the instigation of, and supported by, the Council, the delimitation of competence is governed essentially by the law of the Charter and is unlikely to

[153] Decision refusing Defence Motion for Subpoena, *Prosecutor* v. *Kovačević*, Case No. IT-97-24-PT, ICTY, T. Ch. II, 23 June 1998.

[154] Order for the Production of Documents by the European Community Monitoring Mission and its Member States, *Prosecutor* v. *Kordić and Čerkez*, Case No. IT-95-14/2-T, ICTY, T. Ch. III, 4 August 2000 and Decision on Motion for Judicial Assistance to be Provided by SFOR and Others, *Prosecutor* v. *Simić et al.*, Case No. IT-95-9-T, ICTY, T. Ch. III, 18 October 2000.   [155] Article 87(6) of the ICC Statute.

[156] Article 10 of the UN/Sierra Leone Agreement.

become problematic in practice.[157] The ICC is a truly separate international organization and its mandate may touch upon the mandate of the UN Security Council in two ways. First, there may be a positive overlap, in that in the interests of peace and security the Security Council favours prosecution of a case, while at the same time the situation falls within the mandate of the ICC.[158] In such a scenario, Article 13(b) of the ICC Statute permits the Security Council to submit a 'situation' to the Court, thereby offering it the Court as an instrument in the maintenance of international peace and security.[159] Secondly, in a conflict between the mandates of the ICC and the Council, prosecution by the ICC could in certain circumstances constitute a threat to international peace and security.[160] Therefore, there is in Article 16 of the Statute a limitation on the Court's powers to continue with a prosecution that may be effected by the Council. Such a conflict of mandates is unlikely to occur in practice, as maintenance of international peace and security is one of the objectives of international criminal justice. Yet, even before the Court became truly operational, three resolutions had been adopted by the Council requesting the Court not to commence investigations or prosecutions in respect of UN peacekeeping forces possessing the nationality of non-party states, or having that effect.[161] The legal aspects of those resolutions raise a number of questions that go beyond the scope of this book.[162] It suffices to say that the resolutions may indicate of a troublesome relationship between the UN and the ICC, in spite of the existence of a bilateral agreement between them.[163]

1.6.3 Other international courts

The proliferation of international criminal tribunals raises the question of whether this can be seen as a positive development.[164] Since there is no central and compulsory judicial branch in the international legal order, multiple international judicial

---

[157] Note the respect for the delimitation of competence by the ICTY in *Blaškić*, leaving enforcement of ICTY decisions to the Council.

[158] Berman refers to this as the positive pillar of the ICC/UNSC relationship: F. Berman, 'The Relationship between the International Criminal Court and the Security Council', in H. A. M. von Hebel et al. (eds), *Reflections on the International Criminal Court — Essays in honour of Adriaan Bos*, at 174.

[159] For the first use of this possibility, see Resolution 1593 (2005) referring the situation in Darfur (Sudan) to the Court.

[160] Berman denotes it as the negative pillar of the ICC/UNSC relationship: ibid., at 176.

[161] SC Resolutions 1422 (2002), 1487 (2003), and operative paragraph 7 of 1497 (2003). It should also be noted that Resolution 1593 (2005) referring the situation of Darfur to the Court decides that there is exclusive jurisdictions for states sending troops which are not parties to the ICC. As a result, it has the same effect as operative paragraph 7 of Resolution 1497 and intends to make use of the possibility offered by Article 16 of the ICC Statute.

[162] For a critical commentary, see S. Zappalà, 'The Reaction of the US to the Entry into Force of the ICC Statute: Comments on UN SC Resolution 1422 (2002) and Article 98 Agreements' (2003) 1 *JICJ*, at 114–34.

[163] Article 2 of the ICC Statute. The central provision in that agreement (Negotiated Relationship Agreement between the International Criminal Court and the United Nations) is Article 2(3), according to which the UN and the Court respect each other's status and mandate.

[164] See T. Buergenthal, 'The Proliferation of International Courts and Tribunals: Is It Good or Bad?' (2001) 14 *LJIL*, at 267–75; J. Charney, 'The Impact on the International Legal System of the Growth of International Courts and Tribunals' (1999) 31 (4) *New York University J. of International Law and Politics*, at 697–708.

institutions carry the risk of inconsistent and even contradictory rulings on important questions of law.

The international criminal tribunals are not in any formal relationship with other international courts. This is self-evident for the ICC and the SCSL, which are separate and independent international judicial bodies. However, the ad hoc tribunals are subsidiary organs of the Security Council, which raises the question of whether they are subordinate to the ICJ, the principal judicial organ of the United Nations. In *Kvočka* the ICTY was confronted with a request from the defendant to await an important and relevant ruling of the ICJ regarding the application of the Genocide Convention before proceeding with the trial.[165] In its decision the Appeals Chamber underlined the Tribunal's own mandate and denied a hierarchical relationship with the ICJ.[166] It was said that although the Appeals Chamber will take into consideration other decisions of international courts, it may, after careful consideration, come to a different conclusion. An example of this is the rejection by the Appeals Chamber in *Tadić* of the 'effective control' test set by the ICJ in the *Nicaragua* case and employed by the Trial Chamber with a view to determining the internal or international character of a conflict.[167]

The above cases should, however, not create the impression of a jurisprudence that regularly ignores or contradicts the findings of other international courts. A review of the jurisprudence of the ICTY and the ICTR clearly reveals the analysis of, and respect for, decisions of other international courts, especially human rights courts.[168]

I.7 CONCLUSION

While essentially being examined from a criminal law perspective, the growing numbers of international(ized) criminal tribunals offer an interesting contribution to the international institutional landscape. On the one hand, they must be distinguished from traditional international organizations with states as members that are capable of influencing their functioning in the framework of established (political) procedures. On the other hand, the fact that international criminal tribunals and courts are international organizations has multifaceted consequences for their operation and distinguishes them from national criminal courts.

---

[165] Decision on the Defence 'Motion Regarding Concurrent Procedures before International Criminal Tribunal for the former Yugoslavia and International Court of Justice on the Same Questions', *Prosecutor* v. *Kvočka et al.*, Case No. IT-98-30/1, ICTY, T. Ch. I, 5 December 2000 and Decision on Interlocutory Appeal by the Accused Zoran Zigic against the Decision of Trial Chamber I Dated 5 December 2000, *Prosecutor* v. *Kvočka et al.*, Case No. IT-98-30/1, ICTY, A. Ch., 25 May 2001.

[166] It did so by quoting *Delalić* appeal judgment, para. 24. See Decision on Interlocutory Appeal by the Accused Zoran Zigic against the Decision of Trial Chamber I Dated 5 December 2000, *Prosecutor* v. *Kvočka et al.*, para. 16.

[167] *Tadić* appeal judgment, para. 115 *et seq.* See also critical commentary by T. Gill in Klip and Sluiter, *Annotated Leading Cases, vol. III*, at 868–75.

[168] For details, see G. Sluiter, 'International Criminal Proceedings and the Protection of Human Rights' (2003) 37 *New England Law Review*, at 935–48.

There are important aspects of their entry into the family of international institutions. First, the unique international character of ad hoc tribunals triggered challenges to their legality. While these institutions have generally upheld their own legality, what is far more important is that the community of states has generally endorsed their creation and has welcomed them as new faces in the international legal order. Secondly, the consequences of the legal personality of these tribunals have not always been fully grasped. Judges initially had difficulties in the coherent application of general international law. There is not yet a consistent doctrine elaborated on this point. Thus the judges had to resort to so-called inherent and implied powers. Although extensive use was made of these concepts, it is necessary to ask to what extent they fit within the principle of legality, which is a major element of criminal law. The ensuing judicial restraint has not done the tribunals much harm and has met with increased understanding on the part of the international community. Thirdly, the advent of international criminal tribunals raises issues of coordination of these new institutions with existing subjects of international law — primarily states, but also other international organizations and courts. What matters is a healthy balance between activism and restraint, and this has generally been satisfactorily achieved. However, a sensitive issue is the relationship of the international(ized) courts and tribunals with the Security Council. While the latter is obviously supportive of the ICTY, the ICTR, and the SCSL, it maintains a rather schizophrenic relationship with the ICC. The Council is willing to use the ICC for its own purposes, and has now done so in respect of the situation in Darfur. At the same time it is still guided by its political agenda, and this may even force it to prevent the ICC from exercising jurisdiction over certain situations or certain categories of persons, or to impose other measures that are incompatible with the objectives and interests of international criminal justice.

2

PARTICIPANTS IN INTERNATIONAL CRIMINAL PROCEEDINGS

SUMMARY

2.1 INTRODUCTION

Understanding the nature and content of the international criminal process requires an introduction to the participants in the respective proceedings. This chapter explores the positions and roles of the main actors in international criminal procedure. The institutional position of those actors falls outside the scope of this book, although it may not always be separated from their procedural function. This book does not deal with matters such as the election and selection of judges, prosecutorial staff, and defence counsel and in Chapter 1 we have already looked at the immunities accruing to the personnel of international criminal tribunals as an element of their legal personality.

In order fully to grasp the role and position of participants in international criminal proceedings, we need to understand the organization of those proceedings, and this chapter begins by looking at this issue. Indeed, the contours of international criminal procedure, inspired essentially by the common-law model, are the basis of more detailed rules concerning, for example, the rights and duties of defence counsel. After this preliminary section, the present chapter moves on to the various participants and, as elsewhere, will not merely be descriptive but will illustrate and analyse problems through critical assessment of case law. The role and position of each participant in international criminal proceedings will be assessed in relation to those of the other participants.

2.2 ORGANIZATION OF INTERNATIONAL CRIMINAL PROCEEDINGS

It was noted earlier that the current international criminal tribunals had little precedent at their disposal to shape their criminal proceedings.[1] On the one hand, this may seem a handicap, especially in situations of uncertainty as to the applicable law. On the other hand, the absence of the burden of a legacy enabled the elaboration of a system of international criminal procedure from scratch, corresponding to the specific needs, objectives, and nature of international criminal trials. In other words, an excellent opportunity presented itself to produce a well-thought-through and coherent corpus of procedural rules. One cannot but conclude — after more than ten years of recent international criminal procedural practice — that the opportunity has not been seized. On the contrary, the organization of international criminal proceedings and procedural practice can be characterized as arbitrary and opportunistic. It will be demonstrated that the functioning of the international criminal procedural edifice has been essentially coloured by an almost ideological struggle between common-law and civil-law systems and states. The former clearly prevailed. International procedural practice illustrates shifting interests and approaches. The many changes to the ICTY and ICTR Rules testify to this, as do their conflicting jurisprudence, underlining the common-law or mixed, unique character of the ad hoc tribunals' proceedings, depending on the specific needs of a particular case.

Let us start with the drafting of international criminal procedure via the statutes and rules, before concentrating on its application in practice.

---

[1] The ICTY Trial Chamber in *Tadić* mentioned this for the first time when confronted with the question whether witnesses should be allowed to testify anonymously (*Tadić* protective measures decision, para. 20). It referred to the international military tribunals of Nuremberg and Tokyo as having only rudimentary rules of procedure (Nuremberg rules consisting of 11 rules and covering barely three and a half pages). It has been submitted that the rules of procedure of the Nuremberg and Tokyo tribunals were devised by US lawyers and based on US law; furthermore, the intentionally amorphous nature of those rules left room for unfairness. For those views and for a comprehensive analysis of the procedural rules of the Nuremberg and Tokyo tribunals, see E. J. Wallach, 'The Procedural and Evidentiary Rules of the Post-World War II War Crimes Trials: Did They Provide An Outline For International Legal Procedure?' (1999) 37 *Columbia J. of Transnational Law*, at 851–83.

It is difficult to assess the precedential value of the Nuremberg and Tokyo tribunals' procedure. In 1948 Telford Taylor submitted the following view:

A particularly fruitful field for research and publication is that of legal procedure. Almost all the war crimes trials have presented procedural questions to which different answers might be given depending upon what system of law the court chose to follow. The evidentiary weight to be given hearsay evidence of affidavits is a common example of this type of problem. Furthermore, the unsettled state of the world and the unusual nature of the trials precipitated many novel procedural matters which the tribunals had to determine without much in the way of past practice to guide them. Based upon the records of the Nurnberg trials alone a most useful study could be made, but a full treatment would require examination of the records of many other trials in order to make a comparative study. From such a study, the outlines of international legal procedure should emerge.[2]

Although such an outline did not emerge out of Nuremberg and Tokyo, the current international criminal justice systems are ambivalent towards the post-Second World War procedures. On the one hand, the precedential value of Nuremberg and Tokyo is dismissed for a number of reasons, the most prominent being the lack of guidance in both qualitative terms (no coherent procedure presented by those trials) and quantitative terms (an extremely limited set of rules),[3] and the limited due process character of that procedure, especially in light of present-day standards.[4] On the other hand, when they fitted a certain approach or interpretation, the Nuremberg procedural law and practice were cited as an important precedent. This was done to support the choice of a flexible law of evidence, without, however, any thorough inquiry being made as to the quality of the Nuremberg law on that point.[5]

A sense of urgency prevailed in the establishment of the criminal procedure of the ICTY, since it had been set up by the Security Council to restore international peace and security. The tribunal became a flexible institution especially in terms of the organization of its criminal proceedings. The preference for a common-law-oriented criminal procedure was envisioned, albeit only in outline, in the Statute, because most of the team who drafted the Secretary-General's report and the Statute had a common-law background.[6] The regulation of the details and elements of criminal procedure not addressed in the Statute was delegated to the ICTY's judges via Article 15 of the Statute. It is generally acknowledged that the judges relied heavily on proposals from the

---

[2] T. Taylor, 'An Outline of the Research and Publication Possibilities of the War Crimes Trials' (1949) 9 *Louisiana Law Review*, at 501.

[3] The latter sense, applies to the critical approach of the Trial Chamber in *Tadić* towards the Nuremberg Tribunal's criminal procedure; see *Tadić* protective measures decision, para. 20.

[4] For examples, see E. J. Wallach, 'The Procedural and Evidentiary Rules of the Post-World War II War Crimes Trials: Did They Provide An Outline For International Legal Procedure?' (1999) 37 *Columbia J. of Transnational Law*, at 851–83. It should also be noted that the Tokyo Tribunal provided fewer due process guarantees than the Nuremberg Tribunal. The reason for this difference was cynically, but unfortunately probably correctly, explained by Taylor: 'apparently, in old-line military circles yellow generals did not rank as high in the scale of virtue as Nordic White ones' (T. Taylor, *The Anatomy of the Nuremberg Trials* (New York: Knopf, 1992), at 241).

[5] For more details on the emergence and nature of the contemporary law of evidence in international criminal proceedings, see Chapter 10, section 10.2.   [6] Bassiouni and Manikas, *Law of the ICTY*, at 863.

US government when drafting the rules and thus when organizing the ICTY's criminal procedure.[7]

What has this brought in terms of criminal proceedings and the role and position of its participants? A plethora of scholarly writing has been produced seeking to analyse and characterize international criminal proceedings on the basis of the common law/civil law dichotomy.[8] It comes as no surprise that there are as many views as writings on the nature of ICTY and other international criminal proceedings. However, there are two methodological problems. First, it has been correctly pointed out that characterizing a certain procedure as 'common law' or 'civil law' is frequently based on generalizations and — in many cases — on a misunderstanding of the true nature of (certain) domestic criminal justice systems.[9] It is undoubtedly quite difficult to describe the common-law or civil-law system precisely. Secondly, a survey of the literature shows that the characterization of international criminal proceedings in terms of the common law/civil law dichotomy seems to be rather arbitrary and to depend on the commentator's perception of what the vital elements of the procedure are.

For the purpose of this book we must nevertheless adopt a working definition, however simplified and generalized that may be, of the essential features of common-law and civil-law criminal proceedings, which play such a prominent role in the creation of international criminal procedure. What matters most in criminal procedure is the fact-finding process. As a result of significant political and societal differences between continental Europe and the Anglo-Saxon world, one may distinguish between the fact-finding process as one of dispute resolution and as an official investigation.[10] Both 'dispute resolution' and 'official investigation' approaches claim to yield effective and fair

---

[7] Ibid. and D. D. Ntanda Nsereko, 'Rules of Procedure and Evidence of the International Tribunal for the Former Yugoslavia' (1994) 5 *CLF*, at 508. See also Morris and Scharf: 'Of the several States and organizations that submitted comments and draft provisions for the Rules, the United States submitted by far the most comprehensive set of proposed rules with commentary, numbering approximately seventy-five pages. This proposal was particularly influential because of its detailed coverage of procedural and evidentiary issues, the explanation of the reasons for the proposals contained in the commentary and the timeliness of the submission.' Morris and Scharf, *An Insider's Guide*, at 177.

[8] Just some examples: G. A. McClelland, 'A Non-Adversary Approach to International Criminal Tribunals' (2002) 26 *Suffolk Transnational Law Review*, at 1–38; T. M. Clark, 'Transplant Justice?: The Efficacy of a Purely Common Law Concept in the International Criminal Law Forum' (2003) 9 *Buffalo Human Rights Law Review*, at 75–110; K. Ambos, 'International criminal procedure: "adversarial", "inquisitorial" or mixed?' (2003) 3 *ICLR*, at 1–37; G. Champy, 'Inquisitoire — Accusatoire devant les Juridictions Pénales Internationales' (1997) 68 *International Review of Penal Law*, at 149–93.

[9] See in this respect an article by Kai Ambos pointing out a number of misunderstandings in the common-law/civil-law discussion: K. Ambos, 'International criminal procedure: "adversarial", "inquisitorial" or mixed?', at 2–7.

[10] Mirjan Damaška distinguishes between the conflict-solving type and the policy-implementing type of proceedings. In his authoritative work, *The Faces of Justice and State Authority — A Comparative Approach to the Legal Process* (New Haven: Yale University Press, 1986), he offers a fascinating analysis of the rationales underlying the differences between common-law and civil-law criminal proceedings. The major issue — outside the scope of this book — is whether his theoretical framework can be transplanted into the international criminal justice system. The essential problem is that international criminal justice lacks a societal context which is normally the basis for the organization of criminal proceedings. As a result, while one may discern elements of both common law or civil law in international criminal proceedings, they operate in isolation, in the sense that there is no theoretical framework based on the underlying societal and political considerations and compelling a choice of either system. See M. R. Damaška, *The Faces of Justice and State Authority — A Comparative Approach to the Legal Process*.

fact-finding results.[11] Dispute resolution as a starting point in an adversarial criminal procedure results in the process being dominated by the parties to the dispute, who determine its scope and have the exclusive task of gathering evidence and presenting their case at trial; the judge is passive and does not engage in evidence gathering; the emphasis is on the trial phase, where the evidence is presented by each of the parties and challenged by the opposing side.[12] While jury trials do not fit into the dispute resolution/official investigation dichotomy and occur in civil-law systems as well as common-law ones, the fact is that jury trials are a vital element and a right of the accused in all adversarial systems.[13] Thus the oral nature of trials in these systems and the technical rules of evidence can partially be explained by the need to shield lay adjudicators from irrelevant or unreliable evidence.

The civil-law systems take the official investigation as a starting point in their criminal law and practice. Aspirations for 'objective' fact-finding call for a system where all parties are expected to cooperate impartially in this endeavour. This results in the accused being an object of investigation; the emphasis lies in the pre-trial phase where a dossier, a case file accessible to all parties, is prepared; all authorities, including pre-trial and trial judges, are very active in the ongoing process of discovering the truth; the public hearing is not a contest between parties, but a verification and examination of the contents of the dossier. Also at trial, the judge plays an active role in the fact-finding process; the judges' role as professional adjudicators and the primary aspiration of 'objective' fact-finding result in trials where oral evidence is not a vital element and where no strict evidentiary rules apply.[14]

In both systems the question arises as to the existence of safeguards ensuring the quality of the fact-finding process. In the adversarial system the starting point is that *du choc des opinions jaillit la lumière*; this adage, and as a result the position of the defendant, can only live up to expectations when there is equality of arms between the parties, and when abuse of power or process is strictly and severely sanctioned. In the inquisitorial

---

[11] However, this is not to say that the methods cannot be criticized. In respect of the adversarial dispute-solving approach, see Damaška: 'not all matters that end up in court are reducible to two contrary factual hypotheses. Often a lawsuit requires that the factual predicate be established for the application of a measure that advances the public interest. In this type of lawsuit, is it not better for the adjudicator to examine a wide range of factual scenarios, rather than focus solely on two contrary versions of events?' (M. R. Damaška, *Evidence Law Adrift* (New Haven: Yale University Press 1997), at 100. Regarding the official investigation approach, on the other hand, one may wonder whether the authorities truly extend their investigations to all relevant facts, both inculpatory and exculpatory. This undeniably requires a high degree of confidence in those authorities (cf. N. Jörg et al., 'Are Inquisitorial and Adversarial Systems Converging?', in P. Fennell (ed.), *Criminal Justice in Europe — A Comparative Study* (Oxford: Clarendon Press, 1995), at 43).

[12] For more detailed analyses of major elements of the adversarial procedure, see N. Jörg et al., 'Are Inquisitorial and Adversarial Systems Converging?', at 41–56; A. Orie, 'Accusatorial v. Inquisitorial Approach in International Criminal Proceedings prior to the Establishment of the ICC and in the Proceedings before the ICC', in Cassese et al., *Rome Statute Commentary*, at 1442–56; and M. Langer, 'The Rise of Managerial Judging in International Criminal Law' (2005) 53 *American J. of Comparative Law*, at 838–47.

[13] Cf. A. Orie, 'Accusatorial v. Inquisitorial Approach in International Criminal Proceedings prior to the Establishment of the ICC and in the Proceedings before the ICC', at 1453–4. On the difference between juries in common-law and civil-law systems, see M. R. Damaška, *The Faces of Justice and State Authority — A Comparative Approach to the Legal Process*, at 24–5.

[14] For a more detailed analysis of the main elements of the inquisitorial system, or the 'official investigation' fact-finding model, see the sources referred to in note 12 above.

system, the safeguards lie in confidence in the public authority leading the fact-finding process; the dossier, containing all relevant evidence and keeping track of investigative activities, should be adequate for verifying whether confidence in the authorities has been justified.[15]

Bearing in mind the above observations, general and simplified as they may be, we now turn to an analysis of the ICTY's own view on the organization of its criminal proceedings. The first annual report of the ICTY, following the adoption of the Rules, offered the following observations on the positioning of the ICTY procedure on the common-law/civil-law scale:

Based on the limited precedent of the Nürnberg and Tokyo Trials, the statute of the Tribunal has adopted a largely adversarial approach to its procedures, rather than the inquisitorial system prevailing in continental Europe and elsewhere. There is no investigating judge collecting the evidence. The initial task of inquiring into allegations of offences and obtaining the necessary evidence falls on the Prosecutor (rules 39–43). He is the one who submits indictments to a judge for confirmation and who argues the case before the Chamber (rules 47, 84 and 85). However, at the trial, the prosecution and the defence have been put on the same footing: after confirmation of the indictment, the defence is entitled to collect and to have access to all relevant evidence; and both the prosecution and the defence are reciprocally bound to disclose all documents and witnesses. Each party is entitled to cross-examine the witnesses presented by the other party. Thus the rights of the accused are fully safeguarded and the setting for a fair trial is created (rules 66–67). One can discern in the statute and the rules a conscious effort to avoid some of the often-mentioned flaws of Nürnberg and Tokyo.[16]

In the report three important differences from the common-law system are set out:

The first is that, as at Nürnberg and Tokyo, there are no technical rules for the admissibility of evidence. This Tribunal does not need to shackle itself to restrictive rules which have developed out of the ancient trial-by-jury system. There will be no jury sitting at the Tribunal, needing to be shielded from irrelevancies or given guidance as to the weight of the evidence they have heard. The judges will be solely responsible for weighing the probative value of the evidence before them. Consequently, all relevant evidence may be admitted to the Tribunal unless its probative value is substantially outweighed by the need to ensure a fair trial (rule 89) or where the evidence was obtained by a serious violation of human rights (rule 95).

Secondly, while normally, in the adversarial system, the court must be content with the evidence produced by the parties, the Tribunal may order the production of additional or new evidence proprio motu (rule 98). This will enable the Tribunal to ensure that it is fully satisfied with the evidence on which its final decisions are based. It was felt that, in the international sphere, the interests of justice are best served by such a provision and that the diminution, if any, of the parties' rights is minimal by comparison.

Thirdly, the granting of immunity and the practice of plea-bargaining find no place in the rules. It remains entirely a matter for the Prosecutor to determine against whom to proceed. Cooperation

---

[15] In both systems the safeguards may be inadequate. In adversarial systems situations of inequality can undermine the basic assumptions of the system. In inquisitorial systems not everything is necessarily documented in the dossier or critically supervised.

[16] Annual Report of the International Tribunal for the Prosecution of Persons Responsible for Serious Violations of International Humanitarian Law Committed in the Territory of the Former Yugoslavia since 1991, 29 August 1994, UN Doc. A/49/342-S/1994/1007 (1994), para. 71.

from an accused will also be taken into account by the Chambers as a mitigating factor in sentencing (rule 101), as well as by the President for the purpose of granting pardon or commutation of sentence (rule 125).[17]

We must conclude that the perceived vital differences from common-law systems have withered over time and are in practice not as important as when the first annual report was prepared. In fact, only the law of evidence of the ICTY reminds us of civil-law systems. Rule 98, allowing for a more active role for the judiciary in the fact-finding process, has rarely been used.[18] As to the practice of plea-bargaining, it has found an important place, especially in the practice of the ICTY, due to the recent significant increase in its case load and the presence of a compelling exit strategy.[19] Note that the ICTY Trial Chamber in *Tadić* stressed those three perceived differences, possibly with a view to ridding itself of certain shackles of common-law systems; the result was that certain witnesses could testify anonymously.[20]

With the benefit of hindsight, the general observations of Judge Cassese in a separate and dissenting opinion concerning the nature of the ICTY procedure are equally open to criticism:

international criminal procedure does not originate from a uniform body of law. It substantially results from an amalgamation of two different legal systems, that obtaining in common-law countries and the system prevailing in countries of civil-law (although for historical reasons, there currently exists at the international level a clear imbalance in favour of the common-law approach). It is therefore only natural that international criminal proceedings do not uphold the philosophy behind one of the two national criminal systems to the exclusion of the other; nor do they result from the juxtaposition of elements of the two systems. Rather, they combine and fuse, in a fairly felicitous manner, the adversarial or accusatorial system (chiefly adopted in common-law countries) with a number of significant features of the inquisitorial approach (mostly taken in States of continental Europe and in other countries of civil-law tradition). This combination or amalgamation is unique and begets a legal logic that is qualitatively different from that of each of the two national criminal systems: the philosophy behind international trials is markedly at variance with that underpinning each of those national systems. Also the Statute and Rules of the International Tribunal, in outlining the criminal proceedings before the Trial and Appeals Chambers, do not refer to a specific national criminal approach, but originally take up the accusatorial (or adversarial) system and adapt it to international proceedings, while at the same time upholding some elements of the inquisitorial system. . . . It follows that — unless expressly or implicitly commanded by the very provisions of international criminal law — it would be inappropriate mechanically to incorporate into international criminal proceedings ideas, legal constructs, concepts or terms of art which only belong, and are unique, to a specific group of national legal systems, say, common-law or civil-law systems. Reliance upon one particular system may be admissible only where indisputably imposed by the very terms of an international

---

[17] Ibid., paras 72–4.

[18] An exceptional example: Witness Summons by the Trial Chamber pursuant to Rule 98 of the Rules of Procedure and Evidence, *Prosecutor* v. *Kupreškić et al.*, Case No. IT-95-16-T, ICTY, T. Ch. II, 30 September 1998.

[19] On whether this is a positive development, see, among others, M. P. Scharf, 'Trading Justice for Efficiency: Plea-Bargaining and International Tribunals' (2004) 2 *JICJ*, at 1070–81.

[20] *Tadić* protective measures decision, para. 22.

norm, or where no autonomous notion can be inferred from the whole context and spirit of international norms.[21]

In our opinion, the amalgamation is not unique: the ICTY procedure is in essence of a common-law nature. Reference in the ICTY case law to a unique combination of various elements of both legal traditions is generally not supported by thorough comparative research and seems to be inspired by generalizations which turn out to be false in light of the Tribunal's actual practice. As noted above, the vital differences between adversarial and inquisitorial systems concern the degree of the parties' control over proceedings, the nature and method of fact-finding, and the nature and method of decision-making.[22] On all those vital points the Tribunal's procedure is strongly embedded in the common-law tradition.[23]

The practice of the ICTY and the ICTR openly and consistently displays key common-law concepts of party autonomy, fact-finding conducted by the parties, and a relatively inactive judiciary. Also, in more specific areas, common-law approaches are predominant. One example is the ICTY and ICTR's claims to inherent contempt powers, which is a typical common-law element unknown in this form in continental systems.[24]

The legal history of the ICC reveals no significant departures from the basic tenets of ICTY and ICTR procedure. However, Orie has concluded that 'one could say that the main line of thinking is still more common-law oriented, but at all thresholds a civil-law corrective instrument is implanted'.[25] One should be sceptical as to the value of those corrective elements. It is first of all debatable whether they fundamentally alter the common-law nature of ICC proceedings and, secondly, the extent to which those 'civil-law corrective instruments' will be useful in practice remains to be seen. In this respect, one may mention the far-reaching powers of the Pre-Trial Chamber in the collection of evidence, including the possibility of preserving and collecting evidence in the pre-trial phase at the request of the Prosecutor or *proprio motu* pursuant to Article 56 of the Statute (a unique investigative opportunity).[26] An active role for the Pre-Trial Chamber in this matter touches upon one of the basic elements of common-law proceedings, that is the autonomy of the parties in, and their responsibility for, the collection of evidence. The ICTY and ICTR's lack of practice in respect of Rule 98,

---

[21] *Erdemović* appeal judgment, para. 4.

[22] M. Damaška, *Faces of Justice and State Authority — A Comparative Approach to the Legal Process.*

[23] See note 10 above.

[24] Rule 77(A) of the ICTY and ICTR statutes; *Blaškić* subpoena appeal decision, para. 59; Judgment on Allegations of Contempt against Prior Counsel, Milan Vijun, *Prosecutor* v. *Tadić*, IT-94-1-T, ICTY, A. Ch., 30 January 2000, paras 13 and 15; Judgment on Appeal by Anto Nobilo against Finding of Contempt, *Prosecutor* v. *Aleksovski*, IT-95-14/1-A, ICTY, A. Ch., 30 May 2001, para. 38. For a critical opinion on this claim, see G. Sluiter, 'The ICTY and Offences against the Administration of Justice' (2004) 2 *JICJ*, at 631–41; C. Gane, 'Commentary to Judgment in the Matter of Contempt Allegations against an Accused and his Counsel, *Simić and others*, IT-95-9-R77, ICTY Trial Chamber, 30 June 2000', in Klip and Sluiter, *Annotated Leading Cases, vol. V*, at 236–44.

[25] A. Orie, 'Accusatorial v. Inquisitorial Approach in International Criminal Proceedings prior to the Establishment of the ICC and in the Proceedings before the ICC', in Cassese et al., *Rome Statute Commentary, vol. II*, at 1494.

[26] For the first use of Article 56 of the ICC Statute, concerning the situation in the Congo, see Decision on the Prosecutor's Request for Measures under Article 56, *Situation in the Democratic Republic of the Congo*, Case No. ICC-01/04, PTC I, 26 April 2005.

which permits investigations to be undertaken under the control and direction of the judiciary, foreshadows a strong commitment to a common-law approach.

Two important reasons for the (anticipated) adherence of the ICC to the common-law style of proceedings may be mentioned. The first is the ICTY and ICTR precedent, and to a lesser degree that of Nuremberg and Tokyo. The advantages of those precedents form a first possible basis for compromise. Secondly, one must acknowledge the significant input of common-law countries in the negotiations on the ICC, including on procedural matters. A considerable number of delegations sympathized with many of the views and positions adopted by the United States in the hope — and also expectation — that the result would be approval of the Statute. Under these circumstances, a fundamental move towards civil-law procedure was not an option, in spite of the problems the ICTY and ICTR had already been facing in the conduct of their trials before the conclusion of the Rome Statute. It is not surprising therefore that one of the first acts of the ICC Prosecutor was to seek advice on how to reduce the length of proceedings within the framework of a common-law based procedure.[27]

Information on the essentials of the organization of the criminal proceedings of the recently established internationalized criminal courts is sparse. This is because of their extremely close connection to, or even integration in, specific domestic legal orders. This certainly applies to the East Timor special panels and the Cambodian Extraordinary Chambers. The latter are part of the Cambodian legal order and apply Cambodian procedural law.[28] Similarly, the procedural law applicable to the proceedings of the East Timor special panels consists of the laws applied in East Timor prior to 25 October 1999.[29] However, the Special Court for Sierra Leone has consistently

---

[27] See the informal expert paper drawn up at the request of the ICC Prosecutor entitled 'Measures available to the International Criminal Court to reduce the length of proceedings', available at www.icc-cpi.int/library/organs/otp/length_of_proceedings.pdf (last visited 10 November 2006). The drafters of this paper had the benefit of a prior and broader attempt to improve the functioning of the ICTY and ICTR. See Report of the Expert Group to Conduct a Review of the Effective Operation and Functioning of the International Tribunal for the Former Yugoslavia and the International Criminal Tribunal for Rwanda, UN Doc. A/54/634, S/2000/957, 22 November 1999.

[28] Article 12(1) of the UN/Cambodia Agreement stipulates that the procedure shall be in accordance with Cambodian law, which is of a civil-law nature and origin. This may cause tension with the predominance of common law in international criminal proceedings. This tension may be reinforced by the escape route included in Article 12(1) that 'guidance may be sought in procedural rules established at the international level' when Cambodian law is unclear or where there is a question regarding the consistency of Cambodian law with international standards. This, in our view, opens the door for an interesting but uneasy struggle over applicable procedural law. For a more detailed account, see G. Sluiter, 'Due Process and Criminal Procedure in the Cambodian Extraordinary Chambers' (2006) 4 *JICJ*, at 314–26.

[29] Section 3.1 of UNTAET Regulation 1999/1 of 27 November 1999 on the Authority of the Transitional Administration in East Timor. Specific rules of criminal procedure have subsequently been developed and obviously take priority; they deal, however, essentially with fair trial, due process, and rights of the accused (UNTAET Regulation No. 2000/30 on the Transitional Rules of Criminal Procedure, as amended by Regulation 2001/25 of 14 September 2001). The question arose whether other issues should be governed by Indonesian law or Portuguese law, a matter which centred on the consequences of the unlawful occupation by Indonesia of East Timor for applicable procedural law. In the controversial Decision of the Court of Appeal for East Timor in *Prosecutor v. Armando Dos Santos*, 15 July 2003 (available at www.jsmp.minihub.org/judgmentspdf/courtofappeal/Ct_of_App-dos_Santos_English22703.pdf) the matter was decided in favour of Portuguese law, because of the illegal nature of the Indonesian occupation. Since this decision created major practical difficulties, it was overridden by

presented itself as a truly international tribunal.[30] As far as the organization of its proceedings is concerned, this stems from its copying ICTY and especially ICTR law.[31] It may reasonably be expected that the SCSL's procedural law will be even more coloured by common-law tradition and approaches than the ICTY and ICTR procedures. This is rooted in the common-law legal tradition of Sierra Leone, which serves as guidance for the judges in the interpretation, application, and amendment of the Rules.[32] Furthermore, every visitor to the Special Court notices the overwhelming presence of lawyers with a common-law background in all organs of the Court and on the defence side.[33]

If we move on to the realities of the courtroom, the setting and the allocation of places to the participants perfectly illustrate the common-law nature of international criminal proceedings. The parties to the proceedings, the defence and the prosecution, are placed on an equal footing. There are no outward distinctions, except that the prosecution is placed on the left side of the judges, and the defence on the right. The centre, directly opposite the judges, is reserved for the presentation of evidence; in particular, this is the place where witnesses are seated. This is quite different in civil-law countries. For example, in a Dutch courtroom, both the judges and the public prosecutor are placed on a podium. However, the prosecutor is not at the same table as the judges, but placed at a separate table on the right-hand side. This underlines the position of the prosecutor as part of the magistracy, entailing a different role and responsibility — one which is more objective than in the common-law tradition. The accused and defence counsel are placed at the centre of the courtroom, directly opposite the judges and diagonally opposite the prosecutor. This position perfectly corresponds to the view of an accused as an 'object' of investigations in the context of an impartial fact-finding process. Witnesses are generally offered a seat close to the accused, which illustrates that both are considered primarily as important sources of evidence.

Bearing in mind the common-law nature of international criminal procedure, we will explore in that particular context the roles and positions of the different actors in the respective proceedings. Since in common-law systems the trial is the climax of the fact-finding and decision-making process, the emphasis lies on the roles of participants in that particular phase of the proceedings, with due regard to other parts of the procedure. Again, an exhaustive exploration and analysis exceeds the scope of this book; but, a selection of vital and illustrative issues is unavoidable.

UNTAET legislation declaring Indonesian legislation, unless repealed, one of the applicable sources of law (Law no. 10/2003, published 10 December 2003). For further details, see S. de Bertodano, 'East Timor: Trials and Tribulations', in C. P. R. Romano et al. (eds), *Internationalized Criminal Courts — Sierra Leone, East Timor, Kosovo, and Cambodia* (Oxford: Oxford University Press, 2004), at 90–1.

[30] See Chapter 1, section 1.2.4. See also the commentary on the decision on Taylor's immunity by Claus Kress in Klip and Sluiter, *Annotated Leading Cases, vol. IX*, at 202–8.

[31] For instance, Article 14 of the SCSL Statute stipulates that the ICTR Rules shall be applicable *mutatis mutandis* to the conduct of legal proceedings before the Special Court.

[32] See Article 14(2) of the Statute, referring to the 1965 Criminal Procedure Act of Sierra Leone.

[33] The fact that the only working language of the Court is English (Article 24 of the Statute) undoubtedly plays a role in this respect.

2.3 JUDICIAL BRANCH

The title of this section may seem somewhat misleading in that the judicial branch as such does not exist in the organic structure of international criminal tribunals. The statutes of international criminal tribunals set out the organs of a judicial nature: chambers, comprising trial chambers and an appeals chamber (Article 11 ICTY Statute, Article 10 ICTR Statute, and Article 11 SCSL Statute), the presidency, an appeals division, a trial division, and a pre-trial division (Article 34 ICC Statute).[34] However, the organizational structure set out in the statutes does not reveal much about the nature of the judicial functions within systems of criminal justice and, more importantly, about the relationship of the organs *inter se*.[35] These are vital differences compared to non-judicial international organizations and domestic criminal justice systems, in both of which there are generally clear views of the nature and specific tasks of each organ, and also of their relationship *inter se*.

In the Rules the judges of the ICTY have strengthened the Tribunal's internal organization and have allocated the necessary judicial and administrative functions to the Presidency, the Bureau, the Coordination Council, and the Management Committee.[36] Plenary meetings with all judges are held to adopt and amend Rules of Procedure and Evidence.[37] The ICC Statute contains provisions on the organs of its judicial branch, the Presidency (Article 38), and various Chambers (Article 39). The ICC Regulations establish a Coordination Council (Regulation 3), as well as the *novum* of an Advisory Committee on Legal Texts (Regulation 4).

Before focusing on the position of the trial chamber, we should note the judicial roles of the President, Pre-Trial Judges, and Chambers. As in other fields, the history of the ICTY reveals uncertainties as to the delimitation of tasks and mandates and also some important developments as to the supervision of prosecutorial policy.

The first example is the function of the President pursuant to Article 28 of the ICTY Statute. This provision, further implemented by Rule 124, attributes to the President the power to determine whether pardon or commutation of the sentence is

---

[34] It is not possible to establish a similar organizational structure for the Cambodian Extraordinary Chambers and the East Timor special panels, as they function within the domestic legal order and, although established pursuant to international law, they are not structural parts of an international organization.

[35] In addition to organs which are part of the judicial branch, the (office of the) Prosecutor and the Registry are set out as organs of international criminal tribunals.

[36] Regarding the Presidency, see Rules 18–22 of the ICTY, ICTR, and SCSL Rules; it should be noted that president as an organ is not unknown in the statutes, even if not expressly mentioned in the organizational structure. It is provided that judges shall elect a president and, pursuant to Article 28 of the ICTY Statute, Article 27 of the ICTR Statute, and Article 23 of the SCSL Statute, the president decides on pardons and the commutation of sentence. The other organs are new institutions; on the Bureau, see Rule 23 of the ICTY and ICTR Rules, on the Coordination Council Rule 23 *bis* of the ICTY and ICTR Rules, and on a Management Committee Rule 23 *ter* of the ICTY and ICTR rules. The SCSL is endowed with a Council of Judges instead of the Bureau and Coordination Council (see Rule 23 of the SCSL Rules). Although there is a separate management committee of the SCSL established pursuant to Article 7 of the Agreeemnt, it deals only dealing with non-judicial aspects of the Court, whereas the ICTY and ICTR management committees are exclusively concerned with judicial tasks.

[37] Rule 24(ii) of the ICTY and ICTR Rules; Rule 24(i) of the SCSL Rules.

appropriate. Although Rule 124 provides for a consultation mechanism with judges, the manner in which the President would exercise his powers remains highly speculative, certainly with respect to the initial judgments.[38] Unlike in many national jurisdictions, judges could not, in the determination of a sentence, anticipate any early release practice.[39] For this reason we see in the early sentencing judgments quite robust observations on the (minimum) duration of the sentence. Thus, in the first *Erdemović* sentencing judgment the Trial Chamber demanded full respect for the duration of the penalty from the enforcing state.[40] In a similar vein, in *Tadić* the Trial Chamber, instead of demanding full respect for the duration of the international sentence of 20 years, explicitly provided for a recommended minimum term of 10 years after the issuance of the judgment on 14 July 1997.[41] The above observations may seem to be directed at the enforcing state, but they also inevitably touch upon the role of the President pursuant to Article 28 of the ICTY Statute. They raise pertinent questions as to the relationship between the Trial Chamber, bearing responsibility for the (authority of the) judgment, and the managing role of the President as to the enforcement of sentences at the national level. Those questions could have been addressed more thoroughly in the Rules.[42]

The second example concerns the judicial branch's role in respect of prosecutorial policy. Two levels should be distinguished here. First, the initiation of investigations by the prosecutor has been considered by the judicial branch to be outside the scope of review, as is indicated in the following letter from Judge McDonald:

Article 16(2) of the Statute provides that the Prosecutor shall act independently as a separate organ of the Tribunal; moreover, Article 18 provides that the Prosecutor 'shall initiate investigations'. Therefore, it is clear that only the Prosecutor may initiate an investigation and that the President does not exercise any control in this regard. However, the approach proposed in the Request would result in the President making a quasi-judicial finding regarding the initiation of an investigation, a responsibility vested clearly with the Prosecutor. Rule 7*bis*(B) cannot be interpreted or applied in a manner that is contrary to the Statute; therefore, I do not have the authority to conduct the review proposed in the Request.[43]

This view is diametrically opposed to the approach adopted by the ICC Statute. An independent Prosecutor with the power to initiate investigations *proprio motu* was one

---

[38] If one does the maths in respect of all early release decisions taken to date, it can safely be concluded that gradually a practice of early release after having served two-thirds of the sentence has developed.

[39] In a number of jurisdictions early release is a right under domestic law; see Article 15 of the Penal Code of the Netherlands, which allows for a conditional approach, but is not applied as such in practice.

[40] *Erdemović* sentencing judgment (no. 1), para. 73: 'the Trial Chamber is of the opinion that no measure which a State might take could have the effect of terminating a penalty or subverting it by reducing its length'.

[41] *Tadić* sentencing judgment (no. 1), para. 76: 'The Trial Chamber recommends that, unless exceptional circumstances apply, Dusko Tadic's sentence should not be commuted or otherwise reduced to a term of imprisonment less than ten years from the date of this Sentencing Judgment or of the final determination of any appeal, whichever is the latter.'

[42] The most important argument in favour of a clear and transparent regulation of early release concerns the uniformity of sentences; since a clear policy of early release after serving two-thirds of a sentence has emerged, a trend of increased sentences may be discerned. In this light, a possible strain in relations between president and trial chamber is only of minor relevance.

[43] Letter from the President to the Prosecutor, 16 March 1999, press release, 18 March 1999, JL/PIU/386-E.

of the most controversial issues throughout the negotiation process.[44] The compromise was found in judicial review of both the Prosecutor's initiation of investigations (Article 15(3) of the ICC Statute) and his or her refusal to do so (Article 53(3) of the ICC Statute).[45]

It is self-evident that the exercise of prosecutorial discretion is subjected to increased judicial review. This has everything to do with the general importance of prosecutorial policy, an important aspect of the authority and legitimacy of an international criminal tribunal,[46] as well as with the significant consequences for an indicted individual. The degree of judicial review may, however, raise questions as to the principle of prosecutorial independence. Those questions may be addressed at various stages of the proceedings, and in different forms.

At the individual level, the confirmation of an indictment presents the first direct opportunity for judicial review. However, this review is confined to assessing the individual indictment in light of submitted evidence.[47] The broader question of prosecutorial discretion is therefore not an object of discussion in this procedure. This was expressed in strong terms by Judge Wald in her partial dissenting opinion in the *Jelisić* appeal judgment:

> The Statute provides for an independent Prosecutor as one of three co-ordinate branches of the Tribunal. Article 16 says '[t]he Prosecutor shall act independently as a separate organ of the International Tribunal' and shall be 'responsible for the investigation and prosecution of persons responsible for serious violations of international humanitarian law ... '. Article 19 provides that when the Prosecutor has prepared an indictment, it shall be transmitted to a Judge of the Trial Chamber who 'shall' confirm it if satisfied that a *prima facie* case has been established. The trial Judges are not given any power to reject the indictment because they do not think it is a wise use of the Tribunal's resources or for any other reason other than the lack of a *prima facie* case. Nowhere in the Statute is any Chamber of the ICTY given authority to dismiss an indictment or any count therein because it disagrees with the wisdom of the Prosecutor's decision to bring the case.[48]

Judicial supervision in respect of prosecutorial discretion has turned up, however, after the confirmation stage in judgments and other decisions. In *Delalić et al.*, Landžo

---

[44] See, among others, R. J. Goldstone and N. Fritz, ' "In the Interests of Justice" and Independent Referral: The ICC Prosecutor's Unprecedented Powers' (2000) 13 *LJIL*, at 657.

[45] Article 53 (3) allows for review of the Prosecutor's determination that there is no reasonable basis to proceed with an investigation at the request of a referring State or the Security Council. Furthermore, the Pre-Trial Chamber may on its own initiative review this determination.

[46] See L. Côté, 'Reflections on the Exercise of Prosecutorial Discretion in International Criminal Law' (2005) 3 *JICJ*, at 162–86; D. D. Ntanda Nsereko, 'Prosecutorial Discretion Before National Courts and International Tribunals' (2005) 3 *JICJ*, at 124–44; M. R. Brubacher, 'Prosecutorial Discretion within the International Criminal Court' (2004) 2 *JICJ*, at 71–95.

[47] See Article 19(1) of the ICTY Statute and Article 18(1) of the ICTR Statute. It should be noted that those provisions oblige a judge to confirm an indictment when he or she is satisfied that a prima facie case has been established. In the ICTY jurisprudence a 'prima facie case' is considered to be a 'a credible case which would (if not contradicted by the accused) be a sufficient basis to convict him of that charge'. See, among others, Decision on Review of Indictment and Application for Consequential Orders, *Prosecutor* v. *Milošević et al.*, Case No. IT-99-37-I, ICTY, T. Ch., 24 May 1999, para. 4, and Decision on the Review of the Indictment, *Prosecutor* v. *Kordić et al.*, Case No. IT-95-14-I, ICTY, T. Ch., 10 November 1995, at 3, referring to the Report of the International Law Commission, UN Doc. A/49/10 (1994), at 95. [48] *Jelisić* appeal judgment, para. 4.

argued that he was the victim of a selective prosecution policy, in that his prosecution was only or essentially the result of him being a Muslim.[49] While the Appeals Chamber in that case acknowledged that the Prosecutor has a broad discretion in prosecutorial policy, this is by no means unfettered and prosecution on discriminatory grounds is clearly prohibited.[50] However, the burden of proof in this respect lies on the defendant and, moreover, in case of violation the appropriate remedy is not reversal of the conviction.[51] A similar claim was made by Krajišnik, albeit on the discriminatory ground of nationality.[52] It was dismissed by the Appeals Chamber as not affecting the Tribunal's jurisdiction.[53] Also the ICTR was confronted with an accused complaining about selective prosecution, namely that Hutus are the exclusive target of prosecutorial policy. The respective ICTR chambers developed and affirmed the position that prosecutorial policy is not unfettered and subject to judicial review; prosecution on discriminatory grounds is impermissible, but the defence must meet a high threshold to show such cause and so far has in no case succeeded in doing so.[54]

One may safely conclude that judges initially exercised considerable judicial restraint when reviewing prosecutorial discretion and attached significant weight to prosecutorial independence. In this light and taking into account the Secretary-General's commentary that the Tribunal as a whole will have to perform its functions independently and will not be subject to the authority or control of the Security Council with regard to the performance of its judicial functions,[55] one views with a certain degree of surprise the acceptance of increasing interference by the UN Security Council in prosecutorial policy. The matter came to the fore in the *Milošević* case when the amici curiae pointed out that the language of UNSC Resolution 1160 (1998), urging the prosecutor to commence investigations in Kosovo, was not in keeping with the envisaged independence under Article 16(2) of the ICTY Statute.[56] The Chamber rejected this argument and observed that only the indictment of a particular person on the instruction of any body would vitiate the prosecutor's independence.[57]

The most far-reaching intrusion into prosecutorial independence has arguably been triggered by the tribunals' exit strategy. The first example in this respect is the amendment of Rule 28 of the ICTY Rules in April 2004, pursuant to which the Bureau shall

---

[49] *Delalić et al.* appeal judgment, para. 596.   [50] Ibid., paras 602–5.

[51] Ibid., paras 607 and 618.

[52] Decision on Interlocutory Motion Challenging Jurisdiction, *Prosecutor* v. *Krajišnik*, Case No. IT-00-39-AR72.2, ICTY, A. Ch., 25 May 2001, para. 22.

[53] Ibid., para. 23. A conflicting position was adopted in the *Milošević* case, where a similar argument was examined on its merits in the context of preliminary (jurisdiction) motions. Decision on Preliminary Motions, *Prosecutor* v. *Milošević*, Case No. IT-99-37-PT, ICTY, T. Ch. III, 8 November 2001, paras 12–17.

[54] *Akayesu* appeal judgment, paras 94–6; Decision on the Prosecutor's Motion to Join the Indictments ICTR 96-10-I and ICTR 96-17-T, *Prosecutor* v. *Ntakirutimana et al.*, Case No. ICTR-96-10-I and ICTR 96-17-T, ICTR, T. Ch., 22 February 2001, paras 870–87; Decision on Prosecutor's Motion under Rule 50 for Leave to Amend the Indictment Issued on 20 January 2000 and Confirmed on 28 January 2000, *Prosecutor* v. *Ndindiliyimana et al.*, Case No. ICTR-2000-56-I, ICTR, T. Ch., 26 March 2004, para. 26.

[55] Report of the Secretary-General on the ICTY, para. 28.

[56] Decision on Preliminary Motions, *Prosecutor* v. *Milošević*, Case No. IT-99–37-PT, ICTY, T. Ch. III, 8 November 2001, paras 12–17.

[57] Ibid., para. 15. See also Chapter 8, section 8.5.2, which deals with this matter from the perspective of the right to an independent and impartial tribunal.

determine whether the indictment, prima facie, concentrates on one or more of the most senior leaders suspected of being most responsible for crimes within the jurisdiction of the Tribunal.[58] In line with this example is the amendment of Rule 73 *bis* of the ICTY Rules.[59] The Rule deals with pre-trial conferences, concerning the Prosecutor and after its amendment in 2006 it is especially concerned with restricting the scope of prosecution in order to reduce the length of trials.[60] The most far-reaching power appropriated by the judges is that pursuant to Rule 73 *bis* (E) they may direct the Prosecutor to select the counts in the indictment on which to proceed. According to ICTY President Pocar such powers are appropriate and justified:

The basis for this amendment is the Statutory responsibility of a Trial Chamber to manage the trial with respect for an accused's right to a fair and expeditious trial and the right of those in pre-trial detention to be tried within a reasonable time ... At the same time, the amendment respects Prosecutorial independence in bringing indictments before the Tribunal and seeks the Prosecution's cooperation in shortening the trials through focused indictments.[61]

ICTY Prosecutor Del Ponte protested strongly and considered this rule change to violate the division of powers and prosecutorial independence:

In view of the checks and balances contained in the Statute, and particularly the duties and responsibilities of the Prosecutor under the Statute, such directions by the Chambers can only be interpreted as *purely advisory in nature*. Only the Security Council has the power to modify the ICTY Statute, which guarantees the independence of the Prosecutor and assigns to her the responsibility of determining which charges to bring in a prosecution.[62] (Emphasis added.)

Furthermore she underlined the risk of denial of justice to victims and 'arbitrarily cut[ting] and slic[ing] cases', without any reason connected to the merits of the case or the availability of evidence.[63]

The stand-off between judges and prosecutor remains unresolved at the time of writing. Given the prosecutor's strong opposition, it may be expected that judges will exercise considerable restraint in respect of the new powers set out in Rules 28 and 73 *bis*. The aforementioned rules continue to raise the question of the wisdom of the exit strategy, and also the terms of division of powers between tribunal organs. The amendments to Rules 28 and 73 *bis* were triggered by Security Council Resolutions 1503 and 1534

---

[58] It should be noted that no similar amendment has (yet) been adopted by the ICTR judges, even though the Council's call in this matter was directed to both tribunals.

[59] Note that the ICTR and SCSL Rules have not followed the May 2006 amendments to ICTY Rule 73 *bis*.

[60] See press release, ICTY Plenary Session, 30 March 2006, available at www.un.org/icty/pressreal/2006/p1083-e.htm (last visited 13 November 2006) and Assessment and Report of Judge Fausto Pocar, President of the ICTY, Provided to the Security Council Pursuant to Paragraph 6 of SC Res. 1534 (2004), 31 May 2006, available at www.un.org/icty/publications-e/assessments/documents/2006-531eng.doc (last visited 13 November 2006). 'Under this amendment, Trial Chambers now have the explicit ability, at the pre-trial stage, to invite the Prosecution to reduce the number of counts charged or to direct the Prosecution to select the counts on which the trial should proceed', see Statement by Fausto Pocar to the Security Council, 7 June 2006, available at www.un.org/icty/pressreal/2006/p1084e-annex.htm (last visited 13 November 2006). [61] Ibid.

[62] See Statement by Tribunal's Prosecutor Carla Del Ponte to the Security Council, 7 June 2006; www.un.org/icty/pressreal/2006/p1085e-annex.htm (last visited 13 November 2006).

[63] In more detail, see Assessment and Report of Carla Del Ponte, Prosecutor of the ICTY, Provided to the Security Council Pursuant to Paragraph 6 of the SC Res. 1534 (2004), 31 May 2006, para. 6.

which in the light of the exit strategy called on the ad hoc tribunals in reviewing and confirming any new indictments to ensure that they focus on the top-level leaders bearing most responsibility for serious international crimes. The passing of such resolutions raises pertinent questions as to the independence of the Tribunal as a whole and the prosecutor in particular. It seems to us not to be in keeping with the above-mentioned commentary of the Secretary-General, which was approved by the SC, no less, and the ICTY's jurisprudence on judicial review of prosecutorial discretion. On this last point one must bear in mind the overt acceptance of the twin pillars of prosecutorial policy in *Delalić et al.*: persons holding a high degree of responsibility or persons who have been personally responsible for exceptionally brutal or otherwise extremely serious offences.[64] For these reasons the judges could and should have ignored the Council's call.

Now that the ICTY has adopted a review mechanism for prosecutorial policy via Rule 28, it has come closer to the law of the ICC on this matter, although two vital differences remain. On the one hand, ICC judicial review goes considerably further, in that the ICTY and ICTR judiciary cannot order the prosecutor to prosecute, whereas the ICC Pre-Trial Chamber can request the prosecutor to reconsider a decision not to proceed with an investigation at the request of a referring state or the Security Council and can review on its own initiative a decision not to investigate when the latter is based on the 'interests of justice'.[65] On the other hand, pursuant to Article 15(4) of the ICC Statute, the ICC Pre-Trial Chamber review at the investigation stage is of an exclusively evidentiary and jurisdictional nature and does not impose any conditions as to the position of the investigated persons.[66]

Indeed, in the case of a permanent international criminal justice system, such conditions are not appropriate as they can never anticipate the needs of a specific prosecution strategy. In the context of ad hoc international prosecutions this may be different. However, the standard of independence requires this to be set out in the constitutive document and not to be imposed along the way. In this respect, the approach embodied in the agreement setting up the Cambodian Extraordinary Chambers is to be preferred, although its ambiguous wording is an open invitation to challenges to the scope of judicial review:

The co-prosecutors shall be independent in the performance of their functions ... It is understood, however, that the scope of the prosecution is limited to senior leaders of Democratic Kampuchea and those who were most responsible.[67]

The hierarchically superior position of the judiciary in international criminal proceedings follows logically from its position as decision-maker. In the case of the ad hoc tribunals and the SCSL this is reinforced by the judges' position as (secondary) law-makers. In practical terms, this means that the judges both stipulate and supervise to a significant degree the means whereby the parties to the proceedings realize their procedural rights and competences, and organize and structure the tasks of the Registrar.

---

[64] *Delalić et al.* appeal judgment, para. 614.   [65] See Article 53(3)(a) and (b) of the ICC Statute.

[66] Such conditions are also not imposed with respect to the issuance of an arrest warrant (Article 58 of the ICC Statute).   [67] Article 6(3) of the UN/Cambodia Agreement.

The climax in this respect lies in the power vested in the judges to issue orders to the parties and to hold them in contempt if they violate orders. The power to issue certain orders has been contested on the basis of the 'division of powers' arguments. In the *Milošević* case, the Prosecutor complained that the Trial Chamber's decision to limit the time for presentation of the prosecution case interfered with the prosecutorial discretion guaranteed by Article 16(2) of the ICTY Statute. The argument was rejected by the Appeals Chamber which rightfully pointed out that Article 16(2) does not concern the powers of judges in the management of a case and emphasized in that context the duty of the judiciary pursuant to Article 20 of the Statute.[68] Indeed, this last point, the duty to ensure that a trial is both fair and expeditious, is in our opinion by far the most important substantive ground on which to attribute to the judiciary a dominant position in both the conduct and the organization of trials. The joint power of issuing orders and finding contempt is therefore not unique to the far-reaching claims from ICTY, ICTR, and SCSL judges,[69] but has also been codified by the negotiating states in the ICC Statute. Article 64(2) contains the duty for the Trial Chamber to ensure a fair and expeditious trial and paragraph 8 of that same provision empowers the Chamber to give directions for the conduct of proceedings. Parties who fail to comply with those directions are liable to administrative sanctions, other than imprisonment, but including fines, pursuant to Article 71 of the Statute.[70]

While the joint 'order and contempt power' lies at the heart of the relationship between the judges and parties to the proceedings, the relationship with other tribunal organs outside that context is certainly more ambiguous. This can best be illustrated by the conduct of the ICTR Registrar in the *Ntuyahaga* case.[71] In this case, the indictment was withdrawn, following which the Trial Chamber ordered the immediate release of Ntuyahaga.[72] The Registrar was then instructed by the Trial Chamber to take all the necessary measures to execute this decision and that it should 'take into account considerations that may arise, notably factors pertaining to the security of Bernard Ntuyahaga'. The Registrar must have understood 'security' in a broad sense, because he

---

[68] Reasons for Refusal of Leave to Appeal from Decision to Impose Time Limit, *Prosecutor* v. *Milošević*, Case No. IT-02-54-AR73, ICTY, A. Ch., 16 May 2002.

[69] Those claims are either codified in the Rules or exercised on the basis of the inherent powers doctrine (as was the case with the power to hold individuals in contempt).

[70] Rule 171(4) indicates that a fine for refusal to comply with a direction by the Court shall not exceed €2,000. Although beyond the scope of this book, the question arises as to whether the qualification of the sanction as administrative is not misleading. In fact, the sanction remains penal in nature, triggering the applicability of fair trial rights as set out in Article 14 of the ICCPR and Article 6 of the ECHR for the relevant proceedings. In this respect, it should be noted that the European Court of Human Rights maintains an autonomous interpretation of the notion of 'criminal charge', see *Öztürk* v. *Germany (Article 50)*, Judgment on Application no. 8544/79 [1984] ECtHR 13 (21 February 1984), paras 49–56.

[71] See the following decisions: Decision on the Prosecutor's Motion to Withdraw the Indictment, *Prosecutor* v. *Ntuyahaga*, Case No. ICTR-98-40-T, ICTR, T. Ch. I, 18 March 1999; Decision by the Registrar in Execution of the Decisions by Trial Chamber I ordering the release of Mr Bernard Ntuyahaga, *Prosecutor* v. *Ntuyahaga*, Case No. ICTR-98-40-T, ICTR, Registrar, 29 March 1999; Declaration on the point of law by Judge Laïty Kama, President of the Tribunal, Judge Lennart Aspegren, and Judge Navanethem Pillay, *Prosecutor* v. *Ntuyahaga*, Case No. ICTR-98–40-T, 22 April 1999.

[72] Belgium was interested in his prosecution, but the Rules at that time did not provide for transfer to a state other than the state of arrest.

provided Ntuyahaga with a 'safe conduct' document, by which he requested all UN member states, other states, and international organizations to accord safe conduct to Ntuyahaga and extend to him any necessary cooperation to enable him to move freely in or transit through, without hindrance, any country to his final destination, in accordance with the relevant provisions of international law. In an unprecedented manner,[73] the judges of the *Ntuyahaga* Trial Chamber dismissed the Registrar's safe conduct measure as ultra vires. The judges rightfully claimed that from the perspective of an internal division of powers it should have been clear to the Registrar that the issuance of safe conduct measures is reserved for the judiciary.[74] On the other hand, one notes in this, but also in a significant number of other decisions, that trial chambers delegate the execution of their decisions to the Registrar and may offer the latter a wide discretion in this regard. From this perspective, the *Ntuyahaga* case is certainly a lesson for the judiciary to be more specific in its instructions pertaining to the execution of decisions.

Just as important as the position and powers of judges in criminal proceedings, which is more an institutional matter, is that of professional integrity, including impartiality and independence. In respect of all international criminal tribunals, the selection process obviously aims to provide highly qualified, impartial, and independent judges.[75] However, a significant political element in the election process cannot be denied.

One notes in practically all laws governing the functioning of international criminal tribunals provisions as to the excuse and disqualification of individual judges.[76] They are without exception inspired by the requirements of impartiality and independence. As this is a fundamental element of the right to a fair trial, this will be examined in more detail in Chapter 8. With the exception of the ICC Statute, no specific code of conduct or of judicial ethics has been developed. The judges of the ICC have drafted and adopted a short Code of Judicial Ethics, comprising 11 rather short provisions. They deal again with impartiality and independence, but also with integrity, extra-judicial activity, public expression, and confidentiality. The Code is intended to serve as guidelines (see its Article 11); no enforcement mechanism has been provided for.

---

[73] The judges issued under their own names, not sitting as a chamber, a declaration on a point of law. The Prosecutor objected to the issuance of the safe conduct measure by the Registrar (not only on legal grounds, but the prosecution had withdrawn the indictment with the intention of Belgium taking over the prosecution). However, there was no longer an available legal avenue to file that complaint, as the case was no longer pending before the Trial Chamber. Since the matter was considered of significant importance — a precedent in this field should be avoided — the approach adopted was a declaration.

[74] Notice should be taken of the ICTY precedent: Decision on the Defence Motions to Summon and Protect Defence Witnesses, and on the Giving of Evidence by Video-Link, *Prosecutor* v. *Tadić*, Case No. IT-94-1-T, ICTY, T. Ch., 25 June 1996.

[75] Cf. Article 13 of the ICTY Statute, Article 12 of the ICTR Statute, Article 36(3)(a) of the ICC Statute, and Article 13(1) of the Statute of the Special Court for Sierra Leone.

[76] Article 41 of the ICC Statute, Rule 15 of the Rules of the ICTR, ICTY, and SCSL; see also Section 2 of UNTAET Regulation no. 2000/11 on the Organization of Courts in East Timor, as amended by Regulation 2001/25 of 14 September 2001. With regard to the Cambodian Extraordinary Chambers, neither the UN/Cambodia Agreement nor the Law on the Establishment of the Extraordinary Chambers in the Courts of Cambodia for the Prosecution of Crimes Committed during the Period of Democratic Kampuchea set out the procedures for excusing and disqualification of judges. The motions challenging the impartiality and independence of judges may be brought under the 1962 Code of Criminal Procedure. See S. Linton, 'Safeguarding the Independence and Impartiality of the Cambodian Extraordinary Chambers' (2006) 4 *JICJ*, at 336.

2.4 PROSECUTOR

Unquestionably, the prosecutor is the most dynamic organ in international criminal justice. His role in international criminal proceedings comprises activities at three stages. First, on the basis of received information, the prosecutor may start investigations. Secondly, the conduct of an investigation may result in an indictment. Finally, after confirmation of an indictment the prosecutor will try to convince the chamber beyond reasonable doubt that the accused is guilty as charged. In contrast to the prosecutor's role in certain domestic jurisdictions, like that of the Netherlands, the international prosecutor plays no role in the enforcement of sentences, apart from presenting his or her views during a procedure for review concerning reduction of sentence.[77] In this section we focus on the prosecutor's role in each of those stages, but do not look at prosecutorial policy, which contains important non-legal aspects we are not qualified to analyse fully.[78]

In order to depict adequately the legal procedural position of the prosecutor and to understand the nature and scope of prosecutorial competence, the vital issue to be addressed is the extent to which the prosecutor is *dominus litis* in each of those stages. One may note varying approaches in this respect, which are the result of different methods of establishment and different mandates of international criminal tribunals. Prosecutorial freedom is most restricted in the case of the ICC, which has permanent jurisdiction (starting on 1 July 2002) over indefinite conflicts and territories. The compact mandates of the ICTR, the ICTY, and the SCSL and their role in restoring and maintaining international peace and security have resulted in wide prosecutorial freedom. The Cambodian Extraordinary Chambers occupy a middle position, in that in the constitutive agreement prosecutorial activity is confined to the senior leaders.

At the investigative stage the prosecutor undoubtedly enjoys most freedom. For the ICTR, the ICTY, and the SCSL, the threshold for the conduct of criminal investigations lies in a 'sufficient basis to proceed' after the analysis of information held by the prosecutor.[79] It has already been indicated that this evidentiary standard is not subject to judicial review. The matter is entirely different for the ICC Prosecutor. First of all, the threshold for initiating a criminal investigation lies in a reasonable and not a sufficient basis to proceed.[80] A reasonable standard is not confined to an evidentiary test, but includes the broader concept of the interests of justice.[81] Secondly, as stated in section 2.3 above, the Pre-Trial Chamber plays an important role in supervising the interpretation and application of a reasonable basis to proceed.

Two important questions concerning the role of the prosecutor in the investigative stage are the following. First, to what extent is the prosecutor under an obligation to

---

[77] See Rule 224 of the ICC Statute.

[78] For more details see sources referred to in the discussion of prosecutorial discretion in the preceding section.

[79] In the East Timorese and Cambodian contexts, no specific threshold for the conduct of investigations is set out in international instruments; thus, the relevant and applicable domestic law must be taken into account.

[80] See Article 15(3) and 53(1) of the ICC Statute.   [81] Article 53(1)(c) of the ICC Statute.

establish the objective truth and to look for both inculpatory and exculpatory evidence? Secondly, what are the powers vested in the prosecutor in the investigative stage?

The first question lies at the heart of the already mentioned common law/civil law dichotomy as to the organization of criminal proceedings. One may note that on this point that there is nothing in the legal framework of the ICTY, the ICTR, or the SCSL obliging the prosecutor to investigate incriminating and exonerating circumstances equally. Yet, the general understanding of the position of the prosecutor appears to be that of an officer of the court and thus is not based on the partisan stance in the common-law tradition. In *Kupreškić* the ICTY Trial Chamber expressed this as follows:

it should be noted that the Prosecutor of the Tribunal is not, or not only, a Party to adversarial proceedings but is an organ of the Tribunal and an organ of international criminal justice whose object is not simply to secure a conviction but to present the case for the Prosecution, which includes not only inculpatory, but also exculpatory evidence, in order to assist the Chamber to discover the truth in a judicial setting.[82]

Concrete obligations for the actual investigations are, however, difficult to deduce from this statement. Rather, it is a logical corollary to the disclosure obligation of Rule 68, in the sense that exculpatory evidence *in the possession* of the prosecutor may not be hidden from the defence or the Chamber.

The ICC Statute sets out explicit obligations for the prosecutor in the investigative phase, aiming at an impartial fact-finding process. Pursuant to Article 54(1)(a) of the ICC Statute, the investigation must cover all relevant facts and evidence and in this light the prosecutor must investigate incriminating and exonerating circumstances equally. The legal framework of the East Timor special panels echoes the last part of Article 54(1)(a).[83] This duty has been referred to as building a bridge between common-law and civil-law systems.[84] However, it remains extremely difficult to assess the prosecutor's compliance with that obligation in practice. The ICC prosecutor has — from a civil-law perspective — made a promising start, by resorting to Article 56 with a view to the conduct of *independent* forensic examinations in Congo.[85]

As to the second question, namely the prosecutorial powers in the investigative stage, one notes again the differences between the ICTY, the ICTR, and the SCSL, on the one hand, and the ICC on the other. The broad power to collect evidence attributed to the prosecutors of all international criminal tribunals offers them the possibility of imposing a wide variety of measures of both coercive and non-coercive nature.[86] The

[82] Decision on the Communications between the Parties and their Witnesses, *Prosecutor* v. *Kupreškić et al.*, Case No. IT-95-16-T, ICTY, T. Ch. II, 21 September 1998. In a similar vein on the position of the prosecutor, see: Separate Opinion of Judge Shahabuddeen, *Barayagwiza* II appeal decision, para. 68.

[83] See Section 7.1 of UNTAET Regulation No. 2000/30, as amended by Regulation 2001/25 of 14 September 2001.

[84] M. Bergsmo and P. Kruger, 'Article 54', in O. Triffterer, *Commentary on the Rome Statute*, at 716.

[85] Decision on the Prosecutor's Request for Measures under Article 56, *Situation in the Democratic Republic of the Congo*, ICC-01/04, ICC, PTC I, 26 April 2005.

[86] See Rule 39(i) of the ICTY, ICTR, and SCSL Rules, Article 54(3)(a) of the ICC Statute, Section 7.4.a of UNTAET Regulation No. 2000/30, as amended by Regulation 2001/25 of 14 September 2001, Article 23 of the Cambodian law implementing the UN/Cambodian Agreement (but note the reference to national procedures, which requires understanding of Cambodian law on this point).

vital question from the perspective of respect for individual rights is whether the prosecutor may indeed perform or request coercive measures in the investigative phase.[87] One notes that neither the ICC Statute nor the Rules explicitly attribute coercive powers to the prosecutor. For example, the power to arrest is reserved for the judicial branch.[88] This is a vital difference in respect of the legal frameworks of the ICTY, the ICTR, and the SCSL, which allow for provisional arrest of a suspect in urgent situations, at the sole request of the prosecutor. Although the ICC approach offers a high level of protection of individual liberty, the law of the ad hoc tribunals and the SCSL is more in conformity with domestic practice, where generally the police, acting under the authority of prosecuting services, have a power to arrest in urgent circumstances.[89] As to other coercive measures, such as the interception of telecommunications, search and seizure, none of the legal frameworks of international criminal tribunals contain specific regulations.[90] In the ICTY case law in these matters the prosecutor is guided by general principles of criminal procedure as well as by international human rights law and usually applies for warrants where the imposition of coercive measures is required.[91] In most instances, this appears imperative from a human rights perspective. It follows from the case law of the European Court of Human Rights that, especially when searches, seizures, the interception of telecommunications, and other measures are not governed by laws indicating with reasonable clarity their (manner of) execution, judicial intervention is mandatory.[92] It is in fact a problem with the procedural law of international criminal tribunals that it contains no regulations at all on this matter, let alone any of 'reasonable clarity'. As a result, when acting without a warrant, the prosecutor should refrain from requesting or authorizing the execution of coercive measures.

[87] For a more detailed treatment of that question, see G. Sluiter, *International Criminal Adjudication and the Collection of Evidence: Obligations of States* (Antwerp: Intersentia, 2002), at 109–11.

[88] See Article 58 of the ICC Statute; see also G. Sluiter, 'The Surrender of War Criminals to the International Criminal Court' (2003) 25 *Loyola of Los Angeles International & Comparative Law Review*, at 605–52.

[89] The practical application of Rule 40 *bis* has been challenged by two accused persons before the SCSL. Fofana and Kondewa argued that this rule, allowing for the arrest of suspects under the authority of the prosecutor, is ultra vires the Statute, as the latter contains no provision for the detention of suspects; the argument was dismissed by Judge Boutet on the basis of the fact that the Statute as a rudimentary instrument needs further and effective implementation in the Rules (Decision on the Urgent Application for Release from Provisional Detention, *Prosecutor* v. *Fofana*, Case No. SCSL-2003-11-PD, SCSL, T. Ch., 21 November 2003, paras 24–6; Decision on the Urgent Application for Release from Provisional Detention, *Prosecutor* v. *Kondewa*, Case No. SCSL-2003-12-PD, SCSL, T. Ch., 21 November 2003, paras 24–6. For a defence perspective and thus critical view see J. R. W. D. Jones et al., 'The Special Court for Sierra Leone — A Defence Perspective' (2004) 2 *JICJ*, at 227–9.

[90] This may be different for the Cambodian Extraordinary Chambers and the East Timor special panels, which operate partly on the basis of domestic laws and regulations. Furthermore, it should be taken into account also that the issue and execution of arrest warrants is only subject to minimal rules, certainly in respect of the ICTY, the ICTR, and the SCSL. The ICC Statute contains an improvement in that it regulates in significant detail both the issue and execution of arrest warrants (see Articles 58 and 59).

[91] We mention just one example, as those applications are normally not transparent: Decision Stating Reasons for Trial Chamber's Ruling of 1 June 1999 Rejecting Defence Motion to Suppress Evidence, *Prosecutor* v. *Kordić and Čerkez*, Case No. IT-95-14/2, ICTY, T. Ch. III, 25 June 1999.

[92] *Camenzind* v. *Switzerland*, 21353/93 [1997] ECtHR 99 (16 December 1997), Reports of Judgments and Decisions 1997-VIII, and *Funke* v. *France*, 10828/84 [1993] ECtHR 7 (25 February 1993), Series A, Vol. 256-A.

Although investigations may continue, with the confirmation of the indictment a new phase in criminal proceedings commences. One may note the structural difference between the law of the ad hoc tribunals and the SCSL and the law of the ICC on this point. While confirmation of the indictment is clearly linked to the issue of coercive measures, especially arrest warrants, in the case of the ICTY, the ICTR, and the SCSL,[93] this is not the approach under the ICC Statute. The latter does not connect arrest and other forms of compulsory process to the confirmation of the indictment; pursuant to Article 61, the Pre-Trial Chamber shall only hold a confirmation hearing within a reasonable time after a person's surrender or appearance. The result of this difference is that the ICC prosecutor is expected to maintain his or her position as *dominus litis* longer than her or his ICTY, ICTR, and SCSL colleagues. In fact, all international criminal tribunals have in common that prior to the confirmation of charges the prosecutor may amend or withdraw certain charges or even the entire indictment.[94] The later confirmation time in the case of the ICC may have been agreed in order to avoid or minimize the need for motions to amend, which are common in ICTY and ICTR proceedings.[95] Furthermore, one may indeed distinguish between an individual's right to be informed of the reasons for the arrest and the right to be given specific information on the charges against him or her with a view to the preparation of the trial. The confirmation of a full indictment is more important in the latter situation than in the former.

In the practice of the ICTY and the ICTR the withdrawal of indictments in the pre-trial phase is unproblematic. The most impressive precedent is the simultaneous withdrawal of 14 indictments by the ICTY prosecutor, which was readily accepted by confirming judges Riad and Vohrah.[96] After a trial has commenced, it is only with the Trial Chamber's permission that the indictment or charges may be withdrawn.[97] In the ICTY and ICTR the withdrawal of charges is not subject to serious judicial review, which underlines the position of the prosecutor as *dominus litis* throughout the entire procedure.[98] Illustrative in this respect are the ICTR's considerations regarding the withdrawal of the indictment against Ntuyahaga:

the Chamber stresses that it is the sole duty of the Prosecutor to devise the prosecution strategy and therefore to decide, even before instituting any proceedings, whether such action serves the interests of her mandate as Prosecutor.[99]

[93] See Article 19(2) of the ICTY Statute, Article 18(2) of the ICTR Statute, and Rule 47(h)(i) of the SCSL Rules.

[94] See Rule 51 of the ICTY, ICTR, and SCSL Rules, stipulating that indictments may be withdrawn prior to confirmation without leave; and Article 61(4) of the ICC Statute, allowing the amendment or withdrawal of charges prior to the confirmation hearing. However, in the ICC context the Pre-Trial Chamber must, given its supervisory role in respect of the prosecutorial policy, be notified of the withdrawal of charges.

[95] See Chapter 9, section 9.3.

[96] For more information, see Statement by the Prosecutor following the withdrawal of the charges against 14 accused, 8 May 1998, CC/PIU/314-E.

[97] Article 61(9) of the ICC Statute and Rule 51(A)(iii) of the ICTY, ICTR, and SCSL Rules.

[98] This is certainly different in civil-law jurisdiction, where after the start of the trial the prosecutor may not withdraw the case but instead the trial ends with a final decision.

[99] Decision on the Prosecutor's Motion to Withdraw the Indictment, *Prosecutor* v. *Ntuyahaga*, Case No. ICTR-98-40-T, ICTR, T. Ch. I, 18 March 1999.

One may expect the ICC Trial Chamber, in the broader context of extended judicial supervision of prosecutorial activity, to exercise a greater degree of supervision.

The relationship of the prosecutor with the defence has been a recurring theme in the law and practice of international criminal tribunals. Especially in the context of adversarial proceedings this matter is often approached in the context of the principle of equality of arms. As this is not only a general principle of criminal procedure, but also a right of the accused, we believe it more appropriate to deal with it under that heading.[100]

As to the conduct of the prosecutor in the course of investigations and during a trial, we have already partially dealt with this matter in relation to the judiciary. As already mentioned, the latter may sanction (serious) violations of court orders and misconduct via its 'contempt power'. Yet, this is an extreme situation, and before that stage is reached the prosecutor may be expected to follow certain rules of conduct. There is neither a detailed publicly available code of prosecutorial conduct, nor any similar regulations in the legal frameworks of the ad hoc tribunals.[101] The ICC prosecutor is in the process of finalizing internal regulations, which include rules relating to professional conduct.[102] The Special Court for Sierra Leone represents an innovative approach in that a Code of Conduct has been drafted, which essentially focuses on defence counsel, but also includes four articles containing obligations for prosecution counsel.[103] Yet, in the absence of internal codes of conduct, 'rules of conduct' are applicable to the prosecutor and also binding on this organ, when part of general principles of law. To identify these 'rules of conduct' comparative analysis of domestic systems is generally required.[104] Such comparative analysis, which falls outside the scope of this book, will undoubtedly result in a number of elementary rules, relating to matters such as the use of coercive measures, confidentiality, integrity, and impartiality. These rules have already been codified by the General Assembly of the United Nations, adopting a Code of Conduct for Law Enforcement Officials, in 1979.[105]

The above rules of conduct essentially have an internal effect, but may in certain circumstances have consequences for the trial. In the case law of the ad hoc tribunals and the SCSL the concept of abuse of process has surfaced in respect of the procedural

---

[100] See Chapter 8, section 8.5.1.

[101] See M. Bergsmo et al., 'The Prosecutors of the International Tribunals: the Cases of the Nuremberg and Tokyo Tribunals, the ICTY and ICTR, and the ICC Compared', in L. Arbour et al. (eds), *The Prosecutor of a Permanent International Criminal Court — International Workshop in Co-operation with the Office of the Prosecutor of the International Criminal Tribunals (ICTY and ICTR)* (Freiburg im Breisgau: Ed. Iuscrim, 2000), at 121–54.

[102] Draft Regulations of the Office of the Prosecutor, available at www.icc-cpi.int/library/organs/otp/draft_regulations.pdf (last visited 10 November 2006).

[103] See Articles 23–6 of the Code of Professional Conduct for Counsel with the Right of Audience before the Special Court for Sierra Leone. Those articles deal with the scope of prosecution, impartiality, conflict of interest, and confidentiality. The disciplinary proceedings in case of violations of those obligations also extend to prosecution counsel.

[104] According to Judges McDonald and Vohrah in the *Erdemović* case, the comparative exercise need not necessarily involve a comparison of the specific rules of each of the world's legal systems; in order to discern a general trend, it may suffice, as they argue, to compare those jurisdictions whose jurisprudence is, as a practical matter, available and accessible to the tribunal. See Joint Separate Opinion of Judge McDonald and Judge Vohrah, *Erdemović* appeal judgment, para. 57.

[105] General Assembly Resolution 34/169 (1979) on Code of Conduct for Law Enforcement Officials.

conduct of parties to the proceedings, notably the prosecutor. Under the common-law doctrine of abuse of process, proceedings that have been lawfully initiated may be terminated after an indictment is issued if improper or illegal procedures have been employed in pursuing an otherwise lawful process.[106] Its effect in international criminal proceedings is, however, far from clear. In the *Barayagwiza* case the Appeals Chamber found that there was a case of abuse of process, with prejudice to the prosecutor. It terminated the proceedings on that particular ground, but failed to set out clearly the scope and content of the abuse of process doctrine in international criminal proceedings. On the basis of subsequent cases, one may safely conclude that the abuse of process doctrine has not been solidly established in the context of international criminal proceedings. For example, the *Nikolić* case, dealing with a claim of unlawful arrest, evades the abuse of process doctrine and ponders instead on the continuing exercise of jurisdiction in light of the integrity of the proceedings; obviously, the conduct of the prosecutor plays a significant part in the determination of whether jurisdiction needs to be declined.[107] Interestingly, in the case *Brima et al.* the defence resorted to the abuse of process doctrine, in addition to the more appropriate avenue of challenging jurisdiction; in this light, the substantive analysis of the defence motion seemed unnecessary. Yet the SCSL Trial Chamber did engage in such analysis, and found nothing wrong with the prosecutor's choices in the indictment.[108] Thus it increased confusion as to the appropriate role for the abuse of process doctrine in international criminal proceedings. Furthermore, the ICC Pre-Trial Chamber rendered a decision of comparable effect where it also resorted to this doctrine in the framework of a jurisdictional challenge.[109] In response to the defence position that violation of the accused's rights in the course of arrest detention required his release, the Chamber held that 'the application of this doctrine [abuse of process] ... has been confined to instances of torture or serious mistreatment by national authorities'.[110] What the abuse of process consists of when the prosecutor is not involved, and why it does not apply when the prosecutor *is* involved are issues that remain unresolved. In our view, inappropriate prosecutorial conduct may have repercussions at various stages of the proceedings, for example, in the form of exclusion of evidence or — in the most extreme cases — in the form of declining to exercise further jurisdiction. In these various procedural remedies, the abuse of process doctrine serves no useful purpose.[111]

---

[106] See *Barayagwiza* I appeal decision, para. 74. See also Written Reasons for the Trial Chamber's Oral Decision on the Defence Motion on Abuse of Process due to Infringement of Principles of *Nullum Crimen Sine Lege* and Non-Retroactivity as to Several Accounts, *Prosecutor v. Brima et al.*, Case No. SCSL-04-16-PT, SCSL, T. Ch., 31 March 2004, para. 21. In the latter decision, the Trial Chamber also cited Black's law dictionary on this point, where abuse of process is defined as the improper and tortuous use of legitimately issued court process to obtain a result that is either unlawful or beyond the process's scope.   [107] See *Nikolić* jurisdiction trial decision.

[108] Written Reasons for the Trial Chamber's Oral Decision on the Defence Motion on Abuse of Process due to Infringement of Principles of *Nullum Crimen Sine Lege* and Non-Retroactivity as to Several Accounts, *Prosecutor v. Brima et al.*, Case No. SCSL-04-16-PT, SCSL, T. Ch., 31 March 2004.

[109] Decision on the Defence Challenge to the Jurisdiction of the Court pursuant to Article 19(2)(a) of the Statute, *Prosecutor v. Lubanga Dyilo*, *Situation in the Democratic Republic of the Congo*, Case No. ICC-01/04-01/06, ICC, PTC I, 3 October 2006.   [110] Ibid., at 10.

[111] For a different view, see E. van Sliedregt, 'Commentary', in Klip and Sluiter, *Annotated Leading Cases, vol. IX*, at 130: 'the abuse of process doctrine in international criminal law seems an academic concept. This might

2.5 DEFENCE

While this chapter focuses on the role of various participants in international criminal proceedings, in the case of the organization and conduct of the defence some words need to be said about its institutional position, or rather absence thereof. In none of the statutes has the defence, or a defence unit, reached the status of an organ. In Chapter 1, section 1.4.1 we referred to commentators who regret the exclusion of the defence function, as this may convey the message that this function is not particularly important.

One may indeed be critical of the drafters' permanent failure to make a 'defence office' a (primary) organ of international criminal tribunals. The vital question is, to what extent has this negatively affected the quality of the defence, as a crucial part of the broader right to a fair trial? While the right to a fair trial is discussed in more detail in Chapter 8, at this juncture we offer the following observations.

First of all, the degree to which the lack of institutional status has negatively affected the conduct of the defence in the specific context of international criminal justice is a matter for empirical research and careful analysis that is beyond the scope of this book.[112] The logical follow-up question in this respect is what degree and form of organization of the defence best suits an effective defence and the interests of international criminal justice.[113]

A second and closely related question is whether the forms of organization that have developed over the years and are still developing may have already to a significant degree accommodated concerns as to the quality of the defence. While it is premature to answer this question definitively, we will briefly sketch the various attempts at both internal and external organization of the defence in international criminal justice.

In the context of the ad hoc tribunals, the degree of organization was for a long time very minimal. The registry was and still is responsible for the assignment of defence counsel, pursuant to Rules 44 and 45 of the ICTY and ICTR Rules, as well as the Directive on Assignment of Defence Counsel. The defence unit operating under the registry certainly has its benefits, but its work is generally limited to assignment of counsel. Indeed, the Registry is not equipped and also is not the appropriate organ to represent the interests of the defence in a broader sense and to supervise its performance. Without a separate defence organization, there is only the extreme of contempt

explain the scepticism of some scholars when discussing the abuse of process doctrine in the context of the *ad hoc* Tribunals. This author, however, would argue that abuse of process is a very important and underestimated tool in an international court or tribunal's tool box. Maybe more than on the national level does an international court or tribunal need to guard the integrity of its proceedings.'

[112] For a generally affirmative response to this question, although not based on a comprehensive case-law analysis, see the contributions to H. Bevers and C. Joubert (eds), *Independent Defence before the International Criminal Court* (Amsterdam: Thela Thesis, 2000). It has furthermore been submitted that the organization of the defence is desirable for the following reasons: independence, parity of resources, and training (R. J. Wilson, 'Assigned Defence Counsel in Domestic and International War Crimes Tribunals: The Need for a Structural Approach' (2002) 2 *ICLR*, at 179.

[113] Internally, this may range from an international public defender's office to a defence unit under the registry with an essentially facilitatory task.

proceedings, while what is needed are various forms of training and the possibility of disciplinary measures. As a result, one should welcome the establishment of the Association of Defence Counsel appearing before the ICTY (ADC ICTY) and its counterpart in the ICTR context,[114] although their establishment occurred quite late in the lifespan of the ad hoc tribunals (2002) and their relationship *inter se* as well as their position within a broader 'international criminal bar' leave much to be desired.[115] One indeed wonders why a single association has not been set up for the ICTY and the ICTR. At present, some puzzling differences remain. The most important is that the ICTY association has received recognition from the ICTY: in July 2002 Rule 44 was amended and in its present wording requires defence counsel who wishes to appear before the ICTY to be a member in good standing of an association of counsel practising at the Tribunal recognized by the Registrar, which is the ADC ICTY.[116] No similar requirement exists in the ICTR Rules.

In the course of the negotiations on the ICC, France proposed the establishment of an Office of the Defence to the ICC, but the proposal was rejected.[117] As a result, the initial situation as to the organization of the defence is similar to that of the ad hoc tribunals. Yet the ICC Rules are more instructive in this matter, especially Rule 20 which sets out in significant detail the responsibilities of the registrar in relation to the rights of the defence. Rule 20(3) needs special mention in that in relation to certain tasks of the registrar reference is made to an independent representative body of counsel or legal associations.[118] The fact that the establishment of such a body is envisaged from the beginning represents an improvement on the position of the ad hoc tribunals. At the same time, it seems appropriate not to establish this within the Court itself with a view to its independence[119] and its possible broader role in international criminal justice beyond the ICC.

The body envisaged has already materialized in the form of the International Criminal Bar (ICB).[120] Yet, its recognition in the sense of Rule 20(3) is still on the agenda of the Assembly of States Parties.[121] In addition to the ICB, mention must also be made of the

---

[114] Association des Avocats de la Defense auprès du Tribunal International pour Rwanda.

[115] The ICTY and ICTR associations share the same objectives, which can be summarized as supporting defence counsel, promoting and ensuring quality of defence counsel, advising the tribunals on defence-related matters, such as the code of conduct, and to supervising performance and professional conduct of defence counsel. However, it is unclear whether they are connected and to what extent they are integrated in the 'global' International Criminal Defence Attorney Association or the International Criminal Bar. By organization and law, they are separate associations: the ICTY association was established under Dutch law on 20 September 2002, whereas the ICTR association is based in Arusha, Tanzania. As in other matters of international criminal procedure, the entire endeavour lacks a structural, integrated, and well-thought-through approach.

[116] Rule 44(a)(iii).

[117] S. Kay and B. Swart, 'The Role of the Defence', in Cassese et al., *Rome Statute Commentary, vol. II*, at 1429.

[118] See also Rule 20(1)(f).

[119] J. R. W. D. Jones, 'Composition of the Court', in Cassese et al., *Rome Statute Commentary, vol. I*, at 240.

[120] The ICB was conceived in June 2002, and established under Dutch law on 22 July 2003. It has been set up as an organization both to represent and regulate counsel who will practise before the ICC and to advise the Court on defence-related matters.

[121] 'Report of the Registrar on activities regarding defence counsel, including the legal representation of victims, and the process of consultation followed' appeared in item 12 of the Provisional Agenda of the Third Session of the ASP; it seems that it has not further been discussed at the Fourth and Fourth-resumed sessions. The provisional agenda for the Fifth Session contains no information on this matter.

International Criminal Defence Attorneys Association. It remains to a significant degree unclear how those organizations relate one to another, and whether international criminal justice would not be better served with one single integrated organization, possibly with sub-branches for each distinctive international criminal tribunal.

The Special Court for Sierra Leone has taken an interestingly different and innovative approach to the organization of the defence. It provides a clear vision of and a firm position to the defence in its institutional framework in the form of the Office of the Principal Defender. The latter is set up by the registry and its functions are to ensure an effective defence at the early stages, to assign defence counsel, and to offer assistance to counsel.[122] While innovative, the approach adopted adds to the fragmentation and confusion: for example, is there in the context of the SCSL still room for an independent organization outside the Court, and if so, what would its objectives be?[123] The independence of the Principal Defender vis-à-vis the registrar is uncertain. Arguably, this has to some degree been resolved by the decision dealing with reappointment of counsel. In a complicated and extensive appeal in *Brima et al.* one of the issues was whether the registrar had been acting ultra vires when countermanding a decision of the Principal Defender on the reassignment of the previous lead counsel.[124] The Appeals Chamber's approach was rather formalistic in that it recognized the Principal Defender's not being part of the organic structure of the SCSL and necessarily operating under the authority of the registrar. Furthermore, the Chamber ruled that the registrar could have delegated part of his power to the Defender Office, but had not divested himself of this power and thus could act concurrently with the Principal Defender.[125] In his separate opinion Judge Robertson submitted that until the independence of the Defence Office is recognized by an amendment to the Statute, the Principal Defender works under the administrative supervision of the registrar; in the spirit of the Rule change that created the office, the registrar should allow it to work so far as possible with operational independence.[126]

Having regard to the above, the position of the defence in international criminal justice is in the process of formation. Yet, its development lacks uniformity, coherence, and consistency. The internationalized courts in East Timor and Cambodia present an even more confusing picture.[127] This may all be explained by the embryonic state of

---

[122] See Rule 45 of the SCSL Rules. The Defence Office was initially set up to represent the accused at all stages of the proceedings, but this proved to be unworkable because of conflicts of interests between accused persons who were charged with the same crimes. For a more detailed account of the role of the principal defender, see J. R. W. D. Jones et al., 'The Special Court for Sierra Leone — A Defence Perspective' (2004) 2 *JICJ*, at 211.

[123] The answer is probably in the negative, as the SCSL Rules do not make any mention of an independent defence attorney organization. In this case, the question arises whether, in the absence of an explicit mention to that effect, such an interpretation would be in conformity with the accused's right to defend himself or herself in person or through legal assistance of *his or her own* choosing.

[124] Decision on Brima-Kamara Defence Appeal Motion against Trial Chamber II Majority Decision on Extremely Urgent Confidential Joint Motion for the Re-appointment of Kevin Metzger and Wilbert Harris as Lead Counsel for Alex Tamba Brima and Brima Bazzy Kamara, *Prosecutor* v. *Brima et al.*, Case No. SCSL-2004-16-AR73, SCSL, A. Ch., 8 December 2005.   [125] Ibid., paras 83–7.

[126] Ibid., Separate and concurring opinion of Judge Robertson, para. 102(viii).

[127] For East Timor, the organization of defence services or legal aid is set out in UNTAET Regulation No. 2001/24. The Cambodian legal framework gives almost no clue to the organization of the defence, except for the

international criminal procedure, in combination with the proliferation of distinct international criminal jurisdictions. Once past this phase, the fundamental question to be addressed will be the following: which aspects of the organization and functioning of the defence should as a matter of principle remain within the institutional structure of international criminal tribunals? Other matters can better be left to independent organizations outside that structure, provided that they offer a credible alternative. This is in conformity with the defence's independent position and prevents unnecessary burdens for international criminal tribunals. It is self-evident that appropriate consultation mechanisms need to be introduced.

After an overview of developments in the broader organization of the defence in international criminal justice systems, we now turn to the core of this section: what is the position of the defence in the daily practice of international criminal tribunals? Fundamental to the answer to that question lies the right embodied in Article 14(3)(d) of the ICCPR and reproduced verbatim in the legal frameworks of all international criminal tribunals:

[the right] to defend himself in person or through legal assistance of his own choosing; to be informed, if he does not have legal assistance, of this right; and to have legal assistance assigned to him, in any case where the interests of justice so require, and without payment by him in any such case if he does not have sufficient means to pay for it.[128]

While the content and scope of this provision will be addressed in Chapter 8, its fundamental importance for the concrete and visible conduct of defence in international criminal justice systems merits particular attention in the present context. The 'normal' and desirable situation, especially in adversarial proceedings,[129] is a full defence, namely one or more defence counsel of the accused's choice, who conduct a defence with appropriate consultation with the accused and in accordance with the applicable rules. Deviation from this standard has caused embarrassment for the ICTY, the ICTR, and the SCSL and resulted in a variety of defence constructions: self-representation, amici curiae, standby counsel, and court-assigned counsel.[130] One may distinguish two types of extraordinary procedural conduct on the part of the accused, which have triggered the aforementioned defence constructions. The first scenario is when the accused no longer wish to participate in their trial, because either they do not recognize the trial forum or they do not agree with certain decisions, and as a result they have lost confidence in the trial.[131] Those accused have also instructed their counsel to withdraw, but both the

general rule that Cambodian procedural law applies, unless otherwise regulated or inconsistent with the 'international standard'.

[128] Article 21(4)(d) of the ICTY Statute; Article 20(4)(d) of the ICTR Statute; Article 67(1)(d) of the ICC Statute; and Article 17(4)(d) of the SCSL Statute.

[129] On the position of the defence in an adversarial setting, see M. R. Damaška, 'Assignment of Counsel and Perceptions of Fairness' (2005) 3 *JICJ*, at 3–8.

[130] For an overview of the developments and solutions adopted in the jurisprudence, see N. H. B. Jørgensen, 'The Right of the Accused to Self-Representation before International Criminal Tribunals' (2004) 98 *AJIL*, at 711–26.

[131] See the situations of Barayagwiza (ICTR) and Gbao (SCSL): Decision on Defence Counsel Motion to Withdraw, *Prosecutor v. Barayagwiza*, Case No. ICTR-97-19-T, ICTR, T. Ch. I, 2 November 2000, and Gbao — Decision on Appeal against Decision on Withdrawal of Counsel, *Prosecutor v. Sesay et al.*, Case No. SCSL-04-15-AR73, SCSL, A. Ch., 23 November 2004.

ICTR and the SCSL have refused such withdrawal in the interests of justice;[132] one could make an analogy here with court-assigned counsel, even if the accused Barayagwiza and Gbao started their defence with the assistance of counsel. Secondly, one should mention accused, such as Šešelj, Milošević, and Norman, who have elected to represent themselves.[133] The interests of justice have led Trial and Appeals Chambers to adopt various models to strengthen and thus organize the defence, even against the explicit wish of the accused concerned. They have, however, not been consistent in their approach. In *Norman* and *Šešelj* the Trial Chambers adopted the solution of standby counsel.[134] From an institutional perspective, the defence is still led by the accused himself, with the counsel essentially in a residuary role of assistant. Only in exceptional circumstances, such as disruptive conduct on the part of the accused, is counsel allowed to take over the defence. This latter, drastic, step has been taken with the court-assigned counsel. In the *Milošević* case, the Trial Chamber assigned counsel to the accused and instructed the counsel to 'determine how to present the case for the Accused'.[135] In contrast to the standby counsel model, an assigned counsel is in charge of the defence, given that the accused may continue to participate actively in the trial with leave of the Chamber.[136] The Appeals Chamber approved of this approach, but only if the health situation of Milošević were to deteriorate.[137] Prior to assigning a counsel to Milošević, the Trial Chamber had appointed amici curiae, with a view to strengthening the defence.[138] Although appointed as impartial advisers to the Trial Chamber, the latter were specifically instructed to act as 'pseudo-counsel', for example, by drawing the attention of the Trial Chamber to defences or in any other appropriate way.[139]

What transpires from the developments in this field is the following. The accused and the defence counsel may together constitute the defence but they have different roles and positions. It has repeatedly been emphasized, and with reason, that defence

[132] Ibid.

[133] See Reasons for Decision on Assignment of Defence Counsel, *Prosecutor* v. *Milošević*, Case No. IT-02-54-T, ICTY, T. Ch., 22 September 2004; Decision on Interlocutory Appeal of the Trial Chamber's Decision on the Assignment of Defense Counsel, *Prosecutor* v. *Milošević*, Case No. IT-02-54-AR73.7, ICTY, A. Ch., 1 November 2004; Decision on Prosecution's Motion for Order Appointing Counsel, *Prosecutor* v. *Šešelj*, No. IT-03-67, paras 4, 22 (9 May 2003), and Decision on The Application of Sam Hinga Norman for Self-Representation Under Article 17(4)(d) of the Statute of the Special Court, *Prosecutor* v. *Norman et al.*, Case No. SCSL-04-14-T, SCSL, T. Ch., 8 June 2004.

[134] Decision on Prosecution's Motion for Order Appointing Counsel, *Prosecutor* v. *Šešelj*, Case No. IT-03-67, ICTY, T. Ch., 9 May 2003, paras 4 and 22. It should be noted that the Trial Chamber sought to assign counsel to Šešelj, but was corrected by the Appeals Chamber for not having this assignment preceded by a formal warning: Decision on Assignment of Counsel, *Prosecutor* v. *Šešelj*, Case No. IT-03-67-PT, ICTY, T. Ch., I, 21 August 2006 and Decision on Appeal against the Trial Chamber's Decision on Assignment of Counsel, *Prosecutor* v. *Šešelj*, Case No. IT-03-67-AR73.3, ICTY, A. Ch., 20 October 2006. See also Decision on the Application of Sam Hinga Norman for Self-Representation under Article 17(4)(d) of the Statute of the Special Court, *Prosecutor* v. *Norman et al.*, Case No. SCSL-04-14-T, SCSL, T. Ch., 8 June 2004.

[135] Reasons for Decision on Assignment of Defence Counsel, *Prosecutor* v. *Milošević*, Case No. IT-02-54-T, ICTY, T. Ch., 22 September 2004, para. 69.   [136] Ibid.

[137] Decision on Interlocutory Appeal of the Trial Chamber's Decision on the Assignment of Defense Counsel, *Prosecutor* v. *Milošević*, Case No. IT-02–54-AR73.7, ICTY, A. Ch., 1 November 2004, para. 20.

[138] Order concerning Amici Curiae, *Prosecutor* v. *Milošević*, Case No. IT-99-37-PT, ICTY, T. Ch. III, 11 January 2002.

[139] Ibid. For a critical view of the solution of using amici curiae, see Zappalà, *Human Rights in International Criminal Proceedings*, at 64.

counsel as officers of the court not only have duties towards their clients, but also serve the proper administration of justice. This may imply that they cannot withdraw from the defence at the wish of their client. An important point here is that in adversarial proceedings a true adversarial debate must be ensured.[140] Be this as it may, the solutions adopted will always leave much to be desired from the perspective of an effective defence, since the fact remains that counsel who do not communicate with their clients cannot be expected to perform miracles. The *Šešelj* case is furthermore illustrative of what a truly 'obstructionist' accused is capable of doing, even to the detriment of his or her own interests: Šešelj reportedly insulted his assigned counsel and his family, as a result of which the latter instituted domestic proceedings against his 'client'. In the light of those developments, the deputy registrar replaced standby counsel with a new one, meaning a further delay in the delivery of justice.[141]

The position of the defence in criminal proceedings is generally analysed in terms of equality of arms, in relation to its counterpart — the prosecutor. This is no different in international criminal proceedings. As an element of the right to a fair trial, the principle of equality of arms will be dealt with in Chapter 8, section 8.5.1. It suffices here to emphasize that the principle does not call for full substantive equality between defence and prosecutor.[142] What matters rather is equality from a procedural point of view, offering both defence and prosecutor comparable opportunities to interview witnesses, to gather information, to conduct (on-site) investigations, and so forth. While the institutional inequality between prosecutor and defence inevitably has repercussions here, the judges may remedy the procedural inequality by assisting the defence, in particular in the issuance of warrants and orders and requests for legal assistance, where appropriate.[143]

The possibility for the defence of independently setting out the best defence strategy in the interests of the accused is generally recognized as vitally important.[144] However,

---

[140] Ibid.

[141] For a more detailed account, see N. H. B. Jörgensen, 'The Right of the Accused to Self-Representation before International Criminal Tribunals', at 721–2. On problems related to self-representation see also M. R. Damaška, 'Assignment of Counsel and Perceptions of Fairness' (2005) 3 *JICJ*, at 3–8; G. Sluiter, ' "Fairness and the Interests of Justice": Illusive Concepts in the *Milošević* Case' (2005) 3 *JICJ*, at 9–19; J. Temminck Tuinstra 'Assisting an Accused to Represent Himself: Appointment of *Amici Curiae* as the Most Appropriate Option' (2006) 4 *JICJ*, at 47–63; M. P. Scharf, 'Self-Representation versus Assignment of Defence Counsel before International Criminal Tribunals' (2006) 4 *JICJ*, at 31–46.

[142] It is the scope of this book to explore whether one can still speak of substantive inequality in international criminal proceedings. Such an investigation calls for a case-by-case approach. The prosecutor may be seen as a powerful 'apparatus', consisting of a significant number of highly trained specialists and which has built up expertise in war crimes trials; similarly, the quantity and quality of defence teams has also grown over the years. Defence teams may also comprise highly trained specialists, including lawyers who had previous careers within organs of the tribunal concerned. Furthermore, with the increasing number of prosecutions and simultaneous trials (some of them high profile, such as the *Milošević* case), the prosecutor's office is probably no longer in a position to assign big prosecution teams to each case.

[143] This was also the position of the ICTY Appeals Chamber in *Tadić*, underlining that it is the task and the duty of the judicial branch to redress the inequality of arms that exists under the Statute. It ruled that 'the Chamber shall provide every practicable facility it is capable of granting under the Rules and Statute when faced with a request by a party for assistance in presenting its case' (*Tadić* appeal judgment, para. 52).

[144] T. Spronken, *Verdediging. Een onderzoek naar de normering van het optreden van advocaten in strafzaken* (Defence. A study of the regulation of the professional conduct of advocates in criminal cases) (Deventer: Gouda Quint, 2001), at 633–6.

there are limits to what can be done. For a proper insight into the applicable rules, one should distinguish between the accused and his or her defence counsel.

The accused is not bound by any specific code of conduct. This may seem obvious since codes of conduct concerning defence counsel are generally created by the profession to maintain its honour and dignity as an essential agent of the administration of justice.[145] However, if an accused is conducting his or her own defence, this creates a certain gap in applicable law. It is indeed pertinent to ask in that particular situation to what degree the accused may be considered 'an agent of the administration of justice', which then should have repercussions on applicable rules of conduct.[146] Each accused remains bound by the minimum rules of contempt, prohibiting a variety of conduct which can be labelled as an offence against the administration of justice.[147] The question arises to what degree individuals accused of the most serious crimes are impressed by the consequences of contempt proceedings.[148] Rather, the accused will fear negative inferences that might be drawn from his conduct, for example the intimidation of, or tampering with, witnesses is likely to result in toughening of the detention regime and will affect sentencing.

The conduct of defence counsel is governed by significantly more rules and may occasion more diverse sanctions in case of violations. One should distinguish the following situations.

At the international level, defence counsel are bound by the law of contempt and specific rules of conduct, which are to a large degree contained in specific codes of conduct.[149] While the law of contempt and the codes may overlap, the latter go

---

[145] S. Kay and B. Swart, 'The Role of the Defence', in Cassese et al., *Rome Statute Commentary, vol. II*, at 1432.

[146] In our view, one should attempt to distinguish between rules of conduct which are exclusively or essentially oriented to the conduct of defence counsel towards the client, and rules which are directed at the defence's position as officer of the court, thus his conduct towards the court. The former category is obviously not applicable to an accused conducting his or her own defence. The latter category may to some extent be applicable, certainly from the perspective of the orderly conduct of a trial. On the other hand, one should be cautious about imposing on the accused a cooperative role as an officer of the court which may be at odds with the privilege against self-incrimination. See further below and Chapter 8, section 8.5.4 on the content and scope of the privilege against self-incrimination.

[147] On the 'contempt law' in international criminal justice, see G. Sluiter, 'The ICTY and Offences against the Administration of Justice' (2004) 2 *JICJ*, at 631–41. For an example of the contempt ruling involving an accused, see: Judgment in the Matter of Contempt Allegations against an Accused and his counsel, *Prosecutor v. Simić et al.*, Case No. IT-95-9-R77, ICTY, T. Ch., 30 June 2000 (allegations of contempt dismissed for both Milan Simić and Branislav Avramović as not proven beyond reasonable doubt).

[148] The maximum penalty known to the authors to be imposed to date for contempt is four months' imprisonment; see Judgment on Contempt Allegations, *Prosecutor v. Beqa Beqai*, Case No. IT-03-66-T-R77, ICTY, T. Ch. I, 27 May 2005.

[149] The ICTY and ICTR, meaning the judges without involvement of defence counsel, have adopted Codes of Conduct for Defence Counsel in 1997 and 1998 respectively, pursuant to Rules 44–6 (ICTR: Code of Professional Conduct for Defence Counsel; ICTY: Code of Professional Conduct for Counsel Appearing before the International Tribunal (as amended on 12 July 2002) (IT/125 REV. 1)). The title of the ICTY code may seem to suggest that it is also applicable to prosecution counsel, but the definition section makes clear that it is only applicable to defence counsel. By contrast, the SCSL Code of Professional Conduct for Counsel with the Right of Audience for the SCSL (adopted in May 2005) also applies to prosecution counsel, although the majority of rules focus on defence counsel.

In the context of the ICC, Rule 8 sets out the procedure for the development and adoption of a Code of Professional Conduct for Counsel. The Code was adopted by the Assembly of States Parties, by consensus, on 2 December 2005.

considerably further and contain far more detailed obligations for defence counsel towards their clients and the court and are aimed at maintaining the integrity of the profession.[150] Violation of those obligations may not always meet the contempt standard, but may trigger a disciplinary sanction. In this regard account should be taken of two possible avenues, one set out in Rule 46 of the ICTY, ICTR, and SCSL rules, and the other available in the codes of conduct of the SCSL and the ICTY. Rule 46 had for a long time provided the only disciplinary mechanism for dealing with misconduct by counsel — and still remains so for the ICTR. As to what amounts to misconduct, reference is made to the codes of conduct. Pursuant to Rule 46, disciplinary action in response to violations short of contempt is reserved for a judge or chamber and inter alia consists of replacing counsel or striking him or her from the list, and non-payment of fees in the case of 'frivolous motions'.[151] Interestingly, disciplinary measures in the context of the SCSL and the ICTY may also be taken by special disciplinary panels.[152] It is unclear how those proceedings and ensuing sanctions relate to the Rule 46 avenue. One could consider the disciplinary panels as similar in nature and scope to disciplinary proceedings in domestic bar associations, whereas the Rule 46 proceedings could be seen as a lighter version of contempt proceedings, which essentially are concerned with the integrity of the proceedings and not that of the profession as such. Undeniably, counsel is better off with Rule 46, as the disciplinary proceedings allow for the additional sanction of a maximum fine of €50,000. Such a potentially severe penalty underlines the punitive nature of the proceedings and raises the questions of whether, first of all, the tribunals may lawfully exercise jurisdiction over this category of cases and, secondly, whether exercise of jurisdiction may lawfully be delegated to special panels.[153]

The ICC Code of Conduct regulates disciplinary measures only, as intended by Rule 8. The Code represents the most detailed codification at present. It contains an elaborate disciplinary regime, with clear distinction between the investigative role (for

[150] For a discussion of the proposals the most recent codification of a Code of Conduct by the ICC, see M. Walsh, 'The International Bar Association Proposal for a Code of Professional Conduct for Counsel Before the ICC' (2003)1 *JICJ*, at 490–501.

[151] For an example, see Decision on the Defence Motion for the Interpretation of Rules 89(A), (B), (C), (D), and 90(F) and (G) of the Rules of Procedure and Evidence and for the Recall of a Witness, *Prosecutor* v. *Semanza*, Case No. ICTR-97-20-I, ICTR, T. Ch. III, 1 December 2000, and also the instructive commentary by Chrisje Brants in respect of the wasted cost orders, in Klip and Sluiter, *Annotated Leading Cases, vol. VI* at 458–67.

[152] In the case of the SCSL, the panel is composed of a judge, a lawyer appointed by the Principal Defender, and a lawyer appointed by the Prosecutor (Article 29 of the SCSL Code of Conduct); the ICTY panel consists of a member of the Association of Counsel, a member of the Advisory Panel who has practised at the Tribunal to be appointed by the President of the Advisory Panel, and the Registrar of the Tribunal, or a senior legal officer designated by the Registrar (Article 40 ICTY Code of Conduct).

[153] The question of jurisdiction was also raised in respect of 'ordinary' contempt proceedings (see A. Klip, 'Witnesses before the International Criminal Tribunal for the Former Yugoslavia' (1996) 67 *International Review of Penal Law*, at 277, footnote 40; J. Cockayne, 'Commentary', in Klip and Sluiter, *Annotated Leading Cases, vol. IV*, at 195; M. Bohlander, 'International Criminal Tribunals and Their Power to Punish Contempt and False Testimony' (2001) 12 *CLF*, at 106–7; and G. Sluiter, 'ICTY and Offences against Administration of Justice' (2004) 2 *JICJ*, at 632–5). The matter is even more pertinent here, as the exercise of punitive powers is delegated to a non-judicial panel. We believe that in the case of a possible €50,000 fine this is problematic. It would have been more appropriate to stick to termination or suspension of membership of the relevant association of defence counsel, a condition for practising law with the relevant international criminal tribunal.

'Commissioner', Article 33 of the Code) and the adjudicative role (Disciplinary Board and Disciplinary Appeals Board, Articles 36 and 43). A clear improvement in respect of the disciplinary process is that the ICC Code provides for coordination of disciplinary reaction with national boards.[154] Interestingly, the principle of complementarity applies to this relationship as well, also with an 'unwilling' and 'unable' criterion![155] In contrast with proceedings concerning the subject-matter of the jurisdiction of the Court, one would expect the ICC to have primacy in disciplinary matters; in fact, misconduct by counsel in the course of ICC proceedings primarily concerns the Court justifying primacy.[156]

At the national level, one should bear in mind that defence counsel practising in international criminal justice are generally members of domestic bar associations, with their own rules and disciplinary proceedings. Generally, this is not problematic, as the international rules of conduct tend to be inspired by widely shared domestic rules. Yet, the question of conformity of ICTY and ICTR counsel's conduct with domestic codes of conduct has come to the fore, notably in respect of the conduct of a defence against the wishes of the accused but as ordered by a trial chamber. This issue has already been explored in Chapter 1, section 1.5.2 in relation to immunities for counsel. It seems to us that the matter calls for a clear delimitation between international and domestic disciplinary rules and proceedings.

A closely related question is to what extent the defence counsel, as agent of the administration of justice, should adopt a cooperative position. Undeniably, adversarial proceedings could be considerably expedited if the defence and prosecution were to reach agreement on undisputed facts and the way to proceed with the trial. The Expert Group which focused on expediting ICTY and ICTR proceedings proposed that judges — in the event of no apparent dispute as to certain facts — might require the party declining to accept them to explain the reasons therefor.[157] One should also

---

[154] The need for such coordination may be explained by instances in the context of ICTY and ICTR proceedings where accused have complained about the performance of counsel to their respective national disciplinary boards (see Chapter 1, section 1.5.2, footnote 133). These situations, however, differ from those envisaged by the ICC Code of Conduct, namely that the counsel's conduct qualifies at both the national and international level as misconduct. This is certainly not the case with the aforementioned situations, where the conduct of counsel is lawful according to ICTY and ICTR standards and, moreover, is explicitly called for. The ICC Code of Conduct does not solve this difficult and undesirable situation for counsel. Rather, the solution lies in an expanded attribution of immunities to counsel; this requires both amendment of the APIC (see Chapter 1, section 1.5.2) and Article 30 of the ICC Code.

[155] See Article 38(4) of the Code:
When the alleged misconduct is the basis of a disciplinary procedure which has already been initiated before the relevant national authority, the procedure before the Disciplinary Board shall be suspended until a final decision is reached regarding the former procedure, unless:

(a) the national authority does not respond to communications and consultations in accordance with paragraph 2 of this article within a reasonable time;
(b) the Disciplinary Board considers that the information received is not satisfactory; or
(c) the Disciplinary Board considers that, in the light of the information received, the national authority is unable or unwilling to conclude the disciplinary procedure.

[156] It should be noted that there is primary jurisdiction for the ICC over offences against the administration of justice (Article 70 of the ICC Statute). We see no reason to depart from that regime, which is closely related to disciplinary sanctions for counsel's misconduct.

[157] Report of the Expert Group to Conduct a Review of the Effective Operation and Functioning of the International Tribunal for the Former Yugoslavia and the International Criminal Tribunal for Rwanda, para. 84.

mention Rule 84 *bis* of the ICTY Rules, which allows the defence to make statements at various stages of the trial, including the opening phase. The idea behind this rule is that since the accused is asked to present his or her version of the facts at the outset of the trial, there will be no need to further prove facts that he or she evidently does not contest. One notes in the case law of the SCSL a strong urge for the defence to be cooperative.[158]

All of these efforts appear reasonable in the context of compelling needs to expedite proceedings. However, we have difficulty with obligations that go against the spirit of the privilege against self-incrimination and also with possible negative inferences that might be drawn for an accused if his defence counsel is not sufficiently cooperative.[159]

2.6 REGISTRAR

Although one cannot pass over the registry as one of the organs that exists in all institutions of international criminal justice,[160] we can be brief as to its position as a participant in the proceedings. In fact, there is hardly any, because the registry does not have an independent role in those proceedings. However, its supportive function should not be underestimated. The registry serves the judges and manages court proceedings. A vital difference from registry services in domestic criminal justice systems is that the registry in international criminal tribunals has been allocated a number of tasks which are more than managerial matters and have important legal aspects, including judicial decision-making. In this respect, we mention the registrar's role in the management of detention units, in the context of which the registrar is empowered, inter alia, to restrict communication with detainees.[161] Furthermore, the registrar plays a crucial role in respect of the defence, especially when it comes to assigning, withdrawing, and reassigning counsel.[162] However, it has to be acknowledged that the registry's decisions

[158] See the opinion of Judge Robertson in the *Fofana* case: 'Every counsel for every party appearing in this Special Court has a duty to assist [the Court]: this obligation entails a duty to make admissions, if requested and at an early stage, of facts that they have no reason to dispute later in the trial. This is an *ethical duty* binding professionally on all counsel who appear in this court: it is reflected in the Code of Conduct [of the Special court] recently adopted, but exists from the moment that counsel accepts instructions. . . . The presumption of innocence . . . does not relieve defence counsel of their duty to make admissions, if requested, of matters which cannot or will not be disputed' (Separate opinion of Justice Robertson, Fofana — Decision on Appeal against 'Decision on Prosecution's Motion for Judicial Notice and Admission of Evidence', *Prosecutor v. Norman et al.*, Case No. SCSL-04-14-AR73, SCSL, A. Ch., 16 May 2005, para. 11). See also the Decision on Co-operation between the Parties, *Prosecutor v. Norman et al.*, Case No. SCSL-04-14-PT, SCSL, T. Ch., 26 May 2004, where the defence and prosecutor were ordered to submit a joint statement containing all agreed points of fact and law.

[159] The matter is explored from the perspective of the accused's right to remain silent in Chapter 8, section 8.5.4.

[160] On this matter, see J. R. W. D. Jones, 'Composition of the Court', in Cassese et al., *Rome Statute Commentary*, *vol. I*, at 275–83.

[161] Note the ICTY registrar's measures in respect of Šešelj and Milošević (early 2004) and also Decision Prohibiting Communications and Visits, *Prosecutor v. Norman*, Case No. SCSL-2003-08-PT, SCSL, Registry, 21 January 2004.

[162] See, as an example, Decision, *Prosecutor v. Hadžihasanović et al.*, Case No. IT-01-47-PT, ICTY, Registrar, 19 December 2001.

in those important areas are subject to judicial review.[163] Be this as it may, the important role of the registrar in areas which are normally reserved for the judiciary gives rise to pertinent questions, notably concerning the relationship with the judicial branch. These questions are also triggered by far-reaching and unclear instances of attribution or delegation of tasks by the judiciary to the registrar.

The first example concerns the appointment of amici curiae in the *Milošević* case.[164] The Trial Chamber requested the registrar to appoint the amici. In fact, while the ICTY Rules allow the registrar to assign counsel, the invitation appears to be reserved for the Trial Chamber.[165] One may wonder whether delegation is appropriate here.

Instructions of a more practical nature have at times had significant and undesired legal consequences. We have already alluded to the *Ntuyahaga* case, where the Trial Chamber withdrew the indictment and instructed the registrar to 'take all the necessary measures to execute' that particular decision, including the consequences of the withdrawal.[166] Yet, the origin of the misunderstanding caused by the issuance by the registry of the safe conduct letter for Mr Ntuyahaga lay with the Chamber, gave ambiguous instructions and generally exceeded the scope of appropriate delegation.

In our opinion, the above two examples illustrate the difficulties inherent in the attribution of an amalgam of complex legal tasks to the registrar. While for the judges, both when it comes to the execution of decisions and to the drafting of the rules, the allocation of a significant number of tasks to the registrar may have a certain appeal, they must be alert to preservation of the judicial domain. As a result, instructions should be unambiguous and not require activities that are reserved for the judicial branch.

2.7 VICTIMS

2.7.1 Introductory remarks

The position of victims in criminal proceedings is a complicated matter and may vary from state to state depending upon which notions and purposes of criminal trials are deemed fundamental. Furthermore, while it might be expected that adversarial systems

---

[163] For instance, Decision on Review in Terms of Article 19(E) of the Directive on Assignment of Defence Counsel, *Prosecutor v. Barayagwiza*, Case No. ICTR-97-19-I, ICTR, President, 19 January 2000, and Decision on the Prosecution's Motion for Review of the Decision of the Registrar to Assign Mr. Rodney Dixon as Co-counsel to the Accused Kubura, *Prosecutor v. Hadžihasanović et al.*, Case No. IT-01-47-PT, ICTY, T. Ch. II, 26 March 2002, and Decision on Motion to Reverse the Order of the Registrar under Rule 48(C) of the Rules of Detention, *Prosecutor v. Norman*, Case No. SCSL-2004-14-PT, SCSL, A. Ch., 18 May 2004.

[164] See Order concerning Amici Curiae, *Prosecutor v. Milošević*, Case No. IT-99-37-PT, ICTY, T. Ch. III, 11 January 2002.

[165] See Rules 45 and 74. For a critical view of this point, see Zappalà, *Human Rights in International Criminal Proceedings*, at 63–4.

[166] Decision on the Prosecutor's Motion to Withdraw the Indictment, *Prosecutor v. Ntuyahaga*, Case No. ICTR-98-40-T, ICTR, T. Ch. I, 18 March 1999. For the facts, see note 71 *et seq.* above, and accompanying text.

would be more hostile to giving victims a strong role in criminal proceedings — as this can distort the fact-finding process so that it ceases to be a contest between two equal parties—this is not necessarily the case. In fact, both systems have different roles for victims and generalizations appear to be impossible along the civil law/common law distinction.[167] In international criminal justice systems victims initially played a highly marginal role, but the permanent ICC has embarked upon an extensive and ambitious participatory and reparatory programme for victims. We can safely say that the enhanced status of victims in the ICC is the result of the input in negotiation of civil-law countries, which are familiar with a strong role for victims in criminal proceedings, as well as the input of certain NGOs concerned with victims' rights.[168] Whether this is in all regards a sensible approach will be explored below. A distinction will be made between four roles of the victim in criminal proceedings: (a) victims as witnesses; (b) victims as subjects empowered to initiate and/or join investigations and prosecutions; (c) victims as distinct participants in the proceedings; and (d) victims as beneficiaries of reparation for damages.

2.7.2 Victims as witnesses

The primary role victims have fulfilled until now and will continue to fulfil in international criminal proceedings is that of a source of evidence, namely testimonial evidence. The strong reliance on testimonial evidence in the context of the ICTY, the ICTR, and the SCSL has given rise to the practice whereby witnesses are continually pushed to give testimony in court. Although witnesses have a duty to testify before these tribunals, both parties to the proceedings and judges are generally reluctant to resort to this subpoena power. Not only is it a cumbersome procedure, but implementation of a subpoena is ultimately dependent on state cooperation, which may not be readily given.[169] As a result, in practice witnesses are in a strong bargaining position in respect of prospective testimony. This has given rise to two areas of concern, which tend, for reasons of sympathy towards the victim or witness, to be somewhat neglected.

First, protective measures for witnesses are almost automatically granted in most ICTY, ICTR, and SCSL cases. The trial chambers have gradually substituted a strict 'objective fear test' for more flexible criteria and are generally satisfied by a claim of 'overall volatile security situation'.[170] One may wonder what is problematic about this development, especially if both prosecution and defence benefit from these protective

---

[167] For an overview of the position of victims in a number of criminal jurisdictions, see C. M. Bradley, *Criminal Procedure — A Worldwide Study* (Durham: Carolina Academic Press, 1999).

[168] See Th. van Boven, 'The Position of the Victim in the Statute of the International Criminal Court', in H. A. M. von Hebel et al. (eds), *Reflections on the International Criminal Court. Essays in Honour of Adriaan Bos* (The Hague: TMC. Asser Press, 1999), at 83.

[169] The problem is that the subpoena needs to be implemented via enforcement of sentences imposed by the ICTY, ICTR, or SCSL. States may not have the legal tools to enforce these sentences, as they may comprise penalties not provided for in the Statutes (e.g. fines) and also may be related to 'secondary' crimes not punished by the Statute. For further details, see G. Sluiter, 'The ICTY and Offences against the Administration of Justice' (2004) 2 *JICJ*, at 631–41.

[170] See G. Sluiter, 'The ICTR and the Protection of Witnesses' (2005) 3 *JICJ*, at 968–9.

measures and extensive individual assessment of the need for protective measures would be a significant burden on the legal process.[171] As a result, one gains the impression that the principle of publicity of hearings is not excessively impaired. Yet, a public hearing serves in international criminal law a broader purpose than ensuring the accused's individual right to a fair trial, namely that of making trials accessible and transparent, especially to the societies concerned. This is a sufficient justification for the critical assessment of each individual application for protective measures.

As to the precise implementation of protective measures, there is also some reason for concern. It has to be acknowledged that the *Tadić* decision granting full anonymity to prosecution witnesses[172] was an isolated incident and that the opposing party has been in a position ever since to challenge the testimony provided by a witness benefiting from protective measures. However, the case law of the ICTR and the SCSL has extended the scope of protective measures by providing for so-called 'rolling disclosure'. Pursuant to Rule 69(C) of the SCSL and ICTR Rules, it is possible to withhold the identity of protected witnesses from the opposing party after the commencement of the trial but allowing sufficient time for the preparation of cross-examination.[173] This possibility stemmed from the concern that the time from the disclosure of the identity of protected witnesses prior to the commencement of the trial to the moment when the testimony is actually given may in long international criminal trials amount to a considerable period and have negative effects on the protection offered. However, the drawback of this approach is that the defence — once fully engaged in the trial — has very little opportunity effectively to prepare to challenge the testimony and in fact its right to adequate time and facilities to prepare the defence is impaired.[174]

The second area of concern in relation to witnesses before international criminal tribunals has received less attention, because it is generally not the object of litigation; nevertheless, it is of overriding importance for the fair and effective administration of justice. It concerns the covering of expenses and other agreements that may have been made to encourage the witness to give testimony in court. Undeniably, the strong bargaining position of witnesses is likely to result in some form of financial or other compensation. While this is not by definition problematic, reimbursement of expenses may represent huge sums of money for the witnesses concerned. In these circumstances, one should not take lightly the possibility of witnesses providing evidence that suits the negotiating partner, be it prosecution or defence counsel. The matter was raised by defence counsel in the Dutch *Van Anraat* case, concerning complicity in war crimes

---

[171] Ibid.   [172] *Tadić* protective measures decision.

[173] Note that Rule 69(C) of the ICTY Rules still provides for disclosure of the witnesses' identity prior to trial. It should also be borne in mind that the acceptance of Rule 69(C) at the ICTR was preceded by a controversial decision on this matter (Decision and Scheduling Order on the Prosecution Motion for Harmonisation and Modification of Protective Measures for Witnesses, *Prosecutor* v. *Bagosora et al.*, Case No. ICTR-98–41-I, ICTR, T. Ch. III, 5 December 2001), with a strong and convincing dissenting opinion from Judge Dolenc (Separate Dissenting Opinion of Judge Pavel Dolenc on the Decision and Scheduling Order on the Prosecution Motion for Harmonisation and Modification of Protective Measures for Witnesses, *Prosecutor* v. *Bagosora et al.*, Case No. ICTR-98-41-I, ICTR, T. Ch. III, 5 December 2001).

[174] This fundamental right is protected in Article 21 of the ICTY Statute, Article 20 of the ICTR Statute, and Article 67 of the ICC Statute.

and genocide, where the prosecution had taken testimony from victims of attacks with chemical weapons in Iran.[175] What matters in these situations is consistency and the transparency of compensation schemes. Furthermore, chambers should in assessing the credibility of witnesses be more courageous in taking into account the benefits witnesses derive from giving testimony. Compensation may take the form not only of covering expenses, but also of certain protective measures, like relocation to a more stable and prosperous country, and a significant reduction of sentence as the result of a plea agreement.

The above reasons for caution will come even more strongly to the fore in the ICC. While the ICTY, the ICTR, and the SCSL still have the subpoena power to 'impress' witnesses, there is no such option for the ICC. For reasons that remain incomprehensible, the appearance of witnesses before the ICC is entirely dependent on their own free will.[176] As a result, their bargaining position is very strong and will in all likelihood have consequences for the scope of protective measures and other benefits. In the interests of justice, there is every reason for the greatest caution in bargaining over giving testimony and offering money or other advantages which are likely to cast serious doubt on the testimony's probative value.

2.7.3 Power to initiate and/or join investigations and prosecutions

Unlike the role of victims as witnesses, which is a vital one in all criminal jurisdictions, the right of victims to initiate or join investigations and prosecutions is far more controversial. It goes to the heart of criminal law as a public rather than private matter. At the national level there are diverging approaches ranging from the prosecutorial monopoly of the state to the power of the victim to set a prosecution in motion.[177] In a number of civil-law jurisdictions it is possible for victims to initiate prosecutions.[178]

In addition to the arguments that are generally advanced to withhold from a victim the right to set a prosecution in motion, it is not difficult to see why such a right would be particularly inappropriate in the context of international criminal proceedings. The most important is undeniably that it infringes too much upon the independent position of the prosecutor, who especially in the context of international crimes may

---

[175] The Hague district court, judgment of 23 December 2005, case no. LJN: AU8685; for the English translation use LJN: AX6406.

[176] See Article 93(1)(e) of the ICC Statute on facilitating voluntary appearance and Article 93(7) making the transfer of detained witnesses to the seat of the Court dependent upon their informed consent. In our opinion, parties approaching witnesses should also inform them that they cannot be obliged to give testimony before the ICC.

[177] For a comparative overview, see J. Pradel, *Droit pénal comparé*, 2nd edn (Paris: Dalloz, 2002), at 540–5. Between these extremes is the availability of a corrective mechanism for victims; in the Netherlands, for example, the victim can apply to the Court of Appeal to order the prosecution service to initiate prosecutions (see Article 12 of the Dutch Code of Criminal Procedure).

[178] See G. J. Mekjian and M. C. Varughese, 'Hearing the Victim's Voice: Analysis of Victim's Advocate Participation in the Trial Proceedings of the International Criminal Court' (2005) 17 *Pace International Law Review*, at 16–17 and related footnotes. However, note that the foundation of adversarial criminal procedure is the dispute between private parties; as a result, in the England and Wales victims can prosecute (see section 6 of the Prosecution of Offences Act 1985, as well as J. Pradel, *Droit pénal comparé*, at 541).

have legitimate interests that differ from those of victims.[179] Furthermore, it is highly probable that the drafters of the Rome Statute were not very keen on the idea of having the ICC used, like Belgian courts,[180] as a forum for human rights groups initiating proceedings. As a result, the role of victim at the start of investigations is confined in the context of international criminal proceedings to supplying information. Notably, in the context of the ICC, victims are entitled, on the one hand, to make representations to the Pre-Trial Chamber in connection with the prosecutor's request for authorization of an investigation and, on the other hand, to receive from the prosecutor a follow-up on the preliminary examination where they have provided him with information and this has not resulted in the initiation of investigation (Article 15(3) and (6)).

2.7.4 Victim participation in criminal proceedings

While the ad hoc tribunals and the SCSL do not allow for any participation by victims other than their role as witnesses, the ICC Statute contains an innovation offering victims an independent participatory right in criminal proceedings. Article 68(3) of the ICC Statute provides as follows:

Where the personal interests of the victims are affected, the Court shall permit their views and concerns to be presented and considered at stages of the proceedings determined to be appropriate by the Court and in a manner which is not prejudicial to or inconsistent with the rights of the accused and a fair and impartial trial. Such views and concerns may be presented by the legal representatives of the victims where the Court considers it appropriate, in accordance with the Rules of Procedure and Evidence.

It should be noted that the legal framework of the East Timor special panels also allows for participation but is more specific about what is intended. Section 12 of UNTAET Regulation 2001/25 on transitional rules of criminal procedure provides, among other things, that:

12.3 Any victim has the right to be heard at a review hearing before the Investigating Judge, and at any hearing on an application for conditional release pursuant to Section 43 of the present regulation. In the exercise of this right, the victim may be represented in court by a legal representative. An individual victim has the right to be notified by the prosecutor, or by the police in proceedings pursuant to Section 44 of the present regulation, in advance of the time and place of review hearings referred to in Sections 20, 29.5 and 43 of the present regulation, provided that the victim has previously indicated in a reasonable manner to the court, prosecutor or investigating officer a desire to be so notified. ...

12.5 A victim may request to the court to be heard at stages of the criminal proceedings other than review hearings.

---

[179] Cf. C. Jorda and J. de Hemptinne, 'The Status and Role of the Victim' in Cassese et al., *Rome Statute Commentary*, at 1392.

[180] On the Belgian experience and practice, where the combination of *un droit de poursuite* for victims and universal jurisdiction for international crimes resulted in criminal investigations of foreign (former) heads of states and members of cabinet, see D. Vandermeersch, 'Prosecuting International Crimes in Belgium' (2005) 3 *JICJ*, at 400–21.

12.6   The victim has the right to request the Public Prosecutor to conduct specific investigations or to take specific measures in order to prove the guilt of the suspect. The Public Prosecutor may accept or reject the request. . . .

12.8   The Public Prosecutor shall take reasonable steps to keep the victims informed of the progress of the case.

In relation to the ICC, the broad language of its relevant articles raises numerous questions both as to their underlying rationale and as to their conceivable implementation.

The underlying rationale for victim participation can best be explained by the strong emphasis on the position of victims during the Rome negotiations, among other things, as a result of the prominent role played by NGOs. An example of their views follows.

The Prosecutor's statutory duties and the interests of efficiency mandate that he or she should also represent the rights and interests of victims in the investigation and prosecution. However, given that the Prosecutor's actions most probably will be governed by the desire to gain a successful conviction, it is possible that the victim's interests and the interests of the Prosecutor will not coincide. For this reason, the Rules should recognise and give effect to the independent voice of victims in the process.[181]

This appears rather vague, just as the text of Article 68(3) is. What exactly is intended and is participation really desirable in international criminal proceedings?

A few critical remarks are in order concerning the independent participation of victims in criminal proceedings. In the Netherlands the right of victims to speak out in court and inform the court about the consequences of the crime has recently been introduced.[182] This right has met with criticism in that its use may prejudice the accused, because victims generally introduce negative information which the defence is unable to challenge, and because there is a risk of overburdening the court system. Furthermore, some commentators consider the possibility of submitting reparatory claims in Dutch criminal proceedings to be informative enough for the judges.[183]

These points of criticism also apply to the international criminal justice system. But there are two additional points that make allowing for participation by victims a potentially harmful experiment. First, in contrast to ordinary national proceedings we are dealing with potentially hundreds or even thousands of victims who may very well overburden the system. Secondly, and far more important, the international criminal justice system is still a highly fragile system that should stay clear of experiments until the system has been put in order. In other words, given that trials lasting for a number of years are no exception even without victims participating, modesty in any ambitious experiments seems fitting. The broad language of Article 68(3) of the Statute is all the more surprising in light of the other experiment introduced, namely, the possibility of submitting reparatory claims. Why not, in this initial phase of the ICC, confine ambitions regarding victims' status to claiming reparations?

---

[181]   Views submitted by Human Rights Watch, as cited in C. Jorda and J. de Hemptinne, 'The Status and Role of the Victim', in Cassese et al., *Rome Statute Commentary*, at 1396.

[182]   See Article 302 of the Dutch Code of Criminal Procedure.

[183]   For this possibility, see Article 51a–f of the Dutch Code of Criminal Procedure.

While there is every reason for a cautious approach, the ICC Pre-Trial Chamber has surprisingly set a different tone. In the *Situation in the Congo* victims have been permitted to participate in the investigative phase and in a very broad manner;[184] taking the opposite view to that of the prosecutor, the Pre-Trial Chamber ruled that victims may

in connection with the current investigation:

    (a) Present their views and concerns;
    (b) File documents;
    (c) Request the Pre-Trial Chamber to order specific measures.[185]

The Chamber offered a puzzling and far from reasonable analysis, but also paved the way for fact-finding by victims by recognizing their role in contributing to the clarification of facts and by allowing them to request the Chamber to order specific proceedings.[186] A viable role for the victim in the fact-finding process raises substantive problems of fairness and also accountability. We have no doubt that the victim's role in fact-finding may be damaging to the accused, especially if one bears in mind that the same victim may have a strong (financial) interest in conviction with a view to reparation proceedings. The decision thus goes beyond any reasonable participatory right in what is still a highly fragile system.[187]

2.7.5 Victims submitting reparatory claims

The final role of victims, as beneficiaries of reparations, raises the fundamental question of demarcation between criminal and civil proceedings. In fact, reparation to victims is, as already implied in the terminology, a matter of civil and not criminal law. It has found its way into domestic criminal proceedings of a predominantly inquisitorial nature with the aim of not burdening the victim with expensive and slow civil proceedings. This argument applies equally to international criminal proceedings. An additional argument for inserting reparation proceedings in that context is the lack of credible alternative fora, which is a vital distinction from domestic jurisdictions. The lack of an international civil court raises complicated legal issues.

The Statutes of the ICTY and ICTR under the heading 'penalties' offer the following possibility: 'In addition to imprisonment, the Trial Chambers may order the return of any property and proceeds acquired by criminal conduct, including by means of duress, to their rightful owners.'[188]

---

[184] On the participatory role for victims in the pre-trial phase see C. Stahn et al., 'Participation of Victims in Pre-Trial Proceedings of the ICC' (2006) 4 *JICJ*, at 219–38.

[185] Decision on the Applications for Participation in the Proceedings of VPRS 1, VPRS 2, VPRS 3, VPRS 4, VPRS 5 and VPRS 6, *Situation in the Democratic Republic of the Congo*, Case No. ICC-01/04, ICC, PTC I, 17 January 2006, disposition.   [186] Ibid., paras 63 and 75.

[187] The prosecutor tried to appeal, but leave was denied as was the appeal without such leave; see Judgment on the Prosecutor's Application for Extraordinary Review of Pre-Trial Chamber I's 31 March 2006 Decision Denying Leave to Appeal, *Situation in the Democratic Republic of the Congo*, Case No. ICC-01/04, ICC, A. Ch., 13 July 2006.

[188] Article 24(3) of the ICTY Statute and Article 23(3) of the ICTR Statute.

The provision is restricted to the return of property and thus does not appear to allow for a broader approach to reparation, for example in the form of value confiscation. It has remained a dead letter in the practice of the ICTY and ICTR. In the *Milošević* case an attempt was made to put it into effect, by requesting states to freeze assets of the accused, with a view to ensuring the future return of property to victims.[189] While all UN members were ordered to search and freeze assets of the accused, to our knowledge implementation of the order has left much to be desired and has not been heard of since.[190]

It might have been expected that the drafters of the ICC Statute would have noted that this minimal possibility of reparation was practically never used by the ICTY and ICTR. The underlying message of ICTY and ICTR experience is clearly that every participant in the proceedings has his or her hands full bringing the criminal trial to a satisfactory end.

Yet, Article 75 of the ICC Statute offers the legal basis for an ambitious programme of reparation to victims.[191] According to this provision, reparation is possible in the form of restitution, compensation, or rehabilitation; it may be ordered at the request of the victim or on the Chamber's own motion; the reparation will be paid either directly by the convicted person, or through the Trust Fund (Article 79 of the ICC Statute); with a view to enforcing an order for reparation, cooperation in the sense of Article 93(1) and Article 109 of the ICC Statute may be sought.[192]

The ICC reparation proceedings present opportunities, but also difficulties. First, there is the problem of a criminal court venturing into civil law. This also appears as a problem in domestic proceedings; for example, in the Netherlands claims by victims which are not of a 'simple nature' are declared inadmissible, not suitable for criminal proceedings.[193] In the same vein, we may expect complex claims for reparation to be submitted to the ICC, which raises the question of the capacity of criminal judges to deal with them. In this respect, the possibility referred to in Rule 97 to appoint experts to assess claims is certainly welcome. However, there is still a significant problem regarding the applicable law. In domestic criminal proceedings the application of civil law within the framework of a criminal procedure is possible because of the familiarity with a national system of civil law of which at least the general principles are applicable.

---

[189] Decision on Review of Indictment and Application for Consequential Orders, *Prosecutor* v. *Milošević et al.*, Case No. IT-99-37-I, ICTY, T. Ch., 24 May 1999.

[190] One wonders whether a similar request issued by the ICC's Pre-Trial Chamber I to search for and freeze the assets of the accused Lubanga will share the same fate. See Request to States Parties to the Rome Statute for the Identification, Tracing and Freezing or Seizure of the Property and Assets of Mr. Thomas Lubanga Dyilo, *Prosecutor* v. *Lubanga Dyilo, Situation in the Democratic Republic of the Congo*, Case No. ICC-01/04-01/06, ICC, PTC I, 31 March 2006.

[191] Note that in the case of the East Timor special panels — which looked at the ICC law as a model for both substantive and procedural law — there is no similar possibility of reparation. Section 10 of UNTAET Regulation 2000/15 allows for the forfeiture of proceeds, property, and assets directly or indirectly derived from the crime, without indicating victims as beneficiaries. However, pursuant to Section 25 of the same Regulation the money collected through fines and forfeitures may be ordered to be transferred to the Trust Fund, which is there for the benefit of victims. [192] Details of the reparation procedure can be found in Rules 94–9 of the ICC RPE.

[193] Cf. Article 51a of Dutch Code of Criminal Procedure.

Such a fallback option is absent at the international level. At a more general level, the drafters of the Rome Statute totally overlooked the need to establish principles of direct civil liability under international law. As a result, the decision on reparation, which is a question of civil liability, is to be made without a proper legal framework.

One provision that may be to the benefit of the procedure before the Court is that, in contrast to national proceedings, reparations need not always be paid by the convicted person, but may also be charged to the Trust Fund. While this has the benefit of shielding the convicted person from complex claims, the Court will have to be cautious not to let this blur admissibility and assessment criteria. In other words, the fact that a Trust Fund disposes of some resources to help victims should not influence the determination of civil liability. A final point concerns the enforcement of reparation orders, which only concerns orders directed to the convicted person. Both the regime applicable to this enforcement — Article 109 of the ICC Statute — and the implementation of such orders in the domestic legal orders raise complicated questions.[194]

2.8 CONCLUSION

The above overview of participants in international criminal proceedings warrants a number of conclusions. First, the uncertainty in respect of the nature of international criminal proceedings — adversarial/inquisitorial — is undeniably reflected in the roles and relations *inter se* of all participants in those proceedings. Participants may not feel comfortable with what exactly is expected of them in terms of being more active (more partisan) or more passive (impartial). This impression may be reinforced by changes in the laws and by the creation of new institutions, with different emphases. As far as the ICC is concerned, it will be interesting to see to what extent the prosecutor will develop into a more civil-law-oriented prosecutor. Secondly, the participants in the proceedings also suffer from the international criminal tribunals' nature of 'self-contained' regimes, in the sense that there is neither a clear legal setting nor an institutional or societal framework in which the tribunals are embedded. A clear example is the problematic development of an international criminal bar association. Furthermore, there are no support services available to the tribunals comparable to those at the national level. This has resulted in a registry combining services and powers which tend to be strictly separated in national criminal jurisdictions. Thirdly, as if the aforementioned uncertainties were not problematic enough, the drafters of the ICC have added to the legal confusion by introducing victims as major participants. The role in the proceedings envisaged for victims represents unjustified optimism, given the current poor state of international criminal proceedings.

---

[194] For more details, see C. Kress and G. Sluiter, 'Enforcement', in Cassese et al., *Rome Statute Commentary*, at 1723–810.

3

'CUSTOM' AND OTHER SOURCES OF SUBSTANTIVE INTERNATIONAL CRIMINAL LAW

SUMMARY

3.1 INTRODUCTION

One of the most important areas of controversy and confusion in the practice of the ad hoc tribunals has been their choice and use of sources, to define, among other things, elements of crimes and forms of personal criminal liability. This chapter reviews the various sources of law utilized by the tribunals and the methods employed to interpret them.[1] One should be aware that the law of evidence and procedure is much more flexible than substantive law, since there is no requirement that the former law is fixed and known at the time of the commission of the offence. Procedural innovations, of which there have been many at the tribunals, must conform with the principle of fairness, but the issues they raise are generally not entangled with those examined in this chapter.[2]

---

[1] For a history of the sources of the law of armed conflict up until 1949, see Green, *Contemporary Law of Armed Conflict*, pp. 20–53.

[2] See Part III of this book for a discussion of the development of the law of procedure and evidence at the tribunals.

Traditionally, the sources of international law are taken to be those listed in Article 38 of the 1945 Statute of the International Court of Justice, and in theory this is true of the sources of substantive international criminal law as well:

1. The Court, whose function is to decide in accordance with international law such disputes as are submitted to it, shall apply:

   a. international conventions, whether general or particular, establishing rules expressly recognized by the contesting states;
   b. international custom, as evidence of a general practice accepted as law;
   c. the general principles of law recognized by civilized nations;
   d. subject to the provisions of Article 59, judicial decisions and the teachings of the most highly qualified publicists of the various nations, as subsidiary means for the determination of rules of law.

2. This provision shall not prejudice the power of the Court to decide a case *ex aequo et bono*, if the parties agree thereto.

How does one get from this to *criminal law* with its myriad elements; that is, to a workable criminal law which oils the gears of a busy criminal court and has the more than occasional effect of incarcerating individuals for years? Compared with state jurisdictions, where the whole of the criminal law is found in Acts of Parliament and in judicial decisions that have interpreted and applied the legislature's provisions, the ad hoc tribunals, and in particular the ICTY and ICTR, have lived the life of hunter-gatherers in a legal wilderness. They have had to track down and synthesize for themselves the law to apply to the facts.

3.2 THE UNCERTAIN INSISTENCE ON CUSTOMARY INTERNATIONAL LAW

It is the very ad-hocness of international criminal tribunals (the fact that they post-date the alleged crimes) that places them at a disadvantage in relation to sources of law. The Nuremberg Tribunal suffered from the problem of having to pass judgment as an *ex post facto* court. The same is true of the latter-day tribunals. Their 'statutes' are retrospective and are not themselves *law*; they are, rather, pointers to a law existing in some form in the rarefied sphere of international law at the time of the alleged offences.

The Nuremberg judges would have quibbled over this last claim, yet in the final analysis they too viewed the International Military Tribunal's charter negatively, as a limitation on jurisdiction, not as the law itself. For the latter they were obliged to look elsewhere. This is clear from the IMT judgment, where the court undertakes to excavate the foundations of its charter, revealing first a layer of treaties, and beneath that a layer of general legal principles.

The IMT's approach must be reviewed in some detail, since it is a model that contemporary tribunals have aspired to follow. The tribunal at Nuremberg began from the following position:

The jurisdiction of the Tribunal is defined in the Agreement[3] and Charter,[4] and the crimes coming within the jurisdiction of the Tribunal, for which there shall be individual responsibility, are set out in Article 6. The law of the Charter is decisive, and binding upon the Tribunal.[5]

Despite this remark, the tribunal was to concede that if the charter was law, it was law derived from other sources:

The Charter is not an arbitrary exercise of power on the part of the victorious nations, but in the view of the Tribunal, as will be shown, it is the expression of international law existing at the time of its creation.[6]

There was no reasonable alternative to this concession. The German defendants possessed a powerful argument:

It was urged on behalf of the defendants that a fundamental principle of all law — international and domestic — is that there can be no punishment of crime without a pre-existing law. 'Nullum crimen sine lege. Nulla poena sine lege.' It was submitted that ex post facto punishment is abhorrent to the law of all civilized nations.[7]

The international tribunal agreed with this position. It was not possible, therefore, to take the charter at face value. Not only was it not statutory law, it did not even *evidence* law. The law was evidenced, rather, by treaties.

The IMT indictment listed several international treaties which Germany allegedly had violated, among them the 1899 and 1907 Hague Conventions for the Pacific Settlement of International Disputes, the 1919 Treaty of Versailles, and the 1928 Kellogg–Briand Pact. Numerous bilateral treaties, conventions, and pacts which Germany had entered into with other countries, providing for arbitration, reconciliation, and non-aggression, had also been cast aside by Germany, according to the indictment.[8]

What was the relationship of the 'law of the charter' to these treaties? Was it the charter's role to bring to the fore, and consolidate, treaty-law prohibitions pre-dating the alleged offences? Was it the IMT's role to punish violations of these treaties per se? Or did the charter stand for a different kind of law and the IMT for a different kind of adjudication? The Nuremberg judges wrote:

The nations who signed the [Kellogg–Briand] pact or adhered to it unconditionally condemned recourse to war for the future as an instrument of policy, and expressly renounced it. After the signing of the pact, any nation resorting to war as an instrument of national policy breaks the pact.[9]

So far, this is only about the Pact, but then:

In the opinion of the Tribunal, the solemn renunciation of war as an instrument of national policy necessarily involves the proposition that such a war is illegal in international law; and that those who plan and wage such a war, with its inevitable and terrible consequences, are committing a crime in so doing.[10]

---

[3] London Agreement, 8 August 1945 (1951) *UNTS* 280.   [4] (1951) *UNTS* 284.
[5] 22 IMT Judgment 461.   [6] Ibid.   [7] Ibid., at. 461–2.
[8] 1 IMT Judgment 84–92 (Appendix C of indictment).   [9] 22 IMT Judgment 463.   [10] Ibid.

As for jurisdiction over personal responsibility, while the IMT barely touched on the subject, it said enough to indicate that it was operating outside the sphere of treaties:

It was submitted that international law is concerned with the actions of sovereign states and provides no punishment for individuals; and further, that where the act in question is an act of state, those who carry it out are not personally responsible, but are protected by the doctrine of the sovereignty of the state. In the opinion of the Tribunal, both these submissions must be rejected. That international law imposes duties and liabilities upon individuals as well as upon states has long been recognized.[11]

Beyond the treaties, then, lies the 'international law' which those treaties helped to create.[12] Where this has occurred, the criminal law has, as it were, broken free from its mother treaties between states and has become a body of law in its own right, and a type of law, moreover, that gives rise to individual criminal liability.

But there are also cases where 'international law' pre-existed treaties. The treaties merely gave expression to the older criminal law:

The Hague Convention of 1907 prohibited resort to certain methods of waging war. These included the inhumane treatment of prisoners, the employment of poisoned weapons, the improper use of flags of truce, and similar matters. Many of these prohibitions had been enforced long before the date of the Convention; but since 1907 they have certainly been crimes, punishable as offences against the laws of war; yet the Hague Convention nowhere designates such practices as criminal, nor is any sentence prescribed, nor any mention made of a court to try and punish offenders. For many years past, however, military tribunals have tried and punished individuals guilty of violating the rules of land warfare laid down by this Convention. . . . The law of war is to be found not only in treaties, but in the customs and practices of states which gradually obtained universal recognition, and from the general principles of justice applied by jurists and practiced by military courts.[13]

There is a lot of information in this excerpt about sources of international criminal law, including the suggestion that state military tribunals are an important source. Not everything, however, is perspicuous. The last quoted sentence suggests that treaties may be utilized as sources for the law of war *in addition to* customs and practices of states. (As we shall see, this remains a hotly contested issue at the ICTY.) Moreover, Nuremberg takes the existence of 'customs and practices of states' for granted; if there is a method to determine them, the Second World War tribunal never tells us what it is.

About fifty years later, the UN Secretary-General, in his report on the ICTY Statute, expressed his opinion on the sources of law which are open to an ad hoc international criminal tribunal:

According to paragraph 1 of resolution 808 (1993), the International Tribunal shall prosecute persons responsible for serious violations of international humanitarian law committed in the territory of the former Yugoslavia since 1991. This body of law exists in the form of both conventional law and customary law. While there is international customary law which is not laid

---

[11] Ibid., at. 465.

[12] There is extensive scholarship on this topic. See, for example, G. Fitzmaurice, 'Some Problems Regarding the Formal Sources of International Law' (1958) *Symbolae Verzijl* 153; and R. Baxter, 'Multilateral Treaties as Evidence of Customary International Law' (1965) 41 *Brit. Y'book Int'l Law* 275.   [13] 22 IMT Judgment 463–4.

down in conventions, some of the major conventional humanitarian law has become part of customary international law.[14]

Even though the temporal jurisdiction of the ICTY was to be open-ended ('since 1991'), as noted earlier the ICTY was to be mostly an *ex post facto* court, dealing with offences committed for the most part prior to the ICTY's establishment.

By the time of the Secretary-General's report, the principle of *nullum crimen sine lege* referred to by the IMT had been incorporated into human-rights conventions[15] and had been elaborated in international case law.[16]

The next passage in the Secretary-General's report on the ICTY Statute acknowledged the *ex post facto* nature of the new court. This passage was to become the reference point of controversy about the law the ICTY was to apply:

In the view of the Secretary-General, the application of the principle nullum crimen sine lege requires that the international tribunal should apply rules of international humanitarian law which are beyond any doubt part of customary law so that the problem of adherence of some but not all States to specific conventions does not arise. This would appear to be particularly important in the context of an international tribunal prosecuting persons responsible for serious violations of international humanitarian law.[17]

In the domain of international law it is accepted practice to give weight to interpretations of the law by persons who do not hold a judicial or academic position, such as the head of the UN or the head of the International Committee of the Red Cross, on the assumption that they are neutral and well advised. For different reasons (explained below), the pronouncements of state spokespersons are also regularly accorded some weight.

In the above opinion, the UN Secretary-General appears to draw from the principle of legality the conclusion that the ICTY is bound to apply customary law only. Another possible reading of the opinion is that if the ICTY were to apply *conventional* law it would run into the problem that not every state has signed up to every relevant treaty, for example Additional Protocol I. If the latter reading is correct, then the problem identified by the Secretary-General can be overcome in those cases where the warring states or parties to an armed conflict are signatories to the relevant international convention, or to a local agreement incorporating humanitarian-law provisions, in which

---

[14] Report of the Secretary-General on ICTY, para. 33.

[15] For example, ECHR, Article 7: 'No one shall be held guilty of any criminal offence on account of any act or omission which did not constitute a criminal offence under national or international law at the time when it was committed'; also ICCPR, Article 15.

[16] For example, *Kokkinakis* v. *Greece*, ECtHR, 25 May 1993, para. 52: 'The Court points out that Article 7 para. 1 of the Convention is not confined to prohibiting the retrospective application of the criminal law to an accused's disadvantage. It also embodies, more generally, the principle that only the law can define a crime and prescribe a penalty (*nullum crimen, nulla poena sine lege*) and the principle that the criminal law must not be extensively construed to an accused's detriment, for instance by analogy; it follows from this that an offence must be clearly defined in law. This condition is satisfied where the individual can know from the wording of the relevant provision and, if need be, with the assistance of the courts' interpretation of it, what acts and omissions will make him liable.' Offences must be defined with 'sufficient accessibility and foreseeability' (*Streletz, Kessler, and Krenz* v. *Germany*, ECtHR, 22 March 2001, para. 105).

[17] Report of the Secretary-General on ICTY, para. 34.

case there is no 'problem of adherence,' and therefore enforcement of the agreed law would not in itself be a breach of the *nullum crimen sine lege* principle. This is a question we shall return to below.

The Secretary-General's 1993 report proceeds to identify several sources of law that are safely open to the ICTY:

The part of conventional international humanitarian law which has beyond doubt become part of international customary law is the law applicable in armed conflict as embodied in: the Geneva Conventions of 12 August 1949 for the Protection of War Victims; the Hague Convention (IV) Respecting the Laws and Customs of War on Land and the Regulations annexed thereto of 18 October 1907; the Convention on the Prevention and Punishment of the Crime of Genocide of 9 December 1948; and the Charter of the International Military Tribunal of 8 August 1945.[18]

This conclusion about the transformation of certain parts of conventional law into customary law is only slightly elucidated in later remarks by the Secretary-General, as we shall see. The student of sources will want to know by what path this conclusion was reached. The truth is that there is no simple answer.

When the Secretary-General wrote that the Geneva Conventions 'embodied' customary international law, he particularly had in mind the handful of 'grave breaches' provisions in each Convention.[19] This source, as a source of customary international law, is therefore much more limited than might seem at first. The Secretary-General also gave an indication as to the peculiar effect in this sphere of law of UN resolutions:

The Security Council has reaffirmed on several occasions that persons who commit or order the commission of grave breaches of the 1949 Geneva Conventions in the territory of the former Yugoslavia are individually responsible for such breaches as serious violations of international humanitarian law.[20]

The several reaffirmations are recalled here by the Secretary-General not simply as information but for the purpose of relieving any anxiety about the provision in the Conventions calling on the contracting parties to enact legislation to penalize individuals for the commission of grave breaches.[21] The Secretary-General's point is that, whatever may have been the progress at the state level to that end, the international community has recognized through UN resolutions that there is personal liability for grave breaches.

We may now ask the same question about the IMT Charter: what is the meaning and basis of the Secretary-General's remark that the IMT Charter is beyond doubt part of customary law? Consider the following difficulty. The Charter gave the tribunal jurisdiction over crimes including 'crimes against peace', defining the latter as the waging of a war of aggression, or a war in violation of international treaties, agreements, or assurances.[22] The IMT said in its judgment:

All these expressions of opinion, and others that could be cited, so solemnly made, reinforce the construction which the Tribunal placed upon the Pact of Paris, that resort to a war of aggression is not merely illegal, but is criminal. The prohibition of aggressive war demanded by the

---

[18] Ibid., para. 35.   [19] Ibid., paras 37–8.   [20] Ibid., para. 39.
[21] See, for example, Article 146 of Geneva Convention IV.   [22] IMT Charter, Article 6(a).

conscience of the world finds its expression in the series of pacts and treaties to which the Tribunal has just referred.[23]

Yet in 1998, in the lead-up to the Rome Statute, the international community was unable to agree to a legal definition of the 'crime of aggression'. The ICC Statute draws a blank at this point, promising that the question will be revisited and the gap filled in due course.[24] In what sense, then, is a crime against peace part of international customary law already since 1946, as the Secretary-General implied when he said that the IMT Charter is beyond doubt part of customary law? A healthily sceptical attitude is essential to the study of international criminal law and its sources. Much is made to seem certain when it is not.

The law of grave breaches was linked to Article 2 of the ICTY Statute, whereas 'violations of the laws or customs of war' was linked to Article 3. The Secretary-General commented on the sources for the latter provision:

The 1907 Hague Convention (IV) Respecting the Laws and Customs of War on Land and the Regulations annexed thereto comprise a second important area of conventional humanitarian international law which has become part of the body of international customary law. The Nürnberg Tribunal recognized that many of the provisions contained in the Hague Regulations, although innovative at the time of their adoption were, by 1939, recognized by all civilized nations and were regarded as being declaratory of the laws and customs of war. The Nürnberg Tribunal also recognized that war crimes defined in article 6(b) of the Nürnberg Charter were already recognized as war crimes under international law, and covered in the Hague Regulations, for which guilty individuals were punishable.[25]

The Secretary-General's report noted that the Hague Regulations covered aspects of international humanitarian law which were later written into the 1949 Geneva Conventions, but that the Regulations also recognized that the right of belligerents to conduct warfare is not unlimited and that resort to certain methods of waging war is prohibited under the rules of land warfare. An important point, in respect of sources, is the Secretary-General's stipulation that war-crimes law at the ICTY is to be understood 'as interpreted and applied by the Nürnberg Tribunal'.[26]

On the law of genocide, the Secretary-General wrote that its customary nature is evidenced by the ICJ's 1951 Advisory Opinion on reservations to the Genocide Convention.[27] Genocide law was linked to Article 4 of the ICTY Statute.

Finally, the law of crimes against humanity, which Article 5 of the ICTY Statute was made to stand for, was sourced to the IMT Judgment, but also to the case law of the national military courts that were established in accordance with Control Council Law No. 10, which closely resembled the IMT Charter. The Secretary-General wrote:

Crimes against humanity were first recognized in the Charter and Judgement of the Nürnberg Tribunal, as well as in Law No. 10 of the Control Council for Germany. . . . In the conflict in the territory of the former Yugoslavia, such inhumane acts have taken the form of so-called 'ethnic

---

[23] 22 IMT Judgment 465.

[24] ICC Statute, Article 5. For an overview of the history of the crime of aggression, see Preparatory Commission for the ICC, *Historical Review of Developments Relating to Aggression*, UN Doc. PCNICC/2002/WGCA/L.1, 24 January 2002.   [25] Report of the Secretary-General on ICTY, paras 41–2.

[26] Ibid., para. 44.   [27] Ibid., para. 45.

cleansing' and widespread and systematic rape and other forms of sexual assault, including enforced prostitution.[28]

We have thus seen several sources of international criminal law described in the Secretary-General's 1993 report. In relation to law not relating to subject-matter or personal jurisdiction, it was largely left to the ICTY judges to decide the proper sources. On defences, for example,

the International Tribunal itself will have to decide on various personal defences which may relieve a person of individual criminal responsibility, such as minimum age or mental incapacity, drawing upon general principles of law recognized by all nations.[29]

The rules of procedure and evidence of the IMT[30] and of the military tribunals under Control Council Law No. 10[31] were not mentioned in this connection. The ICTY judges were to come up with their own rules.

The principle of *nullum crimen sine lege* goes hand in hand with that of *nulla poena sine lege*, as noted by the IMT. The UN Secretary-General recognized this in his report on the ICTY when referring to the determination of terms of imprisonment:

Suggestions have been made that the international tribunal should apply domestic law in so far as it incorporates customary international humanitarian law. . . . there is one related issue which would require reference to domestic practice, namely, penalties . . . In determining the term of imprisonment, the Trial Chambers should have recourse to the general practice of prison sentences applicable in the courts of the former Yugoslavia.[32]

In addition to opening up the legal system of the former Yugoslavia as a source of law for the ICTY, this comment signals a relaxation of the requirement that the law applied at the tribunal must be 'beyond any doubt part of customary law'.

The Secretary-General did not produce a similar report for the ICTR until some months after the ICTR Statute was finalized at the end of 1994.[33] The statute had limited the ICTR's temporal jurisdiction to the 1994 period. Its fourth article adopted provisions of conventional law, namely 'serious violations of Article 3 common to the Geneva Conventions of 12 August 1949 for the Protection of War Victims, and of Additional Protocol II thereto of 8 June 1977'. The Secretary-General wrote about this new *ex post facto* court:

the Security Council has elected to take a more expansive approach to the choice of the applicable law than the one underlying the statute of the Yugoslav Tribunal, and included within the subject-matter jurisdiction of the Rwanda Tribunal international instruments regardless of whether they were considered part of customary international law or whether they have customarily entailed the individual criminal responsibility of the perpetrator of the crime. Article 4 of the statute, accordingly, includes violations of Additional Protocol II, which, as a whole, has not yet been universally recognized as part of customary international law, and for the first time criminalizes common article 3 of the four Geneva Conventions.[34]

---

[28] Ibid., paras 47–8.   [29] Ibid., para. 58.   [30] 1 IMT Judgment 19–23.

[31] Uniform Rules of Procedure, 8 January 1948, 15 *TWC* 70–8.

[32] Report of the Secretary-General on ICTY, paras 36, 111.

[33] The ICTR Statute was annexed to UN Resolution 955, 8 November 1994.

[34] Report of the Secretary-General Pursuant to Paragraph 5 of Security Council Resolution 955 (1994), UN Doc. S/1995/134, 13 February 1995, para. 12.

This statement has added to the general confusion about sources. How does a 'more expansive approach' dovetail with the principle of *nullum crimen sine lege* and the prohibition of extension of the law by analogy? How could the statute of an *ex post facto* court — which statute is no more than a constitutive instrument — criminalize anything 'for the first time'? The Secretary-General implied here that an ad hoc tribunal may enforce international treaty provisions per se, as if they were a criminal statute; in other words, as if they were an original source of law.

The UN's philosophy on the law applicable to tribunals with jurisdiction in the sphere of international criminal law found subsequent expression in a report preceding the establishment of the Special Court for Sierra Leone. The Secretary-General wrote in that report of late 2000:

The subject-matter jurisdiction of the Special Court comprises crimes under international humanitarian law and Sierra Leonean law. . . . In recognition of the principle of legality, in particular nullum crimen sine lege, and the prohibition on retroactive criminal legislation, the international crimes enumerated, are crimes considered to have had the character of customary international law at the time of the alleged commission of the crime.[35]

The jurisprudential output of the ICTY and ICTR by this time was already considerable, and any hesitation the Secretary-General might have felt seven years earlier about setting up the ad hoc tribunals of the mid-1990s was no longer in evidence. He was now in a position to trace a line of pedigree between the jurisprudence of Nuremberg and that of Yugoslavia and Rwanda:

The list of crimes against humanity follows the enumeration included in the Statutes of the International Tribunals for the Former Yugoslavia and for Rwanda, which were patterned on article 6 of the Nürnberg Charter. Violations of common article 3 of the Geneva Conventions and of article 4 of Additional Protocol II thereto committed in an armed conflict not of an international character have long been considered customary international law, and in particular since the establishment of the two International Tribunals, have been recognized as customarily entailing the individual criminal responsibility of the accused.[36]

By this time the Rome Statute of the ICC had been agreed, providing the Secretary-General with an additional rhetorical platform when setting up the SCSL. The ICC had codified customary law, but it had also created new law to be used within the framework of this non-retroactive court.

The theory that *ex post facto* tribunals were to apply only customary law called for caution when borrowing from the 1998 ICC Statute. One ICC provision forbids 'Conscripting or enlisting children under the age of fifteen years into armed forces or groups or using them to participate actively in hostilities'.[37] The Secretary-General, writing in October 2000, did not consider this formulation suitable for insertion into the SCSL Statute, preferring instead 'Abduction and forced recruitment of children under the age of 15 years into armed forces or groups for the purpose of using them to

---

[35] Report of the Secretary-General on the Establishment of a Special Court for Sierra Leone, UN Doc. S/2000/915, 4 October 2000, para. 12.   [36] Ibid., para. 14.
[37] Article 2(e)(vii).

participate actively in hostilities'.[38] He explained:

Owing to the doubtful customary nature of the ICC Statutory crime which criminalizes the conscription or enlistment of children under the age of 15, whether forced or 'voluntary', the crime which is included in article 4(c) of the Statute of the Special Court is not the equivalent of the ICC provision. While the definition of the crime as 'conscripting' or 'enlisting' connotes an administrative act of putting one's name on a list and formal entry into the armed forces, the elements of the crime under the proposed Statute of the Special Court are: (a) abduction, which in the case of the children of Sierra Leone was the original crime and is in itself a crime under common article 3 of the Geneva Conventions; (b) forced recruitment in the most general sense — administrative formalities, obviously, notwithstanding; and (c) transformation of the child into, and its use as, among other degrading uses, a 'child-combatant'.[39]

However, finally, the SCSL Statute of January 2002 came to include the same formulation as the Rome Statute.[40] This shift towards including prohibitions that were not beyond doubt part of customary law was, as we have seen nothing new.[41]

The *ex post facto* tribunal that borrowed most heavily from the Rome Statute was the Special Panels of East Timor. This system was created by regulation of the United Nations Transitional Administration in East Timor.[42] The ETSP Statute's provision for war crimes is word for word that of the ICC. Large parts of it are not customary international law. Section 12.1 does provide the guarantee that 'A person shall not be criminally responsible under the present regulation unless the conduct in question constitutes, at the time it takes place, a crime under international law or the laws of East Timor'. But one is left to wonder why the UN took such a different approach in the case of East Timor.

We have seen, then, that both the Nuremberg Tribunal and, decades later, the UN Secretary-General, have insisted, although not without ambiguity and not without significant exceptions, that international or internationalized criminal courts shall apply or prefer customary international law.

3.3 THE BATTLE OVER SOURCES AT THE ICTY

The question whether an international criminal tribunal may enforce treaty provisions binding on the parties to a conflict even if the prohibition as formulated in the treaty is not an offence in customary international law was answered in the affirmative in the

---

[38] Report of the Secretary-General on the Establishment of a Special Court for Sierra Leone, UN Doc. S/2000/915, 4 October 2000, para. 15(c).   [39] Ibid., para. 18.

[40] SCSL Statute, Article 4(c).

[41] Judge Robertson of the SCSL argued that the criminalization of child enlistment only took effect upon the adoption of the Rome Statute, and therefore he declined to find that the SCSL had jurisdiction to deal with charges of child enlistment for acts predating July 1998: *Prosecutor* v. *Sam Hinga Norman*, Decision on Preliminary Motion Based on Lack of Jurisdiction, Dissenting Opinion of Justice Robertson, 31 May 2004.

[42] UNTAET Regulation No. 2000/15 on the Establishment of Panels With Exclusive Jurisdiction Over Serious Criminal Offences, 6 June 2000.

first major decision of the ICTY Appeals Chamber. The pronouncement in the *Tadić* case seems to contradict what the Secretary-General had written in his report (although we have noted the ambiguity in that particular passage, and, as we shall see, *Tadić* latched on to the ambiguity to deny that there was any contradiction).

The issue in *Tadić* was the scope of the ICTY's subject-matter jurisdiction pursuant to Article 3 of its Statute (violations of the laws or customs of war). The court held:

The following requirements must be met for an offence to be subject to prosecution before the International Tribunal under Article 3:

  (i) the violation must constitute an infringement of a rule of international humanitarian law;
  (ii) the rule must be customary in nature or, if it belongs to treaty law, the required conditions must be met . . .
  (iii) the violation must be 'serious', that is to say, it must constitute a breach of a rule protecting important values, and the breach must involve grave consequences for the victim . . .
  (iv) the violation of the rule must entail, under customary or conventional law, the individual criminal responsibility of the person breaching the rule.[43]

The distinction between customary and treaty law was revisited in the same decision under the heading 'May the International Tribunal also apply international agreements binding upon the conflicting parties?':

It should be emphasised again that the only reason behind the stated purpose of the drafters that the International Tribunal should apply customary international law was to avoid violating the principle of nullum crimen sine lege in the event that a party to the conflict did not adhere to a specific treaty. . . . It follows that the International Tribunal is authorised to apply, in addition to customary international law, any treaty which: (i) was unquestionably binding on the parties at the time of the alleged offence; and (ii) was not in conflict with or derogating from peremptory norms of international law, as are most customary rules of international humanitarian law. This analysis of the jurisdiction of the International Tribunal is borne out by the statements made in the Security Council at the time the Statute was adopted. . . . representatives of the United States, the United Kingdom and France all agreed that Article 3 of the Statute did not exclude application of international agreements binding on the parties.[44]

This, one must note, was an obiter dictum. Tadić had not been charged with a violation of any agreement.[45] Another problem, one could say, is that the Appeals Chamber did not explain by which logic a non-treaty-based international tribunal might utilize treaty provisions as the law against which defendants would be judged. Yet, one might retort, why is the proposition that such a tribunal may hold a person accountable for violations of *customary* international law inherently more logical? What is so self-evident about the latter, yet so in need of explanation in the case of the former? *Tadić* had limited itself, after all, to treaties which 'must entail . . . the individual criminal responsibility of the person breaching the rule'.

Most likely, *Tadić* was taking its lead from Article 38 of the ICJ Statute, quoted at the start of this chapter. Article 38 gives greater prominence to treaties — and of course a treaty has the distinct advantage of relative clarity and precision compared with that

---

[43] *Tadić* jurisdiction appeal decision, para. 94.   [44] Ibid., para. 143.   [45] Ibid., para. 144.

body of customary international law which has yet to be incorporated into a treaty. As one commentator has noted:

The advantage of the employment of a treaty as evidence of customary international law, as it was at the time of the adoption of the treaty or as it has come to be, is that it provides a clear and uniform statement of the rule to which a number of States subscribe. There is no problem of reconciling ambiguous and inconsistent State practice of varying antiquity and varying authority. The treaty speaks with one voice as of one time.[46]

Following the *Tadić* pronouncement, two schools emerged at the ICTY, one seeking to undermine it, the other taking advantage of its implied methodological shortcut. Neither school thought it prudent to analyse its own assumptions, or to acknowledge the existence of the other school. Thus more than a decade has passed without any discussion in the tribunal's jurisprudence (or, for that matter, in the academic world)[47] of this weakness in the institution's intellectual foundations.

The anti-*Tadić* school took to reiterating its favourite axiom. Here are three examples from decisions of three differently constituted benches of the ICTY Appeals Chamber:

The scope of the Tribunal's jurisdiction *ratione materiae* may therefore be said to be determined both by the Statute, insofar as it sets out the jurisdictional framework of the International Tribunal, and by customary international law, insofar as the Tribunal's power to convict an accused of any crime listed in the Statute depends on its existence *qua* custom at the time this crime was allegedly committed.[48]

The obligation of the Tribunal to rely on customary international law excludes any necessity to cite conventional law where customary international law is relied on. Contrary to the arguments of the Appellants, there is nothing in the Secretary-General's Report, to which the Statute of the Tribunal was attached in draft, which requires both a customary basis and a conventional one for an incrimination. . . . The Appeals Chamber holds the view that this Tribunal can impose criminal responsibility only if the crime charged was clearly established under customary law at the time the events in issue occurred. In case of doubt, criminal responsibility cannot be found to exist, thereby preserving full respect for the principle of legality.[49]

The Tribunal may enter convictions only where it is satisfied that the offence is proscribed under customary international law at the time of its commission.[50]

The pro-*Tadić* school grew out of uses of Additional Protocol I, especially in the *Kordić and Čerkez* and *Galić* trial judgments.[51] At the time of writing, the Appeals Chamber had not decided Galić's appeal, but a bench of the Appeals Chamber in *Kordić and*

---

[46] R. Baxter, 'Multilateral Treaties as Evidence of Customary International Law' (1965) 41 *Brit. Y'book Int'l Law* 275, 299.

[47] See, e.g., Cassese, *International Criminal Law*, pp. 25–37. Mettraux, *International Crimes*, pp. 5–9, is an advocate of the anti-*Tadić* tendency.

[48] *Prosecutor* v. *M. Milutinović et al.*, Decision (on appeal) on Dragoljub Ojdanić's Motion Challenging Jurisdiction — Joint Criminal Enterprise, 21 May 2003, para. 9.

[49] *Prosecutor* v. *E. Hadžihasanović et al.*, Decision on Interlocutory Appeal Challenging Jurisdiction in Relation to Command Responsibility, 16 July 2003, paras 35, 51.   [50] *Blaškić* appeal judgment, para. 141.

[51] Paras 165–9 and 63–138 of those judgments, respectively.

Čerkez had reaffirmed *Tadić*, and in a strikingly inept act of housekeeping had attempted to sweep the problem of the anti-*Tadić* tendency under the carpet:

The Appeals Chamber notes that the Trial Chamber considered that Article 3 of the Statute covers not only violations which are based in customary international law but also those based on treaties. It found that Additional Protocol I constituted applicable treaty law in the present case, and found that 'whether [Additional Protocol I] reflected customary law at the relevant time in this case is beside the point.' The Appeals Chamber holds that the Trial Chamber's approach is correct.... The Trial Chamber's approach is also in line with the Report of the Secretary-General ... The Trial Chamber's approach corresponds with the Appeals Chamber's early decision on jurisdiction in the *Tadić* case ... Later, in *Čelebići*, the Appeals Chamber relied upon *Tadić* in its finding that Bosnia and Herzegovina was bound by the 1949 Geneva Conventions *qua* treaty obligations at the time of the alleged offences in that case.... The Appeals Chamber wishes to avoid any ambiguity on this issue that may arise from language it used in *Ojdanić*, *Hadžihasanović* and the *Blaškić* Appeal Judgement [quoted above] which, read out of context, could be misunderstood as vesting jurisdiction in this International Tribunal only for crimes based on customary international law at the time of its commission, but not for treaty-based crimes, however listed in the Statute of this International Tribunal.... In each of the three decisions, the legal issues at stake were solved by applying provisions of international customary law. In the present case, however, reference will have to be made to applicable treaty law that established a crime at the time of its commission.[52]

So, unless the Appeals Chamber changes its position again (this will happen, if at all, in the *Galić* appeal judgment, which was not available at the time of writing), the ad hoc tribunals may source their applicable law to any treaty which, in the words of *Tadić*, was unquestionably binding on the parties at the time of the alleged offences and was not in conflict with, or did not derogate from, peremptory norms of international law.

An attractive feature of this result is that it gives teeth to humanitarian-law agreements brokered by the ICRC among warring (non-state) parties. Already, the ICTY, in the *Galić* case,[53] has relied on one such agreement as evidence that the applicable law included parts of Additional Protocol I. The anti-*Tadić* school has not so far been able to articulate why this is the wrong result — that is, why consent evidenced by a treaty is unenforceable by an ad hoc tribunal, whereas consent implicit in customary international law is enforceable.

Our own position is that, given that the Security Council intended that the ICTY should apply rules in international humanitarian law agreements irrespective of their customary-law status, there is no in-principle obstacle to such an application, as long as there is no breach of the principle of legality, and as long as the rule in question is within the jurisdictional framework of the tribunal's statute.

---

[52] *Kordić and Čerkez* trial judgment, paras 41–6.   [53] *Galić* trial judgment, paras 22–5.

3.4 METHODS OF DISCOVERY OR METHODS OF CREATION?

If the choice is made to utilize customary international law, how does one determine its content? This is a question with no simple answer. The tribunals have not articulated a method,[54] with the consequence that if a method exists, it must be abstracted from the practice of the tribunals.[55] But it is safe to say that there is no one method. We have chosen in this section to quote extensively from the jurisprudence of the tribunals, so that the student of this problem is in a better position to appreciate for himself or herself the variety of approaches.

We begin with a typical definition of customary law:

Customary international law is created by State practice. State practice means any act or state-ment by a State from which views about customary law can be inferred; it includes physical acts, claims, declarations *in abstracto* (such as General Assembly resolutions), national laws, national judgements and omissions. Customary international law can also be created by the practice of international organizations and (in theory, at least) by the practice of individuals.

As regards the quantity of practice needed to create a customary rule, the number of States par-ticipating is more important than the frequency or duration of the practice. Even a practice fol-lowed by a few States, on a few occasions and for a short period of time, can create a customary rule, provided that there is no practice which conflicts with the rule, and provided that other things are equal.[56]

Treaties are also part of state practice, of course.

In addition to state practice there must be *opinio juris*:

Not only must the acts concerned amount to a settled practice, but they must also be such, or be carried out in such a way, as to be evidence of a belief that this practice is rendered obligatory by the existence of a rule of law requiring it. The need for such a belief, i.e., the existence of a sub-jective element, is implicit in the very notion of the *opinio juris sive necessitatis*. The States con-cerned must therefore feel that they are conforming to what amounts to a legal obligation.[57]

State practice need not evince rigorous conformity with the identified rule:

[It is sufficient that] the conduct of States should, in general, be consistent with such rules, and that instances of State conduct inconsistent with a given rule should generally have been treated as breaches of that rule, not as indications of the recognition of a new rule. If a State acts in a way prima facie incompatible with a recognized rule, but defends its conduct by appealing to

---

[54] Cf. Cassese, *International Criminal Law*, pp. 28–30, where the suggestion that such a method exists is a mere assumption. For a critical comment on the 'inconsistent and incoherent methodology' of international tribunals in relation to sources of law, see I. Bantekas, 'Reflections on Some Sources and Methods of International Criminal and Humanitarian Law' (2006) 6 *Int'l Crim. L. Rev.* 121.

[55] Mettraux, *International Crimes*, pp. 13–18, implies that there is a method, but does not manage to explain what it is, or indeed convince us that there really is one.

[56] M. Akehurst, 'Custom as a Source of International Law' (1974–75) 47 *Brit. Y'book Int'l Law* 53.

[57] *North Sea Continental Shelf Cases*, ICJ Report 1969, 3, para. 77.

exceptions or justifications contained within the rule itself, then whether or not the State's conduct is in fact justifiable on that basis, the significance of that attitude is to confirm rather than to weaken the rule.[58]

The formula of state practice plus *opinio juris* represents the theory of 'custom' in its elementary form, yet in a world of non-state organizations whose purpose it is to unite, regulate, critique, or compete with states, the notion of customary law and the mechanisms of its formation have been broadened:

Rather than state practice plus *opinio juris*, multilateral forums often play a central role in the creation and shaping of contemporary international law. Those forums include the United Nations General Assembly and Security Council, regional organizations, and standing and ad hoc multilateral diplomatic conferences, as well as international organizations devoted to specialized subjects.[59]

A loosening of the formula of state practice and *opinio juris* may in any case be necessary in international *criminal* law, since practice is likely to relate to domestic criminal law, for which there will be no *opinio juris*.

The *Tadić* jurisdiction appeal decision was the first to make findings on customary international law applicable at the tribunals. With respect to Additional Protocol II, it said that many of its provisions can be considered declaratory of existing rules of international law, or as having 'crystallized' emerging rules:

This proposition is confirmed by the views expressed by a number of States. Thus, for example, mention can be made of the stand taken in 1987 by El Salvador (a State party to Protocol II). After having been repeatedly invited by the General Assembly to comply with humanitarian law in the civil war raging on its territory (see, e.g., G.A. Res. 41/157 (1986)), the Salvadorian Government declared that, strictly speaking, Protocol II did not apply to that civil war (although an objective evaluation prompted some Governments to conclude that all the conditions for such applications were met . . .). Nevertheless, the Salvadorian Government undertook to comply with the provisions of the Protocol, for it considered that such provisions 'developed and supplemented' common Article 3, 'which in turn constituted the minimum protection due to every human being at any time and place' . . . Similarly, in 1987, Mr. M. J. Matheson, speaking in his capacity as Deputy Legal Adviser of the United States State Department, stated that: 'the basic core of Protocol II is, of course, reflected in common article 3 of the 1949 Geneva Conventions and therefore is, and should be, a part of generally accepted customary law. This specifically includes its prohibitions on violence towards persons taking no active part in hostilities, hostage taking, degrading treatment, and punishment without due process.'[60]

This was the extent of the argument: first, evidence of a half-hearted concession by a minor state; secondly, endorsement by a US official. The argument is focused on *opinio juris*; no reference is made to state practice. If there is a method here, it is not evident.

---

[58] *Military and Paramilitary Activities in and against Nicaragua, ICJ Report* 1986, 14, para. 186.

[59] J. Charney, 'Universal International Law' (1993) 87 *Am. J. Int'l Law* 529, 544. See also B. Sloan, 'General Assembly Resolutions Revisited' (1987) 58 *Brit. J. Int'l Law* 93.

[60] *Tadić* jurisdiction appeal decision, para. 117.

In the appeal against the *Erdemović* sentencing judgment — the ICTY's first judgment — the question arose whether duress is a complete defence to the killing of innocent persons. Two of the judges in the majority explained why, in their view, there was no customary-law basis for such a defence:

To the extent that the domestic decisions and national laws of States relating to the issue of duress as a defence to murder may be regarded as state practice, it is quite plain that this practice is not at all consistent. The defence in its Notice of Appeal surveys the criminal codes and legislation of 14 civil law jurisdictions in which necessity or duress is prescribed as a general exculpatory principle applying to all crimes. The surveyed jurisdictions comprise those of Austria, Belgium, Brazil, Greece, Italy, Finland, the Netherlands, France, Germany, Peru, Spain, Switzerland, Sweden and the former Yugoslavia. Indeed, the war crimes decisions cited in the Separate Opinion of Judge Cassese are based upon the acceptance of duress as a general defence to all crimes in the criminal codes of France, Italy, Germany, the Netherlands and Belgium. In stark contrast to this acceptance of duress as a defence to the killing of innocents is the clear position of the various countries throughout the world applying the common law. These common law systems categorically reject duress as a defence to murder. The sole exception is the United States where a few states have accepted Section 2.09 of the United States Penal Code which currently provides that duress is a general defence to all crimes. ... Not only is State practice on the question as to whether duress is a defence to murder far from consistent, this practice of States is not, in our view, underpinned by *opinio juris*.[61]

This was one of the earliest 'surveys' of state jurisdictions. The *Erdemović* judges also, or at the same time, relied heavily on the Nuremberg-inspired European war-crimes cases. Europe's influence on *Erdemović* was indeed strong. The slant is evident from the names of the countries mentioned in the above passage. Judge Cassese unearthed a multitude of minor war-related Italian cases.[62] He repeated the exercise in the appeal from the *Tadić* trial judgment, in a survey aimed at establishing the customary-law basis of the doctrine of joint criminal enterprise.[63] Language and cultural barriers, and the inaccessibility of material, have meant that surveys of state practice are highly selective. There are seldom references to practice in the Russian Federation, India, China, Indonesia, South Africa, or Nigeria, for example.[64] The ICRC's website has made it possible to access humanitarian-law provisions and case summaries from a large number of countries in translation,[65] but the information is of little value to a lawyer with no grounding in a given country's legal system and little or no understanding of the authority that that system attaches to a particular legal proposition.

Another survey was conducted by the *Furundžija* Trial Chamber, with the aim of determining the elements of rape in international law. The chamber did not claim that the resulting definition of rape was the *customary-law* definition, although probably it

---

[61] *Erdemović* appeal judgment, separate opinion of Judges McDonald and Vohra, paras 49–50.

[62] *Erdemović* appeal judgment, separate and dissenting opinion of Judge Cassese, para. 35.

[63] *Tadić* appeal judgment, paras 214–19.

[64] In all of the ICTY and ICTR judgments, there is just one passing reference to Indian legal practice (*Furundžija* trial judgment, fn. 209), one to China's system (*Tadić* trial judgment, para. 538), and none to the other countries mentioned in the text.

[65] ICRC national implementation database (www.icrc.org/ihl-nat).

should be understood as that:

No definition of rape can be found in international law ... to arrive at an accurate definition of rape based on the criminal law principle of specificity ... it is necessary to look for principles of criminal law common to the major legal systems of the world. These principles may be derived, with all due caution, from national laws.

Whenever international criminal rules do not define a notion of criminal law, reliance upon national legislation is justified, subject to the following conditions: (i) unless indicated by an international rule, reference should not be made to one national legal system only, say that of common-law or that of civil-law States. Rather, international courts must draw upon the general concepts and legal institutions common to all the major legal systems of the world. This presupposes a process of identification of the common denominators in these legal systems so as to pinpoint the basic notions they share; (ii) ... account must be taken of the specificity of international criminal proceedings when utilising national law notions. In this way a mechanical importation or transposition from national law into international criminal proceedings is avoided, as well as the attendant distortions of the unique traits of such proceedings.

The Trial Chamber would emphasise at the outset, that a trend can be discerned in the national legislation of a number of States of broadening the definition of rape so that it now embraces acts that were previously classified as comparatively less serious offences, that is sexual or indecent assault. This trend shows that at the national level States tend to take a stricter attitude towards serious forms of sexual assault: the stigma of rape now attaches to a growing category of sexual offences, provided of course they meet certain requirements, chiefly that of forced physical penetration.

In its examination of national laws on rape, the Trial Chamber has found that although the laws of many countries specify that rape can only be committed against a woman, others provide that rape can be committed against a victim of either sex. The laws of several jurisdictions state that the actus reus of rape consists of the penetration, however slight, of the female sexual organ by the male sexual organ. There are also jurisdictions which interpret the actus reus of rape broadly. The provisions of civil law jurisdictions often use wording open for interpretation by the courts. Furthermore, all jurisdictions surveyed by the Trial Chamber require an element of force, coercion, threat, or acting without the consent of the victim: force is given a broad interpretation and includes rendering the victim helpless. Some jurisdictions indicate that the force or intimidation can be directed at a third person ...

It is apparent from our survey of national legislation that, in spite of inevitable discrepancies, most legal systems in the common and civil law worlds consider rape to be the forcible sexual penetration of the human body by the penis or the forcible insertion of any other object into either the vagina or the anus.

A major discrepancy may, however, be discerned in the criminalisation of forced oral penetration: some States treat it as sexual assault, while it is categorised as rape in other States. Faced with this lack of uniformity, it falls to the Trial Chamber to establish whether an appropriate solution can be reached by resorting to the general principles of international criminal law or, if such principles are of no avail, to the general principles of international law.

The Trial Chamber holds that the forced penetration of the mouth by the male sexual organ constitutes a most humiliating and degrading attack upon human dignity. The essence of the whole corpus of international humanitarian law as well as human rights law lies in the protection of the human dignity of every person, whatever his or her gender. . . . This principle is intended to shield human beings from outrages upon their personal dignity, whether such outrages are carried out by unlawfully attacking the body or by humiliating and debasing the honour, the self-respect or the mental well being of a person. It is consonant with this principle that such an extremely serious sexual outrage as forced oral penetration should be classified as rape.

Moreover, the Trial Chamber is of the opinion that it is not contrary to the general principle of nullum crimen sine lege to charge an accused with forcible oral sex as rape when in some national jurisdictions, including his own, he could only be charged with sexual assault in respect of the same acts. It is not a question of criminalising acts which were not criminal when they were committed by the accused, since forcible oral sex is in any event a crime, and indeed an extremely serious crime . . .

Thus, the Trial Chamber finds that the following may be accepted as the objective elements of rape: (i) the sexual penetration, however slight: (a) of the vagina or anus of the victim by the penis of the perpetrator or any other object used by the perpetrator; or (b) of the mouth of the victim by the penis of the perpetrator; (ii) by coercion or force or threat of force against the victim or a third person.[66]

Because surveys of state pactice are difficult to carry out, they are few and far between. As noted, most 'surveys' look to a handful of state systems to make generalizations.[67]

The survey-style approach used by the chambers in *Erdemović* and *Furundžija* is to be contrasted with the method (or, really, non-method) employed at around the same time by the Trial Chamber in the *Čelebići* case to answer the defendants' attack on the status of Common Article 3. The defence had argued that this provision of the Geneva Conventions does not constitute customary international law applicable in all armed conflicts. The Trial Chamber wrote in its judgment:

The prohibitions contained in the first paragraph of common article 3 . . . express 'the fundamental principle underlying the four Geneva Conventions' — that of humane treatment. The perpetrators of violations of this article during internal conflicts cannot, on any level of reasoning, be treated more leniently than those who commit the same acts in international conflicts. It would, therefore, appear that the prohibitions contained in common article 3 are of precisely the nature which may be expected to apply in internal, as well as international, armed conflicts.

While in 1949 the insertion of a provision concerning internal armed conflicts into the Geneva Conventions may have been innovative, there can be no question that the protections and prohibitions enunciated in that provision have come to form part of customary international law. . . . This development is illustrative of the evolving nature of customary international law, which is its strength. Since at least the middle of this century, the prevalence of armed conflicts within the confines of one State or ensuing from the breakdown of previous State boundaries is apparent, and absent the necessary conditions for the creation of a comprehensive new law by means of a multilateral treaty, the more fluid and adaptable concept of customary international law takes the fore.[68]

---

[66] *Furundžija* trial judgment, paras 175–85.

[67] See J. P. Humphrey, 'On the Foundations of International Law' (1945) 39 *Am. J. Int'l L.* 231, at 238, for a possible theoretical basis for this kind of selective approach.

[68] *Delalić et al.* trial judgment, paras 300–1.

These two paragraphs contain no argument; they merely assert the proposition which the court sets out to prove. The continuation is no improvement:

The evidence of the existence of such customary law — State practice and *opinio juris* — may, in some situations, be extremely difficult to ascertain, particularly where there exists a prior multilateral treaty which has been adopted by the vast majority of States. The evidence of State practice *outside* of the treaty, providing evidence of separate customary norms or the passage of the conventional norms into the realms of custom, is rendered increasingly elusive, for it would appear that only the practice of non-parties to the treaty can be considered as relevant.

. . . in the *Nicaragua Case* . . . the ICJ found that common article 3 was not merely to be applied in internal armed conflicts, but that, 'There is no doubt that, in the event of international armed conflicts, these rules also constitute a minimum yardstick, in addition to the more elaborate rules which are also to apply to international conflicts; and they are rules which, in the Court's opinion, reflect what the Court in 1949 called 'elementary considerations of humanity'.

. . . That common article 3 was considered included in the law to be applied by the Tribunal is borne out by the statement of the representative of the United States upon the adoption of Security Council resolution 827, which was not contradicted by any other State representative, that 'it is understood that the "laws or customs of war" referred to in Article 3 include all obligations under humanitarian law agreements in force in the territory of the former Yugoslavia at the time the acts were committed, including common Article 3 of the 1949 Geneva Conventions, and the 1977 Additional Protocols to these Conventions'.[69]

We see that, finally, *Čelebići* based its finding on a legal aside in an ICJ judgment and an uncontradicted statement by a US official.

A more traditional approach which, as indictated in *Erdemović*, can be combined with a survey, is to seek support for a rule in the Second World War case law.

What is the authority of this body of law?

A review by Lippman of twelve trials of German war criminals conducted before US military tribunals under Control Council Law No. 10 gives a positive assessment. By affirming that civilians and military officials, no matter how exalted their status, are subject to criminal punishment for violations of international law, these cases 'made an important contribution', writes the author.[70] But what is more remarkable, according to Lippman, is that the trials, which were unprecedented, were carried out at all, and that they were carried out as exercises in reasoned legal analysis: 'Even the fate of enemy belligerents who have committed unspeakable horrors may be fairly adjudicated. Of course, it is true that the Allies did not subject their own combatants to prosecution.'[71]

This last comment hints at criticisms of the fairness of the trials. The prosecuting states had been guilty of many grave offences against Axis civilians, but the real problem from our perspective, sixty years later, is not the selectivity of prosecution but the question of the judiciary's independence (the judiciary having been constituted, for the most part, of Allied servicemen). A lawyer today is reluctant to rely on the jurisprudence of a tribunal not enjoying the appearance of impartiality.

---

[69] Ibid., paras 302–5.

[70] M. Lippman, 'The Other Nuremberg: American Prosecutions of Nazi War Criminals in Occupied Germany' (1992) 3 *Ind. Int'l & Comp. L. Rev.* 1, at 99.   [71] Ibid., p. 100.

Another problem with the Second World War decisions is that they were produced by a multitude of state military courts applying national laws. Their decisions were not taken within the framework of an international legal system, and no one today believes that they have any binding force on the UN's ad hoc tribunals. Use of such 'case law' in tribunal judgments must therefore be regarded with some suspicion. As Kelsen once remarked, 'If there is no legal rule conferring upon a judicial decision the character of a legally binding precedent, this decision has a certain chance of being followed by other decisions on condition that it is recognised as a worthy example for the decision of subsequent similar cases'.[72] Contemporary utilization of Second World War case law is necessarily selective. It is not a matter of *following* a norm articulated in the courts of the Allies but merely of demonstrating that a given norm favoured today is not without historical support.

The student of sources of international criminal law should therefore not assume that the war-crimes case law of the immediate postwar period is a reliable or consistent body of law.

The *Furundžija* Trial Chamber relied heavily on Second World War cases to draw conclusions about the form of liability known as aiding and abetting.[73] (The chamber itself noted that the law applied by the military courts of the UK was domestic, thus rendering their pronouncements 'less helpful in establishing rules of international law on this issue'.)[74] A more limited and selective use of war-related cases was made by the Appeals Chamber in the *Čelebići* case. The question was whether customary law imposes a duty on a commander to know of his or her subordinates' actions, with the consequence that breach of the duty may give rise to the commander's criminal responsibility for a crime committed by a subordinate:

In the *Yamashita* case, the United States Military Commission found that: 'where murder and rape and vicious, revengeful actions are widespread offences, and there is no effective attempt by a commander to discover and control the criminal acts, such a commander may be held responsible, even criminally liable, for the lawless acts of his troops, depending upon their nature and the circumstances surrounding them'.

. . . On the same case, the United Nations War Crimes Commission commented: 'the crimes which were shown to have been committed by Yamashita's troops were so widespread, both in space and in time, that they could be regarded as providing either prima facie evidence that the accused knew of their perpetration, or evidence that he must have failed to fulfil a duty to discover the standard of conduct of his troops.'

. . . Contrary to the Trial Chamber's conclusion, other cases discussed in the Judgement do not show a consistent trend in the decisions that emerged out of the military trials conducted after the Second World War. The citation from the Judgement in the case of *United States v. Wilhelm List* ('*Hostage case*') indicates that List failed to acquire 'supplementary reports to apprise him of all the pertinent facts'. The tribunal in the case found that if a commander of occupied territory 'fails to require and obtain *complete* information' he is guilty of a dereliction of his duty. List was found to be charged with notice of the relevant crimes because of reports which had been made to him.

---

[72] H. Kelsen, 'Will the Judgment in the Nuremberg Trial Constitute a Precedent in International Law?' (1947) 1 *Int'l L. Q.* 153, at 164. [73] *Furundžija* trial judgment, paras 190–249.
[74] Ibid., para. 196.

Therefore, List had in his possession information that should have prompted him to investigate further the situation under his command.[75]

The Appeals Chamber continued by criticizing the Trial Chamber for its interpretation of another German case:

The Trial Chamber also quoted from the *Pohl* case. The phrase quoted is also meant to state a different point than that suggested by the Trial Chamber. In that case, the accused Mummenthey pleaded ignorance of fact in respect of certain aspects of the running of his business which employed concentration camp prisoners. Having refuted this plea by invoking evidence showing that the accused knew fully of those aspects, the tribunal stated: 'Mummenthey's assertions that he did not know what was happening in the labor camps and enterprises under his jurisdiction does not exonerate him. It was his duty to know.' . . . Any suggestion that the tribunal used that statement to express that the accused had a duty under international law to know would be obiter in light of the finding that he had knowledge.

In the *Roechling* case, which was also referred to by the Trial Chamber, the court concluded that Roechling had a 'duty to keep himself informed about the treatment of the deportees'. However, it also noted that 'Roechling . . . had repeated opportunities during the inspection of his concerns to ascertain the fate meted out to his personnel, since he could not fail to notice the prisoner's uniform on those occasions'. This was information which would put him on notice. It is to be noted that the [Allied] courts which referred to the existence of a 'duty to know' at the same time found that the accused were put on notice of subordinates' acts . . .

On the basis of this analysis, the Appeals Chamber must conclude, in the same way as did the United Nations War Crimes Commission, that the then customary law did not impose in the criminal context a general duty to know upon commanders or superiors, breach of which would be sufficient to render him responsible for subordinates' crimes.[76]

This is a selective use of the Second World War cases. It assumes that their jurisprudence is internally consistent, when there is every reason to think that it is not (there is no institutional reason why it should be). And it brushes aside inconvenient conclusions as 'obiter'. Obviously the Appeals Chamber here had decided that the 'ought to have known' standard was too low for command responsibility, even if that was the test applied in some instances against Axis officials.[77]

An aspiration to fill gaps in the law — to legislate from the bench — is often the only method discernible in the tribunals' efforts to prove the existence of a rule of customary law. Of course, the system of ad hoc tribunals lacks the state-variety democratic controls that make law consensual and legislators accountable. An example of this aspirational method, in which ends justify the means, is found in the *Kupreškić et al.* trial judgment, where the issue was whether military reprisals against civilians are prohibited in customary international law:

With regard to civilians in combat zones, reprisals against them are prohibited by Article 51(6) of the First Additional Protocol of 1977, whereas reprisals against civilian objects are outlawed by

---

[75] *Delalić et al.* appeal judgment, paras 228–9.   [76] Ibid., paras 229–30.

[77] A similar approach was taken in the *Blaškić* trial judgment, paras 219–33, where the question under consideration was whether acts rendered serious not by their obvious cruelty but by the discrimination they seek to effect against members of a group because they belong to a particular cultural community may be characterized as persecution.

Article 52(1) of the same instrument. The question nevertheless arises as to whether these provisions, assuming that they were not declaratory of customary international law, have subsequently been transformed into general rules of international law. In other words, are those States which have not ratified the First Protocol (which include such countries as the U.S., France, India, Indonesia, Israel, Japan, Pakistan and Turkey), nevertheless bound by general rules having the same purport as those two provisions? Admittedly, there does not seem to have emerged recently a body of State practice consistently supporting the proposition that one of the elements of custom, namely *usus* or *diuturnitas* has taken shape.[78]

To avoid this impasse the court sought to rely on the so-called Martens clause of the 1899 Hague Convention II:[79]

This is however an area where *opinio juris sive necessitatis* may play a much greater role than *usus*, as a result of the . . . Martens Clause. In the light of the way States and courts have implemented it, this Clause clearly shows that principles of international humanitarian law may emerge through a customary process under the pressure of the demands of humanity or the dictates of public conscience, even where State practice is scant or inconsistent. The other element, in the form of *opinio necessitatis*, crystallising as a result of the imperatives of humanity or public conscience, may turn out to be the decisive element heralding the emergence of a general rule or principle of humanitarian law . . .

It should be added that while reprisals could have had a modicum of justification in the past, when they constituted practically the only effective means of compelling the enemy to abandon unlawful acts of warfare and to comply in future with international law, at present they can no longer be justified in this manner. A means of inducing compliance with international law is at present more widely available and, more importantly, is beginning to prove fairly efficacious: the prosecution and punishment of war crimes and crimes against humanity by national or international courts.[80]

The assertion that international justice 'is beginning to prove fairly efficacious' is fairly speculative. The court continued:

even before the adoption of the First Additional Protocol of 1977, a number of States had declared or laid down in their military manuals that reprisals in modern warfare are only allowed to the extent that they consist of the use, against enemy armed forces, of otherwise prohibited weapons — thus *a contrario* admitting that reprisals against civilians are not allowed. In this respect one can mention the United States military manual for the Army (*The Law of Land Warfare*), of 1956, as well as the Dutch 'Soldiers Handbook' (*Handboek voor de Soldaat*) of 1974. True, other military manuals of the same period took a different position, admitting reprisals against civilians not in the hands of the enemy belligerent. In addition, senior officials of the United States Government seem to have taken a less clear stand in 1978, by expressing doubts about the workability of the prohibition of reprisals against civilians. The fact remains, however, that elements of a widespread *opinio necessitatis* are discernible in international dealings. This is

---

[78] *Kupreškić et al.* trial judgment, para. 527.

[79] 'Until a more complete code of the laws of war is issued, the High Contracting Parties think it right to declare that in cases not included in the Regulations adopted by them, populations and belligerents remain under the protection and empire of the principles of international law, as they result from the usages established between civilized nations, from the laws of humanity, and the requirements of the public conscience.' (Convention With Respect to the Laws and Customs of War on Land, 29 July 1899.)

[80] *Kupreškić et al.* trial judgment, paras 527, 530.

confirmed, first of all, by the adoption, by a vast majority, of a Resolution of the U.N. General Assembly in 1970 which stated that 'civilian populations, or individual members thereof, should not be the object of reprisals'. A further confirmation may be found in the fact that a high number of States have ratified the First Protocol, thereby showing that they take the view that reprisals against civilians must always be prohibited . . .

Secondly, the States that have participated in the numerous international or internal armed conficts which have taken place in the last fifty years have normally refrained from claiming that they had a right to visit reprisals upon enemy civilians in the combat area. . . . The aforementioned elements seem to support the contention that the demands of humanity and the dictates of public conscience, as manifested in *opinio necessitatis*, have by now brought about the formation of a customary rule also binding upon those few States that at some stage did not intend to exclude the abstract legal possibility of resorting to the reprisals under discussion.[81]

Thus the conclusion is cornered and bagged. As a fallback position, though, the Trial Chamber, revealing its allegiance with the pro-*Tadić* school, stated:

Finally, it must be noted, with specific regard to the case at issue, that whatever the content of the customary rules on reprisals, the treaty provisions prohibiting them were in any event applicable in the case in dispute. In 1993, both Croatia and Bosnia and Herzegovina had ratified Additional Protocol I and II, in addition to the four Geneva Conventions of 1949. Hence, whether or not the armed conflict of which the attack on Ahmići formed part is regarded as internal, indisputably the parties to the conflict were bound by the relevant treaty provisions prohibiting reprisals.[82]

One exception to the rule is the decision in the *Vasiljević* case to dismiss a charge of 'violence to life and person' (Article 3 of the ICTY Statute):

the Trial Chamber must further satisfy itself that the criminal conduct in question was sufficiently defined and was sufficiently accessible at the relevant time for it to warrant a criminal conviction and sentencing under the criminal heading chosen by the Prosecution . . .

From the perspective of the nullum crimen sine lege principle, it would be wholly unacceptable for a Trial Chamber to convict an accused person on the basis of a prohibition which, taking into account the specificity of customary international law and allowing for the gradual clarification of the rules of criminal law, is either insufficiently precise to determine conduct and distinguish the criminal from the permissible, or was not sufficiently accessible at the relevant time . . .

The *Blaškić* Trial Chamber defined 'violence to life and person' as 'a broad offence which, at first glance, encompasses murder, mutilation, cruel treatment and torture and which is accordingly defined by the cumulation of the elements of these specific offences'. The Trial Chamber added that the mens rea for this offence is 'characterised once it has been established that the accused

---

[81] Ibid., paras 532–3.

[82] Ibid., para. 536. For another example of the aspirational method, see *Blaškić* appeal judgment, paras 144–9, where the issue was whether plunder or pillage could constitute the crime of persecution under customary international law. Note, in particular, this extraordinary transition from doubt to certainty: 'There may be some doubt, however, as to whether acts of plunder, in and of themselves, may rise to the level of gravity required for crimes against humanity. The Appeals Chamber finds that the destruction of property, depending on the nature and extent of the destruction, may constitute a crime of persecutions of equal gravity to other crimes listed in Article 5 of the Statute.' (Ibid., paras 148–9.)

intended to commit violence to life or person of the victims deliberately or through recklessness'. Unfortunately, the *Blaškić* Trial Chamber omitted to identify the source of these propositions . . .

The residual character of a criminal prohibition such as Article 3 of the Statute does not by itself provide for the criminalisation by analogy to any act which is even vaguely or potentially criminal . . . The fact that an offence is listed in the Statute, or comes within Article 3 of the Statute through common article 3 of the Geneva Conventions, does not therefore create new law, and the Tribunal only has jurisdiction over any listed crime if it was recognised as such by customary international law . . .

If customary international law does not provide for a sufficiently precise definition of a crime listed in the Statute, the Trial Chamber would have no choice but to refrain from exercising its jurisdiction over it, regardless of the fact that the crime is listed as a punishable offence in the Statute.[83]

Another exception is the decision of the Appeals Chamber in the *Kordić and Čerkez* case that Articles 51 and 52 of Additional Protocol I cannot be said to criminalize attacks on civilians or civilian objects where there is no proof of actual injury to civilians or damage to civilian objects. Note how this analysis, which purports to be an exposition of customary international law, amounts to an interpretation of the text of a treaty, and hardly relies on another source for its conclusion:

it could be argued that the drafters of Articles 51 and 52 of Additional Protocol I intended that one did not have to show a particular result in order for a breach (not a grave breach) to be found, when considered in the context of other separate offences proscribed under Additional Protocol I such as wilful killing, causing serious bodily injury, and wanton destruction. Such reading of Articles 51 and 52 of Additional Protocol I could no doubt be reconciled with the underlying humanitarian purpose of Geneva Convention IV, which is to ensure the protection of civilians when and wherever possible. In that case, punishment of an unlawful attack on civilians or civilian objects itself, regardless of the result, would be based on the concrete endangerment of civilian life and/or property, as the perpetrator can no longer control the result of an unlawful attack once launched; thus the mere undertaking of such an *in concreto* or *in abstracto* extremely dangerous attack would be penalized for good reasons.

However, the Appeals Chamber notes that the omission of a result element for a violation of Articles 51 and 52 of Additional Protocol I appears to be deliberate in light of the language later found in Article 85 of Additional Protocol I, which highlights the elements required where a breach of Article 51(2) of Additional Protocol I amounts to another category of breach labelled a 'grave breach'. Article 85(3)(a) of Additional Protocol I states in relevant part, that 'acts shall be regarded as grave breaches of this Protocol, when committed wilfully, in violation of the relevant provisions of this Protocol, and causing death or serious injury to body or health: making the civilian population or individual civilians the object of attack'. Thus, under Article 85(3)(a) of Additional Protocol I, the drafters expressly included the requirement of a showing of actual injury as an element of the crime of 'making the civilian population or individual civilians the object of attack' when considering it to be a grave breach and not merely 'a breach' of Additional Protocol I. . . . it is not clear from the plain language of Additional Protocol I whether violations of Articles 51 and 52 would constitute crimes under international humanitarian law.

---

[83] *Vasiljević* trial judgment, paras 193–203.

For the reasons set out above, the Appeals Chamber finds that attacks in violation of Articles 51 and 52 of Additional Protocol I are clearly unlawful even without causing serious harm as provided for in Article 85 of Additional Protocol I. Under the language of these articles, their criminalisation as a matter of international law depends on the practice of the Contracting States under Article 85 of Additional Protocol I.

The Appeals Chamber finds that at the time the unlawful attack occurred in this case, there was no basis for finding that, as a matter of customary international law, State practice or *opinio iuris* translated the prohibitions under Articles 51 and 52 of Additional Protocol I into international crimes, such that unlawful attacks were largely penalized regardless of the showing of a serious result. State practice was not settled as some required the showing of serious injury, death or damage as a result under their national penal legislation, while others did not.[84]

In the *Stakić* case, the Trial Chamber attempted to expand the reach of the crime of deportation by diluting the legal element of cross-border transfer, arguing that it encompassed forced population displacements across both internationally recognized borders and de facto boundaries having no international status, and even across constantly changing front lines.[85] The majority of the Appeals Chamber found the lower court too adventurous,[86] but it is the dissenting opinion of Judge Shahabuddeen which merits attention. The old formula of state practice plus *opinio juris* is not simply relaxed, it seems to have been supplanted in Shahabuddeen's approach by the methods of the Cambridge school of analytic philosophy. Shahabuddeen argues that even if precedent has always used the term 'deportation' in relation to the crossing of a border (which he disputes), the term was reasonably capable of applying in relation to the crossing of a front line, or even a constantly changing front line. In other words, the Appeals Chamber's chimerical (to him) distinction between deportation and forced transfer-within-borders is the result of linguistic confusion:

customary international law has not taken the position that deportation cannot refer to the crossing of any front line. In *Cyprus v. Turkey*, the European Commission of Human Rights used the term 'deportation' to describe the forcible displacement of Greek Cypriots from the territory controlled by Turkish Cypriots 'across the demarcation line' separating it from the south of Cyprus. It may be said that what was involved there was a de facto boundary. It seems to me, however, that the Commission would not have spoken differently if the demarcation line existed on the first day of the occupation and the displacement was made on that day. Turkey landed troops in Cyprus on 20 July 1974; the application was presented to the Commission on 19 September 1974 — two months later. So there was scarcely time for any front line, whenever established between those dates, to evolve into a 'de facto boundary'. The demarcation line was not a border; it was a front line.

Note has to be taken of what the International Law Commission said in its 1991 report. There, the Commission expressed the view that 'Deportation, already included in the 1954 draft Code, implies expulsion from the national territory, whereas the forcible transfer of population could occur wholly within the frontiers of one and the same State'. The Appeals Chamber relies on the Commission's view, but the Commission itself cites no supporting authority for the distinction which it makes between what, for the sake of simplicity, may be called internal forcible displacement and what may be called external forcible displacement.

---

[84] *Kordić and Čerkez* appeal judgment, paras 62–6.   [85] *Stakić* trial judgment, paras 671–84.
[86] *Stakić* appeal judgment, paras 288–303.

I doubt that the International Law Commission intended its statement to be interpreted literally; it was simply making a general remark on the usual situations in which the terms would apply. . . . On the language which it was considering, the Commission had to allocate the field of operation of each of the terms 'deportation' and 'forcible transfer' as they appeared in the combined expression before the Commission; it does not follow that the field which the Commission allocated to the operation of the term 'deportation' as used in that combined expression has to apply to 'deportation' as used alone in article 5(d) of the [ICTY] Statute. What happened was that the collocation of words in which the term occurred in the provision before the Commission deprived it in that provision of what I consider to be its natural capacity to extend to a front line. . . .

No dependable guidance can be had from article 49 of the Fourth Geneva Convention. The first paragraph of that article reads: 'Individual or mass forcible transfers, as well as deportations of protected persons from occupied territory to the territory of the Occupying Power or to that of any other country, occupied or not, are prohibited, regardless of their motive'. That provision only illustrates that 'deportation' encompasses the crossing of a border; it does not stipulate that 'deportation' may not also be applied to the crossing of another kind of boundary.

. . . The language of deportation, in the sense of a crossing of a border of the state, was used in several cases connected with the Second World War. That was natural in the circumstances of that supremely international armed conflict. Nevertheless, there was an observable tendency to speak interchangeably of 'deportation', 'transfer', 'evacuation' and 'expulsion'. It does not appear that there was occasion for the courts to focus on any precise distinction between deportation and transfer or to speak of the former alone in respect of external forcible displacement and of the latter alone in respect of internal forcible displacement. In *Greiser*, 'deportation' was used in the indictment in circumstances in which it could be argued, on the opposing thesis, that what was involved was a 'transfer'. The case arose out of World War II and was decided by the Supreme National Tribunal of Poland in 1946. It related to the forcible displacement of civilians from one place to another within the same state. True, there was no crossing of a front line, but neither was there a crossing of a border; yet the term 'deporting' was used. . . .

It is accepted that in the case of several texts 'deportation' is used in relation to forcible displacement across a border. It is also recognised that strict uniformity is not necessary for the maturing of a proposition into customary international law. But to say that 'deportation' has been used in several cases in relation to the crossing of a border is not the same as saying that it can *only* be so used. On the available material, my view is that customary international law includes no rule which precludes the use of 'deportation' in relation to the crossing of a front line even if it has not become a border.[87]

We come now to a key component of Shahabuddeen's method, which avoids the stricture of pre-existing state practice:

In appreciating the 'essence' of a clarification [of the law by the judiciary], the question to be attended to is not whether a particular set of circumstances was ever concretely recognized by the existing law, but whether those circumstances reasonably fall within the scope of the existing law. . . . In other words, the question is not whether the law, as it stands, was ever applied concretely to a particular set of circumstances, but whether the law, as it stands, was reasonably capable of applying to those circumstances.

---

[87] Ibid., dissenting opinion of Judge Shahabuddeen, paras 23–32.

In this matter, I gather that the approach of the majority has been to consider whether customary international law ever applied the concept of deportation in a concrete case to the crossing of a front line such as that in this case, as distinguished from the crossing of a border. It would have been useful to focus on the question whether customary international law included a principle which was reasonably capable as it stood of applying that concept to the crossing of such a front line, even if the concept had never been so applied in a concrete case. In my view, that question has to be answered in the affirmative . . .

My understanding of the literature (including references given in the foregoing analysis) is that what the term 'deportation' indicates is that there is some kind of demarcation line or barrier which, if crossed, effectively prevents or at least seriously inhibits the return of the forcibly displaced population to its accustomed area of residence. The forcible crossing of a border is a deportation but only in the sense that the border represents such a demarcation line or barrier; deportation is exemplified by the case of a crossing of a border, but it is not restricted to that case . . .

At all times material to this case customary international law regarded forcible displacement of civilians across a front line in circumstances not permitted by international law as a punishable crime. As argued above, that front line included a constantly changing front line. In substance, the crime always existed; all that the Security Council was doing in the Statute was to vest the Tribunal with jurisdiction over the crime. The principle nullum crimen sine lege relates to the existence of the crime. As to jurisdiction over the crime, it makes no difference that the Security Council provided for the crime to be prosecuted under a particular name so long as it is clear (as in my view, it is clear) that the intention was to prosecute for that crime: that is a matter of nomenclature.[88]

3.5 CONCLUSION

This chapter has explored the sources of substantive international criminal law from the perspective of three important issues: Are the *ex post facto* tribunals limited to applying customary international law, or can they also draw upon conventional law under certain conditions? Is there a method by which to discover customary international law, or have tribunal judges been legislating new law? And is the Second World War case law good precedent, or has it been used selectively and opportunistically to support current tendencies? It appears that the truth lies with the second alternative in each of these three questions.

---

[88] Ibid., paras 39–40, 46, 66. Cf. the dissenting opinion of Judge Schomburg on the same subject in the *Naletilić and Martinović* appeal judgment, paras 10–32 ('the Trial Chamber was satisfied that "civilians were deliberately transferred to an area outside the occupied territory" and that civilians were transferred across the front line between the Western and the Eastern sides of Mostar. It would have been *a noble obligation* for the entire Appeals Chamber to decide that these findings were sufficient for a conviction for deportation as an underlying act of persecutions': para. 30, emphasis added).

PART II

CRITICAL REVIEW OF THE SUBSTANTIVE LAW

4

WAR-CRIMES LAW IN THE
NEW CENTURY

SUMMARY

4.1 INTRODUCTION: CARTE BLANCHE

Article 2 of the ICTY Statute[1] deals with the class of war crimes known as 'grave breaches' of the Geneva Conventions of 1949 and Additional Protocol I of 1977, rules that were developed to regulate international armed conflicts.[2]

Other war crimes within the jurisdiction of the tribunals are 'violations of the laws or customs of war' (an allusion to the 1907 Hague Convention IV and its regulations),[3] and non-grave-breach infringements of the Geneva Conventions and of Additional Protocol I committed in the course of international armed conflicts. Two other categories to be considered in this chapter are acts recognized as war crimes in non-international armed conflicts, as provided for by Article 3 of the Geneva Conventions (Common Article 3) and by Additional Protocol II, as well as acts prohibited in any conflict, international or internal.[4]

Article 3 of the ICTY Statute[5] is, according to the ICTY Appeals Chamber, addressed to the three categories of war crimes in the previous paragraph. The ICC's categorization differs only slightly from this.[6] Article 4 of the ICTR Statute is limited to Common Article 3 and Additional Protocol II offences. For the most part, this chapter is an account of the war-crimes jurisprudence that has grown around Article 3 of the ICTY Statute.

International criminal law, and more specifically tribunal law, is not a mature science. It is the product of policy, politics, idealism, invention, and compromise, as well as of the conventional application of rules of statutory construction and interpretation to the corpus of international law.

The ICTY Appeals Chamber gave the Trial Chambers what amounted to a free rein to explore the area of war crimes when it declared that Article 3 of the ICTY Statute conferred jurisdiction over 'any' serious infringement of international humanitarian

---

[1] 'The International Tribunal shall have the power to prosecute persons committing or ordering to be committed grave breaches of the Geneva Conventions of 12 August 1949, namely the following acts against persons or property protected under the provisions of the relevant Geneva Convention: (a) wilful killing; (b) torture or inhuman treatment, including biological experiments; (c) wilfully causing great suffering or serious injury to body or health; (d) extensive destruction and appropriation of property, not justified by military necessity and carried out unlawfully and wantonly; (e) compelling a prisoner of war or a civilian to serve in the forces of a hostile power; (f) wilfully depriving a prisoner of war or a civilian of the rights of fair and regular trial; (g) unlawful deportation or transfer or unlawful confinement of a civilian; (h) taking civilians as hostages.'

[2] *Tadić* jurisdiction appeal decision, para. 71; also paras 78, 80, 81–4.

[3] On the broader meaning of 'laws or customs of war' see paras 113–14 of Judge Sidhwa's separate opinion in the *Tadić* jurisdiction appeal decision.   [4] *Tadić* jurisdiction appeal decision, paras 87, 89.

[5] 'The International Tribunal shall have the power to prosecute persons violating the laws or customs of war. Such violations shall include, but not be limited to: (a) employment of poisonous weapons or other weapons calculated to cause unnecessary suffering; (b) wanton destruction of cities, towns or villages, or devastation not justified by military necessity; (c) attack, or bombardment, by whatever means, of undefended towns, villages, dwellings, or buildings; (d) seizure of, destruction or wilful damage done to institutions dedicated to religion, charity and education, the arts and sciences, historic monuments and works of art and science; (e) plunder of public or private property.'   [6] See Article 8(2) of the ICC Statute.

law not covered by the Statute's other provisions on jurisdiction.[7] The preconditions, in addition to the 'seriousness' of the act, are that the rule infringed must be customary or belong to treaty law and that its infringement must entail, under customary or conventional law, personal criminal liability.[8] The Appeals Chamber thus enunciated a broad definition of war crimes, free of any distinction between international and non-international armed conflict. It shifts the semantic burden to such ill-defined or question-begging terms as 'rule of international humanitarian law' and 'violation giving rise to criminal liability'. But it has served a purpose, as we shall see.

Prohibitions of international law effective in all conflicts are of course especially relevant where there is some doubt as to the international or internal character of a conflict, or the applicable conventions, as is often the case. (Was the Yugoslav conflict an international war? Was the East Timorese conflict an internal disturbance?) The ICTY Appeals Chamber has made known its preference for a more consistent, or indeed uniform, approach to the regulation of international and non-international armed conflict, stating for example that 'What is inhumane, and consequently proscribed in international wars, cannot but be inhumane and inadmissible in civil strife'.[9] This is not quite true: what will be inhumane in one will be inhumane in the other, but what will be proscribed in one will only be proscribed in the other if that is what the collectivity of states want. That is how international law works, at least in theory, although as we often see, the tribunals have taken matters into their own hands and have modified or expanded the law.

An example of state-driven transposition of a recognized war crime from its traditional setting into the context of civil strife dates from 1988, when evidence emerged that the central authority in Iraq used chemical weapons against civilian populations within Iraq's borders. Several states declared that the outlawing of such weapons by the 1925 Geneva Protocol[10] effectively also prohibited their use in internal conflicts. This represented an expansion of the law applicable to internal conflicts.[11] Yet it had a formal validity as an expression of collective state opinion.

The ICTY Appeals Chamber, in its effort to support the growth of international humanitarian law in the politically sensitive area of internal armed conflict, lowered the threshold of proof of a rule's criminalization (meaning the legal precedent that outlawed or made certain behaviour illegal), thus facilitating the kind of piecemeal transposition mentioned above. In this case, however, the growth was to be powered not by states but by the tribunals.

The ICTY Appeals Chamber's argument in its seminal 1995 *Tadić* jurisdiction appeal decision, from where its other pronouncements mentioned so far also come,

---

[7] *Tadić* jurisdiction appeal decision, paras 91–2, and Judge Sidhwa's separate opinion, ibid., paras 117–18. Judge Li dissented on this point: see ibid., para. 13 of his separate opinion. The majority's position was affirmed in the *Delalić et al.* appeal judgment, para. 131.

[8] *Tadić* jurisdiction appeal decision, para. 94. Repeated in the *Delalić et al.* appeal judgment, para. 128.

[9] *Tadić* jurisdiction appeal decision, para. 119. Repeated in the *Delalić et al.* appeal judgment, paras 160–1.

[10] *Protocol for the Prohibition of the Use in War of Asphyxiating, Poisonous or Other Gases, and of Bacteriological Methods of Warfare*, 17 June 1925 (1975) 14 ILM 49.

[11] See references in the *Tadić* jurisdiction appeal decision, paras 120–4.

amounted to this: 'No one can doubt the gravity of the acts at issue, nor the interest of the international community in their prohibition.'[12] There was some consideration by the Appeals Chamber of a few states that had given their courts jurisdiction to adjudicate breaches of Common Article 3 and Additional Protocol II.[13] But one is left wondering whether the Appeals Chamber would have reached the same conclusion in the absence of those few examples of 'state practice'. Later tribunal cases have shown that the existence of relevant state practice is not in reality a precondition for criminalization.

In this chapter, the three-way scheme described above for crimes other than grave breaches will not be followed strictly, since the categories have become fluid. Consider, for instance, that parties to an armed conflict can agree to regulation of their conflict within the terms of Additional Protocol I even if the conflict is not understood to be international.[14] Conversely, Common Article 3 can be used to regulate international armed conflict. The theoretical categories do, however, have a continuing value. The *Tadić* jurisdiction appeal decision has been misinterpreted as dispensing with the need to decide the internationality of a conflict for war crimes other than grave breaches.[15] In fact, the distinction is still relevant to the finding of whether personal criminal liability exists for certain purported offences, which may be criminal in one context but not in another.[16] States are naturally inclined to prefer less, rather than more, regulation of internal strife by international law.

In the experience of the tribunals so far the vast majority of war-crime charges not constituting grave breaches have been brought pursuant to Common Article 3 of the Geneva Conventions (close to 90 per cent of all counts in this category).

---

[12] *Tadić* jurisdiction appeal decision, para. 129. This no-frills approach to the law's exposition ('It has to be true that...') would feature time and again in international criminal law, as illustrated in other parts of this book (cf. *Kayishema and Ruzindana* trial judgment, para. 184; *Delalić et al.* appeal judgment, paras 161, 172).

[13] *Tadić* jurisdiction appeal decision, paras 130–3.

[14] The Geneva Conventions and Additional Protocol I can be extended, by agreement and other mechanisms, to any given conflict. The scope of application of Additional Protocol I is given in Article 1 of that protocol as corresponding to the situations referred to in Article 2 common to the Geneva Conventions, namely 'to all cases of declared war or of any other armed conflict which may arise between two or more of the High Contracting Parties', as well as 'to all cases of partial or total occupation of the territory of a High Contracting Party'. Clearly, however, Article 1 of Additional Protocol I and Article 2 common to the Geneva Conventions do not have the effect of limiting the application of the conventions and the protocol to the cases mentioned above. Thus a unilateral declaration pursuant to Article 96 of Additional Protocol I by the representative authority of a people 'fighting against colonial domination and alien occupation and against racist régimes in the exercise of their right of self-determination' may be enough to bring into force the conventions and the protocol, even though the authority is not a state power. And Common Article 3 enables parties to a non-international armed conflict to bring into force all or part of the conventions and, by extension, all or part of the supplementary protocol. So, for example, the 'grave breaches' regime of the Geneva Conventions and Additional Protocol I can be made effective in relation to an armed conflict if the parties to the conflict have made the regime apply by mutual agreement, irrespective of the categorization of the conflict (whether at the time or in retrospect) as international or internal.

[15] For example, the *Delalić et al.* trial judgment states (para. 285): 'the Appeals Chamber found that the International Tribunal may have jurisdiction over offences under Article 3 of the Statute whether the offences alleged were committed in an international or internal armed conflict' — citing para. 137 of the Appeals Chamber's decision. However, the Appeals Chamber's finding on this point was limited to Common Article 3 offences, the only war crimes (other than grave breaches) charged in the *Tadić* case (see also *Tadić* jurisdiction appeal decision, para. 89). The same misapprehension is found in the *Furundžija* trial judgment, para. 132 and the *Blaškić* trial judgment, para. 161.

[16] See the *Delalić et al.* appeal judgment, para. 172, where this was a ground of appeal by the defence.

This unassuming provision has thus had a remarkable ability to sustain a wide range of contemporary war-crime counts.[17]

4.2 COMMON ARTICLE 3 OFFENCES

4.2.1 A law unto itself

Common Article 3 of the Geneva Conventions protects those taking no active part in hostilities, including members of armed forces who have laid down their arms and those placed *hors de combat* by sickness, wounds, detention, or any other cause.[18]

Direct attack on non-combatants, and especially on civilians, has been considered unlawful since the early twentieth century. The ICTY Appeals Chamber quoted British Prime Minister Neville Chamberlain declaring in Parliament in 1938 that 'The one definite rule of international law … is that the direct and deliberate *bombing* of non-combatants is in all circumstances illegal'.[19] Aerial warfare was by then already circumscribed, at least in theory, by the customary rule articulated by the prime minister.[20] Just over a decade later a set of minimum mandatory rules applicable to internal armed conflict found expression in Common Article 3.

The language used for the acts prohibited by Common Article 3 is somewhat outmoded. The prohibited acts are:

(a) violence to life and person, in particular murder of all kinds, mutilation, cruel treatment and torture;

---

[17] For general works on war-crimes law, see G. H. Aldrich, 'The Laws of War on Land' (2000) 94 *Am. J. Int'l L.* 42 ('Reality can be messy, and armed conflicts in the real world do not always fit neatly into the two categories — international and noninternational — into which international humanitarian law is divided'); J. Campanaro, 'Women, War, and International Law: The Historical Treatment of Gender-Based War Crimes' (2001) 89 *Geo. L. J.* 2557; Cassese, *International Criminal Law*, pp. 47–63; Dixon and Khan, *Archbold*, pp. 301–57; H.-P. Gasser, 'The U.S. Decision not to Ratify Protocol I to the Geneva Conventions on the Protection of War Victims' (1987) 81 *Am. J. Int'l L.* 912; Green, *Contemporary Law of Armed Conflict*; Green, *Essays*; T. Meron, *War Crimes Law Comes of Age*, Clarendon Press, 1998; and Mettraux, *International Crimes*, pp. 23–146.

[18] It states: 'In the case of armed conflict not of an international character occurring in the territory of one of the High Contracting Parties, each Party to the conflict shall be bound to apply, as a minimum, the following provisions: (1) Persons taking no active part in the hostilities, including members of armed forces who have laid down their arms and those placed hors de combat by sickness, wounds, detention, or any other cause, shall in all circumstances be treated humanely, without any adverse distinction founded on race, colour, religion or faith, sex, birth or wealth, or any other similar criteria. To this end the following acts are and shall remain prohibited at any time and in any place whatsoever with respect to the above-mentioned persons: (a) violence to life and person, in particular murder of all kinds, mutilation, cruel treatment and torture; (b) taking of hostages; (c) outrages upon personal dignity, in particular humiliating and degrading treatment; (d) the passing of sentences and the carrying out of executions without previous judgment pronounced by a regularly constituted court, affording all the judicial guarantees which are recognized as indispensable by civilized peoples.'

[19] Cited in the *Tadić* jurisdiction appeal decision, para. 100, emphasis added.

[20] See League of Nations, *Official Journal, Special Supplement no. 182, Records of the XIXth Ordinary Session of the Assembly*, pp. 15–17 (resolution outlawing the intentional bombing of the civilian population, passed on 30 September 1938).

(b) taking of hostages;

(c) outrages upon personal dignity, in particular humiliating and degrading treatment.

A fourth category (the passing of sentences and the carrying out of executions without previous judgment pronounced by a regularly constituted court, affording all the judicial guarantees which are recognized as indispensable by civilized peoples) for which the ad hoc tribunals have found no use thus far will not be dealt with further. Neither will mutilation, for the same reason.

In 1986 the International Court of Justice stated that in the event of an international armed conflict, the rules of Common Article 3 'constitute a minimum yardstick, in addition to the more elaborate rules which are also to apply to international conflicts; and they are rules which, in the Court's opinion, reflect what the Court in 1949 [in the *Corfu Channel* case] called "elementary considerations of humanity"'.[21] Thus the character of a conflict is said to be irrelevant to the applicability of Common Article 3.[22] It is a universal prohibition, incorporated by reference in the ICTR Statute (Article 4), and by statutory construction[23] in the ICTY Statute (Article 3).

As suggested earlier, parties to an armed conflict may agree to expand and elaborate (though not derogate from) the customary rules of Common Article 3, whether pursuant to the provision in the article which encourages such agreements or on some other basis.[24] Unilateral declarations and codes of conduct, made in the expectation of corresponding action from the other side, are not unusual.[25]

In earlier times Common Article 3 simply bound contracting parties (the states). There is no hint in the wording of the provision of criminal liability at the level of individual persons. This is said to have changed, as we shall see below.

---

[21] *Nicaragua Case, ICJ Report* 1986, p. 114.

[22] See *Tadić* jurisdiction appeal decision, para. 102; *Delalić et al.* trial judgment, para. 300; affirmed in the *Delalić et al.* appeal judgment, paras 143–50. While Common Article 3 applies to international as much as to internal armed conflict, there is a lingering tendency to identify it with the latter. For example, the ICTY Appeals Chamber inferred from the incorporation of Common Article 3 into a tripartite agreement among parties to the conflict in Bosnia-Herzegovina that the parties regarded the conflict as non-international, even though the agreement also incorporated a significant portion of Additional Protocol I and was silent on Additional Protocol II and on the character of the conflict (*Tadić* jurisdiction appeal decision, paras 73 and 136, making reference to the so-called 22 May 1992 agreement).

[23] *Tadić* jurisdiction appeal decision, paras 88–9. Applied (for instance) in *Prosecutor* v. *Furundžija*, Decision on the Defendant's Motion to Dismiss Counts 13 and 14 of the Indictment (Lack of Subject Matter Jurisdiction), 29 May 1998. Affirmed in the *Delalić et al.* appeal judgment, paras 132–6. It is indeed remarkable that Common Article 3, so central to the ICTY's jurisprudence, is not mentioned in the ICTY Statute. Its absence is a permanent reminder, one might say, of the speculative origins of the tribunal. The ICTY defendant Esad Landžo commented on this problem: 'The limitation is that the ICTY Statute only incorporates the grave breaches provisions of the Geneva Conventions, omitting Common Article 3 from its scope. ... The easy way to have incorporated the provisions of Common Article 3 into the ICTY Statute would have been to adopt the Geneva Conventions without limitation as to grave breaches. This the Security Council clearly chose not to do. It would be unreasonable to say that the Security Council intended to exclude Common Article 3 from Article 2 of the ICTY Statute only to adopt it by way of the residual clause of Article 3 of the ICTY Statute. ... Article 3 of the ICTY Statute is entitled "Violations of the laws or customs of war" because that is the language of the Hague Convention, not because the Security Council intended to incorporate into Article 3 of the ICTY Statute an entire body of international humanitarian law.' (*Prosecutor* v. *Delalić et al.*, Esad Landžo's Final Submission and Motion for Acquittal, 28 August 1998, pp. 155–6.) [24] *Tadić* jurisdiction appeal decision, para. 103.

[25] E.g., ibid., paras 105–7.

As evidence that the class of universal war-crimes prohibitions has not been static, the ICTY Appeals Chamber cited two UN General Assembly Resolutions, from 1968 and 1970.[26] The first, Resolution 2444, unanimously adopted by the General Assembly in recognition of 'the necessity of applying basic humanitarian principles in all armed conflicts', referred — in sub-paragraph (c) — to what is known as the principle of distinction:

(a) That the right of the parties to a conflict to adopt means of injuring the enemy is not unlimited; (b) That it is prohibited to launch attacks against the civilian populations as such; (c) That distinction must be made at all times between persons taking part in the hostilities and members of the civilian population to the effect that the latter be spared as much as possible.[27]

The principle of distinction had been known since at least 1949. But in Resolution 2444 there is no overt affirmation of a criminal sanction, much less of individual criminal liability.

The other resolution, 2675, was also unanimously adopted by the General Assembly, as a restatement of 'basic principles' covering armed conflicts of all kinds.[28] It reiterated the principle of distinction, added a rudimentary version of the 'precautionary' principle ('all necessary precautions should be taken to avoid injury, loss or damage to civilian populations'), declared that civilian populations or individual civilians 'should not' be the object of reprisals or forcible transfers, avoided the issue of criminal liability, and seemed content to leave elaboration of the above to the ICRC.

Resolutions 2444 and 2675 enjoy little of the solidity and respect commanded by Common Article 3, and it would be wrong to think of them as expanding the universal class of war crimes, or even as preparing the ground for an expanded class. The ICTY Appeals Chamber was right to regard them as declaratory of general principles of customary international law at the time, and no more.[29] The existence of such principles is a precondition for the development of determinate war crimes, but it is also true that the principles as restated by the UN in its two resolutions sound vague and tentative (for example, 'spared as much as possible').

Next in line in this series of provisions, Additional Protocol II to the Geneva Conventions represents an attempt to develop Common Article 3 into a statute for the regulation of internal armed conflict. However, many states at the ICRC's 1974–77 Diplomatic Conference were antipathetic to the idea of such regulation, and although consensus on a heavily pruned second protocol was finally possible,[30] Additional Protocol II should be weighed with that in mind. In contrast with Additional Protocol I, it does not explicitly create any war crimes.[31]

The ICTY Appeals Chamber selectively relied on a positive assessment of the legal significance of Additional Protocol II by a US government official.[32] However, the USA has not ratified either protocol, a fact which undermines the official's high praise.

---

[26] Ibid., paras 110–12.   [27] UNGA Res. 2444, 23rd session (1968).
[28] UNGA Res. 2675, 25th session (1970).   [29] *Tadić* jurisdiction appeal decision, para. 112.
[30] On the eleventh-hour consensus see *Official Records*, vol. VII, pp. 59–65 and 191–251. See also *Tadić* jurisdiction appeal decision, para. 80.   [31] Cf. Article 85 of Additional Protocol I.
[32] *Tadić* jurisdiction appeal decision, para. 117.

The *Akayesu* Trial Chamber said that Article 4 of Additional Protocol II ('Fundamental guarantees') was customary law by 1994, but did not give any reasons in support of this assertion.[33] The prosecutorial preference for Common Article 3 is so strong that the tribunals have had very few opportunities to deal significantly with either protocol. The protocols cannot as yet be considered customary law or the source of universal prohibitions, even if they contain certain restatements of customary law.[34]

Despite the importance of Common Article 3 to the ICTY and ICTR the question of how and when the prohibitions of Common Article 3 were criminalized at the level of natural persons has remained a nagging problem. As one defendant put it:

[Another question] is whether Common Article 3 in the process of becoming customary international law somehow picked up a penal aspect. Does it come into customary law in the same package in which it was wrapped by the signers in 1949, or has it acquired some new application in the process? When, if ever, has the international community recognized that Common Article 3 provisions could be criminalized so as to provide individual criminal responsibility?[35]

An international instrument explicitly providing for prosecution of acts prohibited by Common Article 3 (as well as by Additional Protocol II) is the ICTR Statute, Article 4.[36] This may be taken to demonstrate that at least since November 1994 — the date of UN Security Council Resolution 955 establishing the ICTR — Common Article 3 violations have been regarded as prosecutable offences not only by the Security Council but by the UN's member states generally (which are supporting the ICTR financially). The UN Secretary-General, in his first report on the implementation of Resolution 955, said that Article 4 of the ICTR Statute 'for the first time criminalizes common article 3 of the four Geneva Conventions'.[37] Perhaps what he meant to say was that for the first time at the international level an explicit mechanism for the prosecution of Common Article 3 offences had been provided.[38]

---

[33] *Akayesu* trial judgment, para. 610. The *Rutaganda* trial judgment, para. 87 simply followed *Akayesu*, and thus a baseless opinion became the received wisdom at the ICTR.

[34] See *Prosecutor* v. *Kordić and Čerkez*, Decision on the Joint Defence Motion to Dismiss the Amended Indictment for Lack of Jurisdiction Based on the Limited Jurisdictional Reach of Articles 2 and 3, 2 March 1999, paras 30–1.

[35] *Prosecutor* v. *Delalić et al.*, Esad Landžo's Final Submission and Motion for Acquittal, 28 August 1998, pp. 162–3.

[36] Article 4 bestows upon the ICTR 'the power to prosecute persons committing or ordering to be committed serious violations' of Common Article 3 and Additional Protocol II. The offences are: (a) violence to life, health and physical or mental well-being of persons, in particular murder as well as cruel treatment such as torture, mutilation or any form of corporal punishment; (b) collective punishments; (c) taking of hostages; (d) acts of terrorism; (e) outrages upon personal dignity, in particular humiliating and degrading treatment, rape, enforced prostitution, and any form of indecent assault; (f) pillage; (g) the passing of sentences and the carrying out of executions without previous judgment pronounced by a regularly constituted court, affording all the judicial guarantees which are recognized as indispensable by civilized peoples; (h) threats to commit any of the foregoing acts. This set largely coincides with Article 4 of Additional Protocol II ('Fundamental guarantees').

[37] UN Doc. S/1995/134, 13 February 1995, para. 12.

[38] A footnote to the cited text adds: 'Although the question of whether common article 3 entails the individual criminal responsibility of the perpetrator of the crime is still debatable, some of the crimes included therein, when committed against the civilian population, also constitute crimes against humanity and as such are customarily recognized as entailing the criminal responsibility of the individual.' See also *Delalić et al.* trial judgment, para. 310 and *Delalić et al.* appeal judgment, para. 170.

The dates of the few examples of state practice cited by the *Tadić* Appeals Chamber would suggest an earlier date than November 1994 for the actual criminalization of violations of Common Article 3, but whether that date is 1992 (the start of the Yugoslav conflict), or even the late 1950s, the Appeals Chamber did not venture to say.[39] The Trial Chambers in *Tadić* and in some subsequent cases followed the Appeals Chamber on this point without attempting to account for the date of Common Article 3's transformation into an international criminal code, although they implied that this had happened by the required time, that is, by early 1992 (ICTY) or by early 1994 (ICTR).[40]

The Appeals Chamber in the *Delalić* case returned to the question, distinguishing the issue of criminalization from that of jurisdiction and making the claim that while a jurisdictional or enforcement mechanism had not emerged prior to the establishment of the ICTY, the acts enumerated in Common Article 3 were already criminalized in 1949 (at the time the Geneva Conventions were finalized), for already by then they were intended to be branded illegal within the international legal order. The language of Common Article 3 'clearly prohibits fundamental offences such as murder and torture',[41] according to the Appeals Chamber, but such an approach does not account for the status of other acts listed in Common Article 3 (are they not fundamental?), nor does it clarify the legal personality (state or individual) to be held accountable for any of the acts, including for murder and torture. *Delalić* called to its aid the rhetorical pronouncement of the Nuremberg IMT that 'Crimes against international law are committed by men, not by abstract entities, and only by punishing individuals who commit such crimes can the provisions of international law be enforced',[42] a statement which is not necessarily true and which seems to violate the principle of *nullum crimen sine lege* by suggesting that there can be punishment without law.[43]

---

[39] *Tadić* jurisdiction appeal decision, paras 131–3.

[40] *Tadić* trial judgment, para. 613; *Akayesu* trial judgment, para. 615; *Delalić et al.* trial judgment, paras 307–9; *Rutaganda* trial judgment, paras 86–90; *Musema* trial judgment, paras 240–2; *Blaškić* trial judgment, paras 175–6; *Kunarac et al.* trial judgment, para. 408. See also *Prosecutor* v. *Kordić and Čerkez*, Decision on the Joint Defence Motion to Dismiss the Amended Indictment for Lack of Jurisdiction Based on the Limited Jurisdictional Reach of Articles 2 and 3, 2 March 1999, paras 32–3. In the *Kayishema and Ruzindana* trial judgment, paras 156–7, the Trial Chamber failed to distinguish between a prohibition's currency, on the one hand, and its criminalization at the level of individual persons, on the other. It said that since Rwanda had signed up to the Geneva Conventions and to Additional Protocol II by the relevant time, persons breaching their provisions were subject to prosecution. This confusion was then incorporated into the *Rutaganda* trial judgment (para. 89) and the *Musema* trial judgment (para. 238).   [41] *Delalić et al.* appeal judgment, para. 163.

[42] Cited in the *Delalić et al.* appeal judgment, para. 162.

[43] A further twist for Common Article 3 is that even if one could establish the approximate date of criminalization of its rules as they apply to internal armed conflict, the same question must be asked in relation to its application to international conflict, given that Common Article 3 is now regarded as a universal prohibition. The Appeals Chamber's answer (*Delalić et al.* appeal judgment, para. 172) was: 'In light of the fact that the majority of the conflicts in the contemporary world are internal, to maintain a distinction between the two legal regimes and their criminal consequences in respect of similarly egregious acts because of the difference in nature of the conflicts would ignore the very purpose of the Geneva Conventions, which is to protect the dignity of the human person.'

4.2.2 General requirements

A prosecutor proceeds by proving three conditions common to Common Article 3 offences before focusing on the elements of the particular crime.[44]

Armed conflict

One of the earliest definitions developed by the tribunals is that of 'armed conflict', and it has hardly changed over time. The *Tadić* Appeals Chamber said in 1995 that an armed conflict exists whenever there is a resort to armed force between states, or protracted armed violence between governmental authorities and organized armed groups, or between such groups within a state. International humanitarian law applies from the initiation of such conflict and extends beyond the cessation of hostilities until a general conclusion of peace is reached; or, in the case of internal conflicts, a peaceful settlement is achieved. Until that moment, international humanitarian law continues to apply in the whole territory of the warring states or, in the case of internal conflicts, in the whole territory under the control of a party, whether or not actual combat takes place there.[45] This definition can be expected to be simplified over time, as the significance for war-crimes law of the distinction between international and internal armed conflict diminishes.

The test applied for the purposes of the rules contained in Common Article 3 focuses on two aspects of a conflict: its intensity and the organization of the parties to it. Where a purported armed conflict is of a non-international, mixed, or indeterminate character, these criteria are used to distinguish armed conflict from banditry, non-organized and short-lived insurrections, or terrorist activities, which do not come under the purview of international humanitarian law.[46]

The geographical and temporal frame of reference for armed conflict is broad. The rules contained in Common Article 3 apply outside the narrow geographical context of the theatre of combat operations. This is because the beneficiaries of Common Article 3 are those taking no active part in hostilities (see below). And so the *Delalić* Trial Chamber said that it was not required to find that there existed an 'armed conflict' in the municipality where the alleged crimes were committed, but, rather, in the larger territory of which the municipality was part.[47] The temporal scope also extends

---

[44] Proof of discriminatory intent is *not* required in relation to Common Article 3 offences, nor is it required, more generally, as a precondition for proof of offences falling under Article 3 of the ICTY Statute: *Aleksovski* appeal judgment, paras 17–26.   [45] *Tadić* jurisdiction appeal decision, para. 70.

[46] For applications of this test, see *Tadić* trial judgment, paras 563–8; *Delalić et al.* trial judgment, paras 186–92; *Furundžija* trial judgment, para. 59; *Kayishema and Ruzindana* trial judgment, para. 172; *Musema* trial judgment, paras 970–1. The *Akayesu* trial judgment, para. 603, emphasizes that the intensity test is objective and not reducible to the subjective judgment of a party to the conflict. However, *Akayesu*'s finding on the existence of an armed conflict (para. 174) surprisingly comes before its discussion of the law, where we find one test for Common Article 3 and another for Additional Protocol II (paras 619–27). See also *Rutaganda* trial judgment, paras 94, 435, where the same error is unreflectively carried over.

[47] *Delalić et al.* trial judgment, para. 185. For a misapplication of this test, see *Kayishema and Ruzindana* trial judgment, para. 603 ('evidence was not produced that the military operations occurred in Kibuye Prefecture when the alleged crimes were committed'), and para. 610 (the victims were not 'affected' by military operations under way elsewhere).

beyond the exact time of hostilities, although this point has not been developed in the case law.[48]

Protected persons

Common Article 3 protects more than the 'protected persons' of Geneva Conventions III and IV, that is, there is no requirement that persons, in order to be considered protected, should have 'fallen into the power of the enemy' or should find themselves 'in the hands of a party to the conflict'.

As this extended notion of protection was a feature of Common Article 3 in its original application to internal armed conflict, it must undoubtedly be carried over to international armed conflict when Common Article 3 is accepted as a universal prohibition in accordance with the current tendency.[49]

The test applied by the *Tadić* Trial Chamber was to ask whether, at the time of the offence, the victim was directly taking part in the hostilities, that is, the hostilities in the context of which the alleged offences were committed. If the answer is negative, the victim was protected by Common Article 3.[50] This is preferable to asking whether the victim was a civilian, for a civilian may intermittently take part in hostilities (whereupon he or she becomes a combatant), only to return to long stretches of being a civilian.[51]

Nexus

The existence of an armed conflict and the applicability of international humanitarian law to a territory are not sufficient to give the tribunals jurisdiction over a serious offence committed in the territory against a protected person. For a crime to fall within the jurisdiction of the tribunals, a nexus must be established between the offence and the armed conflict.

It is sufficient, according to the ICTY Appeals Chamber, that the alleged crimes were *closely related* to the hostilities occurring in the territories controlled by the parties to the conflict.[52] The *Tadić* Trial Chamber elaborated this test, stating that it would be sufficient to prove that the crime was committed in the course of or as part of the hostilities in an area controlled by one of the parties.

Consistent with what was said above, to show a nexus it is not necessary to show that armed conflict was occurring at the exact time and place of the alleged offence, nor is it necessary that the offence took place during combat, that it was part of a practice officially endorsed or tolerated by one of the parties to the conflict, or that it was in furtherance of a policy associated with the conduct of war, or even in the interest of a party to the conflict. To assist this conclusion, the *Tadić* Trial Court pronounced that 'the obligations of individuals under international humanitarian law are independent

---

[48] *Tadić* jurisdiction appeal decision, paras 67, 69.
[49] Cf. *Delalić et al.* appeal judgment, paras 171–2.
[50] *Tadić* trial judgment, paras 615–16. Followed in *Blaškić* trial judgment, para. 177.
[51] As implied by Articles 51(3) and 13(3) of Additional Protocol I and II, respectively.
[52] *Tadić* jurisdiction appeal decision, para. 70.

[of] and apply without prejudice to any questions of the responsibility of States under international law'.[53]

Despite the above, at the ICTR the *Akayesu* Trial Chamber purported to fortify the nexus element, finding that a nexus is required not only between the offence and the conflict but also between the *perpetrator* and a party to the conflict. Citing no authority, the Trial Chamber said that the 'duties and responsibilities' set down by the Geneva Conventions and the Additional Protocols apply only to members of the armed forces of the belligerent parties, or to individuals 'legitimately mandated and expected, as public officials or agents or persons otherwise holding public authority or de facto representing the Government, to support or fulfil the war efforts'.[54] Because the prosecutor did not prove that Akayesu held one of those positions, the Trial Chamber acquitted him of all five Common Article 3 counts, including three for murder.[55] This precipitated, at the ICTR, an extraordinary series of acquittals for war crimes,[56] an error which took almost five years to rectify.[57]

---

[53] *Tadić* trial judgment, para. 573. For applications of this test, see *Tadić* trial judgment, paras 574–5, *Delalić et al.* trial judgment, paras 196–8, *Furundžija* trial judgment, para. 65, *Blaškić* trial judgment, para. 70. For an application of the *wrong* test ('direct link' instead of 'closely related') see *Kayishema and Ruzindana* trial judgment, paras 185–8, 603–4, 610.

[54] *Akayesu* trial judgment, para. 631; repeated in *Rutaganda* trial judgment, para. 98, and *Musema* trial judgment, paras 264–75, 280; and acknowledged as a possible requirement in *Kunarac et al.* trial judgment, para. 407. Another line of erroneous reasoning is found in the *Kayishema and Ruzindana* trial judgment, para. 174, by a differently constituted ICTR Trial Chamber: 'Violations of Common Article 3 and Protocol II could be committed during, or as a result of, military operations. This means that the Parties to an armed conflict should be responsible for such breaches.' Ultimately the Trial Chamber adopted and applied the *Akayesu* test (paras 175, 602–3, 616–19).   [55] *Akayesu* trial judgment, paras 641–3.

[56] Kayishema and Ruzindana had eight murder counts dismissed. Three murder counts were dismissed in *Rutaganda* because the prosecutor supposedly failed to show that Rutaganda, a political leader connected with a youth militia, acted in 'support' of the war effort: see *Rutaganda* trial judgment, para. 442, a barely comprehensible paragraph. In *Musema* the ICTR Trial Chamber summarily dismissed the two Common Article 3 counts because no 'nexus' was shown between the acts of this well-connected and influential businessman and the armed conflict (it is not clear whether the 'second' nexus requirement, invented in *Akayesu* and carried over to *Musema*, was also not proven): *Musema* trial judgment, paras 973–5.

[57] One possible explanation is that the ICTR Trial Chambers persisted in seeing the alleged genocide in Rwanda as an operation conceptually and logistically distinct from the war fought between government forces and rebels. Thus, in the *Akayesu* trial judgment, paras 127–8, we read: 'the Chamber . . . holds that the genocide did indeed take place against the Tutsi group, alongside the conflict. . . . it was, evidently, fundamentally different from the conflict'. And in *Kayishema and Ruzindana* trial judgment, para. 621: 'It is true that these atrocities were committed during the armed conflict. However, they were committed as part of a distinct policy of genocide; they were committed parallel to, and not as a result of, the armed conflict. Such crimes are undoubtedly the most serious of crimes which could be committed during or in the absence of an armed conflict. In any event, however, these crimes are beyond the scope of Common Article 3 and Protocol II which aim to protect victims of armed conflict.' Contrast this with the *Rutaganda* trial judgment, para. 443, where 'genocide' and 'conflict' are said to have been 'linked'. The *Akayesu* theory of a second nexus requirement was refuted on appeal: *Akayesu* appeal judgment, paras 430–45. (For a related discussion at a more general level, which serves as an alternative refutation of *Akayesu*'s theory, see *Kunarac et al.* trial judgment, paras 488–95.) The Appeals Chamber in late May 2003 restored two of the *Rutaganda* murder counts and convicted Rutaganda of war crimes. The tide had already turned by the time of the aforementioned *Akayesu* appeal judgment, and certainly at the Trial Chamber level by the time of *Semanza* (May 2003).

4.2.3 'Violence to life and person'

The *Blaškić* Trial Chamber did not hesitate to convict Tihomir Blaškić for this rather vague-sounding offence, which in Common Article 3 is followed by the explanation 'in particular murder of all kinds, mutilation, cruel treatment and torture'. The *Blaškić* court said that the offence 'is accordingly defined by the cumulation of the elements of these specific offences' — a hazy statement, for which no authority was cited.[58] Surprisingly, the judges in *Kordić and Čerkez* embraced *Blaškić* without any discussion, except to say that where the alleged act results in injury but not in the death of the victim, it may be better characterized as the grave breach of inhuman treatment or wilfully causing great suffering.[59]

A far more critical approach was taken in the *Vasiljević* case, which dismissed the *Blaškić* result as 'unfortunate'.[60] The Trial Chamber asked whether the purported offence of violence to life and person was sufficiently defined and sufficiently accessible in 1992 to warrant a criminal conviction. It noted that such a conviction must never be based upon a norm of which an accused could not reasonably have been aware at the time of the acts. The norm must make it sufficiently clear what act or omission could lead to individual criminal responsibility.[61]

The *Vasiljević* Trial Chamber declared itself unable to find any conclusive evidence of state practice prior to 1992 which would point towards a definition of the purported offence. It noted that both 'life' and 'person' are protected in various ways by international humanitarian law, and that some infringements upon each are regarded as criminal under customary international law. This is clear, for instance, of murder, cruel treatment, and torture, as discussed later in this chapter. But the Chamber quite rightly pointed out that not every violation of those protected interests had been criminalized; and those that have — for example, the three offences just mentioned — have usually been given a definition, so that both the individual who commits the act and the court called upon to judge that conduct are in a position to make a determination as to its legal consequences.[62]

Vasiljević went on to state, correctly, that the fact that an offence is listed in the ICTY Statute, or comes within Article 3 of the Statute through Common Article 3, does not create new law. Yet, *Vasiljević* added, more dogmatically, that the tribunal has jurisdiction over a crime only if it was recognized as such by customary international law at the relevant time.[63] This principle has been reiterated elsewhere — for example, in the *Milutinović et al.* case, where the ICTY Appeals Chamber quoted the UN Secretary-General's foundational report on the ICTY, which said that the tribunal should not concern itself with crimes which are not 'beyond any doubt part of customary

---

[58] *Blaškić* trial judgment, para. 182.

[59] *Kordić and Čerkez* trial judgment, para. 260. The Trial Chamber acquitted the two accused on one count each of violence to life and person, but convicted them, on the same facts, for the grave breach of inhuman treatment. [60] *Vasiljević* trial judgment, para. 194.

[61] Ibid., para. 193. [62] Ibid., paras 194–5. [63] Ibid., para. 198.

international law,' from which the *Milutinović* Appeals Chamber concluded that 'the Tribunal's power to convict an accused of any crime ... depends on its existence *qua* custom at the time this crime was allegedly committed'.[64] The sentence from the Secretary-General's report was the sole basis for this conclusion, as discussed in more detail in Chapter 3.

A quite different, but much more plausible, gloss on the Secretary-General's remark was provided by the *Tadić* Appeals Chamber in 1995: 'It should be emphasised again that the only reason behind the stated purpose of the drafters that the [ICTY] should apply customary international law was to avoid violating the principle of nullum crimen sine lege in the event that a party to the conflict did not adhere to a specific treaty.' The passage cited to the relevant segment of the Secretary-General's report. The Appeals Chamber continued:

It follows that the [ICTY] is authorised to apply, in addition to customary international law, any treaty which: (i) was unquestionably binding on the parties at the time of the alleged offence; and (ii) was not in conflict with or derogating from peremptory norms of international law, as are most customary rules of international humanitarian law.[65]

Where such a treaty clearly specifies the elements of a purported offence, and where the two conditions mentioned by the *Tadić* Appeals Chamber are fulfilled, the tribunal may have jurisdiction, despite the suggestions in *Vasiljević* to the contrary.

Nevertheless, this is of no help to 'violence to life and person,' which has not been defined with sufficient clarity in any treaty. The defendant was therefore acquitted on this count.[66]

4.2.4 Murder

The first findings on murder under Common Article 3 were in the *Tadić* case. The accused was acquitted for lack of evidence, without discussion of the law.[67] Next, Dražen Erdemović was convicted of Common Article 3 murder upon pleading guilty to the count.[68] Again there was no discussion of the law. As explained above, the murder charges against Akayesu, which were decided next by the ICTR, were dismissed because a supposed background element for war crimes had not been proven. So it was not until the end of 1998, in the *Delalić* judgment, that a Trial Chamber pronounced on this offence.

---

[64] *Prosecutor v. Milutinović et al.*, Decision (Appeals Chamber) on Dragoljub Ojdanić's Motion Challenging Jurisdiction — Joint Criminal Enterprise, 21 May 2003, para. 9. See also *Prosecutor v. Kordić and Čerkez*, Decision on the Joint Defence Motion to Dismiss the Amended Indictment for Lack of Jurisdiction Based on the Limited Jurisdictional Reach of Articles 2 and 3, 2 March 1999, para. 20; repeated in *Prosecutor v. Kvočka et al.*, Decision on Preliminary Motions Filed by Mlado Radić and Miroslav Kvočka Challenging Jurisdiction, 1 April 1999, para. 26 (paragraph enumeration corrected).   [65] *Tadić* jurisdiction appeal decision, para. 143.

[66] *Vasiljević* trial judgment, para. 204.

[67] *Tadić* trial judgment, paras 241, 341, 373 (facts); and paras 721, 757, 761 (legal findings). The Nuremberg Tribunal also dealt with murder and ill-treatment of the civilian population: 22 IMT Judgment 475–81.

[68] *Erdemović* sentencing judgment (no. 2), para. 11.

In *Delalić*, Common Article 3 murder was charged cumulatively with 'wilful killing' (a grave breach) and the Trial Chamber chose to understand the former in terms of the latter. It said that given that it is prohibited to kill protected persons during an international armed conflict, therefore it is prohibited to kill those taking no active part in hostilities which constitute an internal conflict. 'In this spirit of equality of protection, there can be no reason to attach meaning to the difference of terminology utilised in common article 3.'[69]

The Trial Chamber spent little time on the material elements of the offence. It said that in relation to homicide of all kinds, the actus reus to be proven is that the death of the victim resulted from the actions of the accused, that is, the conduct of the accused must have been a substantial cause of the death of the victim.[70]

The Trial Chamber found more to say about the mens rea, as the accused had argued for the exclusion of recklessness from the fault requirement. The less than satisfactory practice of falling back on the ICRC's commentary is evident here. The Trial Chamber observed that the commentary on Articles 11 and 85 of Additional Protocol I brings the concept of 'recklessness' into that of 'wilfulness'. Mere negligence is excluded from its scope.[71] It also noted that in most common-law jurisdictions the mens rea requirement for murder is satisfied where the accused is aware of the likelihood or probability of causing death, or is reckless as to the causing of death; and in many civil-law jurisdictions the foreseeability of death is relevant, and awareness of the likelihood that death will occur is generally sufficient to fulfil the requisite intention to kill.[72] The Trial Chamber concluded that the necessary mens rea required to establish the crime of wilful killing or the crime of murder as recognized by the Geneva Conventions is the intention to kill or to inflict serious injury in reckless disregard of human life.[73]

4.2.5 Cruel treatment and torture

Cruel treatment as a Common Article 3 offence was first considered in *Tadić*. The Trial Chamber acknowledged that no international instrument defined cruel treatment, but an indication of what was covered by it could be found in Article 4 of Additional Protocol II which makes 'torture, mutilation or any form of corporal punishment' into instances of cruel treatment.[74] (But note that Common Article 3 has mutilation and torture at the same level as cruel treatment and does not mention corporal punishment.)

---

[69] *Delalić et al.* trial judgment, para. 423. Followed in *Blaškić* trial judgment, para. 181.

[70] *Delalić et al.* trial judgment, para. 424. Followed in *Jelisić* trial judgment, para. 35, and subsequent cases.

[71] *Delalić et al.* trial judgment, para. 432. [72] Ibid., paras 434–5.

[73] Ibid., para. 439. For application to the facts, see paras 823, 833, 845, 855, 872 (not proven), 877, 885 (not proven), 890, 894, 898 (not proven), 903, 909. The convictions for murder were later quashed for improper cumulation with the convictions for grave breaches. Six counts of Common Article 3 murder were dismissed in *Kupreškić* on the same technical ground, in this instance that the prohibition of murder as a crime against humanity (which was cumulatively charged) is *lex specialis* in relation to the prohibition of murder as a war crime, and must therefore prevail: *Kupreškić et al.* trial judgment, para. 823. For further discussion and findings on Common Article 3 murder, see *Jelisić* trial judgment, paras 36–40; and *Blaškić* trial judgment, paras 181, 414–17.

[74] *Tadić* trial judgment, paras 724–5.

The Trial Chamber concluded that since 'cruel treatment' was not given a narrow or special meaning in Additional Protocol II, the words were to be given their ordinary sense in Common Article 3.[75] The beatings that Duško Tadić was found to have administered to prisoners 'involved, because of their nature and consequences, *and on any meaning of the words*, acts that caused serious injury and great suffering to the victims', and therefore amounted to cruel treatment.[76] (This could be called the ordinary-language approach to interpretation of statutory prohibitions. It is, perhaps, simplistic.)

A more careful approach was taken in *Delalić*, where the Trial Chamber had to deal with numerous cruel-treatment counts, most of which were charged as alternatives to Common Article 3 torture. Added to this was a variety of cumulatively charged grave breaches (torture, inhuman treatment, and wilfully causing great suffering). Faced with this thicket of related concepts, the Trial Chamber decided to impose order by reducing the proliferation. It started with the more specialized item in the group, torture. Cruel treatment will be discussed after we examine the law on torture.

Torture

The *Delalić* Trial Chamber found that the prohibition of torture is a norm of *jus cogens*, absolute and non-derogable in any circumstance.[77] Since no definition of this offence is given in the Geneva Conventions, its elements must be retrieved from other sources of law. In its generally well-reasoned inquiry into the elements of the crime,[78] greatly assisted by the 1984 Torture Convention and case law of the European Court of Human Rights, the *Delalić* Trial Chamber proceeded on the assumption that there is no difference between torture as a grave breach and torture as an offence under Common Article 3. In either case it consists of intentional acts or omissions by, or at the instigation of, or with the consent or acquiescence of, a public official, which are committed for a particular prohibited purpose and cause a severe level of mental or physical pain or suffering.[79]

'Prohibited purpose' means obtaining information or a confession from the victim or a third person, punishing the victim for an act he or she or a third person has committed or is suspected of having committed, intimidating or coercing the victim or a third person, or (rather too broadly) having any kind of discriminatory purpose.[80] Officials of states that are not parties to a conflict are counted as 'public officials' in

---

[75] Ibid., paras 725–6.

[76] Ibid., para. 243, emphasis added; see also para. 303. Tadić was convicted of five out of six cruel treatment counts.

[77] For more on the universality of this prohibition, see *Furundžija* trial judgment, paras 137–9, 144, 151–7 (much of this discussion consisting of obiter dicta). *Furundžija* was a case where the single torture charge was laid pursuant to Common Article 3. See also *Kunarac et al.* trial judgment, para. 466.

[78] *Delalić et al.* trial judgment, paras 452–96. The main weakness, which took more than two years to come to the surface, is discussed below in the context of the *Kunarac* case.

[79] *Delalić et al.* trial judgment, para. 442. Approved in *Furundžija* trial judgment, para. 160. The *Furundžija* Trial Chamber added that the torture must be linked to an armed conflict (para. 162), but of course all crimes falling within Article 3 of the ICTY's Statute must be so linked.

[80] *Delalić et al.* trial judgment, para. 494. 'Humiliating the victim' should also be on this list, according to the *Furundžija* Trial Chamber, which saw the prohibition of torture as safeguarding human dignity: *Furundžija* trial judgment, para. 162.

order to cover situations of internal conflict, as well as international conflict involving non-state entities.[81]

It is well established that persons who engage in torture are individually accountable under international criminal law since at least the Second World War.[82]

While rape undoubtedly constitutes torture when the required conditions are met,[83] the *Delalić* Trial Chamber overstated its case when it declared itself hard-pressed to envisage any situation in which rape by or at the instigation of or with the consent or acquiescence of a public official could be considered as occurring for a purpose that does not, in some measure, involve punishment, coercion, discrimination, or intimidation, especially when it occurs in armed conflict.[84] Given that at least one of these factors is always present in cases of rape, it does not follow that that factor must always reflect the accused's *purpose* (or even be a part of the motivation behind the conduct) when committed in the context of armed conflict. The onus should be on the prosecutor to prove the nexus of the act with the armed conflict, and it should not be presumed, as the Trial Chamber here suggests.

One of the earliest convictions for Common Article 3 torture with a sexual assault component was in the case of *Furundžija*.[85] The accused interrogated the victim, who was being kept undressed. The accused's assistant rubbed a knife against the inner thighs of the victim and threatened to mutilate her if she did not tell the truth. The interrogation by the accused and the activities of his assistant had merged into one process. Their intention was to obtain information which they believed would benefit the fighting force they belonged to.[86]

The *Kunarac* Trial Chamber disagreed with one aspect of the analysis of the elements of torture undertaken in *Delalić* and approved in *Furundžija*. *Kunarac's* argument is decisive and a model of accurate reasoning which should ideally be read and appreciated as a whole.[87] The Trial Chamber observed that *Delalić* had sourced its analysis to human rights instruments and decisions. While this was, according to the court, unavoidable, the definition of torture under international human rights law should not be assumed to be the same as that under international humanitarian law. This is because the role of the state is completely different in the two regimes. Human rights law has emerged in response to abuses of citizens by their states and is a check on state-sponsored violence, whereas humanitarian law aims at placing restraints on the conduct of warfare so as to diminish its effects on civilians and others.

---

[81] *Delalić et al.* trial judgment, para. 473. Approved in *Kunarac et al.* trial judgment, para. 485 (although allowing that other purposes may have come to be recognized under customary international law). For application to the facts, see paras 923–4, 940–2, 962–4, 976, 988 (not proven), 998, 1007.

[82] Torture was one of the acts expressly classified as a crime against humanity under Article II(1)(c) of Control Council Law No. 10. On the distinction between individual and state responsibility for torture, see *Furundžija* trial judgment, paras 142, 145–6.

[83] See, for example, the incident described in the *Delalić et al.* trial judgment, paras 940–2.

[84] *Delalić et al.* trial judgment, para. 495.

[85] That this was a Common Article 3 case is not evident from the judgment itself. However, see, in the same case, Decision on the Defendant's Motion to Dismiss Counts 13 and 14 of the Indictment (Lack of Subject Matter Jurisdiction), 29 May 1998.   [86] *Furundžija* trial judgment, paras 264–5.

[87] See *Kunarac et al.* trial judgment, paras 466–96.

Delalić uncritically embraced notions developed in a different legal context, according to *Kunarac*. A careful reading of human rights authorities, such as the ECHR and the UN Human Rights Committee, reveals that these authorities did not intend to limit acts of torture to those committed by or at the instigation of public officials.[88] Provisions of the Geneva Conventions, the Additional Protocols, and the ICRC's commentary on the two instruments, lead to the conclusion (in the words of the ICRC) that 'the act of torture is reprehensible in itself, regardless of its perpetrator, and cannot be justified in any circumstances'.[89]

Thus *Kunarac* held that the presence of a state official, or of some other authority-wielding person, in the torture process is not necessary for the offence to be characterized as torture under international humanitarian law. This must now be regarded as settled law. The crime is therefore constituted of just three core elements: an intentional act, committed for a particular prohibited purpose (as defined above), causing a severe level of mental or physical pain or suffering.[90]

Cruel treatment

According to the *Delalić* Trial Chamber, for the purposes of Common Article 3, torture is fully encapsulated by the offence of cruel treatment. The difference is that this more general offence extends to all acts against protected persons which cause serious mental or physical suffering or injury, and which at the same time constitute a serious attack on human dignity.

In its attempt to reduce the apparent multiplicity of similar concepts raised by the charges in the indictment, the *Delalić* Trial Chamber proposed that cruel treatment has the same meaning as the grave breach of *inhuman* treatment.[91] Its inquiry into the latter was extensive,[92] relying on the ICRC's commentary to navigate the multitude of prohibitions of inhuman treatment in the Geneva Conventions, but also drawing attention to the scrutiny of the concept by the European Court of Human Rights. Violations of human dignity are the essential target of the prohibition of inhuman treatment, which is mentioned alongside cruel treatment in Article 5 of the Universal Declaration of Human Rights, Article 7 of the ICCPR, Article 5, paragraph 2, of the Inter-American Convention of Human Rights, and Article 5 of the African Charter of Human and Peoples' Rights.

On the assumption that cruel treatment has the same residual function for the purposes of Common Article 3 as inhuman treatment has in relation to grave breaches, the Trial Chamber concluded that cruel treatment constitutes an intentional act which causes serious mental or physical suffering or injury and constitutes a serious attack on human dignity. Treatment that does not meet the purposive requirement for torture in Common Article 3 constitutes cruel treatment.[93]

---

[88] Ibid., paras 478–81.   [89] Ibid., paras 490–2 and citations therein.

[90] Ibid., para. 497. For application to the facts of the case, see paras 630–87, 688–98 (not proven), 705–15, 784–98 (not proven), 799–822. The facts that went to prove torture were the same, as far as it is possible to tell, as the facts that went to prove rape. See also *Limaj et al.* trial judgment, para. 235.

[91] *Delalić et al.* trial judgment, para. 443.   [92] See ibid., paras 516–44.

[93] Ibid., para. 552. Approved in *Jelisić* trial judgment, para. 41, *Blaškić* trial judgment, para. 186.

The meaning of cruel treatment may be better appreciated with reference to some of the *Delalić* Trial Chamber's legal findings on the facts. Newly arrived detainees at Čelebići camp, in Bosnia-Herzegovina, were made to stand with their hands up against a wall inside the compound while they were beaten. One of the victims who was unable to stand on account of previously inflicted injuries was hit several times before being pulled away. The court said that although the evidence was not enough to assess the level of severity of the beating, the act of hitting a person who is so seriously injured that he is unable to stand necessarily entails a serious affront to human dignity.[94] The Trial Chamber found that one of the accused used an electric shock device on numerous detainees. Its use caused pain, burns, convulsions, twitching, and scarring. It had the effect of frightening the victims and reducing them to begging the accused for mercy. Their suffering and humiliation gave the accused a 'sadistic pleasure'. This made for a clear case of an attack on human dignity.[95] In another instance, the Trial Chamber found that the act of forcing a father and his son to beat one another repeatedly over a period of at least ten minutes constituted cruel treatment.[96] A fortiori the act of forcing two brothers to perform fellatio on one another was an attack on human dignity, qualifying as cruel treatment.[97] (According to the Trial Chamber it also constituted rape, which however had not been pleaded.)

The victim of cruel treatment *must have suffered*.[98] Thus persons who are, unbeknownst to them, used as human shields are not the victims of cruel treatment. The situation will change as soon as they become aware of their actual condition.[99]

While *Delalić* equated cruel treatment and inhuman treatment (a grave breach), the Trial Chamber in *Kupreškić*, which had to decide three counts of cruel treatment but no grave breaches, equated cruel treatment with *inhumane acts* (a crime against humanity). Its definition of an inhumane act is generally the same as *Delalić*'s definition of inhuman treatment.[100] Thus a close family of offences was formed, each member of the family conceived in a different substantive provision of the ICTY's Statute. Because the *Kupreškić* Trial Chamber perceived cruel treatment and inhumane acts as alternatives, it had to dismiss one set of counts. It was clear, in the court's view, that each time an inhumane act is committed, cruel treatment is ipso facto also inflicted.[101] But the reverse is not true if the element of widespread or systematic attack is not proven. Thus inhumane acts must be preferred if that condition is satisfied; if not, cruel treatment will be considered.[102]

---

[94] *Delalić et al.* trial judgment, paras 1025–6.

[95] Ibid., para. 1058.   [96] Ibid., para. 1070.

[97] Ibid., para. 1066. For other findings on cruel treatment, see, ibid., paras 866, 1018, 1033–4, 1040, 1044–5, 1119; *Jelisić* trial judgment, paras 42–4; *Blaškić* trial judgment, paras 688–700, 713–16 (detainees made to dig trenches at the front line; used as human shields; mock executions; engine oil given to detainees to 'wash' in; exposure to harsh weather; oppressive and unhygienic conditions of detention; terrorization by guards).

[98] See, e.g., *Limaj et al.* trial judgment, paras 250–5, 310–18.

[99] *Blaškić* trial judgment, para. 715.   [100] *Kupreškić et al.* trial judgment, para. 566.

[101] Note that the ICTY Statute limits the jurisdiction for crimes against humanity to those committed in armed conflict.   [102] *Kupreškić et al.* trial judgment, para. 711.

It follows from the above that forcing a family to witness the murder of a relative, expelling the family from its home, and destroying the home, amounts to cruel treatment, for it was found in *Kupreškić* to amount to an inhumane act.[103]

Article 23 of Geneva Convention III provides that 'No prisoner of war may at any time be sent to, or detained in areas where he may be exposed to the fire of the combat zone, nor may his presence be used to render certain points or areas immune from military operations'. In *Blaškić*, the Trial Chamber found that the defendant ordered the use of detainees as human shields to protect the defendant's headquarters and that this 'inflicted considerable mental suffering upon the persons involved'.[104] The reasoning was as follows: the detainees (numbering 247) were detained in front of Blaškić's headquarters for about three hours on 20 April 1993; Blaškić was present in the building for a large part of that afternoon; and the Bosnian-government army began an offensive on that day, and the defendant knew about that offensive. The Trial Court was 'therefore convinced beyond all reasonable doubt' that Blaškić ordered civilians to be used as human shields in order to protect his headquarters.[105] The ICTY Appeals Chamber commented on this finding:

> Using protected detainees as human shields constitutes a violation of the provisions of the Geneva Conventions regardless of whether those human shields were actually attacked or harmed. Indeed, the prohibition is designed to protect detainees from being exposed to the risk of harm, and not only to the harm itself. To the extent that the Trial Chamber considered the intensity of the shelling of Vitez on 20 April 1993, that consideration was superfluous to an analysis of a breach of the provisions of the Geneva Conventions, but may be relevant to whether the use of the protected detainees as human shields amounts to inhuman treatment for the purposes of Article 2 of the Statute.[106]

The Appeals Chamber agreed that the use of the detainees as human shields caused them serious mental harm and constituted a serious attack on human dignity.[107] The analysis of the problem of human shields in terms of the law of 'cruel treatment' can be extended, for example, to the problem of forced labour, such as trench-digging. It has been said that compelling persons taking no active part in hostilities to dig trenches or to prepare other forms of military installations, in particular when such persons are ordered to do so against their own forces in an armed conflict, constitutes cruel treatment.[108]

4.2.6 'Outrages upon personal dignity' including rape

A species of this Common Article 3 offence came up for the first time in a conviction for aiding and abetting rape in the *Furundžija* case.[109] The Trial Chamber there declared that Common Article 3 refers to rape 'implicitly'.[110] How this insight was

---

[103] Ibid., para. 819.   [104] *Blaškić* trial judgment, para. 716.

[105] Ibid., paras 742–3.   [106] *Blaškić* appeal judgment, para. 654.

[107] However, the Appeals Chamber recharacterized Blaškić's responsibility as an omission: ibid., para. 670.

[108] Ibid., para. 597.

[109] That this was a Common Article 3 case is not evident from the judgment itself, as noted in footnote 85 above.   [110] *Furundžija* trial judgment, para. 166.

attained we are not told, but most probably the Trial Chamber reasoned backwards, from Article 4 of the 1977 Additional Protocol II, which mentions rape as an example of an outrage upon personal dignity, to the 1949 Geneva Conventions.

Rape

There is no doubt that the prohibition of rape in war has long ago matured into customary international law. The Lieber Code contains both a prohibition of rape (Article XLIV, which is cited by the *Furundžija* court) and its punishment (Article XLVII, which is not).[111] At least since the Second World War, superiors who tolerate the commission of rape or other serious sexual assault by their subordinates in armed conflict are liable to be held criminally responsible.[112] However, despite an overall sense of certainty that the ground is well trodden, the ICTY Trial Chamber could not produce any other decided cases, and conceded that there was no established definition of rape in international law.

The *Furundžija* Trial Chamber set out to define rape by first dismissing *Akayesu*'s claims on this point.[113] *Akayesu* had dealt with the definition of rape in three short paragraphs in a manner that can at best be described as intuitive. Not a single authority or other citation underpinned the Trial Chamber's decision that 'rape is a form of aggression and that the central elements of the crime of rape cannot be captured in a mechanical description of objects and body parts. ... The Chamber defines rape as a physical invasion of a sexual nature, committed on a person under circumstances which are coercive.'[114] *Furundžija* considered this a subversion of the *nullum crimen sine lege* principle and turned for guidance 'to the major legal systems of the world'.[115]

It would seem that most legal systems consider rape to be the forcible sexual penetration of the human body by the penis, or the forcible insertion of any other object into either the vagina or the anus. Forced oral penetration by the penis has not been widely criminalized as rape[116] — even less so a decade ago, in 1992 (*Furundžija* made no effort to tie its survey to dates). In Yugoslavia the defendant in such a case would have been charged with sexual assault, not rape. Faced with this lack of uniformity, the Trial Chamber could have given up on the uncertain element, but instead held on to it.

---

[111] It is reasonably clear from the immediate context of the word 'rape' in Article XLIV of the Code that it was being used in the sense relevant here (as opposed to its archaic sense of 'violent seizure of property'). See also Article II(1)(c) of Control Council Law No. 10, Article 27 of Geneva Convention IV, Article 76(1) of Additional Protocol I, and, as already mentioned, Article 4(2)(e) of Additional Protocol II.

[112] *Furundžija* trial judgment, para. 168, and references given therein. The United States Military Commission in the *Yamashita* case stated that 'where murder and rape and vicious, revengeful actions are widespread offences, and there is no effective attempt by a commander to discover and control the criminal acts, such a commander may be held responsible, even criminally liable, for the lawless acts of his troops, depending upon their nature and the circumstances surrounding them' (*US* v. *Yamashita*, (1947) 4 LRTWC 1, 35).

[113] Akayesu was convicted of rape as a crime against humanity.

[114] *Akayesu* trial judgment, paras 597–8.

[115] *Furundžija* trial judgment, paras 178–82.   [116] Ibid., para. 182.

The only thing clear about *Furundžija's* reasoning on this point is that the judges were well intentioned:

This principle [of respect for human dignity] is intended to shield human beings from outrages upon their personal dignity, whether such outrages are carried out by unlawfully attacking the body or by humiliating and debasing the honour, the self-respect or the mental well being of a person. It is consonant with this principle that such an extremely serious sexual outrage as forced oral penetration should be classified as rape.[117]

It is also 'consonant' that it is classified not as rape but more broadly, as an outrage upon personal dignity. The Trial Chamber's explanation of why its admitted 'broadening [of] the definition of rape' does not offend the *nullum crimen sine lege* principle[118] illustrates a central theme of this book, namely that in international criminal law the ends often justify the means, and thus as a legal system it is fundamentally different from the settled national criminal systems where, generally speaking, the reverse logic applies, which is that the available legal means are generally used to justify the ends.

The actus reus of rape finally developed by the *Furundžija* court had two elements: (1) the sexual penetration, however slight of (a) the vagina or anus of the victim by the penis of the perpetrator or any other object used by the perpetrator; or (b) the mouth of the victim by the penis of the perpetrator; (2) by coercion or force or threat of force against the victim or a third person.[119] The Trial Chamber found that Furundžija's assistant committed rape by penetrating the victim's mouth, vagina, and anus with his penis.[120]

The *Kunarac* Trial Chamber did not approve of item (2) of the actus reus developed in *Furundžija*, which it found too limiting.[121] International law, according to *Kunarac*, does not limit acts of rape to sexual penetration accompanied by coercion or force, or threat of force — these are sufficient but not necessary factors. Other factors exist which render an act of sexual penetration non-consensual or non-voluntary, thereby qualifying it as rape. The Trial Chamber's opinion was based on its own survey of national legal systems.[122] According to its interpretation of this survey, sexual penetration is understood in law to constitute rape if it is not consensual or voluntary on the part of the victim. 'The true common denominator' which unifies the various systems, according to the Trial Chamber, is a principle penalizing violations of 'sexual autonomy'.[123] Sexual autonomy is violated when the person subjected to the act has not freely agreed to it or is otherwise not a voluntary participant.[124]

Kunarac's argument on this point is a model of clarity and accuracy. Item (2) of *Furundžija's* definition must therefore be considered to have been supplanted by the element 'where such sexual penetration occurs without the consent of the victim'. Consent must be given voluntarily, as a result of the victim's free will, assessed in the context of the surrounding circumstances. The mens rea of the crime is the intention

---

[117] Ibid., para. 183. See the ICTY Appeals Chamber's endorsement in the *Kunarac et al.* appeal judgment, para. 128, of the definition given in the *Kunarac et al.* trial judgment, para. 412, which is the same as that in the *Furundžija* trial judgment, para. 181.   [118] *Furundžija* trial judgment, para. 184.
[119] Ibid., para. 185.   [120] Ibid., para. 271.   [121] *Kunarac et al.* trial judgment, para. 438.
[122] Ibid., paras 443–56.   [123] Ibid., paras 440, 457.   [124] Ibid., para. 457.

to effect sexual penetration with the knowledge that penetration occurs without the consent of the victim.[125]

To take an example from *Kunarac*'s application of this doctrine to the facts, the Trial Chamber found that one detained victim, D. B., had sexual intercourse with Kunarac in which she took an active part by taking off his trousers and kissing him all over before having vaginal intercourse with him. The defendant claimed that he had not been aware that D. B. had not had sex with him of her own free will but rather had complied out of fear. D. B., on the other hand, testified that prior to the intercourse she had been threatened by a person named Gaga that he would kill her if she did not satisfy the desires of his commander, Kunarac. The Trial Chamber accepted that D. B. initiated sexual intercourse with Kunarac only because she was afraid of being killed by Gaga if she did not do so. The court dismissed as fanciful the claim that Kunarac could have been 'confused' by the behaviour of D. B. This was not credible in the context of the wartime situation, the specific situation of the detained Muslim girls, and the accused's knowledge that D. B. had been raped by other soldiers. Moreover, to the court it was irrelevant that Kunarac might have been unaware of Gaga's threat against D. B. What mattered was that D. B. did not freely consent to sexual intercourse with Kunarac. She was in captivity and in fear for her life. Kunarac knew enough to know that D. B.'s conduct was involuntary.[126]

The broader category of 'outrages'

On the heels of *Furundžija* came *Aleksovski*, another prison-camp case. The court, citing the character of the conflict, dismissed two grave-breach counts, leaving Aleksovski with just one count, formulated as 'outrages upon personal dignity, in particular humiliating and degrading treatment', one of the four prohibitions of Common Article 3.

The court, having no precedent to guide it, began by interpreting Common Article 3, as a whole, as being against 'inhuman treatment'.[127] It then recalled *Delalić*'s discussion of inhuman treatment (as a grave breach), which was reviewed above in connection with cruel treatment. With little more, the Trial Chamber declared: 'An outrage upon personal dignity within Article 3 of the Statute is a species of inhuman treatment that is deplorable, occasioning more serious suffering than most prohibited acts falling within the genus.'[128] This is both imprecise and ambiguous ('more serious suffering'?).

The law's growth in this instance is assisted. The *Aleksovski* Trial Chamber quoted the ICRC's commentary — 'outrages upon personal dignity refer to acts which, without directly causing harm to the integrity and physical and mental well-being of persons, are aimed at humiliating and ridiculing them' — as holding the key to establishing the elements of the offence.[129] The student of substantive crimes is left to wonder why a court would find a mere commentary intellectually so compelling?

---

[125] Ibid., para. 460.
[126] Ibid., paras 644–6. For other findings on the charges of rape, see paras 630–87, 688–98 (not proven), 699–704, 705–15, 716–45, 746–65, 784–98 (not proven), 799–822. Some of the facts supporting rape also went to prove torture. [127] *Aleksovski* trial judgment, para. 51.
[128] Ibid., para. 54.   [129] Cited in ibid., para. 55.

But the Trial Chamber did not look into this question, nor did it inquire into the criminalization of the prohibition at the level of individual actors. Instead, it elaborated the elements without precision and without citing any source or authority. It claimed that an outrage upon personal dignity is an act which is 'animated by contempt' for the human dignity of another person and causes serious humiliation or degradation to the victim. 'It is not necessary for the act to directly harm the physical or mental well-being of the victim. It is enough that the act causes real and lasting suffering to the individual arising from the humiliation or ridicule. . . . the humiliation to the victim must be so intense that the reasonable person would be outraged.'[130] The Trial Chamber added that the accused must have committed the act with the *intent* to humiliate or ridicule the victim.

As discussed above, cruel treatment constitutes an act which causes serious mental or physical suffering or injury and which constitutes a serious attack on human dignity. This raises the question whether cruel treatment is different from outrages upon personal dignity — is there perhaps a difference between 'human' dignity and 'personal' dignity? Not only did the *Aleksovski* Trial Chamber not try to explain the difference, it went on to convict the accused for acts closer to cruel treatment than to its definition of outrages upon personal dignity. It based its finding of guilt essentially on these facts:[131] soldiers would go into the cells of the prison camp at night to assault and insult the detainees and to demand money; recordings of songs and the screams of people being beaten were played at night over a loudspeaker, keeping the detainees awake;[132] psychological violence included direct threats (holders of military identity papers were threatened with death) and systematic assaults (by soldiers entering the cells at night, the screams broadcast over the loudspeaker, etc.). Detainees also worried about whether they would be dispatched to dig trenches and whether they would ever be released.[133] The element of physical violence in this case means that cruel treatment provided a more apposite categorization of these facts, and while the Trial Chamber was not called upon to make a choice, since cruel treatment was not charged, the problem should not have gone without comment.[134]

Aleksovski's pioneering work on 'outrages' was first criticized on appeal. The ICTY Appeals Chamber, after concluding its discussion on whether discriminatory intent is an element of Common Article 3 offences (it is not), noted politely that the Trial Chamber's reasoning in relation to the mental element of the offence of outrages upon personal dignity 'is not always entirely clear'.[135] The Appeals Chamber declared that it did not interpret the observation in the ICRC's commentary (quoted above), that the term outrages upon personal dignity refers to acts 'aimed at humiliating and ridiculing'

---

[130] Ibid., para. 56.   [131] Ibid., para. 228.

[132] Ibid., para. 187.   [133] Ibid., para. 226.

[134] While expressing no opinion on this point, the ICTY Appeals Chamber (*Aleksovski* appeal judgment, para. 37) observed that the victims of the incidents referred to above 'were not merely inconvenienced or made uncomfortable — what they had to endure, under the prevailing circumstances, were *physical and psychological abuse and outrages* that any human being would have experienced as such' (emphasis added).

[135] *Aleksovski* appeal judgment, para. 27.

the victim, as necessarily supporting a requirement of a *specific intent* on the part of a perpetrator to humiliate, ridicule, or degrade. The ICRC's statement, according to the Appeals Chamber's interpretation, simply describes the conduct which Common Article 3 seeks to prevent. Thus the Trial Chamber's indication that the mens rea of the offence is the intent to humiliate or ridicule the victim imposes a requirement that the prosecutor is not, in fact, obliged to prove.[136]

A harsh critique of the *Aleksovski* trial judgment followed in the *Kunarac et al.* case. The *Kunarac* Trial Chamber did not agree that the humiliation or degradation inflicted must cause 'lasting suffering' for the victim. The humiliation or degradation must be real and serious, that is, *objectively* serious.[137] But the fact that a victim has recovered, or is overcoming the effects of the acts in question, does not force the conclusion that the acts did not constitute an outrage upon personal dignity. If the humiliation and suffering were only fleeting in nature, it may be difficult to accept that they were real and serious. But this, according to *Kunarac*, does not add a requirement of perseverance of the effects of an act of 'outrage' to the elements of the offence.[138]

In a further comment on the mens rea, the *Kunarac* Trial Chamber observed that it is a necessary aspect of a true intention to perform a particular act that there is an awareness of the nature of the act. The relevant act for an outrage upon personal dignity is an act which would be generally (that is, objectively) considered to cause serious humiliation or degradation, or to be a serious attack on human dignity. The accused must have known that the act or omission was of that character.[139]

And so *Kunarac* put forth the following two elements as constituting the offence of outrages upon personal dignity: that the accused intentionally committed or participated in an act which would generally be considered to cause serious humiliation, degradation, or otherwise be a serious attack on human dignity; and that he or she knew that the act could have that effect.[140] The *Kunarac* Trial Chamber entered both an acquittal and a conviction for outrages upon personal dignity. Concerning the former, it said that while the evidence went to prove rape and enslavement, there was no evidence upon which it would have been appropriate to convict for outrages upon personal dignity that was not already 'covered' by the other two convictions.[141] This indicates that while rape is part of the notion of an 'outrage', where the two are charged together over the same range of facts a tribunal will acquit for the latter unless some behaviour can be isolated which is incidental to the rape and which warrants the supplemental conviction.

The Trial Chamber was able to isolate evidence of 'outrages' in relation to the second such charge.[142] Three captive girls, one as young as twelve, were forced to strip and dance naked on a table while one of the defendants watched them from a sofa and aimed weapons at them. The Trial Chamber noted that the defendant certainly knew

---

[136] Ibid. Approved in *Kunarac et al.* trial judgment, para. 509.

[137] The *Kunarac* Trial Chamber (*Kunarac et al.* trial judgment, paras 504–7) refuted *Aleksovski's* uses of tautology and psychology where it sought to establish a subjective measurement for 'seriousness' in relation to an act of outrage upon personal dignity (*Aleksovski* trial judgment, para. 56).

[138] *Kunarac et al.* trial judgment, paras 500–3.

[139] Ibid., para. 512.   [140] Ibid., para. 514.

[141] Ibid., para. 743.   [142] Ibid., paras 766–74, 775–81.

that having to dance naked on a table while being watched in the situation described was a painful and humiliating experience for the three girls, even more so on account of their young age.

The offence of outrages upon personal dignity must nevertheless be considered imperfectly understood. The Appeals Chamber and the *Kunarac* Trial Chamber purported to correct *Aleksovski*, but all three chambers took the same ordinary-language approach to the statute, mixing intuition in liberally with their literal method, while making few external references which would root the offence in legal history. And as a result, we cannot say that we know where the difference lies between the offence of outrages and that of cruel treatment.

4.2.7 Taking of hostages

The ICRC commentary was the only source used by the *Blaškić* Trial Chamber to lay the foundation for the crime of hostage-taking for which Blaškić was convicted. (The same offence exists as a grave breach, listed in Article 2 of the ICTY Statute, for which Blaškić was also convicted.) The Trial Chamber said that hostages are persons unlawfully deprived of their freedom, often arbitrarily and sometimes under threat of death, for the purpose of obtaining a concession or gaining an advantage.[143] The *Blaškić* Appeals Chamber agreed that the essential element in the crime of hostage-taking is the use of a threat concerning detainees so as to obtain a concession or gain an advantage. Thus a situation of hostage-taking exists when a person seizes or detains and threatens to kill, injure, or continue to detain another person in order to compel a third party to do or to abstain from doing something as a condition for the release of that person.[144] The Appeals Chamber reversed the Trial Court's conviction for lack of evidence.[145]

Hostage-taking as a grave breach of the Geneva Conventions and as a violation of the laws or customs of war was also considered by the Trial Chamber in the *Kordić and Čerkez* case.[146]

4.3 RESIDUAL CATEGORIES OF WAR CRIMES

4.3.1 Introduction

Except for the crime of plunder, on which a fair amount had been said, there was very little 'residue' prior to 2003. It was in this year that Additional Protocol I was tested essentially for the first time, with the elaboration of two offence types based on Article 51 of the Protocol:[147] the crime of attack on civilians and the crime of terror.

---

[143] *Blaškić* trial judgment, para. 158. [144] *Blaškić* appeal judgment, para. 639.
[145] Ibid., para. 646. [146] *Kordić and Čerkez* trial judgment, paras 311f.
[147] Article 51:

1. The civilian population and individual civilians shall enjoy general protection against dangers arising from military operations. To give effect to this protection, the following rules, which are additional to other

The list of residual categories is open-ended. It will surely grow, if not on account of the ad hoc tribunals (whose years are numbered), then through the work of the ICC. One need only glance at the list of 'laws and customs' under Article 8(2)(b) of the ICC Statute to appreciate the potential richness of this group. Many rules in this group concern not infringements of the Geneva Conventions (protection of civilians and other non-combatants) but the regulation of the conduct of hostilities, for example by prohibiting the use of certain kinds of weapon.

The ICTR has not had to deal with any residual categories.[148] Article 3 of the ICTY Statute, by contrast, lists five offences from the Regulations to the 1907 Hague Convention IV, intended to apply to international conflict only. They form part of customary international law:[149] (1) employment of poisonous weapons or other weapons calculated to cause unnecessary suffering;[150] (2) wanton destruction of cities, towns, or villages, or devastation not justified by military necessity;[151] (3) attack or bombardment by whatever means of undefended towns, villages, dwellings, or buildings;[152] (4) seizure of, destruction of, or wilful damage done to institutions dedicated to religion, charity,

applicable rules of international law, shall be observed in all circumstances. 2. The civilian population as such, as well as individual civilians, shall not be the object of attack. Acts or threats of violence the primary purpose of which is to spread terror among the civilian population are prohibited. 3. Civilians shall enjoy the protection afforded by this section, unless and for such time as they take a direct part in hostilities. 4. Indiscriminate attacks are prohibited. Indiscriminate attacks are: (a) those which are not directed at a specific military objective; (b) those which employ a method or means of combat which cannot be directed at a specific military objective; or (c) those which employ a method or means of combat the effects of which cannot be limited as required by this Protocol; and consequently, in each such case, are of a nature to strike military objectives and civilians or civilian objects without distinction. 5. Among others, the following types of attacks are to be considered as indiscriminate: (a) an attack by bombardment by any methods or means which treats as a single military objective a number of clearly separated and distinct military objectives located in a city, town, village or other area containing a similar concentration of civilians or civilian objects; and (b) an attack which may be expected to cause incidental loss of civilian life, injury to civilians, damage to civilian objects, or a combination thereof, which would be excessive in relation to the concrete and direct military advantage anticipated. 6. Attacks against the civilian population or civilians by way of reprisals are prohibited. 7. The presence or movements of the civilian population or individual civilians shall not be used to render certain points or areas immune from military operations, in particular in attempts to shield military objectives from attacks or to shield, favour or impede military operations. The Parties to the conflict shall not direct the movement of the civilian population or individual civilians in order to attempt to shield military objectives from attacks or to shield military operations. 8. Any violation of these prohibitions shall not release the Parties to the conflict from their legal obligations with respect to the civilian population and civilians, including the obligation to take the precautionary measures provided for in Article 57.

[148] Attempts by the prosecutor to rely on Additional Protocol II, for example in *Kayishema and Ruzindana*, are reducible to Common Article 3.

[149] The UN Secretary-General, in his report on the ICTY Statute (Report of the Secretary-General on ICTY, para. 42), mentioned that the Nuremberg IMT recognized that many of the provisions contained in the Hague Regulations, although innovative at the time of their adoption, were, by 1939, regarded as being declaratory of the laws and customs of war. The IMT itself said, indeed, that war crimes defined in Article 6(b) of its Charter had been fixed as war crimes under international law, and were covered in the Hague Regulations. See also *Blaškić* trial judgment, para. 168.

[150] Hague Regulations 1907, Article 23(a): 'To employ poison or poisoned weapons.'

[151] Hague Regulations 1907, Article 23(g): 'To destroy or seize the enemy's property, unless such destruction or seizure be imperatively demanded by the necessities of war.'

[152] Hague Regulations 1907, Article 25: 'The attack or bombardment, by whatever means, of towns, villages, dwellings, or buildings which are undefended.'

and education, the arts and sciences, historic monuments, and works of art and science;[153] and (5) plunder of public or private property.[154]

Of these offence categories, (1) and (3) will not be considered further, as the tribunals have yet to pronounce on them.

The general requirements for residual offences are the same as for Common Article 3 (see section 4.2.2, above), except that the persons protected may be defined more narrowly, or differently, as the case may be. This question will be dealt with as it arises.

4.3.2 Attack on civilians

The war crime of 'attack on civilians' has been carved out of Article 51, paragraph 2, of Additional Protocol I, whose first sentence reads: 'The civilian population as such, as well as individual civilians, shall not be the object of attack.' As mentioned above, direct attack on civilians has been considered unlawful since the early twentieth century, and therefore the rule in Additional Protocol I must be regarded as a restatement of customary international law. While much has been said about this prohibition, it was not until the ICTY's *Galić* case (2003) that certain aspects of the offence were given concrete form. This delay is largely the result of the prosecutor's preference for the arsenal of Common Article 3.

However, in the *Kupreškić* case, where there were nine counts of Common Article 3 offences (murder and cruel treatment) but none charging 'attack on civilians' (even though at the core of the case was the attack on the village of Ahmići), the Trial Chamber was prepared to make some general observations on the subject. It noted that the legal protection for civilians may be diminished when the object of an attack consists of military objectives and the attacking side cannot avoid causing 'collateral damage'. In such a case the prevailing principle (found in Articles 51 and 57[155] of

---

[153] Hague Regulations 1907, Article 27: 'To spare, as far as possible, buildings dedicated to religion, art, science, or charitable purposes, historic monuments.'

[154] Hague Regulations 1907, Article 28 (conduct of hostilities): 'The pillage of a town or place, even when taken by assault'; and Article 47 (occupied territories): 'Pillage is formally forbidden.'

[155] Article 57:

1. In the conduct of military operations, constant care shall be taken to spare the civilian population, civilians and civilian objects. 2. With respect to attacks, the following precautions shall be taken: (a) those who plan or decide upon an attack shall: (i) do everything feasible to verify that the objectives to be attacked are neither civilians nor civilian objects and are not subject to special protection but are military objectives within the meaning of paragraph 2 of Article 52 and that it is not prohibited by the provisions of this Protocol to attack them; (ii) take all feasible precautions in the choice of means and methods of attack with a view to avoiding, and in any event to minimizing, incidental loss of civilian life, injury to civilians and damage to civilian objects; (iii) refrain from deciding to launch any attack which may be expected to cause incidental loss of civilian life, injury to civilians, damage to civilian objects, or a combination thereof, which would be excessive in relation to the concrete and direct military advantage anticipated; (b) an attack shall be cancelled or suspended if it becomes apparent that the objective is not a military one or is subject to special protection or that the attack may be expected to cause incidental loss of civilian life, injury to civilians, damage to civilian objects, or a combination thereof, which would be excessive in relation to the concrete and direct military advantage anticipated; (c) effective advance warning shall be given of attacks which may affect the civilian population, unless circumstances do not permit. 3. When a choice is possible between several military objectives for obtaining a similar military advantage, the objective to be selected shall be that, the

Additional Protocol I) is that reasonable care must be taken so that civilians are not injured, and that, in any event, incidental harm to civilians must not be out of proportion to the direct military advantage gained by the attack.[156] The Trial Chamber expressed the view that this precautionary principle was part of customary international law, but rightly remarked on the wide margin of interpretation left by its terms. Not only are Articles 51 and 57 of Additional Protocol I laconically drafted, very little case law exists to assist with their interpretation.

The first to decide a charge of 'attack on civilians' (labelled, overemphatically, *unlawful* attack on civilians) was the Trial Chamber in the *Blaškić* case. Article 51 of Additional Protocol I was said to have been given effect by the parties to the conflict by way of a special agreement among them. The Trial Chamber took the view that it was empowered to apply any law being part of an agreement which incontestably bound the parties at the date a crime was perpetrated (whether or not that law was customary in nature).[157] This approach had been adumbrated by the Appeals Chamber in its 'carte blanche' decision, discussed above, on the proviso that the law agreed to by the parties did not derogate from customary international law.[158] The fact that *Blaškić* went along with this approach placed the Trial Chamber in the pro-*Tadić* school (discussed in Chapter 3).

As we have seen, the tribunals have generally been flexible in demonstrating that a prohibition they seek to enforce has been criminalized at the level of individual persons, and the effort in *Blaškić* is an example of this. The Trial Chamber said that violations of Article 3 of the ICTY Statute were 'by definition' serious violations of international humanitarian law, and thus 'likely' to give rise to individual criminal responsibility.[159] Obviously this was insufficient. So the Trial Chamber added that the provisions of the Yugoslav criminal code adopted by Bosnia-Herzegovina in April 1992 created individual criminal responsibility for 'war crimes'. Did this include 'attack on civilians' or any of the other purported war crimes for which Blaškić was indicted? The court did not say.

As to the definition of attack on civilians, the *Blaškić* Trial Court adopted the prosecutor's proposal without further explanation.[160] It said that the attack, in order to be regarded as a crime, must have caused death or serious bodily injury to civilians — even though paragraph 2 of Article 51 of Additional Protocol I says no such thing.[161] The Trial Chamber added that the parties to a conflict are obliged to 'attempt' to distinguish between military targets and civilians; that targeting civilians is an offence when not justified by military necessity; and that the attack must have been conducted intentionally in the knowledge that civilians are being targeted not through military necessity. There is much here that calls for clarification. No clarification was given by

---

attack on which may be expected to cause the least danger to civilian lives and to civilian objects. 4. In the conduct of military operations at sea or in the air, each Party to the conflict shall, in conformity with its rights and duties under the rules of international law applicable in armed conflict, take all reasonable precautions to avoid losses of civilian lives and damage to civilian objects. 5. No provision of this article may be construed as authorizing any attacks against the civilian population, civilians or civilian objects.

[156] *Kupreškić et al.* trial judgment, paras 522, 524.   [157] *Blaškić* trial judgment, paras 169–73.
[158] *Tadić* jurisdiction appeal decision, paras 143–4.   [159] *Blaškić* trial judgment, para. 176.
[160] Ibid., para. 180.   [161] In contrast with Article 85(3) of the Protocol, which does.

the Trial Chamber. Blaškić was convicted of one count of 'unlawful attack on civilians' for having ordered attacks against several villages in April 1993 which caused hundreds of civilian deaths and injuries.[162]

Dario Kordić and Mario Čerkez were also convicted of the offence of unlawful attack on civilians. The Trial Chamber in that case said, on the basis of very little discussion, that attacks launched deliberately against civilians in the course of an armed conflict are prohibited if not justified by military necessity. It added that, for the crime to be proven, the attack must have caused death or serious bodily injury to civilians.[163] The court did not explain its remarkable proposition that deliberate attacks on civilians are justifiable through military necessity. This can only be a drafting error which escaped the judges' attention. It was corrected on appeal.[164]

The first significant discussion of the crime of 'attack on civilians' appears in the *Galić* trial judgment. The prosecution in *Galić* threw caution to the winds, leaving the safe territory of Common Article 3 for the relative unknown of the Additional Protocols (in particular, Article 51 of Additional Protocol I and Article 13 of Additional Protocol II). But the task of the Trial Court turned out to be relatively simple. Article 85 of Additional Protocol I supplements the Geneva Conventions by criminalizing attacks on civilians 'causing death or serious injury to body or health'.[165] This was a solid foundation on which to base the remaining analysis. The court noted that the legal elements of the crime of attack on civilians had yet to receive a definitive statement. Because the *Galić* indictment was limited to sniping and shelling attacks causing death or serious injury, the Trial Court was not required to consider whether the crime existed in international law in a broader sense (extending, for example, to victimless attacks).[166] For the mens rea, the Court drew on the ICRC's commentary on Additional Protocol I, which incorporated the concept of recklessness into that of 'wilful' action. A consequence of this is that an *indiscriminate* attack, that is, an attack which strikes at civilian and military tagrets without distinction, may qualify as a direct attack on civilians. The same is true of a *disproportionate* attack, that is, an attack which targets a military objective but which is carried out in the knowledge that excessive civilian casualties are likely to result.[167]

---

[162] See, for example, *Blaškić* trial judgment, paras 417, 428, 437, 495, 510, 512, 529–31, as well as findings relating to several other attacks proven against Blaškić, with the exception of the attack on Zenica (for which he was acquitted: see, ibid., paras 662–78). [163] *Kordić and Čerkez* trial judgment, para. 328.

[164] *Kordić and Čerkez* appeal judgment, para. 54.

[165] Article 85:

> ...3. In addition to the grave breaches defined in Article 11 [of the Additional Protocol], the following acts shall be regarded as grave breaches of this Protocol, when committed wilfully, in violation of the relevant provisions of this Protocol, and causing death or serious injury to body or health: (a) making the civilian population or individual civilians the object of attack; (b) launching an indiscriminate attack affecting the civilian population or civilian objects in the knowledge that such attack will cause excessive loss of life, injury to civilians or damage to civilian objects, as defined in Article 57, paragraph 2 (a)(iii); (c) launching an attack against works or installations containing dangerous forces in the knowledge that such attack will cause excessive loss of life, injury to civilians or damage to civilian objects, as defined in Article 57, paragraph 2 (a)(iii); (d) making non-defended localities and demilitarized zones the object of attack; (e) making a person the object of attack in the knowledge that he is hors de combat; ...

[166] *Galić* trial judgment, paras 42–3. [167] Ibid., paras 57–60.

The *Galić* court settled on the following definition of the crime of attack on civilians:

1. An act of violence directed against the civilian population or individual civilians not taking direct part in hostilities causing death or serious injury to civilians.

2. The offender wilfully made the civilian population or individual civilians not taking direct part in hostilities the object of that act of violence.[168]

The Trial Court's approach to the crime of attack on civilians was in some respects superficial. The Court said that the prohibition in the Additional Protocols

explicitly confirms the customary rule that civilians must enjoy general protection against the danger arising from hostilities. The prohibition against attacking civilians stems from a fundamental principle of international humanitarian law, the principle of distinction, which obliges warring parties to distinguish *at all times* between the civilian population and combatants and between civilian objects and military objectives and accordingly to direct their operations only against military objectives.[169]

Here there is too much emphasis, too little exposition, and not enough attention given to practical realities. For example, what does 'to distinguish' mean — not as an armchair concept but in armed conflict? To distinguish with certainty? To distinguish on the balance of probabilities? To have some reason to think that the target is a military objective? To obey your instinct that the figure approaching you through the haze of the front line is not an innocent civilian but an enemy combatant who will take you out unless you act to stop him? The *Galić* judges wrote:

In order to promote the protection of civilians, combatants are under the obligation to distinguish themselves at all times from the civilian population; the generally accepted practice is that they do so by wearing uniforms, or at least a distinctive sign, and by carrying their weapons openly. In certain situations it may be difficult to ascertain the status of particular persons in the population. The clothing, activity, age, or sex of a person are among the factors which may be considered in deciding whether he or she is a civilian. *A person shall be considered to be a civilian for as long as there is a doubt as to his or her real status.*[170]

The source of this rule is unclear. This risks that members of the armed forces who are meant to comply with international humanitarian law will come to dismiss tribunal developments in this area as irrelevant. Rules that are unrealistic or so imprecise as to be meaningless will be ignored or derided. The above rule is either too restrictive (if 'as long as there is a doubt' is understood to mean nothing short of certainty) or too loose ('doubt' could mean 'some doubt', 'reasonable doubt', 'overwhelming doubt', and so forth). The Court finally resiled from the above position, adopting (although again without legal argument) a more sensible test, that 'a person shall not be made the object of attack when it is not reasonable to believe, in the circumstances of the person contemplating the attack, including the information available to the latter, that the potential target is a combatant'.[171]

---

[168] Ibid., para. 56.   [169] Ibid., para. 45, emphasis in original.

[170] Ibid., para. 50, emphasis added.

[171] Ibid., paras 50, 55. For an application of the test resulting in a finding that the civilian victim of a shooting incident was *not* unreasonably attacked, see ibid., paras 556–7.

Galić's definition of the crime of attack on civilians was questioned by the more idealistic *Strugar* Trial Court:

the imminent risk of falling victim of an unlawful attack is in itself an acute experience for civilians, who, unarmed and defenceless, find themselves facing an army that has chosen them as its target. The Chamber emphasises that the categorical nature of the prohibition of such attacks and its prominent place among the rules of international humanitarian law make it evident that the purpose of this prohibition is not only to save lives of civilians, but also to spare them from the risk of being subjected to war atrocities. The Chamber is of the opinion that the experiencing of such a risk by a civilian is in itself a grave consequence of an unlawful attack, even if he or she, luckily, survives the attack with no physical injury.[172]

No authority is cited for the proposition that a person may be convicted for 'attack on civilians' as a violation of the laws or customs of war absent death or serious injury. In the event, *Strugar* applied *Galić*'s definition of the crime to the facts of that case.[173] (For the facts in *Strugar*, see the crime of 'attack on civilian objects', below.)

4.3.3 Terror

As with attack on civilians, the war crime of terror has been founded on Article 51, paragraph 2, of Additional Protocol I, whose second sentence reads: 'Acts or threats of violence the primary purpose of which is to spread terror among the civilian population are prohibited.' The *Galić* Trial Chamber, by a majority of the judges, took this modest proposition and expanded it into a war crime with its own unique position in international law. The result is highly instructive for two reasons: it represents a spectacular clash of the pro-*Tadić* and anti-*Tadić* tendencies (discussed in Chapter 3) in the framework of a single judgment (with the dissenting judge, Nieto-Navia, speaking for the anti-*Tadić* school); and it contains an unusually detailed justification for the assumption of jurisdiction over a crime in international law.

The *Galić* indictment covered the period from September 1992 to August 1994. Stanislav Galić was the commander of a branch of the Bosnian-Serb armed forces (the SRK) which kept a stranglehold on the city of Sarajevo throughout much of this period. Hundreds of civilians in the city were killed by SRK snipers or in mortar attacks on residential neighbourhoods. What was the purpose of such attacks? The prosecution's theory, which the Trial Chamber seemed to accept,[174] was that the Serbs, unable to take the city through direct attack, sought to undermine the morale of the Bosnian-Muslim army and bring down the Bosnia-Herzegovina government through psychological pressure involving the infliction of terror upon the city's population.

Consider the following incident. On 22 January 1994, two mortar shells hit a street in rapid succession in a residential area, killing six children who were playing outside and seriously injuring several others. A third shell landed in a nearby park, causing no

---

[172] *Strugar* trial judgment, para. 221.   [173] Ibid., para. 283.
[174] *Galić* trial judgment, paras 576–7.

casualties. The particular neighbourhood had been shelled before, and altogether ten persons (nine of them children) from just one apartment block in the affected street had been killed in such attacks. There was no legitimate military target in the immediate vicinity. In each apartment block there lived one or two soldiers, according to the evidence, but there was no barracks or group of soldiers or even police station close to the site of the explosions. The closest possible legitimate target was at least 200 metres away. The three shells did not land progressively closer to that possible target (which might have suggested an attempt to correct a targeting error), and the attack ceased after the three shells were fired (suggesting that the exercise was aimless).[175] The intention, it seems, was merely to terrorize.

Is there a 'crime of terror'? The *Galić* Trial Chamber majority said that it was not required to decide whether an offence of terror broadly defined falls within the jurisdiction of the tribunal, but only whether a specific offence of killing and wounding civilians in time of armed conflict with the intention to inflict terror on the civilian population is an offence over which the tribunal has jurisdiction.[176] The majority judges latched on to the *Tadić* jurisdiction appeal decision, which expanded the jurisdiction of the ICTY by transforming Article 3 of the ICTY Statute into a non-exhaustive list of war crimes, as discussed at the beginning of this chapter. They also relied on an agreement among the warring factions, brokered by the ICRC, which made Article 51 of Additional Protocol I, including the prohibition of 'terror', applicable to the Bosnia-Herzegovina conflict.[177]

The *Galić* majority declared itself opposed to the anti-*Tadić* tendency when it claimed that it was not required to pronounce on whether the Additional Protocol's rule against terror was a rule of customary international law. However, it also argued that since the crime of 'attack on civilians' *is* customary in nature, attacking civilians with the intent to terrorize them can logically be no less a rule of customary international law, even if the majority was not obliged to decide the question.[178]

The majority reviewed the negotiations underlying the Additional Protocol. The ICRC's delegate to the committee to which Article 51 of the Protocol was assigned in draft form said that the rule 'merely reaffirmed existing international law'. The states' concerns were for the most part limited to whether the object of the prohibition against terror should be the actor's intent or the capacity of the methods employed to spread violence. Several states simply approved the draft provision without proposing changes. The drafting committee reported to the plenary:

The prohibition of 'acts or threats of violence which have the primary object of spreading terror' is directed to intentional conduct specifically directed toward the spreading of terror and excludes terror which was not intended by a belligerent and terror that is merely an incidental effect of acts of warfare which have another primary object and are in all other respects lawful.[179]

---

[175] Ibid., paras 331–45.   [176] Ibid., para. 87.
[177] Ibid., paras 22–5, 95–6, 124.   [178] Ibid., paras 97–8.
[179] *Official Records of the Diplomatic Conference on the Reaffirmation and Development of International Humanitarian Law Applicable in Armed Conflicts* (17 vols), ICRC, 1974–77, vol. XV, p. 274.

The *Tadić* conditions for jurisdiction include the requirements that the violation constitutes a breach of a rule protecting important values, and that the breach must involve grave consequences for the victim. The *Galić* majority observed that a campaign of shelling and sniping of civilians is bound to cause death and injury to civilians over time. Obviously this is a grave consequence, and doing the same with the primary purpose of spreading terror among civilians is no less a grave act. Another requirement for jurisdiction is prior criminalization. The first conviction for terror against a civilian population was delivered in July 1947 by a court martial sitting in Makassar, in the Netherlands East Indies. The offences alleged in *Motomura et al.*[180] were charged in the indictment as 'systematic terrorism against persons suspected by the Japanese of punishable acts . . . this systematic terrorism taking the form of repeated, regular and lengthy torture and/or ill-treatment, the seizing of men and women on the grounds of wild rumours, repeatedly striking them . . . the aforesaid acts having led or at least contributed to the death, severe physical and mental suffering of many'.[181] The *Motomura* court martial convicted 13 of the 15 defendants of 'systematic terrorism practiced against civilians' for acts including unlawful mass arrests. The court found that those arrests had the effect of terrorizing the population, 'for nobody, even the most innocent, was any longer certain of his liberty, and a person once arrested, even if absolutely innocent, could no longer be sure of health and life'. The associated torture and ill-treatment of interned civilians was also found to be a form of systematic terror. Seven of those convicted were sentenced to death and the rest to prison sentences ranging from one to twenty years.[182]

As noted by the *Galić* majority, the first international-level postwar rule against 'terror' is found in Article 33 of the fourth Geneva Convention of 1949: 'No protected person may be punished for an offence he or she has not personally committed. Collective penalties and likewise all measures of intimidation or of terrorism are prohibited.' This protection extends only to persons 'in the hands of a Party to the conflict' (Article 4 of the Convention). Civilians in territory not occupied by the adversary were therefore not protected by the fourth Convention against 'measures of intimidation or of terrorism' which the adversary might decide to direct against them. *Galić*, in one of the most interesting observations in the judgment, argued that Article 51 of Additional Protocol I was meant to close this gap in international humanitarian law. The Additional Protocol as a whole elaborated and extended the protections of the Geneva Conventions, including those of the fourth Convention on the protection of civilians in times of war. The scope of application of the Additional Protocol is found in its first article, which states that the Protocol 'shall apply in the situations referred to in Article 2 common to [the Geneva] Conventions'. Common Article 2 states that the Convention 'shall *also* apply to all cases of partial or total occupation of the territory of a High Contracting Party, even if the said occupation meets with no armed resistance'. Consequently, Additional Protocol I applies to the aforementioned situations to the extent feasible, as well as to the kind of situation dealt with in the *Galić* case, in which

---

[180] *Trial of Shigeki Motomura and 15 Others*, 13 LRTWC 138.
[181] Ibid., pp. 138–9.   [182] Ibid., pp. 140–3.

civilians not in the hands of an attacking force become victims of attacks by that force. In other words, whereas the cited part of Article 33 of Geneva Convention IV brought protection from intimidation or terrorism to only a subset of civilians in the context of armed conflict (namely, those in the hands of a party to the conflict), Article 51 of the Protocol elaborated and extended the protection from terror to civilians whether or not in the hands of the party to the conflict conducting the attack.[183]

In its inquiry into the prior criminalization of 'terror', the *Galić* majority took account of pre-conflict initiatives by the state authorities in the region to implement the Geneva law. The 1960 Criminal Code of the Federal Republic of Yugoslavia, Article 125, provided that 'Whoever, in violation of the rules of international law in times of war, armed conflict or occupation issues orders for or performs . . . the application of intimidating measures and terror . . . shall be punished with severe imprisonment of at least five years or with the penalty of death'.[184] The source of this was probably Article 33 of Geneva Convention IV, although the Yugoslav version of the prohibition is formulated quite generally and does not seem to be limited to protected persons, in the sense of the Geneva Conventions. Following Yugoslavia's ratification of Additional Protocol I on 11 March 1977, the new treaty was incorporated into Yugoslavia's '[Armed Forces] Regulations on the Application of International Laws of War'. An order from the Federal President prefaces the regulations and makes unit commanders responsible for the application of the international laws of war. The applicable laws include Additional Protocol I. The regulations state that 'serious' violations of the laws of war constitute criminal offences. These include war crimes against a civilian population, namely 'attack on civilians . . . inhuman treatment [of civilians] inflicting great suffering or injury to bodily integrity or health . . . application of measures of intimidation and terror' and 'deliberate bombardment of the civilian population'. In a later part, on means and methods of combat, the regulations state: 'Attacking civilians for the purpose of terrorising them is especially prohibited.' Moreover, ignorance of the provisions of the laws of war 'does not exonerate the transgressors from responsibility'; perpetrators of war crimes 'may also answer before an international court, if such a court has been established'; and the Criminal Code had been updated to criminalize and punish the aforementioned war crimes against the civilian population. When the authorities of Republika Srpska, under whom Galić served, sought to break away from Bosnia-Herzegovina, in early 1992, they incorporated the above codes into their own legal system.[185]

The *Galić* majority narrowed its exercise to terror attacks causing death or serious injury to civilians. Thus it did not deal with terror 'threats', nor did it pronounce upon terror attacks which do not cause death or serious injury.[186] This cautious approach sought to forge a link with the grave-breach provisions of the Geneva Conventions, whose criminalization is not in doubt. The rationale was that if a charged violation is of the same nature as a grave breach, individual criminal responsibility would thereby

---

[183] *Galić* trial judgment, para. 120.
[184] *Criminal Code 1960* (Belgrade: Union of Jurists' Associations, 1960), pp. 48–9.
[185] *Galić* trial judgment, paras 122–3.
[186] Ibid., para. 132. See also the discussion by the ICTY Appeals Chamber in the *Kordić and Čerkez* appeal judgment, paras 55–68, where the crime of 'attack on civilians' requires proof of death or serious injury.

have been established. Terror in *Galić* was not charged as a grave breach of Additional Protocol I. But with regard to whether there was, in 1992, individual criminal responsibility for a person committing a serious violation of the rule prohibiting terror, this is answerable in the affirmative where the violation took the form of death or serious injury caused to civilians. In such cases the acts of violence qualified, in themselves, as grave breaches of the Protocol. Therefore, according to the *Galić* majority, it would make no sense to qualify the terror attacks as less criminal than a grave breach.[187]

The majority concluded that terror in the narrow sense had been criminalized in a precise and accessible manner by 1992, and that this was known or should have been known to Galić. The elements of the crime were said to be (note that proof of *actual* infliction of terror is not among them):

1. An act of violence directed against the civilian population or individual civilians not taking direct part in hostilities which causes death or serious injury within the civilian population.

2. The defendant wilfully made the civilian population or individual civilians not taking direct part in hostilities the object of that act of violence.

3. The defendant committed the act with the primary purpose (*dolus eventualis* is not sufficient) of spreading terror among the civilian population.[188]

The dissenting judge, Nieto-Navia, wrote in response:

The Prosecution and the Majority cited few examples indicating that the criminalization of such an offence was an admitted state practice at such a time. In my view, these limited references do not suffice to establish that this offence existed as a form of liability under international customary law and attracted individual criminal responsibility under that body of law. I therefore conclude that the offence of inflicting terror on a civilian population does not fall within the jurisdiction of this Trial Chamber. By concluding otherwise without establishing that the offence of inflicting terror on a civilian population attracted individual criminal responsibility under international customary law, the Majority is furthering a conception of international humanitarian law which I do not support.[189]

The ICTY Appeals Chamber set the following limits on the creation of new law:

This fundamental principle [of *nullum crimen sine lege*] does not prevent a court from interpreting and clarifying the elements of a particular crime. Nor does it preclude the progressive development of the law by the court. But it does prevent a court from creating new law or from interpreting existing law beyond the reasonable limits of acceptable clarification. This Tribunal must therefore be satisfied that the crime or the form of liability with which an accused is charged was sufficiently foreseeable and that the law providing for such liability must be sufficiently accessible at the relevant time, taking into account the specificity of international law when making that assessment.[190]

Did the *Galić* majority exceed these limits? At the time of writing, the ICTY Appeals Chamber had yet to deliver its judgment in the *Galić* case. Whatever the final result, the

---

[187] *Galić* trial judgment, para. 127.   [188] Ibid., paras 133–7.

[189] Ibid., para. 113 of the dissenting opinion.

[190] *Prosecutor* v. *Milutinović et al.*, Decision (Appeals Chamber) on Dragoljub Ojdanić's Motion Challenging Jurisdiction — Joint Criminal Enterprise, 21 May 2003, para. 38.

ICTY's jurisprudence on the 'crime of terror' will certainly be remembered as one of the most interesting chapters in the history of that institution, not least because it would have forced the Appeals Chamber to reconsider fundamental questions about jurisdiction and legal methodology which the judges of the Appeals Chamber had until that time dealt with superficially.[191]

4.3.4 Unlawful labour

Naletilić and Martinović is the first case in this area. It convicts both defendants of unlawful labour, brought pursuant to Article 51 of Geneva Convention IV and Articles 49, 50, and 52 of Geneva Convention III. The Trial Chamber concluded, simply, that the offence of unlawful labour against a prisoner of war is defined as an intentional act by which a prisoner of war is forced to perform labour prohibited under Articles 49, 50, 51, or 52 of Geneva Convention III.[192] For example, compelling a prisoner of war to turn a private property into a military headquarters amounts to unlawful labour.[193] The same is true, a fortiori, of the act of dressing up a prisoner of war in camouflage uniform, equipping him with a fake rifle carved from wood, and ordering him into the battlefield to recover the bodies of fallen soldiers.[194]

4.3.5 Slavery

Milorad Krnojelac was charged with slavery as a violation of the laws or customs of war on the basis of both the 1926 Slavery Convention and customary international law.[195] The court relied, among other things, on the *Kunarac et al.* trial judgment, which held that enslavement constitutes a crime against humanity under customary law.[196] (Sourcing war-crimes law to the law of crimes against humanity, and vice versa, is a common practice at the ICTY.) There is no real difference between slavery, as analysed in the *Krnojelac* case, and unlawful labour.[197] Krnojelac was acquitted of the slavery charges.[198]

4.3.6 Plunder of public or private property

The ICTY's *Delalić* judgment was the first to deal with this subject, and in particular with plunder of *private* property.[199] The Trial Chamber stated that the prohibition of plunder is part of customary international law.[200] The basic norms are contained in the Regulations to the 1907 Hague Convention IV: Articles 46 to 56 are broadly aimed at preserving the inviolability of public and private property during military occupation.

---

[191] See, e.g., *Kordić and Čerkez* appeal judgment, paras 45–6.
[192] See the analysis in *Naletilić and Martinović* trial judgment, paras 250–61.
[193] Ibid., para. 311.   [194] Ibid., paras 288–9.
[195] The Nuremberg Tribunal also dealt with slave labour: see 22 IMT Judgment 486–91.
[196] *Krnojelac* trial judgment, para. 353.
[197] Ibid., paras 359–60.   [198] Ibid., paras 425–30.
[199] The Nuremberg Tribunal dealt with pillage: see 22 IMT Judgment 481–6.
[200] *Delalić et al.* trial judgment, paras 587–8.

(*Delalić*, being a prison-camp case, was not concerned with the other anti-pillaging provision of the Hague Regulations, namely Article 28, which applies to the conduct of hostilities.)[201]

In relation to private property, the fundamental principle is contained in Article 46 of the Regulations, which provides that private property must be respected and must not be confiscated. This rule is reinforced by the unequivocal Article 47: 'Pillage is formally forbidden.'[202] The Nuremberg Charter and Control Council Law No. 10 both included the offence of 'plunder of public and private property'. (No significant distinction between pillage and plunder has emerged, so the two should be regarded as synonymous.) The principle is further reflected in the Geneva Conventions of 1949. For example, Article 18 of the third Convention protects the personal property of prisoners of war from arbitrary appropriation, and Article 33 of the fourth Convention categorically affirms that pillage is prohibited. This latter prohibition is of general application, extending to the entire territories of the parties to a conflict, and is thus not limited to acts committed in occupied territories.[203]

As to individual criminal responsibility for plunder, the *Delalić* Trial Court observed that 'organized seizure' of property undertaken as part of a 'systematic economic exploitation' of occupied territory was the subject of prosecutions before the International Military Tribunal and subsequent proceedings before the Nuremberg military courts. On the other hand, mundane acts of looting of enemy property committed by soldiers for private gain also have been criminalized, according to the Trial Chamber, under the same rubric of unjustified appropriation. Such 'isolated instances' of theft of personal property of modest value were treated as war crimes in a number of trials conducted by French military tribunals following the Second World War.[204]

Clearly this odd history of the offence of plunder raises the question whether the appropriation must be *substantial* in some sense to constitute the crime, but the *Delalić* court did not acknowledge this issue. Instead it found that the ICTY prosecutor had failed to demonstrate that property taken from detainees at the Čelebići camp was of 'sufficient monetary value' for its unlawful appropriation to involve 'grave consequences' for the victims. The Trial Chamber accordingly concluded that it lacked jurisdiction, and dismissed the charge.[205]

This result is not convincing. What do 'sufficient monetary value' and 'grave consequences' mean in a context where detainees are stripped of their last valuable belongings? What about the *sentimental* value of stolen property having little monetary value, yet which has become psychologically so important that the consequences of

---

[201] Article 28 of the Regulations provides that: 'The pillage of a town or place, even when taken by assault, is prohibited.'

[202] The wording of Articles 28, 46, and 47 is taken unchanged from the Regulations to the 1899 Hague Convention II.

[203] The Trial Chamber maintained that the terminological differences in the cited sources should be regarded as unimportant and that plunder should be understood to embrace all forms of unlawful appropriation of property in armed conflict, including those acts traditionally described as 'pillage' (para. 591).

[204] See *Delalić et al.* trial judgment, para. 590, and the extensive references given therein.

[205] Ibid., para. 1154.

appropriation are more serious than the theft of items with monetary value? The Trial Chamber said it had considered the evidence of plunder in the light most favourable to the prosecutor. It accepted, therefore, that the theft of private property took place in the Čelebići prison-camp between May and September 1992; that it was carried out on a systematic basis; and that it concerned money, or jewellery of sentimental value. Several former detainees described how, either immediately upon their arrival at the prison-camp or subsequently during their detention, any valuable property in their possession was taken from them. For example, one witness described an incident where money and gold watches were taken from the detainees by two persons in uniform. Another two witnesses testified that detainees were ordered to put their valuables into a helmet that was passed around; property taken in this way included watches, rings, bracelets, chains, and crosses.[206]

In the *Jelisić* case, which included a guilty plea to one count of plunder, the Trial Chamber defined the offence as the fraudulent appropriation of public or private 'funds' belonging to the enemy or the opposing party, perpetrated during, and in connection with, an armed conflict.[207] (Why it chose to focus on 'funds' is not clear.) The Trial Chamber expressed agreement with the exposition of the law in *Delalić*. Yet it convicted Jelisić for stealing money, watches, jewellery, and other valuables from detainees upon their arrival at the camp, without considering *Delalić*'s criterion of 'grave consequences'.[208]

Blaškić also followed the law in *Delalić*.[209] In convicting the accused, the *Blaškić* court found that soldiers under the defendant's command had set fire to stables, slaughtered livestock, and looted houses. They had also stolen money from civilians. One Croatian soldier had seized 2,000 German marks and jewellery from an inhabitant of a village under attack. Two soldiers had confiscated money from a person's wallet after he had surrendered. And 400 German marks had been taken from the dead body of another Muslim victim.[210] Whether grave consequences resulted in every case (including the last finding) is not clear from the facts.

In another case, the *Kunarac* Trial Chamber acquitted an accused charged with a count of plunder because the prosecutor had not adduced evidence that the theft was 'widespread.'[211] The Trial Chamber noted that in both *Delalić* and *Blaškić* the plunder allegations concerned large-scale activities, and moreover in *Blaškić* the activities covered a large geographical area. *Kunarac* saw in the 'ordinary meaning' of the ICTY Statute a requirement that appropriation of property, if it is to be characterized as plunder, must victimize more than a small number of people. The Trial Chamber's decision to acquit the defendant followed from the fact that the case at hand was limited to evidence of theft from only a few persons in one building.[212] This approach implicitly dispenses with *Delalić*'s requirement of grave consequences — it is the systematic nature of the theft that makes the crime, not its individual or overall impact. Thus we encounter considerable confusion in this area.

---

[206] Ibid., paras 1147–9.   [207] *Jelisić* trial judgment, para. 48.
[208] Ibid., para. 49.   [209] *Blaškić* trial judgment, para. 184.   [210] Ibid., para. 424.
[211] *Prosecutor* v. *Kunarac et al.*, Decision on Motion for Acquittal, 3 July 2000, paras 14–16.
[212] Ibid., para. 16.

The ICTY Appeals Chamber has said that the crime of plunder is applicable in both international and non-international armed conflict. Violations of the prohibition against plunder entail, under customary law, the individual criminal responsibility of the person breaching the rule.[213] The prohibition against pillage is found in numerous military manuals, and constitutes an offence under the legislation of a large number of states.[214] As for the threshold test, the Appeals Chamber added:

> The question remains at what point the breach actually involves grave consequences for the victim. ... there is a consequential link between the monetary value of the appropriated property and the gravity of the consequences for the victim. ... the assessment of when a piece of property reaches the threshold level of a certain value can only be made on a case-by-case basis and only in conjunction with the general circumstances of the crime.[215]

But whereas the above proposition is unhelpful because it is broad and unprincipled, the Appeals Chamber's next statement, which does purport to state a principle, is unhelpful because it is not supported reasoning: 'a serious violation could be assumed in circumstances where appropriations take place vis-à-vis a large number of people, even though there are no grave consequences for each individual. In this case it would be the overall effect on the civilian population and the multitude of offences committed that would make the violation serious.'[216]

4.3.7 Attack on civilian objects

The *Blaškić* Trial Chamber spent one summary paragraph dealing with the crime of attack on civilian objects.[217] The prohibition is relatively clearly set out in Article 52 of Additional Protocol I, although once again there is plenty of room for interpretation, and the question whether a violation of the prohibition in 1992 or at a later time attracted individual criminal responsibility is not adequately addressed in *Blaškić*.

Article 52 defines a 'civilian object' negatively: in this category fall all objects which are not 'military objectives'. The latter comprise 'those objects which by their nature, location, purpose or use make an effective contribution to military action and whose total or partial destruction, capture or neutralization, in the circumstances ruling at the time, offers a definite military advantage'. Where there is doubt (but how much doubt is doubt?) the object must be treated as if it were a civilian object.

The *Blaškić* Trial Chamber adopted the prosecutor's definition of attack on civilian objects, according to which the attack must have caused damage to civilian property. Parties to the conflict are obliged to 'attempt' to distinguish between military targets and civilian property; targeting civilian property is an offence when not justified by military necessity; and the attack must have been conducted intentionally in the knowledge that civilian property was being targeted not out of military necessity.[218]

---

[213] *Prosecutor* v. *Hadžihasanović and Kubura*, Decision on Joint Defence Interlocutory Appeal of Trial Chamber Decision on Rule 98 *bis* Motions for Acquittal, 11 March 2005, para. 37. [214] Ibid., para. 38.
[215] *Kordić and Čerkez* trial judgment, para. 82. [216] Ibid., para. 83.
[217] *Blaškić* trial judgment, para. 180. [218] Ibid.

Blaškić was convicted of one count of attack on civilian objects for ordering a series of attacks on villages which resulted in extensive destruction to civilian property. For example, in the course of a single attack, 180 out of 200 Muslim houses in the village of Ahmići were set alight.[219] Moreover, several mosques were destroyed without military justification.[220]

The *Strugar* Trial Court said that the prohibition of attack on civilian objects is a necessary complement to the protection of civilian populations. There must be 'damage'.[221] The indictment in *Strugar* was confined to an artillery attack on the Old Town of Dubrovnik on 6 December 1991. The Trial Court noted that the Old Town is a physically distinct part of the larger city. Its clearly visible boundaries are marked by the medieval walls that surround the Old Town. The demarcation is plain to see at a distance, and would have been obvious to the attacking forces of the Yugoslav People's Army (JNA). The Old Town had a World Heritage listing, with the consequent protections and immunities. Though a World Heritage site, it had a substantial resident population of between 7,000 and 8,000. Religious communities lived within the walls of the Old Town. Some people from the larger Dubrovnik area had been able to take up temporary residence in the Old Town during the blockade in the belief that its World Heritage listing would give them protection from military attack. There were no Croatian military positions in the Old Town on 6 December 1991, and the court found that the JNA officers were aware of this fact. The population was thus properly characterized as a civilian population, and the 'objects' located in the Old Town were civilian objects.[222] The JNA's shelling of the Old Town on 6 December 1991 resulted in the death of two civilians, injuries caused to civilians, and extensive damage to civilian objects. The Court found Pavle Strugar guilty of the crimes of attack on civilians and destruction or wilful damage to cultural property; the elements of the crime of 'attack on civilian objects' were proven, but a conviction was not entered due to the rule against the cumulation of convictions.[223]

4.3.8 Wanton destruction or devastation not justified by military necessity[224]

The drafters of the *Blaškić* judgment seem to have been more preoccupied with the facts than with the law. Why become entangled in fine legal distinctions (they must have thought) when the facts tell you that the accused, through his actions, wrought massive destruction to whole villages, torching homes and causing populations to flee or perish?

This would explain why *Blaškić* dealt with the above offence in one line, calling it 'similar' to the grave breach of Article 2(d) of the ICTY Statute ('extensive destruction and appropriation of property, not justified by military necessity and carried out

---

[219] Ibid., para. 418. See also, ibid., paras 499, 572, 610, 750.
[220] Ibid., paras 418, 419, 421, 500.   [221] *Strugar* trial judgment, para. 225.
[222] Ibid., paras 279, 285.   [223] Ibid., paras 289, 452–5, 478–9.
[224] ICTY Statute, Art. 3(b).

unlawfully and wantonly').[225] If the ICTY Statute's Article 3 provision is only similar, it must also be different in some respect, but the Trial Chamber did not say in which respect. About the grave breach it said, citing only the ICRC commentary, that an occupying power is prohibited from destroying property except where such destruction is made absolutely necessary by military operations. To constitute a *grave breach*, the destruction not justified by military necessity must be extensive, unlawful and wanton, the Court declared.[226]

Must the destruction be 'extensive' to qualify also as a violation of the laws or customs of war? How is this offence different from that of 'attack on civilian objects'? Despite the existence of basic unresolved questions, the Trial Chamber convicted Blaškić of two counts of devastation not justified by military necessity.

The ICTY Appeals Chamber has said that the wanton destruction of cities, towns, or villages reflects the customary international law prohibition on unlawful attack against civilian objects which is found in conventional and customary international law applying to situations of international and non-international armed conflict. The rule against devastation not justified by military necessity includes the customary international law prohibition that destruction of the property of an adversary is prohibited, unless required by imperative military necessity. This rule also applies in international and non-international armed conflict, according to the Appeals Chamber.[227] The prohibition is contained in numerous military manuals that are applicable in or have been applied in international and non-international armed conflict, and numerous states have adopted legislation making it an offence to attack civilian objects during any armed conflict.[228]

In the most recent ICTY case to deal with this charge, the elements of the crime are given as: the destruction of property occurred on a large scale; the destruction was not justified by military necessity; and the perpetrator acted with the intent to destroy the property in question.[229] This is one of a series of definitions produced at the tribunals to give trial courts a structure to work with. This particular list of elements, intuitive as it may be, was invented in the *Kordić and Čerkez* trial judgment.[230] The absence of relevant case law from which to derive general principles has meant that much of the jurisprudence of the tribunals is adrift, as illustrated by the following, convoluted, announcement in *Orić*:

A different situation arises if a military attack is launched against a settlement from which previously, due to its location and its armed inhabitants, a serious danger emanated for the inhabitants of a neighbouring village who are now seeking to remove this danger through military action. It may be the case that, after such a settlement has been taken, destruction of houses occurs in order to prevent the inhabitants, including combatants, to return and resume the attacks. A submission that such destruction is covered by 'military necessity' will be entertained on a case-by-case basis. Except for the rare occasions in which such preventive destruction could arguably fall within the

---

[225] *Blaškić* trial judgment, para. 183.   [226] Ibid., para. 157.

[227] *Prosecutor* v. *Hadžihasanović and Kubura*, Decision on Joint Defence Interlocutory Appeal of Trial Chamber Decision on Rule 98 *bis* Motions for Acquittal, 11 March 2005, para. 29.

[228] Ibid., para. 30.   [229] *Orić* trial judgment, para. 581.

[230] *Kordić and Čerkez* trial judgment, para. 346. See also *Strugar* trial judgment, para. 292.

scope of 'military necessity', the principle must be upheld that the destruction of civil settlements, as a rule, is punishable as a war crime.[231]

4.3.9 Destruction or wilful damage to institutions dedicated to religion or education[232]

This is, unfortunately, another prohibition that had not been adjudicated prior to *Blaškić*. The court gave it unceremonious treatment. It said only that the destruction or damage must have been committed intentionally to institutions clearly identified as dedicated to religion or education, and which were not being used for military purposes and were not located in the 'immediate vicinity' of military objectives.[233] No authorities were cited. The accused was convicted pursuant to this purported offence for ordering attacks resulting in the destruction of mosques.[234]

In relation to this provision of Article 3 of the ICTY Statute, the Appeals Chamber has said that the rule is derived from conventional and customary international law and applies in both international and non-international armed conflict.[235] The ICTY provision reproduces the core of Articles 27 and 56 of the 1907 Hague Regulations. According to the Appeals Chamber, there are two types of protection for cultural, historical, and religious monuments embodied in Article 3 of the ICTY Statute: general and special. General protection stems from Article 52 of Additional Protocol I, and applies to a building or monument, such as a school or a place of worship, with the effect that it may not be destroyed 'unless it has turned into a military object by offering the attacking side "a definite military advantage" at the time of the attack'.[236] Special protection stems from Article 53 of Additional Protocol I, which provides protection to three categories of objects: historic monuments, works of art, and places of worship, on the condition that they constitute 'the cultural or spiritual heritage of peoples'.[237] Buildings dedicated to education are also protected.[238] The *Strugar* Appeals Chamber found that these conventional rules represent statements of a core principle of customary international law that protects cultural property during armed conflict and that provides a sufficient basis for charging individuals with criminal responsibility in situations of both international and non-international armed conflict.[239]

As for the *Strugar* Trial Chamber, it said that even though the victim of the crime of destruction of cultural property is to be understood broadly as a 'people', rather than any particular individual, the destruction, if it is grave, can be said to involve grave consequences 'for the victim'.[240] After a discussion highlighting the absence of case law in this area, the trial court concluded that an act will fulfil the elements of the crime of

---

[231] *Orić* trial judgment, para. 588.   [232] ICTY Statute, Art. 3(d).

[233] *Blaškić* trial judgment, para. 185.   [234] Ibid., paras 418–23, 500, 600, 618, 626, 750.

[235] *Prosecutor* v. *Hadžihasanović and Kubura*, Decision on Joint Defence Interlocutory Appeal of Trial Chamber Decision on Rule 98 *bis* Motions for Acquittal, 11 March 2005, para. 44.

[236] *Kordić and Čerkez* appeal judgment, para. 89.

[237] Ibid., paras 90–1.   [238] Ibid., para. 92.

[239] *Prosecutor* v. *Strugar et al.*, Decision on Interlocutory Appeal, 22 November 2002, paras 10, 14.

[240] *Strugar* trial judgment, para. 232.

destruction or wilful damage to cultural property if, (1) it has caused damage or destruction to property which constitutes the cultural or spiritual heritage of peoples; (2) the damaged or destroyed property was not used for military purposes at the time when the act of hostility directed against this object took place; and (3) the act was carried out with the intent to damage or destroy the property in question.[241]

4.4 GRAVE BREACHES OF GENEVA LAW IN INTERNATIONAL ARMED CONFLICT

The four 1949 Geneva Conventions define a number of serious violations of its provisions as 'grave breaches'. These breaches are limited to acts against 'persons or property protected' by the Conventions. The term 'protected persons' applies to wounded, injured, or shipwrecked combatants,[242] prisoners of war,[243] and civilians.[244] With respect to the latter category, Article 4 of Geneva Convention IV limits protection to persons who find themselves in the hands of a party to the conflict of which they are not nationals. The term 'protected property' generally applies only to property found in occupied territory.[245]

Grave breaches prohibit wilful killing, torture, or inhuman treatment of protected persons, including biological experiments and wilfully causing great suffering or serious injury to body or health.[246] Geneva Conventions I, II, and IV also proscribe the extensive destruction or appropriation of property not justified by military necessity.[247] Compelling a prisoner of war or a civilian to serve in the armed forces of the hostile power or depriving him or her of the right to a fair and regular trial constitute grave breaches under Geneva Conventions III and IV. Pursuant to Article 147 of Geneva Convention IV, the unlawful deportation, transfer, or confinement of a protected person, and the taking of hostages, are also considered grave breaches. The four Geneva Conventions apply in international armed conflict only,[248] and so the grave breaches system is formally inapplicable to internal armed conflict, although there has been a great amount of cross-fertilization, both within the broader category of war crimes[249]

---

[241] Ibid., para. 312.

[242] See Geneva Convention I, Art. 13, and Geneva Convention II, Art. 13, for general definitions of who is protected under these treaties.

[243] See Geneva Convention III, Art. 4, for a description of who constitutes a prisoner of war.

[244] Geneva Convention IV, Art. 4.

[245] Ibid., Art. 53; *Brđanin* trial judgment, para. 125. Concerning 'occupied territory', see the Hague Regulations 1907, Art. 42.

[246] The grave breaches provisions are set forth in Geneva Convention I, Art. 50, Geneva Convention II, Art. 51, Geneva Convention III, Art. 130, and Geneva Convention IV, Art. 147.

[247] *Brđanin* trial judgment, paras 584–90.

[248] Except for Common Article 3, as discussed above.

[249] See, e.g., *Prosecutor* v. *Furundžija*, Decision on the Defendant's Motion to Dismiss Counts 13 and 14 of the Indictment (Lack of Subject Matter Jurisdiction), 29 May 1998; and, more recently, the following exchange: L. Zegveld, 'Dutch Cases on Torture Committed in Afghanistan: The Relevance of the Distinction Between

and between the categories of war crimes and crimes against humanity,[250] which is the result of the tribunals' almost exclusive focus on war crimes committed against civilians and non-combatants.

The ICTY Appeals Chamber said about grave breaches:

The grave breaches system of the Geneva Conventions establishes a twofold system: there is on the one hand an enumeration of offences that are regarded [as] so serious as to constitute 'grave breaches'; closely bound up with this enumeration a mandatory enforcement mechanism is set up, based on the concept of a duty and a right of all Contracting States to search for and try or extradite persons allegedly responsible for 'grave breaches'. The international armed conflict element generally attributed to the grave breaches provisions of the Geneva Conventions is merely a function of the system of universal mandatory jurisdiction that those provisions create. The international armed conflict requirement was a necessary limitation on the grave breaches system in light of the intrusion on State sovereignty that such mandatory universal jurisdiction represents. State parties to the 1949 Geneva Conventions did not want to give other States jurisdiction over serious violations of international humanitarian law committed in their internal armed conflicts — at least not the mandatory universal jurisdiction involved in the grave breaches system.[251]

Concerning the existence of an international armed conflict, the ICTY Appeals Chamber has held that an armed conflict exists whenever there is resort to armed force between states.[252] The grave breaches regime applies from the initiation of such armed conflict until a general conclusion of peace is reached.[253] This body of law applies throughout the entire territory of the parties to the armed conflict — even to those parts of the territory where no active combat occurs.[254] Cases before the ICTY have required the establishment of a nexus between the armed conflict and the underlying criminal act.[255]

The ICTY Appeals Chamber has taken an expansive view with respect to the scope of the requirement that the victim be a protected person.[256] The protections to which such individuals are entitled attach only when they 'fall into the hands of the adverse party'. Because grave breaches may only be committed in international armed conflict, the reference to the 'adverse party' must mean forces of a state of which the victim is not a national. Secondly, grave breaches generally cannot be committed during the actual course of combat, since the victims usually will not have fallen into the hands of the adversary during the course of the hostilities.[257]

Internal and International Armed Conflict' (2006) 4 *J. Int'l Crim. J.* 878; W. Ferdinandusse, 'On the Question of Dutch Courts' Universal Jurisdiction' (2006) 4 *J. Int'l Crim. J.* 881; and G. Mettraux, 'Response to the Comments by Zegveld and Ferdinandusse' (2006) 4 *J. Int'l Crim. J.* 884.

250 See Chapter 6.   251 *Tadić* jurisdiction appeal decision, para. 80.

252 Ibid., para. 70; *Brðanin* trial judgment, para. 124.

253 *Tadić* jurisdiction appeal decision, para. 70.   254 Ibid.

255 See *Delalić et al.* trial judgment, para. 193. In the *Tadić* jurisdiction appeal decision, para. 70, the Appeals Chamber stated that the 'alleged crimes were closely related to the hostilities'.

256 *Tadić* jurisdiction appeal decision, para. 81.

257 The grave breaches provisions in Additional Protocol I, Art. 85, seek to avoid this problem.

In *Tadić*, the ICTY Appeals Chamber interpreted the phrase 'adverse party' broadly, taking into account the fact that modern conflicts are often between different ethnic groups — 'ethnicity rather than nationality may become the ground for allegiance'.[258] In a later case, the Appeals Chamber said:

> depriving victims, who arguably are of the same nationality under domestic law as their captors, of the protection of the Geneva Conventions solely based on that national law would not be consistent with the object and purpose of the Conventions. Their very object could indeed be defeated if undue emphasis were placed on formal legal bonds, which could also be altered by governments to shield their nationals from prosecution based on the grave breaches provisions of the Geneva Conventions. ... the nationality of the victims for the purpose of the application of the Geneva Convention IV should not be determined on the basis of formal national characterisations, but rather upon an analysis of the substantial relations, taking into consideration the different ethnicity of the victims and the perpetrators, and their bonds with the foreign intervening State.[259]

Because grave breaches are essentially a sub-component of the more general category of war crimes, the ICTY Trial Chambers typically find that the elements of the underlying offences are the same for grave breaches as for other war crimes, even though the terms employed may differ.[260]

4.5 CONCLUSION

Developments in war-crimes law have been exclusive to the ICTY. By 2006 this institution had abandoned the rigid distinction it had upheld in its early jurisprudence between crimes committed in international armed conflict and crimes committed in civil war. Instead, war-crimes law became identified with the expansion of Common Article 3 as supplemented by the Additional Protocols. The demands of practice, the paucity of precedent, and the tribunal's primary focus on war crimes committed against civilians and non-combatants broke down theoretical divisions to such an extent that not only has war-crimes law become internally homogenized, the distinction between it and the law of crimes against humanity has become increasingly elusive.

---

[258] *Tadić* appeal judgment, para. 166.
[259] *Delalić et al.* appeal judgment, paras 80, 84. See also *Blaškić* appeal judgment, paras 167–82.
[260] For example, 'wilful killing' is a grave breach whereas 'murder' is a war crime.

5

GENOCIDE LAW: AN EDUCATION IN SENTIMENTALISM

SUMMARY

Genocide is a denial of the right of existence of entire human groups, as homicide is the denial of the right to live of individual human beings; such denial of the right of existence shocks the conscience of mankind, results in great losses to humanity in the form of cultural and other contributions represented by these human groups, and is contrary to moral law and to the spirit and aims of the United Nations. (Opening paragraph of Resolution 96(I) of the UN General Assembly, 11 December 1946.)

5.1 INTRODUCTION

Genocide was 'codified' as a crime in the Genocide Convention of 1948,[1] a rare gift to international criminal law where the nascent UN tribunals generally have had to struggle to give shape to ill-defined crimes:

Article II: In the present Convention, genocide means any of the following acts committed with intent to destroy, in whole or in part, a national, ethnical, racial or religious group, as such:

(a) Killing members of the group;

(b) Causing serious bodily or mental harm to members of the group;

(c) Deliberately inflicting on the group conditions of life calculated to bring about its physical destruction in whole or in part;

(d) Imposing measures intended to prevent births within the group;

(e) Forcibly transferring children of the group to another group.

Article III: The following acts shall be punishable:

(a) Genocide;

(b) Conspiracy to commit genocide;

(c) Direct and public incitement to commit genocide;

(d) Attempt to commit genocide;

(e) Complicity in genocide.

The above key elements of genocide's codification were added, unchanged, to the statutes of the ICTY, the ICTR, the ICC, and the Special Panels of East Timor. The Special Court for Sierra Leone does not have jurisdiction over genocide.

From its inception the crime of genocide was considered to be a species of a crime against humanity.[2] It has since been accepted, in general formulation, but also in the specific form given to it by the Convention, as part of customary international law.[3]

---

[1] A brief history of the preparation of the Genocide Convention may be found in the *Report of the Sixth Committee*, 3 December 1948, UN Doc. A/760. For a more detailed account, see Robinson, *Genocide Convention*, and Schabas, *Genocide*, pp. 14–101. More generally, see M. Lippman, 'Genocide: The Crime of the Century. The Jurisprudence of Death at the Dawn of the New Millennium' (2001) 23 *Houston J. Int'l L.* 467.

[2] See reports on the trials of Josef Altstötter and others, 6 LRTWC 4, 9, and 48; Amon Goeth, 7 LRTWC 9; Franz Hoess, 7 LRTWC 24–6; Ulrich Greifelt and others, 13 LRTWC 2–3, 39 (making direct reference to the Genocide Convention); and Artur Greiser, 13 LRTWC 112–14. The *Jelisić* case of the ICTY termed genocide a specialized form of persecution (a crime against humanity): *Jelisić* trial judgment, para. 68; see also *Sikirica et al.* no-case-to-answer decision, para. 58.

[3] The UN General Assembly's Resolution 96(I) of 11 December 1946 affirmed that genocide, in the general formulation given at the start of this chapter, is a crime under international law. This proposition was received not without some controversy (Robinson, *Genocide Convention*, pp. 55–7). By 1951, however, it was possible for the ICJ to declare: 'the principles underlying the Convention are principles which are recognized by civilized nations as binding on States, even without any conventional obligation' (Reservations to the Convention on the Prevention and Punishment of the Crime of Genocide: Advisory Opinion of 28 May 1951, 1951 *ICJ Reports* 23). See also *Kayishema and Ruzindana* trial judgment, para. 88; *Jelisić* trial judgment, para. 60; and *Krstić* trial judgment, para. 541.

To the contemporary eye the Convention is far from perfect. It has allowed the tribunals to diverge — not always for good reason — in their interpretation of the law in several respects. But its enduring strengths should be noted: it does not require a showing that a genocide was associated with 'war' — in the quaint language of the Convention genocide can happen in a time of 'peace'. The Convention moreover supplies the mens rea of the crime of genocide, as well as five categories of actus reus, and five modes of agency or commission. 'Rulers', public officials, and private individuals are all punishable. The Convention envisaged that trials for genocide would be conducted by both municipal and international courts.[4]

By the end of 2006, the tribunals had convicted 25 persons of various forms of responsibility for genocide, 23 of them at the ICTR and two at the ICTY.

To appreciate the current state of the law, which is dominated by the ICTR's output, it is apposite to begin with an examination of the *Akayesu* case, the ICTR's first judgment, and the first treatment of genocide by an international tribunal.[5] From a jurisprudential point of view, the most striking aspect of the *Akayesu* judgment is the slightness of its legal sources. The bibliographical citations in the judgment suggest that research facilities in Arusha were scarce at the time. But *Akayesu* also makes several pronouncements on the law that are not reasoned and were not necessary. Many of these were reaffirmed in later cases by the same panel of judges which decided *Akayesu* (of the five ICTR cases which followed *Akayesu*, four were decided by that same panel). Thus contingencies peculiar to international criminal justice led to the creation of legal precedents which remain formally in effect and are difficult to eliminate except through the direct action of the Appeals Chamber.

By the end of this section, the student of genocide law will be in a position to identify the weaknesses and obiter dicta in the jurisprudence and to contrast them with the elements of the law that may now be considered settled.

5.2 *AKAYESU* AND ITS INFLUENCE

The *Akayesu* judgment managed two findings on genocide where only one was called for. The Trial Chamber entitled a section of its judgment, 'Genocide in Rwanda in 1994?',[6] and proceeded to answer the question in the affirmative even though the indictment did not aim so broadly as to allege that there had been a genocide throughout Rwanda in that period. The judges may have felt they were discharging a 'historical'

---

[4] Genocide Convention, Arts I–VI.

[5] See, however, the above references to genocide in the Second World War trials by national military tribunals pursuant to Control Council Law No. 10. See also the *Eichmann* case, 36 ILR 18–342, 30, in which the relevant provision of Israeli Law 5710/1950 was modelled on Article II of the Genocide Convention.

[6] *Akayesu* trial judgment, paras 112–29.

burden by tackling this larger question upfront — international justice's long-awaited verdict on that sorry affair in central Africa.[7]

In any case it is remarkable that the Arusha court answered the general question even before it had a chance to set out its views on the law of genocide.

5.2.1 The problem of the group

In making its preliminary determination on whether a genocide occurred in Rwanda in 1994, the *Akayesu* Trial Chamber treated the Tutsi 'group' as an ethnic group.[8] The Convention protects only national, ethnic, racial, or religious groups,[9] and since no Tutsi group is distinguishable with reference to religious belief or national aspirations, the choice left to the court was between ethnicity and race; outright dismissal of the genocide charges on the grounds that the victims did not form a protected group was never entertained by these judges.

It is fair to note that there was disagreement about the meaning of 'ethnic group' among the framers of the Genocide Convention[10] and that *Akayesu* as a result did not have a settled definition to work with. But nor was the *Akayesu* Trial Chamber able clearly to explain the meaning to be attached to the expression 'ethnic group' in the Rwandan context.

In an introductory section of the *Akayesu* judgment, which offers a potted history of Rwanda, we are told that in the early twentieth century the distinction between Hutu and Tutsi was based on *lineage* rather than ethnicity.[11] We are also told, not fully consistently, that the demarcation line was blurred ('one could move from one status to another'); that in the minds of the colonizers, the Tutsi, because of their height and colour, looked more like the colonizers themselves (which might suggest a 'racial' difference); that in the early 1930s the Belgian authorities instituted a fixed division of

---

[7] On this see A. Zahar and S. Rohol, 'The International Criminal Tribunal for Rwanda', in S. Totten (ed.), *Genocide at the Millennium: A Critical Bibliographic Review* (Transaction, 2005), pp. 209–39.

[8] *Akayesu* trial judgment, paras 122, 124.

[9] UN Resolution 96(I) declared that international law protected also 'political' groups. This was reflected in the draft genocide convention prepared by the UN's Economic and Social Council in May 1948 (UN Doc. E/794). In October 1948, the UN's Sixth Committee retained the reference to political groups by a vote of 29 in favour to 13 against, with 9 abstentions (see *Report of the Sixth Committee*, 3 December 1948, UN Doc. A/760, para. 10). However, on 29 November 1948, the matter was raised again, and the Committee this time decided to exclude political groups by a vote of 22 to 6, with 12 abstentions (ibid., para. 21). See also *Study of the Question of the Prevention and Punishment of the Crime of Genocide*, UN Doc. E/CN.4/Sub.2/416, 4 July 1978, paras 79–87.

[10] Ibid., paras 69–75.

[11] This is a lawyer's, not a historian's, history. It is simplistic, tendentious, at times incoherent, and full of inaccuracies. The main fault is not so much the absence of a historical methodology as the very thin evidential basis for the court's claims. The same tendency to make grand statements about the causes of Rwanda's 1994 conflict, based on very little evidence, is found in the *Kayishema and Ruzindana* trial judgment (paras 275–84, 289–91). For much better accounts of the relevant history, see M. Mamdani, *When Victims Become Killers: Colonialism, Nativism, and the Genocide in Rwanda* (Princeton University Press, 2001); and B. Jones, 'The Arusha Peace Process', in H. Adelman and A. Suhrke (eds), *The Path of a Genocide: The Rwanda Crisis from Uganda to Zaire* (Transaction, 1999), pp. 185–208.

the population into three groups which they called ethnic groups; and that by the 1950s the Tutsi and the Hutu had come to represent different *political* forces, the former supporting the monarchy, the latter opposed to it.[12] In 1956 the electorate apparently voted 'on strictly ethnic lines',[13] but this division could just as well have been described by the Trial Chamber as political.[14]

By 1993 'the bond built on Hutu kinship once again began to prevail over political differences'.[15] The notion of kinship is of a blood relationship, suggesting that the court returned to the idea of 'lineage'. Yet in the next breath it switched again to a political colouration of the divisions, claiming that in order to make '*the economic, social and political conflict* look more like an ethnic conflict', those in power launched propaganda campaigns and fabricated events.[16] These were the 'extremists' in the court's judgment,[17] and while apparently they identified as 'Hutu', their extremism was very much political (nationalist, republican, anti-monarchist, and in support of a one-party state) rather than ethnocentric. Both Tutsi and ordinary (non-extremist) Hutu were massacred by the extremists,[18] further complicating any attempt to cast the conflict as one between two ethnic groups.

The problem of construction of a victim group which plausibly coincides with a group protected by the Genocide Convention haunts the *Akayesu* judgment and is never satisfactorily resolved. If applied genocide law starts with *Akayesu*, it also starts with the problem of who (or what) is 'the group'.

When the *Akayesu* Trial Chamber turned to the specifics of the indictment, which alleged that the victims belonged to one of the four groups without specifying which one, the court seemed intent on an ethnic categorization. It said that while the Tutsi population did not have a culture distinct from the rest of the population, government-issued identity cards identified their holders as belonging to one of three *ethnies* (in French).[19] Laws in force up until the events of 1994 identified a citizen in terms of his or her *ethnie*, among other attributes. As already indicated, this was a legacy of the colonial administration, which no more proves that there were ethnic groups in Rwanda in 1994 than does Belgium's enforcement of *ethnies* in the 1930s prove that ethnic groups existed then.

The *Akayesu* Trial Chamber added that, besides the ID cards, 'customary rules existed in Rwanda governing the determination of ethnic group, which followed patri-lineal lines of heredity'.[20] This begs the question: did those so-called customary rules determine *ethnie*, or did they involve another concept, for example the Kinyarwanda concept of *ubwoko*, which has no simple equivalent in English (but which includes the notions of race and clan)? Equally question-begging was the Trial Chamber's assertion that 'the Tutsi were conceived of as an ethnic group by those who targeted them for killing'.[21] Granted that the enemy or victims were conceived of, in large part, as Tutsi,

---

[12] *Akayesu* trial judgment, paras 81–3, 86.   [13] Ibid., para. 87.
[14] In effect the court did exactly that at ibid., para. 88.   [15] Ibid., para. 97.
[16] Ibid., para. 99, emphasis added.   [17] Ibid., para. 103.
[18] Ibid., paras 105, 107, 159.   [19] Ibid., para. 170.   [20] Ibid., para. 171.
[21] Ibid. A remark to the same effect is found in the *Kayishema and Ruzindana* trial judgment, para. 525.

it does not follow that they were conceived of as members of an ethnic group unless that is what 'Tutsi' represented at the time.

The judgment accepted the opinion of a human-rights activist, Alison Desforges. She had written:

the primary criterion for an ethnic group is the sense of belonging to that ethnic group. It is a sense which can shift over time. . . . But, if you fix any given moment in time, and you say, how does this population divide itself, then you will see which ethnic groups are in existence in the minds of the participants at that time. . . . In Rwanda, the reality was shaped by the colonial experience which imposed a categorisation which was probably more fixed, and not completely appropriate to the scene. . . . The categorisation imposed at that time is what people of the current generation have grown up with. . . . This practice was continued after independence by the First Republic and the Second Republic in Rwanda to such an extent that this division into three ethnic groups became an absolute reality.[22]

Desforges's opinion neglects to examine whether the colonial attempt to ethnically categorize Rwandans had, by 1994, given way to a political construction of the enemy or victim group. There is a mass of evidence that the broad term 'Tutsi' was being used by activists on one side of the conflict interchangeably with the more specific term 'Inyenzi' to denote, first, the invading force (which was composed of people classified in the terms of the colonial system as Tutsi and, to a lesser extent, as Hutu) and, secondly, the sympathizers or presumed sympathizers of the invading force within the country (a group also composed of people labelled Tutsi and, to a lesser extent, Hutu on their identification cards). The meaning of 'Tutsi' had shifted in certain wartime uses to mean 'the enemy', without necessarily meaning the ethnic other.

At the very least, this is a theory which to this day is open to reasonable disagreement. There had been a flurry of political activity in Rwanda in 1992 to 1994, with a dozen or so parties and factions forming to reflect a spectrum of political views. It was well known that many with a 'Tutsi' identification on their ID cards were actively opposed to the revolutionary politics of the invading force (famously among them the leader of the much-maligned Interahamwe militia). The 'Tutsi' of the extremists arguably was not intended to denote all the Tutsi in the country, for that would have been self-defeating, but rather that portion supporting regime change. *Akayesu* elided the complexities and pronounced the war of 1994 an ethnic conflict.[23]

It therefore comes as a surprise when three-quarters of the way through the *Akayesu* judgment a new theory is put forth, as if by an invited guest, proposing in effect that the Tutsi were *not* one of the four groups explicitly protected by the Convention, but were nevertheless protected because the Tutsi group shared the essence, as it were, of the

---

[22] Quoted in the *Akayesu* trial judgment, para. 172.

[23] *Akayesu* also carefully avoided the epithet 'racial', presumably because, since 1948, it has gradually fallen out of fashion. Yet Rwandan witnesses often make references to racial stereotypes, as the following courtroom incident from a later case illustrates. The witness was a former gendarme: Q. 'What ethnic origin do you claim?' A. 'It is difficult for me to answer your question. In any case, it is the father who procreates. My father is a Hutu and my mother is Tutsi. It is, therefore, clear I am a Hutu, or I am a mixture of Hutu and Tutsi. So I am of mixed origin. . . . I am not a blood group expert but I say I am from mixed origin.' (*Prosecutor* v. *Eliézer Niyitegeka*, Witness KJ, 15 October 2002.)

four listed types of group. The court defined an *ethnic* group as one whose members share a common language or culture[24] (which, as already mentioned, is not sufficient to distinguish Tutsi from Hutu), and proceeded to introduce its jurisprudential innovation thus:

[From] the travaux préparatoires of the Genocide Convention, it appears that the crime of genocide was . . . perceived as targeting only 'stable' groups, constituted in a permanent fashion, and membership of which is determined by birth, with the exclusion of the more 'mobile' groups which one joins through individual voluntary commitment, such as political and economic groups. Therefore, a common criterion in the four types of groups protected by the Genocide Convention is that membership in such groups would seem to be normally not challengeable by its members, who belong to it automatically, by birth, in a continuous and often irremediable [*sic*] manner.[25]

It continued:

the question that arises is whether it would be impossible to punish the physical destruction of a group as such under the Genocide Convention, if the said group, although stable, and membership is by birth, does not meet the definition of any one of the four groups expressly protected . . . In the opinion of the Chamber, it is particularly important to respect the intention of the drafters of the Genocide Convention, which according to the travaux préparatoires, was patently to ensure the protection of any stable and permanent group.[26]

The court later added, ambiguously:

The Chamber further noted that all the Rwandan witnesses who appeared before it invariably answered spontaneously and without hesitation the questions of the Prosecutor regarding their ethnic identity. Accordingly, the Chamber finds that, in any case, at the time of the alleged events, the Tutsi did indeed constitute a stable and permanent group and were identified as such by all.[27]

Thus the Court found that even if the Tutsi were not really an ethnic group, they were at least protected as a stable and permanent group. (It was inaccurate of the Trial Chamber to say that the witnesses who appeared before it invariably answered unhesitatingly the prosecutor's questions regarding their ethnic identity. These questions were posed in English and were translated into Kinyarwanda. The witnesses were responding to questions in Kinyarwanda, and their answers were reconceptualized in the course of their translation into English. The word 'ethnic' became 'ubwoko' in translation. The latter is a pre-colonial concept with no direct English translation. In dictionaries it has come to encompass several different English concepts.)

Subsequent ICTR cases retreated from the 'stable and permanent group' theory,[28] but otherwise took their cue from *Akayesu*, never seriously re-examining the question of the group, and never seriously reconsidering whether it was an ethnic group, as such, which had been persecuted in Rwanda. In *Kayishema and Ruzindana* a different panel

[24] *Akayesu* trial judgment, para. 513.   [25] Ibid., para. 511.
[26] Ibid., para. 516 (reiterated at para. 701).   [27] *Akayesu* trial judgment, para. 702.
[28] Although see *Rutaganda* trial judgment, para. 57, and cf. *Krstić* trial judgment, para. 556. For a critique of this theory, see Schabas, *Genocide*, pp. 130–3. See also Editorial, 'Defining Protected Groups Under the Genocide Convention' (2001) 114 *Harv. L. Rev.* 2007.

of ICTR judges accepted the testimony of André Guichaoua, a professor of sociology and economics at the University of Lille, that 'all Rwandans share the same national territory, speak the same language, believe in the same myths and share the same cultural traditions. The Trial Chamber opines that these shared characteristics could be tantamount to a common ethnicity.'[29] And this, presumably, would have been the Trial Chamber's conclusion had it not been for the Belgians' introduction of ID cards in 1931: 'Although prior to the arrival of the European colonisers the Rwandans had referred to themselves as Hutus, Tutsis or Twas, it was after this point that the group identity solidified and this former sociological categorisation became a means of ethnic identification.'[30]

Kayishema and Ruzindana considered also the possibility that the Genocide Convention protects groups having no recognized existence outside of the perceptions of certain ideological movements or criminal groups: 'An ethnic group is one whose members share a common language and culture; or, a group which distinguishes itself, as such (self identification); or, a group identified as such by others, including perpetrators of the crimes (identification by others).'[31] No legal authority was cited for these propositions.

The *Akayesu* bench of judges picked up this theme in their judgment in the *Rutaganda* case, which followed *Kayishema and Ruzindana*, and where, again without reference to any authority, the situation was confused further:

for the purposes of applying the Genocide Convention, membership of a group is, in essence, a subjective rather than an objective concept. The victim is perceived by the perpetrator of genocide as belonging to a group slated for destruction. In some instances, the victim may perceive himself or herself as belonging to the said group.[32]

This suggests that genocide can be committed against a 'group' existing only in the mind of the perpetrator — an indefensible notion. Or it suggests that genocide is committed when individuals who are not members of a protected group are eliminated in the mistaken belief that they are members of that group — equally indefensible. There was no reason for the ICTR Trial Chambers to engage in speculation which was of no relevance either to the concerns of the framers of the Genocide Convention or to the facts under consideration in each case. The objective/subjective issue in the constitution of a protected group remains ill-defined to this day.[33]

---

[29] *Kayishema and Ruzindana* trial judgment, para. 34.

[30] Ibid., para. 35; cf. also paras 523, 526.   [31] Ibid., para. 98.

[32] *Rutaganda* trial judgment, para. 56; repeated in *Musema* trial judgment, para. 161. Cf. *Krstić* trial judgment, para. 557; *Brđanin* trial judgment, paras 683–4; *Stakić* appeal judgment, para. 25.

[33] Although it has found some support at the ICTY. For example, in the *Jelisić* trial judgment, para. 70: 'Although the objective determination of a religious group still remains possible, to attempt to define a national, ethnical or racial group today using objective and scientifically irreproachable criteria would be a perilous exercise whose result would not necessarily correspond to the perception of the persons concerned by such categorisation. Therefore, it is more appropriate to evaluate the status of a national, ethnical or racial group from the point of view of those persons who wish to single that group out from the rest of the community. The Trial Chamber consequently elects to evaluate membership in a national, ethnical or racial group using a subjective criterion. It is the stigmatisation of a group as a distinct national, ethnical or racial unit by the community which allows it to be

5.2.2 Genocide's 'special' intent

The *Akayesu* Trial Chamber began its discussion of the legal elements of genocide with the crime's so-called special intent.[34] It is not clear why genocide's intent is referred to as 'special', as opposed to merely specific or unique to the crime. The Trial Chamber's explanation was this:

> Special intent is a well-known criminal law concept in the Roman-Continental legal systems. It is required as a constituent element of certain offences and demands that the perpetrator have the clear intent to cause the offence charged. According to this meaning, special intent is the key element of an intentional offence, which offence is characterized by a psychological relationship between the physical result and the mental state of the perpetrator.[35]

This is difficult to understand and philosophically uninformed. The words 'clear intent' may have been meant by the court to exclude recklessness.[36] They reoccur in the text soon afterwards, once again suggesting the insufficiency of knowledge of likely outcome or *dolus eventualis*. But this interpretation is contradicted by the court's pronouncement: 'The offender is culpable because he *knew or should have known* that the act committed would destroy, in whole or in part, a group'[37] — close enough to the mental element of recklessness.[38] Is this to be brushed aside as an error?[39]

As a result of *Akayesu* the appellation 'special intent', or *dolus specialis*, in relation to genocide, stuck. There is no reason why it should have. Murder is also a crime of special intent (inasmuch as the mens rea of murder is not general, but specific). A passage from a UN report on genocide presents an instructive contrast:

> A proposal [in the Convention's drafting committee] to replace the words 'committed with the intent to destroy' by the words 'aimed at the physical destruction of' groups was not accepted. It was explained that the proposal stemmed from the fact that the perpetrators of acts of genocide would in certain cases be able to claim that they were not guilty of genocide, having had no intent to destroy a given group, either wholly or partially. Accordingly, the purpose of the amendment was to guard against the possibility that the presence in the definition of the word 'intent' might be used as a pretext, in the future, for pleading not guilty on the grounds of absence of intent. In the circumstances, the objective concept seemed to be more effective than the subjective concept. Acts of genocide should therefore be defined as acts 'resulting in' the destruction of a group.

---

determined whether a targeted population constitutes a national, ethnical or racial group in the eyes of the alleged perpetrators.' Here the Trial Chamber lumps everything that is not 'scientifically' objective into the subjective category. (It was nevertheless approved in the *Sikirica et al.* no-case-to-answer decision, paras 88–9.)

[34] *Akayesu* trial judgment, para. 498.

[35] Ibid., para. 518; repeated in *Musema* trial judgment, para. 166.

[36] See also *Rutaganda* trial judgment, para. 59 and *Musema* trial judgment, para. 164, where these words recur.

[37] *Akayesu* trial judgment, para. 520, emphasis added.

[38] The *Akayesu* trial judgment also equivocated between intent and motive (para. 522): 'The perpetration of the act charged therefore extends beyond its actual commission, for example, the murder of a particular individual, for the realisation of an ulterior motive, which is to destroy, in whole or part, the group.' A motive is not normally a legal element of a crime.

[39] There was authority at the time for the thesis that *dolus eventualis* is not sufficient for genocide (e.g. Robinson, *Genocide Convention*, pp. 58–9). But the *Akayesu* Trial Chamber did not cite any authority.

In opposition to the proposal, it was observed that elimination of the intent to destroy a group would make it impossible to draw a distinction between genocide and ordinary murder.[40]

The intent of genocide is the crime's distinguishing mark, but there is a tendency in ICTR jurisprudence to take the matter further, mystifying rather than clarifying the law.[41]

5.2.3 Determination of intent against a backdrop of genocide

The *Akayesu* court worried about the supposed inscrutability of intent: 'intent is a mental factor which is difficult, even impossible, to determine'.[42] This Cartesian sentiment is hard to associate with a professional fact-finding panel, which would be expected to regard intent as being as perspicuous as any other aspect of human conduct.[43] Indirectly through this comment the Trial Chamber raised the question of whether it is necessary to prove a background of genocide for an individual to be convicted of the crime — in the same way that a background of widespread or systematic attacks on civilians must be proven for an individual to be held responsible for a crime against humanity. The court said about its preliminary finding on a Rwanda-wide genocide: 'the fact that genocide was indeed committed in Rwanda in 1994 and more particularly in Taba [Akayesu's home region], cannot influence it in its decisions in the present case'.[44] This would indicate a negative answer to the above question about the need to prove a context of genocide. Later in the judgment, though, Akayesu's supposedly elusive intent was allowed to be fixed against a background finding of genocide:

the Chamber has already established that genocide was committed against the Tutsi group in Rwanda in 1994 ... [From] the very high number of atrocities committed against the Tutsi, their widespread nature not only in the commune of Taba, but also throughout Rwanda, and the fact that the victims were systematically and deliberately selected because they belonged to the Tutsi group, with persons belonging to other groups being excluded,[45] the Chamber is also able to infer, beyond reasonable doubt, the genocidal intent of the accused in the commission of the above-mentioned crimes.[46]

The judgment's position on the question is therefore inconsistent.[47] It is also much less cautious than might be expected, as the Rwandan conflict featured war crimes and

---

[40] *Study of the Question of the Prevention and Punishment of the Crime of Genocide*, UN Doc. E/CN.4/Sub.2/416, 4 July 1978, para. 98.

[41] See, for example, *Kambanda* sentencing judgment, para. 16 (repeated in *Serushago* sentencing judgment, para. 10): 'The crime of genocide is unique because of its element of dolus specialis ... hence the Chamber is of the opinion that genocide constitutes the crime of crimes, which must be taken into account when deciding the sentence.' It is not clear how the two points, which are part of the same sentence, relate, unless the *Kambanda* court (consisting of the same judges as the *Akayesu* chamber) had come to view the *dolus specialis* of genocide as being not only unique but also uniquely evil. See also the *Musema* trial judgment, para. 164.

[42] *Akayesu* trial judgment, para. 523.

[43] Yet it was repeated in the *Kayishema and Ruzindana* trial judgment, para. 93, and the *Rutaganda* trial judgment, paras 61, 398.   [44] *Akayesu* trial judgment, para. 129.

[45] This last claim is not accurate: as mentioned above, many Hutu were targeted along with the Tutsi.

[46] *Akayesu* trial judgment, para. 730.

[47] The same confusion is evident in the *Kayishema and Ruzindana* trial judgment, paras 273, 276. In the *Rutaganda* trial judgment, paras 399–400, the Trial Chamber used its finding that genocide was taking place throughout Rwanda to confirm that Rutaganda acted with the intent to commit genocide.

crimes against humanity as well as acts of genocide, which is to say that several background conditions could have been utilized to 'infer' Akayesu's intent.[48]

The proven backdrop to an individual's acts does have the potential to severely weaken his or her defence. As an ICTY Trial Chamber said in the course of its discussion of the mens rea of genocide, 'an individual knowingly acting against the backdrop of the widespread and systematic violence being committed against only one specific group could not reasonably deny that he chose his victims discriminatorily'.[49] Whatever the theoretical possibilities, the practical advantage here lies with the prosecutor. The early ICTR cases muddied the waters, expending energy on trying to prove that a genocide occurred in Rwanda, while professing in parallel the primacy of proof of an individual's mens rea. In fact, proof of the former became a precondition for the latter. This problem was resolved, to some extent, in the ICTY's *Jelisić* case (see below).

5.2.4 Complicity in genocide contrasted with aiding and abetting

Another theory put forth in *Akayesu* and later contradicted in the same judgment concerns complicity in genocide. Article III(e) of the Genocide Convention lists complicity as one of the punishable forms of participation in genocide. The ICTR Statute incorporates this article, and as well contains a separate, global, provision on forms of participation in the statutory crimes (Article 6 of the ICTR Statute). This provision includes aiding and abetting. There is thus an overlap between the Convention's article and the ICTR's 'participation' provision. To be precise, the overlap exists if aiding and abetting are understood in the usual way,[50] as varieties of complicity.

However, the *Akayesu* Trial Chamber attempted to distinguish complicity from aiding and abetting, presumably because it wanted to convict Akayesu for full genocide and not merely for complicity for those acts which Akayesu did not directly commit himself (chiefly sexual assault).[51] *Akayesu*'s unexpected distinction was based on the mental element: 'in many legal systems, aiding and abetting constitute acts of complicity. However, though akin to the constituent elements of complicity, they themselves constitute one of the crimes referred to in Articles 2 to 4 of the [ICTR] Statute, particularly, genocide.' This is, unfortunately, difficult to understand, and we quote it here only as evidence of the condition of this foundational judgment.

The judges went on to say:

The Chamber is consequently of the opinion that when dealing with a person accused of having aided and abetted in the planning, preparation and execution of genocide, it must be proven that such a person did have the specific intent to commit genocide, namely that he or she acted with the intent to destroy in whole or in part, a national, ethnical, racial or religious group, as such; whereas . . . the same requirement is not needed for complicity in genocide.[52]

[48] The same error is found in the *Kayishema and Ruzindana* trial judgment, para. 528.

[49] *Jelisić* trial judgment, para. 73.

[50] See, e.g., A. P. Simester and G. R. Sullivan, *Criminal Law: Theory and Doctrine*, 2nd edn (Hart, 2003), pp. 199–203.　　[51] See *Akayesu* trial judgment, paras 727–34.

[52] Ibid., para. 485; also paras 546–7 and 726, where this same proposal is repeated.

No further explanation was given of this conclusion.

It is a fair question whether a person aiding and abetting genocide with the intent to commit genocide should be treated differently from the accomplice who is aware of the principal's intent to commit genocide but does not share that intent himself or herself. Put differently, if the prosecutor has managed to prove that the accomplice's contribution to the crime of genocide was made with intent, and not just with knowledge of intent, how does this affect the characterization of the defendant's role, if at all?

One answer would be to allow the difference to be reflected in the sentence given. A more intricate, but also more accurate, legal manoeuvre would be to find, in the case of complicity with intent, that there was a joint criminal enterprise between the defendant and the person or persons being aided and abetted by the defendant — and on this basis convict the defendant for genocide proper and not just for complicity in genocide. (The overall advantage of the joint enterprise doctrine is that every member of the enterprise may be convicted of the offence committed by the principal perpetrator; see Chapter 7.) The ICTR was very slow to realize the utility of joint criminal enterprise. In *Akayesu*'s time it was not even on the ICTR's horizon.

A third answer, which was entirely within *Akayesu*'s reach, would have been to avoid conceptualizing the defendant's role in the sexual assaults as one of aider and abettor.[53] According to the Trial Chamber's findings, Akayesu *led* the protracted attacks against the Tutsi — by ordering, instigating, and facilitating them.[54] The sexual assaults formed part of the violence. Akayesu condoned them. In this context he became responsible for them, even if he did not participate more directly (physically) in their commission, or did not, literally, order them. In *Kayishema and Ruzindana* the Trial Chamber characterized Kayishema's responsibility in relation to one of the four massacre sites in that case as 'aiding and abetting' because 'Kayishema's presence prior [to] and during the major attack and the participation of those under his control encouraged the killings of the Tutsi refugees assembled there'.[55] To describe this as aiding and abetting[56] is either to misapply the concept or to use it in such a loose sense as to attribute to Kayishema the highest form of responsibility for the commission of a crime.

The *Akayesu* Trial Chamber was finally to take the least plausible course and create two categories of accomplice liability, with aiding and abetting supposedly implying intent, and complicity implying no more than knowledge of the principal's intent. As late as 2003 an ICTR Trial Chamber relied on this distinction to convict Pastor Ntakirutimana for 'aiding and abetting genocide' (and thus for genocide proper) and to dismiss the charge of complicity in genocide.[57] The *Ntakirutimana* Trial Chamber

---

[53] Contrary to what was done, for example, in the *Akayesu* trial judgment, para. 694: 'the Accused, having had reason to know that sexual violence was occurring, aided and abetted the following acts of sexual violence, by allowing them to take place on or near the premises of the bureau communal and by facilitating the commission of such sexual violence through his words of encouragement in other acts of sexual violence which, by virtue of his authority, sent a clear signal of official tolerance for sexual violence, without which these acts would not have taken place'.

[54] See, e.g., ibid., paras 648, 656, 657, 664, 665, 704.

[55] *Kayishema and Ruzindana* trial judgment, para. 560.

[56] Ibid., para. 562; see also *Rutaganda* trial judgment, paras 386, 391.

[57] See *Ntakirutimana* trial judgment, paras 787–90. The elements of aiding and abetting (at para. 787) are said to require proof of intent to commit genocide. There is no authority for this analysis of aiding and abetting other than *Akayesu*. The elements of aiding and abetting were stated correctly in *Furundžija* trial judgment, para. 249.

did not notice that a later section of *Akayesu*, after discussing English authorities to the effect that proof of the defendant's knowledge of the principal's intent is sufficient for aiding and abetting, seemed to deny its earlier distinction: 'As far as genocide is concerned, the intent of the accomplice is thus to knowingly aid or abet one or more persons to commit the crime of genocide. Therefore, the Chamber is of the opinion that an accomplice to genocide need not necessarily possess the dolus specialis of genocide'.[58]

What is lacking in *Akayesu* is a legal methodology to guide the court in its exposition of a crime which, while arguably recognized as such in customary law, had received little attention prior to 1998. A well-known methodology for the discovery of principles and rules of international law is that outlined in Article 38 of the ICJ Statute. The *Krstić* Trial Chamber at the ICTY recognized that it was bound to interpret the Genocide Convention with due regard to the principle of legality.[59] In *Jelisić*, another ICTY case, the Trial Chamber outlined a methodology tailored to the interpretation of the Convention.[60] But *Akayesu* does not acknowledge that a credible legal exposition must rest on a firm and painstakingly constructed foundation. It follows no particular methodology. Its tendency instead is to assert the law.

Another example of this tendency is *Akayesu*'s remark, which has had a continuing influence, that 'the Chamber finds that it is not justifiable to convict an accused of two offences in relation to the same set of facts where . . . one offence charges accomplice liability and the other offence charges liability as a principal, e.g. genocide and complicity in genocide'.[61] No reasonable explanation[62] was given of this proposition.[63]

5.2.5 Direct and public incitement to commit genocide

The *Akayesu* Trial Chamber was the first international tribunal to pronounce on the crime of direct and public incitement to commit genocide. The indictment alleged that Akayesu 'urged the population to eliminate the accomplices of the RPF [the invading force], which was understood by those present to mean Tutsi'. The Court accepted a generalized notion of incitement (not specific to genocide) which it attributed to common-law systems: an act of encouragement or persuasion to commit an offence.[64]

---

[58] *Akayesu* trial judgment, para. 540; restated in para. 545. *Akayesu*'s last-ditch effort (para. 548) to explain the earlier distinction only makes the confusion more obvious. *Akayesu*'s distinction was first explicitly attacked by an ICTY Trial Chamber, in the *Stakić* case (*Stakić* no-case-to-answer decision, para. 60). It was also rejected, less explicitly, in *Semanza* trial judgment, para. 394.   [59] *Krstić* trial judgment, para. 580.

[60] *Jelisić* trial judgment, para. 61.   [61] *Akayesu* trial judgment, para. 468.

[62] Ibid., paras 528–32.

[63] A person who commits genocide together with others but who also supplies the means for those other persons to commit the crime is guilty not only of genocide but also of complicity. Why then would it not be justified to enter two convictions? The *Akayesu* Trial Chamber's remark seems not to be confined to genocide, and it may be that the court considered that where a person is committing a crime there is no room left for, in addition, assisting its commission, but this is not necessarily true in cases where the lapse of time between the act of complicity and the act of commission is such as to render the acts distinct. Neither *Akayesu* nor any ICTR judgment repeating *Akayesu*'s determination on this point (e.g. *Musema* trial judgment, para. 175) has attempted to explain why a double conviction for genocide and complicity in genocide 'in relation to the same set of facts' is never appropriate.

[64] *Akayesu* trial judgment, para. 555. Only one secondary source on English law is cited for this generalization.

This is a dictionary-based analysis: a legal element is substituted with an equivalent term from a dictionary.

It is difficult to follow *Akayesu* on the (French) civil-law position. According to the Trial Chamber, a notion similar to incitement, albeit under a different name, exists in civil-law systems.[65]

Akayesu accepted the International Law Commission's understanding of the terms 'direct' and 'public'.[66] According to the ILC:

The element of direct incitement requires specifically urging another individual to take immediate criminal action rather than merely making a vague or indirect suggestion. The . . . element of public incitement requires communicating the call for criminal action to a number of individuals in a public place or to members of the general public at large . . . such as by radio or television.[67]

The Trial Chamber proceeded to state its 'opinion' that 'the direct element of incitement should be viewed in the light of its cultural and linguistic content'.[68] The explanation of this unsourced pronouncement was that 'a particular speech may be perceived as "direct" in one country, and not so in another, depending on the audience'. This presumably means that when a statement in one language is translated literally into another it may lose much or all of its 'directness', if the translation — because it is literal — fails to convey to the new audience the meaning it had for the original audience. But this is obvious, and irrelevant. The Trial Chamber's comment concerns an extra-legal issue: the shortcomings of literal translation.

The *Akayesu* court did follow up with a legal proposition: *incitement may be direct and nonetheless implicit*.[69] This is based on only one source: 'at the time the Convention on Genocide was being drafted, the Polish delegate observed that it was sufficient to play skillfully on mob psychology by casting suspicion on certain groups, by insinuating that they were responsible for economic or other difficulties in order to create an atmosphere favourable to the perpetration of the crime'.[70] But this cannot be a sufficient foundation for the above proposition. Creating an atmosphere favourable to the perpetration of a crime through brainwashing or indoctrination may well be unlawful conduct, but it is not incitement. (It does not correspond, in *Akayesu*'s own terms, with 'encouragement or persuasion to commit an offence'.) And while the 'observation' of one state delegate cannot carry much weight, what is worse is that the Polish position, if that is what it is, seems to contradict the stance of the ILC, adopted by the Trial Chamber, that 'merely making a vague or indirect suggestion' is not sufficient for incitement. It makes little sense to say that incitement may be implicit, but must not be *in*direct. If it must be *direct*, it must also be explicit, even if couched in an allegory or another rhetorical device.

Akayesu's formulation served a purpose, which was to allow the ICTR to enter convictions for incitement to commit genocide in cases where the utterance could be said to have merely *alluded* to the average Tutsi civilian, whilst on the surface its venom was

---

[65] Cf., *Akayesu* trial judgment, paras 552 and 555, where the exposition is inconsistent.
[66] Ibid., paras 556–7.   [67] ILC Draft Code of Crimes, para. 16 of the commentary on Article 2.
[68] *Akayesu* trial judgment, para. 557.   [69] Ibid., para. 557.   [70] Ibid.

directed, in a sense legitimately, at the invading force and its collaborators within the country. We are entitled *to read between the lines*. This is *Akayesu*'s idea. But while it is understandable that a court in the position of having to clarify the law will hesitate to articulate a rule against incitement in such a way as to encourage offenders to fall back on implicit meanings to protect themselves, if an audience has to puzzle over the meaning of a speech, or takes away from it two or more quite different meanings, this is no longer a case of incitement.

Akayesu did ultimately propose a reasonable test for directness: that 'the persons for whom the message was intended immediately grasped the implication'.[71] This is another way of saying that only a clear and unambiguous call to commit a crime will count as incitement, something quite different from the Polish idea of psychological manipulation.[72]

The person who incites genocide intends the substantive offence to be committed, and thus intends to realize both the mens rea and the actus reus of the offence. Incitement not only 'implies a desire on the part of the perpetrator to create by his actions a particular state of mind necessary to commit such a crime'[73] — as *Akayesu* would have it — it presupposes an intent (and optionally a desire) to have the audience complete the crime. In contrast with complicity, whose centre of gravity is the normally material assistance rendered to the perpetrator, incitement is chiefly about the genocidal intent of the writer or speaker, which is brought directly into the public domain by the act of incitement. The prosecutor does not have to prove that the crime incited was committed. Again, this is in contrast with complicity where the law requires a completed offence.

The *Akayesu* Trial Chamber accepted, at one point, the categorization of incitement as inchoate.[74] On the factual side it found that:

with regard to the allegation that the Accused urged the population, during the gathering, to eliminate the accomplices of the RPF [the invading rebel group]...the Chamber is satisfied beyond a reasonable doubt that the Accused clearly called on the population to unite and eliminate the sole enemy: accomplices of the Inkotanyi [another term for the RPF]. On the basis of consistent evidence...and the information provided by...an expert witness on linguistic issues, the Chamber is satisfied beyond reasonable doubt that the population construed the Accused's call as a call to kill the Tutsi. The Chamber is satisfied beyond reasonable doubt that the Accused was himself fully aware...that his call to wage war against Inkotanyi accomplices *could* be construed as one to kill the Tutsi in general.[75]

Was 'could' an ill-chosen word or does it betray a weak grasp of the issues?

Having declared incitement inchoate, the Trial Chamber nevertheless added: 'the Chamber is satisfied beyond a reasonable doubt that there was a causal link

---

[71] Ibid., para. 558.

[72] According to Robinson, the Convention 'restricts "incitement" to cases of "direct" action, i.e., incitement which *calls* for the commission of acts of Genocide, not such which *may result* in such commission' (*Genocide Convention*, p. 67, emphasis in original).   [73] *Akayesu* trial judgment, para. 560 (cf. para. 674).

[74] Ibid., paras 561–2.   [75] Ibid., para. 361 (reiterated at para. 673), emphasis added.

between the statement of the Accused at the 19 April 1994 gathering and the ensuing widespread killings'.[76] The resulting ambiguity (must a causal link be proven or not?) remained in the jurisprudence until 2003, when the *Nahimana* trial judgment (also by the ICTR) explicitly removed it.[77]

5.2.6 Rape as genocide

Akayesu's most remarked-upon contribution to genocide law is its interpretation of Article II(b) of the Genocide Convention (causing serious bodily or mental harm to members of the group) to include sexual assault.

It is probably true that few people prior to *Akayesu* had seriously considered sexual assault — a staple of armed conflict since ancient times — to amount to genocide in certain circumstances, unless it should take the form of forced procreation or sterilization, acts which are specifically covered by other provisions of the Convention.[78]

The Trial Chamber found that 'numerous Tutsi women were forced to endure acts of sexual violence, mutilations and rape, often repeatedly, often publicly and often by more than one assailant'. They were 'systematically raped, as one female victim testified . . . "each time that you met assailants, they raped you". Numerous incidents of such rape and sexual violence against Tutsi women occurred inside or near the bureau communal' of the commune of Taba, where Akayesu was the mayor. The Trial Chamber continued:

It has been proven that some communal policemen armed with guns and the accused himself were present while some of these rapes and sexual violence were being committed. . . . it is proven that on several occasions, by his presence, his attitude and his utterances, Akayesu encouraged such acts, one particular witness testifying that Akayesu, addressed the [militia] who were committing the rapes and said that 'never ask me again what a Tutsi woman tastes like'.

This was 'tacit encouragement to the rapes that were being committed'.[79] (Hardly tacit.)

The Trial Chamber then declared the following: 'rape and sexual violence . . . constitute genocide in the same way as any other act as long as they were committed with the specific intent to destroy, in whole or in part, a particular group, targeted as such'. No source was cited. 'Any other act' was left ambiguous. The Trial Chamber continued:

Rape and sexual violence certainly constitute infliction of serious bodily and mental harm on the victims and are even, according to the Chamber, one of the worst ways of inflict harm . . . the Chamber is satisfied that the acts of rape and sexual violence described above, were committed solely against Tutsi women, many of whom were subjected to the worst public humiliation, mutilated, and raped several times, often in public . . . and often by more than one assailant. These rapes resulted in physical and psychological destruction of Tutsi women, their families and their communities. Sexual violence was an integral part of the process of destruction . . . of the Tutsi group as a whole.[80]

---

[76] Ibid., para. 362 (reiterated at para. 675).   [77] *Nahimana et al.* trial judgment, para. 1015.

[78] See paras (c) and (d) of Article II of the Convention.

[79] *Akayesu* trial judgment, para. 706 (see paras 692–4 for a summary of findings on sexual violence).

[80] Ibid., para. 731.

These considerations supplied one of the supports for the court's ultimate conviction of Akayesu for genocide.[81]

There is a great deal of inaccuracy in the above proposals, starting with the notion that Article II(b) of the Convention creates jurisdiction to punish sexual assault in cases where serious bodily or mental harm results. The five acts of genocide listed in Article II must be interpreted in the context of the article, and in the context of the Convention itself, as being limited to acts which conceivably *could* destroy a protected group (in whole or in part), and therefore to acts whose performance *could* threaten the existence of a protected group.[82] The *Akayesu* Trial Chamber said that rape and sexual violence cause serious bodily or mental harm, which is indisputable.[83] But it did not consider whether such harm could destroy a group, or contribute to its destruction, and therefore constitute an actual threat to the existence of the group. It resorted instead to assertions and metaphors ('sexual violence was a step in the process of destruction . . . of the spirit, of the will to live, and of life itself')[84] and to conclusions of fact that went well beyond the evidence heard by the court ('rapes resulted in physical and psychological destruction of Tutsi women, their families and their communities').

This is not to say that *Akayesu* was completely off the mark. But the Trial Chamber did not manage to explain why its position must be accepted as right. (It would have been relatively simple to argue that evidence of systematic rape may be used to bolster evidence of a defendant's genocidal *intent*, rather than try to broaden the actus reus of genocide to include rape.) So much in this field of law depends on rational persuasion, yet a streak of legal activism persists in the work of the tribunals. The *Akayesu* judges perhaps felt that they were in tune with the times, but the uncharted reaches of international criminal law demand a far more conservative attitude. This type of activism should be left to governments and human-rights NGOs which have the means to effect changes to conventional law.

A further ambiguity was introduced by the court's observation that sexual assaults were usually followed by the murder of the victims of the assaults:

in most cases, the rapes of Tutsi women in Taba, were accompanied with the intent to kill those women. Many rapes were perpetrated near mass graves where the women were taken to be killed.

---

[81] See, ibid., para. 734.

[82] See Robinson, *Genocide Convention*, p. 63: ' "Serious harm" (subparagraph (b)), however, is already a matter of interpretation to be decided in each instance on the basis of the intent *and the possibility of implementing this intent by the harm done*' (emphasis added).

[83] Note, however, that the words 'or mental' were added to the Convention to address China's concern that acts of genocide could be performed through the administration of 'narcotics' (*Report of the Sixth Committee*, 3 December 1948, UN Doc. A/760, para. 10). An 'understanding' appended to the Convention's ratification by the United States states that 'the term "mental harm" in [A]rticle II(b) means permanent impairment of mental faculties through drugs, torture or similar techniques' (see www.icrc.org/ihl.nsf). *Akayesu*'s approach to the phrase 'serious bodily or mental harm' is superficial and probably wrong. The Trial Chamber said: 'Causing serious bodily or mental harm to members of the group does not necessarily mean that the harm is permanent and irremediable' (para. 502; repeated in *Rutaganda* trial judgment, para. 51; *Musema* trial judgment, para. 156; *Semanza* trial judgment, paras 320–2; and *Stakić* trial judgment, para. 516). Why so? The only explanation is a reference (*Akayesu* trial judgment, para. 503) to a passage in the *Eichmann* case which talks about conditions which might *cause* serious bodily or mental harm, but not what *counts as* such harm. [84] *Akayesu* trial judgment, para. 732.

A victim testified that Tutsi women caught could be taken away [to be raped] by peasants and men with the promise that they would be collected later to be executed. Following an act of gang rape, a witness heard Akayesu say 'tomorrow they will be killed' and they were actually killed ... the acts of rape and sexual violence, as other acts of serious bodily and mental harm committed against the Tutsi, reflected the determination to make Tutsi women suffer and to mutilate them even before killing them, the intent being to destroy the Tutsi group *while inflicting acute suffering* on its members in the process.[85]

In typical *Akayesu* fashion we are thus confronted with two very different theories on the role of sexual assault in genocide. The former construes sexual assault to be a separate act of genocide. The latter ties it to the killing of members of the group as a kind of perverse expression of loathing preceding the act of destruction. The result is that it is not possible to tell from the *Akayesu* judgment whether persons who sexually assault members of a protected group with the intent to commit genocide can be convicted of genocide if the victims are not also murdered. The *Kayishema and Ruzindana* trial judgment read the second theory into *Akayesu*, viz. it understood that sexual violence could contribute to the process of physical destruction, not that it was a separate actus reus of genocide.[86]

Despite the shortcomings summarized above, the *Akayesu* trial judgment was to be highly influential. It set the format and narrative style for many subsequent ICTR judgments, it pronounced on most aspects of the law of genocide (even when not called upon to do so), but more importantly it undertook, an intuitive and commonsensical approach to legal reasoning, neither scholarly nor informed by comparative law, confident rather than cautious, declamatory rather than inquisitive — qualities not expected of a text occupying a foundational position in international law.[87]

The above critique of *Akayesu* reinforces a central thesis of this book, that several elements of international criminal law are — or start out as being — castles built on sand. It is a disservice to this new field of jurisprudence and legal practice, which is still trying to find its feet and gain credibility in a not-so-welcoming political world, to pretend otherwise. The student should have the courage to identify the weaknesses in the edifice.

5.3 POST-*AKAYESU* DEVELOPMENTS AND PROBLEMS

To prove genocide the prosecutor must prove at least three elements: (1) that one or more of the acts listed in Article II of the Genocide Convention was performed; (2) that the act was performed against one or more members of a protected group, that is to say, a

---

[85] Ibid., para. 733, emphasis added. On a critical note, see M. A. Lyons, 'Hearing the Cry Without Answering the Call: Rape, Genocide, and the Rwandan Tribunal' (2001) 28 *Syracuse J. Int'l L. & Com.* 99.

[86] *Kayishema and Ruzindana* trial judgment, para. 95.

[87] For the deleterious influence of *Akayesu* at the level of a state exercising universal jurisdiction — a case heard in Switzerland — see L. Reydams, 'Niyonteze v. Public Prosecutor' (2002) 96 *Am. J. Int'l L.* 231.

national, ethnic, racial, or religious group; and (3) that the act was performed with the intent to destroy the group, as such, in whole or in part. The previous section reviewed theoretical issues, triggered by the *Akayesu* trial judgment, related to all three elements. New issues and positions emerged in later judgments of the Arusha and Hague tribunals.

5.3.1 Proving the intent of genocide: a wider plan

The intent of genocide is apparent in, or otherwise inferred from, the defendant's conduct. The intent may be found in what the defendant is alleged to have said at the relevant time, or in the number and category of the defendant's victims. An ICTR Trial Chamber has said that:

> the number of Tutsis killed in the massacres, for which Kayishema is responsible . . . provides evidence of Kayishema's intent. [An] enormous number of Tutsis were killed in each of the four crime sites. . . . they were also killed regardless of gender or age. Men and women, old and young, were killed without mercy. Children were massacred before their parents' eyes, women raped in front of their families. No Tutsi was spared, neither the weak nor the pregnant.[88]

For obvious reasons, the killing of children, pregnant women, and elderly persons is strong evidence of genocidal intent.

Georges Rutaganda was overheard ordering members of his militia 'to work', adding that there was 'a lot of dirt that needed to be cleaned up' in the commune.[89]

'Dirt' was also how Goran Jelisić regarded Muslims in Bosnia-Herzegovina.[90] The *Jelisić* case was the first ICTY case to deal with genocide. The accused had pleaded guilty to various other crimes, for which he was convicted and sentenced to forty years' imprisonment. But he had pleaded not guilty to genocide. The Trial Chamber decided that there was no case to answer on the charge of genocide, and acquitted Jelisić at the close of the prosecutor's case.[91]

One of the ideas that the *Jelisić* Trial Chamber floated in the process was that genocide's intent element implies that the accused must have committed his crimes 'as part of a wider plan to destroy the group as such'.[92] No source was cited for this interpretation. The Trial Chamber seems to have been influenced by the strong family resemblance between genocide and persecution as a crime against humanity, and by the fact that the latter requires proof of a widespread or systematic attack against civilians: 'By killing an individual member of the targeted group, the perpetrator does not thereby only manifest his hatred of the group to which his victim belongs but also knowingly commits this act as part of a wider-ranging intention to destroy the national, ethnical, racial or religious group of which the victim is a member.'[93]

---

[88] *Kayishema and Ruzindana* trial judgment, paras 531–2.

[89] *Rutaganda* trial judgment, para. 198.

[90] *Jelisić* trial judgment, para. 75. The distinction between Muslims, Serbs, and Croats in Bosnia-Herzegovina was never any trouble for the ICTY. Unlike the Tutsi and Hutu, the three Bosnian groups were distinguishable at once as national, ethnic, and religious groups, and even as political groups (see, e.g., *Krstić* trial judgment, para. 559). [91] *Jelisić* trial judgment, para. 15.

[92] Ibid., para. 66.   [93] Ibid., para. 79.

The Trial Chamber did not find sufficient evidence that the killings performed by Jelisić were associated with a plan to destroy the Muslim group. According to one witness, 'Jelisić seemed to select the names of persons at random from a list. Other witnesses suggested that the accused himself picked out his victims from those in the hangar. . . . It is not therefore possible to conclude beyond all reasonable doubt that the choice of victims arose from a precise logic.'[94] Moreover, no clear information was provided concerning the military authority to which Jelisić answered, or whether he acted 'beyond the scope of the powers entrusted to him'.[95] The Trial Chamber concluded that the prosecutor had failed to prove that there existed 'a plan to destroy the Muslim group in Brčko [a municipality in Bosnia-Herzegovina] or elsewhere within which the murders committed by the accused would allegedly fit'.[96]

At the same time, the court sought to limit the impact of these statements by conceding the 'theoretical possibility' that a person could have harboured a plan (and thus the intent) to destroy a group without this intent having been supported by any organization in which other individuals participated.[97] Indeed, the framers of the Genocide Convention had not ruled out this possibility. However, in terms of the practical application of the law, the *Jelisić* case suggests (as *Akayesu* did before it) that it will be very difficult to prove the genocidal intent of an individual if the crimes committed were not widespread and were not backed by an organization or a system.[98]

This is a plausible point of view. Indirectly it recalls for us the truism that the project of genocide is so far removed from normality, or from the average experience of morality and immorality, that it is looked upon as a case of utter irrationality, even in the context of war. Unless the prosecutor can make a prima facie case that a plan of genocide was being implemented with the defendant's knowledge and involvement, there will be little to stop the court from dismissing the defendant's intentionality as merely deranged. The individual is regarded as simply insane. This is what the *Jelisić* Trial Chamber did. Jelisić had presented himself to the ICTY, at his initial hearing, by his adopted nickname 'Adolf' — which must have raised a few eyebrows.[99] Despite the evidence that he claimed to hate Muslim women, that he found them dirty and that he wanted to sterilize them in order to prevent an increase in the number of Muslims, or that before exterminating them he would begin with killing the men in order prevent any proliferation — or perhaps *because* such claims were left by the prosecutor to hang in a contextual void — the Trial Chamber concluded that 'the words and attitude of Goran Jelisić as related by the witnesses essentially reveal a disturbed personality'.[100] (The judges recommended psychiatric treatment.)[101]

It did not help the prosecutor's case that Jelisić was not as bent on destruction as his words would suggest, sometimes allowing his victims to live or escape.

---

[94] Ibid., para. 93.   [95] Ibid., paras 96–7.

[96] Ibid., para. 98. Incidentally, the Trial Chamber for procedural reasons was not entitled to this conclusion, which it reached through a critical assessment of the prosecution evidence. At the no-case-to-answer stage of proceedings a court must take prosecution evidence at its highest. The Appeals Chamber detected the mistake, but did not reverse the finding: *Jelisić* appeal judgment, paras 53–77.   [97] *Jelisić* trial judgment, para. 100.

[98] Ibid., para. 101.   [99] Ibid., para. 102.   [100] Ibid., para. 105.   [101] Ibid., para. 140.

Thus, the intent to commit genocide will be difficult to prove against an individual acting alone, the evidence tending to establish mental instability rather than the necessary resolve.[102] At the same time, the present position is that a plan or policy, even on a small scale, is not a legal ingredient of genocide.[103] If a plan *can* be demonstrated, it will of course be given pride of place.[104]

The student of genocide must be particularly careful to distinguish the actus reus of genocide from evidence going to the mens rea of genocide. This problem is illustrated in the following section.

5.3.2 Meaning of 'in whole or in part'

In its Draft Code of Crimes the ILC said that the perpetrator of genocide must have the intent to destroy a group in whole or in part, which means that 'it is not necessary to intend to achieve the complete annihilation of a group from every corner of the globe. None the less the crime of genocide by its very nature requires the intention to destroy at least a substantial part of a particular group.'[105] The United States' ratification of the Convention is subject to the understanding that 'the term "intent to destroy, in whole or in part, a national, ethnical, racial, or religious group as such" . . . means the specific intent to destroy, in whole or in *substantial* part, a national, ethnical, racial or religious group as such'.[106] The *Kayishema and Ruzindana* Trial Chamber, in obiter dicta, accepted this view, and concluded that ' "in part" requires the intention to destroy a considerable number of individuals who are part of the group'.[107] In the ICTY case of *Sikirica* the Trial Chamber said it preferred the expression 'reasonably substantial' over 'reasonably significant' number.[108]

It should be emphasized that 'in whole or in part' qualifies the intent, not the action, although of course it is often in the action that one discerns the intent.

An early authority on the Convention gave a helpful account of the issue:

Genocide is not necessarily characterized by the intent to destroy a whole group; it suffices if the purpose is to eliminate portions of the population marked by specific racial, religious, national, or ethnic features. The restriction to a 'group,' as an assemblage of persons regarded as a unit because of their comparative segregation from others, would have left open the question whether the aim must be the destruction of the group in the whole of a country, in a part of it, in a single town, etc. The addition of the words 'in part' indicates that Genocide has been committed when acts of homicide are joined with a connecting purpose, i.e. directed against persons with specific

---

[102] This is true even taking into account the Appeals Chamber's officious chastisement of the *Jelisić* Trial Chamber, that 'there is no *per se* inconsistency between a diagnosis of the kind of immature, narcissistic, disturbed personality on which the Trial Chamber relied and the ability to form an intent to destroy a particular protected group. Indeed, as the prosecution points out, it is the borderline unbalanced personality who is more likely to be drawn to extreme racial and ethnical hatred than the more balanced modulated individual without personality defects' (*Jelisić* appeal judgment, para. 70). [103] *Jelisić* appeal judgment, para. 48.

[104] E.g. *Krstić* trial judgment, paras 572–3; *Stakić* no-case-to-answer decision, paras 50–1; and *Semanza* trial judgment, para. 424. [105] Draft Code of Crimes, para. 8 of the commentary on Article 17.

[106] Emphasis added; see www.icrc.org/ihl.nsf.

[107] *Kayishema and Ruzindana* trial judgment, para. 97.

[108] *Sikirica et al.* no-case-to-answer decision, para. 65.

characteristics (with intent to destroy the group or a segment thereof). Therefore, the intent to destroy a multitude of persons of the same group because of their belonging to this group, must be classified as Genocide even if these persons constitute only part of a group either within a country or within a region or within a single community, provided the number is substantial; the Convention is intended to deal with action against large numbers, not individuals even if they happen to possess the same group characteristics. It will be up to the courts to decide in each case whether the number was sufficiently large.[109]

The point is well made that the intent of genocide is formed when the perpetrator intends to destroy a number of individuals 'joined with a connecting purpose', that is, on account of their group characteristics. Whether that number represents the whole group or some part of it is a secondary matter, albeit an important one in certain situations, as will be seen below.

The interpretation of 'in part' first came up for decision in the *Jelisić* case. According to the Trial Chamber, the question which arose was 'what proportion of the group is marked for destruction, and beyond what threshold could the crime be qualified as genocide?' In particular, the Trial Chamber 'will have to verify whether genocide may be committed within a restricted geographical zone'.[110] The prosecutor had contended that the zone within which acts to eliminate a group are performed, or intended, may be limited to the size of a region within a country or a municipality. The Trial Chamber accepted, in view of the object of the Convention (but of very little else), 'that international custom admits the characterisation of genocide even when the exterminatory intent only extends to a limited geographic zone'.[111] One wonders whether 'limited geographic zone' is really an improvement over 'in part'.

The court did manage greater specificity when it said, in obiter dicta, that the intent to eliminate the group's *leadership* — or more generally the 'most representative' members of the targeted community — could satisfy the 'in part' requirement, provided that elimination of the subgroup would destroy the chances of survival of the group as such.[112] And thus the position attained in *Jelisić*, although without great accuracy, is that the intent to commit genocide may be manifested where the actor intends to exterminate a substantial number of the members of the group, or a more limited number selected for the impact that its annihilation would have upon the survival of the group, even when the intent is to commit these destructive acts within a 'limited geographic zone'.

Yet the case which dominates the subject in this regard is *Krstić*. General Krstić was charged with genocide (and in the alternative with complicity in genocide) in relation to the mass executions of Bosnian-Muslim men in Srebrenica in July 1995. The prosecutor contended that the Bosnian-Serb forces had planned and intended to kill all of Srebrenica's Bosnian-Muslim men of military age. The large-scale murders, coupled with this intent, constituted genocide, according to the prosecutor, because the intent to destroy part of the Bosnian-Muslim group, as such, comes within the meaning of the Genocide Convention.[113]

---

[109] Robinson, *Genocide Convention*, p. 63. See also Schabas, *Genocide*, pp. 230–40.
[110] *Jelisić* trial judgment, para. 80.   [111] Ibid., para. 83.   [112] Ibid., para. 82.
[113] *Krstić* trial judgment, para. 545.

Here one is called upon to notice the distinction between 'part of the Bosnian-Muslim group', and 'part of *Srebrenica's* Bosnian-Muslim group' (namely, the men) — the latter being only a part of a lesser part.

The Trial Chamber found that the murders and the infliction of serious bodily or mental harm were indeed committed with the intent to kill all members of the male subgroup, without regard as to whether they were civilians or soldiers. Bosnian-Muslim women, children, and the elderly were bused out of the area with little harm. But, as the Trial Chamber put it, the desire to capture all the Bosnian-Muslim men was so great that Bosnian-Serb forces stopped the departing buses to check that no men were hiding on board. The men captured in and around Srebrenica were executed in small groups, or in carefully orchestrated mass killings, where they were lined up and shot in rounds. Others were jammed into buildings and killed by machine-gun fire or hand-grenades. Bulldozers were brought in to bury the dead. Soldiers returned to the execution sites to check that no one had survived.[114]

Did this group of victims represent a sufficient part of the Bosnian-Muslim group, as a whole, so that the intent to destroy it qualifies as an 'intent to destroy the group in whole or in part'? The *Krstić* trial court answered yes, but its reasoning is not clear.

The problem is that 'in part' may be understood territorially. To intend to destroy the group in a region may be enough. 'Destroy' has to mean physically destroy, not deport to another region,[115] the latter more accurately to be described as ethnic cleansing and dealt with as a crime against humanity. From the facts of *Krstić* one does not immediately apprehend the intent to physically destroy the Bosnian-Muslim group territorially (in the area of Srebrenica), or, for that matter, to destroy it in substantial part. This is because everybody but the military-aged men were given safe passage out of the area. The killing of the men may be reasonably interpreted as an intent to eliminate both armed opposition and the threat of military re-infiltration. The killing was savagely carried out and was certainly a war crime. Thus we have crimes against humanity (killing of non-combatant men and ethnic cleansing) and war crimes (killing of men in captivity), not quite adding up to the specific intent of genocide.

Another way of putting the problem is that either the Bosnian Serbs intended to physically destroy the Bosnian-Muslim group *in the area of Srebrenica* (that is, in *territorial* part) — which they seem not to have intended because they gave safe passage to most of the group; or they intended to destroy *the Bosnian-Muslim group* by killing many thousands of military-aged men (that is, to destroy the group in *substantial* part) — which they possibly did intend, although it is not the only reasonable inference from the evidence (it is just as likely that they intended to eliminate military resistance).

The *Krstić* Trial Chamber mentioned several sources confirming that the intent to 'eradicate' a group within a limited geographical area of a country may be characterized as genocide.[116] As we have already seen, this is not controversial, since 'limited

---

[114] Ibid., paras 546–7.
[115] E.g. *Semanza* trial judgment, para. 315; and *Stakić* trial judgment, paras 518–19, 557.
[116] *Krstić* trial judgment, paras 585–9.

geographical area' is one way of saying 'in part'. But then the court said:

the object and purpose of the Convention . . . is to criminalise specified conduct directed against the existence of protected groups, as such. The Trial Chamber is therefore of the opinion that the intent to destroy a group, even if only in part, means seeking to destroy a distinct part of the group as opposed to an accumulation of isolated individuals within it. Although the perpetrators of genocide need not seek to destroy the entire group protected by the Convention, they must view the part of the group they wish to destroy as a distinct entity which must be eliminated as such. A campaign resulting in the killings, in different places spread over a broad geographical area, of a finite number of members of a protected group might not thus qualify as genocide, despite the high total number of casualties, because it would not show an intent by the perpetrators to target the very existence of the group as such.[117]

The Court gave no reason to depart from a plain reading of the Convention, that the intent to destroy in *substantial* part is sufficient, even when the intended part is not 'distinct'. The court's innovation, which is a testament to the infancy of applied genocide law, would unaccountably lessen the Convention's protection.[118]

The Trial Chamber continued by contrasting the above with its interpretation of *territorial* part:

Conversely, the killing of all members of the part of a group located within a small geographical area, although resulting in a lesser number of victims, would qualify as genocide if carried out with the intent to destroy the part of the group as such located in this small geographical area. Indeed, the physical destruction may target only a part of the geographically limited part of the larger group because the perpetrators of the genocide regard the intended destruction as sufficient to annihilate the group as a distinct entity in the geographic area at issue.[119]

It was by this assertion that *Krstić* arrived at the conclusion that the intent to destroy *part of a part* of a group, namely a distinct part of a territorial part, could be sufficient as the intent of genocide. In its final comment the Trial Chamber talked not about destruction, but about 'disappearance', and the line between genocide and ethnic cleansing was again allowed to blur: 'The Bosnian Serb forces knew, by the time they decided to kill all of the military aged men, that the combination of those killings with the forcible transfer of the women, children and elderly would inevitably result in the physical disappearance of the Bosnian Muslim

---

[117] Ibid., para. 590. Approved, without explanation, in *Stakić* trial judgment, para. 524.

[118] In *Sikirica*, a decision handed down one month after the *Krstić* trial judgment and apparently not influenced by it, the Trial Chamber suggested that where the *numbers* were too small to suggest an intent to destroy a group in substantial part, that intent could nevertheless be discerned if the persons killed formed a 'significant' subgroup, e.g. the leadership. (*Sikirica et al.* no-case-to-answer decision, paras 65–6.) The only source relied on (ibid., paras 65, 77) is a UN report (*Revised and Updated Report on the Question of Prevention and Punishment of the Crime of Genocide*, E/CN.4/Sub.2/1985/6, 2 July 1985, paras 29, 94) and the obiter dicta in the *Jelisić* case referred to in the main text. These can hardly be treated as authorities, yet the *Sikirica* Trial Chamber proceeded as if it had been well established that the intent to destroy a group's leadership or other 'significant section' is sufficient for genocide (*Sikirica et al.* no-case-to-answer decision, paras 76–85). See also the *Krstić* trial judgment, para. 587, where the same UN report is quoted with approval.   [119] *Krstić* trial judgment, para. 590.

population at Srebrenica.'[120] The ICTY Appeals Chamber tried to find a way out for the Trial Chamber:

The Trial Chamber stated that the part of the group Radislav Krstić intended to destroy was the Bosnian Muslim population of Srebrenica. The men of military age, who formed a further part of that group, were not viewed by the Trial Chamber as a separate, smaller part within the meaning of Article 4. Rather, the Trial Chamber treated the killing of the men of military age as evidence from which to infer that Radislav Krstić and some members of the VRS Main Staff had the requisite intent to destroy all the Bosnian Muslims of Srebrenica.[121]

In the case of *Sikirica*, the question was whether 1,000 to 1,400 Bosnian-Muslim 'victims' (broadly defined) out of an estimated total Bosnian-Muslim population of 49,351 in Prijedor municipality (2 to 2.8 per cent) qualified as a 'reasonably substantial' part of the Bosnian-Muslim group in Prijedor. The Trial Chamber said that it did not.[122]

One of the most important lessons under this heading is that 'destruction', as a component of the mens rea of genocide, is not limited to physical or biological destruction of the group's members, since the group (or a part of it) can be destroyed in other ways as well, such as by transferring children out of the group (or the part), or by severing the bonds among its members. This follows from the simple grammatical observation that it is not accurate to speak of 'the group' as being amenable to physical or biological destruction. Members of the group are, of course, physical or biological beings, but the bonds among the members, as well as such aspects of the group as its members' culture and beliefs, are neither physical nor biological. Hence the Genocide Convention's 'intent to destroy' the group cannot sensibly be regarded as reducible to an intent to destroy the group physically or biologically, as has occasionally been said. On this basis, it becomes easy to see why one may rely, for example, on evidence of deliberate forcible transfer as evidence of the mens rea of genocide, even though forcible transfer is not an actus reus of genocide.[123]

5.3.3 Motive, and the meaning of 'as such'

The words 'as such' appended to the intent requirement of genocide have attracted little comment in the jurisprudence of the tribunals. The Genocide Convention's drafting committee gave an explanation of their origin.[124] The question had arisen whether the

---

[120] Ibid., para. 595. See also W. A. Schabas, 'Was Genocide Committed in Bosnia and Herzegovina? First Judgements of the International Criminal Tribunal for the Former Yugoslavia' (2001) 25 *Fordham Int'l L. J.* 23.

[121] *Krstić* appeal judgment, para. 19.

[122] *Sikirica et al.* no-case-to-answer decision, paras 70–2. The *Stakić* Trial Chamber responded: 'any mathematical calculation of the number of victims relative to the total population of the group in this context is rather unhelpful' (*Stakić* no-case-to-answer decision, para. 29) — without explaining why that is so. Yet, in its judgment proper, the same Trial Chamber, in determining that it had not been proven that Stakić had the intent to commit genocide, 'noted' that approximately 23,000 people were registered as having passed through various detention centres in Prijedor municipality, yet the total number of killings in the municipality had not exceeded 3,000 (*Stakić* trial judgment, para. 553).

[123] See *Krstić* appeal judgment, para. 33; *Blagojević and Jokić* trial judgment, paras 657–66 (where there is some confusion between the concepts of actus reus and mens rea); and *Krajišnik* trial judgment, para. 854.

[124] See *Report of the Sixth Committee*, 3 December 1948, UN Doc. A/760, para. 10.

committee should retain, as motives of the acts of genocide, the words 'on grounds of the national or racial origin, religious belief, or political opinion of its members', which formed part of the draft text at the time. The issue was dealt with when the committee adopted an amendment (27 votes to 22, with two abstentions) submitted by Venezuela, whereby the above phrase was deleted and the words 'as such' were added.

Those opposed to a statement of motives thought that such a statement would allow perpetrators of genocide to claim in their defence that they had not acted under the impulse of one of the motives held to be necessary to prove the crime.[125] Venezuela and some other members of the drafting committee nevertheless insisted that the replacement words 'as such' should be construed as making reference to motives. This difference in opinion led the committee to include a statement in its report to the effect that Venezuela's interpretation was not necessarily the committee's interpretation.[126] Thus, in the words of an early commentator, 'the question of whether the motives of the crime . . . are included in the text of Article II or not will remain a matter of interpretation'.[127]

According to Schabas, interpreters of Article II 'cannot simply ignore the words "as such", which were inserted as a compromise to take account of views favouring recognition of a motive component'.[128] He proposed a distinction between the 'collective motive' ('organizers and planners must necessarily have a racist or discriminatory motive, that is, a genocidal motive, taken as a whole') and the individual or personal motive ('individual participants may be motivated by a range of factors, including financial gain, jealousy and political ambition'). Schabas argues that the prosecutor must establish that genocide, taken in its collective dimension, was committed *on the grounds* of nationality, race, ethnicity, or religion, but that individual offenders should not be entitled to raise personal motives as a defence to genocide.[129]

In the *Rutaganda* trial judgment we find the view that an act of genocide 'extends beyond its actual commission, for example, the murder of a particular person, to encompass the realization of the ulterior purpose to destroy, in whole or in part, the group of which the person is only a member'[130] — a clear reference to motives. But this proposition was neither explained by the trial court nor based on any authority, and since the question had not arisen in the case, the court's opinion belongs to that stream of obiter dicta that flows from ICTR judgments.

It was Obed Ruzindana who first complained before the ICTR Appeals Chamber that the Trial Chamber had not found any motive in him to commit genocide. If he had committed certain crimes, he said, it was for profit and vengeance, and evidence to back this up was in the record.[131] The Appeals Chamber summarily dismissed his plea, saying that criminal intent must not be confused with motive, and that where the mens rea of genocide is proven, 'personal motive does not exclude criminal responsibility'.[132]

---

[125] See *Study of the Question of the Prevention and Punishment of the Crime of Genocide*, UN Doc. E/CN.4/Sub.2/416, 4 July 1978, para. 104.　　　　　　　　[126] Ibid., para. 105.

[127] Robinson, *Genocide Convention*, p. 61.　　[128] Schabas, *Genocide*, p. 254.

[129] Ibid., pp. 255–6.　　[130] *Rutaganda* trial judgment, para. 60.

[131] *Kayishema and Ruzindana* appeal judgment, para. 161.　　[132] Ibid.

In the ICTY's *Krstić* case we find the Trial Chamber acceding to the view that the victims of genocide must be targeted *by reason* of their membership in a group, but it seems that this was not an affirmation of a motive so much as a repudiation of the view that mere knowledge that the victims belong to a certain group is sufficient to prove an intent to destroy the group.[133] It was not until the ICTR Appeals Chamber delivered its judgment in the *Niyitegeka* case, in July 2004, that the term 'as such' was given an in-house interpretation: its purpose was to draw 'a clear distinction between mass murder [on the one hand] and crimes in which the perpetrator targets a specific group because of its nationality, race, ethnicity or religion', on the other.[134]

5.3.4 Complicity in genocide on appeal

As explained earlier (at section 5.2.4), the *Akayesu* trial judgment made a confused and erroneous contribution to this subject. That case finally left open the question whether the specific intent of genocide has to be proven in relation to every punishable form of participation in genocide, including complicity. As late as the end of 2002 an ICTY Trial Chamber felt that the question was still open, and said that it preferred not to depart from what it called 'the strict pre-requisite of *dolus specialis* related to all forms of committing and participation in genocide'.[135]

This view cannot be regarded as well founded, and although the issue has still not been properly analysed, some Trial Chambers have understood complicity in genocide in keeping with the general notion of accomplice liability, as illustrated by the ICTR case of *Semanza*. According to that Trial Chamber, 'complicity to commit genocide in Article 2(3)(e) [of the ICTR Statute] refers to all acts of assistance or encouragement that have substantially contributed to, or have had a substantial effect on, the completion of the crime of genocide. The accused must have acted intentionally and with the awareness that he was contributing to the crime of genocide, including all its material elements.'[136]

Laurent Semanza was convicted of complicity in genocide and acquitted of genocide proper. Yet he was found not just to have had *knowledge* of the genocidal intent of the principal perpetrators, but to have possessed 'an independent intent' to destroy the Tutsi group. This intent coupled with the fact that Semanza was found to have 'directed' the separation of Tutsi and Hutu, and to have 'instructed' the militia to kill the former, which the militia then did,[137] makes it hard to understand why the Trial Chamber did not convict him of genocide but settled for complicity. In any event, this means that Semanza's conviction for complicity in genocide (historically the first in a tried case) was conditioned on proof of the specific intent of genocide.

Following *Semanza*, the question of how to understand complicity in genocide came up again in *Stakić*, an ICTY case. Liability for genocide was pleaded here within the

---

[133] *Krstić* trial judgment, para. 561; although see para. 571, where the term 'goal' introduces ambiguity.

[134] *Niyitegeka* appeal judgment, para. 53; see also *Stakić* appeal judgment, para. 20.

[135] *Stakić* no-case-to-answer decision, para. 67; according to *Stakić*, the *dolus specialis* of genocide is required also for command responsibility (ibid., para. 92). [136] *Semanza* trial judgment, para. 395.

[137] See ibid., paras 426, 429–30.

framework of a joint criminal enterprise. The common purpose of the enterprise of which Stakić was allegedly a part was said to have included genocide, or alternatively genocide was the natural and foreseeable consequence of the execution of the common purpose.[138] The latter variant of the joint criminal enterprise doctrine is known as JCE 3 (see Chapter 7) and while it is not particularly controversial in relation to other crimes, the *Stakić* Trial Chamber refused to contemplate the possibility that it could work with genocide: 'Conflating the third variant of joint criminal enterprise and the crime of genocide would result in the *dolus specialis* being so watered down that it is extinguished.'[139] In a decision following the *Stakić* judgment by a few months, another Trial Chamber remarked that:

genocide, as a specific-intent crime, cannot be found against a person who merely foresees geno-cide to be the natural consequence of another crime he or she committed personally or as part of a joint criminal enterprise. Nothing less than the intent to commit genocide must be present in the mind of the perpetrator of genocide.[140]

Since then, the Appeals Chamber of the ad hoc tribunals has twice found occasion to pronounce the above view erroneous.[141]

When *Stakić* insists that the intent of genocide must *always* be met,[142] one is reminded of the corrosive effect of the *Akayesu* judgment, which placed genocide on a pedestal, without taking into account how this would affect its conceptual relations with other components of the law. The *Stakić* Trial Chamber was unable to find that any one of the persons whom the defendant was associated with possessed the 'core element' of the crime of genocide — the *dolus specialis* — but more fundamentally did not find that the defendant himself possessed that intent, and so acquitted him of both genocide and complicity in genocide.[143] We can be certain that the court would have acquitted him of both these counts even had it found that his associates (but not he himself) possessed the *dolus specialis*.[144]

On the subject of complicity in genocide, the ICTY Appeals Chamber has made pronouncements that neither seem consistent nor are easy to understand. In *Krstić* the Appeals Chamber said:

There is support for a position that Article 4(3) [of the ICTY Statute] may be the more specific provision (*lex specialis*) in relation to Article 7(1). There is, however, also authority indicating that modes of participation enumerated in Article 7(1) should be read, as the Tribunal's Statute directs, into Article 4(3), and so the proper characterization of such individual's criminal liability would be that of aiding and abetting genocide.

The Appeals Chamber concludes that the latter approach is the correct one in this case. Article 7(1) of the Statute, which allows liability to attach to an aider and abettor, expressly applies that

---

[138] *Stakić* trial judgment, para. 529.   [139] Ibid., para. 530.

[140] *Prosecutor* v. *Radoslav Brđanin*, Decision on Motion for Acquittal Pursuant to Rule 98 *bis*, 28 November 2003, paras 30, 57.

[141] *Prosecutor* v. *Radoslav Brđanin*, Decision on Interlocutory Appeal, 19 March 2004, paras 5–10; and *Prosecutor* v. *André Rwamakuba*, Decision on Interlocutory Appeal Regarding Application of Joint Criminal Enterprise to the Crime of Genocide, 22 October 2004.   [142] E.g. *Stakić* trial judgment, para. 530.

[143] Ibid., para. 546.   [144] See, e.g., ibid., paras 555, 559, 561.

mode of liability to any 'crime referred to in articles 2 to 5 of the present Statute', including the offence of genocide prohibited by Article 4. Because the Statute must be interpreted with the utmost respect to the language used by the legislator, the Appeals Chamber may not conclude that the consequent overlap between Article 7(1) and Article 4(3)(e) is a result of an inadvertence on the part of the legislator where another explanation, consonant with the language used by the Statute, is possible. In this case, the two provisions can be reconciled, because the terms 'complicity' and 'accomplice' may encompass conduct broader than that of aiding and abetting. Given the Statute's express statement in Article 7(1) that liability for genocide under Article 4 may attach through the mode of aiding and abetting, Radislav Krstić's responsibility is properly characterized as that of aiding and abetting genocide.[145]

It is an indication that the Appeals Chamber has reached an impasse when it falls back on vague propositions such as 'the terms "complicity" and "accomplice" may encompass conduct broader than that of aiding and abetting'. In the event, the Appeals Chamber held that complicity in genocide, 'where it prohibits conduct broader than' aiding and abetting, requires proof that the accomplice had the specific intent to destroy a protected group. The reasoning, such as it is, is entirely superficial.[146] The implication of *Krstić* is that the Genocide Convention did not foresee convictions for genocide absent the specific intent; such convictions *are* possible at the ad hoc tribunals, according to the Appeals Chamber, because the Statutes (Article 6 of the ICTR, Article 7 of the ICTY) incorporate a broader zone of personal liability. In *Ntakirutimana*, the Appeals Chamber said, again, that 'complicity in genocide . . . encompasses aiding and abetting'.[147] Schabas has offered his own theory of complicity, which is worth noting.[148]

5.3.5 Conspiracy to commit genocide

In the ICTR case of *Musema* the defendant was charged with, and eventually acquitted of, conspiracy to commit genocide. The indictment cast the charge of conspiracy, like the other charges in this case, over the factual allegations generally, without specifying the acts which the prosecutor thought pointed to a conspiracy.[149] Thus the charge of conspiracy and the charge of genocide were referenced to the same set of acts. In its discussion of the law, the Trial Chamber said that conspiracy to commit genocide consists of an agreement between two or more persons to commit genocide.[150] The intent of the conspirators must be to commit genocide, that is, to destroy, in whole or in part, a national, ethnic, racial, or religious group, as such. The Trial Chamber concluded that the prosecutor had not adduced evidence of an agreement between Musema and others. It did not ask whether such an agreement could be inferred from the evidence.[151]

The Trial Chamber's real reason for dismissing the charge of conspiracy was that it possessed enough evidence to convict Musema of genocide proper — what it called 'the substantive offence in relation to conspiracy'.[152] *Musema* interpreted the records of the

---

[145] *Krstić* appeal judgment, paras 138–9.   [146] Ibid., para. 142.

[147] *Ntakirutimana* appeal judgment, para. 371; see also *Semanza* appeal judgment, paras 260 ff.

[148] Schabas, *Genocide*, pp. 285–303.   [149] *Musema* trial judgment, para. 937.

[150] Ibid., para. 191.   [151] Ibid., para. 940.   [152] Ibid., para. 941.

Genocide Convention's drafting committee as suggesting that the reason for the inclusion of conspiracy was to ensure, in view of the serious nature of the crime of genocide, that 'mere agreement' to commit genocide would be punishable even if no 'preparatory act' had taken place.[153] The Trial Chamber did not explore the meaning of these concepts in the context of the law of genocide. It argued that a notion similar to the common-law notion of conspiracy existed in civil-law systems: *complot*, it said, is punishable in those (unidentified) systems where the purpose of the *complot* is to commit crimes regarded as extremely serious, such as undermining state security.[154]

The court proposed that at least within the limits of this notion of *complot*, civil- and common-law systems both considered conspiracy to be an *inchoate* offence, punishable as an act in itself and not for any harm that might result from it.[155] The *Musema* court also suggested, again without citing sources, that in civil-law systems, if the conspiracy is successful, and the substantive offence is carried out, the accused will be convicted only of the substantive offence and not of the conspiracy.[156] (Doubts have been expressed as to the accuracy of these propositions.)[157] This stands in supposed contrast with the common law, where according to *Musema* one may be convicted of both conspiracy and the substantive offence in certain circumstances.[158]

The Trial Chamber said in conclusion that it would adopt 'the definition of conspiracy most favourable to Musema, whereby an accused cannot be convicted of both genocide and conspiracy to commit genocide on the basis of the same acts. ... no purpose would be served in convicting an accused, who has already been found guilty of genocide, for conspiracy to commit genocide.'[159] One problem with this is that the same panel of judges, just over a year earlier, had convicted Kambanda of both genocide *and* conspiracy to commit genocide. *Kambanda* involved a guilty plea, and guilty-plea judgments at the ad hoc tribunals are generally brief. But in *Niyitegeka*, a trial case, the court also found the defendant guilty of the same two offences.[160] And the same result is found again in the *Nahimana* case.[161]

Of greater concern is *Musema*'s assumption that for the purposes of exposition of international law it is open to a court to adopt the interpretation or definition most favourable to the defendant. One should note, in relation to the application of this principle of fair interpretation, that it is not a matter of finding the interpretation most favourable to the first defendant who comes along. The choice made concerns all persons, for it effectively becomes a new statement of the law. The *Musema* court was of the view that there is no clear answer in law to the question whether a charge of conspiracy to commit genocide must be dismissed where a charge of genocide is proven. However, the court did not engage with the question analytically. Therefore its answer is of little value as precedent.

---

[153] Ibid., para. 185.
[154] Ibid., para. 186. There is no indication that the Trial Chamber looked beyond French law.
[155] Ibid., para. 193.   [156] Ibid., para. 196.
[157] See Schabas, *Genocide*, pp. 259–66. See also ILC Draft Code of Crimes, Article 2, where conspiracy can be punished only if the intended crime 'in fact occurs'.   [158] *Musema* trial judgment, para. 196.
[159] Ibid., para. 198.   [160] *Niyitegeka* trial judgment, paras 429, 480, 502.
[161] *Nahimana et al.* trial judgment, paras 1043–55.

5.3.6 Direct and public incitement revisited

In December 2003 the ICTR convicted three radio and newspaper executives, Ferdinand Nahimana, Jean-Bosco Barayagwiza, and Hassan Ngeze, for direct and public incitement to commit genocide, sentencing them to life imprisonment.[162] In many ways, the so-called 'media judgment' of the ICTR is not a helpful precedent in international criminal justice, as we endeavour to explain in this section.

Nahimana was not the first judgment of an international tribunal to decide a charge of direct and public incitement to genocide. As we saw above (5.2.5), the ICTR's very first trial judgment convicted Jean-Paul Akayesu of the same charge. Juvénal Kajelijeli was convicted next.[163] Perhaps the best known precedent is the Nuremberg IMT's case of Julius Streicher, who was convicted in 1946 essentially for the same crime.[164] Yet in *Nahimana* the centrality of the incitement charge to the case, the wealth of the material underpinning it, the size of the written judgment — with its 1,110 paragraphs and pioneer narrative voice — ensure that any future litigation on the subject, in an international or domestic setting, will start here.

Article II of the Genocide Convention provides:

Genocide means any of the following acts committed with intent to destroy, in whole or in part, a national, ethnical, racial or religious group, as such: (a) Killing members of the group; (b) Causing serious bodily or mental harm to members of the group . . . The following acts shall be punishable . . . (c) direct and public incitement to commit genocide . . .

Thus a person may be punished for direct and public incitement to commit genocide when he or she incites others, directly and publicly to kill or to seriously harm members of a national, ethnic, racial, or religious group, with the intent to destroy that group as such, in whole or in part. The speaker's (or the writer's) intent need not be revealed in these very words, as long as the hallmark intent of genocide and its target are plain in the circumstances. The speaker must intend that the recipient of the message will react to the stimulus of the words by committing the crimes (of killing, etc.) with the genocidal intent to destroy the group. Whether the recipient of the message finally commits any crime is not an ingredient of the crime of incitement.[165]

We are confident to recognize this sort of conduct when we see it. Because it is *linguistic* conduct, we must understand the language, or have it translated for us. The party official who in a time of social unrest and fear calls upon the crowd at the militarized rally to excise the national cancer represented by a particular ethnic or religious group is inciting the crowd to commit genocide (unless something about the speech or

---

[162] *Nahimana et al.* trial judgment.   [163] *Kajelijeli* trial judgment, paras 850–61.

[164] See 22 IMT Judgment 547–9. The conviction was for incitement to murder and extermination, a species of persecution (itself as a crime against humanity).

[165] On the law of incitement generally, see Ashworth, *Principles*, pp. 480–2; on direct and public incitement to commit genocide, see Schabas, *Genocide*, pp. 266–80. In the post-*Nahimana* ICTR case of *Muvunyi*, the defendant was convicted of incitement to commit genocide for calling the Tutsi 'snakes' at a public gathering: *Muvunyi* trial judgment, paras 507–9.

the circumstances at the time admit of a different interpretation). If a news agency retransmits the official's speech, in a broadcast or in print, in such a way as to adopt it rather than just report it, the agency's own culpability for incitement to genocide will also be obvious to us.

All of this follows from the logical observation that direct and public incitement to commit any crime is, by definition, evident for what it is — a publicly meaningful call to commit a crime. For if it is not thus understood, it will fail as incitement.[166] You may be disinclined to do what you are called upon to do, but you know (you must know) when you are being incited. You may need a lawyer to tell you what an act of genocide consists of, but if you know the legal definition of genocide, you also know direct and public incitement to commit genocide when you come across it; a lawyer knows nothing more about it than you do. The Nuremberg Tribunal did not need to explain in its judgment why the following passage from Streicher's May 1939 issue of *Der Stürmer* qualified as a call to genocide: 'The Jews in Russia must be killed. They must be exterminated root and branch.'[167]

A certain amount of non-legal background is required at this point in order to appreciate the issues in *Nahimana*. Rwanda's 1994 civil war flared on 7 April of that year and ran its course in three months and ten days, the time it took for the rebel invading force (RPF) to topple the cautiously reformist government and install the regime that holds power to this day.[168] The RPF rebels were ethnically mostly Tutsi. They were commonly known as the *Inkotanyi* (a *nom de guerre*),[169] or *Inyenzi* ('cockroaches'), or often as the *Inkotanyi-Inyenzi*. (Today's rulers of Rwanda still call themselves *Inkotanyi*, but seem to have dropped the older *Inyenzi*, perhaps because it is no longer descriptive of their survival tactics.)[170] Much about *Nahimana* turns on the semantics of these sobriquets. The Inkotanyi/Inyenzi invaded from Uganda, where they had built up their strength in the course of thirty years of exile (their monarchist forebears were defeated and chased out of Rwanda in 1959, after which the country's First Republic came into being).[171]

In 1994, the majority ethnic group in Rwanda was the Hutu. About 8 per cent of the population was Tutsi. Large numbers of Rwandan civilians — disproportionately Tutsi — were killed in the course of the April–July 1994 war, especially between April and

---

[166] In *Leon Mugesera* v. *Minister of Citizenship and Immigration*, [2004] 1 FCR 3, Canada's Federal Court of Appeal said that in assessing whether an utterance constitutes direct and public incitement to commit genocide, the meaning of the utterance is to be assessed in terms of the speech as a whole, in terms of the context in which the speech was made, and in terms of a reasonable listener; in other words, the 'assessment' is to be in accordance with the ordinary way in which ordinary language is ordinarily understood.   [167] 22 IMT Judgment 547–9.

[168] It is now recognized that, most probably, the shooting down of the aircraft carrying the Rwandan President, on the night of 6 April 1994, which led to the outbreak of the war the next day, was carried out by the RPF. See interview with A. Guichaoua, in S. Smith, 'Révélations d'un expert de la justice internationale', *Le Monde*, 7 May 2004, p. 8.

[169] The *Dictionnaire Rwandais-Français* (I. Jacob, ed., 1987) defines 'inkotanyi' as '*le batailleur acharné qui ne capitule pas*' and as '*personne zélée, acharnée*'.   [170] See www.rpfinkotanyi.co.rw, the official RPF website.

[171] See also our discussion in section 5.2.1, above. Post-1994 historical works on Rwanda are tarnished by the misconceptions and mythologies surrounding the war of that year. The work with the fewest flaws, and the deepest insight into the history of modern Rwanda, is M. Mamdani, *When Victims Become Killers: Colonialism, Nativism, and the Genocide in Rwanda* (Princeton University Press, 2001).

mid-May.[172] The murder of these people is said to have been incited, in part, by segments of the media.

Prior to the war, news was transmitted in Rwanda primarily by radio and tabloid newspaper. By the beginning of 1994, two nationwide radio stations were in operation, Radio Rwanda (owned by the government) and the newly established RTLM (a private venture in which the defendants Nahimana and Barayagwiza had a stake). Several magazines and newspapers were in print, but due to the general illiteracy of Rwandans (only about 30 per cent of adults could read and write), and the peasantry's extreme poverty, the print runs were very small. *Kangura*, the weekly tabloid published by Hassan Ngeze, had a circulation of between 1,500 and 3,000 (in a country of eight million). *Kangura* did not publish during the war. Its last pre-war issue, number 59, is from March 1994. Radio broadcasts — by RTLM and Radio Rwanda, but also by the RPF's Radio Muhabura — continued intermittently during the war.

The prosecutor placed before the ICTR the 59 pre-war issues of *Kangura*. A minuscule portion of this material (13 passages of a few lines each) formed the basis of Ngeze's conviction by the tribunal.[173] The ICTR was presented also with several hundred tape-recordings of RTLM broadcasts, running to several thousand transcript pages. The conviction of Nahimana and Barayagwiza was based on a tiny fraction of this material (37 excerpts).[174]

Certain human-rights activists,[175] journalists, and academics[176] have been so successful in forging a common wisdom that radio was the daily purveyor of genocide in Rwanda in the April–July 1994 period, that many who dutifully waded through the *Nahimana* judgment's copious regurgitation of the evidence in search of the chilling exhortations to fill the graves with the innocent Tutsi must have been puzzled by the court's inability to come up with a single example — whether broadcast on RTLM or printed in *Kangura* — of a blatant call on Hutu to hunt down and destroy the Tutsi ethnic group.[177]

---

[172] For population and victim estimates, see A. J. Kuperman, *The Limits of Humanitarian Intervention: Genocide in Rwanda* (Brookings Institution Press, 2001), pp. 121–2. Kuperman is the first scholar to have attempted a significant revision of the received account concerning responsibility for the 1994 war and its consequences; see his 'Provoking Genocide: A Revised History of the Rwandan Patriotic Front' (2004) 6 *J. Genocide Research* 61.

[173] See *Nahimana et al.* trial judgment, paras 122 ff. Ngeze, as well as Nahimana and Barayagwiza, were convicted also of other forms of genocide, and of crimes against humanity.

[174] The prosecutor also invited some witnesses to testify on their recollections of the content of RTLM broadcasts. The best evidence, however, is the recordings. Since they are plentiful, they must take precedence over what some people say they remember hearing.

[175] A. des Forges, *'Leave none to tell the story': Genocide in Rwanda* (Human Rights Watch, 1999), pp. 248–57; J.-P. Chrétien, *Rwanda: Les médias du génocide* (Karthala, 1995). See also G. Prunier, *The Rwanda Crisis: History of a Genocide* (Columbia University Press, 1995), pp. 189, 224; and Article 19, *Broadcasting Genocide: Censorship, Propaganda, and State-Sponsored Violence in Rwanda, 1990–1994* (Article 19, 1996), pp. 109–46.

[176] E.g. P. Gourevitch, *'We wish to inform you that tomorrow we will be killed with our families': Stories from Rwanda* (Farrar, Straus, and Giroux, 1998), pp. 110–44; Frank Chalk, 'Hate Radio in Rwanda', in H. Adelman and A. Suhrke (eds), *The Path of a Genocide: The Rwanda Crisis from Uganda to Zaire* (Transaction, 1999), pp. 93–107.

[177] There is a tendency in humanitarian circles to assume that mass atrocities are planned and executed from above, and that the locus of evil is thus centralized. This tendency is evident in almost all writings on Rwanda, where the genocide is presented as centrally planned. For a critique, see the reviews by A. Zahar on some of the literature on Rwanda in (2001) 3 *J. Genocide Research* 293, (2002) 4 *J. Genocide Research* 461, (2002) 4 *J. Genocide Research* 590,

Two or three of the 37 RTLM fragments quoted in the *Nahimana* judgment are sufficiently brutal and ambiguous to raise an eyebrow and invite a court's disapprobation, or even a penal response, even after allowing for the patriotic fervour that enfeebles the intellect of many a broadcaster in time of war. Yet the fragments do not read like direct and public incitement to commit genocide and cannot possibly justify a punishment of life imprisonment.[178]

Here is the first of these passages, translated from the original Kinyarwanda language:

One hundred thousand young men must be recruited rapidly. They should all stand up so that we will kill the Inkotanyi and exterminate them, all the easier that . . . the reason we will exterminate them is that they belong to one ethnic group. Look at the person's height and his physical appearance. Just look at his small nose and then break it. Then we will go on to Kibungo, Rusumo, Ruhengeri, Byumba, everywhere. We will rest after liberating our country.[179]

Whether the Tutsi were ever typically tall and slim, with fine noses, distinguishable from a Hutu group whose members were typically short and stocky, with flaring nostrils, is not a question one needs to consider in order to accept that in 1994 Rwanda differentiations between the two groups were sometimes signalled by reference to these stereotypes.[180] But while the radio presenter in this instance calls on people to kill Tutsi, he does not unambiguously call on them to kill *the* Tutsi. He does not say — nor is there evidence of anyone at RTLM or *Kangura* saying — that the Hutu should get out and trawl neighbourhood and field, making sure no Tutsi child, mother, or grandparent is left alive.

What the presenter does say is that the Inkotanyi (that is, the RPF rebels) should be eliminated, that people cannot expect to rest before liberation (by the date of this broadcast, on 4 June 1994, around half the country had been overrun by the rebels), and that the elimination of the RPF-Inkotanyi is made easier for the reason that its members are all of the Tutsi ethnic group. This last point is inaccurate, for the RPF had some Hutu members, but allowing that the RPF was overwhelmingly Tutsi, a person

---

and (2004) 6 *J. Genocide Research* 286. In the received model, the influence of the presumed centralized evil on the masses is achieved through a public-communications system controlled by the conspirators, hence the need to locate and condemn an RTLM or a *Kangura*. Without this link the centralized model collapses and criminal responsibility shifts down and out into the regions.

[178] The prosecutor recommended life imprisonment for each count on which a conviction was entered. The tribunal pronounced a single sentence of life imprisonment for each defendant, without stating the penalty attaching to each ground of conviction; see *Nahimana et al*. trial judgment, paras 1097 ff. We are left to assume that the court accepted the prosecutor's recommendation.

[179] Ibid., para. 396. Unless otherwise indicated (by use of square brackets), ellipses belong to the judgment text.

[180] As is evident from the *Nahimana et al*. trial judgment, Ngeze, a natural caricaturist, could poke fun at this aspect of his culture. The tribunal stated (para. 304): 'Witness ABE [a pseudonym] recalled that he had asked Ngeze once if he could attend a CDR [nationalist political party] meeting. Ngeze told him it was not possible, because the party was exclusively for one ethnic group. He asked Witness ABE to put two of his fingers into one nostril, saying if those fingers could enter his nostril, he could be a member. Thereafter, as he was calling others to the meeting, Ngeze kept on saying "remember, remember" and would hold up two fingers close to his nose. It was his way of saying that the party was exclusively for pure-blooded Hutus. Witness ABE recalled seeing in Rwandan newspapers a cartoon of a gorilla with two fingers in its nose, and it was said that if someone did not have a nose like that he could not participate in the CDR.'

with an identity card showing him to be a Hutu would most probably not be working undercover for the RPF. This is, perhaps, what the presenter meant to suggest — look for the RPF among the minority Tutsi. Nevertheless, the presenter does stray from his already disagreeable path — and he strays twice. He seems to say that the Inkotanyi should be eliminated *because* they are Tutsi; and he seems to call on his audience to kill everyone denoted by the physical stereotype, that is, every Tutsi — as if every Tutsi might be an Inkotanyi. Overall there is ambiguity, but no doubt it is too close for comfort. Perhaps in this specific instance a case of direct and public incitement to commit genocide brought against the presenter *himself* would succeed, although something more would be needed to net the radio's director. (A series of such broadcasts with evidence that the director knew about them and did nothing to stop them, would certainly come within reach of the Streicher precedent.)

The next example of an insolent and dangerous broadcast is from 31 May 1994, also late in the war, long after the mass killings of civilians had wound down. The presenter says:

He [General Dallaire, the head of the UN peacekeeping force in Rwanda] is a pretentious fellow. Simply, I told him that his favorite ethnic group, known as the Inyenzi-Inkotanyi, Tutsis, will disappear from the face of the earth in the end. We then had a discussion and a Senegalese soldier who was there separated us, but I told them in no uncertain terms that a minority ethnic group, which commits suicide by declaring war on the majority ethnic group will end up by disappearing once and for all, because it's committing mass suicide. I don't know whether Dallaire will tell his friends about it, but it's inevitable.[181]

The first passage we examined called on its audience to act. This second one does not. It is in the form of an opinion. If it is incitement at all, it is not particularly 'direct'. But there are other problems with the tribunal's reliance on this passage.

In a footnote the judges noted, without comment, that Nahimana had objected to the formulation 'known as the Inyenzi-Inkotanyi, Tutsis', on the ground that in the original utterance the last word was, according to Nahimana, rendered adjectivally, and thus the translation should have been 'known as the Tutsi Inyenzi-Inkotanyi'. This adds significantly to the overall ambiguity of the passage. We might assume that the defendant's objection was overruled, but if so, it is not clear on what basis this was done (none of the judges had any knowledge of Kinyarwanda), or why the objection was allowed to stand in a footnote to the translated text. The consequence is that the qualification introduced by Nahimana lingers over the face of the text.

For a case which turned not on physical acts, but on the semantics of Kinyarwanda utterances, the Nahimana judgment betrays a complete lack of sophistication in matters of translation and cultural difference. In commenting on an RTLM broadcast from 2 July 1994, which enjoined listeners to, among other things, 'sing "Come, let us rejoice: the Inkotanyi have been exterminated! Come dear friends, let us rejoice, the Good Lord is just",'[182] and which was — even to the tribunal's one-track mind — mostly just about wiping out the RPF rebels, the tribunal said: 'These references are evocative of combatants, not civilians. For this reason they might suggest an association

---

[181] *Nahimana et al.* trial judgment, para. 432.   [182] Ibid., para. 403.

with the RPF rather than with the Tutsi population as a whole, *although the word "extermination" is one generally associated with civilians rather than military operations.*[183] In the *Nahimana* judgment, as is apparent from this last comment, a catch is never too small. Here the tribunal reels in the item in evidence just as we have come to believe that it has been judged to be inconsequential and will be let go.

The problem in this instance is, of course, that the tribunal's claim that 'the word "extermination" is one generally associated with civilians rather than military operations' shows that the tribunal is thinking English semantics, not Kinyarwanda semantics. This interpretative error could have been avoided had the tribunal remained alert to its unusually difficult task: to pass judgment, in English, on alleged incitement, in Kinyarwanda, before defendants who were following the proceedings in Kinyarwanda or French translation, before defence counsel who were following in English or French translation, using texts which are (plainly) second-rate English translations which were based on French translations of the original Kinyarwanda audio recordings.[184] An acknowledgement of this extraordinary situation and its attendant dangers is nowhere to be found in the *Nahimana* judgment. This is inexcusable in a case decided on shades of meaning, in which, moreover, the prosecutor was not able to arrange for a single witness to testify that he or she was incited by appeals or hints, such as those examined here, to commit genocide.

Even if one were to accept Nahimana's correction to the second RTLM passage quoted above, the presenter's remarks do cut very close to the bone. It is, on its face, a warning to the 'minority ethnic group' to desist from its war on the 'majority ethnic group', or face annihilation. This can be read in two ways, as incitement to commit genocide or as a comment on the hopelessness of the rebels' cause. Five days later, on 5 June 1994, RTLM snarled:

Our country, the Tutsi clique has plunged it into mourning; [...] Thus when day breaks, when that day comes, we will be heading for a brighter future, for the day when we will be able to say 'There isn't a single Inyenzi left in the country'. The term Inyenzi will then be forever forgotten, and disappear for good... that will only be possible if we continue exterminating them at the same pace. As we have told you time and again, it would be unimaginable for this clique, which does not make up 1%, to drive us out of the country and rule it.[185]

The tribunal made no connection between this broadcast and the one above, from 31 May, even though the latter is relevant to understanding the former. The 'Tutsi clique', which in size is not even equal to 1 per cent of the country's population, is undoubtedly a reference to the RPF. Surely it is suicide — we understand the presenter to be saying — for this clique to continue to fight, when it is so decisively outnumbered. This is the radio's bravura, in the face of imminent defeat, but it is not a call to genocide.[186]

---

[183] Ibid., para. 404, emphasis added.

[184] At the ICTR, due to a shortage of Kinyarwanda-to-English interpreters, the evidence of Kinyarwanda-speaking witnesses is first translated into French; the French translation is then fed into the French-to-English interpretation booth. The judges thus receive the oral translation of an oral translation.

[185] *Nahimana et al.* trial judgment, para. 405.

[186] See also the broadcast from 30 May 1994, to the same effect, at ibid., para. 395. For the tribunal, however, a cigar is never just a cigar, as its commentary on the quoted passage shows (para. 407): 'The Chamber considers that in reference to the context of what was happening at the time, the number of Tutsi civilians who had

There is a third and very nasty RTLM broadcast quoted in the *Nahimana* judgment, from 23 May, the mid point in the war:

Let me congratulate thousands and thousands of young men I've seen this morning on the road in Kigali doing their military training to fight the Inkotanyi . . . At all costs, all Inkotanyi have to be exterminated, in all areas of our country. Whether they reach at the airport or somewhere else, but they should leave their lives on the spot. That's the way things should be . . . Some (passengers) [*sic*] may pretext that they are refugees, others act like patients and other like sick-nurses. Watch them closely, because Inkotanyi's tricks are so many . . . Does it mean that we have to go in refugee camps to look for people whose children joined the RPA [that is, RPF] and kill them? I think we should do it like that. We should also go in refugee camps in the neighbouring countries and kill those who sent their children within the RPA. I think it's not possible to do that. However, if the Inkotanyi keep on acting like that, we will ask for those whose children joined the RPA among those who will have come from exile and kill them. Because if we have to follow the principle of an eye for an eye, we'll react.[187]

We have here a crystal-clear call on RTLM listeners to commit a crime against humanity (which, technically, is the killing of innocent civilians as part of a widespread or systematic attack upon them). What the presenter expresses is comparable to the instantly recognizable model incitement experience we discussed at the start, which has little to gain in sharpness from the explanations of a lawyer. The presenter invites his audience to hunt down and kill the parents of RPF recruits. We know that RPF agents operating inside Rwanda in the years prior to the 1994 war secretly recruited hundreds of young men to the rebels' ranks. When the recruits finally joined the rebels, disappearing from their villages overnight, everyone got to know which families they came from.[188] The broadcast in effect is telling you to go into your neighbour's house — and into other houses in your village from which the RPF is known to have recruited — and to kill its elderly occupants.

However appalling this instance of incitement, it is not a Streicherean case of incitement to commit genocide. The vengeful words target those who are perceived as having contributed to the RPF's strength — persons of supposedly split allegiances whose treachery must be addressed with the machete. But the words do not target the Tutsi ethnic group as such. They cannot, therefore, support an inference beyond reasonable doubt to the existence of genocidal intent in the maker of the utterance.

actually been killed by then, the Inyenzi who it was said could be forever forgotten "if we continue exterminating them at the same pace" could well have been understood as a reference to the Tutsi population as a whole. This understanding would be based, however, not on any language intrinsic to the text but rather [on] a juxtaposition of the phrase referencing the extermination of the Inyenzi to the external context, the fact that the Tutsi population was being exterminated, as well as the fact that other broadcasts equated the term Inyenzi with Tutsi.' This tendentious interpretation is not supported by the recorded broadcasts, which, far from 'equating' the Inyenzi with the Tutsi, nearly always distinguish them, often for the purpose of warning the latter not to give support to the former, as in the following broadcast from 14 May 1994 (para. 398): 'Which is the numerically weak family in Rwanda? It is the Inkotanyi family, because for it is a groupuscule [*sic*] which stems from those known as Tutsis. The Tutsis are very few in number. They were initially estimated at 10%, but the war must have reduced that figure to 8%. Will they really continue to commit suicide by locking horns with people who are by far numerically superior to them?'

[187] Ibid., para. 425.
[188] See the *Bagilishema* trial judgment, paras 123 ff. for more information on the RPF's recruitment activities.

RTLM radio often directed its attacks against individuals, taking its populist 'investigative journalism', which distinguished it from the dull programming of Radio Rwanda, one odious step further, transforming itself into a kind of bush radio for the vigilantes. In March 1994 (a month prior to the commencement of the war) it said:

> There are others who have become Inkotanyi, Marc Zuberi, good day Marc Zuberi (laughter), Marc Zuberi was a banana hauler in Kibungo. With money from the Inkotanyi he has just built himself a huge house there.[189]

The ICTR Trial Chamber seized on this development, concluding that the evidence 'indicates a pattern of naming people on vague suspicion, without articulated grounds, or in those cases where the grounds were articulated they were highly speculative or in some cases entirely unfounded. In these cases, the only common element is the Tutsi ethnicity of the persons named, and the evidence in some cases clearly indicates that their ethnicity was in fact the reason they were named.'[190]

These words are an indictment not of RTLM but of the tribunal, which by this stage in its judgment seems to have forgotten that RTLM was accused not of sloppy investigative journalism but of direct and public incitement to commit genocide. In criminal matters the burden is always on the prosecutor to prove the allegation, which in this instance is that the named person, Marc Zuberi, was not in fact an Inkotanyi. By censuring RTLM for not having given proper reasons, the Court shifted the burden to the defence. The presenter may not have stated his basis, but no stated basis is not the same as no basis at all.

Perhaps the most remarkable of all the Trial Chamber's glosses on RTLM broadcasts is its condemnation of the station for the station's censure of the RPF's use of child soldiers in the war. The tribunal quotes an RTLM presenter as saying:

> Some moments ago, I was late due to a small Inkotanyi captured in Kimisagara. It is a minor Inkotanyi aged 14. I don't know whether he is not less than that. So Inkotanyi who may be in Gatsata or Gisozi were using this small dirty Inkotanyi with big ears who would come with a jerrican pretending to go to fetch water but he was observing the guns of our soldiers, where roadblocks are set and people on roadblocks and signal this after. It is clear therefore, we have been saying this for a long time, that this Inkotanyi's tactic to use a child who doesn't know their objective making him understand that they will pay him studies; that they will buy him a car and make him do for their war activities, carry ammunitions on the head for them. And give him a machine to shoot on the road any passenger while they have gone to dig out potatoes. Truly speaking it is unprecedented wickedness to use children during the war, because you know that a child doesn't know anything.[191]

Child soldiers are hardly a rarity in Africa. It is not known for certain whether the RPF recruited children for its attack on Rwanda in April–July 1994, but the rebels did fight as dirty as any armed group in that part of Africa,[192] so it certainly is a possibility. But the

---

[189] *Nahimana et al.* trial judgment, para. 375.   [190] Ibid., para. 1026.   [191] Ibid., para. 413.
[192] See A. Zahar and S. Rohol, 'The International Criminal Tribunal for Rwanda', in S. Totten (ed.), *Genocide at the Millennium: A Critical Bibliographic Review* (Transaction, 2005), pp. 209–39. All efforts to prosecute RPF members for war crimes before the ICTR have been blocked by the Rwandan government.

Court's commentary on the above passage is disbelieving and burden-reversing: 'This broadcast linked a small child to espionage without citing any evidence that the child was doing anything other than fetching water and looking around . . . RTLM promoted the idea that [RPF] accomplices were everywhere.'[193] In light of the new liability threshold created here by the ICTR, a patriotic radio which fails to shut itself down prior to a war is leaving itself wide open to postwar prosecution for criminal incitement.

Kangura did shut itself down prior to the war, but this somehow was not enough to save Ngeze from a life sentence. It must be said that *Kangura* did nothing to lessen the tensions inside Rwanda prior to the war. It was a Hutu-nationalist rag, hateful of the RPF and the threat it posed to what Ngeze saw as the glorious Hutu revolution of 1959, when the masses threw off the Tutsi yoke, founded the Republic, regained their dignity, and set Rwanda on the path to modernity. Ngeze attempted to blend Hutu chauvinism with democratic institutions — '*Kangura* is not denying the Tutsis or the Twa the right to form their own democratic political parties or associations . . . With our democratic Hutu movement which we wish to be born, we hope to hear a new slogan: Long live Diversity!'[194] — but succeeded only in stamping out the latter. In pushing the agenda of Hutu survival, *Kangura* felt no compunction about sowing doubt about the trustworthiness of Rwanda's Tutsi population:

when it comes to spying, the Inkotanyi enlist the help of their worldly sisters and daughters. You find them everywhere in all the institutions, in the Ministries, in the private sector, in legal and illegal drinking-places, as well as in our own houses, which many of them have managed to infiltrate through marriage. Having husbands does not prevent them from being accomplices and extracting secrets from people by using their worldly wiles. Hutus do not abuse others, they are taken advantage of. The Hutus must understand that they are not all waging the war as the Tutsis, because everyone can see that, the Tutsis want to regain the power that was taken from them by the Hutus. If you look closely, you will see that 85% of the Tutsis who live in the country are somehow linked with the refugees from which come the Inyenzi-Inkotanyi who attack us.[195]

This piece of paranoid drivel from July 1991 is typical not only of *Kangura*'s tone, but more generally of the level of civility (or lack thereof) in Rwandan public discourse at the time. Rwanda was a society with loudly racist elements. In this and other passages *Kangura* glides from the subject of the RPF to the subject of a fifth column inside the country. The *Nahimana* judgment would have us believe that, by April 1994, *Kangura* and RTLM had succeeded in collapsing the notions of 'Inyenzi-Inkotanyi' and 'Tutsi' into one indivisible whole in the minds of their audiences, so that the wartime calls to exterminate the Inyenzi-Inkotanyi were semantically equivalent to incitement to commit genocide against the Tutsi.[196]

The main reason why this theory never gets off the ground is that it is, finally, *Kangura* and RTLM which insist on maintaining the distinction between the Inyenzi-Inkotanyi and the Tutsi.[197] These 'media' were nothing if not realistic when it came to

---

[193] *Nahimana et al.* trial judgment, para. 413.   [194] Ibid., para. 186.
[195] Ibid., para. 177.   [196] See ibid., para. 473.
[197] Nahimana, a history professor, explained the meaning of 'Inyenzi' in an RTLM broadcast on 20 November 1993, distinguishing the Inyenzi from the resident Tutsi population (ibid., para. 357): 'There is no difference

the true source of the danger to the Republic; they were nothing if not pragmatic about the need to maintain a vigilant, or in any case vigilantist, law-and-order within the country, so as to deal with the ruthlessly efficient external forces. Both *Kangura* and RTLM sensed very well that if a minimum level of internal control were not maintained, or if central control were finally to collapse under pressure from the RPF, the resulting destruction would be universal.[198]

The continuing distinction between the Inyenzi-Inkotanyi and the Tutsi is evident practically in every *Kangura* and RTLM excerpt cited by the tribunal. Neither of these opinionated outlets felt anything but contempt for the Tutsi, as a collectivity, as a historical identity, if not as individuals. But there is a wide gap between the expression of such contempt — what the *Nahimana* judgment calls 'ethnic resentment' — and direct and public incitement to commit genocide. It is *this* charge, not some looser notion of aiding and abetting genocide, which must be made out on the evidence.

The *Nahimana* judgment's discussion of what it considers the applicable jurisprudence is problematic. Critics have already attacked this aspect of the judgment.[199] The trial court reiterated the *Akayesu* judgment's *ex cathedra* pronouncements on incitement law and reviewed at length human-rights cases from the UN and European systems.[200] The latter are only marginally relevant to the charge of direct and public incitement to commit genocide. The only conclusion of any note is that causation between the act of incitement and resulting crimes need not be proved (correcting the ambiguity in *Akayesu*).[201] There is also an obscure paragraph, which on the one hand acknowledges the general irrelevance of the human-rights jurisprudence cited by the Trial Chamber, and on the other hand draws a conclusion from that same jurisprudence, that where the incitement is used by a state against a minority living within the state's borders, the threshold for incitement is lower:

the Chamber considers that the 'wider margin of appreciation' given in European Court cases to government discretion in its restriction of expression that constitutes incitement to violence should be adapted to the circumstance of this case. At issue is not a challenged restriction of expression but the expression itself. Moreover, the expression charged as incitement to violence was situated, in fact and at the time by its speakers, not as a threat to national security but rather in defence of national security, aligning it with state power rather than in opposition to it. Thus there is justification for adaptation of the application of international standards, which have

---

between the RPF and the Inyenzi because the Inyenzi are refugees who fled Rwanda after the mass majority Revolution of 1959, the fall of the monarchy and the establishment of a democratic Republic. Those who refused the Republic and the democracy went into self-imposed exile. Not long after, between 1962 and 1967, those refugees tried to replace the new Republic by the former monarchy. They launched attacks that killed people. However, Rwanda had then a national army, the national guard. Those sons of the nation did their best and drove those attacks out and in 1967, the Inyenzi stopped their attacks . . . You understand that the RPF that attacked us is made of those people, has its origin in those Tutsis who fled in 1959, those who attacked us until 1967. So, they got organized and named themselves RPF.'

[198] See, for example, the texts cited in *Nahimana et al.* trial judgment, paras 225, 400.

[199] See, for example, H. R. Davidson, 'The International Criminal Tribunal for Rwanda's Decision in *The Prosecutor* v. *Ferdinand Nahimana et al.*: The Past, Present, and Future of International Incitement Law' (2004) 17 *Leiden J. Int'l L.* 505.　　　　　　　　　　[200] *Nahimana et al.* trial judgment, paras 983–99, 1011–15.

[201] Ibid., para. 1007.

evolved to protect the right of the government to defend itself from incitement to violence by others against it, rather than incitement to violence on its behalf against others, particularly as in this case when the others are members of a minority group.[202]

Yet substantive law is not the *Nahimana* judgment's most serious error. The provision in the Genocide Convention codifying the crime (now a part of customary international law) enjoys a plain meaning, both as an everyday concept (incitement) and as a legal term of art, with Streicher's example providing the historical reference point. There was little left for the ICTR to say about the substantive offence.

Where the 'media judgment' fails is in convincing us that any one of the passages it cites — tasteless, vile, and occasionally criminal though they might be — unambiguously incites genocide. The tribunal often drifts into condemnation of the media for failing to take a robust stance *against* genocide.[203] But that is not what this case was meant to be about. It was not a question of complicity, but of direct and public incitement. The most disturbing texts, which number less than half a dozen, are from late in the war. The absence of an outright call to commit genocide against the Tutsi in the critical month of April 1994 is a point on which scholars of the period, who have staked so much on the postulate of *Kangura* and RTLM as the driving forces of genocide, ought to reflect further.

The ICTR's findings that Nahimana, Barayagwiza, and Ngeze are guilty of direct and public incitement to commit genocide[204] are unsustainable on the evidence. The sources of the ICTR's errors have been mentioned before in this book: the international judiciary is not checked by a legislature or by a normative and textured tradition of international criminal justice; basic legal concepts remain ill-defined; and some tribunal judges have been inexperienced not only in international criminal law (which is understandable) but in criminal litigation generally. All this, coupled with a prevailing sense that a new world order is being forged, in which impunity for large-scale atrocities in armed conflict is eradicated, has facilitated legal activism.[205]

---

[202] Ibid., para. 1009.

[203] See, for example, ibid., paras 419–20, where RTLM's exhortation of its listeners that 'Your neighbour is not our adversary, simply because he is this or that other way. You know our adversaries. No one should be victimized on account of his appearance, no one should be victimized because of his height, people should be judged based only for their acts' (25 June 1994) is dismissed by the tribunal as merely 'politically correct'. Also merely politically correct, we are told, is this broadcast from 15 May 1994 (para. 423): 'Whenever the RPF fights us, we consider him as our enemy, the enemy of all Rwandans, whenever it attacks us and fights us we consider him as such and we fight him like that. The reason why I say that the enemy is the RPF is to distinguish it with another who they call an enemy although he is not really an enemy. You are asked to train and explain to the population to avoid whatever can lead them to fight each other because of their ethnic groups. Some people think that a person of different ethnic groups is your enemy. To be an enemy he must belong to RPF . . . A Tutsi, a Hutu, a Twa who is not a RPF soldier is not our enemy we cannot say that the one who is from a different ethnic group is our enemy, the one from another region is our enemy.' [204] See ibid., paras 1033, 1034, and 1038.

[205] This section is based on an article by A. Zahar, 'The ICTR's "Media" Judgment and the Reinvention of Direct and Public Incitement to Commit Genocide' (2005) 16 *Crim. L. Forum* 33. While our criticism of the *Nahimana et al.* judgment is focused on the Trial Chamber's use of the texts allegedly evidencing incitement, the student is encouraged to explore other weaknesses in the judgment, such as the finding that Nahimana and Barayagwiza had 'command responsibility' for RTLM radio and its output during the relevant period; see *Nahimana et al.* judgment, paras 1033–4.

5.4 CONCLUSION

With regard to the range of crimes by which genocide may be committed, the case law of the tribunals is at the present time limited to the interpretation and application of Article II(a) of the Convention (the underlying crime of killing members of the group), even though the wording of Article II(b) (serious bodily or mental harm) has come up in passing. By contrast, most forms of participation (Article III of the Convention), except for attempt, have been dealt with, to some extent, in the case law. The bulk of the work on genocide has been performed at the ICTR. The subject has been emotionally and politically charged, with the result that genocide law rests on weak foundations and is inconsistent.

6

RISE TO PROMINENCE OF CRIMES AGAINST HUMANITY AND CODIFICATION OF 'ETHNIC CLEANSING'

6.1 INTRODUCTION

The recent history of the law of crimes against humanity begins with the *Tadić* trial judgment of May 1997. This law and its application to facts have received an enormous amount of judicial attention since that time, with hundreds of counts considered at the ad hoc tribunals, more than for any other category of crime. The notion of 'ethnic cleansing' — non-technical, but also singularly apt as a general characterization of the outcome and the purpose of the Yugoslav wars — finds a conceptual home in the law of crimes against humanity, for it is synonymous with persecution.[1] Major ICTY judgments, such as the *Krajišnik* judgment of September 2006 describing ethnic cleansing in Bosnia-Herzegovina, are focused entirely on crimes against humanity. Within the class of crimes against humanity, the crime of persecution is a unifying notion. It is the picture that emerges from the concurrence of several lesser crimes, such as armed attack on civilians, unlawful detention, cruel treatment, and forced transfer of civilians, as well as precursory or ancillary acts, such as ethnic vilification and discriminatory propaganda, dismissal from employment, and restrictions on movement, this latter group of acts serving generally as an introduction to the more violent forms of persecution. Whereas war crimes are amenable to piecemeal treatment (as when a member of an armed force with an otherwise law-abiding individual or collective record commits a war crime), and genocide is an all-too-specific and exceptional offence, crimes against humanity capture the broad middle ground of criminal activity in cases where the civilian population and non-combatants more generally are systematically victimized in the course of an armed conflict, as happened, for example, in Bosnia-Herzegovina, Rwanda, East Timor, Sierra Leone, and Darfur.

The law of crimes against humanity which has emerged from the tribunals is only as secure as its foundations. While this proposition verges on being a truism, and is true of all tribunal law, it captures a theme, or critical approach, that runs through this book. It is not a proposition without alternatives. There are those who prefer a more pragmatic assessment of the practice of international criminal law in the last decade. The pragmatists will say that the momentum, internal coherence, and general acceptance of tribunal law since 1995 is an argument for its legitimacy. Pre-1995 procedural and substantive law might be obscure or worse, but this does not mean that tribunal law is baseless — for it *works*, and it works with international consensus, and not only for the ICTY and the ICTR but also for the several institutions that have been modelled on the original tribunals. For pragmatists, the basis of contemporary international criminal law to a large extent *is* just the 1995–2005 case law.

It would be churlish to say that the pragmatists' argument is question begging, because this is the mark of pragmatism. If a legal system functions more or less smoothly, and if it is generally accepted, then it is legitimate, even if it has no historical depth, is expedient, and made on the fly. Lack of *that* kind of foundation is not tantamount to a lack of legitimacy in the pragmatists' view. Witness the hold Nuremberg has had on the popular imagination, despite what scholars might say about victors' justice and the other shortcomings of that process. In international criminal law, where there is no constitution, there is intuition about what is right and what is wrong. Pragmatism would have us brush aside the dominant rhetoric of the tribunals, namely the principle of legality, and simply accept what works.

Despite the availability of this alternative view, we prefer the proposition that tribunal law must, in the first place, be assessed with reference to its foundations. The

---

[1] The UN Secretary-General, in discussing crimes against humanity, wrote that 'In the conflict in the territory of the former Yugoslavia, such inhumane acts have taken the form of so-called "ethnic cleansing" and widespread and systematic rape and other forms of sexual assault, including enforced prostitution' (Report of the Secretary-General on ICTY, para. 48).

creation or discovery of legal principles by tribunal judges judges should be identified for what it is in the course of a piecemeal critical analysis. Where there is a fog of legality, this should also be identified. Pragmatism may well be the only realistic response to many questions of legitimacy, but it is a philosophy that has nothing to say about those situations where actual foundations in prior law are found to exist.

6.2 THE EARLY DECISIONS

A convenient starting point for an enquiry into the foundations of the contemporary law of crimes against humanity is the October 1995 jurisdiction appeal decision in the *Tadić* case. As noted there by the ICTY Appeals Chamber, the law of crimes against humanity originates in Second World War case law.[2] In particular, Article 6(c) of the Nuremberg Tribunal's 1945 Charter defines crimes against humanity as murder, extermination, enslavement, deportation, 'and other inhumane acts committed against any civilian population, before or during the war; or persecutions on political, racial or religious grounds in execution of or in connection with any crime within the jurisdiction of the Tribunal, whether or not in violation of the domestic law of the country where perpetrated'.

The IMT's provision was novel, awkward in its formulation (very much a compromise solution, it seems), and duplicative insofar as it overlaps with the Charter's provision on war crimes (in particular the war crime of 'ill-treatment or deportation to slave labor or for any other purpose of civilian population of or in occupied territory'). On its face, Article 6(c) of the Charter afforded jurisdiction to punish any serious crime against civilian populations by the defeated powers, irrespective of time of commission.

From the pespective of a later age, when vague enactments are out of favour, the IMT's provision is simplistic. For example, it introduced, circumscribed, but failed to further define the notion of persecution, a shortcoming that, as we shall see, has given the tribunals of today a free hand to develop and expand the law to fit the circumstances of the end-of-century Balkan and Rwandan wars and the requirements of contemporary morality.

The IMT in its judgment did not define or explore the legal foundations of crimes against humanity, preferring what was perhaps felt to be a robust, pragmatic approach to the question. Alternatively, the silence may reflect a preference not to draw attention to the novelty of the idea. The Tribunal read down the plain meaning of Article 6(c) of the Charter — it said that 'To constitute crimes against humanity, the acts relied on before the outbreak of war must have been in execution of, or in connection with, any crime within the jurisdiction of the Tribunal'[3] — found that no such crimes had been shown to have been committed in that connection, and proceeded to create a scheme

---

[2] *Tadić* jurisdiction appeal decision, para. 107 (quoting the Report of the Secretary-General on ICTY, paras 47–8); also *Tadić* trial judgment, para. 618.   [3] 22 IMT Judgment 498.

in which crimes against humanity were to be those crimes falling outside the better understood category of war crimes:

insofar as the inhumane acts charged in the Indictment, and committed after the beginning of the war, did not constitute war crimes, they were all committed in execution of, or in connection with, the aggressive war, and therefore constituted crimes against humanity.[4]

This negative definition is doubly unhelpful, since the elements of war crimes are themselves nowhere accurately articulated in the IMT judgment. The result is that whatever might distinguish a crime against humanity from a war crime is not clear in a precise legal sense. Moreover, the IMT did not specifically distinguish war crimes from crimes against humanity in its findings,[5] meaning that it is finally for the reader to decide if there is a difference. At times the difference seems to come down to a lack of any nexus with the ongoing armed conflict, as for example in the case of the German SS and their role in the persecution of Jews:

Himmler wanted to rotate guard battalions so that all members of the SS would be instructed as to the proper attitude to take to inferior races. After 1942, when the concentration camps were placed under the control of the WVHA, they were used as a source of slave labor.... The evacuation of the Jews from occupied territories was carried out under the directions of the SS with the assistance of SS Police units. The extermination of the Jews was carried out under the direction of the SS central organizations. It was actually put into effect by SS formations. The Einsatzgruppen engaged in wholesale massacres of the Jews. SS Police units were also involved. For example, the massacre of Jews in the Warsaw ghetto was carried out under the directions of SS Brigadeführer and Major General of the Police Stroop. A special group from the SS central organization arranged for the deportation of Jews from various Axis satellites, and their extermination was carried out in the concentration camps run by the WVHA.[6]

Included here are the key notions of murder, extermination, enslavement, and deportation, crimes committed against a civilian population of 'inferior race'. The acts had no acceptable military purpose, and, for the most part, were not even incidental to military action. That, today, is the core idea of persecution, but the IMT's superficial approach to the new offence category of crimes against humanity cannot be sidestepped, and any suggestion that the law of today rests on the foundation of Second World War case law is wishful thinking. The IMT's cornerstone is superciliousness, not legal analysis, which is to be expected of a victors' court applying *ex post facto* law without the possibility of appeal. The raft created by the IMT gave the Supreme Court of Israel something to hold on to in the 1962 *Eichmann* case, even though its gratitude to the IMT was qualified. The Israeli court reconceptualized the Charter crimes, remarking that war crimes, genocide, and crimes against humanity are 'interdependent, and

---

[4] Ibid.

[5] The only significant exceptions are found in the sections discussing the responsibility of Julius Streicher and Baldur von Schirach. The IMT said that Streicher's incitement to murder and extermination at the time when Jews in the East were being killed 'clearly constitutes persecution on political and racial grounds in connection with War Crimes', meaning that it was a crime against humanity in the terms of the Charter (ibid., p. 549). As for von Schirach, he was convicted for the deportation to the East of Vienna's Jews (ibid., pp. 564–6).

[6] Ibid., pp. 514–15.

we may, therefore, for the purpose of our reasoning at this stage, group them within the broad category of "crimes against humanity" '.[7]

Despite the absence of a foundation for the Nuremberg case law, the *Tadić* Appeals Chamber proceeded on the assumption that the law of crimes against humanity had, by 1995, been elevated to *customary law*,[8] that realm of true law which has been postulated by the ad hoc tribunals, often drawn upon, but barely ever explained (see Chapter 3).

The *Tadić* Trial Chamber did attempt to find some support for the Appeals Chamber's original contention about the law's customary status. The Trial Chamber started off frankly, if inauspiciously, with the remark that the IMT, in taking on crimes against humanity, had created a 'new' crime category. A footnote reference directs the reader to a book by Antonio Cassese from 1988.[9] There is little elaboration,[10] with the result that questions as to the entitlement of the Allies to create new crimes, and the repercussions of such action for future utilization of the new categories, are left to the reader to consider. The Trial Chamber resiled from the observation, which is evident to any lawyer reading the IMT judgment, that nowhere does the judgment define crimes against humanity, except, as noted above, by way of a passing contrast with war crimes. The Trial Chamber's adoption of the IMT's question-begging and self-serving assessment of its Charter as being 'the expression of international law existing at the time of its creation',[11] is an expression of deference unaccompanied by legal analysis.[12]

The *Tadić* Trial Chamber wrote[13] that the prohibition of crimes against humanity was affirmed by the UN General Assembly in a 1946 resolution[14] and then 'confirmed' by the International Law Commission in a 1950 report.[15] These observations are inaccurate. At the end of 1946 the General Assembly had just 53 members. It was dominated by the former Allies. And while this is not to say that its pronouncements on international law may be ignored today, the weight to be given to them must be in proportion to the stature of the world body at the time, and should take account of the political climate at the time. As for the ILC in 1950, it explicitly *refrained* from considering whether the principles in the IMT Charter and judgment constituted principles of international law. It explained that since the Nuremberg principles had been affirmed by the General Assembly, the task entrusted to the ILC was not to express any appreciation of those principles as principles of international law, but merely to formulate them. So it proceeded to formulate them. The jurisprudential weight of that exercise in abstraction is precisely zero. It serves only as a reminder that, a good five

---

[7] *Attorney General of Israel* v. *Eichmann*, 36 ILR 277, 287.

[8] *Tadić* jurisdiction appeal decision, paras 141–2.   [9] *Tadić* trial judgment, para. 618.

[10] See, ibid., paras 619–20.   [11] 22 IMT Judgment 461; *Tadić* trial judgment, para. 620.

[12] The same unexplained deference to the IMT was expressed in 1962 by the Supreme Court of Israel in *Attorney General of Israel* v. *Eichmann*, 36 ILR 277, 294, and in 1989 by a judge of the High Court of Canada in *R.* v. *Finta*, 82 ILR 424, 439.   [13] *Tadić* trial judgment, para. 621.

[14] Resolution 95(I), Affirmation of the Principles of International Law Recognized by the Charter of the Nürenberg Tribunal, 11 December 1946.

[15] *Yearbook of the International Law Commission 1950*, Vol. II, pp. 374–8.

years after the London Agreement, a need was still felt to formulate the principles pursuant to which the leadership of Germany had been tried.

In addition to the aforementioned sources, the *Tadić* Trial Chamber found nothing more significant to cite than the UN Secretary-General's 1993 framework report on the ICTY. The pronouncements of the UN's chief executive are often accorded significant weight, but they are not directly authoritative sources of international law, and since the Secretary-General's report merely asserted the foundational status of the IMT Charter and judgment for crimes against humanity, without a word of analysis,[16] the Trial Chamber should have declined to rely on it at all.

Other cited 'confirmations' of the customary-law status of the prohibition of crimes against humanity are so lacking in authority or relevance that the *Tadić* judgment confines them to a footnote.[17]

Upon these weak sources the *Tadić* court rested its finding that 'since the Nürnberg Charter, the customary status of the prohibition against crimes against humanity and the attribution of individual criminal responsibility for their commission have not been seriously questioned'.[18] Certainly, no questioning is ever undertaken, or even considered, by the Trial Chamber.

May the law of crimes against humanity be characterized as customary international law? The ICJ Statute ('international custom, as evidence of a general practice accepted as law')[19] gives the general, accepted conditions for the establishment of a customary rule of law: existence of a general practice of states, and acceptance of that practice as law by states (see Chapter 3). This is an elegant statement, simple without being simplistic. Principle must be rooted in practice, it says, and the practice must be general and necessitated by law.[20]

Crimes against humanity have seen very little state practice since Nuremberg and the lesser Second World War trials. *Tadić* does not rely on any case law to establish the proposition that the rules governing this category of crime had, by the early 1990s, achieved customary status. In the little state practice there is, the law is in a state of flux. The French *Barbie* case, decided in 1984, is a case in point. The Court of Cassation of France purported to give the 'meaning' of Article 6(c) of the IMT Charter, in what amounted to a new definition of crimes against humanity:

inhumane acts and persecution committed in a systematic manner in the name of a State practising a policy of ideological supremacy, not only against persons by reason of their membership of a racial or religious community, but also against the opponents of that policy, whatever the form of their opposition.[21]

---

[16] Report of the Secretary-General on ICTY, para. 47. [17] *Tadić* trial judgment, para. 622, fn. 104.
[18] Ibid., para. 623. [19] ICJ Statute, Art. 38(1)(b).
[20] This is preferable to the formulation found in human-rights conventions, as in Article 7 of the ECHR, which echoes Article 38(1)(c) of the ICJ Statute: 'This article shall not prejudice the trial and punishment of any person for any act or omission which, at the time when it was committed, was criminal according to the general principles of law recognized by civilized nations.' The threshold here is much lower, and while the principle might be serviceable in a system in which there is a legislature to limit the law-making activities of the courts, it is not a threshold that the ad hoc tribunals in the laissez-faire environment of international criminal practice should be allowed to appropriate to themselves.
[21] *Fédération Nationale des Déportés et Internés Résistants et Patriotes and Others* v. *Barbie*, 78 ILR 125, 137.

The element of *supremacist* policy seems foreign to a mind attuned to the later jurisprudence of the ICTY,[22] even though 'policy' was an element in some of the early ad hoc tribunal decisions (as discussed below). But the point about *Barbie* is the fluidity of the notion of crimes against humanity as late as 1984, a fact acknowledged by the French Advocate General, who had made submissions before the court for an unrestricted definition of the victim class of the crime: 'I freely admit that it was a thankless task to have to deduce a rule, just as it is a thankless task for this Court today to fix the principle. . . . To my knowledge it is the first occasion when a supreme court anywhere in the world has been called upon to give a precise definition of crimes against humanity.'[23] (We shall further discuss the victim-class issue, as well as the *Barbie* case, in the next section.)

Shortly after *Barbie* was decided, a US District Court was seized of an action for damages for the alleged involvement of the defendant in atrocities, including crimes against humanity, against the Jewish population of Yugoslavia during the Second World War.[24] One question was whether such a claim could arise under US law. For this it was necessary, according to the court, to show an express or implied grant of a right of action. The plaintiff argued that a right of action could be inferred from international law. The court disagreed. To imply a cause of action from international law would, in the court's words, 'completely defeat the critical right of the sovereign to determine whether and how international rights should be enforced in that municipality'.[25] International law does not determine, at the state level, the actionability of conduct condemned by that body of law.[26] It was for the US Congress to give effect to the substantive international law concerning crimes against humanity. The fact that the US had not done so by the mid-1980s is another indication of the poverty of relevant state practice at the onset of the Yugoslav wars in the early 1990s. In Canada, the drawn-out litigation and extensive judicial disagreement in the *Finta* case argues for the same conclusion.[27]

How is it, then, that an international bench of judges, such as that in the *Tadić* case, will proceed as if on solid legal ground in a case where the attentive reader sees no support at all? The explanation of intellectual feebleness is too reductive if limited to the level of individuals in the system (the authors will not undertake here a discussion of the inappropriateness of certain judicial appointments). At the systemic level, however, it is accurate. The feebleness of the system is the direct result of conflicts of interest built into it. The deleterious results are plain to see in the foundational decisions of the ad hoc tribunals in the *Tadić* and *Akayesu* cases. These decisions are intellectual compromises.

---

[22] It has been suggested that the element of supremacist policy was inserted by France into the definition of crimes against humanity in order to exonerate, in advance of prosecution, members of the Vichy government. See L. Sadat Wexler, 'The Interpretation of the Nuremberg Principles by the French Court of Cassation: From Touvier to Barbie and Back Again' (1994) 32 *Colum. J. Transnat'l L.* 289, 343–4.

[23] *Fédération Nationale des Déportés et Internés Résistants et Patriotes and Others* v. *Barbie*, 78 ILR 125, 141 and 147.

[24] *Handel and Others* v. *Artukovic*, 79 ILR 396.   [25] Ibid., 403.   [26] Ibid., 402.

[27] *R.* v. *Finta* [1994] 28 CR (4th) 265; this split decision by the Supreme Court of Canada reflects the case's stormy history in the lower courts.

In sum, the *Tadić* case put in place a superficial and erroneous assessment of the state of the law at the time the crimes in Yugoslavia were committed, with the result that questions of jurisdiction were left unanswered.[28]

6.3 CONSTRAINTS IN THE MANNER OF PERPETRATION

The ICTY Statute contains the first working codification of crimes against humanity since Nuremberg:

The International Tribunal shall have the power to prosecute persons responsible for the following crimes when committed in armed conflict, whether international or internal in character, and directed against any civilian population: (a) murder; (b) extermination; (c) enslavement; (d) deportation; (e) imprisonment; (f) torture; (g) rape; (h) persecutions on political, racial and religious grounds; (i) other inhumane acts.[29]

The eight crimes (including deportation and imprisonment, which need additional elements to become crimes) and the cryptic 'other inhumane acts' of this succinct provision, will be discussed later in this chapter, but clearly the main character of a crime against humanity, or of this family of crimes, is to be found in the introductory sentence, which specifies a factual and legal context in which otherwise mundane crimes (or even mere acts not being crimes in themselves) may be conceptualized as crimes of much greater consequence.

6.3.1 When committed in armed conflict

The key phrase 'when committed in armed conflict, whether international or internal in character, and directed against any civilian population' has from very early on been treated as unsatisfactory. The *Tadić* Trial Chamber read into the provision several unstated elements, notably that the acts must be undertaken in a widespread or systematic manner, and in furtherance of a policy.[30] The *Tadić* court hesitated at the words 'when committed in armed conflict', for it was concerned that this qualification went beyond the relevant rule of customary law as it supposedly stood in the early

---

[28] For general works on the law of crimes against humanity, see Cassese, *International Criminal Law*, pp. 64–95; Dixon and Khan, *Archbold*, pp. 359–86; and Mettraux, *International Crimes*, pp. 147–92.

[29] ICTY Statute, Art. 5.   [30] *Tadić* trial judgment, para. 626.

1990s. In this respect the court was not helped by the UN Secretary-General, who had said in his report on the tribunal that crimes against humanity are 'prohibited regardless of whether they are committed in an armed conflict',[31] and yet proceeded to propose the provision quoted above, which includes that very restriction.

One way to resolve the apparent contradiction is to read the Secretary-General's remark in full, together with an associated footnote, to mean that while armed conflict *is* an element, it does not matter whether the character of the armed conflict is international or internal. A drafting error would be to blame, then. It is another sign of how muddled international criminal law was in the mid-1990s.

In coming to terms with the formulation in the ICTY Statute, the *Tadić* Trial Chamber was also not helped by its own Appeals Chamber, which had erased 'when committed in armed conflict' from the (supposed) customary definition of crimes against humanity, on the mere ground that it did not appear in the December 1945 Control Council Law No. 10.[32] That law's provision on crimes against humanity is drafted more economically and more perspicuously than the IMT's, but one cannot plausibly maintain that it gave jurisdiction over crimes committed outside the context of war, in general, and the Second World War, in particular. This is evident from the opening paragraph of Control Council Law No. 10: its purpose is to enable the prosecution of *war criminals and other similar offenders*, in order to complete the work of the IMT.

In brief, the qualification 'when committed in armed conflict' survives at the ICTY, but only grudgingly, as an artificial limitation.[33] It was left out of the statutes of the ICTR and ICC, and consequently is not a factor at the Sierra Leone and East Timor courts, which reproduce the ICTR and ICC provisions, respectively.

6.3.2 Directed against any civilian population

We now turn to the interpretation of the above words. Despite the announcement of the *Tadić* Trial Chamber that crimes against humanity are governed by law so entrenched as to be considered customary, the court struggled through its explanation of the meaning of 'civilian population'. To derive that meaning, it tapped the limited case law of crimes against humanity, to the extent of relying on the French case of *Barbie*. The court tried to find another foothold in international humanitarian law, particularly Common Article 3 of the Geneva Conventions, which was the solution also proposed by the prosecutor in *Tadić*.[34] With respect to the latter proposal, the logic seems to be that the words 'when committed in armed conflict' in the ICTY Statute open the door to the stock of war-crimes concepts. This is a problematic idea — under what rationale may elements of one family of crimes be transposed to another? — as the court itself acknowledged.

---

[31] Report of the Secretary-General on ICTY, para. 47.
[32] *Tadić* jurisdiction appeal decision, para. 140.   [33] *Tadić* trial judgment, paras 630–5.
[34] Ibid., para. 637.

Nevertheless, the *Tadić* chamber's first contribution on the subject of 'civilian population' is a direct borrowing from Geneva law. Almost a decade later, the confusion generated by this step is palpable. The court said that 'the targeted population must be of a predominantly civilian nature. The presence of certain non-civilians in their midst does not change the character of the population.'[35] This Geneva rule, which defines neither 'civilian' nor 'civilian population', is merely an elaboration of the principle of distinction.[36] The point of the rule is that the presence of fighters in a civilian settlement does not necessarily transform the site into a legitimate military target. To put it simply, if the fighters are relatively few in number and do not pose a significant military threat, the site remains a civilian object that should be regarded as immune to attack. If those fighters must be neutralized, the operation may be undertaken only in a precise surgical manner, or after the evacuation of the civilians, or through negotiations; in other words, in ways not likely to harm the civilian population.

Thus the rule which the *Tadić* court sought to import into the law of crimes against humanity is of no relevance to this branch of the law. At the general level, in a case where a civilian population is under 'widespread or systematic attack' in a territory, such as Rwanda, it is *irrelevant* to the concept of civilian population that armed forces are also present in that territory, whatever their numbers might be — for the intended victim of a crime against humanity *is just* the civilian (or non-combatant) population. And at the level of the specific incident, a crime against humanity can be committed against the last remaining child in a village swarming with fighters; again, it is irrelevant that the village at some point became, in terms of Geneva law, a legitimate military target, as this does not exclude a crime against humanity on the child in this example. What *is* required is that civilians are under attack in the general territory, in a manner which will be discussed below. The Geneva rule deployed in *Tadić*'s discussion of crimes against humanity had the effect of throwing several cases off course, as we shall see.

On the definition of 'civilian population' *Tadić* hesitated. Here again we notice the temptation to fall back on the better understood category of war crimes. The court said that the definition of 'civilian' contained in Common Article 3 'is not immediately applicable to crimes against humanity because it is a part of the laws or customs of war and can only be applied by analogy'.[37] In this context 'by analogy' signifies a process of reasoning from parallel cases; but because *Tadić* never established that the law of crimes against humanity has a parallel in the law of war crimes (whatever that might mean), reasoning by analogy was not open to the court.

The basic error, however, is not the form of syllogism employed, but the idea that a syllogism is needed to derive the meaning of 'civilian population'. The term 'civilian' in the *chapeau* of Article 5 of the ICTY Statute is, as a matter of statutory interpretation, to be taken in its ordinary sense; that is, as signifying a person not being a member of the armed forces or reduced by illness or injury to non-combatant status. A 'population' of civilians is also a concept with a clear meaning, as is the notion that a civilian population comes under attack. *Tadić*, in a state of confusion, went for a 'wide' definition of the term, according to which 'the presence of those actively involved in the conflict

---

[35] Ibid., para. 638.   [36] See Chapter 4.   [37] *Tadić* trial judgment, para. 639.

should not prevent the characterization of a population as civilian and those actively involved in a resistance movement can qualify as victims of crimes against humanity'.[38] This kind of statement commits a category mistake, confusing a contextual require-ment of a crime against humanity (that the attack should be directed against a civilian population) with the victim class of the crime (which might be more broadly consti-tuted). These are separate questions, and having dealt with the former, which is the simpler by far, we shall now address the latter.

Tadić contains a significant proposition which is still awaiting doctrinal clarification and deliberate application. It is that the victim class of crimes against humanity is open. Referring to Common Article 3 and Additional Protocol I, the *Tadić* court said that these provisions give 'guidance' on the question whether acts against an individual who is not a non-combatant (because he or she is an active member of an armed force involved in the conduct of hostilities) 'can nevertheless constitute crimes against humanity if they are committed in furtherance or as part of an attack directed against a civilian population'.[39] The court again failed to explain the rationale by which Geneva law could be said to have any bearing on the law of crimes against humanity. But ultimately the judges relied on the case of *Barbie*.

We have already cited the rule articulated and applied in *Barbie*, that a condition for a crime against humanity is that it be committed 'in the name of a State practising a policy of ideological supremacy'.[40] Klaus Barbie was charged with crimes against humanity committed against both Jews and members of the French Resistance. The case reached the French Court of Cassation after an appellate court upheld a decision that crimes such as torture, deportation, and murder committed against members or supposed members of the Resistance, even if they were Jews, could be classified only as war crimes. The lower courts had formed the view that these combatants could legitimately be considered by a German officer as 'dangerous adversaries requiring elimination', whether or not this hypothetical German was a member of the Nazi party, and therefore regardless of any ideology.[41] In other words, since by definition a crime against humanity could not be said to have been committed unless in furtherance of a policy of ideological supremacy, and since that ideology was barred from application to combatants by another imperative, viz. the elimination of combatants (whether by legal means or not) in the name of victory in the war, it followed in the view of the French lower courts that a crime deliberately committed against combatants or suspected combatants could not be a crime against humanity.

The ruling of the French Court of Cassation was that the lower courts were wrong to think that the wartime imperative barred a mens rea proceeding from a policy of supremacy. A finding that a defendant rationalized politically, through the nationalist-socialist ideology, crimes committed against persons who were members or might have been members of the Resistance, sufficed to establish the intent necessary for the com-mission of a crime against humanity.[42] The Court of Cassation said little to justify this

---

[38] Ibid., para. 643.   [39] Ibid., para. 639.
[40] *Fédération Nationale des Déportés et Internés Résistants et Patriotes and Others* v. *Barbie*, 78 ILR 125, 137.
[41] Ibid., 139.   [42] Ibid., 140.

assertion, another sign that as late as 1984 the law of crimes against humanity was so unsettled that it could be restated in response to social exigencies (in this case to appease the Fédération Nationale des Déportés et Internés Résistants et Patriotes, who brought the action, and who enjoyed broad popular support). The same kind of thing happened at the IMT. From 1946 to the present, excursions into international criminal law have been feats of political power, with the law often relegated to the position of dressing up, rationalizing, and perhaps to some extent moderating the effects of that power.

It was the French Advocate General in the *Barbie* case who hinted at the rationale that almost certainly underlies the ruling of the Court of Cassation. He said that what was most frightful about crimes against humanity was the deliberate moral degradation of the victims, 'the debasement of those detained to the point of making them lose, if that were possible, all character as human beings'.[43] Those deported to concentration camps, combatants and non-combatants alike, suffered the same debasement. 'I cannot accept,' declared the Advocate General, 'once such a stage is reached, that a legal choice should be made between different victims.'[44] The moral reprobation which an advocate was (and still is) free to express, and which the IMT judges themselves often expressed in their judgment, had by 1984 been expunged from judicial narrative, as evidenced in the subdued language of the Court of Cassation itself and in the work of the tribunals established a decade later, where crimes against humanity and other serious crimes are generally discussed with the cool-headedness befitting a clinical and constitutional approach to criminal law. Beneath the surface, however, a moral revulsion for depraved and dehumanizing acts has driven the expansion of international criminal law.

From a definitional point of view, finally what matters is that the French case rendered the victim class of crimes against humanity open (it encompassed Resistance members), and this definition was adopted by the *Tadić* trial court. Statutory interpretation of the IMT Charter does not support this conclusion, because Article 6(b) (war crimes) distinguishes between 'civilian population' and persons rendered *hors de combat* (let alone active combatants), whereas Article 6(c) (crimes against humanity) mentions the civilian population only, which suggests that persons rendered *hors de combat* fall outside the Article 6(c) victim class. Later statutes, like that of the ICTY and ICC, do not explicitly restrict the victim class, but this is of little help, at least in the case of the retroactive ICTY, since interpretation of the ICTY Statute as to the law of crimes against humanity must in principle be guided by customary law, to avoid a breach of the principle of legality.

The only argument in favour of an unrestricted conception of the victim class is a *reductio ad absurdum*: if the victim class were limited to civilians, or to civilians and persons *hors de combat*, there will be cases where the intentional killing of a person, committed in the course of the commission of crimes against humanity, is not punishable as a crime against humanity, or at all, under international law. For example,

---

[43] Ibid., 144.   [44] Ibid., 146.

a civilian of nationality A who kills a guard (an active-duty member of the armed forces) also of nationality A, as the latter interposes himself between the assailant and captive civilians of nationality B, who are under attack as part of a widespread or systematic attack against nationality-B civilians, commits no offence under international law (only the lesser offence of murder under domestic law) if the victim class of crimes against humanity is closed to active-duty members of the armed forces. And this result, one might say, is illogical, since it mutes the law's response to the killing of the guard who is the sole person in this example capable of averting a crime against humanity upon the detained civilians.

6.3.3 Widespread or systematic attack

The third general constraining element in crimes against humanity, which is explicit in the ICTR and ICC Statutes, which has had to be read into the ICTY Statute, and which was absent from the IMT Charter, is that the attack against the civilian population must be 'widespread or systematic'.

This phrase first appears in the UN Secretary-General's 1993 framework report on the ICTY. The words had been put into circulation by the ILC at least since 1991, and are found in the ILC's 1996 Draft Code of Crimes, which predates the *Tadić* trial judgment. In the Draft Code the ILC stated, intuitively, that crimes under international law 'by their very nature often require the direct or indirect participation of a number of individuals at least some of whom are in positions of governmental authority or military command'. The tone is not one of legal analysis, but then the ILC's task — to draft a code at the request of the UN for an international criminal jurisdiction — was legislative rather than judicial. The ILC continued:

This is particularly true with respect to the crimes under international law which are of such gravity or magnitude, are committed on such a massive or widespread scale or are committed on such a planned or systematic basis as to constitute a threat to international peace and security and thereby qualify for inclusion in the Code.[45]

Here the words 'widespread' and 'systematic' define a desired threshold of seriousness, articulated in terms of Article 39 of the UN Charter ('threat to . . . international peace and security'). In imputing the phrase 'widespread or systematic' to the ICTY Statute, the *Tadić* Trial Chamber relied entirely on the work of the ILC,[46] an unacceptable methodology, as the ILC's Draft Code is not a restatement of customary international law, but, as we have noted, a non-retroactive code, developed for the most part in parallel with the unfolding atrocities against civilians in Yugoslavia. To insist, as the Trial Chamber does,[47] on the Code's acceptance among UN members, is to misunderstand what the Code was accepted *as*.

Related to the question of 'widespread or systematic' is that of 'policy' and the role of the state. The *Tadić* trial court acknowledged that 'the traditional conception' was not

---

[45] ILC Draft Code of Crimes, para. 50, commentary on Art. 5.
[46] *Tadić* trial judgment, paras 647–8.   [47] Ibid., para. 655.

only that a policy must be present, but that the policy must be that of a state, as was the case in Nazi Germany. The further qualification, according to *Tadić*, is no longer necessary. The law of crimes against humanity 'developed to take into account forces which, although not those of the legitimate government, have de facto control over, or are able to move freely within, defined territory'.[48] The Trial Chamber did not cite any jurisprudence demonstrating that the law had developed in this way. Its sole source again was the ILC's Draft Code, which contains the recommendation that the qualification 'instigated or directed by a Government or by any organization or group' be included in the notion of a crime against humanity. The Trial Chamber concluded from this that a policy, not necessarily that of a state, must be proven as part of the *chapeau* elements. The ICTY Appeals Chamber rejected this conclusion, dispensing with the policy element altogether, and thus wholly dispensing with 'the traditional conception'. Case law played no part in its reasoning, either.[49]

6.4 MENS REA ELEMENTS

The methodology of the *Tadić* trial court might be described as selective. It involves choosing elements and setting thresholds that fit the court's conception about how a crime should be constituted. References to the supposed customary law are added to the exercise. Because the question is one of choice, problems encountered along the way are easier to evade. The same method of selection was used in the *Akayesu* judgment (see Chapter 5). In the wake of these judgments, intuitive selectivity became a common method in international criminal justice. The approach of *Tadić* to the mens rea of crimes against humanity is an illustration of this method at work.

The *Tadić* trial court asked whether all crimes against humanity, and not only persecution (for which discriminatory intent is an explicit requirement in the ICTY Statute), were constituted of discriminatory intent on national, political, ethnic, racial, or religious grounds. Faced with a choice between reading this requirement into the Statute, despite its absence from the IMT Charter and its offshoots,[50] and accepting the Statute at face value, which would mean ignoring the UN Secretary-General's commentary suggesting that it is a general requirement, the Trial Chamber chose the former.[51] This was soon reversed by the Appeals Chamber, relying on principles of statutory interpretation,[52] but the point is that neither the Trial Chamber nor the Appeals Chamber explored 'customary law' on this question. Their different answers merely hinged on different

---

[48] Ibid., paras 654–5.

[49] *Jelisić* appeal judgment, para. 48; *Kunarac et al.* appeal judgment, paras 98–101. The revised position ignores relatively recent case law, such as *Quinn* v. *Robinson* (1986) 783 F.2d 776, 799–801, where a US court asserted that crimes against humanity are 'by definition' carried out by, or with the toleration of, authorities of a state.

[50] As acknowledged by the Trial Chamber, *Tadić* trial judgment, paras 651–2.

[51] Ibid., para. 652.   [52] *Tadić* appeal judgment, paras 281–305.

preferences. The requirement of discriminatory intent was added to the *chapeau* of the ICTR's provision on crimes against humanity,[53] further exacerbating differences in the case law. It is not found in the corresponding chapeau of the ICC statute.[54]

In *Finta*, a majority of the Supreme Court of Canada held that the mens rea required for a crime against humanity is, as for a war crime, more than the mens rea required for the underlying offence. The additional element is awareness of the circumstances of the offence which make it a crime against humanity; in other words, awareness of a nexus with the attack on the civilian population. The jury, according to the Canadian court, in order to convict, must find that the defendant knowingly participated in conduct that reached the level of a crime against humanity. The trial judge had correctly emphasized that

it was not sufficient that the jurors thought that what had happened constituted a violation of the laws of war or were crimes against humanity. Finta himself had to be aware of those conditions and factual circumstances that raised the crimes to the level of crimes against humanity or war crimes.[55]

This is not to say that a defendant must have been aware that he or she was committing a crime against humanity (as knowledge of illegality is not required in criminal law), only of the contextual elements that go with the crime.

That is another way of saying that the defendant must be shown to have known that his or her act was not isolated, but was associated with other such acts, through, for example, a common purpose.[56] The minority in *Finta* took as its only reference point domestic criminal practice, which left it unable to accept that international criminal law was so different from state practice as to require proof of the higher standard of mens rea entailed by knowledge of the contextual (*chapeau*) elements.[57] The international tribunals have followed the *Finta* majority.[58]

6.5 PERSECUTION AND ETHNIC CLEANSING

We have already noted that persecution at its core is about acts of murder, unlawful imprisonment, torture, enslavement, and deportation committed against civilians considered to be of 'inferior race' (as the IMT found against Nazi Germany), or on political or religious grounds.[59]

---

[53] 'The International Tribunal for Rwanda shall have the power to prosecute persons responsible for the following crimes when committed as part of a widespread or systematic attack against any civilian population on national, political, ethnic, racial or religious grounds: . . .'.

[54] 'For the purpose of this Statute, "crime against humanity" means any of the following acts when committed as part of a widespread or systematic attack directed against any civilian population, with knowledge of the attack: . . .'.   [55] *R. v. Finta* [1994] 28 CR (4th) 265, para. 105.

[56] Cf. *Tadić* trial judgment, para. 644.

[57] *R. v. Finta* [1994] 28 CR (4th) 265, para. 294 (dissenting opinion of Judge La Forest).

[58] E.g. *Tadić* trial judgment, paras 656–7.

[59] On the persecution of the Jews by the Nazis, see 22 IMT Judgment 491–6.

Tadić was the first case in which persecution was considered by an international tribunal, and *Tadić*'s first observation on the subject (for which it relied on an opinion by Cherif Bassiouni) was that the crime of persecution was not clearly defined in international criminal law. As for its status in municipal systems, persecution was largely unknown.[60]

There are limits to how much 'clarification' a court may give to the law, even within a tradition that allows judges the facility to manufacture or adapt a certain amount of the law. In the English case of *R. v. R.*, Lord Chief Justice Lane said:

> The remaining and no less difficult question is whether, despite that view [namely the court's finding that the supposed marital exception in rape forms no part of the law of England], this is an area where the court should step aside to leave the matter to the Parliamentary process. This is not the creation of a new offence, it is the removal of a common law fiction which has become anachronistic and offensive and we consider that it is our duty having reached that conclusion to act upon it.[61]

This indicates the limits of judicial 'clarification' in a parliamentary system. Modification of the elements of an offence through the removal of inaccuracies, which have been rendered so, for example, by a change in social attitudes, is a permissible clarification; beyond that, parliamentary action is necessary. The same limits presumably apply in international criminal law. The appellant in *R. v. R.* took his case to the European Court of Human Rights, with a complaint under Article 7 of the applicable Convention. The ECtHR endorsed the English approach, and added, in relation to the prohibition against *ex post facto* law:

> the Convention cannot be read as outlawing the gradual clarification of the rules of criminal liability through judicial interpretation from case to case, provided that the resultant development is consistent with the essence of the offence and could reasonably be foreseen.[62]

The question, then, is whether the law of persecution, despite not being clearly defined in international law by 1992, as *Tadić* recognized, emerges in the court's discussion to have had a clearly defined 'essence'. In addition, the elements which were appended to the notion by the court must have been reasonably foreseeable in 1992.

The perennial question for the law of persecution is the degree to which it encompasses elements of the lay notion of persecution, fixed in the contemporary imagination by the retelling of the Nazi persecution of the Jews, and in particular by such details as the exclusion of Jews from the professions, anti-Semitic insults and demeaning practices, the burning of books symbolizing Jewish culture and history, and the wearing of the yellow star. When the IMT judgment described the persecutory precursors to the murder, extermination, enslavement, and deportation of Jews during the war, it drew on a non-technical notion of persecution, for the acts it referred to figured neither in the Charter nor in the convictions handed down:

> With the coming of the Nazis into power in 1933, persecution of the Jews became official state policy. On 1 April 1933, a boycott of Jewish enterprises was approved by the Nazi Reich Cabinet,

---

[60] Ibid., para. 694.   [61] *R. v. R.* [1991] 93 Cr. App. R. 1, 8.

[62] *C.R.* v. *United Kingdom*, Appl. 2019/92, November 1995, ECtHR, Series A, para. 34.

and during the following years a series of anti-Semitic laws were passed, restricting the activities of Jews in the Civil Service, in the legal profession, in journalism and in the Armed Forces. In September 1935 the so-called Nuremberg Laws were passed, the most important effect of which was to deprive Jews of German citizenship. In this way the influence of Jewish elements on the affairs of Germany was extinguished, and one more potential source of opposition to Nazi policy was rendered powerless.[63]

Is there any lawful basis for treating acts of this kind as crimes against humanity if they are not followed by murder, extermination, enslavement, or deportation? And if this is too academic a question, may such acts be punished as crimes against humanity when they *are* committed in combination with murder, etc.? An affirmative answer to the second question — and perhaps even to the first — comes from a most unexpected source, ICTY defendant Mario Čerkez:

Persecution of civilians on political, racial or religious grounds means conscious and deliberate killings, encouraging murder, encouraging economic deprivations, plundering of property, passing discriminatory laws and implementing discriminatory legal practice, denying family life, dismissing and removing civilians from certain professions, denying citizenship, ghettoization; all very serious crimes which restrict and deprive basic human rights; discriminatory intent is required.[64]

Čerkez, having put forth this definition, went on to attack it for lack of clarity and foundation, complaining that criminality must be connected to a 'determined, clearly defined factual substrate which encompasses the illegal act', and so on.[65] It could be said that Čerkez conflated the legal and the lay notions of persecution, and that his attack was therefore directed against a straw man. Yet a trend does exist to expand the restrictive definition of persecution to include elements of the lay notion.

The second question posed above — may peripheral acts of persecution be punished as crimes against humanity when committed in combination with core persecutory acts listed in the IMT Charter and ICTY Statute — is answered to some extent by the Second World War case law. The problem with this case law, however, is that it is so lacking in uniformity, due to its articulation by the military commissions of several states, mostly without appellate review, that inconsistent propositions could be supported through selective quotation. Be that as it may, the following cases may be cited in favour of a wider notion of persecutory acts.

Starting with the IMT itself, the Tribunal found Wilhelm Frick, Reichminister of the Interior, responsible for promulgating many laws designed to eliminate Jews from German life and the economy. A decree he signed in 1943 placed Jews 'outside the law'.[66] Walter Funk, Minister of Economics, was held responsible for his involvement in

---

[63] 22 IMT Judgment 421. As the Tribunal acknowledged, 'It was contended for the Prosecution that certain aspects of this [pre-war] anti-Semitic policy were connected with the plans for aggressive war' (ibid., p. 492). But the Tribunal did not accept this contention, moving quickly to focus on the atrocities of wartime persecution. 'The Tribunal therefore cannot make a general declaration that the acts before 1939 were Crimes against Humanity within the meaning of the Charter' (ibid., p. 498).

[64] *Prosecutor* v. *Čerkez and Kordić*, Defendant Mario Čerkez's Final Trial Brief, 13 December 2000, pp. 93–4.

[65] Ibid., p. 97.   [66] 22 IMT Judgment 545–6.

the Nazi programme of economic discrimination against Jews, in particular a decree banning Jews from business activities.[67] Hans Frank, Governor-General of Occupied Poland, was found to have participated in the persecution of Jews, who had been 'forced into ghettos, subjected to discriminatory laws, deprived of the food necessary to avoid starvation', before finally being exterminated.[68] The IMT held against Constantin von Neurath, Reich Protector for Bohemia and Moravia, his institution in that territory of anti-Semitic policies and laws. This led to Jews being barred from leading positions in government and business, among other consequences.[69] Arthur Seyss-Inquart, Reich Commissioner for the Occupied Netherlands, was held responsible for putting into effect a series of laws imposing economic discrimination against Jews; these were followed by decrees requiring the registration of Jews and compelling them to live in ghettos and to wear the Star of David, as well as arbitrary arrests and detention in concentration camps, prior to mass deportation and the 'final solution'.[70] About Martin Bormann the IMT said that he had been extremely active in the persecution of Jews. In July 1943 he had signed an ordinance withdrawing Jews from the protection of the laws and placing them under the exclusive jurisdiction of the Gestapo.[71]

Thus denial of freedom of movement, denial of employment, and denial of the right to judicial process have been treated as forms of persecution, at least when leading to deportation and extermination.

This rule is evident also in the case law of the tribunals operating under Control Council Law No. 10. In the *Justice* case, in which members of the judiciary of Nazi Germany were tried for war crimes and crimes against humanity, a US military tribunal wrote:

The record contains innumerable acts of persecution of individual Poles and Jews, but to consider these cases as isolated and unrelated instances of perversion of justice would be to overlook the very essence of the offence charged in the indictment. . . . lesser forms of racial persecution were universally practised by governmental authority and constituted an integral part in the general policy of the Reich. We have already noted the decree by which Jews were excluded from the legal profession. . . . By other decrees Jews were almost completely expelled from public service, from educational institutions, and from many business enterprises. . . . Poles and Jews convicted of specific crimes were subjected to different types of punishment from that imposed upon Germans who had committed the same crimes. Their rights as defendants in court were severely circumscribed. Courts were empowered to impose death sentences on Poles and Jews even where such punishment was not prescribed by law . . . And, finally, the police were given carte blanche to punish all 'criminal' acts committed by Jews without any employment of the judicial process.[72]

Denial of equal access to public services was also dealt with in the case of Hans Albin Rauter before the Netherlands Special Court in The Hague. Rauter had been in charge of the police in the Occupied Netherlands. He was convicted for his participation in the persecution of Jews. The Special Court concluded that Rauter had

issued orders under which Jews were subjected to discriminatory treatment and gradually segregated from the rest of the population, which facilitated their being detected and apprehended

---

[67] Ibid., p. 551.   [68] Ibid., p. 543.   [69] Ibid., p. 581.   [70] Ibid., p. 576.
[71] Ibid., p. 586.   [72] *US* v. *Alstötter et al.* (1947) 3 TWC 954, 1063–4.

at a later date for slave labour and eventual extermination. Jews were ordered to wear a Star of David in public, and were forbidden to take part in public gatherings, to make use of public places for amusement, recreation or information, to visit public parks, cafes and restaurants, to use dining and sleeping cars, to visit theatres, cabarets, variety shows, cinemas, sports clubs, including swimming baths, to remain in or make use of public libraries, reading rooms, and museums. A special curfew was introduced for all Jews between the hours of 8 p.m. and 6 a.m. Later orders banned them from railway yards and the use of any public or private means of transport. These measures were followed by the erection of concentration camps in various places. They culminated in systematic round-ups of Jews, who were sent to the concentration camps in order to be deported to Germany or Poland, where they were to be used for slave labour or exterminated.[73]

Joseph Buhler, who served in various roles in Occupied Poland, including that of deputy Governor-General, was convicted by the Supreme National Tribunal of Poland for war crimes and crimes against humanity committed between 1939 and 1945. He was held responsible for issuing orders and regulations restricting access of Poles to schools and universities.[74] Artur Greiser, who had served as Governor of the province of Poznan between 1939 and 1945, was convicted by the Supreme National Tribunal for the persecution of Jews, primarily by removing them from their homes without prior notice, and 'Constant visitations by day and night on all sorts of pretexts, during which the victims would be insulted and often robbed'.[75]

When the *Tadić* court came to look at the same question, it did not approach it through an analysis of precedent, as we have illustrated above, but again utilized a selective method. After sampling the opinions of the Rapporteur in the *Barbie* case and two academic authors, the court concluded: 'it is evident that what is necessary is some form of discrimination that is intended to be and results in an infringement of an individual's fundamental rights'.[76] This is a remarkable broadening of the crime of persecution. It suggests an affirmative answer to the first question posed above, namely whether there is any lawful basis for treating peripheral acts of persecution as crimes against humanity if they are not followed up with murder, extermination, enslavement, or deportation. *Tadić* attempted to create such a basis by shifting the emphasis, in the case of persecution, from the inhumane nature of the act to the presence of discriminatory intent in the actor: 'it is not necessary to have a separate act of an inhumane nature to constitute persecution; the discrimination itself makes the act inhumane'.[77] This goes so far beyond clarification of the law of crimes against humanity as it stood in 1992 as to amount to a new crime. The fact that in tribunal law such an expansion can be carried out over the course of a single paragraph in a judgment can be expected to raise questions about the credibility and viability of the tribunal system of justice.

---

[73] *Trial of Hans Albin Rauter* (1948) 14 LRTWC 89, 92–3.
[74] *Trial of Dr Joseph Buhler* (1948) 14 LRTWC 23, 29.
[75] *Trial of Artur Greiser* (1946) 13 LRTWC 70, 94, 105. The authors are indebted to Jonas Nilsson for his original survey of this material.   [76] *Tadić* trial judgment, para. 697.
[77] Ibid.

6.6 EXTERMINATION

Extermination has had its own peculiar history at the ad hoc tribunals. The *Krstić* Trial Chamber acknowledged that the Second World War jurisprudence had not thrown any light on the crime, that rarely had the crime been defined by national courts since then, and that until the *Krstić* judgment was pronounced (2001), extermination had not been defined at the ICTY.[78] (At the ICTR, the *Akayesu* Trial Chamber had commented on the offence in a superficial manner.)[79] Finding no useful precedent, *Krstić* relied on the definition of the crime given in the 1998 ICC Statute — a remarkable choice![80] *Krstić* also offered its own, intuitive, explanation: 'The very term "extermination" strongly suggests the commission of a massive crime, which in turn assumes a substantial degree of preparation and organisation. . . . while extermination generally involves a large number of victims, it may be constituted even where the number of victims is limited.'[81]

The *Vasiljević* Trial Chamber disagreed, noting that 'The Trial Chamber is not aware of cases which, prior to 1992, used the phrase "extermination" to describe the killing of less than 733 persons'.[82] Without staking too much on this very high number, the court concluded rather generally that the actus reus of extermination consists of an 'act or combination of acts which contributes to the killing of a large number of individuals'.[83] However, 'large' changed to 'vast' when the trial court came to explain why it would acquit Mitar Vasiljević of the charge of extermination:

The Prosecution has . . . failed to establish that the Accused knew that his acts were part of a vast collective murder in which a large number of individuals were systematically marked for extermination or were in fact exterminated. As far as the evidence in this case is concerned, the Accused is showed to have intended to kill only the seven Muslim men who were the victims of the Drina River incident.[84]

By the time of the *Krajišnik* trial judgment in 2006, the terminology had changed; now the killings must have occurred on a 'mass scale', with corresponding intent. Mass scale refers 'primarily' to the number of killings, 'but does not suggest a numerical minimum'. The killings constituting extermination must form part of the same incident.[85] The trial court found in the evidence a large number of extermination incidents. For example:

Between 150 and 200 Muslim and Croat detainees in Keraterm shot dead in one room by Serb guards between 24 and 26 July.

Approximately 130 Muslim women, children, and elderly persons waiting to be evacuated from Gacko municipality killed by Serb forces during the attack on Fazlagića Kula on 17 June 1992.

---

[78] *Krstić* trial judgment, para. 492. [79] *Akayesu* trial judgment, paras 591–2.
[80] *Krstić* trial judgment, para. 498. [81] Ibid., para. 501.
[82] *Vasiljević* trial judgment, fn. 587. [83] Ibid., para. 229. [84] Ibid., para. 232.
[85] *Krajišnik* trial judgment, para. 716. See also *Ntakirutimana* appeal judgment, paras 516, 522, 542; *Stakić* appeal judgment, para. 260.

Eighty-eight Muslim male detainees at Dom Kulture in Drinjača taken out in groups of ten and executed by the White Eagles on 30 May 1992.

Thirty-six Muslim detainees from the Foča area killed at KP Dom by Serb guards between 28 June and 5 July 1992.

Twenty-four Muslim male detainees from an ammunition warehouse in Jelašačko Polje executed by Serb soldiers and the police in a stable in Ratine on 5 August 1992, after having been severely mistreated, bound, and stripped of their valuables. Twenty were killed first and the remaining four ordered to place the dead bodies in the stable after which they were killed as well.

Nineteen Muslim men from Donji Begići brought to Vrhpolje bridge by 50 Serb soldiers, beaten, ordered to jump off the bridge and shot dead in the water on or about 31 May 1992.

Eighteen Muslim men interrogated by Serb soldiers on or about 27 June 1992 and then taken to a house in Blaževići whereupon the soldiers threw explosives into the house and opened fire on those trying to escape.

Approximately 17 Muslim and Croat detainees from Betonirka camp killed in Kriva Cesta by Serb soldiers on 22 June 1992 after being forced at gunpoint to dig their own graves.[86]

6.7 DEPORTATION AND FORCED TRANSFER

The broadening of the notion of crimes against humanity happened not only under the heading of persecution, but also under the last clause in Article 5 of the ICTY Statute, the seemingly open-ended 'other inhumane acts'. Tadić's defence complained in this connection that crimes defined in other parts of the Statute, for example in the provisions on war crimes, should not be imported into crimes against humanity through the loophole of 'other inhumane acts'.[87] One of the crimes commonly charged under 'other inhumane acts' is forced transfer. This is distinguished from deportation, which is a listed crime in the tribunals' provisions, by the state-border element, which is present in the latter. As stated in *Krajišnik*, deportation and forcible transfer both entail the forcible displacement of persons from the area in which they are lawfully present, without grounds permitted under international law. (This law recognizes certain circumstances under which the displacement of civilians during armed conflict is permitted, namely if it is carried out for the security of the persons concerned, or for imperative military reasons.)[88] 'Forcible' includes situations where the fear of violence, unlawful detention, psychological oppression, and other such circumstances of intimidation create an environment where there is little choice but to leave. The additional element for deportation is that a person is displaced across a *de jure* state border, or, in certain circumstances, a de facto border.[89] This has been a cause of considerable controversy at the ICTY.[90]

---

[86] *Krajišnik* trial judgment, para. 720.   [87] Ibid., para. 698.
[88] Geneva Convention III, Art. 19; Geneva Convention IV, Art. 49; Additional Protocol II, Art. 17.
[89] *Krajišnik* trial judgment, paras 723–6.
[90] *Stakić* appeal judgment, paras 278, 300, and Judge Shahabuddeen's partially dissenting opinion.

6.8 CONCLUSION

Like war-crimes law, the law of crimes against humanity has been a growth area at the ICTY. But the growth has been poorly regulated. One striking illustration is provided by the *Kordić and Čerkez* appeal judgment. In the course of this one judgment the Appeals Chamber formulated — presumably without realizing it — four different jurisdictional tests for an act alleged to constitute persecution. The first test was that the act must be criminalized in *customary* law.[91] The second test was that the act must be a *war crime*.[92] The third test was that the act must be *as grave as other persecutory acts* listed in the ICTY Statute.[93] And the fourth test was that the act must be criminalized in customary *or treaty* law.[94] More than the law of war crimes and genocide, the law of crimes against humanity has been the brainchild of the ad hoc tribunals. Prior to the establishment of these tribunals, the UN Secretary-General assured the Security Council that there exised a sufficiently rich legal framework for the tribunals to operate within. We now know that this was wishful thinking. The framework was a bare outline. The tribunals have had to create for themselves the details of their legal system.

[91] 'The Appeals Chamber finds that the Trial Chamber erred when it considered that "educational institutions are undoubtedly immovable property of great importance to the cultural heritage of peoples". The Trial Chamber did not consider whether and under which conditions the destruction of educational buildings constituted a crime *qua custom* at the time it was allegedly committed' (*Kordić and Čerkez* appeal judgment, para. 92, emphasis in original).

[92] 'To the extent that the alleged crimes against humanity were committed in the course of an armed conflict, the laws of war provide a benchmark against which the Chamber may assess the nature of the attack and the legality of the acts committed in its midst' (ibid., para. 96).

[93] 'The acts underlying persecutions as a crime against humanity, whether considered in isolation or in conjunction with other acts, must constitute a crime of persecutions of gravity equal to the crimes listed in Article 5 of the Statute' (ibid., para. 102). Note that the construction 'whether considered in isolation or in conjunction with other acts' could mean (1) 'both in isolation and in conjunction' (= they must be serious enough in isolation), or (2) 'in isolation, or, if not in isolation, then in conjunction' (= they need not be serious enough in isolation if they are serious enough in conjunction). Here is an example which seems to suggest that sense (1) is the correct interpretation: the act 'must constitute a denial of or infringement upon a fundamental right laid down in international customary or treaty law; not every act, if committed with the requisite discriminatory intent, amounts to persecution as a crime against humanity' (ibid., para. 103). And here is an example which seems to suggest that sense (2) is the correct interpretation: 'The underlying acts include killings, beatings, unlawful attacks on civilians and civilian objects, the unlawful imprisonment of civilians, destruction of civilian objects, and looting. All of them, *considered in conjunction*, amount to a criminal conduct of gravity equal to crimes listed in Article 5 of the Statute' (ibid., para. 672, emphasis added).

[94] 'It must be demonstrated that the acts underlying the crime of persecutions constituted a crime against humanity in customary international law or in international treaty law at the time the accused is alleged to have committed the offence' (ibid., para. 103).

7

FACETS OF PERSONAL LIABILITY
FOR PARTICIPATION IN CRIMES

SUMMARY

7.1 INTRODUCTION

In the ICTY Statute, the crimes are covered by Articles 2 to 5, whereas the modes of liability are covered by Article 7. This separation, which is seen in the statutes of all international tribunals, has reinforced a particular narrative in tribunal jurisprudence.

From the outset, the tribunals have treated the definition of crimes, and the definition of forms of responsibility for crimes, as separate questions. In tribunal judgments, the two questions are invariably dealt with in separate and essentially unrelated sections. The underlying logic is that a crime, for example genocide, consists of a set of legal elements (actus reus, mens rea) which must be proven. In addition to this, there is the alleged way in which the defendant was associated with the crime — for example, through aiding and abetting its commission. The form of association — aiding and abetting — is constituted of a set of legal elements of its own (which also may be divided into material and mental elements), to be proven additionally to the elements of the crime.

The distinction between proof of the crime itself and proof of the forms of responsibility for it is plausible, although it is not a necessary distinction, nor is it always workable. For example, in tribunal indictments, complicity in genocide is charged as a crime, not as a form of commission of a crime. This has something to do with the wording of Article 3 of the Genocide Convention, which seems to create five crimes, one of which is complicity. (It could also be said that these are five modes of liability for the one crime of genocide. Recently, complicity has indeed been stripped away from genocide and recast as a mode of participation in genocide akin to aiding and abetting.)[1]

The inchoate offences of conspiracy, attempt, and incitement to commit *genocide* (which seems to be the only crime in tribunal law for which a conviction under one of these three headings is permitted) also fall outside the crime/responsibility model. In these cases, responsibility *is* the crime, and vice versa. As for the case of what might be called unmediated commission (principal in the first degree), the distinction between crime and responsibility is of no significance: it is enough to prove the elements of, say, torture against a person who committed torture as a principal, to find that person responsible for torture.

Thus the ad hoc tribunals have grappled with a question in this form: 'Having decided what a crime consists in, what forms of responsibility exist for that crime?' Perhaps a more accurate way to pose the question is, '*Who else*, besides the person who committed the crime as a principal, may be found responsible in the commission of the crime, and why?' The critical distinction should not be one between a disembodied legal profile of a crime and the legal profile of embodied forms of participation in it, but between the responsibility of the principal perpetrator of the crime and the responsibility of other persons variously associated with the crime's commission. The perpetrator being conceptually and indistinguishably at the core of the crime, how far should the waves of punishable responsibility be allowed to spread? What types of conduct will make persons other than the principal liable for the same crime?

To answer these questions, it is necessary to consider the principles according to which personal criminal liability exists for certain acts in international law. What 'exists' here, has been almost entirely constructed by the tribunals themselves over the past decade.

---

[1] See Chapter 5, section 5.3.4.

The study of the law of personal liability is hugely rewarding. In the context of the types of cases dealt with at the international tribunals, the question of personal liability is, in many ways, more interesting than the study of the law of the crimes themselves. 'Leadership cases', such as the ICTY's *Krajišnik* case, are all about the responsibility of a person far removed from the crimes on the ground.[2] It is this frequently encountered distance between the defendant and the crimes, which personal liability must bridge, which has sharpened the crime/responsibility distinction at the tribunals.

The international criminal tribunals, which are not unaware that their powers are essentially unchecked, have had to exercise self-restraint, as seen in occasional efforts to limit the reach of the personal-liability provisions in their statutes. However, in two extraordinarily influential areas of personal liability, namely joint criminal enterprise (JCE) and command responsibility, there has been the opposite effect. And in both cases the tribunals have attempted to base their elaborations of the law on a platform of international custom.[3]

7.2 JOINT CRIMINAL ENTERPRISE

7.2.1 Differential utilization at ICTY and ICTR

The doctrine of joint criminal enterprise was developed early in the history of the ICTY, by the ICTY Appeals Chamber, and has found extensive use at that institution ever since. By the end of 2005, 19 out of the 37 ICTY cases that had been completed at least at first instance involved a question of joint criminal enterprise. Major trials under way at the time, such as those of Slobodan Milošević and Momčilo Krajišnik, alleged JCE as the chief mode of participation in the crimes. Milošević's trial was never completed, due to his death, but Krajišnik's was, in September 2006. The *Krajišnik* judgment was the only ICTY trial judgment in 2006 to have utilized JCE, but nevertheless 2006 was a most important year in the history of the doctrine. For it was with *Krajišnik* that JCE became established as a workable doctrine in large and complex leadership cases.

---

[2] See *Krajišnik* trial judgment, paras 870–1124.

[3] For the main forms of liability not discussed in the present chapter, see *Furundžija* trial and appeal judgments (for aiding and abetting); *Krnojelac* trial judgment (for aiding and abetting); *Nahimana et al.* trial judgment (for conspiracy and for incitement to commit genocide); *Krstić* appeal judgment (for aiding and abetting contrasted with complicity); *Blaškić* appeal judgment (for ordering); *Brđanin* trial judgment (for planning and for instigating); *Ntakirutimana* appeal judgment (for aiding and abetting contrasted with complicity); *Semanza* appeal judgment (for aiding and abetting contrasted with complicity, and for instigation contrasted with ordering); *Kamuhanda* appeal judgment (for aiding and abetting and for ordering); *Gacumbitsi* appeal judgment (for committing); and *Muvunyi* trial judgment (for incitement to commit genocide). See also Cassese, *International Criminal Law*, pp. 189–99; Dixon and Khan, *Archbold*, pp. 285–9; and Mettraux, *International Crimes*, pp. 279–87, 293–5.

Despite the fact that the UN's two original criminal tribunals shared the same prosecutor until 2003, the JCE doctrine spread from The Hague to Arusha late in the history of the ICTR. This was presumably the result of a lack of coordination between the prosecutor's offices. Prosecution staff in The Hague prepared indictments largely independently of their ICTR counterparts, with the result that importantly different practices emerged. In 2004 the ICTR Office of the Prosecutor sought to claw back lost ground, arguing that an ICTR Trial Chamber had erred in not utilizing the JCE doctrine to determine the criminal responsibility of the Ntakirutimanas (father and son), even though JCE had not been charged in their indictments.[4] The Appeals Chamber, after taking the opportunity to formally recognize the doctrine's foothold in the ICTR Statute,[5] rejected the prosecutor's argument:

In the present case, the Trial Chamber does not appear to have considered joint criminal enterprise liability at any time in determining the responsibility incurred by Gérard and Elizaphan Ntakirutimana . . . As such the Appeals Chamber does not accept that the authorities relied upon by the Prosecution lend the assistance the Prosecution claims. In the *Tadić* Appeal Judgment, the ICTY Appeals Chamber found the accused liable under the third form of joint criminal enterprise for the killing of five men from the village of Jaskići, even though neither this form of liability nor any other form of joint criminal enterprise was expressly pleaded in the indictment. However, in that case and, unlike here, the trial chamber had considered joint criminal enterprise liability and, on appeal, the Prosecution was actually arguing that the trial chamber had misdirected itself as to the application of that doctrine. In the *Furundžija* case, also relied upon by the Prosecution, although the indictment did not expressly include joint criminal enterprise or even co-perpetration as to the charge of torture, the Prosecution pleaded at trial that liability pursuant to Article 7(1) of the Statute can be established by showing that the accused had the intent to participate in the crime, that his acts contributed to its commission and that such contribution did not necessarily require participation in the physical commission of the crime.[6]

As we shall see, the two elements which the prosecutor is said to have pleaded at trial in the *Furundžija* case (intent to participate in the crime, and a contribution to the crime's commission) are core elements of JCE responsibility. But the important and unstated moral of this story is not that JCE need not be pleaded explicitly in an indictment in order to be utilized at trial level, but that the ICTR prosecutor in the *Ntakirutimana* case realized too late that the JCE doctrine could generate a much higher level of responsibility for the two accused persons than the mundane charges of straightforward commission of the crimes and of aiding and abetting others to commit them. JCE promises greater returns because it creates a class of equally responsible co-perpetrators of an *expanded* set of crimes, a set which moreover consists not only of the co-perpetrators' intended crimes, but also of the crimes foreseen by them.

And so, for example, whereas under one conception of commission — the one actually employed by the *Ntakirutimana* Trial Chamber — the younger Ntakirutimana committed only one murder in the course of the massacre at the Mugonero complex on

---

[4] The ICTR prosecutor had attempted this also in 2003, during closing arguments in the *Ntagerura et al.* case. This was blocked by the Trial Chamber; see *Ntagerura et al.* trial judgment, para. 34.

[5] *Ntakirutimana* appeal judgment, para. 468.   [6] Ibid., para. 474.

16 April 1994, under the looser conception made possible by JCE he may have 'committed' hundreds of murders, as well as any number of other crimes suffered during the attack, depending on proof of a small number of additional elements. JCE thus functions as a multiplier of individual criminal responsibility. Had the theory been used against Gérard Ntakirutimana, it is a safe bet that he would have received a stiffer sentence than the 25-year jail term handed down by the Trial Chamber, a lenient penalty by ICTR standards.[7]

Poor coordination between the two branches of the prosecutor's office aside, the *Ntakirutimana* incident raises the question of how it can be that a mode of responsibility said by the Appeals Chamber to be implicit in the Statutes of the two Tribunals, and available in customary law, is neglected for so long at the ICTR. The first ICTR Trial Chamber judgment utilizing JCE theory came out only at the end of 2005.[8] A second one followed in just under a year.[9]

To conceptualize JCE as a form of commission, which has been the standard position at the ICTY, is neither obvious nor necessary. For example, the ICC Statute has different provisions for commission and JCE.[10] One possible explanation is that the ICTY, feeling hemmed in by its Statute, proceeded to expand its jurisdiction unilaterally (without reference to the Security Council), encompassing a mode of liability largely of its own making.

7.2.2 Origins of the JCE doctrine

Prosecutors have viewed the Appeals Chamber decision in *Tadić* as a golden opportunity. Though it only concerned the killing of five men in the small village of Jaskići, the words and concepts used, viewed in abstraction, seemed to hold great unspoken potential.[11]

The JCE doctrine received its first detailed treatment in the *Tadić* appeal judgment.[12] The ICTY Appeals Chamber held in broad terms that a person who in execution of a common criminal purpose contributes to the commission of crimes by a group of persons may be held criminally liable for those crimes, subject to certain conditions.[13]

---

[7] We note in passing that the JCE doctrine is not the only doctrine which could have been used by the prosecutor or by the *Ntakirutimana* Trial Chamber to expand the responsibility of the younger Ntakirutimana. The Trial Chamber was clearly in error in holding him responsible for only one killing. As a member of an attacking force or large gang, with an unlawful objective, he is responsible for all that eventuated. Yet, as we shall see, this does not require recourse to the JCE doctrine as developed by the ICTY.

[8] *Simba* trial judgment, 13 December 2005.   [9] *Mpambara* trial judgment, 11 September 2006.

[10] See ICC Statute, Art. 25(3)(a) and (d).

[11] *Prosecutor* v. *Krajišnik*, Defence Final Brief Pursuant to Rule 86(B), 18 August 2006, para. 132.

[12] *Tadić* appeal judgment, paras 172–85. The issue on appeal was whether the accused Tadić, who as a member of a group of armed men had entered a certain Bosnian village and committed atrocities against its inhabitants, could be held responsible for the killing of five men from the village, even though there was no evidence that he had personally killed any of them — all that could be inferred from the evidence was that the men had been killed by the armed group to which Tadić belonged.   [13] *Tadić* appeal judgment, para. 190.

Where the conditions are satisfied, each of the persons carrying out the JCE is responsible for the acts of the others who are part of the criminal enterprise.[14]

As we have noted, the conditions of liability under this doctrine are not found on the face of the ICTY Statute, but in the argument of the Appeals Chamber they may be derived with precision from customary international law.[15]

On several occasions, and in particular in Chapter 3, we have remarked on the confusion surrounding the concept of customary international law in the jurisprudence of the tribunals. Not only is the concept and its use poorly explained by the judges, the relationship of the tribunals to the realm of customary law is itself ill-defined. For example, is it sufficient that a criminal-law principle enjoys customary status for it to be utilized by the tribunals? And in the case of the ICTY, is this also a necessary condition?

We have also expressed our own preference for the ICJ's threshold for a rule of customary law: existence of a general practice of states, and acceptance of that practice as law by states.[16] A first step, then, is to determine whether the *Tadić* Appeals Chamber funnelled its proposed JCE doctrine through this stricture.

At the time of the *Tadić* appeal judgment, in July 1999, there was no indictment alleging JCE, and only one Trial Chamber had utilized a liability theory similar to what would become *Tadić*'s doctrine of JCE. This had happened in the *Furundžija* case, decided in December 1998. The concept there had been called co-perpetration in a joint criminal enterprise and it was dealt with under the heading of aiding and abetting, from which co-perpetration was distinguished.[17] (The Trial Chamber bench included Cassese and Mumba, who went on to join the bench of the Appeals Chamber which decided *Tadić*.)

In *Furundžija* the factual situation was as follows. Anto Furundžija, a military commander, interrogated Witness A in a room. She was forced by Accused B, also a commander, to undress and remain naked before a number of soldiers (Accused B had been indicted but was not on trial). As Furundžija interrogated her, Accused B threatened her with assault. Witness A was left by Furundžija in the custody of Accused B, who proceeded to rape her. The interrogation resumed in another room, once more before an audience of soldiers. Witness A was again kept naked. She was raped again by Accused B. In parallel, another person, Witness D, was interrogated by Furundžija and assaulted by Accused B. When not in the room, Furundžija was just outside the open door to the room. As the court found, Furundžija and Accused B effectively divided the process of interrogation between them. Furundžija's role was to question, while Accused B's role was to assault and threaten, with the aim to elicit information from witnesses A and D.[18]

Once the execution of a crime or series of crimes is parcelled out to two or more persons in this way, each perpetrator, or co-perpetrator, is individually responsible for

---

[14] *Prosecutor* v. *Milorad Krnojelac*, Decision on Form of Second Amended Indictment, 11 May 2000, para. 15.

[15] *Tadić* appeal judgment, para. 194. Subsequently confirmed in *Prosecutor* v. *Milan Milutinović et al.*, Decision (Appeals Chamber) on Dragoljub Ojdanić's Motion Challenging Jurisdiction — Joint Criminal Enterprise, 21 May 2003, paras 18–19, 21.   [16] See ICJ Statute, Art. 38(1)(b).

[17] *Furundžija* trial judgment, para. 216.   [18] Ibid., paras 124–30.

the crimes jointly committed, even if, as in the case of Furundžija, the particular defendant happened to remain at arm's length from the violence. In such situations the co-perpetrators all have the same mens rea. It is only their acts that differ. This notion of co-perpetratorship is a simple derivative of the basic notion of individual commission, an almost logical extension. (A joint project can be made out of any actus reus.) The only real issue for such cases is the threshold of contribution, or participation, in the combined realization of the actus reus of the crime. How much action (or what degree of omission) must accompany the mens rea?[19]

The issue of the threshold of contribution grows in significance with every person who is added to the association of co-perpetrators. (For a given offence, the more people involved, the less for them to do.) When the crimes committed by members of the perpetrator group are also multiple in kind, the mens rea of the alleged co-perpetrators will tend to diverge. More actors, and more crimes, favour an analysis utilizing multiple schemes, rather than a single enterprise. A priori, then, co-perpetratorship, as an extension of the notion of individual commission, quickly becomes unstable as more persons and crimes are added to the picture. In *Furundžija*, where the perpetrators of the crimes were never more than two (the liability of the on-looking soldiers did not come into consideration), and where they committed the crimes for the most part in each other's company, neither the equivalence of their intentions nor the contribution threshold was a difficult issue for the Trial Chamber.

The *Furundžija* Trial Chamber therefore went further than it needed to go when it took account of the Dachau concentration camp case, heard by a US military court under Control Council Law No. 10.[20] The defendants in that case had held positions in the hierarchy of Dachau camp, ranging from camp commander to guards and prisoner-functionaries. The prosecution's case was that the defendants had participated in a common plan to run the camp in such a manner that the greater number of prisoners would die or suffer severe injury.[21] Three elements were identified by the military court as necessary to establish guilt for the commission of crimes at the camp: that there was in force a system to ill-treat the prisoners; that a given defendant was aware of the nature of the system; and that the defendant 'encouraged, aided and abetted or participated' in enforcing the system.[22] All 40 accused persons were found guilty, with sentences reflecting their degree of participation.

The criminal enterprise in the *Dachau* case was contained within the camp's perimeter. The camp was the 'system', and everyone who was part of it was held responsible for the crimes committed therein, no matter how attenuated the mens rea of a particular defendant or how slight his or her contribution to the commission of the crimes.

While the circumstances in *Dachau* and *Furundžija* are very different, the notional embankment provided by the camp setting in *Dachau* might suggest a conceptualization of responsibility for the *Dachau* defendants in terms similar to that of the co-accused in *Furundžija*: co-perpetration, although at a much higher level of

[19] Ibid., paras 252, 257.
[20] *Trial of Martin Gottfried Weiss and Thirty-Nine Others* (13 December 1945), 11 LRTWC 5 (*Dachau* case).
[21] Ibid., p. 7.   [22] Ibid., p. 13.

complexity. At least, this is how the *Furundžija* judges saw the matter.[23] But their interpretation is strained. The *Dachau* court gave paramount significance to the existence of a system. ('The accused did not all know each other, nor were they all at Dachau at the same time, but as they came and went the system remained and as each of them took over his position, he adhered to the system.')[24] The court did not see all responsibility in terms of 'co-perpetration', but apportioned responsibility also to those who aided and abetted the system (such as the perimeter guards). *Furundžija* was a case of a joint offence, and so was *Dachau*, but this does not make the latter a jurisprudential basis for the former. If A can be responsible for a crime, then so can A and B together, and so on and so forth, but it will depend on the facts of each case whether all persons involved shared responsibility in the same way and to the same degree.

We have seen other examples of Second World War cases being utilized selectively by today's ad hoc tribunals. The *Dachau* case does not help to broaden the elemental notion of co-perpetration, which fits the facts of *Furundžija* so well, and which is, as we have noted, a mere logical extension of the notion of individual commission.

In *Tadić*, the prosecutor appealed on the ground that the Trial Chamber did not avail itself of the 'common purpose doctrine' in reaching its decision that there was no proof that Duško Tadić killed any of five men during an attack by Bosnian-Serb forces on the village of Jaskići, on 14 June 1992. Tadić had participated in the attack on the village as an ordinary member of an armed group. It was proven that he had rounded up and severely assaulted several villagers. But there was no evidence that he had killed, and no evidence that he had intended to kill. In the prosecutor's view, regardless of which member or members of the attacking force had killed the men, Tadić should have been held responsible for their deaths for the reason that such killings were a predictable consequence of the attack on the village in which he participated.[25]

The Appeals Chamber's first task was to recast Article 7 of the ICTY Statute as an open-ended provision, so that the doctrine of common purpose, however it might turn out, could be absorbed into the Statute. This resulted in one of the most remarkable assertions in tribunal history:

An interpretation of the Statute based on its object and purpose leads to the conclusion that the Statute intends to extend the jurisdiction of the International Tribunal to *all* those 'responsible for serious violations of international humanitarian law' committed in the former Yugoslavia (Article 1). As is apparent from the wording of both Article 7(1) and the provisions setting forth the crimes over which the International Tribunal has jurisdiction (Articles 2 to 5), such responsibility for serious violations of international humanitarian law is not limited merely to those who actually carry out the actus reus of the enumerated crimes but appears to extend also to other offenders.[26]

---

[23] *Furundžija* trial judgment, para. 212.   [24] *Dachau* case, p. 14.

[25] *Tadić* appeal judgment, para. 175.

[26] Ibid., para. 189, emphasis in original. That this is a mere assertion, not an argument, is made plain by the immediately following paragraph in the judgment, where key words are italicized by the Appeals Chamber to add thunder to an opinion of the UN Secretary-General: 'It should be noted that this notion is spelled out in the Secretary General's Report, according to which: "The Secretary-General believes that *all* persons who *participate* in the planning, preparation or execution of serious violations of international humanitarian law in the former Yugoslavia are individually responsible for such violations." '

This exercise in statutory interpretation prepared the ground for the incorporation of JCE, but other forms of responsibility also made their way into the case law through this opening, as we shall see later in the chapter.

For a theory under which to convict Tadić for the murders, the *Tadić* Appeals Chamber turned to 'customary international law',[27] and in particular to the Second World War cases. The first case it relied on was *Almelo*,[28] decided by a British military court. Three of the defendants in that case were found to have taken part in the execution of a British prisoner of war. There was no dispute that they had taken the prisoner to a wood for the purpose of having him killed. The party was under the command of one of the defendants, and one of the two subordinates shot the prisoner in the presence of the other two.[29]

Almelo involved a gang crime, and this is how it was seen by the court. Reference was made to the military-equivalent statutory provision pertaining to gang crimes: 'Where there is evidence that a war crime has been the result of concerted action upon the part of a unit or group of men, then evidence given upon any charge relating to that crime against any member of such unit or group, may be received as prima facie evidence of the responsibility of each member of that unit or group for that crime.'[30]

The problem with citing *Almelo* against Tadić is that the latter was not shown to have been involved in any 'concerted action' to kill villagers. In addition to lack of proof that Tadić intended to kill, Tadić might not even have seen the killings take place. *Almelo* is thus precedent for the conviction of Furundžija, a militarized gang rape (and this is the case which the *Furundžija* Trial Chamber should have cited, not *Dachau*). More was needed than simple co-perpetration to find Tadić responsible.

The *Tadić* Appeals Chamber proceeded to cite several Second World War cases in the *Almelo* vein, before pausing briefly on the trial of Franz Schonfeld and others by a British military court.[31] Schonfeld and his co-accused were charged with killing three pilots pursuant to a plan. Only four of the ten accused were convicted, the very four who had raided the apartment where the pilots had been hiding. One of those four had committed the killings.

The judge advocate explained the applicable law, in words quoted by the *Tadić* Appeals Chamber:

if several persons combine for an unlawful purpose or for a lawful purpose to be effected by unlawful means, and one of them, in carrying out the purpose, kills a man, it is murder in all who are present, whether they actually aid or abet or not, provided that the death was caused by a member of the party in the course of his endeavours to effect the common object of the assembly.[32]

Several phrases in this text ('combine', 'all who are present', 'the party', 'common object', 'the assembly') alert us to a precondition of the doctrine, which is the physical and intellectual proximity and coordination of the actors. This is still the basic idea of

27 *Tadić* appeal judgment, para. 194.
28 *Trial of Otto Sandrock and Three Others* (26 November 1945), I LRTWC 35 (*Almelo* case).
29 Ibid., p. 40.   30 Ibid., p. 43.
31 *Trial of Franz Schonfeld and Nine Others* (26 June 1946), XI LRTWC 64.
32 Ibid., p. 68.

a gang crime, whose underlying logic is that if A can commit a crime, then so can A and B together, and so on.

The *Tadić* Appeals Chamber purported to base its conclusions as to JCE on *Schonfeld*, without remarking on the fact that the judge advocate focused primarily on forms of accessoryship, or aiding and abetting. In this respect, the judge said:

> if a man is present whilst a felony is committed, if he takes no part in it and does not act in concert with those who commit it, he will not be a principal in the second degree, merely because he did not endeavour to prevent the felony. It is not necessary, however, to prove that the party actually aided in the commission of the offence; if he watched for his companions in order to prevent surprise or remained at a convenient distance in order to favour their escape, if necessary, or was in such a situation as to be able readily to come to their assistance the knowledge of which was calculated to give additional confidence to his companions, he was, in contemplation of law, present, aiding and abetting.[33]

On the facts of the ICTY case, Tadić did not aid and abet the murder of the Jaskići villagers. The Appeals Chamber was aware of this, of course, hence its search for another doctrine by which to connect Tadić with the killings. The *Schonfeld* convictions, on the other hand, were achievable by use of standard notions such as principalship in the first or second degree, or, if there had been a plan, the notion that those who pursue a plan to commit murder are all guilty of the murder committed by one among their number. Reading the report on the case, it is not possible to tell which doctrine was applied in *Schonfeld* for the convictions,[34] so the suggestion that another idea (JCE) was afoot in that case is speculation.

The *Tadić* Appeals Chamber concluded its discovery in customary law of the first form of JCE — the form which would come to be referred to, simply, as JCE 1 — with another Second World War case 'worthy of mention':[35] *Einsatzgruppen*.[36]

It was perhaps the biggest murder trial in history. The case involved 23 defendants and more than a million victims. The US military tribunal observed at the outset that the accused persons were not central planners, distant from the crimes, but 'in the field, actively superintending, controlling, directing, and taking an active part in the bloody harvest'.[37] There were four Einsatzgruppen, each 800 to 1,200 men strong, which followed the German armies into Poland and the Soviet Union. Their purpose was to liquidate opposition to National Socialism in the occupied territories. The defendants held senior positions in the four units, with, for instance, Otto Ohlendorf commanding Einsatzgruppe D, which took over the Ukraine, the Crimea, and the Caucasus.

We note in passing that the biggest murder trial in history had possibly the shortest prosecution phase in history for a sizeable murder case: two days. The evidence was entirely documentary.[38] The Einsatz units had painstakingly documented all, or most, of their crimes. The Führer Order had tasked them to shoot, specifically, all the Jews; and so they shot all the Jews they could find and reported their accomplishments back to their headquarters.

---

[33] Ibid., p. 70.   [34] Ibid., p. 71.   [35] *Tadić* appeal judgment, para. 200.
[36] *United States* v. *Otto Ohlendorf et al.* (8 April 1948), 4 TWC 3 (*Einsatzgruppen* case).
[37] Ibid., p. 412.   [38] Ibid., p. 455.

Some of the Einsatz defendants pleaded non-involvement. The attorney of Heinz Schubert asked what was criminal about his client's actions:

Schubert first goes to the gypsy quarter of Simferopol and sees them being loaded aboard and shipped off. Then he drives to the place of execution, sees the rerouting of traffic, the roads blocked off, persons being unloaded, valuables handed over, and the shooting. Finally he drives back once more along the way to the gypsy quarter and there again sees them being loaded aboard and carried off, and then returns to his office. That is what he did.[39]

What could be wrong about that? The tribunal commented: 'There is no realization here that Schubert was taking an active part in mass murder.' It concluded that even though men like Schubert were not in command of the executioners, they could not escape the fact that they were members of Einsatz units 'whose express mission, well known to all the members, was to carry out a large scale program of murder. Any member who assisted in enabling these units to function, knowing what was afoot, is guilty of the crimes committed by the unit.'[40] As for those defendants who *were* in command and who did not participate personally in the executions, but rather devoted themselves to directing the overall operations of the Einsatzgruppen, this 'only serves to establish their deeper responsibility for the crimes of the men under their command'.[41]

It is true that these pronouncements are not served by a simple theory of gang crime, but the presumption of the *Tadić* judges, that a unified theory of responsibility — the JCE doctrine — underlies them, has no force when one considers that Schubert's conviction may have been effected as a variety of aiding and abetting (the words 'assisted in enabling these units to function, knowing what was afoot', makes that more than likely), whereas those commanders with the 'deeper responsibility' compared with other defendants may have been dealt with according to a standard notion of ordering or procuring. One must also keep in mind that the *Einsatzgruppen* tribunal wished to make a distinction between individual responsibility, on the one hand, and responsibility arising from membership in an IMT-defined criminal organization, on the other.[42] The JCE doctrine, for all its qualifications, steers blithely away from the former and worryingly close to the latter. All of the Einsatz defendants were SS men (five generals, five colonels, six lieutenant colonels, three majors, and three junior officers),[43] and all were convicted for membership of the SS, Gestapo, or SD. But not all were convicted for individual responsibility.

The two who were acquitted in this respect were Felix Rühl and Matthias Graf. Rühl was an administrative officer with no proven executive functions. He was with the unit for only a short period. In that time he was informed of the unlawful operations of the unit, but it was not established that he was in a position 'to control, prevent or modify' them.[44] Graf remained a non-commissioned officer throughout 13 months of service with an Einsatz unit. He did not command any of its subdivisions. When assigned a command, he refused to accept it and was arrested. The court had no doubt that Graf

---

[39] Ibid., p. 502.   [40] Ibid., p. 373.   [41] Ibid.   [42] Ibid., pp. 494–6.
[43] One of the defendants, Rasch, was eventually severed from the case due to the onset of parkinsonism.
[44] *Einsatzgruppen* case, p. 580.

knew about the unit's systematic killing of civilians. Yet knowledge is not enough for guilt, and the evidence did not show that Graf had acted to further — or omitted to act to prevent — the unit's unlawful operations. It is clear from the following comment of the military tribunal that it was looking to apply traditional notions of individual liability to Graf, and that there is no justification for deriving an underlying JCE doctrine from the *Einsatzgruppen* case:

it is not to be assumed that the commander of the organization would take Graf into his confidence in planning an operation. As a non-commissioned officer he would not participate in officers' conferences. Since there is no evidence in the record that Graf was at any time in a position to protest against the illegal actions of others, he cannot be found guilty as an accessory... Since there is no proof that he personally participated in any of the executions or their planning, he may not be held as a principal.[45]

The professed excavation of a basic doctrine of JCE (namely, JCE 1) from the field of customary law was of no immediate application to Tadić, but the *Tadić* Appeals Chamber believed that with a little more digging an extended form of the doctrine (JCE 3) would be revealed. The extended form would take care of cases involving 'a common design to pursue one course of conduct where one of the perpetrators commits an act which, while outside the common design, was nevertheless a natural and foreseeable consequence of the effecting of that common purpose'.[46] This attenuation had the potential to link Tadić with the murders, according to the Appeals Chamber.

7.2.3 The outer limits of liability

We now turn to *Tadić*'s analysis of the *Essen Lynching* case.

The seven accused in *Essen Lynching*[47] were charged with having been 'concerned in the killing' of three British airmen. Very little information is available about the case, with much of what we have representing the prosecutor's submissions, hence it must be treated with circumspect. We know that defendant Erich Heyer was an army captain in whose custody the German police had placed the three airmen. We also know that Heyer ordered Peter Könen, an army private, to escort the prisoners on foot to a nearby unit for interrogation. The other five accused were civilian inhabitants of Essen. It was established that Heyer called out loudly to Könen not to intereftere with the crowd that was gathering should anyone in the crowd mistreat the prisoners. The men were marched down the street, and soon they were being hit and pelted with various objects by onlookers. An unnamed soldier fired a shot, wounding one of the airmen. When they reached a bridge, the prisoners were cast over the parapet and killed.[48]

---

[45] Ibid., p. 585.   [46] *Tadić* appeal judgment, para. 204.
[47] *Trial of Erich Heyer and Six Others* (22 December 1945), 1 LRTWC 88 (*Essen Lynching* case).
[48] Ibid., p. 89.

The prosecutor had characterized the seven accused as either accessories before the fact or principals in the unlawful killing of the three airmen.[49] Heyer was sentenced to death by the military court, which indicates the use of a doctrine that creates liability for crimes not specifically ordered. Such a doctrine was nothing new to British law; it was articulated, for example, by the judge advocate in the *Schonfeld* case:

> The accessory is . . . liable for all that ensues upon the execution of the unlawful act commanded; that is to say, if A commands B to beat C, and B beats C so that he dies, A is accessory to the murder of C. There must be some active proceeding on the part of the accessory, that is, he must procure, incite or in some other way encourage the act done by the principal.[50]

Heyer's relevant action was to (in effect) incite the crowd to mistreat the prisoners. There is no requirement in the *Schonfeld* formulation that the ultimate act is foreseeable, and a fortiori the prosecutor is not required to prove the mens rea of murder in person A. Absent mens rea, Heyer was guilty of manslaughter, but manslaughter in this context was still construable as a war crime; in view of Heyer's role as the custodian of the prisoners of war and the instigator of the lynching, capital punishment would have seemed justified to the British military court.

The *Tadić* Appeals Chamber erroneously concluded, however, that 'The inference seems therefore justified that the court assumed that the convicted persons who simply struck a blow or implicitly incited the murder could have *foreseen* that others would kill the prisoners; hence they too were found guilty of murder.'[51] An inference to an assumption is a weak basis for a doctrine. In any event, this aspirational statement is derived from a case which is distinguishable on the facts from *Tadić*. Tadić was not shown to have participated in any prior mistreatment of the five Jaskići villagers who were eventually killed; possibly he was at a different location in the village when the five victims were assaulted and finally shot in the head — we simply do not know.

The *Tadić* Appeals Chamber proceeded to press several Second World War cases into service in this manner.[52] The chamber's aim was to modify existing doctrine, substituting the element of interconnected action with the element of foreseeability. If Tadić was not liable under the old doctrine, because he was insufficiently connected by the evidence with the actions of the persons who killed the villagers, he was liable under the new construct because it was foreseeable to him that the expedition he had joined might have ended up having people unlawfully killed.

The *Tadić* Appeals Chamber concluded that JCE is 'firmly established in customary international law', in both its first and its third forms, and is 'upheld, albeit implicitly', in the ICTY Statute.[53] This is *despite* the fact, the chamber argued, that contemporary municipal systems apparently differ on whether the unplanned crime of the third JCE form is solely the responsibility of the person who committed it.[54] Customary law, here, is a very malleable notion.[55]

---

[49] Ibid., p. 91.   [50] *Schonfeld* case, p. 69.

[51] *Tadić* appeal judgment, para. 209, emphasis added.

[52] Ibid., paras 210–19.   [53] Ibid., para. 220.   [54] Ibid., para. 224.

[55] For a sustained critique of the JCE doctrine, see *Prosecutor* v. *Kvočka et al.*, Final Trial Brief [for Zoran Žigić], 29 June 2001, paras 243–64; and A. Bogdan, 'Individual Criminal Responsibility in the Execution of a "Joint

The Appeals Chamber thus put foward the scheme below, and it is this scheme that the Trial Chambers and the differently composed Appeals Chambers which succeeded the *Tadić* bench have struggled to make sense of ever since:

i. A plurality of persons. They need not be organised in a military, political or administrative structure...

ii. The existence of a common plan, design or purpose which amounts to or involves the commission of a crime provided for in the Statute. There is no necessity for this plan, design or purpose to have been previously arranged or formulated. The common plan or purpose may materialise extemporaneously and be inferred from the fact that a plurality of persons acts in unison to put into effect a joint criminal enterprise.

iii. Participation of the accused in the common design involving the perpetration of one of the crimes provided for in the Statute. This participation need not involve commission of a specific crime under one of those provisions (for example, murder, extermination, torture, rape, etc.), but may take the form of assistance in, or contribution to, the execution of the common plan or purpose.

Then comes a distinction between the first and third forms of the doctrine, as well as a variety of the first form, known as JCE 2:

the mens rea element differs according to the category of common design under consideration. With regard to the first category, what is required is the intent to perpetrate a certain crime (this being the shared intent on the part of all co-perpetrators). With regard to the second category (which...is really a variant of the first), personal knowledge of the system of ill-treatment is required...as well as the intent to further this common concerted system of ill-treatment. With regard to the third category, what is required is the intention to participate in and further the criminal activity or the criminal purpose of a group and to contribute to the joint criminal enterprise or in any event to the commission of a crime by the group. In addition, responsibility for a crime other than the one agreed upon in the common plan arises only if, under the circumstances of the case, (i) it was foreseeable that such a crime might be perpetrated by one or other members of the group and (ii) the accused willingly took that risk.[56]

There is much that is flawed about this pronouncement, most obviously its imprecision — expressions such as 'common plan or purpose may materialise extemporaneously', 'participation need not involve...but may take the form of', and '...contribute to the joint criminal enterprise or in any event to the commission of a crime'. The threshold of participation or contribution is unspecified. A 'plurality'

Criminal Enterprise" in the Jurisprudence of the Ad Hoc International Tribunal for the Former Yugoslavia' (2006) 6 *Int'l Crim. L. Rev.* 63.

   [56] *Tadić* appeal judgment, paras 227–8. There has been some discussion at the ICTY on whether a conviction for genocide is possible under the extended form of JCE (*Stakić* trial judgment, paras 529–30; reiterated at para. 558. The same view was taken in *Prosecutor* v. *Radoslav Brđanin*, Decision on Motion for Acquittal Pursuant to Rule 98 *bis*, 28 November 2003, paras 30, 55–7). The issue has now been settled by the Appeals Chamber, which has held that the extended form of JCE applies to genocide as much as to any other crime as long as the required conditions are met. These conditions are that it was reasonably foreseeable from the JCE's objective that an act specified in Article 4 of the ICTY Statute would be committed with genocidal intent; and that the defendant was aware of this possibility when he or she participated in the JCE (*Prosecutor* v. *Radoslav Brđanin*, Decision on Interlocutory Appeal, 19 March 2004, para. 6).

introduces infinite variability, and can signify a closed class, with a stable (known or identifiable) membership, or an open class, whose boundaries are porous, ever-changing, or simply unidentifiable.

A less obvious, but in retrospect critical flaw, is the failure to explain the relationship among the 'plurality' of persons in the JCE. It is said that the plurality 'need not be organized', and that there is 'no necessity' for the plan, design, or purpose upon which the plurality acts 'to have been previously arranged or formulated'. Yet in some sense the plurality 'acts in unison' to put into effect a 'common concerted system'. The plurality is not referred to as a 'group', with 'members', until the last quoted paragraph, where 'group' is used three times. The last sentence of that paragraph suggests that the plurality is defined through an agreement ('crime other than the one agreed upon'), even though we have seen that the second of the above-quoted paragraphs allows that 'There is no necessity for this plan, design or purpose to have been previously arranged or formulated' — strongly implying that agreement is not required.

7.2.4 The 'plurality' of a joint criminal enterprise

In the Second World War cases considered by the *Tadić* Appeals Chamber the 'plurality' was characterized, as we have seen, by proximity to the scene of the crime. Some of the cases involved a tight-knit group (for example, *Schonfeld*), whereas others involved an accidental gathering of strangers (for example, *Essen Lynching*). *Einsatzgruppen* was broken down into its constituent operational units. The concentration camp cases were confined, literally, to the area within the perimeter of the camp. Persons far from the location of the criminal activity could be made to share responsibility with the on-site perpetrators through links of ordering, procuring, and aiding and abetting.

In the Second World War cases, the physical location of the actors or their bonds within a military hierarchy determined how responsibility was conceptualized in multiple-defendant cases. The common plan or purpose of an ad hoc lynching party, where there is no hierarchy, may well 'materialize extemporaneously', but this is possible only because the persons who momentarily coalesce into a lynching party happen to be in the same place at the same time. In *Tadić*'s eventual definition of JCE, by contrast, the locative element was omitted, except in JCE 2, and the hierarchical element was omitted entirely, casting the notion of 'plurality' adrift. The uncertainty which is the result of this omission could have been corrected through the insertion of a requirement of mutual agreement (explicit or implicit) among those comprising the plurality. 'Jointness' would no longer be referenced to location or hierarchy, but rather to some variety of agreement. JCE would thus have emerged as a variety of conspiracy. But this was not to be.

The legal risk in *Tadić*'s definition of JCE is simple to illustrate. Take persons A and B, who believe that area R in Bosnia-Herzegovina must be cleansed of members of a given ethnic group. The area in question includes the municipality where A and B live. A and B succeed in forcibly removing members of the targeted ethnic group from this municipality. Persons C and D live in a neighbouring municipality; it, too, is part of area R. Like A and B, C and D believe that R must be cleansed of members of the given ethnic group. C and D take action forcefully to remove members of the targeted group from their municipality. In the process of doing so, D kills a member of the group. Whereas A and B are acquaintances, who go about their ethnic cleansing together, C and D do not know of each other at all. Assume, moreover, that neither C nor D has ever heard of A or B, and vice versa.

It follows from the *Tadić* definition that a joint criminal enterprise obtains among A, B, C, and D. The four are a plurality; they have a common purpose, or at least a purpose in common; and each contributes something, with the necessary intent, to realize the common purpose. Because a JCE obtains, each of the perpetrators in the above example is responsible for the forced transfer committed by the other three. Moreover, because it is foreseeable that a person might be killed in such circumstances, A, B, and C share responsibility with D for the killing he committed.

This conclusion is absurd. It is absurd because it takes more than an idea in common to turn several acts into a 'joint enterprise'. The sharing of an idea is, very often, a matter of coincidence, or, for many ideas, simply inevitable. Whereas 'joint' implies coordination, *Tadić*'s definition fails to distinguish coincidental from coordinated action. It renders criminal responsibility unpredictable.

The absence of a requirement of a glue to hold together the plurality in *Tadić*'s definition is bound also to cause a problem in cases where the plurality is very large. The Einsatzgruppen formed a large plurality, and even though they were well defined as an enterprise through their unified hierarchy and the Führer Order, the tribunal which heard the case analysed the whole into several smaller operations, and determined responsibility within those lesser schemes using conventional grounds of liability. Where a large plurality does not have the singular structure and purpose of the Einsatzgruppen, the crimes committed by members of the perpetrator group are likely to be multiple in kind, and the mens rea of the alleged co-perpetrators will tend to diverge. As noted earlier, more actors and more crimes favour an analysis utilizing multiple schemes, rather than a single enterprise. Here again, JCE, lacking a robust definition, is likely to prove unworkable.

7.2.5 Application of the JCE doctrine

In applying the JCE doctrine to Tadić, the Appeals Chamber said that he had actively taken part in a common criminal objective of ridding a region of Bosnia-Herzegovina of its non-Serb population by committing inhumane acts. To this end he had participated in an attack on Jaskići village, as a member of an armed group. In the course of the attack he rounded up and severely assaulted several villagers. (From this the court found Tadić's intention to further the JCE objective of ridding the region of non-Serbs by committing inhumane acts.) That non-Serbs might be killed in effecting this objective was foreseeable, since many had been killed up to this point in similar incidents. Tadić knew about this history, and so was aware that the actions of the group he had joined were likely to result in killings; he willingly took the risk.[57] The Appeals Chamber convicted him of a count of wilful killing and of two counts of murder.[58]

---

[57] *Tadić* appeal judgment, paras 231–2.   [58] Ibid., paras 235–7.

The Appeals Chamber's conviction of Tadić for the Jaskići killings was the right result, for the wrong reasons. In the course of presenting those reasons, the Appeals Chamber put in place a new, vaguely defined, open-ended doctrine which it did not need. The original Trial Chamber had clearly made a mistake. Jaskići was a settlement of 11 houses; the attacking force was a small one; there was overwhelming evidence that Tadić was present in Jaskići beating villagers shortly before the force departed; and immediately after the force departed, the surviving villagers found five bodies in the streets.[59] This was a gang crime, Tadić was present as one of the gang, and it would have been enough for the Appeals Chamber to confine itself to the established law, which as we saw was recalled by the judge advocate in the *Schonfeld* case: 'if several persons combine for an unlawful purpose... and one of them, in carrying out the purpose, kills a man, it is murder in all who are present'.

One year after the Appeals Chamber's *Tadić* judgment, a reconstituted bench of the Appeals Chamber (although with Shahabuddeen still presiding) reviewed the Trial Chamber judgment in the *Furundžija* case. It pronounced that the Trial Chamber had in effect relied on the joint criminal enterprise doctrine, subsequently brought to light by the *Tadić* Appeals Chamber.[60] By this simple device, the co-perpetration argument relied on by the Trial Chamber was declared a variety of JCE, the apparent divergence in the jurisiprudence was brushed aside as terminological, and the foothold of the JCE doctrine in the jurisprudence of the tribunal was strengthened.

The JCE doctrine was next used to determine liability in August 2001, in the *Krstić* case. (A passing reference had been made to JCE in the *Kordić and Čerkez* judgment; it is not clear, however, that that ICTY Trial Chamber finally utilized the doctrine.)[61] As with all cases up to this point, and several cases beyond, JCE was not specifically pleaded in the indictment in the *Krstić* case.[62] The Trial Chamber found Krstić to be a member of two joint criminal enterprises, both of which were directed against the Bosnian-Muslim inhabitants of Srebrenica town. One concerned the women, children, and elderly members of this group, while the other concerned the men.

The two enterprises grew out of a plan to rid Srebrenica of its Bosnian-Muslim inhabitants. The Bosnian-Serb offensive on the town began on 6 July 1995. Five days later, General Mladić, accompanied by General Živanović (then commander of the Drina Corps), and General Krstić (then deputy commander and chief of staff of the Corps), took a notorious stroll, widely televised, through the empty streets of Srebrenica.[63] The women, children, and elderly people, as well as some military-aged men, had fled to Potočari, in the same municipality, where there was a small UN presence. The rest of the men retreated in a column through the woods.

The first JCE aimed to precipitate a humanitarian crisis in Potočari, by witholding food, shelter, and basic services from the displaced persons. The main objective of this JCE was forced transfer. Having heightened the fear and panic of the displaced persons, on 12 and 13 July the Bosnian-Serb forces (VRS) bused the women, children, and

---

[59] *Tadić* trial judgment, paras 348–72.   [60] *Furundžija* appeal judgment, para. 119.
[61] See *Kordić and Čerkez* trial judgment, para. 829.   [62] *Krstić* trial judgment, para. 602.
[63] Ibid., para. 36.

elderly people out of Potočari to Bosnian-Muslim-held territory in a neighbouring municipality.[64] Krstić was found responsible under JCE 1 for the forced transfer, and under JCE 3 for incidental murders, rapes, beatings, and other abuses committed in the execution of the primary objective.[65]

Until the evening of 13 July, that is, until the end of the Potočari evacuation, Krstić remained deputy commander and chief of staff of the VRS Drina Corps; then Mladić promoted him to Corps commander.[66] The second JCE aimed to kill the captured military-aged men of Srebrenica with the intention to destroy the Bosnian-Muslim community of the town. In the Trial Chamber's finding, by implementing this action, the VRS destroyed, in part, the Bosnian-Muslim group as such.[67] (For genocide 'in part', see Chapter 5.)

As mentioned earlier, the JCE doctrine is imprecise in relation to two thresholds: the level of contribution of the defendant to the enterprise; and the strength of the link among members of the enteprise, including the defendant. We shall briefly review how these questions were dealt with by the *Krstić* Trial Chamber.

In relation to the first JCE, the court characterized Krstić's contribution as 'significant' — without discussing what it understood to be the required threshold. Krstić was, according to the Trial Chamber, aware that the shelling of Srebrenica would drive thousands of civilians from the town into the small area of Potočari.[68] When this indeed occurred, Krstić 'subscribed', in the language of the court, to the creation of a humanitarian crisis in Potočari.[69] What this comes down to, it seems, is that Krstić was present in Potočari, was aware of the suffering of the Bosnian Muslims assembled there, and did nothing to allay it. If he had a duty to allay it, and if his contribution was therefore an omission to act, the Trial Chamber did not discuss these matters.

Krstić was more proactive when it came to transfer. He ordered the procurement of buses for the transportation of the Muslim population out of Potočari. He also ordered his subordinates to secure the road along which the buses would travel, and he generally supervised the operation.[70] He knew that the displaced persons were being transferred out of the municipality against their will.[71]

In relation to the second JCE, whose target was the male population, Krstić's involvement began in Potočari, where military-aged men were separated from the rest of the displaced persons, and not transferred.[72] Krstić was 'kept fully informed' of developments relating, in addition, to the column of men fleeing Srebrenica through the woods. By the evening of 13 July 1995, thousands of those men had been captured by VRS forces within the zone of Krstić's responsibility.[73] On the morning of 15 July, according to the Trial Chamber, Colonel Beara asked Krstić for soldiers to help with the execution of the Bosnian-Muslim men. Krstić undertook to arrange for members of a particular VRS unit to be used; that unit commenced the execution of the captive Muslim men on 16 July.[74]

---

[64] Ibid., para. 48.   [65] Ibid., para. 617.   [66] Ibid., para. 461.
[67] Ibid., para. 644.   [68] Ibid., para. 462.   [69] Ibid., para. 615.
[70] Ibid., para. 464.   [71] Ibid., paras 608–9.   [72] Ibid., para. 621.
[73] Ibid., para. 471.   [74] Ibid., para. 473. (This finding was rejected on appeal. See below.)

In the court's view, the Drina Corps rendered 'substantial assistance' in the detention and killing of the men, as well as in their burial.[75] Krstić exercised 'effective control' over the Drina Corps throughout the territory in which the crimes were committed.[76] While the evidence did not show that Krstić had devised the plan to kill the men, he 'fulfilled a key co-ordinating role' in the implementation of the plan.[77] Because the *Tadić* Appeals Chamber did not define the contribution threshold in its formulation of JCE, it becomes necessary to divine it from court practice. In the *Krstić* case, the level of the accused's contribution to each of the joint criminal enterprises was rather high.

On the question of who constituted the enterprises and what kinds of link existed among their members, the findings of the *Krstić* Trial Chamber are unclear. The Court does not seem to have considered the question at all. What we see is that Krstić worked 'in close co-operation with other military officials of the VRS Main Staff and the Drina Corps',[78] that he was present in Potočari with 'other VRS officers, including General Mladić', overseeing the operation,[79] that the Main Staff directed the deployment of Drina Corps units,[80] that Krstić monitored the activities of his subordinate officers taking part in the executions,[81] and other remarks on this level. Was the JCE made up of Krstić, General Mladić, and 'key members of the VRS Main Staff and the Drina Corps' *alone*?[82] Or was it even more ill-defined, encompassing the 'political leadership' of the VRS,[83] namely the supreme commander of the armed forces, Radovan Karadžić, and possibly other politicians?[84] And what about the soldiers who carried out the executions? Were they members of the JCE, and, if so, what was the status of their comrades in the Drina Corps or the VRS as a whole who did not contribute to the enterprises because at the relevant time they were assigned to other duties or happened to be located outside Srebrenica municipality? Where did responsibility for the crimes against humanity of forced transfer and murder, and, indeed, genocide, begin and end? The Trial Chamber may have felt that it did not need to answer this question in relation to anybody other than Krstić, but in that case it should have relied on a liability doctrine other than JCE. When a choice is made to use the JCE lens, one must accept that the focus becomes a plurality, not an individual.

Upon review, the Appeals Chamber dismissed aspects of the *Krstić* Trial Chamber's findings on the second JCE. The Trial Chamber had wrongly concluded that certain men participating in the executions were members of the Drina Corps and that Krstić had assigned them to carry out the executions. Drina Corps personnel had merely facilitated the executions.[85] For the Appeals Chamber, which took great care to affirm that in July 1995 a genocide was committed against Bosnian Muslims in Srebrenica,[86] this reassessment of the evidence raised a question not about the existence of a criminal enterprise to commit genocide, but about Krstić's intent: did he share the JCE's objective to commit genocide? The JCE was treated as a black box in the Trial Chamber's

75 Ibid., para. 624. 76 Ibid., para. 631. 77 Ibid., para. 644.
78 Ibid., para. 612. 79 Ibid., para. 465. 80 Ibid., para. 437.
81 Ibid., para. 474. 82 Ibid., para. 610. 83 Ibid., para. 612.
84 Ibid., para. 101. 85 *Krstić* appeal judgment, paras 68–78. 86 Ibid., para. 39.

judgment, and so it remained in the judgment of the Appeals Chamber.[87] The question on appeal was whether to locate Krstić inside or outside this box.

The Appeals Chamber noted that an important consideration for the Trial Chamber for placing Krstić inside the black box of JCE was the amount of contact Krstić had had with Mladić during the relevant period. The Trial Chamber had assumed that Mladić's intention to execute the Bosnian Muslims was made known to Krstić in the course of such contact, but upon examination there was no evidence to back up the assumption.[88] Nor was the inference justified that Krstić was put on notice early on that the detained Bosnian-Muslim men would all be killed; he may easily have concluded that other plans were afoot.[89] Shortly after the killings started, on 13 July 1995, Krstić most likely found out about them; but his reaction (anger, followed perhaps by passivity) should have precluded the attribution to him of genocidal intent, according to the Appeals Chamber. The most that the evidence shows is that Krstić 'had knowledge of the genocidal intent of some members of the VRS Main Staff'. He was not a co-perpetrator in the JCE.[90]

For a student of the JCE doctrine, the state of the doctrine may at this point begin to seem intolerable. The *Krstić* Trial Chamber constructed an ill-defined JCE out of facts tending to focus on Krstić himself. The rest of the JCE was largely out of focus. With the Appeals Chamber extracting Krstić from the JCE, the enterprise with the genocidal purpose, to which the Srebrenica massacres were attributed, was reduced to a phantom, albeit one to which the Appeals Chamber accorded a central role in fixing Krstić's responsibility. His responsibility, according to the Appeals Chamber, is that he knew that by allowing Drina Corps resources to be used by the JCE he was making a substantial contribution to the execution of the Bosnian-Muslim detainees.[91] He therefore aided and abetted the crimes committed by the JCE. But whose genocidal intent was he aware of? 'The fact that the Trial Chamber did not identify individual members of the Main Staff of the VRS as the principal participants in the genocidal enterprise does not negate the finding that Radislav Krstić was aware of their genocidal intent.'[92] It is as if we are watching shadows pass before us in Plato's cave; the actual JCE is obscured to such a degree that it differs little from an outline projected on to the cave wall.

The next application of the JCE doctrine was in the *Kvočka* case, which involved the same bench as *Krstić*. Once again, JCE was not pleaded in the indictment.[93] The Trial and Appeals Chambers came to disagree fundamentally about JCE doctrine, further undermining tribunal rhetoric that this theory of criminal liability was appropriated in developed form from the shelf of customary law.

The evidence against four of the *Kvočka* defendants related to crimes committed at Omarska camp. The evidence against the fifth, Zoran Žigić, related to camps at Keraterm and Trnopolje, in addition to Omarska. The Trial Chamber said that it was

---

[87] In this regard, consider the almost paradoxical statement in the *Krstić* appeal judgment, para. 143: 'The fact that the Trial Chamber did not identify individual members of the Main Staff of the VRS as the principal participants in the genocidal enterprise does not negate the finding that Radislav Krstić was aware of their genocidal intent. A defendant may be convicted for having aided and abetted a crime which requires specific intent even where the principal perpetrators have not been tried or identified.'   [88] Ibid., para. 98.

[89] Ibid., para. 100.   [90] Ibid., paras 104, 111, 121, 129, 134.   [91] Ibid., para. 137.

[92] Ibid., para. 143.   [93] *Kvočka et al.* trial judgment, para. 246.

Tadić's second category of the JCE doctrine which 'resonated' best with the facts of the case.[94] Yet the Trial Chamber's very next step was to destroy the unitary scheme which the *Tadić* Appeals Chamber had professed to abstract from the Second World War cases: 'The criminal intent of persons who establish or design a criminal enterprise does not necessarily have to be shared by all who knowingly participate in its execution';[95] in particular, 'liability on the basis of a joint criminal enterprise requires a knowing assistance or encouragement for an aider or abettor, and an intent to advance the goal of the enterprise in the case of a co-perpetrator'.[96] Thus the Trial Chamber created two classes of offenders, on the basis of two thresholds of intent. According to this modification, the doctrine of joint criminal enterprise encompasses both classes. The enterprise is still supposedly 'joint', even though the responsibility of a member of one class (co-perpetrators) differs from that of a member of the other (aiders and abettors).

One sympathizes, to some extent, with *Kvočka*'s effort to find elbow room inside the straitjacket imposed by *Tadić*.[97] We noted earlier that the judges in the Second World War cases cited in *Tadić* were more eclectic in their choices of theory than the Appeals Chamber gave them credit for. Yet *Kvočka* is misleading insofar as it encourages the perception that the trial judges remained wholly within the realm of a JCE doctrine. What makes an enterprise 'joint' is never clear in *Tadić*, but *Kvočka*'s division of the offender group into two classes renders the JCE doctrine derivative, a kind of umbrella term for large-scale criminality, responsibility for which is resolved, nevertheless, on a case-by-case basis and in a theoretically eclectic manner.[98]

No less than *Tadić*, the *Kvočka* judges engaged in straitjacketing the Second World War cases.[99] This is symptomatic of an absence of a developed and rational method for identifying principles of customary law.

---

[94] Ibid., para. 268.   [95] Ibid., para. 294.   [96] Ibid., para. 271; elaborated in ibid., para. 284.

[97] The Trial Chamber remarked:

> It must be conceded that the *Tadić* formula for joint criminal enterprise responsibility appears to contain an inherent contradiction. On the one hand, it expressly allows for contribution to the commission of the crime through aiding or abetting which, as we have discussed, requires only knowledge, not shared intent. At other times, *Tadić* defines participation in terms of shared intent and it is not clear that this is limited to co-perpetrators. The [*Kvočka*] Trial Chamber believes that the Nuremberg jurisprudence and its progeny allow for "aiding and abetting" in its traditional form to exist in relation to a joint criminal enterprise and in the case of such an aider or abettor, knowledge plus substantial contribution to the enterprise is sufficient to maintain liability. Once the evidence indicates that the participant shares the intent of the criminal enterprise, he graduates to the level of a co-perpetrator of the enterprise. (Ibid., para. 273.)

[98] The reduction of 'joint criminal enterprise' to a conceptually empty shell is evident in the following remark by the *Kvočka* Trial Chamber:

> Within a joint criminal enterprise there may be other subsidiary criminal enterprises. For example, were the entire Nazi regime to be considered a joint criminal enterprise, that would not preclude a finding that Dachau Concentration Camp functioned as a subsidiary of the larger joint criminal enterprise, despite the fact that it was established with the intent to further the larger criminal enterprise. Within some subsidiaries of the larger criminal enterprise, the criminal purpose may be more particularized: one subset may be established for purposes of forced labor, another for purposes of systematic rape for forced impregnation, another for purposes of extermination, etc. (Ibid., para. 307.)

These remarks about the actual applicability of JCE doctrine to 'a vast criminal regime comprising thousands of participants' (ibid.) are, of course, entirely speculative. The JCE alleged in the *Kvočka* case was much smaller.

[99] Ibid., paras 290–306.

The *Kvočka* Trial Chamber also made pronouncements on the contribution thresh-old, which had been left undefined in *Tadić*.[100] The Trial Chamber sought to rely on the *Einsatzgruppen* case (which of course was not a concentration-camp case), where the threshold for a low-ranking member was 'significant contribution' to the commission of the enterprise crimes, whereas the role of a high-ranking member could, according to the Trial Chamber, be presumed to have been significant.[101] In other words, *Kvočka* set the JCE contribution threshold for all persons at 'significant'. It is a relatively clear threshold (being identical to that of aiding and abetting in general), although the same cannot be said of the court's further explanation, which reintroduced unpredictability into the law: 'By significant, the Trial Chamber means an act or omission that makes an enterprise efficient or effective; e.g., a participation that enables the system to run more smoothly or without disruption.'[102] (An obvious riposte is to ask whether 'more smoothly' is to be understood as '*significantly* more smoothly'.)

The *Kvočka* trial judgment concluded that the evidence had established that Omarska camp — but not any other camp or plurality — had functioned as a joint criminal enterprise. The common purpose 'pervading' the camp was the intent to per-secute non-Serb detainees through crimes such as murder, torture, and rape.[103] The defendants' role had been to keep the detainees in the camp. For example, of Miroslav Kvočka, who was a police officer, the Trial Chamber noted that, while it had not been shown that he himself had abused any detainees, his employment at Omarska camp as a senior guard over a period of three weeks 'sent a message of approval to other partici-pants in the camp's operation', especially the subordinate guards, which amounted to 'a condonation of the abuses and deplorable conditions there'.[104] The court added up the high position which Kvočka held in the camp, the authority and influence which he enjoyed over the guards, his negligible attempts to prevent crimes or alleviate the suffering of detainees, and his role in maintaining the functioning of the camp despite knowing that it was a criminal endeavour, and concluded that Kvočka had been a 'co-perpetrator' of the JCE at Omarska.[105] The same conclusion was reached in respect of the other four defendants.

The *Kvočka* judges were not to utilize, finally, their idea of 'aiding and abetting a joint criminal enterprise'.

The ICTY/ICTR Appeals Chamber has jolted wayward Trial Chambers into line without acknowledging that the first-instance courts might have been led astray by earlier expositions of the Appeals Chamber itself. The Appeals Chamber's review of the *Kvočka* trial judgment was laconic on the subject of JCE. It dismissed the lower court's scheme of two classes of offenders within a JCE, giving no argument, except to say that a JCE 'is simply a means of committing a crime;

---

[100] *Tadić*'s omission was noted by the *Kvočka* Trial Chamber in ibid., para. 289.
[101] Ibid., paras 281–2.   [102] Ibid., para. 309.   [103] Ibid., para. 320.
[104] Ibid., para. 405.   [105] Ibid., para. 414.

it is not a crime in itself'.[106] In other words, *to aid and abet a JCE* is a category mistake, because one cannot aid and abet a form of commission. But this grammatical point does not affect the Trial Chamber's argument that joint criminal enterprises have, historically, been constituted of primary and secondary actors. One would have expected the Appeals Chamber to pinpoint errors in the Trial Chamber's analysis of Second World War cases, and not merely to reaffirm its own judgment in *Tadić*, whose basis — a different selection of Second World War cases — is no more secure than *Kvočka's*.

The Appeals Chamber dismissed, moreover, the *Kvočka* Trial Chamber's attempt to define a contribution threshold for JCE liability. There is, it said, 'no specific legal requirement' that the defendant must have made a substantial or significant contribution to the JCE. The Appeals Chamber allowed exceptions to this rule (for reasons set out below), and concluded: 'In practice, the significance of the accused's contribution will be relevant to demonstrating that the accused shared the intent to pursue the common purpose.'[107] This confuses evidentiary and threshold issues: undoubtedly the accused's actions are relevant to determining his or her intent; but it is not sufficient for JCE liability to subscribe to the criminal enterprise's common purpose. Different elements are involved. A guilty mental state must be linked also with 'a contribution to the execution of the common plan', as *Tadić* put it. Evidence of the latter may serve as evidence of the former, but the substantive point regarding the contribution threshold for JCE remains unresolved. The Appeal Chamber's response to the *Kvočka* Trial Chamber is inadequate in this respect as well.

We noted earlier that the second significant imprecision in *Tadić's* formulation of the JCE doctrine concerns the nature of the link among members of a 'joint' enterprise. Three years and four months separate the judgments of the *Kvočka* lower and upper courts. About halfway along this period the Appeals Chamber delivered its judgment in the *Krnojelac* case. We shall return to this case later on; for the moment it is sufficient to note that the Appeals Chamber in *Kvočka* recited the words it had used in *Krnojelac*,

that, by requiring proof of an agreement in relation to each of the crimes committed with a common purpose, when it assessed the intent to participate in a systemic form of joint criminal enterprise, the Trial Chamber went beyond the criterion set by the Appeals Chamber in the *Tadić* case. Since the Trial Chamber's findings showed that the system in place at the KP Dom sought to subject non-Serb detainees to inhumane living conditions and ill-treatment on discriminatory grounds, the Trial Chamber should have examined whether or not Krnojelac knew of the system and agreed to it, without it being necessary to establish that he had entered into an agreement with the guards and soldiers — the principal perpetrators of the crimes committed under the system — to commit those crimes.[108]

The 'joint' in joint criminal enterprise thus being deliberately kept undefined, the *Kvočka* Appeals Chamber was faced with the task of having to explain who was a member and who was not a member of the Omarska JCE. The Trial Chamber had found one of the accused, Zoran Žigić, responsible 'for the crimes committed in the Omarska camp generally', with respect to the counts of persecution, murder, and torture. Žigić

---

[106] *Kvočka et al.* appeal judgment, para. 91.   [107] Ibid., para. 97 (also paras 104, 187, 421).
[108] Ibid., para. 118 (also para. 209), citing *Krnojelac* appeal judgment, para. 97.

held no official position at Omarska; he was not even a guard. His participation in the functioning of the camp amounted to several — at most ten — visits to the camp. He was shown on two occasions to have participated in the mistreatment of detainees. The Appeals Chamber, on the basis of no argument at all, said of 'opportunistic visitors' like Žigić, who had committed crimes at Omarska, that while it would not be 'appropriate' to hold every one of them responsible as a participant in the Omarska JCE, 'a substantial contribution to the overall effect of the camp is necessary to establish responsibility' under the JCE doctrine, despite 'the general rule that a substantial contribution to the joint criminal enterprise is not required'.[109]

This pronouncement contains arbitrary elements. It cannot be extrapolated from any accepted element of JCE. The Appeals Chamber had persisted in leaving unexplained the general criteria of JCE membership beyond the requirement of intent-in-common. Yet in *Kvočka* it bestowed JCE membership on opportunistic visitors through a participation threshold created for them alone.

It follows from the *Kvočka* appeal judgment that a person may be joined to a criminal enterprise based on his or her intent and on the severity (that is, substantial contribution) of his or her acts relative to (ordinary) members of the system, even if, in other respects, the person has no links to the system. In principle, there is no reason why this arbitrary loosening of the notion of a joint criminal enterprise should be confined to prison-camp settings. It implies a secondary class of JCE actors. Thus the *Kvočka* Appeals Chamber dismissed one secondary class (aiders and abettors of JCE), only to replace it with another (opportunistic participants in a JCE). The effect is that the very notion of a joint criminal enterprise is weakened and its application by the courts is rendered even less predictable.

The Appeals Chamber determined that Žigić's acts did not meet the threshold for opportunistic visitors but 'formed only mosaic stones in the general picture of violence and oppression'.[110] He had not participated in a 'significant way' in the functioning of Omarska camp. Thus the Trial Chamber's conviction of Žigić for the crimes committed in Omarska 'in general' was overturned.

The ICTY issued just two trial judgments in 2002. Both dealt with JCE and both were presided over by Judge David Hunt. In the first, *Krnojelac*, the Trial Chamber opened its discussion of the doctrine with criticisms of certain minor aspects of its formulation.[111] It then seized upon a phrase lying in the periphery of the *Tadić* definition ('a crime other than the one agreed upon in the common plan') and spun it out, without the assistance of any case law or other argument, into a separate element of the doctrine: 'A joint criminal enterprise exists where there is an understanding or arrangement amounting to an agreement between two or more persons that they will commit a crime.'[112] This was rejected, as we have seen, by the *Krnojelac* Appeals Chamber; it does, however, suggest that the Trial Chamber was considering casting JCE as a kind of realized conspiracy. Conspiracy requires an agreement to commit a crime, which is

---

[109] *Kvočka et al.* appeal judgment, para. 599. [110] Ibid.
[111] *Krnojelac* trial judgment, paras 74–8. [112] Ibid., para. 80.

more demanding to prove than 'existence of a common plan' or 'a common state of mind'. While the reader readily agrees with the statement of the *Krnojelac* trial court that, 'If the agreed crime is committed by one or other of the participants in that joint criminal enterprise, all of the participants in that enterprise are guilty of the crime regardless of the part played by each in its commission',[113] according to the Appeals Chamber this is not the JCE doctrine, because JCE does not encompass the elements of conspiracy.

Or so it would seem. In Tribunal jurisprudence occasionally the waves of one judicial tendency will collide with those of another. In a 2003 decision of the Appeals Chamber — which in the meantime had been joined by Judge Hunt, who was the advocate of 'agreement' — the JCE doctrine was described as conspiracy with an additional element:

Joint criminal enterprise and 'conspiracy' are two different forms of liability. Whilst conspiracy requires a showing that several individuals have agreed to commit a certain crime or set of crimes, a joint criminal enterprise requires, in addition to such a showing, that the parties to that agreement took action in furtherance of that agreement.[114]

Only a few months after this decision, the panel of the Appeals Chamber reviewing the *Krnojelac* trial judgment (excluding Judge Hunt), reached the opposite conclusion, cited above.

The *Krnojelac* Trial Chamber's statement that, to prove a JCE of type 1, the prosecutor must show that each of the persons charged as well as the principal offenders (assuming the latter are not also charged) 'had a common state of mind',[115] directs our attention to another set of issues. If a JCE allegedly involved hundreds of co-perpetrators, but only one or two of them are being tried at a given time (as is typically, and necessarily, the case), how much must be proven against the absent alleged co-perpetrators? The answer, evident from the ICTY cases we have reviewed so far, is that the actions of co-perpetrators who are not on trial are generally described superficially, if at all. There are two reasons for this: the practical impossibility of calling probatively complete evidence against each alleged co-perpetrator in a large JCE; and the undesirability of drawing explicit conclusions about the role (and therefore responsibility) of persons who are not present to defend themselves or who are in detention awaiting their own, separate, trials.

The *Krnojelac* indictment alleged that Milorad Krnojelac had acted pursuant to a joint criminal enterprise with guards and soldiers at the KP Dom prison camp in Foča, in Bosnia-Herzegovina, to persecute Muslim civilian detainees. While the indictment did not state any particular form of JCE, it was interpreted by the Trial Chamber as alleging JCE 2, but not an extended (type 3) JCE relating to crimes falling outside the 'agreed' aspects of the basic criminal enterprise.[116]

---

[113] Ibid., para. 82.

[114] *Prosecutor* v. *Milutinović et al.*, Decision on Dragoljub Ojdanić's Motion Challenging Jurisdiction — Joint Criminal Enterprise, 21 May 2003, para. 18.   [115] *Krnojelac* trial judgment, para. 83.

[116] Ibid., paras 84, 86.

Krnojelac was the warden of the prison for over a year beginning in April 1992.[117] He knew that the Muslim men at the KP Dom were being detained because they were Muslim, and for no other reason. As warden, he did not decide their detention and had no power to release them.[118] According to the trial court, the prosecution failed to establish that Krnojelac shared the intent of the joint criminal enterprise to illegally imprison Muslim civilians. While the court did convict him for illegal imprisonment, it was on the basis that his criminal conduct was that of 'an aider and abettor to the principal offenders' of the JCE.[119] The same result was reached in relation to the charges of inhumane living conditions, beatings and torture, and persecution.[120]

What is remarkable, however, is that the Trial Chamber did not make a finding that there *was* a JCE, whose 'principals' Krnojelac aided and abetted. The court *assumed* that the KP Dom stood for a JCE, confining its analysis to the question of whether the defendant had entered into an agreement with JCE members to further the enterprise objectives. The JCE, as an entity consisting of persons linked together by mental or behavioural attributes, was left up to the reader of the *Krnojelac* judgment to imagine. The added uncertainty this created is that, absent any specification of the threshold link or contribution among members of the KP Dom's JCE, it is not possible to understand what separated Krnojelac from that threshold.

The prosecutor's appeal against the first-instance judgment argued that a person like Krnojelac, who held the highest position of authority in a system where detainees were being ill-treated on discriminatory grounds, who knew that crimes were being committed within it, and who contributed to those crimes, cannot be considered a mere aider and abettor to the crimes but must be characterized as a co-perpetrator.[121] This ground of appeal is a reaction to the very weaknesses in the Trial Chamber's exposition which we identified above. The Appeals Chamber allowed the appeal, stating that the Trial Chamber should have examined whether Krnojelac 'knew of the system [of ill-treatment] and agreed to it, without it being necessary to establish that he had entered into an agreement with the guards and soldiers... to commit those crimes'.[122] The choice of words is unfortunate, yet it is clear that 'agreed to it' means whether Krnojelac went along with the operation of the system, or, more precisely, whether he shared the intent to commit the crimes. It is an inquiry into a personal attribute of the defendant, at the time of the events, not an inquiry into links among persons said to constitute a joint criminal enterprise.

7.2.6 JCE doctrine at the brink

The *Krnojelac* incident calls attention to the consequences of a poorly defined liability theory: in this case, a Trial Chamber was not sure how to apply the theory, the Appeals Chamber usurped the role of the Trial Chamber and applied the

---

[117] Part of the KP Dom had been leased to the military for its own use. The lease did not affect the unitary hierarchy within the prison; there was no significant division between military and civilian personnel: ibid., paras 102–4.

[118] Ibid., para. 126.   [119] Ibid., para. 127.   [120] Ibid., paras 170–1, 315, 487–92.

[121] *Krnojelac* appeal judgment, para. 85.   [122] Ibid., para. 97.

(reformulated) theory to factual findings it had not itself made, and the defendant Krnojelac had his seven-and-a-half-year sentence increased — 18 months later — to 15 years by the Appeals Chamber.[123] In these circumstances even the Appeals Chamber had to admit that, leaving aside the adequacy of its definition of the JCE doctrine in *Tadić*, there was no rule in circulation as to the *application* of the doctrine. This admission is found in its remarks quoted below. We have seen that the idea of JCE originates in municipal theories of gang crime utilized by military tribunals in Second World War cases. *Tadić* read into those simple conceptual extensions a grander doctrine, which the Appeals Chamber has since allowed the prosecutor to rely on in all cases, irrespective of complexity. But a legal doctrine requires a tradition — or, alternatively, a rule — as to the effect it should be given. In the following paragraphs from the *Krnojelac* appeal judgment we find the Appeals Chamber attempting to formulate such a rule:

The Appeals Chamber holds that the search for the common denominator in its evidence should have led the Prosecution to define the common purpose of the participants in the system in place at the KP Dom from April 1992 to August 1993 as limited only to the acts which sought to further the unlawful imprisonment at the KP Dom of the mainly Muslim, non-Serb civilians on discriminatory grounds related to their origin and to subject them to inhumane living conditions and ill-treatment in breach of their fundamental rights. The system worked because the camp staff and the military personnel who were involved in committing the crimes or who assisted the perpetrators were aware that the KP Dom facility had stopped operating as an ordinary prison when the Serb authorities arbitrarily incarcerated non-Serb civilians there following the fall of the town of Foča. From that point on, in the minds of the participants, the KP Dom had become a system for subjecting the mainly Muslim, non-Serb civilian detainees to inhumane living conditions and ill-treatment . . .

Additionally, it is undeniable that the decision arbitrarily to arrest the region's male, non-Serb civilians, imprison them at the KP Dom and then deport them from the region, or even physically eliminate some of them, must be linked to the criminal purpose of ethnically cleansing the Foča region pursued by some of its military and civilian authorities. This does not necessarily mean that all the co-perpetrators responsible for the living conditions and ill-treatment inflicted upon the non-Serb detainees at the KP Dom intended to take part in the ethnic cleansing of the region or were even aware of it at the time that they were physically committing the crimes and/or furthering the system in place.

Accordingly, the Appeals Chamber finds that the most appropriate approach in this case would have been to limit the definition of the common purpose within the KP Dom 'system' to the commission of those crimes which, given the context and evidence adduced, could be considered as common to all the offenders beyond all reasonable doubt. This amounts to selecting the common denominator discussed above. As for the crimes which do not plainly fit into the common

---

[123] Questionable intellectual shortcuts are utilized in connection with such exercises. Consider the following contortion: 'the Appeals Chamber will now examine whether no trier of fact could reasonably have concluded that Krnojelac shared the intent of the co-perpetrators of those crimes' (ibid., para. 109). The correct question is quite different; it is whether no reasonable trier of fact could have concluded (as the Trial Chamber had) that Krnojelac did *not* share the intent of the co-perpetrators. But twisting the applicable test, the Appeals Chamber was able effortlessly to reach its desired conclusion: 'a trier of fact should reasonably have inferred from the above findings that he [Krnojelac] was part of the system and thereby intended to further it' (ibid., para. 111). 'Should reasonably have inferred' is a semantically nebulous phrase.

purpose of this system, the Prosecution should, at least as an alternative, have stated on what basis it considered that the responsibility of the Accused could be established. The Appeals Chamber suggests that the following approach could be considered.

For alleged crimes, such as the killings, which albeit committed at the KP Dom clearly go beyond the system's common purpose, liability [JCE 3] may be imputed to a person participating in the system for crimes of this kind committed by another participant if it was foreseeable that a crime of this sort was likely to be committed by that other participant and the former willingly took the risk (or was indifferent to it) . . .

For alleged crimes which, whilst implicating several co-perpetrators at the KP Dom, do not appear beyond all reasonable doubt to constitute a purpose common to all the participants in the system, they should be considered as coming under a first category joint criminal enterprise without reference to the concept of system. The Appeals Chamber holds that the alleged crime of forced labour must be dealt with in this way. A person who participated in its commission may be regarded as a co-perpetrator of a joint criminal enterprise whose purpose was to commit the crime, provided that the individual concerned shared the common intent of the principal offenders. Alternatively, the individual concerned may be considered an aider and abettor if he merely had knowledge of the perpetrators' intent and lent them support which had a significant effect on the perpetration of the crime.

For alleged crimes which fit into a broader plan, such as imprisonment and deportation, they should be distinguished on the basis of whether they form part of the common purpose of all the participants in the system and other co-perpetrators outside of it or whether they form part of a common purpose shared by only some of the participants in the system and the persons outside that system. In the first case, into which the crime of imprisonment falls, the concept of system may be applied to all the participants. However, the distinctive nature of the crimes stems from the fact that some of the principal offenders are persons outside the system in place at the camp, that is, in the case of imprisonment, certain civilian and/or military authorities who ordered the arbitrary arrests and detention at the KP Dom. In the second case, into which the deportation or transfer of some of the non-Serb detainees falls, the crimes in question should be considered without applying the concept of system and a person who participated in their commission may be regarded as a co-perpetrator of a joint criminal enterprise whose purpose was to commit the crimes, provided that the individual concerned shared the common intent of the principal offenders. Alternatively, the individual concerned may be considered an aider and abettor if he merely had knowledge of the perpetrators' intent and lent them support which had a significant effect on the perpetration of the crimes.[124]

It is not clear to whom these complex instructions, reminiscent of pre-trial decisions on preliminary motions on the form of the indictment, are being addressed. Obviously they cannot have been meant for the prosecutor in the *Krnojelac* case, but they may have been meant as future guidance for the Office of the Prosecutor as a whole. One senses, however, that the primary target of the message is the *trial judges*, as well as their colleagues in other trial chambers, which would be only logical, given that the Appeals Chamber was reviewing the work of a Trial Chamber, including its solidification and interpretation of the indictment.

---

[124] Ibid., paras 118–23.

Vasiljević, the second of the two ICTY trial judgments of 2002, was by the same three judges who tried Krnojelac. The bench returned the JCE doctrine to its roots in gang crime. The defendant was a waiter in Višegrad, Bosnia-Herzegovina. He associated himself with a small paramilitary group upon the outbreak of the conflict, although it was not shown that he was a 'member' of that group.[125] The indictment alleged that, around 7 June 1992, Vasiljević and three members of the group led seven Bosnian-Muslim men to the bank of the Drina river. There, they forced the men to line up on the bank and shot them. Five of the seven were killed; two suffered minor injuries and were able to swim away.

The Trial Chamber found no proof that Vasiljević had fired his weapon. There was, instead, proof of 'an understanding amounting to an agreement' among Vasiljević and his three companions to kill the captive men. The defendant was found to have participated in the joint criminal enterprise by keeping watch to prevent the Muslim men from fleeing, by pointing his gun at them at the time they were being detained,[126] by escorting them to the bank of the Drina river while again pointing his gun at them to dissuade them from escaping, and by standing behind them, armed, alongside the members of the paramilitary group shortly before the shooting started. On these grounds the Trial Chamber found Vasiljević guilty as a co-perpetrator in the murder of the men, dismissing the alternative charge of aiding and abetting.[127]

The Appeals Chamber quashed the JCE conviction, substituting for it a conviction for aiding and abetting.[128] The reasoning behind this reversal is worth exploring. The Appeals Chamber maintained that no reasonable trier of fact could find (as the Trial Chamber did) that the only reasonable inference available on the evidence was that the appellant shared the intent to murder the Muslim men.[129] This question of intent, which in *Vasiljević* is about an inference from circumstantial evidence, returns us to the main problem areas of JCE doctrine, namely the threshold of participation (or contribution) and the threshold of association. The Appeals Chamber recited the vague old adage that 'it is sufficient for a participant in a joint criminal enterprise to perform acts that in some way are directed to the furtherance of the common design'.[130] Vasiljević's participation in the shooting incident, as summarized above, seems rather effortlessly to rise above that threshold.

Vasiljević admitted that, by the time the vehicle carrying the gang members and their captives pulled up at the Drina river, he was aware that the purpose of the excursion was to kill the Muslim men. Rather than attempt to talk his three companions out of their pursuit, instead of remaining in the vehicle or walking off in a different direction, Vasiljević acted in unison with them through to the completion of the executions. Even if he was not a paramilitary group member, for the purposes of the Drina river incident he was a member of the gang, there and then, and was responsible for the cumulative

---

[125] *Vasiljević* trial judgment, para. 75.
[126] This particular finding was overturned on appeal: *Vasiljević* appeal judgment, para. 57.
[127] *Vasiljević* trial judgment, paras 206–10.   [128] Ibid., paras 134–5.
[129] *Vasiljević* appeal judgment, para. 131. Contrast the formulation of the test in this instance with the flawed version of the test cited in footnote 123 above.   [130] Ibid., para. 102.

acts of the gang members, which he had foreseen well in advance. The fact that the prosecutor failed to prove that Vasiljević had fired his weapon at the men lined up on the bank should not change the characterization of his responsibility. But the Appeals Chamber reached a very different conclusion:

The Appeals Chamber is satisfied that no reasonable tribunal could have found that the only reasonable inference available on the evidence, as cited above, is that the Appellant had the intent to kill the seven Muslim men. The Trial Chamber found that the Appellant assisted Milan Lukic [the leader of the paramilitary group] and his men by preventing the seven Muslim men from fleeing. It did not find, however, that the Appellant shot at the Muslim men himself, nor that he exercised control over the firing. Compared to the involvement of Milan Lukic and potentially one or both of the other men, the participation of the Appellant in the overall course of the killings did not reach the same level. The above-mentioned acts of the Appellant were ambiguous as to whether or not the Appellant intended that the seven Muslim men be killed.[131]

The Appeals Chamber's comment that, 'Compared to the involvement of Milan Lukic and potentially one or both of the other men, the participation of the Appellant in the overall course of the killings *did not reach the same level*' — which leads to the finding of 'ambiguity' as to Vasiljević's real intent — introduces an unexpected new element: that even evidence of a strong association of the defendant with the group (in this instance co-location and coordinated action) and a relatively high level of contribution (participation in the arrest of the victims, transfer, and so forth) will not be sufficient to prove the defendant's *intent*. One might conclude, therefore, that where intent must be proven from circumstantial evidence (as is almost always the case), the participation and association thresholds for joint criminal enterprise responsibility, which in the *Tadić* judgment of the Appeals Chamber and elsewhere are in theory kept low or undefined, will in practice need to be proven at a high level if co-perpetrator responsibility is to be made out.

One aspect of this development — if indeed it is intentional — is that a post-*Vasiljević* trial court must use evidence of participation (that is, contribution) and association to prove, in the first place, the defendant's intent to commit the crimes of the common design; the intent threshold is exacting; if the evidence proves the intent, the trial court must go on to consider whether the contribution of the defendant to the execution of the common design is sufficient for co-perpetratorship. The latter threshold remains as vague as it was in *Tadić*. Yet, if the defendant's intent has already been proven by way of circumstantial evidence, by implication the defendant's contribution must have been significant.

In an interlocutory appeal from early 2003, the accused Dragoljub Ojdanić, whose case was still in the pre-trial phase, complained that the drafters of the Tribunal's Statute would have referred explicitly to joint criminal enterprise had they intended to include such a form of liability within the Tribunal's jurisdiction. The Appeals Chamber, in dismissing the motion, wrote that the ICTY's Statute 'is not and does not purport to be, unlike for instance the Rome Statute of the International Criminal Court, a

---

[131] Ibid., para. 131.

meticulously detailed code providing explicitly for every possible scenario and every solution thereto. It sets out in somewhat general terms the jurisdictional framework within which the Tribunal has been mandated to operate.'[132] Upon the handing down of the *Stakić* trial judgment two months later, the Appeals Chamber might have come to regret these words, along with all that they implied.

The indictment against Milomir Stakić alleged 'commission', which the prosecutor represented as meaning, in context, JCE. Nothing unusual with this kind of codicil (it had been given effect many times before), except that the prosecutor cannot have foreseen that the Trial Chamber in this case would find that the JCE model was perhaps not derivable, after all, from the ICTY Statute. The trial judges wrote:

joint criminal enterprise is only one of several possible interpretations of the term 'commission' under Article 7(1) of the Statute and . . . other definitions of co-perpetration must equally be taken into account. Furthermore, a more direct reference to 'commission' in its traditional sense should be given priority before considering responsibility under the judicial term 'joint criminal enterprise'.[133]

They proceeded to articulate a model of co-perpetratorship based on no analysis whatsoever, and on only one source, a German criminal-law textbook from 1994 (the presiding judge in *Stakić* was German):

For co-perpetration it suffices that there was an explicit agreement or silent consent to reach a common goal by coordinated co-operation and joint control over the criminal conduct. . . . These can be described as shared acts which when brought together achieve the shared goal based on the same degree of control over the execution of the common acts. In the words of Roxin [the author of the German textbook]: 'The co-perpetrator can achieve nothing on his own . . . The plan only "works" if the accomplice works with the other person.' Both perpetrators are thus in the same position. As Roxin explains, 'they can only realise their plan insofar as they act together, but each individually can ruin the whole plan if he does not carry out his part. To this extent he is in control of the act.' . . . The Trial Chamber is aware that the end result of its definition of co-perpetration approaches that of the aforementioned joint criminal enterprise and even overlaps in part. However, the Trial Chamber opines that this definition is closer to what most legal systems understand as 'committing' and avoids the misleading impression that a new crime not foreseen in the Statute of this Tribunal has been introduced through the backdoor.[134]

It may come as a surprise that as late as July 2003 a Trial Chamber dispensing international justice could simply opine away a liability doctrine that had already found some use at the ICTY and replace it with a theory borrowed from *one* municipal legal system. This is a reflection of the difficulties trial courts have had in understanding and applying the JCE doctrine of the *Tadić* Appeals Chamber.

The notion of co-perpetration which supplants JCE doctrine in *Stakić* conditions the realization of the crime upon the acts of the defendant (*sine qua non*). The Trial Chamber named Stakić's co-perpetrators as the authorities of the self-proclaimed Serb

---

[132] *Prosecutor* v. *Milutinović et al.*, Decision on Dragoljub Ojdanić's Motion Challenging Jurisdiction — Joint Criminal Enterprise, 21 May 2003, para. 18.　　[133] *Stakić* trial judgment, para. 438.

[134] Ibid., paras 440–1.

assembly of Prijedor municipality (Bosnia-Herzegovina), the SDS political party, the Serb crisis staff of Prijedor, and the Serb police, Territorial Defence forces, and military. The Trial Chamber singled out for mention the chief of police, certain 'prominent members' of the military, the president of the municipal assembly, and the commander of the Territorial Defence forces.[135] This large and indefinite number of co-perpetrators is reminiscent of a problem we encountered in the *Krstić* case: with the exception of the defendant, who dominates the foreground of the case, it is hard to tell who else is a member of the JCE (or co-perpetrator collective) and why. The *Stakić* court's assertion that the statutory notion of commission imposes the additional constraint that the acts of a co-perpetrator must have been *necessary* for the realization of the crimes committed by the collective (a requirement not further explained by the court) implies that a full accounting of the co-perpetrators' individual acts is a condition for the application of the 'German' doctrine. Yet, compared with Stakić, they were cardboard cut-outs.

In applying the new doctrine, the *Stakić* Trial Chamber said that the goal of the collective of Serb co-perpetrators was to take control of the Muslim-majority municipality of Prijedor and join it to Serb territories in Bosnia-Herzegovina.[136] The test of necessary contribution (which, in Roxin's words, was that 'each individually can ruin the whole plan if he does not carry out his part') was, in its application, changed by the Trial Chamber into the much less precise test of capacity to frustrate the common goal:

> The common goal could not be achieved without joint control over the final outcome and it is this element of interdependency that characterises the criminal conduct. No participant could achieve the common goal on his own, although each could individually have frustrated the plan by refusing to play his part or by reporting crimes. If, for example, the political authorities led by Dr. Stakić had not participated, the common plan would have been frustrated.[137]

The main problem with this assertion is that the 'political authorities' led by Stakić were not on trial; would the plan have been 'frustrated' had Stakić himself opposed it? This asks for speculation, which a legal test should not do. The *Stakić* formulation of co-perpetratorship is no advance on *Tadić*'s notion of JCE. It clarifies neither the association threshold nor the contribution threshold.

The Appeals Chamber diplomatically noted that the *Stakić* formulation 'appears to be new to the jurisprudence of this Tribunal'.[138] Neither party appealed against the Trial Chamber's use of the German doctrine, yet the Appeals Chamber proceeded to dismiss it with these few remarks:

> Upon a careful and thorough review of the relevant sections of the Trial Judgment, the Appeals Chamber finds that the Trial Chamber erred in conducting its analysis of the responsibility of the Appellant within the framework of 'co-perpetratorship'. This mode of liability, as defined and applied by the Trial Chamber, does not have support in customary international law or in the settled jurisprudence of this Tribunal, which is binding on the Trial Chambers. By way of contrast, joint criminal enterprise is a mode of liability which is 'firmly established in customary

---

[135] Ibid., para. 469.   [136] Ibid., paras 470–1.   [137] Ibid., para. 490.
[138] *Stakić* appeal judgment, para. 58.

international law' and is routinely applied in the Tribunal's jurisprudence. Furthermore, joint criminal enterprise is the mode of liability under which the Appellant was charged in the Indictment, and to which he responded at trial.[139]

The phrase 'does not have support in customary international law' is a subterfuge. It implies the existence of a method of determining the content of that body of law, yet, if there is such a method known to the tribunals, the Appeals Chamber has done little to articulate it (see Chapter 3). The remark would also suggest that the Appeals Chamber applied its litmus test and found that customary international law does not include the German doctrine. But no evidence of such an analysis exists.

In the Appeals Chamber's palimpsest of the Trial Chamber's factual findings, Stakić's responsibility was rewritten as JCE 1 and JCE 3.[140]

In the case of *Simić et al.*, the much amended indictment charged the defendants with 'acting in concert together, and with other Serb civilian and military officials, planned, instigated, ordered, committed, or otherwise aided and abetted the planning, preparation, or execution of a crime against humanity'.[141] If this is ungrammatical, it is because of the late and careless insertion of the phrase *acting in concert together*. The background to this modification is that the third amended indictment, having been confirmed in May 2001, was amended again after the start of the trial in September of the same year. The prosecutor's motion asked for the insertion of the above phrase into several sentences of the May indictment. The Trial Chamber granted the amendments in December 2001.[142] The prosecutor evidently was trying to secure a footing for the JCE doctrine, but such was the confusion more than four years after *Tadić* that a phrase was chosen, and effected, which failed to denote any particular theory of liability, let alone JCE.

To the defence's complaint at the end of the trial that it had not been given adequate notice of an allegation of JCE, the *Simić* court recognized that,

> The Prosecution in its Pre-Trial Brief did not refer specifically to a joint criminal enterprise or any of its possible scenarios, or to any of the material basis upon which it is based. While it does contain some mention of the role of the Accused, the information is very general and largely a repetition of what is in the Amended Indictment. The Prosecution Pre-Trial Brief seemed rather to be directed at a discussion of the elements of aiding and abetting. The matter was not clarified at the Pre-Trial Conference. Neither did the Prosecution refer in its Opening Statement to any form of joint criminal enterprise.[143]

This seemingly insurmountable difficulty did not deter the Trial Chamber, which proceeded with practically no dicussion to apply the test of 'material impairment' — a vague and lenient test:

> Although it is generally expected that the Prosecution case should be made clear to a defendant before his trial starts, the relevant test, regarding whether a defendant was properly notified of the

---

[139] Ibid., para. 62. [140] Ibid., paras 66–98. [141] *Simić et al.* trial judgment, para. 139.
[142] Ibid., paras 1136–7. [143] Ibid., para. 152.

nature of the case against him, is whether the preparation of his defence was materially impaired. Although the Prosecution did not include the words 'joint criminal enterprise' in the Fourth Amended Indictment, reference by the Prosecution to a joint criminal enterprise was explicitly clarified at the time of the third amendment of the Indictment in December 2001.[144]

The prosecutor's only penalty was to suffer the third form of JCE being put out of bounds.[145]

There has been some criticism surrounding the tribunals' acceptance of plea agreements as part of the guilty-plea process, but no comment on the difficult if not impossible relationship between this process and the doctrine of joint criminal enterprise. Predrag Banović is one of several accused at the ICTY who pleaded guilty to a JCE indictment. According to the factual basis agreed to between Banović and the prosecutor, the Keraterm camp in Prijedor municipality, Bosnia-Herzegovina, was established and operated as part of a joint criminal enterprise, the purpose of which was to subject persons of Muslim or Croat ethnicity to dehumanizing conditions so as to force them to leave the municipality.[146] Besides Banović, who was a guard at the camp, other persons mentioned in the plea agreement are Duško Sikirica, the camp commander; guards (a category left open), including reserve police officers organized into shifts of 10–15 guards; and the shift commanders Dragan Kolundžija, Damir Došen, and Dušan Fuštar.[147]

On what rationale may a court convict a person pursuant to a plea agreement for a form of liability which presupposes that several other persons are also held, by implication, guilty? What effect is to be given by a court to the 'agreement' between Banović and the prosecutor that Fuštar, for example, was one of the persons forming the criminal enterprise of which Banović was a member? These rather obvious questions have never been raised at the tribunals. They touch on a problem (the guilt of third parties

---

[144] Ibid., para. 154.

[145] Ibid., para. 155. The Trial Chamber went on to find the existence of JCE 1. Whether the enterprise effectively was a closed or open class of persons is not possible to tell from the imprecise finding of the Trial Chamber (ibid., para. 984): 'The Trial Chamber is satisfied upon the evidence that members of the Crisis Staff, including Blagoje Simić as President; the Serb police, including the Chief of Police, Stevan Todorovic, who was also a member of the Crisis Staff; Serb paramilitaries, including "Debeli" (Srcko Radovanovic, "Pukovnik"), "Crni" (Dragan Djordevic), "Lugar" (Slobodan Miljkovic), and "Laki" (Predrag Lazarevic); and the 17th Tactical Group of the JNA; were participants in a joint criminal enterprise, responsible for executing the common plan to persecute non-Serb civilians in the Bosanski Samac Municipality.' The Trial Chamber surely knew that it did not have the evidence necessary to determine beyond reasonable doubt the mens rea (or even, one suspects, the names) of all of these persons. In relation to the contribution threshold, the *Simić* court (ibid., para. 159) followed *Kvočka* in requiring a 'substantial' contribution for JCE membership. This led to a finding of non-membership for one of the defendants: 'While Miroslav Tadić had knowledge of the discriminatory intent of the joint criminal enterprise, the actions or omissions of Miroslav Tadić cannot be considered to have had a substantial effect on the perpetration of the offence of unlawful arrests and detention, and as such did not aid and abet the joint criminal enterprise. He was not in a position with power to prevent the work of the joint criminal enterprise and the corresponding criminal activity.' (Ibid., para. 999.) It was the same result for the third defendant, Simo Zarić (ibid., para. 1000). Zarić and Tadić were imprisoned for six and eight years, respectively, whereas Simić received a 17-year sentence.

[146] *Banović* sentencing judgment, paras 7, 22, 39.

[147] Ibid., para. 23.

in the multilayered and overlapping cases tried at the international level) which is not limited to plea agreements or the joint criminal enterprise doctrine, but appears at its starkest when these two circumstances coincide.[148]

The raft of joint criminal enterprise was rocked again in the *Brðanin* case, where the trial court flatly refused to apply the received doctrine. The prosecutor had alleged that Radoslav Brðanin, a regional strongman, had participated in a joint criminal enterprise to forcibly remove Bosnian-Muslim and Bosnian-Croat inhabitants from territory which had been earmarked by Bosnian-Serb leaders for a Bosnian-Serb state. A vast and indefinite number of persons were alleged to have joined this JCE:

A great many individuals participated in this joint criminal enterprise, including . . . Momir Talić, other members of the ARK [Autonomous Region of Krajina] Crisis Staff, the leadership of [Republika Srpska] and the SDS [Serbian Democratic Party], including Radovan Karadžić, Momčilo Krajišnik and Biljana Plavšić, members of the Assembly of the Autonomous Region of Krajina and the Assembly's Executive Committee, the Serb Crisis Staffs of the ARK municipalities, the army of the Republika Srpska, Bosnian Serb paramilitary forces and others.[149]

The *Brðanin* judges brushed aside the pronouncements of the *Krnojelac* Appeals Chamber[150] and declared (without argument) that in cases where a defendant is not said to have 'physically perpetrated' the crimes of which he or she is charged, the prosecutor must establish 'that between the person physically committing a crime and the Accused, there was an understanding or an agreement to commit that particular crime'.[151] The Trial Chamber meant the link between the hands-off member of the JCE and the person who committed the crime as a principal to be a *personal* one:

The Trial Chamber in this context emphasises that for the purposes of establishing individual criminal responsibility pursuant to the theory of JCE it is not sufficient to prove an understanding or an agreement to commit a crime between the Accused and a person in charge or in control of a military or paramilitary unit committing a crime. The Accused can only be held criminally responsible under the mode of liability of JCE if the Prosecution establishes beyond reasonable doubt that he had an understanding or entered into an agreement with the [principal perpetrator of the crime] to commit the particular crime eventually perpetrated.[152]

. . . Moreover, the fact that the acts and conduct of an accused facilitated or contributed to the commission of a crime by another person or assisted in the formation of that person's criminal

---

[148] The *M. Nikolić* sentencing judgment, which conducted a purpotedly critical assessment of guilty-plea practice at the international level (ibid., paras 57–73), completely missed the difficulty we have identified above and proceeded to sentence Momir Nikolić for taking part in a vast JCE (ibid., para. 174). Yet once the particular difficulty becomes apparent, a statement such as the following (ibid., para. 76) is difficult to comprehend: 'The Trial Chamber considered Momir Nikolić's acknowledgment of the crimes committed following the fall of Srebrenica and his role therein, as well as the role of other Bosnian Serbs members of the joint criminal enterprise, to be significant in verifying that these crimes were in fact committed and who was responsible for their commission.' Here, the convicted person is treated not only as a witness to his own acts, but as proving the acts of others. See also *Obrenović* sentencing judgment, para. 85; *Deronjic* sentencing judgment, paras 125–8; and *Babić* sentencing judgment, para. 98.

[149] *Prosecutor* v. *Radoslav Brðanin*, Fourth Amended Indictment, 5 October 2001, para. 27.2.

[150] *Krnojelac* appeal judgment, para. 97. [151] *Brðanin* trial judgment, para. 344.

[152] Ibid., para. 347.

intent is not sufficient to establish beyond reasonable doubt that there was an understanding or an agreement between the two to commit that particular crime. An agreement between two persons to commit a crime requires a *mutual* understanding or arrangement with each other to commit a crime.[153]

This requirement would reduce JCE to a realized conspiracy among a small number of people. The *Brđanin* chamber sensed the ambiguity in *Tadić*'s element of a 'common plan'. As noted earlier, a common plan can come about through design, or its commonality may be fortuitous (two unrelated groups happen to have the same plan). Thus there is a need for a linkage threshold to distinguish between the two:

the Trial Chamber is of the view that the mere espousal of the Strategic Plan by the Accused on the one hand and many of the [principal perpetrators of the crimes] on the other hand is not equivalent to an arrangement between them to commit a concrete crime. Indeed, the Accused and the [principal perpetrators of the crimes] could espouse the Strategic Plan and form a criminal intent to commit crimes with the aim of implementing the Strategic Plan *independently from each other* and without having an understanding or entering into any agreement between them to commit a crime.[154]

... Yet another reasonable inference to be drawn would be that the [principal perpetrators of the crimes] committed the crimes in question in execution of orders and instructions received from their military or paramilitary superiors who intended to implement the Strategic Plan, whereby the [principal perpetrators of the crimes] did not enter into an agreement with the Accused to commit these crimes.[155]

The result was that the *Brđanin* court dismissed the relevance of the joint criminal enterprise doctrine to the case. In so doing, the court offered little or no analysis, yet its concluding observations are — as our own analysis shows — to some extent accurate:

JCE is not an appropriate mode of liability to describe the individual criminal responsibility of the Accused, given the extraordinarily broad nature of this case, where the Prosecution seeks to include within a JCE a person as structurally remote from the commission of the crimes charged in the Indictment as the Accused. Although JCE is applicable in relation to cases involving ethnic cleansing, as the *Tadić* Appeal Judgment recognises, it appears that, in providing for a definition of JCE, the Appeals Chamber had in mind a somewhat smaller enterprise than the one that is invoked in the present case.[156]

Thus, by the end of 2004, JCE was a problem-riven doctrine. In certain later applications, a simplified approach was preferred, which ignored the accumulated problems.[157] But at the end of 2006, the doctrine was given a new lease of life, in the *Krajišnik* case.

---

[153] Ibid., para. 352 (emphasis in original).   [154] Ibid., para. 351 (emphasis in original).

[155] Ibid., para. 354.

[156] Ibid., para. 355. The Trial Chamber convicted Brđanin for aiding and abetting or instigating several crimes: ibid., paras 471–5 (wilful killing), 530–8 (torture), 577–83 (deportation and forced transfer), 669–78 (wanton destruction of property), and 1054 (persecution constituted of the above crimes). For a critique of *Brđanin*, see K. Gustafson, 'The Requirement of an "Express Agreement" for Joint Criminal Enterprise Liability', 3 *J. Int'l Crim. Just.* 1 (web version).

[157] For simplified approaches to the JCE doctrine, see *Blagojević and Jokić* trial judgment, paras 709–14, 720–25; *Simba* trial judgment, paras 386–8, 402–9.

7.2.7 'The most appropriate mode of liability': JCE in the *Krajišnik* case

The trial of Momčilo Krajišnik promised to deliver the first ICTY trial judgment on a 'leadership' indictment. More eagerly anticipated, of course, was the judgment in the *Milošević* case (a joinder of three indictments concerning events in three countries and a period of many years), which had been informally scheduled for early 2007, but the death of Slobodan Milošević on 11 March 2006 meant that the *Krajišnik* judgment not only would be a defining moment in ICTY jurisprudence, but would hold on to this title for a considerable period of time.

Krajišnik formally held the position of president (speaker) of the assembly (parliament) of Republika Srpska, a breakaway territory of Bosnia-Herzegovina. He was a close friend of Radovan Karadžić, the president of the three-member presidency of Republika Srpska, which in May 1992 was expanded to include Krajišnik himself and Branko Đerić, the prime minister of the presumptive state. (Biljana Plavšić, who in 2003 pleaded guilty to a count of crimes against humanity and was sentenced to 11 years' imprisonment, was also a member of the Bosnian-Serb presidency at that time.) Đerić described Krajišnik as Karadžić's private prime minister,[158] but a more accurate assessment is that Krajišnik, Karadžić, and General Ratko Mladić, the leader of the Bosnian-Serb armed forces, formed a triumvirate; together they ran Republika Srpska as a personal fief.[159] In an ideal world, they would have been joined and tried on a single indictment, but Karadžić and Mladić have managed (as at the time of writing) to remain in hiding.

The importance of the *Krajišnik* judgment may be reduced to four elements: the defendant was a parliamentarian, although he also had a parallel, de facto, foothold in the executive branch (the presidency); he was physically and causally a long way removed from the crimes against Bosnian Muslims and Bosnian Croats, which were committed by an assortment of Bosnian-Serb forces (as well as forces crossing the border from Serbia proper) in the claimed territories between April and December 1992; the crimes committed by the Serbs in Bosnia-Herzegovina numbered in the thousands (many thousands of murders; over one hundred thousand deportations and unlawful transfers; etc.); and whereas the *Brđanin* court had jettisoned JCE and had used other modes of liability to effect a conviction, the *Krajišnik* court did not waste a word on the other modes, declaring the JCE doctrine to be 'most appropriate' to the nature of the case.[160]

How did the trial court prove the defendant's responsibility within this highly complex factual situation?

The *Krajišnik* judges first tackled the *Brđanin* issue. As explained earlier, this issue can be traced to the looseness of *Tadić*'s original definition of a JCE constituted of three elements — plurality, common objective, and contribution. The problem is, to put it simply, that there may exist a plurality of persons (bank robbers) with a common

---

[158] *Krajišnik* trial judgment, para. 1085.   [159] Ibid., para. 987.   [160] Ibid., para. 877.

objective (to rob banks in The Hague) which nevertheless consists of two unrelated groups (those robbing banks in the south of the city and those robbing banks in the north of the city). Proof of the three JCE elements is not sufficient, in other words, to prove a joint criminal enterprise in which each member of the plurality is responsible for acts committed by other members pursuant to the 'common' objective (a member of the south-robbing group cannot be convicted of a robbery of the north-robbing group).

Brđanin had sought to sharpen the elements of plurality and common objective by imposing a requirement of one-on-one agreement among members of the plurality, and in particular between the leadership figures and the principal perpetrators of the crimes. This focused *mental* link would then account for the 'joint' in joint criminal enterprise. The *Krajišnik* judges took a different approach:

> In relation to the first two elements of JCE liability, it is the common objective that begins to transform a plurality of persons into a group or enterprise, as this plurality has in common the particular objective. It is evident, however, that a common objective alone is not always sufficient to determine a group, as different and independent groups may happen to share identical objectives. Rather, it is the interaction or cooperation among persons — their joint action — in addition to their common objective, that makes those persons a group. The persons in a criminal enterprise must be shown to act together, or in concert with each other, in the implementation of a common objective, if they are to share responsibility for the crimes committed through the JCE. A concern expressed by the Trial Chamber in *Brđanin* about the issue of alleged JCE participants acting independently of each other, is sufficiently addressed by the requirement that joint action among members of a criminal enterprise is proven.[161]

> A person not in the JCE may share the general objective of the group but not be linked with the operations of the group. Crimes committed by such a person are of course not attributable to the group. On the other hand, links forged in pursuit of a common objective transform individuals into members of a criminal enterprise. These persons rely on each other's contributions, as well as on acts of persons who are not members of the JCE but who have been procured to commit crimes, to achieve criminal objectives on a scale which they could not have attained alone.[162]

The notion of agreement was thus subordinated to the much wider notion of joint action, provable by a multitude of evidence, including evidence of agreement. The Trial Chamber proceeded to explore the links between Krajišnik, persons in the central administration, and persons in positions of authority in the regional and municipal administrations, and concluded that the linkages were strong enough to prove joint action.[163] Indeed, Krajišnik's main contribution, according to the court, was to ensure that these people worked together in a coordinated fashion.[164]

The *Krajišnik* court did not find it necessary, or possible, to specify fully the membership of the JCE in that case. According to the court, JCE doctrine does not require that the principal perpetrators of the crimes of a JCE be shown to be members of the JCE, sharing the common objective of the enterprise. This is because the JCE may procure its crimes through third parties who are, for example, unaware of the larger picture, or are mere instruments of the JCE.[165] Thus, in a complex case, while a

---

[161] Ibid., para. 884.   [162] Ibid., para. 1082.   [163] Ibid., paras 894–1075.
[164] Ibid., para. 1120.   [165] Ibid., paras 883, 1086–8.

court is required to list the main figures of the JCE and explain how they were linked to the principal perpetrators of the crimes, it is not required to explore the intentionality of each principal perpetrator with a view to determining the capacity in which this person was acting for the JCE.

Ironically, while *Brđanin* did not find that Radoslav Brđanin was a member of a JCE, *Krajišnik* did.[166]

The *Krajišnik* judgment relied entirely on the JCE 1 form of the doctrine. In accordance with the following reasoning, with the passage of time foreseeable crimes changed character and became intended crimes:

> the crimes of deportation and forced transfer . . . were necessary means of implementing the common objective of removal by force of Bosnian Muslims and Bosnian Croats from large areas of Bosnia-Herzegovina. The Chamber will refer to these crimes as 'original' crimes. These were the crimes which constituted the JCE's common objective as of late March 1992, when the Accused called for 'implementing what we have agreed upon, the ethnic division on the ground'.[167]

> Whether other crimes were 'original' to the common objective or were added later is of course a matter of evidence, not logical analysis. The Chamber's preference is for a strictly empirical approach which does not speculate about the crime-profile of the original JCE objective, but conceptualizes the common objective as fluid in its criminal means. An expansion of the criminal means of the objective is proven when leading members of the JCE are informed of new types of crime committed pursuant to the implementation of the common objective, take no effective measures to prevent recurrence of such crimes, and persist in the implementation of the common objective of the JCE. Where this holds, JCE members are shown to have accepted the expansion of means, since implementation of the common objective can no longer be understood to be limited to commission of the original crimes. With acceptance of the actual commission of new types of crime and continued contribution to the objective, comes intent, meaning that subsequent commission of such crimes by the JCE will give rise to liability under JCE form 1.[168]

And so, for example, unlawful detention, inhumane treatment of detainees, sexual violence, killings, and extermination were, if not original crimes, gradually accepted by Krajišnik, in the trial court's theory, as crimes associated with his programme of ethnic cleansing.[169] He was sentenced to 27 years' imprisonment (five years less than the term of imprisonment given to Brđanin).

7.3 COMMAND RESPONSIBILITY

This officer [Yamashita], of proven field merit and entrusted with a high command involving authority adequate to his responsibility, has failed this irrevocable standard; has failed his duty to his troops, to his country, to his enemy, and to mankind; he has failed utterly his soldier faith.[170]

---

[166] Ibid., para. 1088.   [167] Ibid., para. 1097.   [168] Ibid., para. 1098.
[169] Ibid., paras 1100–18.
[170] General MacArthur, describing General Yamashita's failure as a leader; 'Order of General Douglas MacArthur Confirming Death Sentence of General Tomoyuki Yamashita', 6 February 1946, reprinted in L. Friedman, *The Law of War: A Documentary History* (Random House, 1972), pp. 1598–9.

We shall focus next on the second most controversial doctrine of criminal liability at the tribunals — 'command' or 'superior' responsibility. In contrast with JCE, the tribunal Statutes explicitly provide for this form of liability.

7.3.1 Statutory provisions

The command responsibility provisions of the Statutes of the ad hoc tribunals state that the fact that a statutory offence was committed by an accused's subordinate does not relieve his or her superior of criminal responsibility if the latter knew or had reason to know 'that the subordinate was about to commit such acts or had done so and the superior failed to take the necessary and reasonable measures to prevent such acts or to punish the perpetrators thereof'.[171]

The ICC Statute's provisions on this form of liability are more complex than those of the ad hoc tribunals:

In addition to other grounds of criminal responsibility under this Statute for crimes within the jurisdiction of the Court:

(a) A military commander or person effectively acting as a military commander shall be criminally responsible for crimes within the jurisdiction of the Court committed by forces under his or her effective command and control, or effective authority and control as the case may be, as a result of his or her failure to exercise control properly over such forces, where:
  (i) That military commander or person either knew or, owing to the circumstances at the time, should have known that the forces were committing or about to commit such crimes; and
  (ii) That military commander or person failed to take all necessary and reasonable measures within his or her power to prevent or repress their commission or to submit the matter to the competent authorities for investigation and prosecution.

(b) With respect to superior and subordinate relationships not described in paragraph (a), a superior shall be criminally responsible for crimes within the jurisdiction of the Court committed by subordinates under his or her effective authority and control, as a result of his or her failure to exercise control properly over such subordinates, where:
  (i) The superior either knew, or consciously disregarded information which clearly indicated, that the subordinates were committing or about to commit such crimes;
  (ii) The crimes concerned activities that were within the effective responsibility and control of the superior; and
  (iii) The superior failed to take all necessary and reasonable measures within his or her power to prevent or repress their commission or to submit the matter to the competent authorities for investigation and prosecution.[172]

7.3.2 The neglected element of duty

It is well established that three basic ingredients of command responsibility are: (1) a superior–subordinate relationship, (2) knowledge or notice of the subordinate's

---

[171] Articles 7(3) of the ICTY and 6(3) of the ICTR Statutes. The same wording is adopted in the SCSL Statute, Art. 6(3), and the ETSP Statute, Section 16.　　　　[172] ICC Statute, Art. 28.

offence or its imminent commission, and (3) failure by the superior to prevent or punish the act.[173] Two obvious and unproblematic additional conditions are that the committed or imminent offence is within the tribunals' substantive jurisdiction; and that the offence was in fact committed (or about to be committed) by the alleged subordinate of the accused.

There is a *sixth* element to command responsibility, but it is an element that deserves to be ranked first. The tribunals have never paid proper attention to this sixth element, presumably because it is an obstacle to the expansion of criminal liability, as will be explained below. In the meantime, however, the tribunal judges — the free-wheeling architects of international criminal law — have significantly expanded the application of command responsibility.

Command responsibility is a form of omission liability, for it is based on proof of failure to restrain the actions of others. A general legal principle is that an omission will give rise to liability only if it is possible to establish a duty to act.[174] For criminal liability to arise, the duty must be enforceable through the criminal code. Positive duties to act are rare, since they constitute incursions on individual liberty. To have legal effect, a positive duty must be widely publicized and known. An ICTR Trial Chamber put the matter in this way:

> Liability for an omission may arise in a third, fundamentally different context: where the accused is charged with a duty to prevent or punish others from committing a crime. The culpability arises not by participating in the commission of a crime, but by allowing another person to commit a crime which the Accused has a duty to prevent or punish. . . . On any view, liability for failing to discharge a duty to prevent or punish requires proof that: (i) the Accused was bound by a specific legal duty to prevent a crime; (ii) the accused was aware of, and wilfully refused to discharge, his legal duty.[175]

The ad hoc tribunals' common provision on command responsibility does not list the duty requirement as a separate element; it remains implicit in the provision. Its effect, when properly analysed, is to narrow the class of relevant superior–subordinate relationships to those relationships in which the superior is under a legal obligation to restrain illegal acts of his or her subordinates.[176]

It is undisputed that a military commander is duty-bound to control his or her subordinates and may be held responsible for their violations of the laws and customs of war.[177] This duty was customary by the end of the nineteenth century and is reflected

---

[173] See, e.g., *Delalić et al.* trial judgment, para. 346.

[174] Cf. the US Uniform Code of Military Justice, Art. 77(b)(ii): 'inaction may make one liable as a party, where there is a duty to act. If a person (for example, a security guard) has a duty to interfere in the commission of an offense, but does not interfere, that person is a party to the crime if such a noninterference is intended to and does operate as an aid or encouragement to the actual perpetrator.'

[175] *Mpambara* trial judgment, paras 25, 27. Other ICTR Trial Chambers take the same position: see, e.g., *Rutaganira* sentencing judgment, paras 67–91, and *Ntagerura et al.* trial judgment, paras 659–60.

[176] See A. Zahar, 'Command Responsibility of Civilian Superiors for Genocide' (2001) 14 *Leiden J. Int'l L.* 591.

[177] In *United States* v. *Wilhelm von Leeb et al.* (*High Command* case), 11 TWC 462, 512, the tribunal declared that, 'Under basic principles of command authority and responsibility, an officer who merely stands by while his subordinates execute a criminal order of his superiors which he knows is criminal violates a moral obligation under international law. By doing nothing he cannot wash his hands of international responsibility.' In *Yamashita* v. *Styer*

in Article 1 of the Regulations to the Hague Convention of 1899.[178] In a later example, the term 'armed forces' in Additional Protocol I to the 1949 Geneva Conventions is to be understood according to the Protocol as comprising all organized armed forces, groups, and units under a command responsible to the signatory for the conduct of its subordinates.[179] The duty of military superiors to ensure the lawful conduct of those under their command is the central component of the mechanism laid out in the Protocol for the repression of grave breaches.[180]

It is much less clear whether persons who are not military commanders, and who might be referred to as civilian superiors, are also in certain circumstances affected by the obligation, or legal duty, which is a precondition for command responsibility — and, if so, by what rationale? The tribunals have not dealt with this important question, but instead have assumed that it follows from (mere) proof of the existence of a superior–subordinate relationship that the superior in question had the relevant duty to prevent or punish illegal actions of subordinates.[181] The ICTY Appeals Chamber engaged in word-games when it said: 'It is evident that there cannot be an organized military force save on the basis of responsible command. It is also reasonable to hold

(1946) 327 US 1, 15, the US Supreme Court held that, 'It is evident that the conduct of military operations by troops whose excesses are unrestrained by the orders or efforts of their commander would almost certainly result in violations which it is the purpose of the law of war to prevent. Its purpose to protect civilian populations and prisoners of war from brutality would largely be defeated if the commander of an invading army could with impunity neglect to take reasonable measures for their protection. Hence the law of war presupposes that its violation is to be avoided through the control of the operations of war by commanders who are to some extent responsible for their subordinates.' And, as stated in the Second World War case of *Toyoda* (referred to in *Delalić et al.* trial judgment, para. 373), 'The responsibility for discipline in the situation facing the battle commander cannot, in the view of practical military men, be placed in any hands other than his own'.

178 Convention (II) with Respect to the Laws and Customs of War on Land, 29 July 1899.

179 Additional Protocol I, Art. 43.

180 Ibid., Arts 86–7. See also the 'Final Report of the Commission of Inquiry Into the Events at the Refugee Camps in Beirut' (Kahan Commission) (1983) 22 ILM 473, where the disposition turns on the duty of commanders and military superiors (e.g. p. 496: 'it was their duty, by virtue of their position and their office, to warn of the danger, and they did not fulfill this duty. It is also not possible to absolve of such indirect responsibility those persons who, when they received the first reports of what was happening in the camps, did not rush to prevent the continuation of the Phalangists' actions and did not do everything within their power to stop them . . . it is the duty of the occupier, according to the rules of usual and customary international law, to do all it can to ensure the public's well-being and security . . . as far as the obligations applying to every civilized nation and the ethical rules accepted by civilized peoples go, the problem of indirect responsibility cannot be disregarded').

181 E.g. *Delalić et al.* trial judgment, para. 377. Academic writers have also failed to recognize this problem. See I. Bantekas, 'The Contemporary Law of Superior Responsibility' (1999) 93 *Am. J. Int'l L.* 573; Cassese, *International Criminal Law*, pp. 203–11; A. B. Ching, 'Evolution of the Command Responsibility Doctrine in Light of the Celebici Decision of the International Criminal Tribunal for the Former Yugoslavia' (1999) 25 *N. C. J. Int'l L. & Comp. Reg.* 167; M. Damaska, 'The Shadow Side of Command Responsibility' (2001) 49 *Am. J. Comp. L.* 455; M. Lippman, 'Humanitarian Law: The Uncertain Contours of Command Responsibility' (2001) 9 *Tulsa J. Comp. & Int'l L.* 1; R. May and S. Powles, 'Command Responsibility: A New Basis of Criminal Liability in English Law' (2002) *Crim. L. Rev.* 363; Mettraux, *International Crimes*, pp. 296–309; A. Singh, 'Criminal Responsibility for Non-State Civilian Superiors Lacking De Jure Authority: A Comparative Review of the Doctrine of Superior Responsibility and Parallel Doctrines in National Criminal Laws' 28 *Hastings Int'l & Comp. L. Rev.* 267; G. R. Vetter, 'Command Responsibility of Non-Military Superiors in the International Criminal Court' (2000) 25 *Yale J. Int'l L.* 89; and T. Wu Yong and S. J. Kang, 'Criminal Liability for the Actions of Subordinates: The Doctrine of Command Responsibility and its Analogues in United States Law' (1997) 38 *Harv. Int'l L. J.* 272.

that it is responsible command which leads to command responsibility.'[182] This (1) begs the question (does the leader of *any* organized military force, for example the Sudanese Janjaweed militia, have command responsibility?); (2) reaches the desired conclusion through a syntactical device ('command responsibility' substituted for 'responsible command'); and (3) commits the is/ought fallacy, for the normative conclusion is derived from a mere empirical observation (the Appeals Chamber reiterated: 'military organization implies responsible command and . . . responsible command in turn implies command responsibility').[183]

As illustrated below, superior–subordinate relationships exist in which no legal duty to prevent or punish is present, and indeed where such a duty is inconceivable. Therefore, other factors besides the superior–subordinate relationship account for the duty to prevent, where such a duty exists.

7.3.3 The superior–subordinate relationship

The *Delalić* trial judgment of the ICTY contains the first tribunal conviction for command responsibility after a full trial.[184] The Trial Chamber reviewed at some length the origins and use of the doctrine of command responsibility, as well as its extension to civilians. The court's exposition and specific application of the doctrine was upheld on appeal. All subsequent judgments have followed *Delalić*'s basic definition of the superior–subordinate relationship.

Three of the *Delalić* defendants were charged with command responsibility for crimes committed by camp guards and by others entering the Čelebići prison-camp in Bosnia-Herzegovina. Zdravko Mucić was the 'commander' of the camp; Hazim Delić was his 'deputy' (they held these posts de facto, without formal appointment). Zejnil Delalić held senior positions related to the war effort in an area which included the Čelebići camp.[185]

Delalić's main conceptual task was to resolve what the court referred to as the issue which lies 'at the very heart' of the doctrine of command responsibility — that is, the character of the superior–subordinate relationship.[186] Basing itself on Second World War cases, the court said that the imposition of command responsibility necessarily was limited to persons in positions of *command*.[187] Such positions need not have been formally created, and an incumbent need not have been regularly appointed to the position in question, whether by official act or instrument, etc.[188]

How is a position of command to be conceptualized, according to *Delalić*? It cannot be the *position* itself that matters because any occupant under any circumstances would

---

[182] *Prosecutor* v. *Hadžihasanović et al.*, Decision on Interlocutory Appeal Challenging Jurisdiction in Relation to Command Responsibility, 16 July 2003, para. 16.   [183] Ibid., para. 17.

[184] Kambanda's conviction by the ICTR was pursuant to a guilty plea; there was no discussion of the command responsibility doctrine.   [185] *Delalić et al.* trial judgment, paras 11, 19–20.

[186] Ibid., para. 364.   [187] Ibid., para. 370.

[188] Cf. *Kunarac* trial judgment, para. 397: 'The relationship between the commander and his subordinates need not have been formalized; a tacit or implicit understanding between them as to their positioning vis-à-vis one another is sufficient.'

then be a commander, even if, for some reason, he or she enjoyed no real power. Hence a position of command must be understood as a position from which 'powers of command' are exercised; and 'command' is to be analysed into the notion of 'control', that is, 'the actual possession . . . of powers of control' over the actions of others.[189] Because of the differences to be expected in degree and quality of 'control', the *Delalić* court proceeded to say that, while de facto control would suffice, 'there is a threshold at which persons cease to possess the necessary powers of control over the actual perpetrators of offences'. The *Delalić* Trial Chamber used the term *effective control* to denote the applicable standard. When effective control is demonstrated, international law imposes 'an obligation to take action to prevent the commission of war crimes', and the defendant is brought within the grasp of the command responsibility doctrine.[190]

Delalić did not explain how an 'obligation to take action' might flow from mere demonstration of effective control. While there is no doubt that a lack of effective control must cancel out any pre-existing obligation to control subordinates, the existence of effective control cannot be presumed to be a sufficient condition for the existence of a duty to control. The case of a purely criminal group under the knowing, effective control of a criminally minded individual cannot conceivably create a legal obligation upon that person to suppress the group's unlawful activities. One might think of the Mafia, or the Lord's Resistance Army in Uganda, or ETA's armed forces, or even the Lebanese Hezbollah. The leader of such a criminal or terrorist or ad hoc militarized group may well be responsible for the crimes of members of the group in accordance with the joint criminal enterprise doctrine or another appropriate form of liability, depending on the facts, but he or she will not be held responsible because of a breach of a special legal duty. Common criminals and terrorists and certain brands of revolutionary do not have special legal duties. On the contrary, such duties attach to privileged positions in legitimate society, positions that give rise to an expectation of action to *prevent* — in this case — a criminal offence. They do not attach to persons who come together for the very purpose of committing crimes.

In addition to this apparent oversight regarding the source of the requisite duty, the *Delalić* court did not elaborate the meaning of effective control other than by stating that the alleged superior must have had 'the material ability to prevent and punish the commission of [the alleged subordinates'] offences'.[191] For a more detailed understanding, it becomes necessary, therefore, to consider how the concept was applied by the Trial Chamber to the facts.

One accused, Zejnil Delalić, was acquitted because he was not found to have had responsibility for the operation of the camp, and a fortiori had no superior authority over its personnel.[192] The second accused, Hazim Delić, was convicted, although not for command responsibility; he was not found to have been a superior within the meaning of the Statute.

The court's reasons for this conclusion on Delić's non-liability as a superior reveal a careful attempt to limit the applicability of the doctrine. Concerning Delić's relationship

---

[189] Ibid., paras 368, 370, 377.   [190] Ibid., paras 371–5, 377.
[191] Ibid., para. 378.   [192] Ibid., paras 686, 698, 721.

to the camp guards, the Trial Chamber concluded: 'this evidence is indicative of *a degree of influence* Hazim Delić had in the Čelebići prison-camp on some occasions, in the criminal mistreatment of detainees. However, this influence could be attributable to the guards' fear of an intimidating and morally delinquent individual... and is not, on the facts before this Trial Chamber, of itself indicative of the superior authority of Mr. Delić sufficient to attribute superior responsibility to him.'[193] Thus bare 'influence' — even the considerable degree of influence that Delić exercised within the camp — was not determinative for the court. In fact, it was not even regarded as particularly significant, probably because it was the wrong *kind* of influence ('fear of an intimidating and morally delinquent individual').

The court also considered the sense in which Delić was Zdravko Mucić's deputy. It found that the evidence indicated that 'Delić was tasked with assisting... Mucić by organising and arranging for the daily activities in the Čelebići prison-camp. However, it cannot be said to indicate that he had actual command authority in the sense that he could issue orders and punish and prevent the criminal acts of subordinates.'[194] In other words, Delić was not part of the prison's chain of command, whose primary link was that between Mucić and the guards.

Mucić was convicted as a superior for crimes committed by the guards (he was also found directly liable for the unlawful confinement of civilians).[195] He was not a military commander, but neither was he a civilian. He was informally appointed to head the Čelebići prison-camp, itself hurriedly established to accommodate civil-war detainees.[196] There was evidence that Mucić could use the neighbouring barracks to detain guards for misbehaviour, and that he reported to military headquarters.[197] But he did not have a military rank and it was not alleged that he took part in military operations in the ordinary sense. He administered an operation ancillary to the military campaign.

The court found that the guards and Delić obeyed and executed Mucić's orders;[198] that on a large number of matters having to do with the prison's operations, the guards sought Mucić's permission;[199] that Mucić was in charge of order in the prison and had the means to enforce it; that he had the power to discipline the guards, as mentioned above, by confining them to barracks, or by making reports about them to his own superiors;[200] that he was 'in a position to assist those detainees who were mistreated';[201] and that he was perceived by detainees and by guards as 'the embodiment of authority'.[202] One witness stated that he had 'felt the authority of Mr. Mucić when... guards stopped mistreating two prisoners when they heard that Mr. Mucić was coming'.[203] Mucić was found to have manifested 'all the powers and functions of a formal appointment', even though neither his position nor his appointment to it were 'de jure'.[204]

---

[193] Ibid., paras 798–806, emphasis added.   [194] Ibid., para. 809.

[195] Ibid., para. 1237. The court found no evidence against Mucić of active or direct participation in any violence or mistreatment (paras 1239–40). 'The criminal liability of Mr. Mucić has arisen entirely from his failure to exercise his superior authority for the beneficial purpose of the detainees' (para. 1248).

[196] Ibid., paras 737, 752–3.   [197] Ibid., para. 767.   [198] Ibid., para. 739.

[199] Ibid., para. 765.   [200] Ibid., para. 767.   [201] Ibid., para. 741.

[202] Ibid., paras 743–50.   [203] Ibid., para. 747.   [204] Ibid., para. 750.

7.3.4 Application to non-military superiors

The *Delalić* court argued, with reference to Mucić's status, that the expansion of the command responsibility doctrine to include non-military superiors was in accordance with customary law.[205] In fact, the chamber did not seem to consider that there had been any expansion at all — at least not one that had not been completed already by 1945 — because its argument that the doctrine applies equally to persons in positions of civilian authority was based on judgments rendered against certain German and Japanese defendants, such as the industrialists Flick and Weiss and Japan's foreign minister Koki Hirota.[206] Yet the *Delalić* Trial Chamber additionally stated that it shared the view expressed by the International Law Commission that the doctrine of superior responsibility extends to civilian superiors 'only to the extent that they exercise a degree of control over their subordinates which is *similar to that of military commanders*'.[207]

The court did not explain the sense of 'similar' in this context. However, at a later point, in reply to the prosecutor's contention that it is sufficient for a finding of responsibility that there exists, on the part of the defendant, a de facto exercise of authority even in the absence of de jure authority, the Trial Chamber said that it agreed with this view, 'provided the exercise of de facto authority *is accompanied by the trappings of the exercise of de jure authority*. By this, the Trial Chamber means the perpetrator of the underlying offence must be the subordinate of the person of higher rank and under his direct or indirect control.'[208] The chamber was not explicit about the required 'trappings', merely referring the reader to its concept of the superior–subordinate relationship.

The ICTY Appeals Chamber seems to have agreed with the lower court that de facto subordination must share much of the character of de jure subordination for the doctrine of command responsibility to apply: 'Although the degree of control wielded by a de jure or de facto superior may take different forms, a de facto superior must be found to wield *substantially similar powers* of control over subordinates to be held criminally responsible for their acts.'[209] The same idea is implicit in the Appeals Chamber's decisive rejection of the theory that the superior–subordinate relationship may be founded on anything less than effective control:

> The Prosecution . . . espouses . . . a theory that in fact 'substantial influence' alone may suffice, in that 'where a person's powers of influence amount to a *sufficient* degree of authority or control in the circumstances to put that person in a position to take preventative action, a failure to do so may result in criminal liability.' This latter standard appears to envisage a lower threshold of control than an effective control threshold; indeed, it is unclear that in its natural sense the concept of 'substantial influence' entails any necessary notion of control at all.[210]

---

[205] Ibid., para. 357.   [206] Ibid., paras 357–62.

[207] Ibid., para. 378, emphasis added. The ILC's Draft Code of Crimes contained a provision similar to Articles 7(3) and 6(3) of the ICTY and ICTR Statutes, respectively, with the following comment: 'The reference to "superiors" is sufficiently broad to cover military commanders or other civilian authorities who are in a similar position of command and exercise a similar degree of control with respect to their subordinates' (UN Doc. A/51/10 (1996), para. 4 of commentary to Art. 6).   [208] *Delalić et al.* trial judgment, para. 646, emphasis added.

[209] *Delalić et al.* appeal judgment, para. 197, emphasis added.   [210] Ibid., para. 257.

Thus, while the *Delalić* case left a number of concepts — not least that of effective control — underdeveloped, it introduced the important idea that a non-military superior may be held personally responsible for crimes of his or her subordinates where he or she exercises a degree of control over subordinates 'similar' to the control regularly enjoyed by military commanders; which means, among other things, that the control must be characterized by the 'trappings' of military authority.

The logical development of this idea, which unfortunately was never undertaken at the tribunals, is that effective control entails not only a *degree* but also a *quality* of control. It is one thing to say that a superior holds his or her position de facto, suggesting that the position has been assumed, and quite another to say that the character of the authority exercised from that position is itself purely de facto, suggesting that the 'authority' is a kind of unstructured or arbitrary brute force or powerful influence. An accused whose authority fits the latter description, which strays notably from the military paradigm, may not have effective control in the statutory sense.

The idea introduced by *Delalić* would lead to the general proposition that the legal notion of effective control requires proof that the defendant belonged to a purposeful organization of individuals in the form of a hierarchical unit;[211] that there existed an acknowledged chain of command and a generally accepted practice of issuing and obeying orders;[212] that those alleged to have been subordinates of the accused knew that disobedience or insubordination could trigger a disciplinary response; and that the superior had the means to effectively suppress or punish unauthorized action. While this proposition does not distinguish between military and non-military superiors, it incorporates the principle that the position of the latter will in practice have to be very similar to that of the former. Several attempts by defence teams to help the ICTY/ICTR Appeals Chamber to see the point have not removed the intellectual blind spot.[213]

The question remains as to what is the source of the duty to control subordinates and prevent offences in the case of non-military superiors. One argument that could be advanced with respect to the ICTY prison-camp cases (for example, *Delalić et al.*, *Aleksovski*, *Kvočka et al.*, *Sikirica et al.*, *Krnojelac*) is that states traditionally have held that superintendents of prisons have a legal duty to prevent the abuse of prisoners by guards, at pain of being held responsible for such abuse. The ICTY, according to this argument, has not been bringing forth duties, as it might seem, like rabbits out of the hat of the superior–subordinate relationship, but has rather relied (albeit implicitly) on the long-standing obligation that is the lot of prison wardens and persons in equivalent positions to take measures to prevent the abuse of those under their charge. While this does not help explain the result in the ICTY's other non-military cases involving command responsibility, such as that of Stevan Todorovic, a police chief — nor does it explain the ICTR results, involving the convictions of several civilians — it does

---

[211] 'The Appeals Chamber understands the necessity to prove that the perpetrator was the "subordinate" of the accused . . . to mean that the relevant accused is, by virtue of his or her position, senior in some sort of formal or informal hierarchy to the perpetrator' (*Delalić et al.* appeal judgment, para. 303).

[212] For more on the importance of orders to the constitution of the relationship, see *Aleksovski* trial judgment, paras 104, 135.   [213] E.g. *Kajelijeli* appeal judgment, paras 83–7.

highlight a pre-existing general duty sufficient to meet the requirements of the doctrine of command responsibility in a specific class of cases.

Another argument, more open to dispute but also more general, is that where the 'similarity' between the control exercised by military and non-military superiors is sufficiently strong, international law will impose the same duty on non-military superiors as it does on military commanders. Under this proposal the source of the duty is, as ever, the military tradition and, once again, is extraneous to the superior–subordinate relationship, although it is the character of the latter which will determine whether the duty will be imposed upon a non-military superior.

Does the requirement of similarity extend to the 'lawfulness' of the organization to which the non-military superior belongs? This indeed would seem to be the implication of the words 'if he or she knew or had reason to know that the subordinate was about to commit such acts' in the Statutes of the ad hoc tribunals — such acts being any of the statutory crimes. Commission of proscribed acts cannot be the organization's *purpose*, for if that were its purpose there would be no question about the superior not knowing, or not having reason to know, about illegal activities. In other words, application of the doctrine of command responsibility must be understood to be limited to organized groups whose overall objectives are prima facie legitimate, and whose members commit crimes exceptionally rather than routinely. Again, the armed forces of a state provide the limiting paradigm. Military personnel cannot shrug off international duties, not even when they participate in an illegal war of aggression, for the organization to which they belong does not thereby become a criminal enterprise (whatever might be said of its choice of campaigns and methods), and its members remain sworn to abide by the laws of war.

At the ICTR, the unquestioning approach to the command responsibility doctrine is most extreme in the case of *Nahimana et al.*, where Ferdinand Nahimana and Jean-Bosco Barayagwiza were found guilty of direct and public incitement to commit genocide for their supposed superior-subordinate relationship to the radio station RTLM, whose broadcasts allegedly instigated genocide. The reader of the judgment may be surprised to learn that *Nahimana* nowhere discusses the law of command responsibility. One would have expected the court to give a lengthy explanation of the nature of Nahimana's and Barayagwiza's control over the staff at RTLM, especially since they were mostly absent during the relevant period, but instead all we get is this offering:

Nahimana and Barayagwiza were, respectively, 'number one' and 'number two' in the top management of the radio. They represented the radio at the highest level in meetings with the Ministry of Information; they controlled the finances of the company; and they were both members of the Steering Committee, which functioned in effect as a board of directors for RTLM. . . . While the Chamber recognizes that Nahimana and Barayagwiza did not make decisions in the first instance with regard to each particular broadcast of RTLM, these decisions reflected an editorial policy for which they were responsible. . . . all the RTLM broadcasters down the chain of command were ultimately accountable to the Steering Committee.[214]

---

[214] *Nahimana et al.* trial judgment, para. 970.

Note the suggestive placement of the radio journalists in a 'chain of command,' which is not otherwise explained. The court continued:

After 6 April 1994, although the evidence does not establish the same level of active support, it is nevertheless clear that Nahimana and Barayagwiza knew what was happening at RTLM and failed to exercise the authority vested in them as office-holding members of the governing body of RTLM, to prevent the genocidal harm that was caused by RTLM programming. That they had the de facto authority to prevent this harm is evidenced by the one documented and successful intervention of Nahimana to stop RTLM attacks on UNAMIR and General Dallaire. Nahimana and Barayagwiza informed [a witness] when they met him in June 1994 that RTLM was being moved to Gisenyi. . . . this conversation indicates the sense of continuing connection with RTLM that Nahimana and Barayagwiza maintained at that time.[215]

Little more than this weak analysis underlies Nahimana's and Barayagwiza's conviction for command responsibility by the court.

In respect of the question about the reach of the command responsibility doctrine, it may be argued that the ICC finds itself in a different position than the ad hoc tribunals. The latter require pre-existing law to enable a finding of command responsibility in the case of a civilian. Hence the inquiry above into the source of the duty in the case of civilians. But the ICC Statute is not retrospective in its application, and so it may be more easily interpreted as extending the law at the time of the adoption of the treaty. On this reasoning, the ICC Statute *creates* a duty in civilians, modelled on the duty of military commanders. Still, the ICC will need to look at the facts of each case to determine whether such a duty can be sensibly attributed to the defendant. Logically, it will still never do to attribute such a duty to the leader of a purely criminal gang. As the words of the ICC's provision directed at civilians imply — 'as a result of his or her failure to exercise control properly over such subordinates' — the duty exists where there is an expectation created by the special position held by the defendant and recognized in criminal law that there shall be 'proper control'.

7.3.5 The knowledge element

Commanders must have had a level of awareness that their subordinates' crimes had been committed or were imminent, as there is no question of strict liability even in the doctrine's original setting. The US military tribunal in the *High Command* case wrote that criminality 'does not attach to every individual in this chain of command from that fact alone. There must be a personal dereliction. That can occur only where the act is directly traceable to him or where his failure to properly supervise his subordinates constitutes criminal negligence on his part.'[216]

The statutory standard of awareness applied by the tribunals ('knew or had reason to know') is met where the alleged commander had actual knowledge, proven by means of direct or circumstantial evidence;[217] or where the accused had information placing him

---

[215] Ibid., para. 972. See also, ibid., paras 1033–4. [216] *High Command* case, pp. 543–4.
[217] *Delalić et al.* trial judgment, paras 384–6.

or her on notice of a likelihood that such offences were being committed, or were about to be committed, and indicating the need for additional investigation.[218] Proof of negligence amounting to 'wilful blindness' will also be sufficient to establish awareness.[219] Tribunal judgments subsequent to *Delalić* suggest that where the purported lack of knowledge is attributable to negligence in the discharge of a commander's duties in circumstances where he or she *should* have known about the offences, the knowledge requirement may be made out.[220] Whether the tribunals would ever enforce a standard so closely approaching strict liability is doubtful.[221]

The awareness must follow the outline of the criminal offence with which the defendant is charged, or the prosecution for that particular offence will fail:

in order to determine whether an accused 'had reason to know' that his subordinates had committed or were about to commit acts of torture, the court must ascertain whether he had sufficiently alarming information... to alert him to the risk of acts of torture being committed, that is of beatings being inflicted not arbitrarily but for one of the prohibited purposes of torture. Thus, it is not enough that an accused has sufficient information about beatings inflicted by his subordinates; he must also have information — albeit general — which alerts him to the risk of beatings being inflicted for one of the purposes provided for in the prohibition against torture.[222]

In this particular case, the ICTY Appeals Chamber reversed the trial court and convicted Milorad Krnojelac, a detention camp warden, through the doctrine of command responsibility, for torture of detainees committed by the camp guards.[223]

7.3.6 Failure to prevent or punish

In considering whether the commander failed to prevent imminent illegal acts, suppress crimes in progress, or punish completed offences, the commander's material ability to restrain or to impose sanctions on subordinates is critical. A commander may be held responsible only if there has been a failure to take those measures which were within his or her powers.[224] The Statutes of the tribunals require that a commander take *necessary and reasonable* measures.[225] This test has a long history. In 1947, in the so-called *Medical* case, a US military tribunal sitting in Nuremberg held that, 'The law of war imposes on a military officer in a position of command an affirmative duty to take such steps as are within his power and appropriate to the circumstances to control those under his command'.[226] In 1948, the International Military Tribunal for the Far East found General Iwane Matsui responsible for crimes at Nankin as 'he did nothing

---

[218] Ibid., paras 390–3.   [219] *Blaškić* trial judgment, para. 307.

[220] Ibid., paras 314–32; cf. *Aleksovski* trial judgment, para. 80. Both judgments depart from the *Delalić et al.* trial judgment (para. 393) by taking a more expansive view. Note the decision in *Delalić* (paras 389–90) not to follow the postwar case law of the military tribunals on this point, and its reluctance to pronounce on the state of the law at the time judgment was rendered (para. 393), as opposed to the time when the crimes were committed.

[221] For an argument against taking this route, see M. L. Smidt, 'Yamashita, Medina, and Beyond: Command Responsibility in Contemporary Military Operations' (2000) 164 *Mil. L. Rev.* 155.

[222] *Krnojelac* appeal judgment, para. 155.   [223] Ibid., para. 171.

[224] *Delalić et al.* trial judgment, para. 395.   [225] *Blaškić* trial judgment, para. 333.

[226] *United States* v. *Karl Brandt et al.*, 2 TWC 212.

or *nothing effective* to abate these horrors'.[227] The same tribunal found War Minister Hideki Tojo responsible for not taking 'adequate steps to punish offenders and to prevent the commission' of offences.[228] In the case *US* v. *Medina* (1971), a US court martial stated that, 'A commander is also responsible if...he wrongfully fails to take the necessary and reasonable steps to insure compliance with the law of war'.[229]

The obligation to 'prevent, suppress, or punish' does not provide a defendant with alternative and equally satisfactory options. Where the defendant knew or had reason to know that his or her subordinates were about to commit crimes and failed to prevent them, he or she cannot make up for the failure to act preventively by punishing the subordinates afterwards.[230] However, case law on these matters is minimal.

While a commander may be found liable for failing to punish a particular act of a subordinate, cases before the tribunals are more likely to involve failure on the part of the commander to create or sustain among those under his or her control an environment of discipline and respect for the law. In *Delalić*, the trial court cited evidence that Mucić, the defendant warden, never punished guards, was frequently absent from the camp at night, and failed to enforce any instructions which he did happen to give out.[231] In *Blaškić* the accused had led his subordinates to understand that certain types of illegal conduct were acceptable and would not result in punishment.[232] A commander who in this way tolerates indiscipline among subordinates, giving them cause to believe that their illegal acts will go unpunished (which indeed they do), will be in a much weaker position than a commander who periodically fails to punish isolated acts.[233]

7.3.7 Erroneous decisions involving command responsibility

Alfred Musema and Clément Kayishema were, according to the ICTR prosecutor, at the head of bands formed for no other purpose than to murder Tutsi civilians, and therefore they cannot have been acting within the sphere of application of the command responsibility doctrine. The ICTR Trial Chambers which heard these two cases miscalculated the status of the two defendants by using the wrong standard. By way of a loose notion of 'influence' or 'control', and by failing to see that the command responsibility doctrine in consequence of its conceptual underpinnings must be confined to structures strongly resembling relationships of military command, the Trial Chambers did not systematically seek evidence to satisfy the above-mentioned essential ingredients of the superior–subordinate relationship. It would have been of interest to know whether Musema did in fact appropriate a ready-made civil hierarchy of tea-factory workers, twisting it into a private militia. Similarly, it would have been useful to articulate the argument, if there was one, showing that Kayishema transformed

---

[227] B. V. A. Röling and C. F. Rüter, *The Tokyo Judgement: The International Military Tribunal for the Far East* (Amsterdam University Press, 1977), p. 454, emphasis added.   [228] Ibid., p. 462.

[229] Reproduced in K. A. Howard, 'Command Responsibility for War Crimes' (1982) 21 *J. of Pub. L.* 7, at 8–12.

[230] Ibid., para. 336.   [231] *Delalić et al.* trial judgment, paras 772 ff.

[232] *Blaškić* trial judgment, paras 487, 494–5.

[233] E.g. *Yamashita* v. *Styer* (1946) 327 US 1, 14–16; *Akayesu* trial judgment, para. 691; *Delalić et al.* trial judgment, paras 772 ff.; *Blaškić* trial judgment, paras 487 ff.

ordinary public administration personnel (among others) into a killing machine under his control. But there was no proof on these points, and so neither defendant should have been burdened with the international duty affecting commanders.

The command responsibility doctrine was so misunderstood at the tribunals that for several years the Trial Chambers were quite prepared to convict a defendant for both direct responsibility *and* command responsibility for the same acts. An indictment alleged that 'Kayishema is *also or alternatively* individually responsible as a superior for the criminal acts of his subordinates in the [prefectural] administration, the Gendarmerie Nationale, and the communal police with respect to each of the crimes charged, pursuant to Article 6(3)'.[234] Both Article 6(1) and Article 6(3) of the ICTR Statute were thus covered in relation to each count. The problem arising from this practice is illustrated in the following excerpt from the indictment:

On about 17 April 1994, Clement Kayishema *ordered* members of the Gendarmerie Nationale, communal police of Gitesi commune, members of the Interahamwe and armed civilians to attack the Complex, and *personally participated in the attack....* The attack resulted in thousands of deaths... Before the attack on the Complex, Clement Kayishema did not take measures to prevent an attack, and after the attack Clement Kayishema did not punish the perpetrators.[235]

The juxtaposition of Article 6(1) liability with Article 6(3) liability is almost absurd. How *could* Kayishema have taken measures to prevent the attack when he was *the leader of it*? And how could he later have punished the perpetrators, when he was a perpetrator himself? Nevertheless, the Trial Chamber in *Kayishema and Ruzindana* went along with this thesis:

The finding of responsibility under Article 6(1) of the statute does not prevent the chamber from finding responsibility additionally... under Article 6(3). The two forms of responsibility are not mutually exclusive.... Where it can be shown that the accused was the de jure or de facto superior and that *pursuant to his orders* the atrocities were committed, then the chamber considers that this must suffice to found command responsibility.[236]

The court thus convicted Kayishema on four counts of genocide, in each case pursuant to both direct and command responsibility.[237]

The mistake was repeated in the *Musema* case. The indictment charged Musema with genocide for '[bringing] to the area of Bisesero armed individuals and direct[ing] them to attack the people seeking refuge there. In addition... and often in concert with others Alfred Musema personally attacked and killed persons seeking refuge in Bisesero.'[238] The prosecutor alleged liability 'pursuant to Article 6(1) *and* 6(3)' of the ICTR Statute, dropping the 'also or alternatively' construction used against Kayishema. How Article 6(3) might be raised against someone who is 'directing' and 'personally' participating in genocidal acts is, once again, not a question that the prosecutor stopped to consider; and, as a result, the *Musema* Trial Chamber was led into the same conceptual contortions as *Kayishema and Ruzindana*.

---

[234] *Kayishema and Ruzindana* trial judgment, para. 5, which reproduces the indictment; the excerpt is from para. 22 of the indictment (emphasis added). [235] Ibid., indictment, paras 28–30.
[236] Ibid., para. 210. [237] Ibid., paras 551–71. [238] *Musema* trial judgment, annex A, para. 4.6.

The ICTY did not escape the initial confusion:

The Chamber is satisfied that Mladen Naletilić ordered the destruction of the houses in Doljani and that he is responsible under Article 7(1) of the Statute. The Chamber is further satisfied that the destruction was carried out by KB soldiers under the command of Mladen Naletilić. Mladen Naletilić knew about the destruction, since he himself had ordered it; he did not prevent it and, therefore, he is also responsible under Article 7(3) of the Statute.[239]

In the *Blaškić* case, the Appeals Chamber said:

the provisions of Article 7(1) and Article 7(3) of the Statute connote distinct categories of criminal responsibility. However, the Appeals Chamber considers that, in relation to a particular count, it is not appropriate to convict under both Article 7(1) and Article 7(3) of the Statute. Where both Article 7(1) and Article 7(3) responsibility are alleged under the same count, and where the legal requirements pertaining to both of these heads of responsibility are met, a Trial Chamber should enter a conviction on the basis of Article 7(1) only, and consider the accused's superior position as an aggravating factor in sentencing.[240]

7.3.8 Conclusions on command responsibility

The ad hoc tribunals have been uncertain about how to express and apply the law of command responsibility,[241] and in the process they have pushed it beyond its limits. The limits may be summarized as follows: The superior–subordinate relationship must have the appearance of a formal relationship of authority (even if it is not formally constituted), and it must subsist within a goal-directed hierarchical organization or institution (even if it is ad hoc or transitory). There must be a power in the superior to give orders to the subordinates, such power resting on a mutual expectation (as between the superior and the subordinates) that the superior's orders will be obeyed — something to be distinguished from obedience achieved through bullying, or by submission to 'an intimidating and morally delinquent individual' (the above-cited characterization of Hazim Delić).[242] Moreover, there must be a known power in the superior to control and discipline the criminal behaviour of subordinates in meaningful and effective ways, such as by intervening to restrain a subordinate or by directly suspending his or her services to the unit, at least until such time as the matter is reviewed by another (higher) authority. More generally, a superior must be able 'to take every appropriate measure to ensure the maintenance of order' in the ranks.[243] Proof of the superior–subordinate relationship in the case of non-military superiors is likely to be difficult unless the defendant was part of a prima facie legitimate quasi-martial organization, such as a prison-camp, or in control of a militia-like unit with a prima facie legitimate role, such as a police force.

---

[239] *Naletilić and Martinović* trial judgment, para. 596.

[240] *Blaškić* appeal judgment, para. 91. See also *Blaškić* trial judgment, para. 337; *Krstić* trial judgment, para. 605; *Krnojelac* trial judgment, para. 173; *Stakić* trial judgment, fn. 1013.

[241] See, in particular, the recent, surprising, discussion of command responsibility in the *Halilović* trial judgment, paras 42–54.   [242] At fn. 193. *Delalić et al.* trial judgment, para. 806.

[243] Ibid., para. 767.

PART III

PROCEDURE, EVIDENCE, AND DEFENCES

8

DUE PROCESS AND HUMAN RIGHTS

8.1 INTRODUCTION

International criminal tribunals are considered important tools for improving the protection of human rights. And rightly so. However, the important mandate of international criminal tribunals should not make us lose sight of the fact that as *criminal* tribunals in the first instance these institutions may potentially violate human rights themselves. In this respect, one can immediately think of the various fair trial rights and the right to liberty and security of persons. Other rights may be at stake as well. For example, when the ICTY or ICTR judges issue a search warrant, the right to privacy and inviolability of the home may be compromised. Likewise, in one case an ICTY Trial Chamber curtailed the right to freedom of expression when a newspaper was ordered not to publish names of protected witnesses.[1]

As exemplars of international criminal justice, the ICTY and ICTR may be expected to fully respect internationally protected human rights. In the long run, the support for, and confidence, in the organs of international criminal adjudication, including the recently established permanent International Criminal Court (ICC) will depend on whether or not the tribunals can live up to this expectation.

The present chapter concentrates on due process and human rights protections in the context of international criminal proceedings. Before dealing with a variety of rights — which can, however, only be selective in the context of this book — we devote two sections to the applicability of human rights law to international criminal proceedings and its scope of application in general to international criminal proceedings (sections 8.2 and 8.3). Next, we explore habeas corpus rights (section 8.4), fair trial rights (section 8.5), and rights of detained persons (section 8.6).

8.2 APPLICABILITY OF HUMAN RIGHTS STANDARDS

A central and crucial question is to what extent international criminal tribunals are bound by international human rights law. This question needs to be dealt with before we concentrate on some practical problems in the application of this body of law.

Human rights 'enter' the legal framework of the ad hoc tribunals in a number of ways. The most direct application of human rights law is the resort to the rights explicitly set out in the Statutes and the rules of procedure and evidence (RPE) of the Tribunals. Article 21 of the ICTY Statute and Article 20 of the ICTR Statute contain the rights of the accused.[2] Both provisions derive their language almost directly from Article 14 of the International Covenant on Civil and Political Rights (ICCPR).[3] Rule 42 common to the ICTY, ICTR, and SCSL RPE contains the rights of suspects during investigation.[4] The statutes and rules are far from complete and omit some important

---

[1] See Decision on Prosecution Motion for an Order for Publication of Newspaper Advertisement and an Order for Service of Documents, *Prosecutor* v. *Mrkšić et al.*, Case No. IT-95-13a-PT, ICTY, T. Ch. II, 19 December 1997.

[2] Cf. Article 17 of the SCSL Statute.

[3] See Morris and Scharf, *Insider's Guide*, at 226; id., *International Criminal Tribunal for Rwanda*, at 513–14; and Bassiouni and Manikas, *Law of the ICTY*, at 957 *et seq*.

[4] For a discussion of the right to counsel as one of the rights contained in Rule 42, see Decision on Zdravko Mucić's Motion for the Exclusion of Evidence, *Prosecutor* v. *Delalić et al.*, Case No. IT-96-21-T, ICTY, T. Ch. II *quater*, 2 September 1997.

rights, such as the right not to be subjected to arbitrary arrest and detention, which is contained in Article 9 of the ICCPR.

In a more indirect way human rights enter the legal framework of the Tribunals on the basis of the oft-quoted commentary by the UN Secretary-General to Article 21 of the ICTY Statute: 'It is axiomatic that the International Tribunal must fully respect internationally recognized standards regarding the rights of the accused at all stages of its proceedings.'[5] The report of the Secretary-General was approved by the Security Council when establishing the ICTY and can therefore be considered an authoritative interpretation of the ICTY Statute.[6]

Human rights must be respected and applied by the tribunals as organs of the United Nations, and to achieve international cooperation in promoting and encouraging respect for human rights and for fundamental freedoms is a purpose of the United Nations proclaimed in Article 1(3) of its Charter.[7] However, the determination of the scope of application of these human rights and fundamental freedoms under the Charter, as well as their relationship *inter se* proves problematic. More specifically, it is uncertain *which* human rights are alluded to in the purposes clause of the Charter referred to above.[8]

Finally, human rights law binds the tribunals in their activities to the extent that it is part of customary international law or general principles of law. International organizations, including their subsidiary organs, are creations of international law and are, as such, subjected to international law.[9] A practical application of this view can be found in the case law of the European Court of Justice, according to which 'the European Community must respect international law in the exercise of its powers'.[10] There is no reason why this should be different for the UN, including the Security Council and the ad hoc tribunals. Thus, they should abide by peremptory norms of international law under all circumstances and respect other rules of international law when they have not been empowered to deviate from these rules.[11]

---

[5] Report of the Secretary-General on ICTY, para. 106.

[6] Given the practically identical language of Article 20 of the ICTR Statute, the commentary by the Secretary-General to Article 21 of the ICTY Statute is equally applicable to the ICTR provision.

[7] Morris and Scharf, *International Criminal Tribunal for Rwanda*, at 513.

[8] Morris and Scharf in this respect refer to the most important human rights instruments, the International Bill of Human Rights, consisting of the Universal Declaration of Human Rights (UDHR), the ICCPR, and the International Covenant on Economic, Social and Cultural Rights (ICESCR) (ibid.). They do not address the question, however, whether all the rights contained therein fall under Article 1(3) of the UN Charter.

[9] See the ruling of the International Court of Justice (ICJ) in *Interpretation of the Agreement of 25 March 1951 between the WHO and Egypt*, Advisory Opinion, *ICJ Reports* 1980, at 73, 89–90: 'international organizations are subjects of international law and, as such, are bound by any obligations incumbent upon them under general rules of international law'. For in our view compelling arguments as to why international organizations should be considered bound by international law, even without their consent, see H. Schermers and N. Blokker, *International Institutional Law — Unity within Diversity* (The Hague: Martinus Nijhoff, 1995), at 983–4.

[10] Case C–286/90, *Anklagemyndigheden* v. *Poulsen and Diva Navigation Corp.* [1992] ECR I-6019, para. 9; Case C–162/96, *Racke* v. *Hauptzollamt Mainz* [1998] ECR I-3655, para. 45. The latter case related to the suspension of the operation of a cooperation agreement between the Socialist Federal Republic of Yugoslavia and the European Economic Community (EEC). The Court held that the 'rules of customary international law concerning the termination and suspension of treaty relations by reason of a fundamental change of circumstances are binding upon the Community institutions and form part of the Community legal order' (ibid.).

[11] For more detail on the applicability of international law to the Security Council, see T. Gill, 'Legal and Some Political Limitations on the Power of the UN Security Council to Exercise Its Enforcement Powers Under Chapter VII of the Charter' (1995) 26 *Netherlands Y'book Int'l Law*, at 33–138, in particular at 61–4.

The application of human rights norms as part of customary international law or general principles of law raises a number of problems for international criminal tribunals. A major difficulty is the identification of human rights falling within those categories. Not all of the rights set out in the various international and regional human rights treaties reflect customary international law or general principles of law. A further complicating factor in making that determination is that a considerable number of human rights may be derogated from under certain conditions, for example when this is 'necessary in a democratic society',[12] or 'in time of public emergency which threatens the life of the nation'.[13] These conditions, however, concern the application of human rights within national societies and may not fit easily into the application of human rights by international criminal tribunals. For these reasons, when confronted with questions as to the exact scope of application of human rights law, resort to customary international law and general principles may be a highly complicated and time-consuming matter for the tribunals. Application of human rights treaties, and in particular well-developed interpretations of the treaty provisions by supervisory bodies of a judicial and quasi-judicial nature, is a far more attractive alternative. This is what the tribunals have been doing so far. It is true that in the initial case law, for example, in the *Tadić* protective measures decision, the ICTY was reluctant to take into account human rights treaty law, including decisions of supervisory bodies.[14] However, subsequent decisions display a greater ease with sources of law outside the Tribunal's Statute and RPE and have increasingly referred to the treaty-based human rights law.[15] In the *Mucić* case, for example, the Trial Chamber gave ample regard to the case law of the European Court of Human Rights in order to determine the scope of the right to counsel under Rule 42 of the ICTY RPE.[16] In the *Dokmanović* decision dealing with the legality of arrest the Trial Chamber attentively considered relevant case law of the European Court of Human Rights and, to a lesser extent, of the Human Rights Committee.[17] At the appellate level, account may be taken of the decision of the Appeals Chamber in the *Blaškić* case. When considering the power of the Tribunal to hold contempt proceedings against individuals not complying with a subpoena *in absentia*, the Appeals

---

[12] Language used in the second sections of various provisions in the ECHR; see e.g. Article 8(2) of the ECHR.

[13] See Article 4 of the ICCPR.

[14] *Tadić* protective measures decision, para. 27, where it held that 'the interpretation given by other judicial bodies to Article 14 of the ICCPR and Article 6 of the ECHR is only of limited relevance'. It also ruled that 'the International Tribunal must interpret its provisions within its own legal context and not rely in its application on interpretations made by other judicial bodies' (para. 28).

[15] Affolder found that the *Tadić* protective measures decision 'uncovers a deep uncertainty about the sources of international procedural law and the relevance of international standards in making procedural decisions'. N. Affolder, 'Tadic, the Anonymous Witness and the Sources of International Procedural Law' (1998) 19 *Michigan J. Int'l Law*, at 448.

[16] Decision on Zdravko Mucić's Motion for the Exclusion of Evidence, *Prosecutor* v. *Delalić et al.*, Case No. IT-96-21-T, ICTY, T. Ch. II *quater*, 2 September 1997, paras. 50–1. The analysis of the ECtHR case law contained some flaws and its impact on the outcome of the case may be very limited, but the Trial Chamber nevertheless took it into account. See also the commentary of G. Sluiter to that case in Klip and Sluiter, *Annotated Leading Cases, vol. I*, at 242–3.

[17] Decision on the Motion for Release by the Accused Slavko Dokmanović, *Prosecutor* v. *Mrkšić et al.*, Case No. 95-13a-PT, ICTY, T.Ch. II, 22 October 1997, paras. 62–8.

Chamber held that the guarantees provided for in the context of the ECHR should be respected.[18] More recently, the Appeals Chamber applied human rights treaties and decisions of supervisory bodies in the *Barayagwiza* case.[19] Concerning the legality of Mr Barayagwiza's arrest and his detention, the Appeals Chamber considered which provisions it should apply. It held that:

The International Covenant on Civil and Political Rights is part of general international law and is applied on that basis. Regional human rights treaties, such as the European Convention on Human Rights and the American Convention on Human Rights, and the jurisprudence developed thereunder, are persuasive authorities which may be of assistance in applying and interpreting the Tribunal's applicable law. Thus, they are not binding of their own accord on the Tribunal. They are, however, authoritative as evidence of international custom.[20]

This citation is indicative of the role of international human rights law in the framework of the tribunals. Nevertheless, it raises a number of questions. For example, what is meant by declaring the ICCPR part of general international law? Does it reflect customary international law, or general principles of law? Is it part of general international law in its entirety? Furthermore, if the regional instruments are evidence of international custom,[21] do they bind the tribunals on the basis of customary international law? Notwithstanding these questions, the citation conveys sufficient clarity. It is desirable[22] and legitimate to apply fully the ICCPR as a universal instrument because the accused benefits from this protection in most national jurisdictions as well. Full application of the ICCPR should include paying due attention to the views of the Human Rights Committee, as authoritative interpretations of the provisions contained in this instrument.

Problems relating to the ICCPR's exact scope of application will nonetheless subsist, especially since the provisions address the protection of human rights by states. As was already mentioned, whereas states are permitted to derogate from certain human rights standards on limited and specific grounds, one can hardly imagine how these grounds could apply to the tribunals.[23] The emphasis that the rights contained in the ICCPR and other instruments are *minimum* rights is found in *Barayagwiza*[24] and *Nikolić*.[25] This fact can be expected to play an important role in passing judgement on their applicability.

---

[18] *Blaškić* subpoena appeal decision, para. 59.   [19] *Barayagwiza* I appeal decision.

[20] Ibid., para. 40.

[21] In particular, the ECHR can be considered to reflect customary international law. It is true that this is only a regional convention and therefore the ensuing state practice is by definition limited, but this Convention dates from 1950 and served as a model for the ICCPR.

[22] In this vein, see the commentary on the ICTR Trial Chamber's decision in *Barayagwiza* by Bert Swart, referring to the the tribunals as institutions inevitably providing role models for national systems of criminal justice (B. Swart, 'Commentary', in Klip and Sluiter, *Annotated Leading Cases, vol. II*, at 197).

[23] In this respect it may seem understandable that the majority in the *Tadić* protective measures decision ruled that 'the interpretation given by other judicial bodies to Article 14 of the ICCPR and Article 6 of the ECHR is only of limited relevance in applying the provisions of the Statutes and Rules of the International Tribunal as these bodies interpret their provisions in the context of their legal framework, which do not contain the same considerations'. *Tadić* protective measures decision, para. 27.

[24] See *Barayagwiza* I appeal decision, para. 79: 'suspects held at the behest of the Tribunal . . . are entitled, at a bare minimum, to the protections afforded under these international [human rights] instruments'.

[25] *Nikolić* jurisdiction trial decision, para. 110: 'This Chamber observes that these norms [provisions from the ICCPR and the ECHR] only provide for the absolute minimum standards applicable.'

The ICC Statute seeks to regulate the applicable sources of law in a hierarchical manner in Article 21. According to its third section, the application and interpretation of the sources of law mentioned above must be consistent with internationally recognized human rights.[26] As a result, internationally recognized human rights appear to occupy the highest place in the hierarchy of norms, even above the Statute, as some sort of constitutional review yardstick for all applicable law. As a result, in case of a conflict between a provision in the ICC Statute or RPE with an internationally recognized human right, the latter shall prevail.[27]

It is uncertain, however, what is to be understood by 'internationally recognized human rights'. Given the universal aspiration of the Court, this notion first and foremost includes universal human rights law, such as the ICCPR, the Convention against Torture (CAT), and the Convention on the Rights of the Child. Regional human rights treaties play in principle a less prominent role, but may frequently be applied in practice, because of the highly developed character of certain regional human rights systems, such as the ECHR. With respect to all of the above human rights norms, however, the same question arises as in relation to the ad hoc tribunals: what should be their scope of application in an international criminal prosecution?

For the internationalized criminal tribunals for East Timor, Sierra Leone, and Cambodia the application of human rights norms outside the context of their statutes is somewhat more complex. The SCSL has proclaimed itself as a truly international institution, as a result of which it is in our opinion fully bound by internationally accepted human rights norms.[28] The East Timor panels and the Cambodian Extraordinary Chambers are, however, formally part of the domestic legal order. As a result, the applicability of human rights law depends, from a legal perspective, on two things: (1) the formal commitment of East Timor and Cambodia to human rights instruments through ratification and taking into account reservations made; and (2) the national constitutional arrangements in respect of (direct) application of international (human rights) law before national courts. As important is the national culture and legal conscience in respect of the importance of human rights protection. For example, Cambodia offers excellent constitutional arrangements for the application of human rights norms, including the ICCPR, but does not have a good reputation for practical enforcement of those norms.[29] Equally important is the possibility of nationals submitting individual complaints to the Human Rights Committee, concerning compliance with the ICCPR.[30] In both the East Timor and Cambodian contexts this is not

---

[26] There was virtual unanimity among delegations regarding the desirability of such a provision: M. McAuliffe deGuzman, 'Applicable Law', in Triffterer, *Commentary on the Rome Statute*, at 445.

[27] A clear conflict is a highly theoretical possibility. More likely is that the *exercise* of discretionary powers attributed by the Statute can conflict with human rights norms.   [28] See Chapter 1, sections 1.2.4 and 1.3.2.

[29] See G. Sluiter, 'Due Process and Criminal Procedure in the Cambodian Extraordinary Chambers' (2006) 4 *JICJ* 314–26.

[30] This is conditional upon whether the state has ratified the First Optional Protocol to ICCPR: Optional Protocol to the International Covenant on Civil and Political Rights, GA Res. 2200A (XXI) of 16 December 1966, 21 UN GAOR Supp. (No. 16) at 59, UN Doc. A/6316 (1966), 999 *UNTS* 302, entered into force 23 March 1976.

possible;[31] we wonder whether any support by the UN to the national legal order for the prosecution of international crimes should not be conditional on prior ratification of the Optional Protocol to the ICCPR.

8.3 SCOPE OF APPLICATION

The criminal procedure of international criminal tribunals generally takes place in two or even more jurisdictions. For example, evidence is collected in different states, the accused is arrested by persons other than tribunal officers, and finally the sentences are enforced by states. This fragmentation is a vital distinction between international and national criminal procedures. Of course, in national cases it may be necessary to request another jurisdiction to collect evidence or to arrest and extradite the accused, but it is not standard practice, as it is with international criminal tribunals.

The dispersal of the criminal procedure over various jurisdictions raises some pertinent questions about the scope of application of human rights law. From a practical point of view, the most vital question is to what extent an international criminal tribunal should bear responsibility (in the sense of providing remedies) for human rights violations that have occurred in the framework of its proceedings.

It is undisputed that the tribunals bear full responsibility for all conduct within the courtroom or within detention units, which are within their 'exclusive domain'. Thus, violation of the right to counsel or ill-treatment of prisoners constitutes unlawful conduct fully attributable to these institutions.

The situation is much more complicated as regards conduct that occurs outside this exclusive domain. One view is that (human rights) violations that occur outside the trial forum's jurisdiction are of no concern to the trial forum, or have no consequences for the trial. The argument in favour of this view is that the trial forum lacks the competence to supervise acts of criminal procedure that take place in another sovereign state. This argument has its roots in the rule of non-inquiry and seems also to have been used by a trial chamber of the ICTR refusing to review the legality of a number of searches, seizures, and arrests by national authorities.[32]

---

[31] Cambodia signed the Protocol on 27 December 2004, but has not ratified it as at the time of writing. East Timor has not even signed the Protocol.

[32] See the following decisions: Decision on the Defence Motion for Exclusion of Evidence and Restitution of Property Seized, *Prosecutor* v. *Nyiramasuhuko*, Case No. ICTR-97-21-T, ICTR, T. Ch. II, 12 October 2000, para. 26; Decision on the Defence Motion challenging the Lawfulness of the Arrest and Detention and seeking Return or Inspection of Seized Items, *Prosecutor* v. *Ngirumpatse*, Case No. ICTR-97-44-I, ICTR, T. Ch. II, 10 December 1999, para. 56; Decision on the Defence Motion concerning the Arbitrary Arrest and Illegal Detention of the Accused and on the Defence Notice of Urgent Motion to Expand and Supplement the Record of 8 December 1999 Hearing, *Prosecutor* v. *Kajelijeli*, Case No. ICTR-98-44-I, ICTR, T. Ch. II, 8 May 2000, para. 34; Decision on the Defence Motion for the Restitution of Documents and other Personal or Family Belongings Seized (Rule 40(C) of the Rules of Procedure and Evidence), and the Exclusion of such Evidence which may be used by the Prosecutor in preparing an Indictment against the Applicant, *Prosecutor* v. *Karemera*, Case No. ICTR-98-44-I, ICTR, T. Ch. II, 10 December 1999, para. 4.2; Decision on the Defence Motion challenging the Legality of the Arrest and Detention of the Accused and requesting the Return of Personal Items Seized, *Prosecutor* v. *Nzirorera*, Case No. ICTR-98-44-T, ICTR, T. Ch. II, 7 September 2000, para. 27.

Another argument, which has been used in a national decision, is that laws have only territorial application and 'foreigners' do not benefit from their protection. This was the position of the US Supreme Court majority in the *Verdugo-Urquidez* case, dealing with the question whether or not the US Constitution governed a search of a home in Mexico by US law enforcement officials.[33]

Our view, however, is that the trial forum must take account of every human rights violation that occurs in the framework of the criminal proceedings. This view is based on the requirement of fairness and the specific nature of the relationship between the accused and the trial forum. Justice Brennan in his dissenting opinion to the *Verdugo* case coined the notion of mutuality:

[i]f we expect aliens to obey our laws, aliens should be able to expect that we will obey our Constitution when we investigate, prosecute, and punish them. . . . Mutuality is essential to ensure the fundamental fairness that underlies our Bill of Rights.[34]

The same argument can be used with respect to the institutions of international criminal justice, meaning that the individuals appearing before them should enjoy the protection of their legal framework, including internationally protected human rights. The statutes of all international(ized) criminal tribunals specify that trial chambers have a duty to ensure the fairness of trials.[35]

The obligation not to disregard human rights violations that occurred prior to trial follows from these tribunals' statutes. Article 20(1) of the ICTY Statute and Article 19(1) of the ICTR Statute explicitly obligate a trial chamber to ensure that a trial is fair and expeditious. This implies that pre-trial human rights violations must be addressed, since they can affect the fairness of the trial.

In the jurisprudence of the ICTY and ICTR one notes that the chambers are generally aware of their obligation to ensure the fairness of the trial as a whole. The decisions of the ICTR mentioned above[36] should be seen as unfortunate exceptions to this rule. In at least three cases, the ICTY and ICTR chambers have reviewed the legality of pre-trial investigative and other measures in the light of internationally protected human rights.

In the *Čelebići* case the ICTY Trial Chamber was confronted with the question whether a statement obtained in the absence of the accused's counsel could be admitted into evidence.[37] The accused, Zdravko Mucić, was prior to his transfer interrogated by Austrian police, not at the request of the ICTY, but with a view to his transfer to the ICTY or even his extradition to another state. Under Austrian law there is no right for

---

[33] *United States* v. *Verdugo-Urquidez*, (1990) 494 US 259, 108 L.Ed 2d 222, 110 S. Ct. 1056. For a commentary, see B. Albrecht, '*United States* v. *Verdugo-Urquidez*: The Reach of United States Law Enforcement Agents Abroad — Are there Any Fourth Amendment Limits?' (1991) 22 *UWLA Law Rev.,* at 303–34, and D. Haug, 'Comment on United States v. Verdugo-Urquidez' (1991) 32 *Harvard Int'l. Law J.,* at 295–301.

[34] *United States* v. *Verdugo-Urquidez* (1990) 494 US 284, 108 L.Ed 2d 222, 110 S. Ct. 1056.

[35] Article 20(1) of the ICTY Statute, Article 19(1) of the ICTR Statute, Article 64(2) of the ICC Statute, Article 17(2) of the SCSL Statute, Article 13 of the UN/Cambodia Agreement, and Section 2(2.1) of the UNTAET Regulation 2001/25 amending UTAET Regulations 2000/11 and 2000/30.   [36] See note 32 above.

[37] Decision on Zdravko Mucić's Motion for the Exclusion of Evidence, *Prosecutor* v. *Delalić et al.,* Case No. IT-96-21-T, T. Ch. II *quater*, 2 September 1997.

counsel to be present at such interrogations. The ICTY prosecutor essentially adopted the position that the Tribunal, including its organs, had not violated the right to counsel protected by Rule 42 of the ICTY Rules and international human rights instruments, and as a result, there was no reason to exclude the evidence.[38] The Trial Chamber, however, emphasized that the exclusion of evidence obtained in violation of internationally protected human rights is mandatory under Rule 95.[39] In this respect it is irrelevant whether the Tribunal in any way requested, or was involved in, the collection of evidence, although involvement of the prosecutor in obtaining evidence in violation of human rights could result in remedies additional to the exclusion of evidence.

Two other relevant cases concern alleged violations of the human rights pertaining to arrest and pre-trial detention. The first case relates to the arrest of and pre-trial detention in Cameroon of Jean-Bosco Barayagwiza.[40] Barayagwiza's arrest was lawful, but following a long period of detention in Cameroon the accused's right to be promptly informed of the charges against him and the right to challenge the legality of his detention before a court of law were violated. The complexity of the *Barayagwiza* case lies not so much in the facts of the case as in the question of responsibility for these various facts. The prosecutor tried to diminish her own role in the prolonged pre-trial detention of the accused in Cameroon and the related violations of the accused's rights, and to allocate much of the responsibility to Cameroon. It is true that the conduct of the prosecutor was of great significance for the choice of remedies in the *Barayagwiza* I appeal decision: termination of the proceedings, based on the prosecutor's significant role in the continuous violation of the accused's rights. However, in the *Barayagwiza* II appeal decision the Appeals Chamber decided that, on the basis of new information, the violations of Barayagwiza's rights were due more to Cameroon than to the prosecutor, and, therefore, the remedies adopted previously were reversed. Be this as it may, the question of allocation of responsibilities between the prosecutor and Cameroon is irrelevant to the question whether the violations should be addressed by the court. The Appeals Chamber made it clear that it would fully exercise its supervisory powers over pre-trial human rights violations. According to the Chamber, '[t]he use of such supervisory powers serves three functions: to provide a remedy for the violation of the accused's rights; to deter future misconduct; and to enhance the integrity of the judicial process'.[41]

The Appeals Chamber also considered it self-evident that the trial forum is the appropriate place to address human rights violations that occurred in the framework of the criminal proceedings:

At this juncture, it is irrelevant that only a small portion of that total period of provisional detention is attributable to the Tribunal, since it is the Tribunal — and not any other entity — that is currently adjudicating the Appellant's claims. Regardless of which other parties may be responsible, the

---

[38] Ibid., para. 22.   [39] Ibid., para. 43.

[40] See *Barayagwiza* I appeal decision and *Barayagwiza* II appeal decision. For a critical commentary on the first decision, see B. Swart, 'Commentary', in Klip and Sluiter, *Annotated Leading Cases, vol. II*, at 197–208, for a note on *Barayagwiza* I and II appeal decisions, see W. A. Schabas, '*Barayagwiza v. Prosecutor*' (2000) 94 *AJIL*, at 563–71.

[41] *Barayagwiza* I appeal decision, para. 76.

inescapable conclusion is that the Appellant's right to be promptly informed of the charges against him was violated.[42]

The first *Barayagwiza* decision was altered in a highly questionable review procedure.[43] However, this review only concerned the choice for the remedies. The *Barayagwiza* II appeal decision did not in any way affect the guiding principles established in the *Barayagwiza* I appeal decision,[44] which can be summarized as follows: the ICTY or ICTR Trial Chamber should supervise every violation of individual rights that occurs in the framework of its proceedings, with the aim of preserving the integrity and the fairness of the proceedings.

Although both *Barayagwiza* appeal decisions can be criticized on many points, they should be welcomed for having established the above principle, which aims to prevent unacceptable gaps in the protection of human rights.

The final decision we would like to address concerns the method of arrest of the accused Dragan Nikolić.[45] The accused in this case claimed that his arrest and subsequent detention were unlawful, because he had been abducted, by unknown individuals, from the territory of the Federal Republic of Yugoslavia and put in the hands of SFOR. The case raises a classical issue of *male captus bene detentus*: can jurisdiction still be lawfully exercised over an unlawfully arrested individual?[46] Put in this way, the focus is placed immediately on the remedy, namely the termination of the proceedings. However, another question must be addressed first: to what extent should the ICTY review the legality of the arrest of the accused? The ICTY Trial Chamber here followed the *Barayagwiza* jurisprudence, recognizing that violations of the rights of the accused in the pre-trial phase can negatively affect the fairness and integrity of the entire proceedings. It is worth quoting the most relevant paragraph of the decision:

There exists a close relationship between the obligation of the Tribunal to respect the human rights of the Accused and the obligation to ensure due process of law. Ensuring that the Accused's

---

[42] Ibid., para. 85.

[43] *Barayagwiza* II appeal decision. The circumstances surrounding these decisions are extremely controversial and have provoked considerable criticism of the tribunals' authority and legitimacy. On 3 November 1999 the Appeals Chamber ordered Barayagwiza's release, as a result of the dismissal of the case with prejudice to the prosecutor. However, although this was a final decision, the Appeals Chamber reviewed it on the basis of an extremely controversial interpretation of Article 25 of the Statute dealing with review proceedings (this provision can hardly be interpreted otherwise than as a review of a final judgment of acquittal or conviction, and not of other decisions). Furthermore, one may indeed wonder whether the new facts underlying the review should not have been known to the prosecutor at the time of the first decision. Although the suggestion was vehemently denied by the judges, some commentators have concluded that political pressure, in the form of a threat by Rwanda to halt all cooperation with the ICTR, played a vital role in reversing the first Appeals Chamber decision. See the criticism by Schabas: W. A. Schabas, 'Barayagwiza v. Prosecutor' (2000) 94 *AJIL*, at 567–8.

[44] See Declaration by Judge Nieto-Navia, *Barayagwiza* II appeal decision, para. 28: 'Human rights treaties provide that when a state violates fundamental human rights, it is obliged to ensure that appropriate domestic remedies are in place to put an end to such violations and in certain circumstances to provide for fair compensation to the injured party. Although the Tribunal is not a State, it is following such a precedent to compensate the Appellant for the violation of his human rights.'   [45] *Nikolić* jurisdiction trial decision.

[46] On the applicability of the *male captus bene detentus* doctrine to international criminal tribunals see S. Lamb, 'The Power of Arrest of the International Criminal Tribunal for the Former Yugoslavia' (1999) 70 *Brit. Y'book Int'l Law*, at 167–244, and M. Scharf, '*The Prosecutor* v. *Slavko Dokmanovic*: Irregular Rendition and the ICTY' (1998) 11 *LJIL*, at 369–82.

rights are respected and that he receives a fair trial forms, in actual fact, an important aspect of the general concept of due process of law. In that context, this Chamber concurs with the view expressed in several national judicial decisions, according to which the issue of respect for due process of law encompasses more than merely the duty to ensure a fair trial for the Accused. Due process of law also includes questions such as how the Parties have been conducting themselves in the context of a particular case and how an Accused has been brought into the jurisdiction of the Tribunal. The finding in the *Ebrahim* case that the State must come to court with clean hands applies equally to the Prosecution coming to a Trial Chamber of this Tribunal. In addition, this Chamber concurs with the Appeals Chamber in the *Barayagwiza* case that the abuse of process doctrine may be relied on if 'in the circumstances of a particular case, proceeding with the trial of the accused would contravene the court's sense of justice'. However, in order to prompt a Chamber to use this doctrine, it needs to be clear that the rights of the Accused have been egregiously violated.[47]

Thus, like the Appeals Chamber in *Barayagwiza*, the Trial Chamber in *Nikolić* considers it imperative to address pre-trial human rights violations.[48] However, the question in *Nikolić* was whether the violation should result in the termination of the proceedings. It now seems accepted that this remedy is not excluded, but should not be taken lightly in view of the nature of the accusations we are dealing with here. Crucial factors in determining whether or not this remedy should be provided for are the following:

(1) the degree of attribution of the violation to the tribunal, in particular the prosecutor (significant involvement in the violation by the prosecutor could damage the integrity of the proceedings to such an extent that the trial cannot be continued);

(2) the nature of the violation of individual rights (violation of individual rights of an egregious nature, such as subjecting the individual to inhuman or degrading treatment bordering on torture, may constitute a legal impediment to exercise of jurisdiction by the tribunal, regardless of whether or not the tribunal, in particular the prosecutor, had anything to do with the violation).

In the *Nikolić* case the Chamber ruled that the Tribunal and its 'special police force' SFOR were not involved in the abduction, and that, furthermore, the manner in which the accused was abducted did not amount to serious mistreatment.[49] We agree with the Chamber that in such circumstances release of the accused would be a disproportionate remedy. However, one wonders why the Trial Chamber did not consider alternative remedies, as the Appeals Chamber did in *Barayagwiza*, such as reduction of the sentence, in case of conviction, or financial compensation, in case of acquittal.

What transpires from the above is that human rights apply fully to international criminal trials, as to any domestic trial. Moreover, international criminal tribunals have full responsibility for the respect of human rights within their exclusive domains. When other entities bear primary responsibility for violations of human rights, what

---

[47] *Nikolić* jurisdiction trial decision, para. 111.

[48] Cf. also the other ICTY decision dealing with the legality of arrest, in which the method of apprehension was reviewed, inter alia, in light of ECtHR jurisprudence: Decision on the Motion for Release by the Accused Slavko Dokmanović, *Prosecutor* v. *Mrkšić et al.*, Case No. 95-13a-PT, ICTY, T Ch. II, 22 October 1997.

[49] *Nikolić* jurisdiction trial decision, paras 67 and 114.

matters is the duty of every tribunal bench to protect the fairness and integrity of the trial by determining an appropriate remedy. Obviously, the trial does not start at the seat of the tribunal but extends to every act connected with it. While this may be a heavy and seemingly unfair burden on the tribunals — they interact with a wide variety of actors, not all of whom may apply the highest standards of justice, and the tribunals are not in a position to change this — the reverse is even more unfair. The decision of the ICTR Trial Chamber not to review national activities is simply untenable from the perspective of the duty to ensure a fair trial.[50]

8.4 HABEAS CORPUS RIGHTS

The right not to be subject to arbitrary arrest and detention plays an important role in international criminal law. Two areas in particular deserve closer examination in respect of international criminal trials: (1) the issue of pre-trial detention; and (2) the consequences of unlawful arrests for the jurisdiction of international criminal tribunals.

8.4.1 Pre-trial detention

One of the weakest spots of the law of international criminal procedure concerns the right not to be subject to arbitrary arrest or detention, the so-called habeas corpus[51] rights. The tribunals have struggled with the issue of pre-trial detention. The circumstances surrounding that struggle are so fundamentally different from national jurisdictions that they need to be set out here.

There are a number of points that support the case in favour of a 'presumption' of detention prior to and during trial. First, trials in the absence of the accused are prohibited in current international criminal law;[52] hence, continued and prolonged detention is more important than in systems where trials *in absentia* are allowed. Secondly, the charges are of the most serious kind, increasing the risk of flight; for a person accused of international crimes to be released and then not return for trial would shake the international legal order.[53] Thirdly, the tribunals have great difficulty in ensuring that a provisionally released person returns for trial or serves a sentence, especially in respect of wealthy and powerful accused persons who still enjoy significant popularity in their countries of origin. Fourthly and finally, the tribunals are not in a position to prevent an accused person who has been released from interfering with witnesses or ongoing investigations.

---

[50] See decisions at note 32 above.

[51] Latin, 'may you have the body', meaning a legal remedy against being wrongly imprisoned.

[52] This was not the case with the Nuremberg and Tokyo tribunals. The most prominent example is of course the death sentence of Martin Bormann handed down in his absence.

[53] This is one of the grounds justifying pre-conviction detention in the Netherlands; see Article 67 of the Dutch Code of Criminal Procedure.

On the other hand, various aspects of the functioning of tribunals may be mentioned in support of the case for provisional release. First, the periods of detention before and during trial are regularly of considerable length, exceeding by far what is permissible under domestic law and making the detention particularly burdensome for the accused. Secondly, release of the accused may seem the easier course in the adversarial procedure — which is predominant in the context of international criminal trials — than in the inquisitorial system, as the accused usually plays an important role in preparing the defence. In current international criminal practice, the release may be of crucial significance for effective collection by the defence side of exculpatory evidence. Thirdly, over the years stability in the former conflict zones under the territorial jurisdiction of the tribunals has improved significantly, as a result of which credible assurances can be obtained that the accused will return for the start of the trial. Fourthly, as a matter of principle, the views of the host state in respect of the personal right to liberty should not carry significant weight.

While there are various reasons why accused persons due to appear before international tribunals should be held on remand, such detention as the rule rather than the exception posed a legal problem in light of the requirement of the reverse by international human rights standards. From the case law of the European Court of Human Rights it follows that a person charged with an offence must always be released pending trial unless the state can show that there are relevant and sufficient reasons to justify continued detention.[54] The European Court has identified in its case law the following reasons for continued detention: the risk that the accused will fail to appear for trial; the risk that the accused would take action to prejudice the administration of justice or commit further offences or cause public disorder; and the risk that release may give rise, by reason of the particular gravity of the accusations and public reaction to them, to a social disturbance.[55] The burden of proof of those circumstances in all cases rests with the state and at no times can the continuation of detention be used to anticipate a custodial sentence.[56] In addition to the ECtHR law one should mention Article 9(3) of the ICCPR according to which it shall not be the general rule that persons awaiting trial shall be detained in custody.[57] Viewing detention on remand as exceptional is of course closely related to the presumption of innocence that is fundamental to criminal proceedings.

In light of these unequivocal standards, the initial version of Rule 65 common to the ICTY and the ICTR as well as case law on provisional release is astonishing.

The first version of Rule 65 read as follows:

(A) Once detained, an accused may not be released except upon an order of a Trial Chamber.

(B) Release may be ordered by a Trial Chamber only in exceptional circumstances, after hearing the host country and only if it is satisfied that the accused will appear for trial and, if released, will not pose a danger to any victim, witness or other person.

---

[54] *Smirnova* v. *Russia*, 46133/99; 48183/99 [2003] ECtHR 397 (24 July 2003), para. 59.

[55] Cf. *Letellier* v. *France*, 12369/86 [1991] ECtHR 35 (26 June 1991), para. 35.   [56] Cf. ibid.

[57] On Article 9, see General Comment 08(16) of the Human Rights Committee (A/37/40 (1982) Annex V (at 95–6): 'Pre-trial detention should be an exception and as short as possible.'

(C) The Trial Chamber may impose such conditions upon the release of the accused as it may determine appropriate, including the execution of a bail bond and the observance of such conditions as are necessary to ensure his presence for trial and the protection of others.

(D) If necessary, the Trial Chamber may issue a warrant of arrest to secure the presence of an accused who has been released or is for any other reason at liberty.

Subparagraph B of this rule raises two fundamental problems, the most important of which is the reference to the exceptional nature of liberty prior to conviction. This cannot be viewed otherwise than as a flagrant violation of international human rights law.[58] The unfairness of this proposition lies to a large degree in the shifting of the burden of proof. It follows from this rule that the accused carries the burden to satisfy the chamber that he or she will appear for trial and will not pose a danger to victims and witnesses.

The uncritical application of Rule 65(B) in initial case law is striking. For example, in *Blaškić* the Trial Chamber held that:

both the letter of this text and the spirit of the Statute of the International Tribunal require that the legal principle is detention of the accused and that release is the exception; that, in fact, the gravity of the crimes being prosecuted by the International Tribunal leaves no place for an other interpretation even if it is based on the general principles of law governing the applicable provisions in respect of national laws which in principle may not be transposed to international criminal law.[59]

Subparagraph B is also problematic from a different perspective. One may read into the conditions for provisional release (assurance of reappearance for trial and non-interference with witnesses) grounds justifying (continued) detention. Yet, this certainly does not correspond to domestic practice, where additional and alternative grounds may be found.[60] Furthermore, the ICC Statute also contains an additional ground in Article 58(1)(b)(iii), aimed at preventing continued commission of the crime.

In this light, the initial formulation of Rule 65 cited above is too modest, justifying its amendment in November 1999. As the grounds for detention were limited to circumstances to which it referred, one might safely claim, on the basis of routine tribunal practice, that release is granted only in exceptional circumstances. However, the result would have been entirely different if other grounds for detention were admitted in Rule 65. Taking into consideration domestic practice, the prosecutor would not have much difficulty in proving that provisionally releasing a person indicted for genocide or

---

[58] See H. Friman, 'Commentary', in Klip and Sluiter, *Annotated Leading Cases, vol. IX*, at 347; D. J. Rearick, 'Innocent until Alleged Guilty: Provisional Release at ICTR' (2003) 44 *Harvard Int'l Law J.*, at 591.

[59] Order Denying a Motion for Provisional Release, *Prosecutor* v. *Blaškić*, Case No. IT-95-14-T, ICTY, T. Ch., 20 December 1996.

[60] E.g. risk of social disturbance in the Netherlands (Article 67a of the Dutch Code of Criminal Procedure); in France: prevention of a fraudulent conspiracy between a person under judicial examination and his or her accomplices, protection of a person under judicial examination, putting an end to an offence and preventing its renewal, putting an end to exceptional and persistent disruption of public order caused by the seriousness of the offence (Article 144 of the French Code of Criminal Procedure); in Germany: suspicion of having committed certain offences (sections 112 and 112a of the German Code of Criminal Procedure).

war crimes would create a serious risk of social disturbance in the societies concerned.[61] This particular ground has met with approval by the European Court of Human Rights in *Letellier* v. *France*.[62] Whereas this could make the line between the criteria set out in Rule 65 and those affirmed by national practices rather fine, the drafters of the rules could have saved confusion and criticism by adopting a rule underscoring the exceptional nature of detention and prescribing the variety of grounds for detention. This would both ensure conformity of Rule 65 with the widely accepted human rights standards and legitimize, from that same perspective, continued provisional detention in the majority of cases before the tribunals.

However, another, and unfortunate, approach has been followed, which has done damage in two ways. First, the old version of Rule 65 has been criticized from a human rights perspective, thereby negatively affecting the image and reputation of the tribunals. Secondly, the change in the rule has undeniably resulted in the unequal procedural treatment of defendants: after the rule amendment defendants benefited from the fact that the burden of proof justifying continued detention lay with the prosecutor, whereas previously defendants had been denied provisional release in comparable situations.

8.4.2 Unlawful arrest

Although there are many aspects of habeas corpus rights, the matter of unlawful arrest deserves special attention. Given the prohibition on trials *in absentia* and the lack of authority of such proceedings whenever they are permitted, the arrest of suspects is of the utmost importance for effective prosecution. From a human rights perspective, the ad hoc tribunals have been plagued by two problems in this regard.

First, indicted persons have been arrested in violation of applicable procedures, for example by abduction. Secondly, the arrest and ensuing detention at the national level may not comply with human rights norms. As will follow from a short survey of case law below, in both situations the difficulty lies in striking a balance between ensuring respect for the right not to be subject to arbitrary arrest and detention, on the one hand,[63] and implementing the international community's interest in arresting and prosecuting major war criminals.

---

[61] For example, in the Netherlands the risk of social disturbance is deemed inherent in the provisional release of a person suspected of a crime punishable with 12 or more years of imprisonment. Regarding such offences (continued) detention is generally imposed as a rule on the basis of that ground. Note that this practice may seem to be at odds with the position of the European Court of Human Rights in the *Letellier* v. *France* judgment: the protection of public order ground is only relevant and sufficient to justify detention if 'based on facts capable of showing that the accused's release would actually prejudice public order', and as long as the latter 'remains actually threatened' (see para. 51).   [62] Ibid.

[63] Both disguised extradition and abductions are generally considered to be violations of the right not to be subject to arbitrary arrest and detention. 'Disguised extradition' has been considered a violation of Article 5 of the ECHR: see *Bozano* v. *France*, 9990/82 [1986] ECtHR 16 (18 December 1986). The Human Rights Committee has ruled on several occasions that cross-border abductions violate Article 9 of the ICCPR. See, inter alia, *Lilian Celiberti de Casariego* v. *Uruguay*, Communication No. 056/1979, views of 29 July 1981, UN Doc. CCPR/C/OP/1 (1984), at 92, and *Cañón García* v. *Ecuador*, Communication No. 319/1988, views of 5 November 1991, UN Doc. CCPR/C/43/D/319/1988 (1991), at 90.

At the national level the balance has often been struck in favour of effective prosecution, embodied in the maxim *male captus bene detentus*. For example, disguised extradition has been considered lawful by the French *Cour de Cassation* in the *Barbie* case in relation to crimes against humanity, to which the 'ordinary extradition rules do not apply'.[64] Other national courts which have accepted forms of disguised extradition and abductions as lawful have generally failed to review these practices in light of international human rights.[65] The ad hoc tribunals, as 'human rights courts', have distanced themselves from *male captus bene detentus* as a matter of principle. Landmarks are the two Appeals Chamber's decisions in *Barayagwiza*, which allow us to distil two fundamental principles relating to the method of arrest and ensuing detention.[66] First, the need to exercise supervisory powers by international criminal tribunals is recognized irrespective of the involvement of one of the organs of the tribunal.[67] Secondly, the need for a response to an unlawful arrest may exist for three reasons: to provide a remedy for the violation of the accused's rights, to enhance the integrity of the judicial process, and — less applicable when no organ of the tribunal is involved — to deter future misconduct.[68] *Barayagwiza* paved the way for a choice of reaction by a chamber to unlawful arrest or detention: either release of the accused or reduction of the sentence in the case of conviction.[69] Litigation on matters of unlawful arrest differs from challenges related to the collection of evidence, where normally exclusion of evidence is the appropriate and only possible remedy.

Barayagwiza offered an important precedent for situations where the arrest is not unlawful as such, but is tainted with the neglect of the person's rights.[70] Equally important is its legacy for situations of unlawful arrest, especially whether, in light of the serious nature of the crimes within the jurisdiction of the tribunals, *male captus bene detentus*

---

[64] *Fédération nationale des déportés et internés résistants et al.* v. *Barbie* (1988) 78 ILR, at 125.

[65] The most notorious example in this respect is the abduction of Alvarez-Machain from Mexico by US law enforcement officials: *United States* v. *Alvarez-Machain* (1992) 112 S Ct. 2188. Many commentaries have appeared in and outside the United States; for example, see A. L. Strauss, 'A Global Paradigm Shattered: The Jurisdictional Nihilism of the Supreme Court's Abduction Decision in Alvarez-Machain' (1994) 67 *Temple Law Review*, at 1209–57; and A. W. Scrimger, '*United States* v. *Alvarez-Machain*: Forcible Abduction as an Acceptable Alternative Means of Gaining Jurisdiction' (1993) 7 *Temple Int'l & Comparative Law J.*, at 369–93.

[66] See *Barayagwiza* I and II appeal decisions.

[67] Cf. *Barayagwiza* I appeal decision, para. 73: 'there are overlapping areas of responsibility between the three organs of the Tribunal and as a result, it is conceivable that more than one organ could be responsible for the violations of the Appellant's rights. However, even if fault is shared between the three organs of the Tribunal—or is the result of the actions of a third party, such as Cameroon—it would undermine the integrity of the judicial process to proceed. Furthermore, it would be unfair for the Appellant to stand trial on these charges if his rights were egregiously violated. Thus, under the abuse of process doctrine, it is irrelevant which entity or entities were responsible for the alleged violations of the Appellant's rights.'

[68] Ibid., para. 76. The right to a remedy was emphasized in *Bayaragwiza* II appeal decision, para. 74: 'The Appeals Chamber reviews its Decision in the light of the new facts presented by the Prosecutor. It confirms that the Appellant's rights were violated, and that all violations demand a remedy.'

[69] See *Barayagwiza* II appeal decision, para. 75. However, the Appeals Chamber did not discuss at all the legal basis for this new remedy.

[70] For instance, in *Semanza* the Appeals Chamber ruled that the right to be informed of the charges in good time and the right to a timely decision on habeas corpus writs had been violated: Decision, *Prosecutor* v. *Semanza*, Case No. ICTR-97-20-A, ICTR, A. Ch., 31 May 2000, paras. 127–8.

should be a guiding principle.[71] Consideration of this question had to wait until *Nikolić*, which will be discussed below.

In *Dokmanović* the luring of the accused into the hands of UNTAES and ultimately of the ICTY prosecutor was not considered to be in violation of the law.[72] In *Todorović* the chamber first established the facts in respect of the accused's alleged abduction and then issued cooperation orders to SFOR; in the face of an escalating cooperation dispute, which would seriously damage the prosecutor's arrest strategy, the accused was in a powerful bargaining position and the matter was settled by a plea agreement.[73] What transpires from both cases is that both prosecutor and certain NATO states adopted the position of *male captus bene detentus*, in the sense that it was argued that the determination of the illegality of arrest served no purpose, as irregularities prior to or during arrest did not affect the jurisdiction of the tribunals.[74]

In *Nikolić* both the Trial Chamber and the Appeals Chamber rejected that position and followed — in part — the *Barayagwiza* precedent.[75] In both instances *male captus bene detentus* as a guiding principle was rejected; yet the test developed for declining to exercise jurisdiction appears a stringent one. To put it simply, only serious injury to state sovereignty complained of by the state and *egregious* violations of human rights may result in dismissal of the case.[76] Compared to *Barayagwiza*, the perspective of analysis in *Nikolić* is rather one-sidedly focused on the court's integrity.[77] The right to a remedy in the case of a violation of human rights, recognized as a matter of principle in the *Barayagwiza* II appeal decision, was passed over in *Nikolić*. This may have to do with the fact that the case centred on the non-exercise of jurisdiction as a remedy, which understandably seems disproportionate in the case of 'less serious' human rights violations. Yet reduction of sentence was not even mentioned as an alternative remedy for human rights violations that failed to meet the 'egregious violation' standard.

Compared to the ICTY, ICTR, and SCSL Statutes, the ICC Statute contains some improvements in respect of arrest and detention at the national level. Before dealing with them, it must be mentioned that the ICC Statute also lacks the attribution of the

---

[71] For more information on this question and other issues surrounding arrest, see S. Lamb, 'The Power of Arrest of the International Criminal Tribunal for the Former Yugoslavia' (1999) 70 *Brit. Y'book Int'l Law*, at 167–244.

[72] Decision on the Motion for Release by the Accused Slavko Dokmanović, *Prosecutor* v. *Mrksić et al.*, Case No. IT-95-13a-PT, ICTY, T. Ch., 22 October 1997.

[73] Decision on Prosecution Motion to Withdraw Counts of the Indictment and Defence Motion to Withdraw Pending Motions, *Prosecutor* v. *Todorović*, Case No. IT-95-9/1, ICTY, T. Ch., 26 February 2001.

[74] Decision on the Motion for Release by the Accused Slavko Dokmanović, *Prosecutor* v. *Mrksić et al.*, para. 78.

[75] *Nikolić* jurisdiction trial decision and *Nikolić* jurisdiction appeal decision.

[76] *Nikolić* jurisdiction appeal decision, para. 26: 'the Appeals Chamber does not consider that in cases of universally condemned offences, jurisdiction should be set aside on the ground that there was a violation of the sovereignty of a State, when the violation is brought about by the apprehension of fugitives from international justice . . . This is all the more so in cases such as this one, in which the State whose sovereignty has allegedly been breached has not lodged any complaint and thus has acquiesced in the International Tribunal's exercise of jurisdiction.' See also para. 28 citing para. 114 of the *Nikolić* jurisdiction trial decision and para. 30: 'certain human rights violations are of such a serious nature that they require that the exercise of jurisdiction be declined . . . Apart from such exceptional cases, however, the remedy of setting aside jurisdiction will . . . usually be disproportionate.'

[77] *Nikolić* jurisdiction trial decision, section VII, 'Conclusion': 'the Tribunal has an inherent right to decide whether there exists a legal impediment to the exercise of jurisdiction over the Accused *in order to ensure the integrity of the entire judicial process*' (emphasis added).

right not to be subjected to arbitrary arrest and detention. Yet, Article 59 of the Statute provides for concrete forms of protection by imposing obligations upon states concerning arrest proceedings. Pursuant to this provision, an arrested person shall be brought promptly before the competent judicial authority, which, among other things, has to determine that the arrested person's rights have been respected; furthermore, the arrested person has the right to apply to the national authorities for interim release. These safeguards to a considerable extent fill in the current legal vacuum in respect of arrests at the behest of international criminal tribunals and set a desired minimum standard. However, several questions in respect of their implementation arise. First, does Article 59 of the ICC Statute apply to arrests performed not by states, but, for example, by entities such as SFOR, and if not, what rights should receive protection in the context of these arrests? Secondly, there seems to be a strong tension between Article 59(3) of the Statute, allowing for interim release, and subsections 4, 5, and 6 of the same provision, which, among other things, make release conditional upon recommendations from the ICC Pre-Trial Chamber. Is this an acceptable interference in domestic legal proceedings? Thirdly, closely related to the previous issue is the question whether violation of the terms of Article 59 of the ICC Statute gives standing before the ICC to apply for remedies. Interestingly, the matter of human rights violations surrounding arrest and national detention is already the object of a motion for release currently pending before the ICC.[78]

8.5 FAIR TRIAL RIGHTS

The right to a fair trial lies at the very basis of criminal procedure.[79] It encompasses all aspects of fairness, and in that capacity occupies a prominent place in the law and practice of international criminal justice. In the discussion below, the fair trial rights are divided into the general notion of a fair trial and specific rights, violations of which inevitably affect the fairness of the trial as such. This division follows the structure of provisions in the major human rights treaties and the statutes of international criminal courts: Article 14 of the ICCPR, Article 6 of the ECHR, Article 21 of the ICTY Statute, and Article 67 of the ICC Statute.

---

[78] On 18 October 2006 the Pre-Trial Chamber denied the defence motion on interim release of Lubanga Dyilo, and this decision was appealed. See Decision on the Application for the Interim Release of Thomas Lubanga Dyilo, *Prosecutor* v. *Lubanga Dyilo, Situation in the Democratic Republic of the Congo*, Case No. ICC-01/04-01/06, ICC, PTC I, 18 October 2006 and Defence Appeal Against the 'Décision sur la demande de mise en liberté provisoire de Thomas Lubanga Dyilo', *Prosecutor* v. *Lubanga Dyilo, Situation in the Democratic Republic of the Congo*, Case No. ICC-01/04-01/06, ICC, A. Ch., 26 October 2006.

[79] In international criminal proceedings this right is protected in Article 21(2) of the ICTY Statute, Article 20(2) of the ICTR Statute, Article 67(1) (*chapeau*) of the ICC Statute, and Article 17(2) of the SCSL Statute; furthermore, there is a duty imposed upon trial chambers to ensure the fairness of the trial: Article 20(1) of the ICTY Statute, Article 21(1) of the ICTR Statute, and Article 64(2) of the ICC Statute.

Unlike the law of the tribunals and the ICC, we make no distinction between the rights of the accused and the rights of suspects. Nor does such distinction exist in human rights law. What matters is an individual's right to liberty and a fair trial, which triggers the applicability of certain rights at different stages of the procedure.

8.5.1 Right to a fair trial in general

The relationship between the specific fair trial rights and the right to a fair trial in a broader sense has yielded two important results. First, the violation of specific rights by definition violates the right to a fair trial in a broader sense, which follows from the reference to them as minimum guarantees.[80] However, the absence of violation of any of the specific minimum guarantees does not automatically warrant the conclusion that the trial as a whole is fair. This brings us to the second point, namely that all the procedural measures bordering on violations of minimum guarantees and elements of a fair trial that have not been translated literally into specific rights may justify the conclusion that there has been no fair hearing. This residual function of the general right to a fair trial serves the useful purpose of making the concept of a fair hearing a dynamic and living reality, capable of adjusting to changing views on fairness and of rectifying omissions that may occur in the law and practice of international criminal courts.[81]

Legal doctrine and practice have given rise to a number of fair trial elements which are not covered by the specific minimum guarantees. In this respect one may mention the right to an adversarial hearing (the principle of *audi alteram partem*), the principle of equality of arms, and the right to a reasoned judgment. In the context of international criminal proceedings the principle of equality of arms deserves our attention.

The very fact that equality of arms does not enjoy the status of a full right, but of a principle is telling of its nature. Full equality between parties to criminal proceedings is an idle aspiration from a practical perspective and not the required standard in the human rights arena. Rather, the principle has a procedural nature and is closely connected to the right to an adequately prepared defence. Thus, the European Court of Human Rights ruled in this respect that 'each party must be afforded a reasonable opportunity to present his case under conditions that do not place him at a disadvantage *vis-à-vis* his opponent'.[82] It also observed that there can be no violation of this principle when both sides are denied something that might have been useful.[83] In this light, the defence's claim in *Tadić* that the principle of equality of arms was

---

[80] Cf. Article 21(4) (*chapeau*) of the ICTY Statute and Article 67(1) (*chapeau*) of the ICC Statute. See also Trechsel, *Human Rights in Criminal Proceedings*, at 86.

[81] An example of the latter is the privilege against self-incrimination, which is part of Article 14 of the ICCPR, Article 21 of the ICTY Statute, and Article 67 of the ICC Statute, but not of Article 6 of the anterior ECHR. The European Court of Human Rights has nevertheless developed progressive case law in respect of this right by considering it a vital element of the right to a fair trial.

[82] *Bulut* v. *Austria*, 17358/90 [1996] ECtHR 10 (22 February 1996), para. 47.

[83] *Jasper* v. *UK*, 27052/95 [2000] ECtHR 90 (16 February 2000), para. 57; *Ekbatani* v. *Sweden*, 10563/83 [1988] ECtHR 6 (26 May 1988), para. 30.

violated as a result of a lack of cooperation from the Bosnian Serbs stood little chance of success.[84] It can convincingly be argued that both sides suffer from this lack of cooperation.

In spite of this unfortunate approach — the defence should have sought to identify inequality of a more structural nature — the Appeals Chamber seized the opportunity to expand on the content and scope of the principle of equality of arms in the context of international criminal proceedings. However, its analysis of the principle leaves much to be desired. It made a distinction between national courts and international criminal tribunals.[85] As the latter are far more dependent on state cooperation than the former, this should, according to the Appeals Chamber, have consequences for the scope of application of the principle of equality of arms.[86] While the lack of state cooperation may raise issues in respect of adequate preparation of the case, its connection to equality of arms is less obvious, as both parties suffer from this. From this perspective, the 'liberal' interpretation of the equality of arms proposed by the Appeals Chamber is unnecessary. Furthermore, it is an approach which might be perceived as damaging to the legitimacy and credibility of the ICTY as a court vested with the mission of promoting respect for human rights. There is nothing in international human rights law suggesting that the applicable rules and principles merit reduced applicability in the context of international criminal proceedings.

The *Tadić* Appeals Chamber rightly elaborated on the possibilities for the chambers to redress any inequality between defendant and prosecutor.[87] Indeed, it is a vital element of the principle of equality of arms to verify the extent to which the difficulties under which the defence labours have been compensated. In this regard, one has to acknowledge that practically all inequalities between the prosecutor and the defendant can — at least from a purely procedural perspective — be redressed by a trial chamber. For example, since the defence has no power to issue directly binding requests for legal assistance to states, it may apply for such a request to a trial chamber.[88] Nevertheless, despite the Appeals Chamber's implicit message in *Tadić* that trial chambers should be generous in offering this type of assistance, practice reveals an opposite trend. Both in case law and the rules[89] stringent admissibility criteria for the issuance of requests of assistance have been developed.[90] While these criteria apply equally to defence and

---

[84] *Tadić* appeal judgment: 'the Defence alleges that the Appellant's right to a fair trial was prejudiced by the circumstances in which the trial was conducted. Specifically, it alleges that the lack of cooperation and the obstruction by certain external entities — the Government of the *Republika Srpska* and the civic authorities in Prijedor — prevented it from properly presenting its case at trial. The Defence contends that, whilst most Defence witnesses were Serbs still residing in the *Republika Srpska*, the majority of the witnesses appearing for the Prosecution were Muslims residing in countries in Western Europe and North America whose governments cooperated fully. It avers that the lack of cooperation displayed by the authorities in the *Republika Srpska* had a disproportionate impact on the Defence. It is accordingly submitted that there was no "equality of arms" between the Prosecution and the Defence at trial, and that the effect of this lack of cooperation was serious enough to frustrate the Appellant's right to a fair trial. The Defence therefore, requests the Appeals Chamber to set aside the Trial Chamber's findings of guilt and to order a re-trial' (*Tadić* appeal judgment, para. 29). [85] Ibid., para. 51.

[86] Ibid. and para. 52. [87] Ibid., paras 53 and 54.

[88] See Article 19 of the ICTY Statute, Article 18 of the ICTR Statute, and Rule 54 of the ICTY and ICTR RPE.

[89] See Rule 54 *bis* of the ICTY.

[90] See G. Sluiter, *International Criminal Adjudication and the Collection of Evidence: Obligations of States* (Antwerp: Intersentia, 2002), at 119–29.

prosecution, it must be borne in mind that there is a far lesser need for the prosecution to call in the assistance of the trial chamber in requesting legal assistance from a state.

There is one element of ICC procedure that amounts in our opinion to a serious violation of the principle of equality of arms and may on that basis jeopardize the fairness of the trial. It concerns the conduct of on-site investigations by the ICC prosecutor pursuant to Article 99(4) of the ICC Statute. In respect of this important procedural advantage over the defendant, the competent chamber has no legal possibility of redress. In other words, nothing can be done to compel a state to cooperate with the defence in its on-site investigations, as the relevant power, pursuant to Article 99(4) of the ICC Statute, is explicitly confined to the prosecutor.[91] In contrast to the aforementioned situation in *Tadić*, it is the present law itself that places the defence at a substantial disadvantage, with no possibility for compensation.

8.5.2 Right to an independent and impartial tribunal

The right to an independent and impartial tribunal occupies an important position in contemporary international criminal procedure.[92] This is not only the result of it being a fundamental human right and a vital element of the rule of law more generally. In a broader sense and not necessarily in a human rights context, independence and impartiality can be considered the weak spots of the Nuremberg and Tokyo tribunals, which were often regarded as the embodiments of victor's justice.[93] The contemporary tribunals are, as a result, quite sensitive to this criticism and have sought ways to underline and strengthen their independence and impartiality. For example, in the ICTY's first appeal decision, in *Tadić*, it was ruled that the tribunals must be considered as having been established by law, in the sense that they offer all the protections associated with the rule of law.[94]

The application of independence and impartiality as a human right to international criminal proceedings is problematic from various perspectives. We look first at independence — which is generally to be understood as lack of subordination to any other state organ, in particular to the executive, in light of the Montesquieuan separation of powers doctrine. The central problem with independence lies in its application to institutions not embedded in state structures.[95] At the international level there is no division of power along the lines of that at national level. Consequently human rights case law dealing with unique national situations is of less relevance. Yet, putting aside this case law, what matters is the absence of undue interference by other organs, both national and international, in the administration of international criminal justice. *In abstracto*, this can be achieved by including norms requiring independence, and by

---

[91] Ibid., at 321, and see also Chapter 10, section 10.5.1.

[92] Article 14(1) of the ICCPR and Article 6 of the ECHR, codified in Article 67(1) (*chapeau*) and 68(1) (last sentence) of the ICC Statute.

[93] See Cassese, *International Criminal Law*, at 332: 'the view must be shared that the two Tribunals were not independent international courts proper, but judicial bodies acting as organs common to the appointing States'.

[94] *Tadić* jurisdiction appeal decision, para. 45.

[95] This problem is similar to the requirement 'established by law' dealt with by the ICTY Appeals Chamber in the *Tadić* jurisdiction appeal decision.

the selection of high-quality judges and other personnel.[96] Whether this suffices depends on enforcement of these norms.[97]

In the case law of the ad hoc tribunals there are challenges to their independence, on account of their particular relationship with the Security Council, and occasional challenges to the independence of individual judges.

Regarding the relationship with the Security Council, in *Kanyabashi* the ICTR Trial Chamber emphasized its own independence:

> This independence is, for example, demonstrated by the fact that the Tribunal is not bound by national rules of evidence as stated under Rule 89A . . .

> Further, the judges of the Tribunal exercise their judicial duties independently and freely and are under oath to act honorably, faithfully, impartially and conscientiously as stipulated in Rule 14 of the Rules. Judges do not account to the Security Council for their judicial functions.

> In this Trial Chamber's view, the personal independence of the judges of the Tribunal and the integrity of the Tribunal are underscored by Article 12(1) of the Statute.[98]

While judges do not account to the Council for their judicial functions, the question of undue interference by the Council in the administration of justice needs to be explored. The amici curiae in *Milošević* challenged the ICTY's jurisdiction because of the Security Council 'urging' the ICTY prosecutor to investigate crimes allegedly committed in Kosovo.[99] The amici saw in the Council's position a violation of Article 16 of the ICTY Statute, according to which the prosecutor shall act independently and not receive instruction from any source.[100] The challenge was dismissed by the Trial Chamber on the understandable ground that there was no evidence of a violation of independence.[101] Obviously, it could not be proved that it was the particular Security Council resolution alone that triggered the investigation.

Nevertheless, the relationship with the Council raises questions of independence, especially concerning the so-called completion strategies. The basis for these strategies can be found in Resolution 1503, which is fairly harmless from the perspective of independence.[102] Resolution 1534 is, however, more problematic. Operative

---

[96] For an overview, see Zappalà, *Human Rights in International Criminal Proceedings*, at 101–2. See also W. A. Schabas, *The UN International Criminal Tribunals — The former Yugoslavia, Rwanda and Sierra Leone* (Cambridge: Cambridge University Press, 2006), at 506–11.

[97] A question beyond the scope of this book is whether perceived independence matters. In the case law of the European Court of Human Rights the importance of perceived bias is often stressed, but only in relation to impartiality. Independence, on the other hand, is to be decided solely on the basis of objective criteria (see Trechsel, *Human Rights in Criminal Proceedings*, at 56). One may wonder whether this should also be the test in international criminal proceedings. As relations between tribunals and outside organs, including the Security Council, may not always be very clear from a legal perspective, it can be argued that perceived independence also matters.

[98] Decision on the Defence Motion on Jurisdiction, *Prosecutor* v. *Kanyabashi*, Case No. ICTR-96-15-T, ICTR, T. Ch. II, 18 June 1997, paras 40–2.

[99] See operative paragraph 17 of Security Council Resolution 1160 (1998): '[u]*rges* the Office of the Prosecutor of the International Tribunal established pursuant to resolution 827 (1993) of 25 May 1993 to begin gathering information related to the violence in Kosovo that may fall within its jurisdiction'.

[100] Decision on Preliminary Motions, *Prosecutor* v. *Milošević*, Case No. IT-02-54, ICTY, T. Ch., 8 November 2001, para. 12.   [101] Ibid., para. 15.

[102] The central provision is operative paragraph 7: '*Calls* on the ICTY and the ICTR to take all possible measures to complete investigations by the end of 2004, to complete all trial activities at first instance by the end of 2008, and to complete all work in 2010 (the Completion Strategies)'.

paragraph 5 of that resolution calls on both ICTY and ICTR to ensure that indictments concentrate on the most senior leaders. This 'instruction' has for the ICTY materialized in the amendment of Rule 28, which now reads in relevant part as follows:

On receipt of an indictment for review from the Prosecutor, the Registrar shall consult with the President. The President shall refer the matter to the Bureau which shall determine whether the indictment, prima facie, concentrates on one or more of the most senior leaders suspected of being most responsible for crimes within the jurisdiction of the Tribunal.

One should also mention new Rule 73 *bis* (D), after its amendment in May 2006:

After having heard the Prosecutor, the Trial Chamber, in the interest of a fair and expeditious trial, may invite the Prosecutor to reduce the number of counts charged in the indictment and may fix a number of crime sites or incidents comprised in one or more of the charges in respect of which evidence may be presented by the Prosecutor which, having regard to all the relevant circumstances, including the crimes charged in the indictment, their classification and nature, the places where they are alleged to have been committed, their scale and the victims of the crimes, are reasonably representative of the crimes charged.[103]

The question of the tribunals' independence also arises here. One must acknowledge that the Council's interference is confined to encouraging the completion of the tribunals' work, a form of interference that cannot be denied to the Council, as the tribunals' founder. Furthermore, this 'call' by the Council does not subordinate the tribunals to a degree amounting to violation of their independence. Yet, leaving aside the human rights framework, the Security Council's interference is surprising, from the perspective of the legitimacy of the tribunals.

When looking at the independence of international criminal tribunals, mention should be made of the situation of Judge Odio Benito. Because the *Čelebići* trial continued beyond her period of nomination, she was for a time both a judge at the ICTY and vice-president of Costa Rica.[104] Although this may have been in violation of independence requirements, it remains an isolated incident, essentially because it was not anticipated that trials would overrun to such an extent.[105]

Impartiality, although closely related to independence, has a distinct definition. It can be described as implying that judges must not harbour preconceptions about the matter put before them, and that they must not act in ways that promote the interests of one of the parties.[106] In the law of international criminal tribunals impartiality is

---

[103] The ICTY prosecutor has criticized this change to the rule; see, for more detail Chapter 2, section 2.3.

[104] See also H. Morrison, 'Judicial Independence: Impartiality and Disqualification', in May et al., *Essays on ICTY Procedure and Evidence*, at 111–20.

[105] A special Security Council resolution (1126) was needed to allow the judges to finish the *Čelebići* trial. The ICTY Bureau did not consider this particular situation to be a ground for disqualification, because Judge Odio Benito was considered as holding the position of vice-president of Costa Rica in name only and the president of Costa Rica had agreed that she would not assume her duties as vice-president until after the completion of the *Čelebići* trial (Decision of the Bureau on Motion on Judicial Independence, *Prosecutor* v. *Delalić et al.*, Case No. IT-96-21-T, ICTY, Bureau, 4 September 1998).

[106] *Karttunen* v. *Finland*, Communication No. 387/1989, Human Rights Committee, UN Doc. CCPR/C/46/D/387/1989 (1992), para. 7.2.

safeguard by the provision for disqualifying judges.[107] Human rights law may be applied more effectively to impartiality than to independence, as case law in this field is not confined to particular internal state structures. Also, in contrast to independence, the test for impartiality is a double one; what matters is both actual bias and perceived bias.[108]

The international setting is more prone to perceived bias than national criminal justice systems, for a number of reasons. First, there are only a limited number of judges at the international criminal tribunals, entailing a greater chance of their involvement in the same or closely related cases. Joint trials have not always been possible, as a result of which there have been several trials dealing with the same or related facts (for example, the various cases involving Omarska, Keraterm, and Trnopolje camps). Secondly, the judges are selected on the basis of their expertise in international criminal law and issues related thereto. This is not a big group of persons, who, moreover, in their 'previous lives' may have adopted positions or have published writings that could be perceived as affecting their impartiality. This was the case with, for example, judges Mumba, Winter, and Robertson. Ironically, the reasons underlying challenges to impartiality in these cases are at the same time seen as indicative of their expertise, and thus a ground for their nomination.[109]

---

[107] See Rule 15 of the ICTY, ICTR, and SCSL Rules, as well as Rule 34(2) of the ICC Rules.

[108] See Trechsel, *Human Rights in Criminal Proceedings*, at 61–3. See also the pronouncement by the European Court of Human Rights in *Incal* v. *Turkey*: 'As to the condition of "impartiality" within the meaning of that provision, there are two tests to be applied: the first consists in trying to determine the personal conviction of a particular judge in a given case and the second in ascertaining whether the judge offered guarantees sufficient to exclude any legitimate doubt in this respect' (*Incal* v. *Turkey*, 22678/93 [1998] ECtHR 48 (9 June 1998), para. 65).
See also ICTY Appeals Chamber in *Furundžija* appeal judgement, para. 189:

    A. A Judge is not impartial if it is shown that actual bias exists.
    B. There is an unacceptable appearance of bias if:
        (i) a Judge is a party to the case, or has a financial or proprietary interest in the outcome of a case, or if the Judge's decision will lead to the promotion of a cause in which he or she is involved, together with one of the parties. Under these circumstances, a Judge's disqualification from the case is automatic; or
        (ii) the circumstances would lead a reasonable observer, properly informed, to reasonably apprehend bias.

[109] Note in this regard the Appeals Chamber in the *Furundžija* appeal judgment:

    The Appeals Chamber does not consider that a Judge should be disqualified because of qualifications he or she possesses which, by their very nature, play an integral role in satisfying the eligibility requirements. Judge Mumba's membership of the UNCSW and, in general, her previous experience in this area would be relevant to the requirement under Article 13(1) of the Statute for experience in international law, including human rights law. The possession of this experience is a statutory requirement for Judges to be elected to this Tribunal. It would be an odd result if the operation of an eligibility requirement were to lead to an inference of bias. Therefore, Article 13(1) should be read to exclude from the category of matters or activities which could indicate bias, experience in the specific areas identified. In other words, the possession of experience in any of those areas by a Judge cannot, in the absence of the clearest contrary evidence, constitute evidence of bias or partiality.

In the same vein, see Decision on the Motion to Recuse Judge Winter from Deliberation in the Preliminary Motion on the Recruitment of Child Soldiers, *Prosecutor* v. *Norman*, Case No. SCSL-2004-14, SCSL A. Ch., 28 May 2004, para. 30:

    each of the grounds relied upon by the Defence Motion, rather than proving any actual or perceived bias on the part of Justice Winter with regard to the question of if and when the recruitment of child soldiers became a crime under international law, are evidence of the internationally recognised qualifications of justice Winter in the general field of juvenile justice.

The cases of Judges Mumba and Winter are very similar. They are both concerned with these judges' active advocacy of certain causes — women's rights in the case of Judge Mumba and children's rights in the case of Judge Winter.[110] As the prosecutions in question dealt with, among other things, the crimes of rape (*Furundžija*) and the recruitment of child soldiers (*Norman*), the challenges do not seem to be without merit.[111] Furthermore, in *Furundžija* the Trial Chamber adopted a broad definition of rape that was unfavourable to the accused; understandably, the defence then tried to connect this to the position of Judge Mumba.[112] The Appeals Chamber dismissed the arguments advanced by the defence, but in a not entirely convincing way. The Chamber concluded that there was no evidence that Judge Mumba was influenced by an expanded definition of rape during armed conflict as propounded in a report in which she participated.[113] But this is not the correct test, as what matters here is the appearance of bias from the perspective of the 'hypothetical fair-minded observer'.[114] With the definition of rape in international criminal law hedged around by many questions, we can imagine this observer having problems with Judge Mumba's participation in that trial.[115] The case is different from that of Judge Winter, where the issue was confined to a motion challenging jurisdiction. In other words, no decision had to be taken on the guilt or innocence of the accused.

A situation where disqualification was an inevitable outcome concerned Justice Robertson, at the time president of the SCSL. In his book entitled *Crimes against Humanity — The Struggle for Global Justice* (2002), Justice Robertson made a number of outspoken comments on accused persons and organizations that were at the time under investigation by the SCSL.[116] These comments betrayed strong views about the

---

[110] Judge Mumba was a member of the UN Commission on the Status of Women prior to nomination as an ICTY judge and Judge Winter participated in a UNICEF report published in September 2002, entitled 'International Criminal Justice and Children', before she became a judge of the SCSL.

[111] An example of unfounded challenges to impartiality is Šešelj who sought the disqualification of judges on account of their nationality (Schomburg) and religion (Agius and Mumba). The accused argued that for him to be tried by a judge who was a national of a NATO country and who held religious beliefs different from his own would prejudice his case. The motion was dismissed as frivolous and an abuse of process: Decision on Motion on Disqualification, *Prosecutor* v. *Šešelj*, Case No. IT-03-67-PT, ICTY, Bureau, 10 June 2003.

[112] On this definition, see Chapter 4, section 4.2.6. The defence alleged that Judge Mumba's bias was shown by the fact that the judgment expanded the definition of rape in a manner that reflected the definition put forward by the UNCSW Expert Group Meeting, in which she had actively participated (*Furundžija* appeal judgment, para. 211). [113] Ibid.

[114] Standard articulated in Decision on the Defence Application for Withdrawal of a Judge from the Trial, *Prosecutor* v. *Krajišnik*, Case No. IT-00-39-PT, ICTY, T. Ch. I, 22 January 2003.

[115] The Appeals Chamber's position that there was jurisprudence available which led the Trial Chamber in the direction it took (*Furundžija* appeal judgment, para. 211) fails to convince, in the sense that that jurisprudence was far from uncontroversial and left many questions unanswered.

[116] Decision on Defence Motion Seeking the Disqualification of Justice Robertson from the Appeals Chamber, *Prosecutor* v. *Sesay*, Case No. SCSL-2004-15-AR15, SCSL, A. Ch., 13 March 2004. Just one extract:

So much for hindsight: a warring faction [referring to the RUF] guilty of atrocities on a scale that amounts to a crime against humanity must never again be forgiven sufficiently to be accorded a slice of power: on the contrary, its leaders deserve to be captured and put on trial [cited in para. 2 of the decision].

guilt of RUF members, and the Appeals Chamber did not doubt that the continuation of his judicial functions would violate the accused's right to an impartial tribunal.[117] One may wonder, however, whether the disqualification, in light of the views expressed in his book, should not go beyond dealings with the RUF. Since these issues may be closely intertwined, and the SCSL deals only with a handful of accused persons, it would better serve the interests of justice for Justice Robertson to be disqualified entirely or to resign from the tribunal.

While the right to impartiality is restricted to 'a tribunal', it has been applied by analogy to participants in the proceedings to whom similar expectations of impartiality apply. In *Milošević* it was alleged that one of the amici curiae, Dutch counsel M. Wladimiroff, in an interview with a Dutch newspaper, expressed his conviction that the accused was guilty on the Kosovo indictment.[118] His appointment was revoked for the following reason:

> Implicit in the concept of an amicus curiae is the trust that the court reposes in 'the friend' to act fairly in the performance of his duties. In the circumstances, the Chamber cannot be confident that the amicus curiae will discharge his duties (which include bringing to its attention any defences open to the accused) with the required impartiality.[119]

8.5.3 Right to be tried within a reasonable time

From a human rights perspective a weak spot in the administration of international criminal justice is the sometimes excessive length of periods of pre-trial detention and trials. There is undeniably a problem bearing upon an individual's right to be tried within a reasonable time (without undue delay).[120] The most extreme example, although this is only one of many, is the course of the prosecution of Théoneste Bagosora. He was arrested on 9 March 1996, and transferred to the ICTR detention facility on 23 January 1997. His trial finally began on 2 April 2002, but as of November 2006 has not yet been concluded. If there is an appeal, this period of more than a decade may be expected to increase by another few years.

While this shocks the sense of justice of every reasonable observer, the relevant question here is whether this and other very long periods pass the test imposed by human rights law. Before dealing with this question, it must be pointed out that in international criminal proceedings, in contrast to certain national cases, it is not difficult to measure the period, in other words to determine when 'the clock starts running'. An

---

[117] Ibid., para. 15. For a critical view on the (absence of) reasoning by the SCSL, see S. Zappalà, 'Commentary', in Klip and Sluiter, *Annotated Leading Cases, vol. IX*, at 644–5.

[118] Decision Concerning an Amicus Curiae, *Prosecutor* v. *Milošević*, Case No. IT-02-54, ICTY, T. Ch., 10 October 2002. The amicus curiae reportedly said: 'The publication in the Haagsche Courant was captioned: "Wladimiroff: Already Enough Evidence Against Milosevic". Mr. Wladimiroff is reported as saying, "If this trial were only about Kosovo and one had to draw up the balance now, Milosevic would certainly be convicted. A link has been established between the army and the police, the warring parties in Kosovo and Milosevic himself."'

[119] Ibid.

[120] Article 21(4)(c) of the ICTY Statute, Article 20(4)(c) of the ICTR Statute, Article 67(1)(c) of the ICC Statute, and Article 17(4)(c) of the SCSL Statute. This right is also safeguarded in Article 14(3) of the ICCPR, Article 6(1) of the ECHR, and Article 8(1) of the ACHR.

arrest at the request of an international criminal tribunal provides sufficient 'notification' of the allegation that the person arrested has committed a criminal offence.[121] What matters is the assessment of the period. No specific time limit exists, and the reasonableness will clearly depend on the circumstances of the case, having regard to the complexity of the case, the conduct of the accused, and the conduct of the relevant authorities.[122] The latter is in fact the most important factor.[123] The highly flexible nature of this assessment has resulted in human rights case law in which an apparently short duration produced a violation, whereas an apparently very long duration was regarded as lawful. The flexible nature of the right is further illustrated by the opportunity open to states to avoid liability for a violation when the affected person is compensated for the excessive length, in the form of a suitable reduction of the sentence.[124]

While the above comments relate to criminal proceedings in general, there are a number of factors unique to international criminal justice that account for the extreme duration of trials in that context. As with other rights, the vital question is whether those factors justify deviation from the standards applicable to national prosecutions. In our view there is no such justification. The three main factors occasioning 'justice delayed' — the complexity of the case, the lack of resources to try all the accused at short notice, and the choice of the adversarial style of proceedings[125] — can all be accommodated under the established criteria. Obviously, the complexity of international cases is a very strong argument in favour of trials of a longer duration. Furthermore, the right to an adversarial hearing is considered a vital element of the right to a fair trial, and cannot in its own right be a factor in assessing the reasonableness of the period.[126] The complicated issue is the lack of resources. In our view, this does not warrant a different standard, nor a balancing exercise based on a contraposition of the rights of the accused to the mandate of tribunals, as was proposed by an ICTR Trial Chamber in *Mugiraneza*.[127] The argument of excessive load has always been dismissed in the national framework.[128] While recognizing the urgency of issuing arrest warrants and

---

[121] For the test adopted by the European Court of Human Rights, see *Kangasluoma* v. *Finland*, 48339/99 [2004] ECtHR 29 (20 January 2004), para. 26: 'the period to be taken into account in the assessment of the length of the proceedings starts from an official notification given to an individual by the competent authority of an allegation that he has committed a criminal offence or from some other act which carries the implication of such an allegation and which likewise substantially affects the situation of the suspect'.

[122] Just one example, from among many decisions of the European Court of Human Rights, is: *Philis* v. *Greece*, 19773/92 [1997] ECtHR 34 (27 June 1997), para. 35. See also Decision on the Defence Extremely Urgent Motion on Habeas Corpus and for Stoppage of Proceedings, *Prosecutor* v. *Kanyabashi*, Case No. ICTR-96-15-T, ICTR, T. Ch. II, 23 May 2000, where these criteria were also adopted.

[123] Trechsel, *Human Rights in Criminal Proceedings*, at 146.   [124] Ibid., at 148.

[125] For more elaborate analysis, see Zappalà, *Human Rights in International Criminal Proceedings*, at 114–19.

[126] On the right to adversarial proceedings as an element of the right to a fair trial, see Trechsel, *Human Rights in Criminal Proceedings*, at 89–94.

[127] Decision on Prosper Mugiraneza's Motion to Dismiss the Indictment for Violation of Article 20(4)(C) of the Statute, Demand for Speedy Trial and for Appropriate Relief, *Prosecutor* v. *Mugiraneza*, Case No. ICTR-99-50-I, ICTR, T. Ch., 2 October 2003, paras 11–13.

[128] The European Court of Human Rights has repeatedly stated that the 'Convention places the Contracting States under a duty to organise their legal systems so as to enable the courts to comply with the requirements of Article 6 §1, including that of trial within a "reasonable time"; nonetheless, a temporary backlog of business does not involve liability on the part of the Contracting States provided that they take, with the requisite promptness,

the importance of the tribunals' mandate, there is no reason why they should be different. The role of the prosecutor in this regard deserves special attention. In *Mugiraneza* the ICTR Appeals Chamber rightly corrected the Trial Chamber when it concluded that there was no need to inquire into any part the prosecutor might have played in the alleged undue delay.[129] In the second instance, the same Trial Chamber ruled that the delay was not attributable to the prosecutor.[130] While it may be difficult to attribute delay directly to the prosecutor, a more critical and progressive approach is needed, for two reasons. First, as established in *Barayagwiza*, the sharing of fault between organs of the tribunal should not affect the application of fundamental rights.[131] Secondly, the prosecutor does bear significant responsibility for delays by submitting indictments in a system that is incapable of handling them within a reasonable period of time. Furthermore, the complexity of prosecutions, which is an important factor causing delay, is in part the result of prosecutorial choices as to the selection of charges.

Especially if the conduct of authorities is seen as the most important criterion for assessing the reasonableness of length of pre-trial detention and trials, the ad hoc tribunals fall short of protecting this right.

8.5.4 Right to be presumed innocent, and the privilege against self-incrimination

The presumption of innocence and the privilege against self-incrimination — also referred to as the right to remain silent — are closely related and will therefore be dealt with under the same heading.[132]

The presumption of innocence has two aspects. First, it concerns the outcome of the proceedings, in the sense that judges are prohibited from doing or saying anything, before the judgment has been delivered, that would imply that the defendant has already been convicted.[133] In this way, there is a direct connection to the right to an impartial tribunal. Secondly, there is the 'reputation-related' aspect, which aims to protect the image of the suspect as 'innocent' in the eyes of the public, which bears some relation to the right to protection against unlawful attacks on honour and reputation, as provided for in Article 17 of the ICCPR.

In international criminal proceedings the first aspect has been dealt with in the context of the right to an impartial tribunal, although the statements by Justice Robertson

---

remedial action to deal with an exceptional situation of this kind'. (See, among many cases, *Baggetta* v. *Italy*, 10256/83 [1987] ECtHR 9 (25 June 1987), para. 23 and *Abdoella* v. *Netherlands*, 12728/87 [1992] ECtHR 70 (25 November 1992), para. 24.)

[129] Decision on Prosper Mugiraneza's Interlocutory Appeal from Trial Chamber II Decision of 2 October 2003 Denying the Motion to Dismiss the Indictment, Demand Speedy Trial and for Appropriate Relief, *Prosecutor* v. *Mugiraneze*, Case No. ICTR-99-50-AR73, ICTR, A. Ch., 27 February 2005.

[130] Decision on Prosper Mugiraneza's Application for a Hearing or Other Relief on his Motion for Dismissal for Violation of his Right to a Trial without Undue Delay, *Prosecutor* v. *Mugiraneza*, Case No. ICTR-99-50-T, ICTR, T. Ch. II, 3 November 2004.   [131] *Barayagwiza* I appeal decision, para. 73.

[132] These rights are provided for, respectively, in Article 21(3) and (4)(g) of the ICTY Statute, Article 20(3) and (4)(g) of the ICTR Statute, Article 66 and 67(1)(g) of the ICC Statute, and Article 17(3) and (4)(g) of the SCSL Statute. See also Article 14(2) and (3)(g) of the ICCPR and Article 6(2) of the ECHR.

[133] Trechsel, *Human Rights in Criminal Proceedings*, at 163.

regarding the atrocities committed by RUF members were apparently at odds with the presumption of innocence.[134]

The second aspect is more problematic, in the sense that there should be an external influence, for example on the media. The risk of 'mediazation' of war crimes trials, including the use of such descriptions of accused persons as the 'butcher of Omarska' (referring to Duško Tadić) and the 'Balkan butcher' (referring to Slobodan Milošević), is very great indeed.[135] But it is difficult to deal with this issue in terms of human rights obligations applied to international criminal tribunals. They operate in 'splendid isolation', being accountable only to themselves for their actions and not to the media or to the public authorities of states.[136]

As to its more concrete effects, the presumption of innocence plays an important role, but rarely in its own right. For example, it is pivotal in respect of habeas corpus rights for persons who have not been convicted. Furthermore, in connection with the privilege against self-incrimination, the presumption of innocence is the basis for the imposition of the burden of proof on the prosecutor. This matter will be examined in more detail in Chapter 10, section 10.4. In the present context suffice it to say that the ad hoc tribunals have in a general sense and on numerous occasions affirmed the presumption of innocence.[137]

The privilege against self-incrimination is one of the most complicated elements of human rights law pertaining to criminal proceedings.[138] Vital questions related to its application, among others, are: whether the right is absolute or not; whether it is confined to testimony or also concerns other forms of cooperation; whether adverse inferences may be drawn from silence; how to ensure protection of the right in interrogations; and how to respond to evidence obtained under duress outside the framework of criminal procedure. These questions have resulted in a somewhat problematic body of international human rights jurisprudence. The matter is further complicated by the question of the applicability of this privilege in an age of terrorism, and whether methods of oppressive questioning are permitted outside the scope of criminal procedure.[139]

---

[134] See above, subsection 8.5.2.

[135] For more detail, see Zappalà, *Human Rights in International Criminal Proceedings*, at 85–6.

[136] Cf. *Allenet de Ribemont* v. *France*, 15175/89 [1996] ECtHR 27 (7 August 1996), para. 37, where France was held liable for a violation of the Convention because of statements by a high-ranking police officer. An interesting but fairly academic exercise concerns the hypothetical situation in which an official of the United Nations, to which the legal persons of the ICTY and ICTR belong, expresses views as to the culpability of persons accused by these tribunals.

[137] See Decision on the Prosecution's Alternative Request to Reopen the Prosecution's Case, *Prosecutor* v. *Delalić et al.*, Case No. IT-96-21, ICTY, T. Ch., 19 August 1998, and Decision on the Prosecutor's Motion to Withdraw the Indictment, *Prosecutor* v. *Ntuyahaga*, Case No. ICTR-98-40-T, ICTR, T. Ch. I, 18 March 1999.

[138] The right to remain silent is protected in Article 21(4)(g) of the ICTY Statute, Article 20(4)(g) of the ICTR Statute, Article 67(1)(g) of the ICC Statute, and Article 17(4)(g) of the SCSL Statute. It is not explicitly mentioned in Article 6 of the ECHR, but is nevertheless considered as a vital element of the right to a fair trial, which is reflected in Article 14(3)(g) of the ICCPR and Article 8(2)(g) and (3) of the ACHR.

[139] See E. Sepper, 'The Ties that Bind: How the Constitution Limits the CIA's Actions in the War on Terror' (2006) 81 *New York University Law Review*, at 1805–43; T. Thienel, 'The Admissibility of Evidence Obtained through Torture under International Law' (2006) 17 *European J. Int'l Law* at 349–67.

International human rights jurisprudence on the right to remain silent has undergone very progressive development, but, at the same time, contains some remarkable loopholes. Let us examine the matter from a thematic perspective.

The first question that arises is whether adequate protection of the privilege against self-incrimination requires protection of the individual's position during (police) interrogation, in the form of assistance by counsel or recording of the interrogation. This matter concerns both the right to remain silent and the right to assistance by counsel. In *Miranda* v. *Arizona* the US Supreme Court ruled in respect of the privilege against self-incrimination, protected by the Fifth Amendment to the US Constitution, that 'the very fact of custodial interrogation exacts a heavy toll on individual liberty and trades on the weakness of individuals'.[140] The Supreme Court deemed it essential for the effective application of the Fifth Amendment to form the so-called 'Miranda rights', including assistance by counsel during (police) interrogation;[141] the 'Miranda' warning and rights lie at the heart of US criminal procedure and have — because of frequent use in films and television series — become part of US national culture.[142] Remarkably, 'Miranda' has not found a place in international human rights law. In many civil-law jurisdictions, including the Netherlands, where the suspect has limited rights in the preliminary investigations, there is no right to assistance by counsel during police interrogation. International human rights courts have never required states to adopt the Miranda rights, neither in the context of the right to counsel, nor in the context of the privilege against self-incrimination.[143] In the view of these courts, the absence of counsel during interviews can be sufficiently compensated for by assistance from counsel at a very early stage and need not affect the fairness of the procedure as a whole.[144]

When confronted with the discrepancies in the various levels of protection for the individual during interrogation, it is interesting to note that international criminal procedure provides the highest level. Rules 42 and 43, derived from a US proposal and implementing Articles 18(3) of the ICTY Statute and 17(3) of the ICTR Statute, clearly transpose 'Miranda' into international criminal law and afford a double protection in that the interrogated person is entitled to assistance by counsel and recording of the interview. In the limited case law both provisions have been strictly applied. In *Mucić* the Trial Chamber excluded from evidence statements obtained from the accused by

---

[140] *Miranda* v. *Arizona*, Case No. 759, 384 US 436 (1966), at 455.

[141] For more detail on these rights, see LaFave et al., *Hornbook on Criminal Procedure* (4th edn, St. Paul: Thomson West, 2004), at 337–79.

[142] Cf. Justice Rehnquist, in *Dickerson* v. *United States*, 530 US 428, 443 (2000).

[143] While the European Court of Human Rights appeared to go in the direction of assistance by counsel during police interrogation in the cases of *Imbrioscia* v. *Switzerland*, 13972/88 [1993] ECtHR 56 (24 November 1993), and the admissibility decision in *J. Murray* v. *UK*, 18731/91 [1996] ECtHR 3 (8 February 1996), the explicit rejection of such a right came in *Dougan* v. *UK*, 44738/98, (14 December 1999): 'Before the Court of Appeal [the defence] argued for the first time that the statements made by the applicant to the police should have been declared inadmissible on account of the absence of a solicitor during interview. However the merits of that argument must be tested against the circumstances of the case. Quite apart from the consideration that this line of defence should have been used at first instance, the Court considers that an applicant cannot rely on Article 6 to claim the right to have a solicitor physically present during interview.'

[144] Cf. *Berlinski* v. *Poland*, 27715/95; 30209/96 [2002] ECtHR 505 (20 June 2002), para. 76.

Austrian authorities in the absence of counsel.[145] Although the prosecutor was not involved in this interview, the chamber saw in it a violation of the accused's rights and this triggered application of Rule 95 of the ICTY RPE.[146] In *Halilović*, the Trial Chamber excluded evidence because Rule 43 was not applied.[147] It considered this rule 'a fundamental provision to protect the rights of a suspect and an accused'.[148]

Although protection of individual rights beyond what is required by human rights law is welcome, the analysis in the cases mentioned above remains puzzling, especially if one bears in mind that in other areas, such as provisional release and the right to an expeditious trial, international criminal tribunals tend to be under- rather than over-protective.

Interestingly, wide-ranging protection during interrogation has rather uncritically been included in the ICC Statute. Article 55 of this Statute elevates the 'Miranda' rights to a fundamental rule of ICC procedure. Furthermore, Rules 111 and 112 of the ICC RPE are detailed provisions on the recording of interviews. One may wonder what aspects of the over-protective position of international criminal procedure on this point could be problematic. Affording this double protection may prove a burden for these international tribunals and difficult to realize in national jurisdictions with widely diverging practices. Furthermore, there may be significant costs involved. One could conceive of a position where evidence may be admissible, depending on the circumstances of each individual case, if at least one of the forms of protection is afforded (either counsel or recording).

The second question that arises is the scope of the right to remain silent. Whereas the US Constitution's Fifth Amendment is restricted to oral testimony, international human rights jurisprudence has adopted a more expansive approach, extending the privilege against self-incrimination to such materials as the defendant produces willingly.[149] This excludes the taking of DNA samples and blood and urine tests,[150] but includes giving testimony and also handing over documents selected by the suspect.[151] In its case law, the European Court of Human Rights has taken the procedure a step further by holding that an undercover operation in a jail, aimed at obtaining evidence from an individual who chose to remain silent during police interrogations, violated the privilege against self-incrimination.[152]

The ICTY was confronted with an interesting application of the scope of the privilege against self-incrimination by the prosecutor in *Mucić*.[153] The prosecutor requested

---

[145] Decision on Zdravko Mucic's Motion for the Exclusion of Evidence, *Prosecutor v. Delalić et al.*, Case No. IT-96-21, ICTY, T. Ch., 2 September 1997.

[146] See also Chapter 10, section 10.7.2. For criticism, see G. Sluiter, 'Commentary', in Klip and Sluiter, *Annotated Leading Cases, vol. I*, at 242–3.

[147] Decision on Motion for Exclusion of Statement of Accused, *Prosecutor v. Halilović*, Case No. IT-01-48-T, ICTY, T. Ch. I, Section A, 8 July 2005.   [148] Ibid., para. 24.

[149] Cf. *J.B. v. Switzerland*, 31827/96 [2001] ECtHR 324 (3 May 2001), para. 29.   [150] Cf. ibid., para. 29.

[151] Ibid., paras 30–2.   [152] *Allan v. UK*, 48539/99 [2002] ECtHR 702 (5 November 2002).

[153] See Decision on the Prosecution's Oral Requests for the Admission of Exhibit 155 into Evidence and for an Order to Compel the Accused, Zdravko Mucic, to Provide a Handwriting Sample, *Prosecutor v. Delalić et al.*, Case No. IT-96-21, ICTY, T. Ch., 19 January 1998.

the Chamber to order the accused to provide a handwriting sample with a view to assessing the authenticity of an exhibit admitted into evidence. In the discussion on the scope of the privilege against self-incrimination, the prosecutor had on her side US case law which allows for orders for handwriting samples, as they are not of a testimonial nature in the sense of the Fifth Amendment.[154] Such a request would not, however, pass the ECtHR test, as provision of the sample is clearly dependent upon the will of the accused.[155] In support of the prosecutor is the language in the Statute, which is taken from Article 14 of the ICCPR and refers to 'testify against himself', which draws very closely upon the Fifth Amendment's reference to 'witness'. Nevertheless, the Trial Chamber came up with a different interpretation, based more on a general sense of what is fair than on any solid legal reasoning:

In construing the provisions of Article 21 sub-paragraph 4(g), it is better to rely on the words of the provision if clear and unambiguous. The words 'to testify against himself' are clear and unambiguous, and require no modification or qualification. Nowhere is the privilege from self-incrimination qualified, or restricted to testimonial evidence. To read such a limitation as is suggested by the Prosecution is to read into the plain words, a condition not contemplated by the law maker. Such a construction will subvert the intention of the protection by introducing a qualification inconsistent with the true basis of the protection. The Trial Chamber cannot deprive the accused of his guaranteed right through construction of the words of the provision given without express limitation.[156]

Differing from one commentator,[157] we do not believe that complying with the prosecutor's application would be unacceptable. It is important in this regard to adopt a balanced approach to the privilege. As international criminal procedure is over-protective regarding the effect of the privilege on police interrogation, a more limited material application seems not unreasonable.

The third question that arises is whether adverse inferences may be drawn from the exercise of the right to remain silent. International criminal procedure is quite adamant in this regard. Article 67(1)(g) of the ICC Statute is explicit: 'without such silence being a consideration in the determination of guilt or innocence'. The ad hoc tribunals have gone one step further, by consistently holding that the right to silence cannot be an aggravating factor in sentencing.[158]

Again, there is a discrepancy with human rights law. The European Court of Human Rights has allowed national courts to draw — in particular circumstances — negative inferences from the exercise of the right to remain silent:

In the Court's view, having regard to the weight of the evidence against the applicant, as outlined above, the drawing of inferences from his refusal, at arrest, during police questioning and at trial, to provide an explanation for his presence in the house was a matter of common sense and cannot

---

[154] Cf. *Gilbert* v. *California*, as cited ibid., para. 52.

[155] However, note that important decisions like *J.B.* v. *Switzerland* and *Allan* v. *UK* are of a later date than the decision discussed in *Prosecutor* v. *Delalić et al.*

[156] Decision on the Prosecution's Oral Requests for the Admission of Exhibit 155 into Evidence and for an Order to Compel the Accused, Zdravko Mucic, to Provide a Handwriting Sample, *Prosecutor* v. *Delalić et al.*, para. 58.

[157] P. Mevis, 'Commentary', in Klip and Sluiter, *Annotated Leading Cases, vol. III*, at 341.

[158] See *Niyitegeka* trial judgment, para. 46; *Čelebići* appeal judgment, para. 738; *Plavšić* sentencing judgment, para. 17.

be regarded as unfair or unreasonable in the circumstances. As pointed out by the Delegate of the Commission, the courts in a considerable number of countries where evidence is freely assessed may have regard to all relevant circumstances, including the manner in which the accused has behaved or has conducted his defence, when evaluating the evidence in the case. It considers that, what distinguishes the drawing of inferences under the Order is that, in addition to the existence of the specific safeguards mentioned above, it constitutes, as described by the Commission, 'a formalised system which aims at allowing common-sense implications to play an open role in the assessment of evidence'.

Nor can it be said, against this background, that the drawing of reasonable inferences from the applicant's behaviour had the effect of shifting the burden of proof from the prosecution to the defence so as to infringe the principle of the presumption of innocence.[159]

Again, the approach by international criminal tribunals is over-protective from a human rights perspective.

Taking the above into account, observers remain puzzled by the over-protective approach of international criminal procedure to the privilege against self-incrimination. One explanation relates to the effective administration of justice. Assistance from the accused, generally in the form of a confession, is at the present stage of international criminal law not as important as in domestic jurisdictions. There is not the situation of immediate arrest followed by interrogation, offering a conducive environment for a confession. The general practice is for an accused person to determine their defence strategy and adequately prepare for a trial beforehand.

8.5.5 Right to be informed of the charges

The right to be informed of the charges against one has both a factual and a legal dimension, and is closely connected to the right to adequate time and facilities to prepare one's defence.[160] Only if accused persons are well informed of the charges against them can they adequately prepare their defence.[161] This is also how the ad hoc tribunals have approached this right. For example, in *Simić* the Trial Chamber ruled that 'this right not only means that he shall be informed about the legal qualification of the charges against him, but also about the facts underlying the charge, in order to prepare adequately his defence'.[162]

This right is thus vital for the requirements concerning the indictment. This matter will be addressed separately in Chapter 9, section 9.3.

---

[159] *J. Murray* v. *UK*, 18731/91 [1996] ECtHR 3 (8 February 1996), para. 54.

[160] The right is protected in Article 21(4)(a) of the ICTY Statute, Article 20(4)(a) of the ICTR Statute, Article 67(1)(a) of the ICC Statute, and Article 17 (4)(a) of the SCSL Statute. See also Article 14(3)(a) of the ICCPR, Article 6(3)(a) of the ECHR, and Article 8(2)(b) of the ACHR.

[161] A distinction should be made between the functional approach to this right and the absolutist approach. The former interprets the right to be informed of the charges in light of the right to have adequate time and facilities to prepare the defence. The latter sees it as a right that stands alone and that can also be violated even if additional information would not have assisted in a better preparation of the defence. See Trechsel, *Human Rights in Criminal Proceedings*, at 193–4.

[162] Reasons for Decision on Prosecution's Motion to Use Telephone Interviews, *Prosecutor* v. *Simić*, Case No. IT-95-9-T, ICTY, T. Ch. II, 11 March 2003, para. 6.

8.5.6 Right to adequate time and facilities

Building upon the right to be informed of the charges, the accused enjoys the right to adequate time and facilities to prepare the defence.[163] This right is also strongly connected with the right to counsel, to such a degree that Article 14 of the ICCPR, which has largely been copied into the statutes of international criminal tribunals, adds to this right the right to communicate with counsel of one's own choosing. This aspect of the right to adequate time and facilities will be dealt with in section 8.5.7.

The two elements of the right are time and facilities. It is virtually impossible to give general criteria for the meaning of 'adequate time', as it is simply too case specific. In this regard, the *Čelebići* Trial Chamber ruled that 'it is impossible to set a standard of what constitutes adequate time to prepare a defence because this is something which can be affected by a number of factors including the complexity of the case, and the competing forces and claims at play, such as consideration of the interests of other accused persons'.[164]

There is more to be said about adequate facilities from a human rights perspective. There are four different aspects of 'facilities': the right of access to the case file under the continental system; discovery under the Anglo-Saxon system; discovery of 'hidden material' under both systems; and investigation by the defence.[165] The latter aspect, investigations by the defence, is closely related to the principle of equality of arms and has already been addressed above in section 8.5.1.

The recurring legal battle in adversarial proceedings is mutual disclosure rights and obligations. In Chapter 10, section 10.6.1 disclosure will be examined from the perspective of the law of evidence. In disclosure in the present context we take as a starting point that it is required 'in principle that the prosecution authorities should disclose to the defence all material evidence in their possession for or against the accused'.[166] The law and practice of international criminal tribunals generally put this adequately into effect. Rule 66 of the ICTY, ICTR, and SCSL rules imposes disclosure obligations on the prosecutor, which comply with human rights standards.[167] Also, because human rights case law is generally quite permissive in respect of withholding disclosure,[168] it will be difficult structurally to assess disclosure in international criminal proceedings in light of human rights law. In Chapter 10, section 10.6.1 reference is made to two problems pertaining to disclosure. First, disclosure obligations are extremely difficult to enforce, as there is no truly effective way to supervise the prosecutor's determination of what information is material to the defence. Secondly, particular demands on international criminal justice, like the protection of witnesses, have impinged on the facilities

---

[163] The right is protected in Article 21(4)(b) of the ICTY Statute, Article 20(4)(b) of the ICTR Statute, Article 67(1)(b) of the ICC Statute, and Article 17(4)(b) of the SCSL Statute. See also Article 14(3)(b) of the ICCPR, Article 6(3)(a) of the ECHR, and Article 8(2)(b) ACHR.

[164] Decision on the Application for Adjournment of the Trial Date, *Prosecutor v. Delalić*, Case No. IT-96-21, ICTY, T. Ch., 3 February 1997.   [165] Cf. Trechsel, *Human Rights in Criminal Proceedings*, at 223.

[166] *Atlan v. UK*, 36533/97 [2001] ECtHR 397 (19 June 2001), para. 40.

[167] For the ICC, see Article 67(2) of the Statute and Rules 76–7 of the ICC RPE.

[168] Cf. Trechsel, *Human Rights in Criminal Proceedings*, at 226.

to prepare a defence. As an example, which is further addressed in section 10.6.1, one may mention the practice of rolling disclosure, which in the interests of protection of witnesses amounts to disclosure of their identities not prior to trial, but in sufficient time prior to them giving testimony.

8.5.7 Right to counsel or to defend oneself in person

In Chapter 2, section 2.5 we dealt with the position of the defence from an institutional perspective. Here we are concerned with the accused's right to assistance from counsel or to defend him- or herself in person.[169] Yet, there is an obvious connection between the right to legal assistance and the institutional environment. International criminal justice suffers in this regard from its isolated position, compared to national jurisdictions, and cannot (yet) count on strong support from some form of bar association to ensure effective representation.[170]

We will address four important aspects of the right to legal assistance in the context of international criminal proceedings: counsel of one's own choice, access to counsel, quality of assistance, and self-representation.

The choice of counsel raises questions of who, and how many, may be appointed, and whether the accused may change counsel. In answering these questions it is generally accepted that the right to counsel of one's choice may be restricted on legal and practical grounds.

Like any national jurisdiction, the international criminal tribunals impose eligibility criteria on persons who wish to act as counsel before them.[171] Compared to national jurisdictions, the eligibility standards are extremely low, in that no knowledge is required — let alone tested in the form of a bar examination — of important aspects of both substantive and procedural international criminal law.[172] As a result, there are numerous examples of poor-quality representation which, as a result, is at odds with other rights and principles of justice in adversarial trials, such as the effective preparation of the defence.[173]

One matter that arises is the choice of defender, from the group of eligible counsel, for indigent accused.[174] While there is no duty imposed on national authorities to appoint the counsel of their choice for indigent accused, they are required to take the

---

[169] The right is protected in Article 21(4)(d) of the ICTY Statute, Article 20(4)(d) of the ICTR Statute, Article 67(1)(c) of the ICC Statute, and Article 17(4)(d) of the SCSL Statute. See also Article 14(3)(d) of the ICCPR, Article 6(3)(c) of the ECHR, and Article 8(2)(e) of the ACHR.

[170] For developments in this regard, see Dixon and Khan, *Archbold*, margin nos 20-233-20-237.

[171] Rule 44 of the ICTY, ICTR, and SCSL RPE, Rule 22 of the ICC RPE. See also J. Ackerman, 'Assignment of Defence Counsel at the ICTY', in May et al., *Essays on ICTY Procedure and Evidence*, at 167–76. For details of qualification requirements, see Dixon and Khan, *Archbold*, margin nos 20-49-20-91.

[172] J. Ackerman, 'Assignment of Defence Counsel at the ICTY', in May et al., *Essays on ICTY Procedure and Evidence*, at 170.

[173] See W. A. Schabas, *The UN International Criminal Tribunals — The former Yugoslavia, Rwanda and Sierra Leone*, at 524–5.

[174] Note that the Directive on Assignment of Counsel says that 'a suspect or an accused shall be considered to be indigent if he does not have sufficient means to retain counsel of choice'. However, a number of accused have been found to be able to contribute to their defence. For more detail on this matter, and on the method used by the registrar to determine indigence, see Dixon and Khan, *Archbold*, margin nos 20-43-20-48.

wishes of the accused into account.[175] This applies even more strongly to international criminal tribunals as they are concerned with a very limited area of legal practice in which counsel have indicated their willingness to serve,[176] and as most of the accused are indigent. As a result, the ad hoc tribunals have endorsed a corresponding practice in which an indigent accused should be permitted to choose counsel from a list kept by the registrar under Rule 45 of the ICTY, the ICTR, and the SCSL RPE, as well as Rule 21(2) of the ICC RPE. The registrar has to take into consideration the wishes of the accused, unless the registrar has reasonable and valid grounds not to grant the request.[177]

In deciding how many counsel may be appointed to indigent accused, a balance must be struck between financial limitations, on the one hand, and ensuring an effective defence and equality of arms on the other. While initially there was only a right to one paid counsel, matters have improved significantly. The Directive on Assignment of Counsel was amended and now allows for assignment of other counsel.[178] Furthermore, allowance is also generally made for recruitment of supporting personnel, such as investigators, case managers, and legal assistants.[179]

The right to change counsel is implied in the right to choose one's own counsel.[180] However, frequent demands to change counsel may not be in the interests of justice and the right to an expeditious trial, as they occasion delays and increased costs. Article 19(A) of the Directive on Assignment of Counsel authorizes a change in counsel in 'exceptional circumstances'. While initially those were held to exist when there was a lack of regular communication and a 'lack of confidence',[181] a more stringent interpretation may be expected to develop in light of the exit strategies.

Access to counsel as an element of the right to counsel is generally unproblematic in international criminal law, especially when compared to national systems. International human rights law, particularly that of the ECtHR, has accepted that the right to confidential contact with counsel at all or important times is substantially restricted. This first instance of this occurs in contact during police interrogations, which we have already examined in the context of the privilege against self-incrimination. Secondly, in

---

[175] *Croissant v. Germany*, 13611/88 [1992] ECtHR 60 (25 September 1992), para. 29.

[176] For example, the practical objection that desired counsel X lives far from the place of the trial (District Court Y) plays no role in international criminal practice, as counsel sign up with a specific tribunal or court.

[177] Decision on the Motions of the Accused for Replacement of Assigned Counsel, Corr., *Prosecutor v. Ntakirutimana*, Case ICTR-96-10-T & ICTR-96-17-T, ICTR, T. Ch. I, 11 June 1997; Decision on Request by Accused Mucic for Assignment of New Counsel, *Prosecutor v. Delalić et al.*, Case No. IT-96-21-T, ICTY, T. Ch., 24 June 1996; *Akayesu* appeal judgment, paras 50–64; Decision on Independent Counsel for Vidoje Blagojević's Motion to Instruct the Registrar to Appoint New Lead and Co-counsel, *Prosecutor v. Blagojević*, Case No. IT-02-60-T, ICTY, T. Ch., 3 July 2003, para. 117, confirmed on appeal: Public and Redacted Reasons for Decision on Appeal by Vidoje Blagojević to Replace his Defence Team, *Prosecutor v. Blagojević*, Case No. IT-02-60-AR73.4, ICTY, A. Ch., 7 November 2003.

[178] See Article 16(C) of the Directive, and para. 106 of the Third Annual Report of the ICTY (1996).

[179] For the system of paying counsel, see Dixon and Khan, *Archbold*, margin nos 20-151-20-169.

[180] Article 19(A) of the Directive provides for three situations of withdrawal of counsel: (a) an accused may request withdrawal of the lead counsel; (b) the lead counsel may request his own withdrawal and/or the withdrawal of co-counsel; and (c) the co-counsel may request his own withdrawal.

[181] See Decision on the Request of the Accused for the Replacement of Assigned Counsel, *Prosecutor v. Akayesu*, Case No. ICTR-96-4-T, ICTR, T. Ch., 20 November 1996 and Decision on the Request by the Accused for Change of Assigned Counsel, *Prosecutor v. Bagosora*, Case No. ICTR-96-7-T, ICTR, T. Ch., 26 June 1997.

the interests of justice and in exceptional circumstances other restrictions may be justified, in particular if there is a risk of collusion or if the 'professional ethics' of the lawyer or the 'lawfulness of his conduct were at any time called into question'.[182] These restrictions do not play a significant role in international criminal practice. Generally, counsel can communicate freely with their clients[183] and have a right to be present during interrogations. The fact that the issue of restrictions was never high on the agenda can be explained by vital differences between national and international criminal law enforcement. For example, the risk of collusion, in the sense that an accused may try to inform a co-accused through a lawyer that the former must remain silent, as the police know nothing, is alien to international criminal practice. The risks of collusion and of violation of protective measures for witnesses through contacts with counsel can hardly be meaningfully addressed by restricting confidential communication between the accused and his or her lawyer. The solution for these problems has been sought in other directions, for example in the above-mentioned rolling disclosure of the identity of witnesses.

The quality of legal assistance is a problematic aspect of the right to legal assistance, as individuals have no standing with international human rights bodies to complain about the performance of their counsel. Furthermore, as to the national authorities, any substantive supervision of the performance of defence counsel may jeopardize the profession's independence.[184] However, there is a minimum threshold of performance under human rights law. Obviously, the absence of any defence activity violates the right to assistance, which goes beyond mere appointment.[185] When defence counsel has been active, the starting point is that the state cannot be held responsible for every shortcoming on the part of a lawyer appointed for legal aid purposes.[186] And national authorities only have to intervene 'if a failure by legal aid counsel to provide effective representation is manifest or sufficiently brought to their attention in some other way'.[187] 'Manifest ineffective representation' is not easily established, as counsel acting against the wishes of his or her client is not necessarily ineffective.[188] In death penalty cases a more demanding standard has been adopted; the state has a positive duty to ensure that the legal assistance provided is effective.[189]

In adversarial systems jurisprudence is better developed, since ineffective representation by counsel seriously undermines the underlying assumption of a struggle between two more or less equal parties, and the judge has to remain passive and can in no way compensate for inadequate representation. Thus, in the USA, according to *Strickland* v. *Washington*, the 'proper standard for [measuring] attorney performance is that of

---

[182] Cf. *S.* v. *Switzerland*, 12629/87; 13965/88 [1991] ECtHR 54 (28 November 1991), para. 49.

[183] Cf. Article 65 of the Rules of Detention of the ICTY, the ICTR, and the SCSL guaranteeing privileged communication with counsel. [184] See Trechsel, *Human Rights in Criminal Proceedings*, at 286.

[185] Cf. *Artico* v. *Italy*, 6694/74 [1980] ECtHR 4 (13 May 1980), and *Goddi* v. *Italy*, 8966/80 [1984] ECtHR 4 (9 April 1984). [186] *Artico* v. *Italy*, para. 36

[187] *Kamasinski* v. *Austria*, 9783/82 [1989] ECtHR 24 (19 December 1989), para. 65.

[188] Ibid., para. 70.

[189] See *Kelly* v. *Jamaica*, Communication 537/1993, Views adopted on 17 July 1996, UN Doc. CCPR/C/57/D/537/1993 UN Doc. Supp. No. 40 (A/46/40) at 241 (1991)) and *Reid* v. *Jamaica*, Communication No. 355/1989, Views adopted on 8 July 1994, UN Doc. CCPR/C/51/D/355/1989 (1994).

reasonably effective assistance', as guided by 'prevailing professional norms' and consideration of 'all the circumstances' relevant to counsel's performance.[190]

The law of international criminal procedure has not yet developed any meaningful jurisprudence on this point. This is somewhat surprising as there are certainly complaints about the quality of counsel. There are two cases, *Kambanda* and *Tadić*, where the performance of counsel was substantially at stake. In *Kambanda* new counsel complained in the appeal hearing about the poor performance of counsel, but did not advance this as a ground for appeal in its own right. He connected this to the ground that Kambanda was denied his first choice of counsel; the point was easily passed over by the Appeals Chamber, precisely because of the restricted scope of the grounds of appeal, and the fact that the defence failed to meet the evidentiary standard for showing incompetence.[191] The Appeals Chamber did not specify what the appropriate standard for showing incompetence would be. In *Tadić* counsel moved to a review procedure pursuant to Article 26 of the Statute, after he learned about the contempt conviction for former counsel of Tadić, Milan Vujin.[192] Defence counsel alluded to the fact that, among other things, Vujin acted against the interests of his client and was 'found guilty of various manipulations throughout his appeal preparations and the investigation conducted at that time with the aim of concealing the real perpetrators'.[193] Interestingly, and also astonishingly, the Appeals Chamber approached the entire matter from a very narrow interpretation of the term 'decisive factor', which is the pivotal element of Article 26 of the ICTY Statute. It confined itself to an analysis of the consequences of Vujin's behaviour for the evidence underlying Tadić's conviction. Not a single word was said about the right to legal assistance, including any violation

---

[190] 466 US 668, 104 S Ct. 2052, 80 L.Ed.2d 674 (1984). The major conclusions of that landmark decision concerning effective representation can be summarized as follows: (1) to establish ineffective assistance requiring reversal of a conviction, a defendant must show both (a) that counsel made errors so serious that counsel was not functioning as counsel guaranteed by the Sixth Amendment, and (b) that the deficient performance prejudiced the defence; (2) the 'proper standard for [measuring] attorney performance is that of reasonably effective assistance', as guided by 'prevailing professional norms' and consideration of 'all the circumstances' relevant to counsel's performance; (3) more specific guidelines in applying that standard are not appropriate; and (4) the proper standard for measuring prejudice is whether there is a reasonable probability that, but for counsel's unprofessional errors, the result of the proceedings would be different. (LaFave *et al.*, *Hornbook on Criminal Procedure*, at 635; for a detailed analysis of the law concerning ineffective representation, see pp. 635–46).

[191] *Kambanda* appeal judgment, see para. 28:

In the instant case, the Appellant considers that the waiver principle must be interpreted in the light of a special circumstance: his Counsel's incompetence. The Appeals Chamber emphasizes firstly that in the Appellant's briefs and oral statements the problem of his counsel's inadequacy never figured as an argument, let alone an independent ground of appeal. The Appellant's allegations on this point are at the very least confused. It is true that in his statement the Appellant did cite, for example, the insufficient number of meetings with his counsel and the latter's lack of interest in and knowledge of the case file. The Appeals Chamber nevertheless finds that the Appellant has not succeeded in showing his Counsel to be incompetent on the basis of solid arguments and relevant facts. Rather, the Chamber has before it documents proving that counsel for the Appellant carried out the functions of his office in the normal manner. The Appeals Chamber therefore cannot accept the Appellant's allegations and concludes that he has not been able to demonstrate the existence of special circumstances capable of constituting an exception to the waiver principle.

[192] Appeal Judgment on Allegations of Contempt against Prior Counsel, Milan Vujin, *Prosecutor v. Tadić*, Case No. IT-94-1-A-R77, ICTY, A. Ch., 27 February 2001.

[193] Decision on Motion for Review, *Prosecutor v. Tadić*, Case No. IT-94-1-R, ICTY, A. Ch., 30 July 2002.

thereof, despite the fact that this was also a decisive factor in the sense of Article 26. This was clearly a case for dealing with the question of ineffective representation, which was also in the framework of review proceedings, and to address it in light of the right to legal assistance.

Another aspect of the right to counsel affecting the quality of the defence is the right to self-representation. In Chapter 2 we dealt with this unique feature of international criminal proceedings, from an institutional perspective.[194] From a human rights perspective, the issue has divided both practitioners and scholars (and continues to do so), depending on one's views on state obligations in respect of human rights. The jury is still out on the question of whether the right to defend oneself in person, as explicitly mentioned in all human rights instruments, should primarily be approached from the perspective of an accused's own informed choice or rather be connected to an effective defence, which may require intervention.[195] Both international human rights law and national law and practice offer support for both approaches, and the rare case law is so divergent that it does not offer much in the way of precedents.[196] Here one encounters the (as yet) rare situation that international criminal law exceeds in scope human rights law on this point and is actually responsible for the most authoritative interpretation of the right to self-representation. By trial and error, the ad hoc tribunals and the SCSL have developed a fairly balanced jurisprudence, which we have already addressed in Chapter 2, section 2.5. The starting point of that case law is the recognition of the right to self-representation. As a result, accused who do not wish to conduct any defence obviously enjoy no protection from the right to self-representation.[197] When accused persons truly want to defend themselves, the right is not absolute but should be balanced against other competing interests, generally referred to as the interests of justice.[198] There are basically two vital competing interests advanced. The first is avoiding the delay and interruption of trials; this may be done intentionally, in the form of disrespectful and disruptive behaviour (Šešelj), or unintentionally, for example because of health problems or simply by not being qualified (Milošević). Secondly, there is the interest of ensuring an 'effective defence'. While these competing interests appear

---

[194] See Chapter 2, section 2.5.   [195] See also Trechsel, *Human Rights in Criminal Proceedings*, at 263.

[196] For an overview of the cases and law we refer to the decisions in the cases of Krajišnik, Šešelj, and Milošević (ICTY), Barayagwiza (ICTR), and Norman (SCSL) and the following articles: G. Sluiter, ' "Fairness and the Interests of Justice": Illusive Concepts in the *Milošević* Case' (2005) 3 *JICJ*, at 9–19; M. P. Scharf, 'Self-Representation versus Assignment of Defense Counsel before International Criminal Tribunals' (2006) 4 *JICJ*, at 31–46; and J. Temminck Tuinstra, 'Assisting an Accused to Represent Himself: Appointment of *Amici Curiae* as the Most Appropriate Option' (2006) 4 *JICJ*, at 47–63; and N. H. B. Jørgensen, 'The Right of the Accused to Self-Representation before International Criminal Tribunals' (2004) 99 *AJIL*, at 711–26, and ibid., 'The Right of the Accused to Self-Representation before International Criminal Tribunals: Further Developments', (2005) 99 *AJIL*, at 663–8.

[197] As in the cases of Gbao (SCSL) and Barayagwiza (ICTR), who refused to put up any defence; in these situations counsel was assigned. See Decision on Defence Counsel Motion to Withdraw, *Prosecutor v. Barayagwiza*, Case No. ICTR-97-19-T, ICTR, T. Ch. I, 2 November 2000, and Gbao — Decision on Appeal against Decision on Withdrawal of Counsel, *Prosecutor v. Sesay et al.*, Case No. SCSL-04-15-AR73, SCSL, A. Ch., 23 November 2004.

[198] See G. Sluiter, ' "Fairness and the Interests of Justice": Illusive Concepts in the *Milošević* Case' (2005) 3 *JICJ*, at 9–19; Decision on Interlocutory Appeal of the Trial Chamber's Decision on the Assignment of Defense Counsel, *Prosecutor v. Milošević*, Case No. IT-02-54-AR73.7 ICTY, A. Ch., 1 November 2004, para. 19; Decision on Appeal against the Trial Chamber's Decision on Assignment of Counsel, *Prosecutor v. Šešelj*, Case No. IT-03-67-AR73.3, ICTY, A. Ch., 20 October 2006.

reasonable factors in a balancing exercise, there are a number of complicating factors. In the case of an accused who unintentionally delays trials because of health problems, the imposition of counsel will not really be helpful, as an accused behaving in good faith cannot be denied the right to be tried in his or her presence.[199] When an accused acts in bad faith and uses his position as his own 'counsel' to obstruct the administration of justice, there is good cause to restrict the right to self-representation. However, even then, formal requirements apply, in the form of an official warning.[200] The assurance of an effective defence is understandable from the perspective of a functional approach to the right to self-representation, but is controversial for two reasons. First, the cure might be worse than the disease, in the sense that the imposition of counsel may in fact lead to a worse defence than the one conducted by the accused. This may be occasioned not only by the fact that the accused generally refuses to communicate with assigned counsel, but also by other elements, like the refusal of witnesses to testify when not examined-in-chief by the accused directly.[201] Secondly, when counsel is assigned to ensure effective defence one wonders how the chamber assesses the 'effectiveness' of defence, and whether similar assessment criteria will be adopted in respect of defences conducted *with* counsel.[202]

In light of these complications, some trial chambers — acting under the pressure of the need for effective trial management — have resorted to assiging counsel. Yet, the Appeals Chamber, mindful of the delicacies inherent in the balancing exercise, has proved to be more cautious. In *Milošević* the Appeals Chamber corrected the Trial Chamber's decision on account of the principle of proportionality[203] and in *Šešelj* the Appeals Chamber basically reproached the Trial Chamber for having been 'slipshod' in giving no formal warning prior to imposing a counsel.[204] This is indicative both of the highly complex balancing exercise developed in the jurisprudence and of the importance attached to self-representation as an element of the right to a fair trial.

8.5.8 Right to examine witnesses

The right to examine witnesses[205] is one of the major human rights difficulties in civil-law criminal jurisdictions.[206] This has to do with the fact that there is no strong tradition

---

[199] See G. Sluiter, ' "Fairness and the Interests of Justice": Illusive Concepts in the *Milošević* Case', at 18.

[200] See Decision on Appeal against the Trial Chamber's Decision on Assignment of Counsel, *Prosecutor* v. *Šešelj*, Case No. IT-03-67-AR73.3, ICTY, A. Ch., 20 October 2006.

[201] The latter was the case in the *Milošević* trial.

[202] See G. Sluiter, ' "Fairness and the Interests of Justice": Illusive Concepts in the *Milošević* Case'.

[203] Decision on Interlocutory Appeal of the Trial Chamber's Decision on the Assignment of Defense Counsel, *Prosecutor* v. *Milošević*, Case No. IT-02-54-AR73.7 ICTY, A. Ch., 1 November 2004, paras 17–18.

[204] Decision on Appeal against the Trial Chamber's Decision on Assignment of Counsel, *Prosecutor* v. *Šešelj*, Case No. IT-03-67-AR73.3, ICTY, A. Ch., 20 October 2006.

[205] The right is protected in Article 21(4)(e) of the ICTY Statute, Article 20(4)(e) of the ICTR Statute, Article 67(1)(e) of the ICC Statute, and Article 17(4)(e) of the SCSL Statute. See also Article 14(3)(f) of the ICCPR, Article 6(3)(d) of the ECHR, and Article 8(2)(f) of the ACHR.

[206] For example, the Netherlands has had a series of painful European Court of Human Rights judgments on this point; see *Kostovski* v. *The Netherlands*, 11454/85 [1989] ECtHR 20 (20 November 1989), *Van Mechelen et al.* v. *The*

of oral presentation of evidence at trial. In adversarial systems this right is fairly unproblematic, in view of the importance attached to cross-examination. And this is also the case with the international criminal tribunals. In Chapter 10 we will examine the right to confront (incriminating) witnesses from an evidentiary perspective and the matter need not be further explored here. Suffice it to say that even with the possibility of admitting 'hearsay evidence', the law and practice of the ad hoc tribunals is still far above the minimum threshold of human rights law. According to the latter, testimonial evidence that the accused has not been able to challenge may still be admitted, provided that the conviction is not solely or to a decisive extent based on that evidence.[207] The ICC presents a very progressive standard, giving full effect to this right. Rule 68 of the ICC RPE sets out a mandatory exclusionary rule for prior recorded testimony that has not been subject to cross-examination.

8.5.9 Right to appeal

The right to appeal is not within the core of fair trial rights, which is evidenced by the fact that it is not part of the ECHR.[208] In international criminal proceedings two questions have arisen in respect of the right to appeal from a human rights perspective. First, is the non-availability of appeal for preliminary motions a violation of this right? Secondly, does the revision of a trial chamber judgment by the appeals chamber increasing the sentence or otherwise aggravating liability deny the accused his right to appeal?

The first matter came to the fore at the SCSL where the judges in order to expedite proceedings decided not to allow interlocutory appeal on preliminary motions.[209] The defence in the case against Norman and others argued that this rule change amounted to a violation of the right to appeal in the sense of Article 14(5) of the ICCPR. The SCSL Appeals Chamber easily disposed of the motion on account of the fact that this provision 'is bestowed only on persons who have been convicted'.[210]

The second matter is more fundamental. The issue came to the fore in the *Rutaganda* and *Semanza* appeal judgments, in which the Appeals Chamber entered new convictions. Judge Pocar dissented in both cases, because this approach would deny the accused an appeal against these new convictions.[211] According to Judge Pocar, the better approach, in spite of the permissive language of Article 24 of the ICTR Statute, would be either to remit the case to a trial chamber or for the appeals chamber to mention the errors, but not to enter new convictions.[212] In the view of Judge Pocar, the

---

Netherlands (Article 50), 21363/93; 21364/93; 21427/93 [1997] ECtHR 90 (30 October 1997), and *Bocos-Cuesta* v. *The Netherlands*, 54789/00 [2005] (10 November 2005).

[207] Cf. *Kostovski* v. *The Netherlands* and *Van Mechelen et al.* v. *The Netherlands*.

[208] The right can be found in Article 14(5) of the ICCPR, Article 2 of the Seventh Protocol to the ECHR and Article 8(2)(h) of the ACHR.

[209] Cf. Rule 73(B) of the SCSL Rules. For the reasons for this departure from ICTY and ICTR law, see Decision on the Applications for a Stay of Proceedings and Denial of Right to Appeal, *Prosecutor* v. *Norman et al.*, Case No. SCSL-2003-08-PT, SCSL, A. Ch., 4 November 2003, paras 3–14.   [210] Ibid., para. 21.

[211] See Dissenting Opinion of Judge Pocar, *Rutaganda* appeal judgment, and Dissenting Opinion of Judge Pocar, *Semanza* appeal judgment.   [212] Ibid., paras 2 and 3.

entry of new convictions by the Appeals Chamber is in violation of Article 14(5) of the ICCPR, but he offers no analysis in support of this conclusion.[213] While at the outset one may have sympathy for an appeal as not being disadvantageous for the accused, there is no unanimous support for this position in human rights law. For example, the ECHR does not contain any prohibition on *reformatio in peius*, and does not protect an appellant from a more severe judgment on appeal.[214] This is also evidenced by the exception set out in Article 2(2) of the Seventh Protocol to the ECHR, according to which the right to appeal need not apply 'in cases in which the person concerned was tried in the first instance by the highest tribunal or was convicted following an appeal against acquittal'. There is a discrepancy between this and Article 14(5) of the ICCPR, in which there is no similar exception and which categorically grants a right to appeal against a conviction. However, this right lies with a higher court and when the Appeals Chamber enters a conviction for the first time this is already the highest court available. Furthermore, in the interests of expedient justice one may question how useful it is to remit a case to a Trial Chamber when the highest judicial instance available has already made up its mind on the outcome of the case.

8.5.10 Right to compensation for wrongful arrest or conviction

A distinction needs to be made between the right to compensation for wrongful arrest, which is part of the habeas corpus body of law, and the right to compensation for wrongful conviction, which is associated with the right to a fair trial.[215]

The law of the ad hoc tribunals is clearly defective on these points,[216] and attempts to improve it have been unsuccessful, which has to do with the financial implications.[217] Acquitted accused, such as the Kupreškić brothers and Delalić, have demanded compensation for wrongful arrest and conviction.[218] Their applications have been unsuccessful because arrest and conviction tend only to be unlawful when they are not based on a reasonable suspicion, i.e only in cases of a miscarriage of justice.[219]

Interestingly, the ICTR Appeals Chamber has allowed for financial compensation in case of human rights violations, giving effect to the right to an effective remedy. In *Barayagwiza* the Appeals Chamber ruled that if the accused had been acquitted he would have received financial compensation for violation of rights during arrest and detention, and in case of conviction the sentence would have been reduced.[220] One

---

[213] Ibid., para. 3.   [214] Trechsel, *Human Rights in Criminal Proceedings*, at 362.

[215] Cf. Article 9(5) of the ICCPR, dealing with the first element, and Article 14(6) of the ICCPR dealing with the second element.

[216] Note that the 'copy and paste' exercise in respect of Article 14 of the ICCPR omitted its sixth paragraph.

[217] In 2000 ICTY and ICTR Presidents requested the UN Secretary General to ask the Security Council to amend the Statutes to deal with this matter, especially in light of the extremely long periods of pre-trial detention; the Security Council has made no such amendments. See W. A. Schabas, *The UN International Criminal Tribunals — The former Yugoslavia, Rwanda and Sierra Leone*, at 537.   [218] Ibid., at 538.

[219] M. Nowak, *UN Covenant on Civil and Political Rights: CCPR Commentary* (2nd rev. edn, Kehl: N. P. Engel, 2005), at 239.   [220] *Barayagwiza* II appeal decision.

wonders where they would have found the compensation money in case of acquittal.[221]

This 'black hole' in the human rights law as applied by the ad hoc tribunals and by the SCSL has been remedied for the ICC by the insertion of Article 85 into its Statute. This provision adopts verbatim in its first two paragraphs the language of Articles 9(5) and 14(6) of the ICCPR. Furthermore, in its third paragraph it allows for discretionary compensation.

8.5.11 Protection against double jeopardy

The protection against double jeopardy,[222] in civil law better known as *ne bis in idem* protection, has for international criminal tribunals two different dimensions. The external dimension concerns the mutual effect of judgments rendered by international criminal tribunals and national courts. This is an important element of the relationship between tribunals and states and will be addressed in Chapter 12, section 12.4. The internal dimension primarily raises the question of subsequent prosecution of the same individual. In the one-dimensional focus of international criminal justice this can be dismissed as a merely theoretical problem. However, the views underlying *ne bis in idem* protection do play a vital role in important matters of substantive criminal law, such as the question of cumulative charging and cumulative convictions.

The question of multiple convictions based on the same set of facts is now settled in the jurisprudence of the ad hoc tribunals, on the basis of the US Blockburger test.[223] This test has been used consistently in the tribunals' case law:

Having considered the different approaches expressed on this issue both within this Tribunal and other jurisdictions, this Appeals Chamber holds that reasons of fairness to the accused and the consideration that only distinct crimes may justify multiple convictions, lead to the conclusion that multiple criminal convictions entered under different statutory provisions but based on the same conduct are permissible only if each statutory provision involved has a materially distinct element not contained in the other. An element is materially distinct from another if it requires proof of a fact not required by the other.

Where this test is not met, the Chamber must decide in relation to which offence it will enter a conviction. This should be done on the basis of the principle that the conviction under the more specific provision should be upheld. Thus, if a set of facts is regulated by two provisions, one of which contains an additional materially distinct element, then a conviction should be entered only under that provision.[224]

The application of the test has given rise to some controversy in the relationship between extermination as a crime against humanity and genocide.[225] The Trial Chamber

---

[221] Barayagwiza's sentence was reduced from life imprisonment to 35 years: *Nahimana et al.* trial judgment.

[222] The right is protected in Article 10 of the ICTY Statute, Article 9 of the ICTR Statute, Article 9 of the SCSL Statute, and Article 20 of the ICC Statute. See also Article 14(7) of the ICCPR.

[223] *Blockburger* v. *United States*, 284 US 299, 52 S. Ct. 180, 76 L.Ed. 306 (1932).

[224] *Čelebići* appeal judgment, paras 412 and 413; see also *Kordić and Čerkez* appeal judgment, para. 1032; *Stakić* appeal judgment, para. 355; *Musema* appeal judgment, para. 360.

[225] On this matter, see F. M. Palombino, 'Should Genocide Subsume Crimes against Humanity? Some Remarks in the Light of the *Krstic* Appeal Judgment' (2005) 3 *JICJ*, at 778–89.

in *Krstić* adopted the position that it could be maintained that a crime against humanity is always subsumed by genocide, on the assumption that the widespread or systematic attack against a civilian population (the contextual element required for a crime against humanity) 'is comprised within the genocide requirement that there be an intent to destroy a specified type of group'.[226] The Appeals Chamber concluded that the test applied in case law as set out above also covers the *chapeau* elements; since genocide and crimes against humanity differ there — intent to destroy versus widespread or systematic attack against a civilian population — it is always possible to enter convictions for both genocide and crimes against humanity.[227] One of the present authors has submitted that the Appeals Chamber's approach is, in light of the historical ties between crimes against humanity and genocide, unduly formalistic, and that its interpretation of the crime of genocide is inconsistent with the ICC Elements of Crimes.[228] The latter in fact stipulate that '[t]he [genocidal] conduct took place in the context of a manifest pattern of similar conduct directed against that group or was conduct that could itself effect such destruction'. In this light, one cannot speak of a materially distinct element between extermination as a crime against humanity and genocide; thus, fairness, in the sense of protection from a double conviction for the same offence, calls for acquittal on the less specific offence, which would be the crime against humanity.

The protection against double jeopardy is sometimes also advanced in respect of the possibility of the prosecutor appealing acquittals, in the sense that this would unduly expose the individual to a new prosecution for the same facts. This view is particularly strong in common law systems, especially in the case of jury trials, and is generally unknown to civil law systems, where an appeal is regarded as a continuation of a single trial. The prevailing view in international human rights law is that it respects national approaches in this regard.[229] In his separate opinion Judge Nieto-Navia rightly concluded that 'there is no general principle of law that would prohibit Prosecution appeals against acquittals'.[230] Yet, the protective function of *ne bis in idem* has led commentators to challenge the appropriateness of appeals by the prosecution against acquittals, especially appeals concerning factual determinations and when an appeal would be detrimental to the accused.[231] While one may, from a protective perspective, sympathize with this view, the reverse side of the coin is the protection of society. Especially in respect of the most serious allegations of genocide, crimes against humanity, and war crimes there is reason to have a higher court also review acquittals.[232]

---

[226] *Krstić* trial judgment, para. 682.   [227] *Krstić* appeal judgment, paras 222 and 223.

[228] See G. Sluiter's commentary on *Musema* appeal judgment in Klip and Sluiter, *Annotated Leading Cases, vol. X* (2006).

[229] Note the language of Article 14(7) from which it follows that each state may define in its laws what it means by 'finally convicted or acquitted'.

[230] *Tadić* appeal judgment, July 1999, Declaration of Judge Nieto-Navia, p. 9.

[231] See M. C. Fleming, 'Appellate Review in the International Criminal Tribunals' (2002) 37 *Tex. Int'l L.J,.* at 139–42, and Zappalà, *Human Rights in International Criminal Proceedings*, at 171.

[232] It is interesting that Fleming in his critique of the possibility of appealing acquittals on factual grounds contends that an acquittal as a result of errors at first instance may indeed harm the interests of society in not convicting, but that this is a price worth paying for not prolonging criminal proceedings against an individual (M.C. Fleming, 'Appellate Review in the International Criminal Tribunals', at 126). Yet, a similar balancing

8.6 RIGHTS OF DETAINED PERSONS

A rather undeveloped and unexplored area of both human rights law and, as a result, also the law of international criminal tribunals concerns the rights of detained persons, not in the sense of habeas corpus rights, but rather with regard to treatment within penitentiary institutions. Interestingly, the law and practice of international criminal tribunals is remarkably progressive on this point. This has to do with the tribunals being institutions of the UN, in the framework of which important instruments on prisoners' treatment have been developed.[233] These instruments do not represent binding law,[234] but it is difficult for UN institutions to ignore them. This has generally resulted in good conditions of detention for persons in the context of international criminal proceedings. This is not widely appreciated, given the inevitable discrepancies with certain national levels of treatment.[235]

When dealing with the rights of detained persons, a distinction should be made between persons detained prior to conviction in specifically designed detention units and persons detained in national detention facilities after conviction.

The situation of pre-conviction detention is quite simple, in the sense that this detention is governed entirely by the law of the relevant tribunal. To protect the rights of detainees adequately 'Detention Rules' have been adopted.[236] These instruments not only provide for a number of substantive rights, concerning, among other things, communications and visits, work and recreational programmes, but also grant a number of procedural rights, like the right to file complaints. In addition to this enforcement mechanism, the treatment of prisoners is supervised by the ICRC, which has been appointed as inspecting authority.[237] While the detention law of international criminal tribunals offers more than satisfactory conditions for treatment,[238] certain rights have

exercise may produce a different result in international criminal proceedings, where the seriousness of the crimes justifies re-examination of acquittals, even at the expense of protracted proceedings.

[233] Standard Minimum Rules for the Treatment of Prisoners (SMR) (Adopted by ECOSOC Res. 663 C (XXIV), 31 July 1957, amended by ECOSOC Res. 2076 (LXII), 13 May 1977); UN Basic Principles for the Treatment of Prisoners (GA Res. 111 (XXXXV), 14 December 1990); UN Body of Principles for the Protection of All Persons under Any Form of Detention or Imprisonment (GA Res. 173 (XXXXIII), 9 December 1988).

[234] For more detail on these instruments, see N. S. Rodley, *The Treatment of Prisoners under International Law* (2nd edn, New York: Oxford University Press, 1999).

[235] Note in this regard the statement by Rwandan President Kagame in an interview: 'I'm sure there are even Rwandese who are innocent who would want to live in those prisons because they will live better than they do here when they are not prisoners' (cited in W. A. Schabas, *The UN International Criminal Tribunals — The former Yugoslavia, Rwanda and Sierra Leone*, at 578).

[236] Rules Covering the Detention of Persons Awaiting Trial or Appeal before the Tribunal or Otherwise Detained on the Authority of the Tribunal, adopted on 5 May 1994, IT/38/REV.9, UN Doc. IT/38/Rev.4 (1995); Rules Covering the Detention of Persons Awaiting Trial or Appeal before the Tribunal or Otherwise Detained on the Authority of the Tribunal, adopted on 9 January 1996.

[237] The agreement on this matter was concluded through an exchange of letters between the ICTY President, Antonio Cassese, and the President of the ICRC, Cornelio Sommaruga, in May 1995.

[238] Van Zyl Smit in this respect submits that 'it appears that most, but not all, of them are positive, in the sense of leading the way towards the more humane implementation of imprisonment' (D. Van Zyl Smit, 'International

been restricted. For example, Norman (SCSL), Milošević, and Šešelj (ICTY) were considered to be abusing communications with the outside world and their rights in this respect were (temporarily) restricted.[239] However, these measures raise few misgivings, especially in light of certain measures adopted at the national level.

The post-conviction situation is more complicated. Pursuant to Article 27 of the ICTY Statute, a sentence of imprisonment is enforced by a state in accordance with its domestic law, subject to supervision by the Tribunal.[240] The ICTY has set the tone by engaging in far-reaching supervision, which included the imposition of substantive norms protecting the rights of the detained person. Both the *Erdemović* sentencing judgment and the enforcement agreements[241] reflect the importance which the tribunals attach to the applicability of international standards regarding conditions of imprisonment. The Trial Chamber in *Erdemović* 'considers that the penalty imposed as well as the enforcement of such penalty must always conform to the minimum principles of humanity and dignity which constitute the inspiration for the international standards governing the protection of the rights of convicted persons'.[242] The Chamber mentions the following instruments and provisions: Article 10 of the ICCPR, Article 5(2) of the ACHR, Article 3 of the ECHR, Article 5 of the Universal Declaration of Human Rights, the Standard Minimum Rules for the Treatment of Prisoners, the Basic Principles for the Treatment of Prisoners, the Body of Principles for the Protection of All Persons under Any Form of Detention or Imprisonment, the European Prison Rules, and the Rules governing the Detention of Persons Awaiting Trial or Appeal before the Tribunal or otherwise Detained on the Authority of the Tribunal. It is noteworthy that enforcement agreements which the ad hoc tribunals conclude with states to regulate enforcement, including the treatment of prisoners, by and large contain references to the same instruments as those referred to in *Erdemović*.[243]

Since the ad hoc tribunals have made it clear, through their case law and enforcement agreements, that, in the execution of the sentence, the rights of the prisoner should be observed, the question of the enforcement of these rights needs to be addressed. Under Article 6 of the Enforcement Agreements with Italy, France, Finland, Norway, and Sweden, pursuant to Rule 104 of the ICTY RPE,[244] as well as Article 6 of the ICTR agreements with Mali and Benin, pursuant to Article 104 of the ICTR RPE, the ICRC

Imprisonment' (2005) 54 *International Comparative Law Quarterly*, at 384) and he deems '[m]ost significant . . . the recognition that has been given to legal standards in the international prison regime, both in the sense of a prison regime that is formally subject to the rule of law, and of one that follows the substantive requirements of international human rights law in its regimes and objectives' (at 378).

[239] Decision on Motion to Reverse the Order of the Registrar under Rule 48(C) of the Rules of Detention, *Prosecutor* v. *Norman*, Case No. SCSL-04-14-PT, SCSL, President, 18 May 2004; Decision, *Prosecutor* v. *Šešelj*, Case No. IT-03-67-PT, ICTY, Registry, 8 January 2004; and Decision, *Prosecutor* v. *Milošević*, Case No. IT-02-54, ICTY, Registry, 6 February 2004.

[240] See also Article 26 of the ICTR Statute and Article 22 of the SCSL Statute.

[241] The ICTY has concluded enforcement agreements with the UK, Denmark, Germany, Spain, France, Sweden, Austria, Norway, Finland, and Italy; with the exception of the UK and Germany, these agreements are available at www.un.org/icty/legaldoc-e/index.htm (last visited 17 November 2006). The ICTR has concluded agreements with Swaziland, Benin, Mali, Italy, France, and Sweden, all available at www.ictr.org (last visited 17 November 2006).   [242] *Erdemović* sentencing judgment (no. 1), para. 74.

[243] E.g., agreements with Italy, Norway, France, Finland, Spain and Sweden, Mali, and Benin.

[244] This rule provides: 'All sentences of imprisonment shall be supervised by the Tribunal or a body designated by it.'

has been given the task of inspecting the conditions of detention and treatment of the prisoners.[245] The agreement with Austria provides for the prison conditions to be monitored but without specifically designating a monitoring body.[246] The agreement with Spain provides for a special monitoring commission, composed of two representatives of Spain and two of the ICTY.[247] The 'monitoring commission', whether the ICRC, a special commission, or representatives of the Tribunal, may, according to the enforcement agreements, inspect the conditions of detention and the treatment of prisoners at any time and on a periodic basis. The findings of the inspections will be submitted, in a confidential report, to the enforcing state and the President of the Tribunal. The President may, after consultations regarding the report with the enforcing state, request the state to report to him or her any changes in the condition of detention suggested by the 'monitoring commission'. It is not stipulated, though, that a prisoner can trigger an inspection by lodging a complaint. The ensuing inspection report may lead to consultations with the enforcing state on appropriate steps to be taken. All the enforcement agreements in force provide that, as an ultimate sanction the Tribunal might request that enforcement of the sentence of imprisonment in that state be terminated, if the 'monitoring commission' had found that the state was mistreating the detainee.

The very high standard of protection of detainees convicted by the ad hoc tribunals has only partially been incorporated into the law of the ICC. The negotiating states were undoubtedly aware that many states would find it difficult to meet the standard of treatment afforded by the ad hoc tribunals, which explicitly recommended UN instruments as applicable law. Add to this a general antipathy to unwritten international law at the Rome negotiations,[248] and the result is the language of Article 106 of the ICC Statute. According to that provision, the standard of treatment to be applied and the object of supervision by the Court is that of widely accepted international treaty standards governing treatment in prisons. This is basically a step backwards from the practice of the ad hoc tribunals, as it excludes all the UN recommendations and leaves us basically with the lower standard of Article 10 of the ICCPR.[249]

8.7 CONCLUSION

The human rights and due process part of international criminal law offers a very mixed picture, where the law varies as easily from under- to over-protective as it does between different tribunals. This makes it virtually impossible to state any firm

---

[245] A. Klip criticizes the choice of the ICRC as inspecting body. He argues that the ICRC has no experience whatsoever in supervising the treatment of prisoners in penitentiary institutions; he would have preferred entrusting this task to the European Committee for the Prevention of Torture and Inhuman or Degrading Treatment or Punishment. See A. Klip, 'Enforcement of Sanctions Imposed by the International Criminal Tribunals for Rwanda and the Former Yugoslavia' (1997) 5 *European J. of Crime, Criminal Law and Criminal Justice*, at 150–1.

[246] See Article 6(1) of that agreement, authorizing 'visits of prisoner(s) by the International Tribunal, or an entity designated by it'.   [247] See Article 4(1) of that agreement.

[248] Cf. R. S. Clark, 'Article 106', in Triffterer, *Commentary on the Rome Statute*, at 1178.

[249] For more detail, see C. Kress and G. Sluiter, 'Enforcement', in Cassese et al., *Rome Statute Commentary*, at 1723–810.

conclusions, but one may nevertheless indicate certain general trends, in terms of strong and weak points.

A first positive note is that tribunals generally have resisted the temptation to restrict the full application of human rights law to elements visible in the courtroom. As a result, methods of arrest are thoroughly reviewed and the ICC has imposed specific obligations for national arrest proceedings. Secondly, international criminal law is over-protective in light of international human rights law concerning typical common-law elements. The most important examples are the privilege against self-incrimination, especially its effect on the protection of individuals in the course of interrogations, and the right to question witnesses. An interesting question is whether this incongruence between international criminal law and human rights law will result in any significant changes in these bodies of law in the future.[250] The status of the ad hoc tribunals as UN institutions has also resulted in a very progressive standard of treatment of detained persons.

In contrast to these positive notes, there are a number of lacunae in human rights protection. The most obvious are undoubtedly the unfortunate approach to habeas corpus rights by the ad hoc tribunals, the extreme length of both pre-trial detention and trials, and the absence of the right to financial compensation for unlawful arrest and conviction. It must be recognized that these lacunae at present concern only the ad hoc tribunals and to a lesser degree the SCSL. The law of the ICC is certainly an improvement on these matters. This may lead one to conclude that the aforementioned short-comings are an inevitable consequence of an initial 'trial and error' period for these new tribunals. In part, this is undoubtedly the case, as certain matters have clearly improved. Yet, there is also the notion, underlying lengthy trials and the view of pre-trial detention as a rule, that the importance of the tribunals' mandate allows for a different level of protection than is available in ordinary trials. This notion should be dismissed, for at least two reasons. First, it is generally unnecessary, as both human rights law regarding habeas corpus and length of trials offers sufficient leeway to discharge an effective mandate. Secondly, human rights courts have generally condemned such an approach on the part of governments, which attempted to justify their actions in light of the serious nature of a certain crime, on the grounds of the 'minimum standards' nature of fundamental human rights.

---

[250] One may think of international criminal law aligning with human rights law, but conversely one can also conceive of the situation that the standards adopted by international criminal tribunals may lead human rights courts to a more progressive interpretation of their standards. On this latter possibility, see G. Sluiter, 'Raadsman bij politieverhoor: De dimensie van het internationale strafprocesrecht', in A. H. E. C. Jordaans et al. (eds), *Praktisch strafrecht. Liber Amicorum J. M. Reijntjes* (Nijmegen: Wolf Legal Publishers, 2005), at 525–40.

9

LITIGATION LANDMARKS IN THE PREPARATION AND CONDUCT OF TRIALS

SUMMARY

9.1 INTRODUCTION

Some of the most interesting legal and factual issues at the international tribunals arise and are dealt with well before the prosecutor's (or the defence's) case goes to trial.[1] Defendants face long pre-trial periods, often much longer than the trial itself. The process begins even before they become defendants, when they are still suspects. Rules govern the prosecutor's pre-indictment investigations.[2] There are litigation opportunities and political obstacles at every step along the way. The indictment must be confirmed by a reviewing judge.[3] Once the indictment and arrest warrant are issued, we enter the arrest phase, which may be rapid or take many years,[4] depending on which state the accused person is residing in, the current political climate in that state, and the

---

[1] The ICTY and the ICTR both have a rule on preliminary motions (Rule 72), which is narrow in its scope. The motions considered in this chapter relate to several other rules also.

[2] See Rules 39 to 43 of the ICTY's Rules of Procedure and Evidence (RPE).   [3] Ibid., Rule 47.

[4] Ibid., Rules 53 *bis*, 55, 60.

state's current relationship with the ad hoc tribunal in question, among other factors. When the accused person is arrested, he or she will be transferred to the seat of the tribunal, which can be a slow process if, for example, the arrest was made in a third country which must first extradite the arestee to his or her home country.[5] Then comes the ceremony of the initial appearance, at which the accused person pleads guilty or not guilty to the charges.[6]

If there is a guilty plea, there will be no trial as such.[7] The tribunal may decide to refer the defendant's case to a municipal court for trial, if it is not a high-profile case.[8] Provisional release (bail) applications are granted, but with difficulty, in the international context.[9] The form that an indictment acquires in the course of pre-trial litigation (during which it may change more than once) will affect the running of the trial all the way through to the end of the appeal stage.[10] Litigation over the tribunal's legality or its jurisdiction over the defendant is common.[11] Discovery and witness protection orders are also major events of the pre-trial stage.[12] The large size of a typical tribunal case, combined with the overlapping 'crime bases' in most cases (the same crimes seen from different vantage points), have provided grounds for introducing evidence in the form of 'facts' adjudicated in prior cases[13] or in the form of written testimony — bundles of transcripts of testimony from prior cases, or written statements by persons not appearing before the tribunals, or appearing only for cross-examination.[14] Several lesser steps must be completed (for example, the filing of pre-trial briefs) before a case is ready to go to trial.[15] If there is no case to answer after

---

[5] Ibid., Rules 56 to 59.   [6] Ibid., Rule 62.

[7] ICTY (RPE), Rules 62 *bis*, 62 *ter*. As at the end of 2006, there had been many more guilty pleas at the ICTY than the ICTR. This is almost certainly due to the unusually harsh treatment (a life sentence) meted out to Jean Kambanda, the former prime minister of Rwanda, who was the first to plead guilty at the ICTR. Five sentencing judgments for guilty pleas have been issued by the ICTR since then (see the cases of Omar Serushago, Georges Ruggiu, Vincent Rutaganira, Paul Bisengimana, and Joseph Serugendo). Over the same period, by contrast, the ICTY prosecutor has managed to have sentenced 19 persons on pleas of guilty.   [8] ICTY (RPE), Rule 11 *bis*.

[9] ICTY (RPE), Rule 65.

[10] ICTY (RPE), Rules 48, 49 (joinder of accused or crimes); Rules 50, 72, 73 *bis* (amendment and reduction of indictment's scope).   [11] ICTY (RPE), Rule 72.

[12] ICTY (RPE), Rules 66, 67, 68 (disclosure); 69, 70, 75 (protective measures).

[13] ICTY (RPE), Rule 94. Hundreds of factual findings can be recycled and used in later cases under certain conditions. These are called 'adjudicated facts'. (The option provided for in Rule 94 of taking judicial notice of 'documentary evidence' from other proceedings had not been tested at the time of writing.) The onus is on the defendant to refute adjudicated facts by calling countervailing evidence. See, e.g., at the ICTY: *Prosecutor* v. *Stanković*, Decision on Prosecution's Motion for Judicial Notice Pursuant to Rule 94(B), 16 May 2003; *Prosecutor* v. *Milošević*, Separate Opinion of Judge Shahabuddeen Appended to the Appeals Chamber's Decision Dated 28 October 2003 on the Prosecution's Interlocutory Appeal Against the Trial Chamber's 10 April 2003 Decision on Prosecution Motion for Judicial Notice of Adjudicated Facts, 31 October 2003; *Prosecutor* v. *Milošević*, Final Decision on Prosecution Motion for Judicial Notice of Adjudicated Facts, 16 December 2003; and *Prosecutor* v. *Popović et al.*, Decision on Prosecution Motion for Judicial Notice of Adjudicated Facts, 26 September 2006. The *Krajišnik* judgment of the ICTY is an example of a judgment which made considerable use of adjudicated facts to reach its own factual conclusions. At the ICTR: *Prosecutor* v. *Karemera et al.*, Decision on Prosecution Motion for Judicial Notice, 9 November 2005. And at the SCSL: *Prosecutor* v. *Norman et al.*, Decision on Prosecution's Motion for Judicial Notice and Admission of Evidence, 2 June 2004; and *Prosecutor* v. *Norman et al.*, Fofana — Decision on Appeal Against 'Decision on Prosecution's Motion for Judicial Notice and Admission of Evidence', 16 May 2005.   [14] ICTY, Rules 92 *bis*, 92 *ter*, 92 *quater*.

[15] ICTY, Rules 65 *ter*, 73 *bis*.

the prosecutor's evidence has been heard, there will be no defence case: the trial will be cut short.[16] Only some of these topics will be considered in detail in this chapter.[17]

9.2 MATTERS OF JURISDICTION

There have been many challenges to the jurisdiction of the tribunals. The early global challenge in the ICTY's *Tadić* case led to the remarkably influential *Tadić* jurisdiction appeal decision of October 1995. First the ICTY, then the ICTR, and more recently the Special Court for Sierra Leone have emerged intact (although not unbruised) from sweeping attacks on their competence.

Jurisdictional issues have been taken up also in narrowly targeted pre-trial motions on the form of the indictment. These are mostly dealt with in the next section.

Duško Tadić alleged before a Trial Chamber of the ICTY that the Tribunal had been illegally founded; that its purported primacy over national courts was wrongful; and that the ICTY lacked jurisdiction *ratione materiae*. His motion was dismissed,[18] and he appealed. The Appeals Chamber, in addressing the first issue, which the Trial Chamber had found (in accordance with the prosecutor's urgings) was not within its legal competence to deal with,[19] defined competence as 'a legal power, hence necessarily a legitimate power', of the tribunal 'to state the law' within the ambit of its temporal, personal, and subject-matter jurisdiction 'in an authoritative and final manner'.[20] The pioneering and thus spare institutional context of international criminal tribunals requires a broad conception of jurisdiction, according to the Appeals Chamber:

International law, because it lacks a centralized structure, does not provide for an integrated judicial system operating an orderly division of labour among a number of tribunals, where certain aspects

---

[16] ICTY, Rule 98 *bis*. There has been a decision pursuant to this rule in almost every case that has gone to trial. The test is whether a prima facie case has been made for each count. Perhaps the most controversial decision was in the early *Jelisić* case: see the *Jelisić* trial and appeal judgments for more details. The rule was changed in December 2004 to force Trial Chambers to hear motions for acquittal and deliver decisions on them orally. Prior to that point, Rule 98 *bis* decisions had begun to evolve into elaborate judgments. See, e.g., *Prosecutor* v. *Milošević*, Decision on Motion for Judgment of Acquittal, 16 June 2004, which is 63,000 words long.

[17] Some of the aforementioned topics are dealt with in other chapters of this book. See also Cassese, *International Criminal Law*, pp. 406–18; Dixon and Khan, *Archbold*, pp. 135–201; and Klip and Sluiter, *Annotated Leading Cases*, *passim*.

[18] *Prosecutor* v. *Tadić*, Decision on the Defence Motion on Jurisdiction in the Trial Chamber of the International Tribunal, 10 August 1995.

[19] The Trial Chamber had said (ibid., para. 8):

it is one thing for the Security Council to have taken every care to ensure that a structure appropriate to the conduct of fair trials has been created; it is an entirely different thing in any way to infer from that careful structuring that it was intended that the International Tribunal be empowered to question the legality of the law which established it. The competence of the International Tribunal is precise and narrowly defined; as described in Article 1 of its Statute, it is to prosecute persons responsible for serious violations of international humanitarian law, subject to spatial and temporal limits, and to do so in accordance with the Statute. That is the full extent of the competence of the International Tribunal.

[20] *Tadić* jurisdiction appeal decision, para. 10. See also *Prosecutor* v. *Kanyabashi*, Decision on the Defence Motion for Interlocutory Appeal on the Jurisdiction of Trial Chamber I, 3 June 1999; Separate Opinion of Judges McDonald and Vohrah, para. 4, and Dissenting Opinion of Judge Shahabuddeen, pp. 2–3.

or components of jurisdiction as a power could be centralized or vested in one of them but not the others. In international law, every tribunal is a self-contained system (unless otherwise provided).[21]

This is not an argument or justification, of course; it is merely an observation.

According to the Appeals Chamber, the ICTY enjoys, moreover, an incidental or inherent jurisdiction which is integral to the exercise of the judicial function. It does not need to be expressly provided for in the constitutive document of the international tribunal.[22] The ICTY's incidental jurisdiction enables it to ascertain whether it is in a position to exercise its primary jurisdiction over the matter before it. The Appeals Chamber thus reasoned that Duško Tadić's first ground could have been heard by the Trial Chamber on the merits.[23]

Prior to examining the first ground, it is instructive to compare the above analysis of *Tadić* with the position taken by the Appeals Chamber in an important decision in the *Blaškić* case. An ICTY Trial Chamber had affirmed the order of a judge purporting to subpoena Croatia and Croatia's defence minister.[24] It was found on appeal that the tribunal has no power to take enforcement measures (as entailed by a subpoena) against states, or against state officials acting in their official capacity. The Appeals Chamber said that, had the drafters of the tribunal's statute intended to vest the ICTY with such a power, they would have expressly provided for it, for this is not a power that may be regarded as inherent in the functions of an international judicial body.[25]

While subpoenas to states are unsustainable, binding orders to states (although not to state officials acting in their official capacity) are, by contrast, allowed by operation of Article 29 of the ICTY Statute. Such orders might enjoin a state to produce documents or to arrest an individual. The Appeals Chamber pointed out, however, that the question is not really one of 'jurisdiction':

The Prosecutor has submitted that Article 29 expressly grants the International Tribunal 'ancillary jurisdiction over States.' However . . . the primary jurisdiction of the International Tribunal, namely its power to exercise judicial functions, relates to natural persons only. . . . To avoid any confusion . . . when considering Article 29 it is probably more accurate simply to speak of the International Tribunal's ancillary (or incidental) mandatory powers vis-à-vis States.[26]

Tadić's argument on the first ground of his appeal was that, for the ICTY to be duly established by law, it should have been created by treaty (the consensual act of nations), or by amendment of the Charter of the United Nations. In any case, it should not have been created through a resolution of the Security Council. The Appeals Chamber answered that Chapter VII of the UN Charter gives the Security Council a wide discretion. It is for the Council to make the determination that there exists a situation

---

[21] *Tadić* jurisdiction appeal decision, para. 11.

[22] The Appeals Chamber here relied on the principle of 'Kompetenz-Kompetenz', also known as 'la compétence de la compétence'; *Tadić* jurisdiction appeal decision, para. 18.

[23] Judge Li dissented on this point. The majority's position was affirmed in subsequent cases; see, e.g., *Prosecutor v. Milošević*, Decision on Preliminary Motions, 8 November 2001, paras 16–17.

[24] *Prosecutor v. Blaškić*, Decision on the Objection of the Republic of Croatia to the Issuance of Subpoenae Duces Tecum, 18 July 1997.

[25] *Prosecutor v. Blaškić*, Judgment (Appeals Chamber) on the Request of the Republic of Croatia for Review of the Decision of Trial Chamber II, 29 October 1997, para. 25.   [26] Ibid., para. 28.

justifying the use of the 'exceptional powers' mentioned in Chapter VII, including a situation of 'threat to the peace'.[27] The armed conflict or series of conflicts under way in the territory of the former Yugoslavia clearly constituted (in 1993, when the resolution in question was passed) a threat to the peace in south-east Europe, in the Appeals Chamber's view. Once such a determination is made, the Security Council again enjoys a wide discretion — though within the limits of Chapter VII of the Charter — in choosing a course of action.[28] Article 41 of the Charter (which is part of Chapter VII) speaks of 'measures not involving the use of armed force'.[29] According to the Appeals Chamber, it was open to the Security Council to read into this the establishment of an international tribunal.[30]

As for the principle that a tribunal must be established by law, this is achieved in the international domain — where there is no legislature to enact laws binding on international subjects — when the court is rooted in the rule of law. If the ICTY were indeed created pursuant to a power in the constitution of the United Nations, and if the ICTY offers the guarantees of fairness and justice in conformity with internationally recognized human-rights instruments, then it is a tribunal established by law.[31] The *Tadić* Appeals Chamber found that both conditions were satisfied. (In a motion many years later raising the same issue, Slobodan Milošević argued that the creation of an ad hoc court directed at events in one country 'corrupts justice and law'. The Trial Chamber in that case responded that international human-rights bodies have stated on several occasions that there is nothing inherently illegitimate in the creation of an ad hoc court, and that the important question is whether it has been established by law.)[32]

Tadić's second ground of appeal was that the creation of an international criminal tribunal violates state sovereignty. Just as no state can assume jurisdiction to prosecute crimes committed on the territory of another state, barring, as Tadić put it, a universal interest justified by treaty or customary international law or an *opinio juris* on the issue, so the establishment of an international tribunal destined to invade an area essentially within the domestic jurisdiction of states must be wrongful.[33] The Trial Chamber said, rather glibly, that the sovereign rights of states should not take precedence over the right of the international community to act appropriately, because serious breaches of international humanitarian law 'affect the whole of mankind and shock the conscience of all nations of the world'.[34] The Appeals Chamber agreed with the Trial Chamber, adding that the ICTY's endowment with primacy over national courts was inevitable: 'human nature being what it is', it said, there is a perennial danger of international crimes being

---

[27] *Tadić* jurisdiction appeal decision, para. 29.   [28] Ibid., para. 32.

[29] The Article reads in full:

> The Security Council may decide what measures not involving the use of armed force are to be employed to give effect to its decisions, and it may call upon the Members of the United Nations to apply such measures. These may include complete or partial interruption of economic relations and of rail, sea, air, postal, telegraphic, radio, and other means of communication, and the severance of diplomatic relations.

[30] *Tadić* jurisdiction appeal decision, paras 35–6.   [31] Ibid., para. 42.

[32] *Prosecutor* v. *Milošević*, Decision on Preliminary Motions, 8 November 2001, paras 8–9.

[33] Cited in *Tadić* jurisdiction appeal decision, para. 55.

[34] *Prosecutor* v. *Tadić*, Decision on the Defence Motion on Jurisdiction in the Trial Chamber of the International Tribunal, 10 August 1995, para. 42.

re-characterized by rogue states as ordinary crimes, or dealt with in state proceedings designed to shield the accused, or being waylaid in cases which are not diligently prosecuted by states.[35]

The reader should be aware that the argumentation in this section of the *Tadić* jurisdiction appeal decision is not persuasive, as will be evident from the following passage:

> It would be a travesty of law and a betrayal of the universal need for justice, should the concept of State sovereignty be allowed to be raised successfully against human rights. Borders should not be considered as a shield against the reach of the law and as a protection for those who trample underfoot the most elementary rights of humanity.[36]

This is akin to a manifesto by a human-rights NGO. No less self-serving is this state-ment: 'True, he will be removed from his "natural" national forum; but he will be brought before a tribunal at least equally fair, more distanced from the facts of the case and taking a broader view of the matter.'[37] This is trivially true — and true of any crime that the defendant may have committed. It is not clear why distance and a broader view should be regarded by a defendant as compensatory.[38]

Tadić maintained on appeal that the alleged crimes were committed in the context of an internal armed conflict. According to Tadić, the ICTY has subject-matter juris-diction over grave breaches of the Geneva Conventions (Article 2 of the ICTY Statute), violations of the laws or customs of war (Article 3), and crimes against humanity (Article 5), only to the extent that they are committed in the context of an *international* armed conflict. The Trial Chamber had concluded that Articles 3 and 5 each apply to both internal and international armed conflict, and that an international armed con-flict is *not* a jurisdictional criterion of grave breaches.[39]

The Appeals Chamber determined, generally, that the armed conflict in the former Yugoslavia could be described as internal or international, depending on the time and place.[40] This was sufficient to dispense with the first part of Tadić's argument. (The holding has not been relied on much in later cases, where greater specificity is required in this respect.) The Appeals Chamber then corrected the Trial Chamber on grave

---

[35] *Tadić* jurisdiction appeal decision, para. 58.   [36] Ibid.   [37] Ibid., para. 62.

[38] From Nuremberg onwards, international criminal tribunals have appealed to the enormity of the crimes they usually deal with, as well as to the (supposed) beneficial impact of the tribunals on peace and reconciliation, to excuse any number of conceptual and procedural shortcuts. For example, the ICTY Appeals Chamber attempted to justify why the kidnapping of one accused, Dragan Nikolić, by unknown individuals who surrendered him to agents of the tribunal, does not preclude jurisdiction *ratione personae*:

> Universally condemned offences are a matter of concern to the international community as a whole. There is a legitimate expectation that those accused of these crimes will be brought to justice swiftly. Accountability for these crimes is a necessary condition for the achievement of international justice, which plays a critical role in the reconciliation and rebuilding based on the rule of law of countries and societies torn apart by inter-national and internecine conflicts. This legitimate expectation needs to be weighed against the principle of State sovereignty and the fundamental human rights of the accused. (*Prosecutor v. Nikolić*, Decision on Interlocutory Appeal Concerning Legality of Arrest, 5 June 2003, paras 25–6.)

[39] *Prosecutor v. Tadić*, Decision on the Defence Motion on Jurisdiction in the Trial Chamber of the International Tribunal, 10 August 1995, paras 50–3. (One can easily forget how little was known about these matters 12 years ago.)

[40] *Tadić* jurisdiction appeal decision, paras 72–7.

breaches, agreeing with Tadić that 'persons or property protected under the provisions' of the Geneva Conventions (the words found in Article 2 of the ICTY Statute) must be given the meaning which they have in the Conventions. Thus, their coverage is limited to persons or objects caught up in an international armed conflict.[41]

Article 3 of the ICTY Statute is also, on its face, all about international armed conflict. Its clauses derive mainly from the 1907 Hague Convention IV and its regulations, and in any case do not post-date 1945.[42] This should mean that they do *not* concern the regulation of internal strife, in the sense that they were not drawn up for this purpose. Yet, the Appeals Chamber was prepared to be much less literal in this instance than it was with Article 2. It is an interpretation tending to promote the development of international criminal law on all fronts.

The Appeals Chamber recognized, on the one hand, that the expression 'violations of the laws or customs of war' (as it occurs in Article 3 of the ICTY Statute) is a traditional term of art from a time when the concepts of 'war' and 'laws of warfare' still prevailed. The Appeals Chamber insisted, on the other hand, that the expression now encompasses two broader notions, 'armed conflict' (introduced by the Geneva Conventions) and the more recent notion of 'international humanitarian law' (which emerged as a result of the influence of human rights doctrines on the law of armed conflict).[43] With no further argumentation worth repeating here, the ICTY Appeals Chamber concluded that Article 3 of the Tribunal's Statute 'may be construed to include other infringements of international humanitarian law. The only limitation is that such infringements must not be already covered' by Article 2 of the ICTY Statute. Accordingly, Article 3 is to be understood to cover *all* violations of international humanitarian law other than grave breaches.[44]

The Appeals Chamber proceeded to limit, somewhat, the use of the carte blanche it had handed the Tribunal,[45] but its point of departure is faulty. If the framers of the ICTY Statute had wanted Article 3 to give the Tribunal broad-ranging jurisdiction over war crimes, including crimes committed in internal armed conflict, why did they choose the very specific — and, according to the Appeals Chamber, *dated* — language of the 1907 Hague Convention? The UN Secretary-General, in his commentary on the draft ICTY Statute, had implied a similarly narrow scope.[46]

---

[41] Ibid., para. 81. See, however, the comment in para. 83 about the 'recent trend' away from the above interpretation, and especially Judge Abi-Saab's separate opinion on the subject.

[42] The wording of Article 3 of the ICTY Statute derives mostly from the 1907 Hague Convention, with the remaining parts taken from the Charter of the Nuremberg Tribunal or from the 1945 Control Council Law No. 10.

[43] *Tadić* jurisdiction appeal decision, para. 87; also paras 96–7.

[44] Ibid., paras 87–91; in particular:

   (i) violations of the Hague law on international conflicts; (ii) infringements of provisions of the Geneva Conventions other than those classified as 'grave breaches' by those Conventions; (iii) violations of common Article 3 and other customary rules on internal conflicts; (iv) violations of agreements binding upon the parties to the conflict, considered qua treaty law, i.e., agreements which have not turned into customary international law (ibid., para. 89).

   See also the Separate Opinion of Judge Sidhwa, paras 117–18.

[45] Ibid., para. 94; see further Chapter 4 in this book.

[46] Report of the Secretary-General on ICTY, paras 41–4.

The alternative view is that it is inconceivable that the framers did not intend (or that they simply forgot) to give the ICTY jurisdiction over crimes so universal as those encompassed by Common Article 3 of the Geneva Conventions. One might therefore sympathize with the Appeals Chamber's effort to find a home for Common Article 3 in Article 3 of the ICTY Statute,[47] even if by doing so the Appeals Chamber did not follow the usual rules of statutory interpretation, giving cause to one defence team to describe this effort as 'carefully manufactured ex post facto history'.[48] (As discussed in Chapter 4, Common Article 3 has in the meantime almost taken over its new home: rarely has the prosecutor used Article 3 of the ICTY Statute to charge an offence which is not a Common Article 3 offence.)[49]

It would surely have been more satisfactory for the Appeals Chamber to have referred the Article 3 question back to the legislator (the Security Council) for possible amendment of the Statute. But the Tribunals have never sought to inconvenience the Security Council with such a request, and from *Tadić* onwards the ICTY Appeals Chamber has remained protective of its purported power to pronounce on the Tribunal's jurisdiction, as the following passage indicates:

The Statute of the International Tribunal sets the framework within which the Tribunal may exercise its jurisdiction. A crime or a form of liability which is not provided for in the Statute could not form the basis of a conviction before this Tribunal. The reference to that crime or to that form of liability does not need, however, to be explicit to come within the purview of the Tribunal's jurisdiction. The Statute of the ICTY is not and does not purport to be, unlike for instance the Rome Statute of the International Criminal Court, a meticulously detailed code providing explicitly for every possible scenario and every solution thereto.[50]

Tadić argued, finally, that crimes against humanity within the ICTY's jurisdiction must be limited to those acts committed 'in execution of or in connection with' a crime against international peace, or a war crime, which recalls the limitation on crimes against humanity in Article 6 of the Charter of the Nuremberg IMT. The resulting condition of an international armed conflict for crimes against humanity is not defeated, according to Tadić, by the presence of the words 'whether international or internal in character' in Article 5 of the ICTY Statute.[51] The Appeals Chamber dismissed this argument, noting, among other things, that the 1945 Control Council Law No. 10 of the Allied administration of Germany did not adopt the Nuremberg Charter's jurisdictional limitation, which is not part of the customary-law definition of the offence.[52]

The jurisdictional challenge directed at the ICTR was answered in a relatively brief decision of no lasting value.[53] The decision claimed to rely on the *Tadić* jurisdiction

---

[47] *Tadić* jurisdiction appeal decision, para. 102.

[48] *Prosecutor* v. *Kordić and Čerkez*, Decision on the Joint Defence Motion to Dismiss the Amended Indictment for Lack of Jurisdiction Based on the Limited Jurisdictional Reach of Articles 2 and 3, 2 March 1999, para. 4. See, similarly, *Prosecutor* v. *Kvočka et al.*, Decision on Preliminary Motions Filed by Mlado Radić and Miroslav Kvočka Challenging Jurisdiction, 1 April 1999, para. 12.   [49] See Chapter 4.

[50] *Prosecutor* v. *Milutinović et al.*, Decision (Appeals Chamber) on Dragoljub Ojdanić's Motion Challenging Jurisdiction — Joint Criminal Enterprise, 21 May 2003, para. 18.

[51] *Tadić* jurisdiction appeal decision, para. 139.   [52] Ibid., paras 140–2.

[53] *Prosecutor* v. *Kanyabashi*, Decision on the Defence Motion on Jurisdiction, 18 June 1997.

appeal decision, even though the ICTR's situation was different in important respects. Rwanda voted *against* Security Council Resolution 955 establishing the ICTR (the only state to do so), giving as one of its reasons that the Tribunal was foreclosed from imposing the death penalty.[54] The answer of the Trial Chamber to Joseph Kanyabashi's claim that state sovereignty had been violated by the Tribunal's establishment was that 'membership of the United Nations entails certain limitations upon the sovereignty of the member States' (without indicating what limitations), and that the ICTR had been brought into being 'with the participation of the Government of Rwanda' — an ambiguous if not misleading statement.[55]

Kanyabashi also argued that in November 1994, when Resolution 955 was passed, the situation in Rwanda did not pose a threat to international peace and security, and thus the precondition for action under Chapter VII of the UN Charter was not fulfilled. The armed conflict in Rwanda had come to an end in July 1994. All ICTR indictments concern the period April to July 1994. The ICTR was not created midway though the conflict, as was the ICTY, but after the event.

The Trial Chamber's answer to this plausible argument was weak. It stated that the Security Council 'has a wide margin of discretion in deciding when and where there exists a threat to international peace and security. By their very nature, however, such discretionary assessments are not justiciable'.[56] This is a paradoxical remark, which moreover contradicts the analysis adopted by the Appeals Chamber in the *Tadić* jurisdiction appeal decision.[57] It also makes decision-making on questions of legality relatively predictable: the defence's motion will almost invariably fail because the Security Council's discretion is 'wide'.

The *Kanyabashi* Trial Chamber then proceeded to undermine its own premise about non-justiciability by taking 'judicial notice' of the fact that the Rwandan conflict had caused a flow of refugees into neighbouring countries. This, the Trial Chamber maintained, could plausibly have been regarded by the Security Council as a threat to the peace.[58] Needless to say, the ICTR was not established to deal with any consequences of the refugee situation, but with the crimes committed in a conflict that had drawn to a close several months earlier.

The ICTR is still the object of allegations of partiality, a point made already in 1997 by Kanyabashi.[59] According to some witnesses and investigators, the killing of two heads of state — the presidents of Rwanda and Burundi — on 6 April 1994, which was immediately followed by widespread violence and chaos in Rwanda, was the work of insurgents under the command of Paul Kagame, the rebel leader who has been in control of

---

[54] *Minutes of the 3453rd Meeting of the Security Council*, 8 November 1994, UN Doc. S/PV.3453, pp. 13–16.

[55] *Prosecutor* v. *Kanyabashi*, Decision on the Defence Motion on Jurisdiction, 18 June 1997, paras 13, 15.

[56] Ibid., para. 20.

[57] *Tadić* jurisdiction appeal decision, paras 29–30. *Kanyabashi* influenced another Trial Chamber to make the same error: see *Prosecutor* v. *Karemera*, Decision on the Defence Motion Pertaining to Lack of Jurisdiction and Defects in the Form of the Indictment, 25 April 2001, para. 25.

[58] *Prosecutor* v. *Kanyabashi*, Decision on the Defence Motion on Jurisdiction, 18 June 1997, para. 21; see also para. 26.

[59] Ibid., para. 47. See also *Prosecutor* v. *Karemera*, Decision on the Defence Motion Pertaining to Lack of Jurisdiction and Defects in the Form of the Indictment, 25 April 2001, paras 26–7.

Rwanda since July 1994. Remarkably, no member of the insurgency has been brought before the ICTR to answer for war crimes.[60]

In a different context, Slobodan Milošević asserted that 'the very psychology of the [ICTY] is persecutorial' — that is, anti-Serb. The *Milošević* Trial Chamber was able to respond, plausibly enough, that the accused had advanced no grounds on which an observer, properly informed, would reasonably apprehend bias on the part of the institution.[61] This cannot be said with the same plausibility about the ICTR. And so the legality question — is the ICTR a tribunal 'established by law'? — was left unresolved.

At the Sierra Leone tribunal the jurisdictional challenge went directly to the Appeals Chamber.[62] The main issues there were whether the SCSL has the competence to determine the lawfulness of its own establishment, and, if so, whether it was lawfully created. The first was dealt with summarily, by reference to the court rules, which state that 'serious' issues relating to jurisdiction are to be referred to the Appeals Chamber — which is not to say, of course, that the Appeals Chamber is competent to address them in every instance. But this point was passed over.[63]

The Special Court agreement between the UN and the Government of Sierra Leone was ratified by the country's Parliament in March 2002 in accordance with the constitution; or, in the submissions of two of the accused, in *breach* of the constitution, which states that the judicial power of Sierra Leone is vested in the judiciary of which the Chief Justice is the head.[64] The Appeals Chamber responded that the SCSL does not form part of the country's judiciary, a clear enough answer, which however does not seem to accord with the UN Secretary-General's description of the SCSL as a 'treaty-based sui generis court of mixed jurisdiction and composition'.[65] The Appeals Chamber's response begs the question whether the Government of Sierra Leone had the power to form a judicial institution which is not part of the country's judiciary.

The purported primacy of the SCSL over the courts of Sierra Leone was said by the appellants also to be unconstitutional, since the final court of adjudication in the constitutional framework is the country's Supreme Court. In its inadequate and vaguely worded reply, the SCSL Appeals Chamber asserted that the SCSL is not part of the national court structure, but is rather an international court with jurisdiction 'in an entirely international sphere'.[66]

Finally, the Special Court's Appeals Chamber stated incorrectly that the Appeals Chamber of the ICTY had agreed with the UN Secretary-General's claim that Common Article 3 of the Geneva Conventions had been for the first time criminalized with the establishment of the ICTR.[67] The SCSL's few comments on its jurisdiction *ratione materiae* are a misstatement of the law.

---

[60] See further A. Zahar and S. Rohol, 'The International Criminal Tribunal for Rwanda', in S. Totten (ed.), *Genocide at the Millennium: A Critical Bibliographic Review* (Transaction, 2005), pp. 209–39.

[61] *Prosecutor* v. *Milošević*, Decision on Preliminary Motions, 8 November 2001, paras 18, 22.

[62] *Prosecutor* v. *Kallon et al.*, Decision (Appeals Chamber) on Constitutionality and Lack of Jurisdiction, 13 March 2004. The bypassing of the Trial Chamber is provided for in Rule 72(E) of the SCSL.

[63] Ibid., para. 37.　　[64] Ibid., para. 47.　　[65] Cited ibid., para. 42.　　[66] Ibid., paras 68–71, 80.

[67] Ibid., para. 81. The reference to para. 178 of the *Delalić et al.* appeal judgment does not support this claim; see, moreover, *Delalić et al.* appeal judgment, para. 163 and the discussion on the criminalization of Common Article 3 in Chapter 4.

In sum, the decisions of the three tribunals on their legality and jurisdiction are unpersuasive.

In the case of the ICTY and the ICTR, the sweeping early defence motions on jurisdiction were succeeded by narrower attacks whose aim was to invalidate or prune the indictments (they are thus not always distinguishable from preliminary motions on the form of the indictment, a topic dealt with in the next section), or to make a special case for why a defendant may not be lawfully tried.

Thus, for example, the amici curiae in the *Milošević* case claimed that the ICTY does not have jurisdiction over former heads of state. This was easily dismissed.[68] Somewhat strained, by comparison, was the Trial Chamber's response to the argument that the ICTY lacks competence by reason of Milošević's unlawful 'surrender' to the tribunal. The arrest warrant was issued not to the Republic of Serbia, which in fact surrendered Milošević to the tribunal, but to the Federal Republic of Yugoslavia, which by the time of the surrender had yet to act on the warrant. The Trial Chamber said that an abuse of process does not create a lack of jurisdiction but merely raises the question of whether the tribunal should exercise its discretion to refuse to try the accused. This it will do if there has been an egregious breach of due-process rights (see Chapter 8), which according to the Trial Chamber was not true in Milošević's situation, who (in the court's view) could not have relied on the laws of his country to shield him from execution of the warrant, just as federal Yugoslavia itself could not have relied on its constitutional arrangements to avoid compliance with an order of the tribunal.[69]

Another Trial Chamber examined the same general issue in *Nikolić*, a case of forced cross-border abduction, and reached what seems to be a different conclusion, that an egregious violation of a defendant's rights *may* bar jurisdiction *ratione personae*, where, for example, the person was seriously (physically) mistreated.[70]

The Kosovo conflict, which flared many years after the ICTY's establishment, and culminated in the NATO bombing campaign against the rump Yugoslavia in 1999, raised jurisdictional questions afresh. The ICTY prosecutor acted on the assumption that the tribunal did have jurisdiction to try NATO personnel for war crimes committed during the campaign, but decided not to proceed with an in-depth investigation because (or at any rate this was the reason given) the applicable law on proportionality in military attacks was murky and evidence on individual responsibility for NATO crimes would have been difficult to come by in the absence of NATO's cooperation.[71]

The alleged murkiness of the law on proportionality did not stop the prosecutor from pursuing charges of disproportionality in attacks against other defendants in ICTY cases (see Chapter 4). Moreover, a Serbian general, Dragoljub Ojdanić, was

---

[68] *Prosecutor* v. *Milošević*, Decision on Preliminary Motions, 8 November 2001, paras 26–34.

[69] Ibid., paras 40–51.

[70] *Prosecutor* v. *Nikolić*, Decision on Defence Motion Challenging the Exercise of Jurisdiction by the Tribunal, 9 October 2002, paras 111–14; confirmed on appeal: *Prosecutor* v. *Nikolić*, Decision on Interlocutory Appeal Concerning Legality of Arrest, 5 June 2003, para. 30.

[71] See *Final Report to the Prosecutor by the Committee Established to Review the NATO Bombing Campaign Against the Federal Republic of Yugoslavia*, 13 June 2000, paras 30–4, 90–1. Available at www.un.org/icty/pressreal/nato061300.htm.

indicted in relation to the events in Kosovo, and arrested. He commenced litigation on the scope of the ICTY's jurisdiction on two fronts. He argued in one motion that the ICTY does not have jurisdiction over crimes committed in Kosovo, because the rump Yugoslavia (then calling itself the Federal Republic of Yugoslavia) was not a member of the United Nations between 1992 and 2000.[72] The Trial Chamber, after reviewing the long period of ambiguity in the FRY's relations with the United Nations, decided that the FRY had functioned in many respects as a UN member throughout. It concluded that Ojdanić could not correctly say that the FRY was untouched by the regime of Security Council resolutions, including the one establishing the ICTY.[73] But according to the trial court, even if, for argument's sake, the FRY had not been a de facto UN member during the period in question, the proper interpretation of the ICTY's territorial jurisdiction is that it takes in the whole of the territory of the former Socialist Federal Republic of Yugoslavia; it has not been affected by the subsequent political divisions. To hold otherwise would be to frustrate the discharge of the Security Council's responsibility for international peace and security in accordance with Chapter VII of the UN Charter. As the judges in Ojdanić's case put it:

> The Chamber does not consider it necessary to pronounce on the general question of the applica-tion of the United Nations Charter to non-member States; on that issue scholarly opinion is divided. . . . It is sufficient for the Chamber to hold that in the particular circumstances of this case, nothing stands in the way of a reading of Chapter VII as enabling the Council to adopt meas-ures under Article 41 of the Charter in relation to a conflict that it has determined to be a threat to international peace and security, and which started [in 1991] in a member State of the United Nations, but which at the time of the measures taken [that is, in 1993] was no longer a United Nations member. The centrality of the goal of the maintenace of international peace and security within the global system established by the Charter underpins this interpretation of Chapter VII.[74]

In the *Hadžihasanović et al.* case the questioning of jurisdiction proceeded on the argu-ment that command responsibility for crimes committed in the course of an *internal* armed conflict did not exist in international humanitarian law in 1993, the period in which the three defendants were senior officers in the Bosnian-Muslim army. The only form of responsibility alleged in the indictment was command responsibility, and therefore the motion implied that the group of counts based on Common Article 3 (which according to the defendants suggested the precondition of an internal armed conflict) had to be dismissed.[75] The court declined to decide the issue as a preliminary motion, urging the parties to return to it again during trial. The reason given was that the parties' submissions on the jurisdictional question were not sufficiently detailed.

---

[72] *Prosecutor* v. *Milutinović et al.*, Decision on Motion Challenging Jurisdiction, 6 May 2003, para. 2.

[73] Ibid., paras 37–9. This was a brash argument by the Trial Chamber, considering that the FRY applied for membership of the UN on 27 October 2000 and was admitted by a General Assembly resolution a few days later — an act which at that point should have dispelled any remaining ambiguity concerning the FRY's UN membership in the period 1992–2000; see, ibid., paras 18, 41–2.

[74] *Prosecutor* v. *Milutinović et al.*, Decision on Motion Challenging Jurisdiction, 6 May 2003, paras 55–6. See also *Prosecutor* v. *Milutinović et al.*, Reasons for Decision Dismissing Interlocutory Appeal Concerning Jurisdiction Over the Territory of Kosovo, 8 June 2004; and the ICJ's decision in *Case Concerning Legality of Use of Force (Serbia and Montenegro* v. *Belgium) — Preliminary Objections*, 15 December 2004, paras 45 ff.

[75] *Prosecutor* v. *Hadžihasanović et al.*, Decision on Challenge to Jurisdiction, 7 December 2001.

Thus while motions on jurisdiction are normally disposed of as part of the pre-trial process, they occasionally will not be decided prior to the mid-term submissions on acquittal for lack of a prima facie case, or prior to the final judgment in the case. And while certain jurisdictional questions have long ago been decided at trial and even on appeal, defendants in later cases have been given the opportunity to reopen these questions, albeit without much success.[76]

The defendants in *Hadžihasanović*, faced with the above setback, did not await the trial stage, but returned with a more detailed preliminary motion disputing the ICTY's jurisdiction over certain forms of command responsibility. The motion was dismissed by the Trial Chamber,[77] and the defendants appealed. In considering the question whether the command responsibility doctrine was, by the relevant time, applicable to crimes in non-international armed conflict, the Appeals Chamber said that the war-crimes provisions encompassed by Article 3 of the ICTY Statute assume the existence of an organized military force, which in turn assumes the existence of 'responsible command'.[78] The Appeals Chamber then executed a remarkable leap from the factual to the normative (what philosophers call the is/ought fallacy): 'It is also reasonable to hold that it is responsible command which leads to command responsibility.' The fallacy is easily demonstrated by considering a criminal group organized as a militia so that it enjoys 'responsible command'. The leader of the group certainly does not have command responsibility, for it is self-contradictory to say that a duty falls upon the leader of a criminal group to prevent or punish the criminal acts of his or her subordinates.[79]

On the wave of this fallacy, the *Hadžihasanović* Appeals Chamber dismissed one part of the motion, reasoning that since international law recognizes that certain war crimes can be committed by a member of an organized military force in the course of an internal armed conflict, it must also be true that there is command responsibility in respect of such crimes.[80] Therefore, according to the Appeals Chamber, jurisdiction over this form of liability exists through the overlap of Articles 3 and 7 of the ICTY Statute.[81]

---

[76] See, e.g., *Prosecutor* v. *Milutinović et al.*, Decision (Appeals Chamber) on Dragoljub Ojdanić's Motion Challenging Jurisdiction — Joint Criminal Enterprise, 21 May 2003; and *Prosecutor* v. *Slobodan Milošević*, Decision on Preliminary Motions, 8 November 2001 ('Although some of the arguments have been dealt with before in the International Tribunal, the Chamber has considered all of them very carefully. Indeed, any judicial body is bound to take seriously a challenge to the legality of its foundation').

[77] *Prosecutor* v. *Hadžihasanović et al.*, Decision on Joint Challenge to Jurisdiction, 12 November 2002.

[78] *Prosecutor* v. *Hadžihasanović et al.*, Decision on Interlocutory Appeal Challenging Jurisdiction in Relation to Command Responsibility, 16 July 2003, para. 16.

[79] See further Chapter 7.

[80] *Prosecutor* v. *Hadžihasanović et al.*, Decision on Interlocutory Appeal Challenging Jurisdiction in Relation to Command Responsibility, 16 July 2003, para. 18.

[81] Other preliminary decisions on jurisdiction worth noting — at the ICTY: *Prosecutor* v. *Nikolić*, Decision on Defence Motion Challenging the Exercise of Jurisdiction by the Tribunal, 9 October 2002 ('the Tribunal has an inherent right to decide whether there exists a legal impediment to the exercise of jurisdiction over the Accused in order to ensure the integrity of the entire judicial process'); *Prosecutor* v. *Vojislav Šešelj*, Decision on the Interlocutory Appeal Concerning Jurisdiction, 31 August 2004 (the jurisdictional requirement of Article 5 of the ICTY Statute does not require the prosecutor to establish that an armed conflict existed within the state or region of the former Yugoslavia in which the charged Article 5 crime is alleged to have been committed); and *Prosecutor* v. *Milutinović et al.*,

9.3 IMPROVING THE INDICTMENT

Ignace Bagilishema, the first ICTR defendant to be acquitted of all charges, wrote in his final trial brief in August 2000:

The Defence unfortunately deplores the attitude of the Prosecution which has continuously violated the basic rights of the accused. Thus, the Defence submits that the Prosecution violated Article 20(a) of the Statute which provides inter alia that the accused 'shall be informed promptly and in detail . . . of the nature and cause of the charge against him or her'.

It is clear from Article 20(a) that the accused is entitled to know the specifics of the charges against him, namely the facts of which he is accused and the legal classification of these facts. In particular, as far as this legal element is concerned, he must be put in a position to know the legal ingredients of the offence charged . . .

In every instance the Prosecution's reliance on a particular set of facts appears to be entirely dependent on the legal case it seeks to make in that instance (although the Prosecution also relies on more than one set of facts for individual allegations). This is an approach born of expediency and resulting from prosecutorial discretion which is dismissive of the right of the accused to know specifically the charges laid against him.[82]

The *Bagilishema* Trial Chamber did not address these complaints — one might say that the judges at the time did not recognize them as real complaints. It was not until after 23 October 2001, when the *Kupreškić et al.* appeal judgment was handed down, that tribunal indictments became not just the springboard of litigation but the very object of it. Here is Ramsey Clark, then counsel for Elizaphan Ntakirutimana, delivering his oral closing argument in the case in August 2002, not long after he became aware of the content, and possible import for his case, of the Appeals Chamber's judgment:

Where's any recognition of . . . the principles involved in *Kupreškić* and some of it is heavy stuff. Nearly all of the so-called murders, the alleged murders, came to us for the first time in the testimony, never mentioned in the statements; . . . I didn't hear the Prosecution address the issue but — and I don't want to give a long analysis. Pat Wald [the Appeals Chamber judge presiding in *Kupreškić*] was in the Department of Justice in the '60s, in the criminal division, doing the happy part of the job, criminal justice reform; brilliant, brilliant person. She lives in the same apartment house as my mother, she and her husband and family. The kids are gone. But when you read, I think particularly paragraph 91 [of the judgment] — there are a whole bunch of

Decision on Ojdanić's Motion Challenging Jurisdiction: Indirect Co-perpetration, 22 March 2006. On the ICTY and jurisdiction, see Klip and Sluiter, *Annotated Leading Cases*, vol. VIII, pp. 15–43. At the ICTR: *Prosecutor v. Karemera et al.*, Decision on the Preliminary Motions by the Defence Challenging Jurisdiction in Relation to Joint Criminal Enterprise, 11 May 2004; and *Prosecutor v. Karemera et al.*, Decision on Jurisdictional Appeals: Joint Criminal Enterprise, 12 April 2006. And at the SCSL: *Prosecutor v. Taylor*, Decision on Immunity from Jurisdiction, 31 May 2004 ('the principle seems now established that the sovereign equality of states does not prevent a Head of State from being prosecuted before an international criminal tribunal'); and *Prosecutor v. Norman*, Decision on Preliminary Motion Based on Lack of Jurisdiction (Child Recruitment), 31 May 2004 (especially the Dissenting Opinion of Judge Robertson). On the SCSL and jurisdiction, see Klip and Sluiter, *Annotated Leading Cases*, vol. IX, pp. 19–62.

[82] *Prosecutor v. Ignace Bagilishema*, Defence Closing Brief, 1 August 2000, paras 20–1, 25.

paragraphs — you see that, . . . as I said earlier, practically none of the murders were named, the victims, the incidents, the time and place.[83]

Clark was better prepared to exploit *Kupreškić* in his appeal against the ICTR trial court's judgment, which convicted and sentenced both Elizaphan and Gérard Ntakirutimana. The appeal led to significant technical victories for the appellants, if not an acquittal or a reduction in sentence.[84] By mid-2004 the lessons from *Kupreškić* had been largely acknowledged and implemented at the ICTR.[85]

The background to the *Kupreškić* judgment was as follows. An ICTY Trial Chamber convicted the three brothers Kupreškić along with two others for crimes against humanity because of their participation in an attack on the Bosnian village of Ahmići on 16 April 1993. On appeal, two of the brothers argued that the Trial Chamber had erred in law by returning convictions on the basis of material facts not pleaded in the indictment. This lack of proper notice, they said, rendered the trial unfair. The Appeals Chamber considered the statutory framework relating to indictments, and the ICTY's interpretation of that body of law. Citing Article 21 of the ICTY Statute, the Appeals Chamber noted the prosecutor's obligation to state the material facts underpinning the charges in an indictment in sufficient detail to inform a defendant 'clearly of the charges against him so that he may prepare his defence'.[86] While materiality cannot be decided in the abstract, in a case where the prosecutor alleges that an accused personally committed the criminal acts, the material facts, such as the identity of the victims, the time and place of the events, and the means by which the acts were committed, must be pleaded in detail.[87]

The Appeals Chamber allowed that there will be instances where the sheer scale of the alleged crimes makes it impracticable to require a high degree of specificity in such matters as the identity of victims or the dates of commission of the crimes — for example, where a defendant is said to have participated as a member of an execution squad in killing hundreds of persons. In such a case the indictment need not identify every victim.[88]

Similarly, where one is accused of having participated in an extensive number of attacks on civilians taking place over a prolonged period of time and resulting in a large number of deaths, the obligation to specify the material facts in the indictment may be met without listing every victim or every relevant date with precision. Nevertheless, since, for example, the identity of victims is information that is valuable to the preparation of the defence case, if the prosecutor is in a position to name the victims, the prosecutor must do so.[89]

Where it would have been *practicable* for the prosecutor to plead, with specificity, the kind of detail mentioned above, except that it happens not to be in the prosecutor's possession, the consequence, according to the Appeals Chamber, is that

doubt must arise as to whether it is fair to the accused for the trial to proceed. In this connection, the Appeals Chamber emphasises that the Prosecution is expected to know its case before it goes

---

[83] *Prosecutor* v. *Ntakirutimana*, transcript of hearing on 22 August 2002, pp. 38, 49–50.

[84] See, e.g., *Ntakirutimana* appeal judgment, paras 71, 79, 85, 88, 91, 99, and 115.

[85] See, e.g., *Prosecutor* v. *Zigiranyirazo*, Decision on the Defence Preliminary Motion Objecting to the Form of the Amended Indictment, 15 July 2004, paras 47–51.   [86] *Kupreškić et al.* appeal judgment, para. 88.

[87] Ibid., paras 88–9.   [88] Ibid., para. 89.   [89] Ibid., para. 90.

to trial. It is not acceptable for the Prosecution to omit the material aspects of its main allegations in the indictment with the aim of moulding the case against the accused in the course of the trial depending on how the evidence unfolds.[90]

Where the evidence turns out differently than expected, the situation 'may require the indictment to be amended, an adjournment to be granted, or certain evidence to be excluded as not being within the scope of the indictment'.[91]

The Appeals Chamber found that the case against the Kupreškić brothers was not one where the sheer scale of the crimes prevented the prosecutor from supplying details. The case was, rather, 'dramatically transformed', from integral involvement of the defendants in the preparation, planning, organization, and implementation of the attack on Ahmići, as alleged in the indictment, to what turned out at trial to be their simple presence in Ahmići on 16 April 1993 and their direct participation in an attack on the house of one Suhret Ahmić, not mentioned in the indictment.[92]

The *Kupreškić* indictment contained the following paragraph, which the prosecutor contended pleaded with sufficient detail the material facts underlying the charge on which the two brothers were found guilty:

21. As part of the persecution, Zoran Kupreškić, Mirjan Kupreškić, Vlatko Kupreškić, Drago Josipović, Dragan Papić and Vladimir Šantić participated in or aided and abetted: (a) the deliberate and systematic killing of Bosnian Muslim civilians; (b) the comprehensive destruction of Bosnian Muslim homes and property; (c) and the organised detention and expulsion of the Bosnian Muslims from Ahmići-Šantići and its environs.[93]

The Appeals Chamber noted the absence of any detailed information about the role of the two accused in the three categories of alleged criminal conduct. The indictment did not particularize what form the alleged participation had taken. By framing the charges against the brothers in such a general way, the indictment failed to fulfil its fundamental purpose.[94] (Many early ICTR indictments are no less vague.)

The Appeals Chamber also noted that the emergent allegation that the Kupreškić brothers were part of a group of soldiers who participated in the attack on Ahmić's house, resulting in the murder of Ahmić and another person, the house being set on fire, and the surviving members of the Ahmić family being expelled, constituted, in retrospect, material facts in the prosecutor's case against them, since this was the sole basis of their conviction. The attack on the house should have been specifically pleaded in the indictment, and the Trial Chamber erred in entering convictions which depended on material facts not pleaded.[95]

Having found the indictment defective, the Appeals Chamber considered whether the prosecutor's pre-trial brief had put the defendants on sufficient notice, but found that the brief's statements to the effect that the Kupreškić brothers joined in the attack on several houses, participating in at least half a dozen murders, were 'extremely

---

[90] Ibid., para. 92.   [91] Ibid.   [92] Ibid., para. 93.   [93] Ibid., para. 83.
[94] Ibid., para. 95.   [95] Ibid., paras 99, 113.

general in nature'.[96] There was, moreover, no reference to the attack on Ahmić's house in the prosecutor's opening address, though specific reference was made to an attack on another house. The Appeals Chamber accepted that around two weeks into the trial the defendants were informed that the allegation concerning Ahmić was relevant to the count of crimes against humanity; nevertheless until the trial's end 'No certain conclusion could be drawn' as to how that evidence was going to be relied upon by the Trial Chamber for the purpose of deciding the issue of the accused's criminal liability.[97]

The *Kupreškić* principles may be summarized as follows:

(1) A defendant enjoys a statutory guarantee 'to be informed promptly and in detail in a language which he or she understands of the nature and cause of the charge against him or her', and 'to have adequate time and facilities for the preparation of his or her defence'.[98]

(2) The indictment is the primary accusatory instrument.[99]

(3) It follows from the above that material facts underpinning the charges must be stated in the indictment clearly and in sufficient detail to inform the defendant of the case against him or her.[100]

(4) An indictment is unacceptably vague and therefore defective if it fails to particularize the material facts of the alleged criminal conduct of the defendant that bear on the defendant's role in the alleged crime.[101]

(5) Vagueness in the indictment constitutes neither a minor defect nor a technical imperfection. It goes to the heart of the substantial safeguards that an indictment is intended to furnish the defendant.[102]

(6) Where the prosecutor alleges that the defendant personally committed criminal acts, the material facts have to be pleaded in the indictment in detail, except where the sheer scale of the crimes makes a high degree of specificity impracticable. In any case, if the prosecutor is in a position to provide details, this must be done.[103]

(7) If the material facts cannot be pleaded in the indictment with the requisite degree of specificity because the prosecutor does not possess the necessary information, doubt must arise as to whether the trial should proceed.[104]

(8) The prosecutor is expected to know the case before the prosecutor goes to trial, not aim to mould it to the unfolding evidence. Where the evidence turns out differently than the prosecutor forecast, it may be necessary to amend the indictment, adjourn the trial, or exclude certain evidence.[105]

(9) A conviction that is critically dependent upon facts not properly pleaded in the indictment is an error in law and cannot be sustained.[106]

---

[96] Ibid., para. 117.   [97] Ibid., para. 199.   [98] See Article 21(4)(a) and (b) of the ICTY Statute.
[99] *Kupreškić et al.* appeal judgment, para. 114.   [100] Ibid., paras 88, 95.   [101] Ibid., paras 98, 114.
[102] Ibid., para. 122.   [103] Ibid., paras 90, 95.   [104] Ibid., para. 92.   [105] Ibid., para. 92.
[106] Ibid., paras 99, 113, 124.

(10) For new evidence to be used at trial, the indictment must be amended. Expediency must never be allowed to override the fundamental rights of the defendant.[107]

There have been many dozens of decisions substantiating the general principles consolidated in the *Kupreškić* case. The most important of these are listed in the notes.[108]

9.4 PROVISIONAL RELEASE

Provisional release at the ICTY may be ordered by a Trial Chamber 'only after giving the host country and the State to which the accused seeks to be released the opportunity to be heard and only if it is satisfied that the accused will appear for trial and, if released, will not pose a danger to any victim, witness or other person'.[109] The rule was more restrictive in the past (prior to an amendment in late 1999), when the applicant for provisional release had to establish 'exceptional circumstances'. The increase in the number of provisional releases granted at the ICTY is also a reflection of the stabilization of the political situation in the territories of the former Yugoslavia and the closer

---

[107] Ibid., para. 100.

[108] It should be kept in mind that some indictments go through several rounds of litigation. At the ICTY: *Prosecutor* v. *Delalić et al.*, Decision on Motion by the Accused Zejnil Delalić Based on Defects in the Form of the Indictment, 2 October 1996; *Prosecutor* v. *Blaškić*, Decision on the Defence Motion to Dismiss the Indictment Based Upon Defects in the Form Thereof (Vagueness/Lack of Adequate Notice of Charges), 4 April 1997; *Prosecutor* v. *Kvočka et al.*, Decision on Defence Preliminary Motions on the Form of the Indictment, 12 April 1999; *Prosecutor* v. *Brđanin and Talić*, Decision on Objections by Momir Talić to the Form of the Amended Indictment, 20 February 2001; *Prosecutor* v. *Brđanin and Talić*, Decision on Form of Further Amended Indictment and Prosecution Application to Amend, 26 June 2001; *Prosecutor* v. *Hadžihasanović et al.*, Decision on Form of Indictment, 7 December 2001; *Prosecutor* v. *Martić*, Decision on the Prosecution's Motion to Request Leave to File a Corrected Amended Indictment, 13 December 2002; *Prosecutor* v. *Mrkšić*, Decision on Form of the Indictment, 19 June 2003; *Prosecutor* v. *Hadžihasanović and Kubura*, Decision on Form of Indictment, 17 September 2003; *Prosecutor* v. *Mrkšić et al.*, Decision on Form of Consolidated Amended Indictment and on Prosecution Application to Amend, 23 January 2004; and *Prosecutor* v. *Sefer Halilović*, Decision on Prosecutor's Motion Seeking Leave to Amend the Indictment, 17 December 2004. On the ICTY and indictments, see Klip and Sluiter, *Annotated Leading Cases, vol. VIII*, pp. 91–138. At the ICTR: *Prosecutor* v. *Kabiligi and Ntabakuze*, Decision on the Defence Motions Objecting to a Lack of Jurisdiction and Seeking to Declare the Indictment Void Ab Initio, 13 April 2000; *Prosecutor* v. *Kanyabashi*, Decision on Defence Preliminary Motion for Defects in the Form of the Indictment, 31 May 2000; *Prosecutor* v. *Karemera*, Decision on the Defence Motions Objecting to the Jurisdiction of the Trial Chamber on the Amended Indictment, 13 April 2000; *Prosecutor* v. *Karemera*, Decision on the Defence Motion Pertaining to Lack of Jurisdiction and Defects in the Form of the Indictment, 25 April 2001; *Prosecutor* v. *Karemera et al.*, Decision on Prosecutor's Interlocutory Appeal Against Trial Chamber III Decision of 8 October 2003 Denying Leave to File an Amended Indictment, 19 December 2003; *Prosecutor* v. *Simba*, Decision on Motion to Amend Indictment, 26 January 2004; *Prosecutor* v. *Bizimungu et al.*, Decision on Prosecutor's Interlocutory Appeal Against Trial Chamber II Decision of 6 October 2003 Denying Leave to File Amended Indictment, 12 February 2004; *Prosecutor* v. *Muvunyi*, Decision on the Prosecutor's Motion for Leave to File an Amended Indictment, 23 February 2005; and *Prosecutor* v. *Karemera et al.*, Decision on Defects in the Form of the Indictment, 5 August 2005. And at the SCSL: *Prosecutor* v. *Kanu*, Decision and Order on Defence Preliminary Motion for Defects in the Form of the Indictment, 19 November 2003. On the SCSL and indictments, see Klip and Sluiter, *Annotated Leading Cases, vol. IX*, pp. 209–80.   [109] Rule 65(B) of the ICTY.

cooperation of their administrations with the tribunal. The same cannot be said about the ICTR or the SCSL.[110] Even at the ICTY, however, the litigation on provisional release remains burdensome and varied.[111]

9.5 EVIDENCE IN LIEU OF ORAL TESTIMONY

Both the ICTY and the ICTR have modified their rules several times to allow for the routine admission of evidence in the form of written statements by witnesses, or transcripts of prior testimony of witnesses, who are not called to give testimony in person, or who are called only for cross-examination.[112] Their written statements usually

[110] At the ICTR the 'exceptional circumstances' clause remained in place long after it was removed from the ICTY rules: see, e.g., *Prosecutor* v. *Kanyabashi*, Decision on the Defence Motion for the Provisional Release of the Accused, 21 February 2001 ('The Trial Chamber is aware of the length of the detention of the Accused since his arrest in 1995, that is, more than five years ago . . . In the present case, the Trial Chamber concludes that . . . the Accused's detention remains within acceptable limits'). As for the SCSL, see *Prosecutor* v. *Norman*, Decision on Motion for Modification of the Conditions of Detention, 26 November 2003 ('The very act of bringing an indictment implies that the Prosecution has a case that is almost ready for trial and can be made ready within 6 to 9 months of the date of arrest . . . Arguments that concern delay in trial fixtures considerably beyond that time period will be carefully scrutinised'); and Klip and Sluiter, *Annotated Leading Cases*, vol. IX, pp. 281–353.

[111] Note that a defendant may take his or her provisional release applications through several rounds of litigation. At the ICTY: for a decision from the era of 'exceptional circumstances', see *Prosecutor* v. *Delalić et al.*, Decision on Motion for Provisional Release Filed by the Accused Zejnil Delalić, 25 September 1996; for decisions after this period, see *Prosecutor* v. *Mrkšić*, Decision on Mile Mrkšić's Application for Provisional Release, 24 July 2002 ('the governments of the FRY and the Republic of Serbia have neither arrested the other two co-indictees in the case, nor arrested other high-ranking individuals indicted by the Tribunal. It is for this reason that the Trial Chamber treats the guarantees from those governments with much caution'); *Prosecutor* v. *Brđanin and Talić*, Decision on the Motion for Provisional Release of the Accused Momir Talić, 20 September 2002 ('The Trial Chamber believes that, given the medical condition of Talić, it would be unjust and inhumane to prolong his detention on remand until he is half-dead before releasing him'); *Prosecutor* v. *Blagojević et al.*, Decision (Appeals Chamber) on Provisional Release of Vidoje Blagojević and Dragan Obrenović, 3 October 2002 ('It was open to the Trial Chamber to assess whether the undertakings by the Republika Srpska constitute, in the cases under consideration, significant assurances that the accused will appear for trial. But an a priori exclusion of such undertakings on the basis that they emanate from an entity not recognised as a state by public international law amounts to an error of law'); *Prosecutor* v. *Šainović and Ojdanić*, Decision on Provisional Release, 30 October 2002 (especially the dissenting opinion of Judge Hunt); *Prosecutor* v. *Blagojević et al.*, Decision (Appeals Chamber) on Provisional Release Application by Blagojević, 17 February 2003 ('Blagojević is thus alleged to be at a high level in the hierarchy of responsibility for the crimes charged. Republika Srpska has so far failed to arrest any persons indicted by the Tribunal, and there is a substantial disincentive for it to arrest this particular accused, who must have substantially valuable information which he could disclose to the Tribunal'); *Prosecutor* v. *Stanišić*, Decision on Provisional Release, 28 July 2004 ('given that the Accused . . . was arrested by Belgrade authorities on 13 March 2003 and was subsequently transferred to the International Tribunal on 11 June 2003, the Trial Chamber is satisfied that the Accused would indeed be re-arrested . . . should the necessity arise'); *Prosecutor* v. *Čermak and Markač*, Decision on Interlocutory Appeal Against Trial Chamber's Decision Denying Provisional Release, 2 December 2004 ('the Trial Chamber erred in exercising its discretion in its assessment of the reliability and effectiveness of the guarantees of Croatia in the instant case'); and *Prosecutor* v. *Stanišić*, Decision on Mićo Stanišić's Motion for Provisional Release, 19 July 2005 ('Although it is to be noted that the Accused's surrender was conditional to him receiving, inter alia, a government guarantee from the Republic of Serbia in support of his provisional release, this is not a basis for doubting the voluntariness of his surrender'). On the ICTY and provisional release, see Klip and Sluiter, *Annotated Leading Cases*, vol. VIII, pp. 45–89.

[112] Up to December 2000, when Rule 92 *bis* was introduced at the ICTY, Rule 90 provided that 'witnesses shall, in principle, be heard directly by the Chambers'. Those words were deleted, but a watered-down version of the

take the form of a few pages of declarative text distilled from interviews given to prosecution investigators. The investigator will have the witness read, correct, and adopt the reduced text.

Motions to admit evidence in this form are decided for the most part in the pre-trial stage. This is because the question is directly related to the number of 'viva voce' witnesses granted to the prosecutor by the pre-trial chamber. The motions are governed, in the case of the ICTY and the ICTR, by Rule 92 *bis* of the tribunals' rules. (At the ICTY, now also by Rule 92 *ter*.)

Use of non-viva voce witnesses raises important issues. In the first place, their statements are, technically, hearsay. The tribunals are not averse to the admission of hearsay, as long as it is deemed reliable on its face, preferring to deal with its drawbacks as a matter of the weight to be given to the evidence. However, a case substantially built on the statements of non-viva voce witnesses is a case substantially built on hearsay sources, and this cannot be satisfactory.

A related problem is that the use of non-viva voce witnesses appears to run counter to the right of the accused 'to examine, or have examined, witnesses against him' (Article 21 of the ICTY Statute). This problem is addressed to some extent by the tribunals' rule that the evidence of non-viva voce witnesses must go to proof of a matter 'other than the acts and conduct of the accused'.[113] (The ICTY's Rule 92 *ter* no longer insists on this condition, but instead requires that an opportunity to cross-examine the witness be given.) The problem is perhaps not so acute where the evidence of a non-viva voce witness is in the form of a transcript of testimony given in another case, a superior source to a mere statement, since the latter is not made under oath and does not involve cross-examination.[114]

A third — and again related — problem is the credibility of non-viva voce witnesses. Credibility affects the weight to be accorded to a witness's evidence. Observation of a witness in court is not the only clue to credibility, although it is one of the most important. A non-viva voce witness's credibility may be assessed from the transcript of his or her cross-examination in another case (if such a record exists, is relevant to the later case, and has been admitted into evidence), or from the extent to which the non-viva voce witness's allegations are consistent with the testimony of other, credible, witnesses. But in practice a determination of credibility is difficult if one has not seen and heard the witness being questioned.

These issues will be examined in more detail below.

Evidence that goes directly to the acts or conduct of the accused (as well as to his or her state of mind) cannot be admitted under Rule 92 *bis* regardless of how repetitive it is of evidence admitted through another witness.[115] This is the explicit test found in the rule; as we shall see, however, it is not the only relevant test. While Rule 92 *bis* is open

---

principle was retained and incorporated into Rule 89: 'A Chamber may receive the evidence of a witness orally or, where the interests of justice allow, in written form.'

[113] Rule 92 *bis* (A) and (D).

[114] See *Prosecutor* v. *Milošević*, Decision on Prosecution Motion for the Admission of Transcripts in Lieu of Viva Voce Testimony Pursuant to [Rule] 92 *bis* (D) — Foča Transcripts, 30 June 2003, paras 38–41.

[115] *Brđanin and Talić*, Confidential Decision [on Rule 92 *bis*], 30 January 2002 para. 30; *Prosecutor* v. *Galić*, Decision on Interlocutory Appeal Concerning Rule 92 *bis* (C), 7 June 2002, paras 10–11.

to use by both parties, it is generally employed by the prosecutor to prove the so-called 'crime base' in cases involving defendants in formerly senior positions who did not themselves commit statutory crimes, but whose decisions are said to have caused, at the ground level, widespread perpetration of such crimes.[116]

For witness statements to be admitted pursuant to Rule 92 *bis* they must comply with certain formalities aimed at increasing their reliability.[117]

In one of the earliest Rule 92 *bis* decisions, a Trial Chamber in the *Sikirica et al.* case said that the rule governing the admission of transcript testimony from prior cases[118] does not supplant or modify the general requirements for the admissibility of evidence, namely that the court may admit 'any relevant evidence which it deems to have probative value' and may exclude evidence if its probative value 'is substantially outweighed by the need to ensure a fair trial'.[119] These conditions also apply to the admission of written statements;[120] they must be met first, before the special conditions of Rule 92 *bis* (for statements or transcripts) are considered.[121]

It has been said that where a transcript from a prior case is put forth for admission in lieu of oral testimony, and the content of the transcript goes to proof of a 'critical element' of the prosecutor's case in the later proceeding, or the cross-examination of the witness in the earlier proceeding (as reflected in the transcript) does not adequately deal with the issues relevant to the defence in the case at hand, the witness should be called for cross-examination.[122]

The 'critical element' test was applied in the *Sikirica* case. The journalist Ed Vulliamy, who had testified in several tribunal cases already, was proposed as a non-viva voce witness. Duško Sikirica objected, saying that the charges against him concerned not only his own acts at a certain detention camp for non-Serbs, but complicity to commit genocide throughout the municipality in which the camp was located. Vulliamy's prior testimony touched upon the intent of the Serb authorities in the municipality in relation to the non-Serb population; this could be used as a basis for fixing Sikirica with knowledge of genocidal acts occurring elsewhere in the municipality. The Trial Chamber agreed, holding that the Vulliamy transcript went to an element of proof of the genocide charge against Sikirica, and ordered the witness to appear for cross-examination.[123] Here, however, the 'critical element' test does not seem any different from the 'acts and conduct of the accused' test.

Another proposed non-viva voce witness dealt with in the same decision was ordered to appear for cross-examination because while his evidence was said to be unrelated to the acts or conduct of the accused, it did bear upon the case in 'a significant and direct

---

[116] *Prosecutor v. Blagojević and Jokić*, First Decision on Prosecution's Motion for Admission of Witness Statements and Prior Testimony Pursuant to Rule 92 *bis*, 12 June 2003, para. 28.

[117] Rule 92 *bis* (B) and (C).   [118] Rule 92 *bis* (D).

[119] Rule 89 (C) and (D), respectively. See *Prosecutor* v. *Galić*, Decision on Interlocutory Appeal Concerning Rule 92 *bis* (C), 7 June 2002, para. 31.   [120] Rule 92 *bis* (A).

[121] *Prosecutor* v. *Sikirica et al.*, Decision on Prosecution's Application to Admit Transcripts Under Rule 92 *bis*, 23 May 2001, para. 3; approved in *Prosecutor* v. *Milošević*, Decision on Prosecution's Request to Have Written Statements Admitted Under Rule 92 *bis*, 21 March 2002, para. 6.

[122] *Prosecutor* v. *Sikirica et al.*, Decision on Prosecution's Application to Admit Transcripts Under Rule 92 *bis*, 23 May 2001, para. 4.   [123] Ibid., paras 8, 11.

way'. This does signal a novel test. The witness was said to be a 'senior Muslim politician' in the municipality and an 'extensive fact witness' in relation to conditions in the detention camps.[124] The Trial Chamber treated as 'critical' in this instance a composite of two elements: the seniority of the position held at the relevant time by the witness made him important in the context of the case; and the witness had experienced a broad cross-section of events.

In the *Milošević* case, the Trial Chamber said that all 19 written statements proffered for admission under Rule 92 *bis*, having to do with attacks by Serb forces in Kosovo resulting in deportation and killing of civilians, related to a 'critical element' of the prosecutor's case, namely the theory that the crimes were committed systematically by the Serbs, not by the Kosovo Liberation Army and NATO, as claimed by Milošević. This was a 'live and important issue between the parties', and so the 23 proposed non-viva voce witnesses would, instead, be called for cross-examination. Had the issue been 'peripheral or marginally relevant', there would have been no need to hear the witnesses.[125]

In another case, the Appeals Chamber articulated what seems to be an alternative version of the 'critical element' test:

Where the evidence is so pivotal to the prosecution case, and where the person whose acts and conduct the written statement describes is so proximate to the accused, the Trial Chamber may decide that it would not be fair to the accused to permit the evidence to be given in written form. An easy example of where the exercise of that discretion would lead to the rejection of a written statement would be where the acts and conduct of a person other than the accused described in the written statement occurred in the presence of the Accused.[126]

This example is *too* easy. Presence is, one might say, nine-tenths of the law in the cases dealt with by the tribunals, since presence establishes knowledge (a mental element of several forms of responsibility) and is a first step towards proof of encouragement.[127] The example given by the Appeals Chamber concerns evidence that would be excluded by the 'acts and conduct' test (which covers the defendant's state of mind) with no assistance from the 'pivotal evidence' test.

In cases involving command responsibility, a Trial Chamber should exercise 'extreme caution' in admitting evidence of non-viva voce witnesses going to the acts or conduct of alleged subordinates of the accused.[128] This implies that such evidence may be inadmissible

---

[124] Ibid., para. 35; approved in *Prosecutor v. Milošević*, Decision on Prosecution's Request to Have Written Statements Admitted Under Rule 92 *bis*, 21 March 2002, para. 7.

[125] Ibid., paras 24–5. See, similarly, *Prosecutor v. Brđanin and Talić*, Third Decision on the Admission of Written Statements Pursuant to Rule 92 *bis*, 3 September 2002, para. 12; *Prosecutor v. Milošević*, Decision on Prosecution Motion for the Admission of Transcripts in Lieu of Viva Voce Testimony Pursuant to [Rule 92] *bis* (D) — Foča Transcripts, 30 June 2003, para. 35; *Prosecutor v. Bagosora et al.*, Decision on Prosecutor's Motion for the Admission of Written Witness Statements Under Rule 92 *bis*, 9 March 2004, para. 16.

[126] *Prosecutor v. Galić*, Decision on Interlocutory Appeal Concerning Rule 92 *bis* (C), 7 June 2002, para. 13.

[127] Consider, for example, the trouble taken by the Trial Chamber in the *Bagilishema* trial judgment (paras 495–530) to show that the evidence did *not* establish beyond reasonable doubt that the defendant was present at a particular massacre site. The Trial Chamber treated this as a precondition for ordering his acquittal.

[128] *Prosecutor v. Brđanin and Talić*, Third Decision on the Admission of Written Statements Pursuant to Rule 92 *bis*, 3 September 2002, paras 17–18.

through Rule 92 *bis*. Another Trial Chamber said, however, that the phrase 'acts and conduct of the accused' should be given its ordinary meaning: no mention is made in the rule of co-perpetrators, subordinates, or anybody else. Where the evidence concerns co-perpetrators or subordinates, the remedy is not to deny admission under the rule but to call the witness for cross-examination.[129] The Appeals Chamber supported the latter interpretation,[130] insisting, somewhat paradoxically, that while the rule's key test ('acts and conduct of the accused') should be interpreted literally, Rule 92 *bis* as a whole is to be interpreted creatively. It is 'but a short step', the Appeals Chamber said, from a finding that the crimes charged were committed by subordinates of the defendant, to a finding that he or she knew or had reason to know of the crimes.[131] In such 'special and sensitive' situations, where the evidence is 'pivotal', admission in written form may not be possible (although nowadays it would be introduced through the new Rule 92 *ter*, instead).[132]

Thus both Trial and Appeals Chambers have found it necessary to read one or more tests into Rule 92 *bis* in order to limit its use by the parties (and by the prosecutor in particular). It is an indication of how poorly drafted the rule is.

According to the case law, then, non-viva voce witness evidence which is 'merely helpful background material' and 'does not bear directly upon the case' against the accused, or which bears upon the case but only to the extent that it concerns events many steps removed from the accused, should be admissible without cross-examination, and Rule 92 *bis* is to that extent appropriate.[133] In the *Galić* case, which dealt with sniping and shelling attacks on civilians under siege in Sarajevo, the written statement of a witness describing the killing of a man by a sniper's shot was found to be straightforwardly admissible through Rule 92 *bis* because it did not indicate the source of fire, and therefore did not implicate a member of the besieging army, namely a subordinate of the accused.[134] Arguably use of the rule makes trials more efficient[135] and saves

[129] *Prosecutor* v. *Milošević*, Decision on Prosecution's Request to Have Written Statements Admitted Under Rule 92 *bis*, 21 March 2002, para. 22. Judge Robinson held, in a Separate Opinion attached to this decision, that 'acts or conduct of the defendant' should be construed as encompassing acts or conduct of subordinates of the defendant (paras 7–10 of Separate Opinion).

[130] *Prosecutor* v. *Galić*, Decision on Interlocutory Appeal Concerning Rule 92 *bis* (C), 7 June 2002, paras 9–10. What is of course beyond doubt is that evidence tending to establish that the accused was the superior of the alleged subordinates counts as evidence going to his or her acts or conduct.   [131] Ibid., paras 14–15.

[132] Ibid., para. 19. A bare reference to 'Serb soldiers' having committed crimes does not produce a 'special and sensitive' situation in a case where not all persons coming under that description were subordinates, let alone proximate subordinates, of the defendants: *Prosecutor* v. *Brđanin and Talić*, Third Decision on the Admission of Written Statements Pursuant to Rule 92 *bis*, 3 September 2002, para. 29 (to be contrasted with the result in paras 35 and 42–4).

[133] *Prosecutor* v. *Sikirica et al.*, Decision on Prosecution's Application to Admit Transcripts Under Rule 92 *bis*, 23 May 2001, para. 16.

[134] *Prosecutor* v. *Galić*, Decision on Interlocutory Appeal Concerning Rule 92 *bis* (C), 7 June 2002, para. 18.

[135] The 'advantages [of] the expeditious disposal of trials which the Rule was designed to achieve' — ibid., para. 16; 'Rule [Rule] 92 *bis* is the most ambitious and far reaching of the measures that have been adopted to expedite proceedings' — *Prosecutor* v. *Milošević*, Decision on Prosecution Motion for the Admission of Transcripts in Lieu of Viva Voce Testimony Pursuant to [Rule] 92 *bis* (D) — Foča Transcripts, 30 June 2003, Dissenting Opinion of Judge Robinson, para. 39. The presumed savings have been exaggerated. While Rule 92 *bis* saves courtroom time, it consumes out of court almost as much time as it saves in court. This is because the admission of each proposed non-viva voce witness is normally litigated between the parties (a time-consuming process), and moreover the judges have to find time out of court to read the witness's statements or transcripts, once for the purposes of admission and then once again with the aim of processing the evidence as evidence in the case.

witnesses the trouble of repetitious court appearances. The fact that a non-viva voce witness's account is 'one-sided' (as one defendant complained) is a matter that can be dealt with by the defence in final submissions, or by calling counteracting evidence, but it is not a ground for ordering the witness's appearance.[136]

Where, however, the proposed non-viva voce evidence concerns a 'live and important issue', a 'special and sensitive situation', or a 'critical element', or is 'pivotal' to the prosecutor's case, then the witness must appear to testify even if the evidence does not literally concern the accused's conduct.[137]

Does this allay the jurisprudential issues adumbrated earlier? There have been cases where the number of non-viva voce witnesses far exceeded that of in-person witnesses. ICTY chambers have hinted that improper use of Rule 92 *bis* could mar a trial (including its public character), but have also defended the rule by saying that reasonable use of the rule does not. Article 21 of the ICTY's Statute is mentioned in this connection.[138] The ICTY chambers have said that the right to cross-examine witnesses 'is not an absolute right',[139] although presumably cross-examination must be closer to the rule than to the exception. The fact remains that Rule 89 of the Tribunal's Rules (to which Rule 92 *bis* is subordinated) makes the admission of non-oral evidence conditional upon 'the interests of justice'.[140] This is to be added to the several tests affecting Rule 92 *bis*. But what does this further test amount to?

Judge Robinson in a Separate Opinion said in effect that a defendant's statutory right to cross-examination is limited to witnesses proffering evidence going to proof of the defendant's acts or conduct or implicating him or her in a 'critical way'.[141] Judge Kwon, of the same Trial Chamber, went further, expressing puzzlement as to 'how the practice of the International Tribunal not to admit witness statements as a matter of course has developed', contrasting this with practice in Korea, and suggesting that a more flexible approach to the admission of non-viva voce witnesses could improve a Trial Chamber's ability 'to manage trials of a vast scale'.[142] (A preliminary question of the highest importance is whether vast trials should be attempted at all, but Kwon did not address it.)

---

[136] *Prosecutor* v. *Sikirica et al.*, Decision on Prosecution's Application to Admit Transcripts Under Rule 92 *bis*, 23 May 2001, para. 21.

[137] In all such cases, if the witness has died, his or her statement cannot be admitted through Rule 92 *bis*: *Prosecutor* v. *Galić*, Decision on Interlocutory Appeal Concerning Rule 92 *bis* (C), 7 June 2002, paras 22–5. For practice at the ICTR, see, e.g., *Prosecutor* v. *Bagosora et al.*, Decision on Prosecutor's Motion for the Admission of Written Witness Statements Under Rule 92 *bis*, 9 March 2004.

[138] See, e.g., *Prosecutor* v. *Sikirica et al.*, Decision on Prosecution's Application to Admit Transcripts Under Rule 92 *bis*, 23 May 2001, para. 4; *Prosecutor* v. *Milošević*, Decision on Prosecution's Request to Have Written Statements Admitted Under Rule 92 *bis*, 21 March 2002, para. 25, as well as the Separate Opinion of Judge Robinson; *Prosecutor* v. *Galić*, Decision on Interlocutory Appeal Concerning Rule 92 *bis* (C), 7 June 2002, para. 16; *Prosecutor* v. *Brđanin and Talić*, Third Decision on the Admission of Written Statements Pursuant to Rule 92 *bis*, 3 September 2002, para. 5.

[139] E.g. *Prosecutor* v. *Blagojević and Jokić*, First Decision on Prosecution's Motion for Admission of Witness Statements and Prior Testimony Pursuant to Rule 92 *bis*, 12 June 2003, para. 14; *Prosecutor* v. *Milošević*, Decision on Prosecution Motion for the Admission of Transcripts in Lieu of Viva Voce Testimony Pursuant to [Rule] 92 *bis* (D) — Foča Transcripts, 30 June 2003, para. 24. [140] See sub-rule (F).

[141] *Prosecutor* v. *Milošević*, Decision on Prosecution's Request to Have Written Statements Admitted Under Rule 92 *bis*, 21 March 2002, Separate Opinion of Judge Robinson, paras 2–5.

[142] Ibid., Separate Opinion of Judge Kwon, paras 2–3.

Both Robinson and Kwon expressed faith in the ability of 'professional judges' to avoid the pitfalls of non-viva voce evidence. Yet they did not explain how this displaces a defendant's 'right' as found in Article 21 of the ICTY Statute to examine witnesses. Kwon, in particular, seems unaware of — or at least does not comment on — the fact that the statements of non-viva voce witnesses at the tribunal are taken by agents of a party to an essentially adversarial system, not by impartial investigative magistrates.[143] Robinson changed his mind in 2003, when he came out with a long dissenting opinion decrying the extensive use of Rule 92 *bis* and emphasizing the right of a defendant to determine the conduct of his or her defence.[144] He argued that 'the threshold for a determination as to whether a matter is in issue such as to warrant cross-examination of a transcript witness should not be unduly high'.[145]

The Appeals Chamber has said in a footnote to one of its decisions that the admission into evidence of written statements in lieu of oral testimony is not inconsistent with human-rights norms, subject to the following condition: that the evidence contained in the statement must not 'lead to a conviction' unless there is 'other evidence which corroborates the statement'.[146] This statement of the norms is imprecise — for what might be included in this notion of 'evidence that would lead to a conviction'? If it means evidence going to the conduct of the defendant, this, as we have seen, is absolutely barred from admission through Rule 92 *bis* and allowed in through Rule 92 *ter* only with cross-examination. Indeed, the relevant ECtHR cases (some of which were cited in the Appeals Chamber's decision) all concern unexamined or untested evidence going to the conduct of the defendant.[147] The general proposition coming out of the ECtHR jurisprudence is well expressed in the case of *A. M.* v. *Italy*:

all the evidence must normally be produced at a public hearing, in the presence of the accused, with a view to adversarial argument. There are exceptions to this principle, but they must not infringe the rights of the defence; as a general rule . . . the defendant [must] be given an adequate and proper opportunity to challenge and question a witness against him, either when he makes his statements or at a later stage . . . In particular, the rights of the defence are restricted to an extent that is incompatible with the requirements of Article 6 [of the Convention] if the

---

[143] This point was noted, however, by two judges of the Appeals Chamber: *Prosecutor* v. *Milošević*, Dissenting Opinion of Judge David Hunt on Admissibility of Evidence in Chief in the Form of Written Statements, 21 October 2003, para. 6; and *Prosecutor* v. *Milošević*, Separate Opinion of Judge Shahabuddeen Appended to Appeal Chamber's Decision Dated 30 September 2003 on Admissibility of Evidence-in-Chief in the Form of Written Statements, 31 October 2003, para. 19.

[144] *Prosecutor* v. *Milošević*, Decision on Prosecution Motion for the Admission of Transcripts in Lieu of Viva Voce Testimony Pursuant to [Rule] 92 *bis* (D) — Foča Transcripts, 30 June 2003, dissenting opinion of Judge Robinson, paras 8–11. [145] Ibid., Dissenting Opinion of Judge Robinson, para. 26.

[146] *Prosecutor* v. *Galić*, Decision on Interlocutory Appeal Concerning Rule 92 *bis* (C), 7 June 2002, fn 34. Followed in *Prosecutor* v. *Blagojević and Jokić*, First Decision on Prosecution's Motion for Admission of Witness Statements and Prior Testimony Pursuant to Rule 92 *bis*, 12 June 2003, para. 25.

[147] E.g. *Unterpertinger* v. *Austria*, 24 November 1986; *Bricmont* v. *Belgium*, 7 July 1989; *Kostovski* v. *Netherlands*, 20 November 1989; *Windisch* v. *Austria*, 27 September 1990; *Delta* v. *France*, 19 December 1990; *Asch* v. *Austria*, 26 April 1991; *Artner* v. *Austria*, 28 August 1992; *Lüdi* v. *Switzerland*, 15 June 1992; *Vidal* v. *Belgium*, 22 April 1992; *Saïdi* v. *France*, 20 September 1993; *Pullar* v. *United Kingdom*, 10 June 1996; *A. M.* v. *Italy*, 14 December 1999; *Luca* v. *Italy*, 27 February 2001; *Sadak and others* v. *Turkey*, 17 July 2001; *Solakov* v. *FYR Macedonia*, 31 October 2001; *Laukkanen and Manninen* v. *Finland*, 3 February 2004; *P.S.* v. *Germany*, 20 December 2001.

conviction is based solely or in a decisive manner on the depositions of a witness whom the accused has had no opportunity to examine.[148]

Because this proposition refers not to evidence in general but to evidence going to the accused's conduct, the use of Rule 92 *bis* at the ICTY does not offend the ECtHR norms. In fact, the bar is set higher at the ICTY, where there are no exceptions to the principle. From a practical point of view, however, it remains to be seen whether Rules 92 *bis* and 92 *ter* make trials more efficient. The evidence admitted in paper form still has to be read by the judges, which means that the effect of the rules is that the judges sit in court less and spend more time out of court reading, but this does not necessarily mean that the trial process overall will be faster (although it will probably be cheaper, and it will certainly free up courtrooms for other cases). A problem with international criminal proceedings, where the 'relevant' evidence is almost limitless, is that the prosecutor, whose prime interest is to gain a conviction, not to make the process more efficient, has a tendency to see innovations such as Rules 92 *bis*, 92 *ter*, 94 (judicial notice), 94 *bis* (testimony of expert witnesses), etc., not as opportunities to present the same amount of evidence more efficiently, but as opportunities to present *even more* evidence in the same amount of time.[149] It is not surprising, therefore, that the ICTY judges assigned themselves the power, in late 2006, to proactively reduce the scope of indictments in the pre-trial stage.[150]

9.6 CONCLUSION

The topics examined in this chapter repay further study. They all address major questions of legality and fairness: Are the tribunals lawfully established? How is fair notice of the factual and legal allegations to be given? Under what conditions is pre-trial detention acceptable? To what extent should the orality of the adversarial system give way to the dossier of the inquisitorial system in international criminal proceedings? The answers to these questions are still being negotiated at the tribunals. The student of pre-trial procedure should attempt to compare this evolving practice with the practice at the ICC.

---

[148] *A. M.* v. *Italy*, 14 December 1999, para. 25.

[149] See, e.g., *Prosecutor* v. *Milošević*, Decision on Admissibility of Prosecution Investigator's Evidence, 30 September 2002 (in which the prosecutor sought, unsuccessfully, to use one of its investigators to summarize the evidence contained in a large number of witness statements); and *Prosecutor* v. *Milutinović et al.*, Decision on Prosecution Motion to Admit Documentary Evidence, 10 October 2006 ('Given the depth and breadth of this case, the Trial Chamber is generally sympathetic to parties presenting documents from the bar table. However, if that is to be the case, the offering party must be able to demonstrate, with clarity and specificity, where and how each document fits into its case . . . the Prosecution has failed in the vast majority to so comply').

[150] See Rule 73 *bis* (D) and (E) of the ICTY RPE.

10

EVIDENCE IN INTERNATIONAL CRIMINAL PROCEEDINGS

SUMMARY

IO.I INTRODUCTION

International criminal trials are no different from domestic criminal trials in that the discovery of the truth lies at their heart. While there are many different legal proceedings to get at the 'truth', they all have in common the determination of fact on the basis of evidence. The established evidential fact then affords a logical basis for inferring other facts or for legal qualification of different matters, like the guilt or innocence of the accused.[1] The process of adducing and evaluating evidence is generally referred to as the law of evidence. This body of law serves three important functions in modern-day criminal procedure: discovering the truth, protecting the innocent from conviction, and maintaining standards of propriety in the criminal process.[2] Its central feature and most difficult task, however, lies in striking a balance between these often competing demands.

In the present chapter, evidence in international criminal proceedings is explored from the perspective of a number of central questions, set out in the order that they emerge in the course of a trial. This selection does not do justice to many aspects of the law of evidence generally, or to the law of evidence of international criminal tribunals in particular.[3] Yet, the study of key issues offers a basic understanding and insight and also reveals trends in the law of evidence in international criminal law.

This chapter is structured in the following manner. First, we briefly explore the origin and development of the law of evidence in international criminal proceedings, in order to enable the reader to grasp fully the subsequent discussion (section 10.2). Next, the question to be addressed preceding the study of the law of evidence proper is which facts require proof in international criminal proceedings (section 10.3). For those matters that require proof it is vital to establish with whom the burden of proof rests (section 10.4). The answer to that question offers the right perspective for the collection of evidence by the parties to the proceedings (section 10.5). The evidence collected then needs to be presented at trial; the rules governing this presentation will be examined (section 10.6). A recurring and generally hard-fought issue in criminal trials concerns the admission of evidence; this is no different in international criminal trials (section 10.7). At the very end of the topic of evidence in criminal proceedings — although foreshadowing the entire prior process — there is the question of the standard of proof and the evaluation of the evidence by triers of fact (section 10.8). The chapter

---

[1] Cf. W. N. Hohfeld, *Fundamental Legal Conceptions as Applied in Judicial Reasoning and other Legal Essays* (New Haven: Yale University Press, 1923), at 34.

[2] A. A. S. Zuckerman, *The Principles of Criminal Evidence* (Oxford: Clarendon Press, 1989), at 6–7.

[3] For an insightful study on principles of evidence, see Zuckerman, note 2 above; Mirjan Damaška approached the law of evidence from a fascinating comparative perspective, thereby illustrating the fundamental differences between common-law and civil-law systems (M. Damaška, *Evidence Law Adrift* (New Haven: Yale University Press, 1997)). As to the international criminal tribunals, we can recommend for further reading R. May and M. Wierda, *International Criminal Evidence* (Ardsley, NY: Transnational Publishers, 2002), and A.-M. La Rosa, *Juridictions pénales internationales: La procédure et la preuve* (Paris: Presses Universitaires de France, 2003).

ends with reflections on the future shape of the law of evidence in international criminal law (section 10.9).

IO.2 ORIGIN AND DEVELOPMENT OF THE LAW OF EVIDENCE: SQUARING INQUISITORIAL LAW OF EVIDENCE IN AN ADVERSARIAL SYSTEM

Generally in discussing the law of evidence, a very rudimentary distinction is made between 'strict' and 'flexible' regimes. The former contains many and stringent rules on matters such as hearsay, corroboration, admission, and cross-examination, and exists in common-law systems. Their most important rationale is the existence of jury trials, where the involvement of lay persons necessitates that they be shielded from evidence lacking in relevance or probative value. Furthermore, the form of the trial as a contest between two partisan parties has also resulted in stricter scrutiny of the collection and presentation of evidence than is the case in non-adversarial proceedings. A 'flexible' law of evidence generally allows for easy admission of evidence, contains no strict corrob-orative rules, and does not strictly regulate the presentation of evidence. It is the common trait of inquisitorial criminal procedure. A flexible evidentiary regime is based on the absence of juries — professional judges are expected to be better able to disre-gard unreliable evidence — and the assumption of a collective truth-finding process, where all information is put in the dossier accessible to all parties. What is the position of the law of evidence in international criminal law in relation to this divide?

While the Nuremberg Tribunal's procedural law was essentially based on the adver-sarial model — given the strong position of the UK/US common-law bloc — it departed significantly from that model in respect of the law of evidence. This resulted not only from accommodating the Russian and French concerns,[4] but also from the existence on the US side of a sense of urgency preventing them from importing the full US law of criminal procedure. The idea was to have a streamlined, simplified procedure that avoided legal niceties; the fear was that a court burdened with the due-process paraphernalia of domestic courts would be ineffectual.[5] This resulted in a flexible law of evidence, as evidenced by the following provisions of the Nuremberg Charter:

Article 18

The Tribunal shall

(a) confine the Trial strictly to an expeditious hearing of the cases raised by the charges,

---

[4] For an insightful account of the negotiations on this point see Telford Taylor, *The Anatomy of the Nuremberg Trials* (New York: Knopf, 1992), at 78–9.

[5] J. A. Bush, 'Lex Americana: Constitutional Due Process and the Nuremberg Defendants' (2001) 45 *St. Louis University L. J.* at 524.

(b) take strict measures to prevent any action which will cause reasonable delay, and rule out irrelevant issues and statements of any kind whatsoever,

(c) deal summarily with any contumacy, imposing appropriate punishment, including exclusion of any Defendant or his Counsel from some or all further proceedings, but without prejudice to the determination of the charges.

Article 19

The Tribunal shall not be bound by technical rules of evidence. It shall adopt and apply to the greatest possible extent expeditious and nontechnical procedure, and shall admit any evidence which it deems to be of probative value.

Article 20

The Tribunal may require to be informed of the nature of any evidence before it is entered so that it may rule upon the relevance thereof.

Article 21

The Tribunal shall not require proof of facts of common knowledge but shall take judicial notice thereof. It shall also take judicial notice of official governmental documents and reports of the United Nations, including the acts and documents of the committees set up in the various allied countries for the investigation of war crimes, and of records and findings of military or other Tribunals of any of the United Nations.[6]

The wish not to apply technical rules of evidence should be seen in the specific context of the Nuremberg trials. Expediency was a key issue, just as was the easy admission of the overwhelming quantity of official government documents without protracted discussions as to their authenticity.[7] Furthermore, (international) human rights law had not yet arisen to prominence, and therefore the impact of a highly flexible law of evidence on the fairness of the proceedings was not as important as it is today. For example, the right to test witness evidence, envisaged in Article 14(3)(f) of the ICCPR, was not yet available as an internationally protected human right. Although defendants at Nuremberg were given the opportunity to cross-examine witnesses testifying at trial, written witness statements were easily admitted.

Remarkably, the judges who produced the ICTY Rules, copied the 'Nuremberg approach' to the law of evidence rather uncritically.[8] This was not only a matter of convenience — the judges thus keeping all options open — but also an important beacon of recognition of civil-law systems. In both the first annual report of the ICTY

---

[6] IMT Charter.

[7] Note in this respect the language of Article 21 of the Nuremberg Charter, which allows for taking judicial notice of government documents. The question of judicial notice has also played — and continues to play — a vital role in the law and practice of current international criminal tribunals (see further below).

[8] The ad hoc tribunals' statutes are silent as to the law of evidence, and the determination thereof was deliberately left to the judges.

and one of the first decisions in the *Tadić* case, the law of evidence is mentioned as a crucial civil-law element in a predominantly adversarial system:

The first is that, as at Nürnberg and Tokyo, there are no technical rules for the admissibility of evidence. This Tribunal does not need to shackle itself to restrictive rules which have developed out of the ancient trial-by-jury system. There will be no jury sitting at the Tribunal, needing to be shielded from irrelevancies or given guidance as to the weight of the evidence they have heard. The judges will be solely responsible for weighing the probative value of the evidence before them. Consequently, all relevant evidence may be admitted to the Tribunal unless its probative value is substantially outweighed by the need to ensure a fair trial (rule 89) or where the evidence was obtained by a serious violation of human rights (rule 95).[9]

Although the Statute adopts a largely common-law approach to its proceedings, it deviates in several respects from the purely adversarial model. For example, there are no technical rules for the admission of evidence and the judges are solely responsible for weighing the probative value of evidence.[10]

The civil-law character of the evidentiary law of the ad hoc tribunals is manifest in the pivotal provision, which in its original version is formulated as follows:

Rule 89 General Provisions

(A) The rules of evidence set forth in this Section shall govern the proceedings before the Chambers. The Chambers shall not be bound by national rules of evidence.

(B) In cases not otherwise provided for in this Section, a Chamber shall apply rules of evidence which will best favour a fair determination of the matter before it and are consonant with the spirit of the Statute and the general principles of law.

(C) A Chamber may admit any relevant evidence which it deems to have probative value.

(D) A Chamber may exclude evidence if its probative value is substantially outweighed by the need to ensure a fair trial.

(E) A Chamber may request verification of the authenticity of evidence obtained out of court.

While this provision may very well reflect the aspirations of a flexible law of evidence, it remains to be seen to what degree the ICTY and ICTR law of evidence truly matches the inquisitorial flexible regimes on this point. In its initial case law the ICTY seemed to wish significantly to distance itself from the law of evidence known in adversarial systems with jury trials. For example, it did not categorically refuse to admit hearsay evidence.[11] However, acceptance of hearsay as a matter of general policy may obscure

---

[9] First annual ICTY report (1994), paras 72–4 (Report of the International Tribunal for the Prosecution of Persons Responsible for Serious Violations of International Humanitarian Law committed in the Territory of the former Yugoslavia since 1991 (UN Doc. A/49/342 and UN Doc. S/1994/1007, 29 August 1994)).

[10] *Tadić* protective measures decision, para. 22.

[11] E.g. Decision on the Defence Motion on Hearsay, *Prosecutor v. Tadić*, Case No. IT-94-1-T, ICTY, T. Ch., 5 August 1996, paras 13 and 14:

In sum, the prohibition on the admissibility of hearsay that fails to meet a recognized exception is a feature of criminal procedure primarily limited to common law systems. In the civil law system, the judge is responsible for determining the evidence that may be presented during the trial, guided primarily by its relevance and its revelation of the truth.

the fact that the demands of relevance, probative value, and fairness exerted significant influence over the law of evidence and certainly moved it away from the inquisitorial systems in this respect. These are in subsequent decisions — all of which recognize that as a matter of principle the admission of hearsay evidence is not excluded — important restrictions and conditions that to a large degree appear to nullify the *Tadić* starting point of admissibility. Still, in February 1999, the Appeals Chamber in *Aleksovski* strongly supported the admission to hearsay evidence from another trial and conceded the disadvantage to a party not being in a position to challenge that evidence to be a logical consequence of hearsay evidence. However, that disadvantage was counterweighed by the benefit of not having relevant and probative evidence excluded.[12] In *Kordić and Čerkez*, the Trial Chamber exercised stricter supervision, attaching more importance to cross-examination, even if the witness had already been cross-examined in another case.[13] But the final blow to a general policy of hearsay admission was delivered by the Appeals Chamber, also in *Kordić and Čerkez*, in respect of the statement of a deceased witness.[14] There can be no doubt that in the flexible law of inquisitorial systems such a statement would be admissible, regardless of its weight. In addition, the obvious unavailability of a witness is an argument in favour of admission, as there is no alternative in the form of live testimony. Yet, the Appeals Chamber ruled that an item of evidence may be so lacking in terms of indicia of reliability that it is not probative and is therefore inadmissible.[15] Furthermore, the deceased witness statement was unsworn and not subject to cross-examination and was therefore excluded from evidence.

What transpires from the jurisprudential developments in respect of hearsay evidence — not to mention of the adoption of specific rules governing written witness statements[16] — is that the law of evidence at the tribunals may not be as flexible — or non-technical — as in civil-law systems. The absence of a jury probably has less impact than one might have anticipated. Rather, the judges were led astray by a doubtful aspiration to combine elements of diametrically opposed systems of criminal procedure.[17] The following discussion may explain the development of stricter evidentiary rules.

> The International Tribunal, with its unique amalgam of civil and common law features, does not strictly follow the procedure of civil law or common law jurisdictions.

See also Decision on Standing Objection of the Defense to the Admission of Hearsay with No Inquiry as to its Reliability, *Prosecutor* v. *Blaškić*, Case No. IT-95-14-T, ICTY, T. Ch., 21 January 1998, para. 5.

[12] Decision on Prosecutor's Appeal on Admissibility of Evidence, *Prosecutor* v. *Aleksovski*, Case No. IT-95-14/1, ICTY, A. Ch., 16 February 1999, para. 27; note also the strong Dissenting Opinion of Judge Robinson.

[13] Decision on the Prosecution Application to Admit the Tulica Report and Dossier into Evidence, *Prosecutor* v. *Kordić and Čerkez*, Case No. IT-95-14/2, ICTY, T. Ch. 29 July 1999.

[14] Decision on Motion by Prosecution for Variation of Time Limit to File a Response to an Application by the Appellants and Permitting Further Response to Be Filed, *Prosecutor* v *Kordić and Čerkez*, Case No. IT-95-14/2, ICTY, A. Ch., 21 July 2000.   [15] Ibid., para. 24.

[16] See below, section 10.7.5.

[17] The following metaphor used by Damaška is instructive:

> In seeking inspiration for change, it is perhaps natural for lawyers to go browsing in a foreign law boutique. But it is an illusion to think that this is a boutique in which one is always free to purchase some items and reject others. An arrangement stemming from a partial purchase — a legal pastiche — can produce a far less

First, the parties to the proceedings collect evidence and do so to support their own case in what might be referred to as a 'subjective truth-finding contest'.[18] Although judges are careful to express views in this vein, the fact that evidence is collected with a view to supporting one side of a dispute does not add to the relevance and probative value of evidence obtained out of court.[19] By contrast, in inquisitorial systems evidence is essentially collected by the police, acting under the supervision of prosecutorial authorities, and investigative judges, who are expected and have sworn to do so impartially, looking for both incriminating and exculpatory evidence.[20]

Secondly, orality in international criminal trials is still considered an important element, not only from the perspective of the rights of the accused, but also in its own right. It is the orality of trials that enables those interested and concerned to follow them.[21]

Thirdly, the right to cross-examination currently occupies an important place as an element of the right to a fair trial.[22] This has had consequences for the law of evidence

satisfactory factfinding result in practice than under either continental or Anglo-American evidentiary arrangements in their unadulterated form' (M. Damaška, 'The Uncertain Fate of Evidentiary Transplants: Anglo-American and Continental Experiments', (1997) 45(4) *American J. Comp. Law*, at 852).

See also the critical article by Fairlie on the pitfalls of combining civil-law and common-law criminal procedure: M. Fairlie, 'The Marriage of Common and Continental Law at the ICTY and its Progeny, Due Process Deficit' (2004) 4 *ICLR*, at 243–319.

[18] By this we mean that the adversarial system is not concerned with facts that can objectively be established, or come as close as possible to this. Rather, one can describe fact-finding in the adversarial system as 'the dialectical process of persuasion in the courtroom which will somehow lead to truth emerging' (N. Jörg, S. Field, and C. Brants, 'Are Inquisitorial and Adversarial Systems Converging?', in P. Fennel (ed.), *Criminal Justice in Europe — A Comparative Study* (Oxford: Clarendon Press, 1995), at 42. For an analysis of the relationship between 'dialectical' theories of rationality and fact-finding in adversarial criminal procedure, see M. Damaška, *Evidence Law Adrift*, at 94–103.

[19] Note in this respect the contempt allegations concerning falsely recording witness statements in Decision on the Prosecutor's further Allegations of Contempt, *Prosecutor v. Nyiramasuhuko, Ntahobali, Nsabimana, Nteziryayo, Kanyabashi and Ndayambaje*, Cases No. ICTR-97-21-T, ICTR-97-29-T, ICTR-96-15-T, ICTR-96-8-T, T. Ch. II, 30 November 2001. In this case, at least one witness reported that the alleged contemnor had 'insisted' that the witness accept a position that the witness disagreed with. It was also reported that the investigator only took notes whenever the witness said something favourable to the accused, but did not note any statements of the witness that were incriminating. The prosecution further produced a declaration of the witness that the alleged contemnor 'went on to hand me a document . . . and he asked me to sign it though he could not let me read its contents. I told him that I could not sign a document whose contents I did not know. I said that if he wanted me to sign he had to come . . . with a document that reflected everything we had discussed and that I would have to read it first before signing' (paras 20 and 35).

We should also take note of the Appeal Chamber's refusal to admit into evidence a summary of witness statements prepared by an OTP investigator, instead of the original witness statements. Not only was there a problem of 'second-hand' hearsay, but also a party to the proceedings was presenting conclusions to the Trial Chamber; see Decision on Admissibility of Prosecution Investigator's Evidence, *Prosecutor v. Milošević*, Case No. IT-02–54-AR73.2, ICTY, A. Ch., 30 September 2002.

[20] In the Netherlands, for example, witness statements are taken by police who sign them as sworn statements. See Article 153 of the Dutch Code of Criminal Procedure.

[21] For more detail on the importance of the principle of orality, see M. Fairlie, 'Due Process Erosion: The Diminution of Live Testimony at the ICTY' (2003) 34 *California Western Int'l. L.J.* at 63–5.

[22] There is extensive jurisprudence of international human rights courts, especially of the European Court of Human Rights, on this point. For a comprehensive overview and analysis, see Trechsel, *Human Rights in Criminal Proceedings*, at 291–326.

in international criminal trials, even though the law of the ad hoc tribunals and the ICC tends to be rather over-protective of this right.[23]

It follows from the above that the law of evidence may in its written form be of a very permissive and flexible nature, but case law — challenged by objections and problems — has set additional rules and principles. This is also likely to be the case for the ICC, where the law of evidence is in its general approach not significantly different from that of the ICTY and ICTR.[24] Yet, one may envisage at least two reasons favouring flexible admission of out-of-court statements, more akin to the inquisitorial law of evidence. First, very practically, the ICC may be much more dependent on those statements, as witnesses cannot be compelled to appear at the seat of the Court.[25] Secondly the ICC prosecutor is obliged under the Statute to 'investigate incriminating and exonerating circumstances equally'.[26] To what extent this affects the adversarial nature of the proceedings, and, as a result, the basic tenets of the ICC's law of evidence remains to be seen.[27]

As for the general aspects of the law of evidence, there is no need to explore other international or internationalized institutions as they either apply primarily national law (e.g. the Cambodia Extraordinary Chambers)[28] or have copied the ICC (e.g. the East Timor Special Panels)[29] or ICTY/ICTR (e.g. the SCSL)[30] law in this respect.

10.3 WHICH FACTS REQUIRE PROOF?

Central to the law of evidence is the question of which facts require proof. When certain facts do not require proof, subsequent questions such as the burden and standard of proof do not need to be addressed. While this offers advantages from the perspective of judicial economy,[31] it bypasses the benefits and safeguards of the evidentiary process, such as the right to dispute evidence. Two categories of facts which may not require proof in the criminal process can be identified. First, in all criminal justice systems there exists a category of facts not considered reasonably disputable, also referred to as facts of common knowledge, of which judicial notice may be taken. Secondly, in adversarial systems, where parties to the proceedings exercise exclusive or far-reaching control over which facts require proof, they can reach agreement on certain or — for example, in the

---

[23] See Chapters 8, section 8.5.7 and section 10.7.5 below.

[24] The ICC Statute contains one general provision on evidence — Article 69. More detailed but still rather general and permissive rules are set out in the RPE (Rules 63–75).   [25] See below, section 10.5.3.

[26] Article 54(1)(a) of the ICC Statute.

[27] Note that Rule 68 of the ICC RPE provides for the mandatory exclusion of written statements of witnesses who could not have been examined by both parties.

[28] Cf. Article 12 of the UN/Cambodia Agreement.

[29] Cf. UNTAET Regulation No. 2000/15 on the Establishment of Panels with Exclusive Jurisdiction over Serious Criminal Offences, UNTAET/REG/2000/15. For more details see S. Linton, 'Cambodia, East Timor and Sierra Leone: Experiments In International Justice' (2001) 12 *CLF*, at 207.

[30] Cf. Article 14(1) of the SCSL Statute.   [31] A. Zuckerman, *The Principles of Criminal Evidence*, at 73.

case of a plea agreement — all of the facts;[32] being no longer in dispute, these facts no longer require proof and judicial notice can be taken thereof.[33]

A number of factors explain why, especially in the context of international criminal proceedings, there is increasing interest in the category of facts which do not — or no longer — require proof. First, especially since the imposition of compulsory exit strategies, the demands of expeditiousness have become even greater at the ICTY and the ICTR.[34] Each contested fact to be proved may require several valuable trial days. Secondly, in order to establish an individual's guilt for war crimes, crimes against humanity, or genocide, important contextual elements need to be proven. One may wonder whether contextual elements — such as the existence of an armed conflict or the identification of the Tutsi as an ethnic group in the sense of the Genocide Convention — are still reasonably in dispute in subsequent cases faced with the same contextual elements. Thirdly, given the circumstances surrounding their establishment and their functioning, the ICTY and the ICTR have most often not been in a position to arrest and try in joint trials those persons alleged to be responsible for the same or overlapping sets of facts. For example, the ICTY has held several trials dealing with the treatment of Bosnian Muslims in the Trnopolje, Keraterm, and Omarska camps. Are matters such as the general level of treatment and the command structure of these camps still reasonably in dispute in later trials?

The applicable rules and jurisprudence in international criminal law reveal the deployment of different approaches which strive for judicial economy; at the same time, the judges have demonstrated awareness that judicial economy should neither result in unfair prejudice against the accused, nor relieve the prosecutor of the burden of proof.[35] The relevant rules distinguish various forms of judicial notice.

In its initial version, Rule 94 of the ICTY and ICTR RPE consisted of a single section obliging a trial chamber to take judicial notice of facts of common knowledge. This provision has been mirrored in Article 69(6) of the ICC Statute, albeit with the important modification that an ICC bench is not under an obligation to take judicial notice of facts of common knowledge. In 1998 (ICTY) and 2000 (ICTR) a section (B) was added in Rule 94 granting a trial chamber the discretion to take judicial notice of 'adjudicated facts or documentary evidence from other proceedings of the Tribunal

---

[32] See on the consequences of control by the parties over facts to be proven for the evidentiary process M. Damaška, *Evidence Law Adrift*, at 103–5.

[33] Unless the facts are not accepted as uncontested, as is possible for the judge to do in common-law systems. Damaška in this respect rightly observes that 'proof-taking in respect to these facts appears artificial or contrived. If parties are compelled to do battle over them, the resulting procedural action is bound to be lifeless or anemic: the wind has gone from the sails of adversary arrangements. Nor can this malfunction be remedied by a unilateral judicial inquiry: it would compromise the basic values of the adversary system.' (Ibid., at 104.)

[34] In respect of the SCSL it can be safely said that there was strong pressure to finalize within a reasonable period of time from the beginning (see Special Court for Sierra Leone Completion Strategy, 18 May 2005, Annex A to identical letters dated May 26 2005, from the Secretary-General to the President of the General Assembly and the President of the Security Council, May 27 2005, A/59/816–S/2005/350).

[35] Decision on the Prosecutor's Motion for Judicial Notice Pursuant to Rules 73, 89, and 94, *Prosecutor v. Bagosora*, ICTR-98-41-T, ICTR, T. Ch. I, 11 April 2003.

relating to matters at issue in the current proceedings'.[36] The legal framework of the ICC does not allow for judicial notice on this basis, which raises the question whether adjudicated facts could be qualified in certain circumstances as facts of common knowledge. The ICC legal framework, however, does provide for agreement as to evidence between the parties. According to Rule 69, a chamber may consider an alleged fact which is agreed upon as proven, unless it is of the opinion that a more complete presentation of the alleged fact is required in the interests of justice, in particular in the interests of the victims. Such a provision is absent in the law of the ICTY and ICTR, while at the same time it is an important aspect of the pre-trial stage to record points of agreement and disagreement on matters of law and fact between the parties.[37] One would have expected better regulation of the evidentiary consequences of an agreement on matters of fact, even if there is no unconditional duty to accept the agreed fact.[38]

The fact that, in contrast with the ad hoc tribunals, the ICC law does not allow for judicial notice to be taken of 'adjudicated facts' represents a serious gap, as the category of adjudicated facts may not be reasonably in dispute between the participants in a certain trial and yet may lack the generality of facts of common knowledge.[39] It is puzzling that this category has been left out of the ICC law, the more so because it has become increasingly important in the practice of the ad hoc tribunals and the SCSL. It does not seem that a fundamental objection — namely that the practice of judicial notice of adjudicated facts usurps the judicial function in a trial — is the reason for this.[40]

The categorization of facts not requiring proof has given rise to confusion concerning how one perceives the very nature of international criminal proceedings. In our view, the vital test is that of facts that are not reasonably in dispute.[41] In *Fofana* Justice Robertson makes a remarkable hierarchical distinction by claiming that judicially noticed facts are 'adjudicated', whereas agreed facts lack this quality; the latter are said to lack that high degree of likelihood that puts them beyond reasonable dispute.[42] But what kind of dispute are we talking about then? The heart of the adversarial trial lies in the dispute between the parties; as a result, any agreement moves elements outside that

---

[36] Note the more extended scope of Article 21 of the Nuremberg Charter in this respect:

> It shall also take judicial notice of official governmental documents and reports of the United Nations, including the acts and documents of the committees set up in the various allied countries for the investigation of war crimes, and of records and findings of military or other Tribunals of any of the United Nations.

[37] See Rule 65 *ter* (H) of the ICTY Rules. Note that Rule 65 *ter* is part of neither the ICTR Rules, nor the SCSL Rules.

[38] Now we can rely on the adversarial nature of international criminal proceedings to consider the evidentiary force of inter-party agreements on facts as self-evident. See the observations in M. Damaška, *Evidence Law Adrift*, at 88–94.

[39] Instructive on the difference between judicial notice of facts of common knowledge and adjudicated facts is Fofana — Decision on Appeal against 'Decision on Prosecution's Motion for Judicial Notice and Admission of Evidence', *Prosecutor* v. *Norman et al.*, Case No. SCSL-2004-14-AR73, SCSL, A. Ch., 16 May 2005, Separate Opinion of Justice Robertson.

[40] See commentary by D. Ntanda Nsereko in Klip and Sluiter, *Annotated Leading Cases, vol. IX*, at 696.

[41] In our view this could also be the only test and replace the different categories — common knowledge, adjudicated facts, and agreed facts — set out in the various statutes and rules.

[42] Fofana — Decision on Appeal against 'Decision on Prosecution's Motion for Judicial Notice and Admission of Evidence', *Prosecutor* v. *Norman et al.*, Case No. SCSL-2004-14-AR73, SCSL, A. Ch., 16 May 2005, Separate Opinion of Justice Robertson, para. 11.

dispute and attributes agreed facts by definition to the highest hierarchical position. Adjudicated facts, on the other hand, may still be in dispute between the parties. While they should not be, according to the court, the fact is that they *are*. From a purely adversarial perspective, the stage of 'adjudicated facts' is never reached in relation to facts that are not in dispute between the parties.[43]

Understandably, the doctrine of judicial notice has surfaced in international criminal law in relation to many of the contextual elements and to the bases of many common crimes that are at the heart of the criminal responsibility of various mid-level and top-level perpetrators. However, there is always the risk of taking judicial notice too easily, to the detriment of the accused's right to a fair trial. While the ad hoc tribunals have generally been aware of this,[44] the doctrine of judicial notice is a handy way of proving complicated issues. In the Dutch *Van Anraat* case, for example, the court ruled that it was a fact of common knowledge that Saddam Hussein exercised absolute power in Iraq in the 1980s.[45] Furthermore, one may wonder to what extent certain facts the SCSL has taken judicial notice of as facts of common knowledge are truly not subject to reasonable dispute, as there is no precedent to rely on.

While the ad hoc tribunals and the SCSL have taken judicial notice of adjudicated facts in a growing number of decisions,[46] they have attached stringent conditions to it.[47] If judicial notice is not taken, the question is whether the evidence from other proceedings may then be easily introduced as hearsay evidence.[48]

---

[43] When judges are not satisfied by the agreed facts, this may give rise to a difficult situation; see M. Damaška, *Evidence Law Adrift*, at 104.

[44] For relevant case law, see Jones and Powles, *International Criminal Practice*, at 751.

[45] However, the court later provided proof for this matter.

[46] ICTY: Decision on Judicial Notice of Adjudicated Facts Following the Motion Submitted by Counsel for the Accused Hadzihasanovic and Kubura on 20 January 2005, *Prosecutor* v. *Hadžihasanović et al.*, Case No. IT-01-47-T, ICTY, T. Ch. II, 14 April 2005; Decision on Third and Fourth Prosecution Motions for Judicial Notice of Adjudicated Facts, *Prosecutor* v. *Krajišnik*, Case No. IT-00-39, ICTY, T. Ch. I, 24 March 2005; *Prosecutor* v. *Krajišnik*, Case No. IT-00-39, Decision on Prosecution Motions for Judicial Notice of Adjudicated Facts and for Admission of Written Statements of Witnesses Pursuant to Rule 92 *bis*, ICTY, T. Ch. I, 28 February 2003; Decision on Motion for Judicial Notice of Adjudicated Facts Pursuant to Rule 94(B), *Prosecutor* v. *Prlić et al.*, Case No. IT-04-74-PT, ICTY, T. Ch. II, 14 March 2006; ICTR: Decision on Prosecutor's Interlocutory Appeal of Decision on Judicial Notice, *Prosecutor* v. *Karemera et al.*, Case No. ICTR-98-44-AR73(C), ICTR, A. Ch., 16 June 2006 ; Decision on Prosecution Motion for Judicial Notice, *Prosecutor* v. *Karemera et al.*, Case No. ICTR-98-44-R94, ICTR, T. Ch. III, 9 November 2005; Decision on the Prosecutor's Motion for Judicial Notice and Presumptions of Facts Pursuant to Rules 94 and 54, *Prosecutor* v. *Semanza*, Case No. ICTR-97-20-I, ICTR, T. Ch. III, 3 November 2000; SCSL: Decision on Prosecution's Motion for Judicial Notice and Admission of Evidence, *Prosecutor* v. *Norman et al.*, Case No. SCSL-04-14-PT, SCSL, T. Ch., 2 June 2004.

[47] Thus, in *Hadžihasanović*, the following were set out: the facts (1) are distinct, concrete and identifiable; (2) are restricted to factual findings and do not include legal characterizations; (3) are contested at trial and form part of a judgment which has either not been appealed or been finally settled on appeal or the facts were contested at trial and now form part of a judgment which is under appeal, but falls within issues which are not in dispute on appeal; (4) do not have any direct bearing on the criminal responsibility of the accused; (5) are not the subject of (reasonable) dispute between the parties in the present case; and (6) do not negatively affect the right of the accused to a fair trial (Final Decision on Judicial Notice of Adjudicated Facts, *Prosecutor* v. *Hadžihasanović*, Case No. IT-01-47-T, ICTY, T. Ch. II, 20 April 2004).

[48] See further details below; at this point it may be noted that in the SCSL proceedings the line of distinction between judicial notice and admission via its highly flexible Rule 92 *bis* is rather thin. See also Fofana — Decision on Appeal against 'Decision on Prosecution's Motion for Judicial Notice and Admission of Evidence', *Prosecutor* v.

Agreement between parties in relation to facts may save valuable time and resources. This raises the question to what extent the parties — especially the defence — may be expected to 'cooperate' in formal admissions.[49] As will be further explored below, the presumption of innocence and the ensuing burden of proof on the prosecutor are serious obstacles to any formal duty in this respect. Yet, in SCSL case law there is bold language. For example, in *Sesay et al.* the parties were *ordered* to intensify their efforts to identify further points of agreement.[50] In his separate opinion in *Norman et al.*, Justice Robertson speaks of an ethical duty of counsel to assist the court, entailing a duty to make admissions, if requested and at an early stage, of facts that they have no reason to dispute later in the trial.[51] We fail to see how this duty can be reconciled with the presumption of innocence and the ensuing burden of proof, to be addressed below.

10.4 BURDEN OF PROOF

In relation to facts that do require proof, the important question of the burden of proof must be addressed.

The fact that the burden of proving the guilt of the accused lies with the prosecutor follows from two fundamental rules. First, as a general principle of law, it is a fundamental requirement that he who alleges must prove.[52] Secondly, it is an internationally accepted human right that everybody is presumed innocent until proven guilty;[53] the logical corollary of this right is the placement of the burden of proof fully and unconditionally on the prosecutor.[54]

Norman et al., Case No. SCSL-2004-14-AR73, SCSL, A. Ch., 16 May 2005, Separate Opinion of Justice Robertson, para. 27.

[49] In practice, prosecutors often invest considerable time and resources in proving matters which the defence later claims were not in dispute. See in this sense Report of the Expert Group to Conduct a Review of the Effective Operation and Functioning of the International Criminal Tribunal for the former Yugoslavia and the International Criminal Tribunal for Rwanda (UN Doc. S/2000/957, 17 June 2000), para. 87.

[50] Decision on Co-operation between the Parties, *Prosecutor* v. *Sesay*, Case No. SCSL-04-15-PT, SCSL, T. Ch., 16 June 2004.

[51] Fofana — Decision on Appeal against 'Decision on Prosecution's Motion for Judicial Notice and Admission of Evidence', *Prosecutor* v. *Norman et al.*, Case No. SCSL-2004-14-AR73, SCSL, A. Ch., 16 May 2005, Separate Opinion of Justice Robertson, para. 11. Justice Robertson infers such a duty from Article 8 of the SCSL Code of Conduct. However, the duty to make formal admissions cannot be inferred from this, as follows from the greater imperatives of the presumption of innocence.

[52] *Delalić et al.* trial judgment, para. 599:

> It is a fundamental requirement of any judicial system that the person who has invoked its jurisdiction and desires the tribunal or court to take action on his behalf must prove his case to its satisfaction. As a matter of common sense, therefore, the legal burden of proving all facts essential to their claims normally rests upon the plaintiff in a civil suit or the prosecutor in criminal proceedings.

[53] Protected in Article 14(2) of the ICCPR, Article 6(2) of the ECHR, Article 21(3) of the ICTY Statute, Article 20(3) of the ICTR Statute, and Article 66 of the ICC Statute.

[54] See Zappalà, *Human Rights in International Criminal Proceedings*, at 91.

In respect of the imposition of the burden of proof, there is no fundamental difference between adversarial and inquisitorial systems.[55] In domestic law and practice there is, on the one hand, an unequivocal attribution of this burden to the prosecution, including the defendant's right not to assist the prosecutor in any manner in discharging his burden of proof.[56] On the other hand, in view of the need for effective prosecution, there arises the question of possible exceptions. For example, may the trier of fact draw negative conclusions from the exercise of the right to silence about the guilt of the accused?[57] Or, to take another example, would it be reasonable and fair to reverse the burden of proof in relation to facts which the defence does not reasonably dispute prior to trial? Generally, domestic criminal law systems provide either explicitly or implicitly for reverse-onus situations, but these may be confined to the particularities of domestic criminal law.[58] From a human rights perspective, the presumption arising from certain facts — for example, that a person who has prohibited goods in his or her possession at customs is guilty of smuggling — is within certain limits acceptable.[59] International criminal law has its own particular issues in relation to the burden of proof. For example, once it is established that a subordinate has committed war crimes, is then the onus on the commander to establish that he or she took all reasonable measures to prevent or repress their commission?[60]

All international criminal tribunals recognize the prosecutor's burden of proof as a fundamental rule and principle of their criminal procedure. However, the post-Second World War tribunals as well as the contemporary ad hoc tribunals and the internationalized criminal courts do not contain a specific rule putting the burden of proof on the

---

[55] Ibid.

[56] See Justice Black's dissent:

> The Framers were well aware of the awesome investigative and prosecutorial powers of government and it was in order to limit those powers that they spelled out in detail in the Constitution the procedure to be followed in criminal trials. A defendant, they said, is entitled to notice of the charges against him, trial by jury, the right to counsel for his defense, the right to confront and cross-examine witnesses, the right to call witnesses in his own behalf, and the right not to be a witness against himself. All of these rights are designed to shield the defendant against state power. None are designed to make convictions easier and taken together they clearly indicate that in our system the entire burden of proving criminal activity rests on the State. The defendant, under our Constitution, need not do anything at all to defend himself, and certainly he cannot be required to help convict himself. Rather he has an absolute, unqualified right to compel the State to investigate its own case, find its own witnesses, prove its own facts, and convince the jury through its own resources. Throughout the process the defendant has a fundamental right to remain silent, in effect challenging the State at every point to: 'Prove it!' (*Williams* v. *Florida*, US Supreme Court, 399 US 78 (1970).)

[57] This is possible in the UK and, remarkably, has found acceptance by the European Court of Human Rights (*Saunders* v. *UK*, 19187/91 [1996] ECtHR 65 (17 December 1996); *Murray* v. *UK*, 14310/88 [1994] ECtHR 39 (28 October 1994); *Beckles* v. *UK*, 44652/98 [2002] ECtHR 661 (8 October 2002); *Condron* v. *UK*, 35718/97 [2000] ECtHR 191 (2 May 2000)).

[58] For examples refer to W. A. Schabas, 'Article 66', in Triffterer, *Commentary on the Rome Statute*, at 839.

[59] *Salabiaku* v. *France*, 10519/83 [1988] ECtHR 19 (7 October 1988).

[60] See Article 28(1)(b) of the ICC Statute. Schabas raises this example, arguing it may amount to a reversal of the burden of proof (W. A. Schabas, 'Article 66', in Triffterer, *Commentary on the Rome Statute*, at 840–1). However, we fail to see that, as this is an element of the crime to be proved by the prosecutor. The mere fact that a subordinate has committed a crime is insufficient to conclude that no reasonable measures were taken. The situation should be distinguished from the common example of the individual possessing large quantities of drugs; the inferred fact that the person must then be a dealer can be drawn, in respect of which the defence has the burden of proving the contrary.

prosecutor. Nevertheless, they apply it as a general rule following from general principles of criminal procedure and the presumption of innocence set out in the Statutes. It has also had a significant impact on the development of international criminal procedure. The adoption and subsequent practice concerning Rule 98 *bis* is the consequence of the burden of proof lying with the prosecutor. Where the latter fails the applicable standard, there is no need to continue the trial.[61]

However, the absence of specific rules has also resulted in some questionable reversals of the burden of proof. For example, according to Rule 92, confessions by the accused shall be presumed to have been free and voluntary unless the contrary is proved.[62] Probably the most criticism has been directed at the original versions of Rule 65 of the ICTY and ICTR Rules, according to which the accused bore the burden of demonstrating 'exceptional circumstances' justifying his or her provisional release. Although this rule was not concerned with the question of the accused's guilt in respect of the charges against him, it is illustrative of the possible results from the absence of stringent rules regarding the burden of proof. The ICC could be seen as constituting in this respect an improvement. Article 66 of the ICC Statute puts the burden of proof on the prosecutor and also sets out the required standard of proof; furthermore, and this is truly innovative, Article 67(1)(i) grants the accused the right not to have imposed on him or her any reversal of the burden of proof or any onus of rebuttal. The question arises what is the precise scope of this provision and how it relates to the ICTY and ICTR law. In *Čelebići* Landžo raised a plea of insanity.[63] The Trial Chamber rightly ruled that criminal law operates on the basis of a presumption of sanity and that the defence carries a burden to prove otherwise, on the balance of probabilities.[64] One may wonder whether this logical finding — and to have concluded otherwise would have put the prosecutor in an impossible position — would still be possible for the ICC, given the combined effect of Articles 66(2) and 67(1)(i) of the Statute.[65] The solution may be found in civil-law jurisdictions where in relation to the 'guilt' of the accused a strict distinction is made between the facts charged in the indictment, on the one hand, and criminal liability and punishability, on the other. The prosecutor carries the full burden of proving the facts charged in the indictment; if proven, criminal liability and punishability are generally presumed, and the defence carries the burden, on the balance of probabilities, of proving the contrary. In our view, it is in this civil-law sense

---

[61] Rule 98 *bis* of the ICTY and ICTR RPE obligates the Trial Chamber to acquit the accused at the close of the prosecutor's case on any count if there is no evidence sufficient to sustain a conviction ('no case to answer'). For some examples of the application of this rule, see: *Jelisić* trial judgment, para. 16; Separate and Concurring Opinion of Judge Williams on Imanishimwe's Defence Motion for Judgment of Acquittal on count of Conspiracy to Commit Genocide Pursuant to Rule 98 *bis*, *Prosecutor* v. *Ntagerura et al.*, Case No. ICTR-99-46-T, ICTR, T. Ch. III, 13 March 2002, paras 4 and 8; Reasons for Oral Decision of 17 September 2002 on the Motions for Acquittal, *Prosecutor* v. *Nahimana et al.*, Case No. ICTR-99-52-T, ICTR, T. Ch. I, 25 September 2002, and so forth. For a detailed discussion of Rule 98 *bis* see Zappalà, *Human Rights in International Criminal Proceedings*, at 91–4.

[62] For critical comment on this reversal of the burden of proof: see ibid., at 94–5.

[63] *Čelebići* trial judgment, paras 1157–60.   [64] Ibid., para. 1157.

[65] In this respect, neither Article 31 of the Statute, setting out grounds excluding criminal responsibility, nor the Rules contain specific provisions on the burden of proving these grounds.

that one should interpret 'guilt' as mentioned in Article 66(2) of the Statute, namely, as confined to the facts charged in the indictment.[66]

This civil-law distinction may also be helpful in better determining the burden of proof remaining on the defence. The latter has a burden of proof in respect of 'special defences' raised, such as the defence of duress or mental incapacity.[67] Rule 67(A)(i)(b) of the ICTY RPE (and Rule 67(A)(ii)(b) of the ICTR RPE) testifies to this, referring to information on which the accused intends to rely to establish the special *defence*. Unfortunately, similar language is used in relation to alibis; they apparently are considered in Rule 67(A)(i)(a) of the ICTY RPE (and Rule 67(A)(ii)(a) of the ICTR RPE) as a defence the accused needs to establish. Obviously this is incompatible with the prosecutor's burden of proof in relation to the facts charged in the indictment, and the tribunals have tried to solve this by not considering an alibi defence as a defence in the true sense.[68] Yet, the defence in certain cases may have been under the impression that it carried a burden of proving its alibi.[69] In this regard, the ICC legal framework constitutes an improvement in that the term 'defences' has been removed from Rule 79 of the ICC RPE, dealing with disclosure by the defence. In that rule, there is only reference to raising the existence of an alibi and raising a ground for excluding criminal responsibility.

10.5 COLLECTION OF EVIDENCE

It is with the burden and standard of proof in mind — the latter being dealt with in more detail below — that evidence is collected. The party carrying the burden of proof should be in a position to do so, as should the party enjoying a right to submit evidence to the contrary.

While this section concentrates on the legal tools for obtaining evidence, it should be noted that this is only a precondition and that practical obstacles and problems often prove to be far more important. In this respect one can think of a state simply refusing

[66] The distinction made by May and Wierda is in our view confusing; they distinguish between a legal or persuasive burden of proof and an evidential burden of proof; the former would then concern the obligation of the prosecution to prove all the facts necessary to establish guilt, and the latter the obligation on either party to establish the facts on a particular issue. It is not clear precisely what this distinction entails in respect of the burden of proof; see May and Wierda, *International Criminal Evidence*, at 121–4.

[67] We confine ourselves now to the guilt or innocence of the accused; in the sentencing phase, for example, the defence also has the burden of proving on the balance of probabilities the existence of mitigating circumstances.

[68] Thus, in *Čelebići* the Appeals Chamber referred to the common misuse of the word to describe an alibi as a 'defence' (*Delalić et al.* appeal judgment, para. 581). In *Kamuhanda*, the ICTR Appeals Chamber concluded that a defence is to be understood as comprising grounds excluding criminal responsibility although the accused has fulfilled the legal elements of the crime (*Kamuhanda* appeal judgment, para. 167). For critical comment on/the defence of alibi, arguing that it does not deserve a special place within the law of international criminal tribunals, see G. Sluiter, 'Commentary', in Klip and Sluiter, *Annotated Leading Cases, vol. X*, at 969–74.

[69] This element came to the fore in a considerable number of cases where the defence of alibi was raised: *Rutaganda* trial judgment; *Kajelijeli* trial judgment; *Kamuhanda* trial judgment; *Ntakirutimana* trial judgment; *Semanza* trial judgment; *Niyitegeka* trial judgment; and *Kayishema and Ruzindana* trial judgment.

to cooperate, or of serious security risks during an ongoing conflict.[70] In *Tadić* the ICTY Appeals Chamber left open the possibility that proceedings might be stayed and the accused provisionally released if such extrajudicial factors might disproportionately affect the accused's ability to defend him- or herself.[71]

Since the collection of evidence covers numerous aspects, we focus on only a few key issues: equal distribution of powers to collect evidence, the need for judicial intervention, and compelling the appearance of witnesses. The question of state cooperation — which is vital to the collection of evidence — will be examined in its own right in Chapter 12, section 12.3.

10.5.1 Equal distribution of powers to collect evidence

While the judicial branch of international criminal tribunals possesses powers to collect evidence (and increasingly so in the case of the ICC), it is obvious that the adversarial international criminal procedure has assigned the task of the collection of evidence to the parties to the proceedings. This implies that the prosecutor should be in a position to discharge the burden of proof effectively and that the defendant is enabled to adequately prepare his or her defence. The principle of equality of arms permeates the analysis of legal tools available to the parties. In this respect, there are some structural problems in international criminal law. Leaving aside the practical aspects, namely that the international prosecutors generally have far more resources at their disposal than do the defence teams, we note in relation to the collection of evidence the following imbalances which are problematic from the perspective of equality of arms.[72]

The prosecutor is one of the main organs of all international criminal tribunals.[73] In that capacity, the prosecutor enjoys three clear advantages over the defence in respect of

---

[70] In respect of the latter see the account of M. Wladimiroff, first defence counsel to Tadić, concerning his first visits to Yugoslavia: 'War Crimes Tribunals: the Record and the Prospects' (1998) 13 *American University Int'l Law Rev.*, at 1450–1. On problems related to state cooperation, see G. Sluiter, *International Criminal Adjudication and the Collection of Evidence: Obligations of States* (Antwerp: Intersentia, 2002); D. Stroh, 'State Cooperation with International Criminal Tribunals for the former Yugoslavia and for Rwanda' (2001) 5 *Max Planck Y'book United Nations Law*, at 249–83; A. Ciampi, 'The Obligation to Cooperate', in Cassese et al., *Rome Statute Commentary, vol. II*, at 1607–8.

[71] Cf. *Tadić* appeal judgment, para. 55:

> The Appeals Chamber can conceive of situations where a fair trial is not possible because witnesses central to the defence case do not appear due to the obstructionist efforts of a State. In such circumstances, the defence, after exhausting all the other measures mentioned above, has the option of submitting a motion for a stay of proceedings. The Defence opined during the oral hearing that the reason why such action was not taken in the present case may have been due to trial counsel's concern regarding the long period of detention on remand. The Appeals Chamber notes that the Rules envision some relief in such a situation, in the form of provisional release, which, pursuant to Sub-rule 65(B), may be granted 'in exceptional circumstances'. It is not hard to imagine that a stay of proceedings occasioned by the frustration of a fair trial under prevailing trial conditions would amount to exceptional circumstances under this rule. The obligation is on the complaining party to bring the difficulties to the attention of the Trial Chamber forthwith so that the latter can determine whether any assistance could be provided under the Rules or Statute to relieve the situation. The party cannot remain silent on the matter only to return on appeal to seek a trial *de novo*, as the Defence seeks to do in this case.

[72] On equality of arms from a human rights perspective, see Chapter 8, section 8.5.

[73] See also Chapter 2, which examines this issue from an international institutional law perspective.

the collection of evidence. First, the statutes and rules have attributed distinct powers to the prosecutor to collect evidence; in the case of the defendant, these powers are to be inferred from his or her right to prepare a defence.[74] Secondly, the prosecutor's being one of the organs of international criminal tribunals, there is a direct relationship of cooperation with states and other subjects of international law; this is not restricted to the power to issue requests for legal assistance and the corresponding duty to comply, but also covers the possibility of entering into cooperation arrangements. Thirdly, again related to the prosecutor's organic position, prosecution staff members enjoy privileges and immunities facilitating their on-site investigations.[75] The above advantages may also be burdens, which favours the defence, however slightly. For example, it may be easier for an individual defence counsel to conduct investigations in a private capacity, travelling on a tourist visa, than for a formally announced prosecution team.[76]

One may easily imagine the possible negative consequences of the above for the collection of evidence and ultimately the fairness of the trial. This raises the question how the position of the defendant in the collection of evidence can be enhanced. An obvious solution lies in the attribution of organic status to the defence in the form of a defence unit. However, this has not been adopted and also has its drawbacks.[77] Rather, the judicial branch plays a vital role in assisting, where necessary, the defence. The Appeals Chamber in *Tadić* rightly said that

It follows that the Chamber shall provide every practicable facility it is capable of granting under the Rules and Statute when faced with a request by a party for assistance in presenting its case. The Trial Chambers are mindful of the difficulties encountered by the parties in tracing and gaining access to evidence in the territory of the former Yugoslavia where some States have not been forthcoming in complying with their legal obligation to cooperate with the Tribunal. Provisions under the Statute and the Rules exist to alleviate the difficulties faced by the parties so that each side may have equal access to witnesses. The Chambers are empowered to issue such orders, summonses, subpoenas, warrants and transfer orders as may be necessary for the purposes of an investigation or for the preparation or conduct of the trial. This includes the power to:

(1) adopt witness protection measures, ranging from partial to full protection;

(2) take evidence by video-link or by way of deposition;

(3) summon witnesses and order their attendance;

---

[74] For more detail see G. Sluiter, *International Criminal Adjudication and the Collection of Evidence: Obligations of States*, at 131. [75] See Chapter 1, section 5.2.

[76] It is reported that members of the OTPs were refused visas to the FRY and Rwanda on a number of occasions. See Address by Judge Gabrielle Kirk McDonald, President of the ICTY, to the UN General Assembly, 18 November 1998, available at www.un.org/icty/pressreal/SPE981119.htm (last visited 20 November 2006); Rwanda refused to cooperate with the ICTR and to allow the prosecutor to enter the territory of Rwanda in protest against the Appeals Chamber's releasing Bayaragwiza (Decision (Prosecutor's Request for Review or Reconsideration), *Barayagwiza* v. *Prosecutor*, Case No. ICTR-97-19-AR72, ICTR, A. Ch., 31 March 2000).

[77] See Chapter 2, section 2.5. In the case of the SCSL, there is a defence office, which is not an independent organ but a part of the Special Court's Registry. While the SCSL Defence Office has claimed a significant degree of independence of other organs, especially the Registrar, the SCSL Appeals Chamber emphasized in *Brima et al.* that the Defence Office is not an independent organ of the Court and remains under the authority of the Registrar

(4) issue binding orders to States for, *inter alia*, the taking and production of evidence; and

(5) issue binding orders to States to assist a party or to summon a witness and order his or her attendance under the Rules.

A further important measure available in such circumstances is:

(6) for the President of the Tribunal to send, at the instance of the Trial Chamber, a request to the State authorities in question for their assistance in securing the attendance of a witness.

In addition, whenever the aforementioned measures have proved to be to no avail, a Chamber may, upon the request of a party or *proprio motu*:

(7) order that proceedings be adjourned or, if the circumstances so require, that they be stayed.[78]

While one may deduce from the above an incentive to trial chambers to offer maximum assistance, they have not always been forthcoming in doing so. At the outset, it should be noted that the process of applying to a chamber for assistance in the collection of evidence is cumbersome in itself. In addition, the ICTY Trial Chambers have developed admissibility criteria, further codified in Rule 54 *bis*.[79] According to these, applications for legal assistance should be duly justified, specific enough (no 'fishing expeditions'!), and not be unduly onerous for states. As reasonable as this may seem, similar conditions do not hinder the prosecutor when directly issuing requests for assistance. Furthermore, strict supervision carries with it the risk of interference with the defence strategy.

While there are in practice problems with the collection of evidence, the judicial branch may at least remedy procedural inequalities in relation to many of these collection activities. Surprisingly, in respect of on-site investigations in the framework of the ICC this is not the case. As will be further explored in Chapter 12, section 12.3 dealing with state cooperation, in the context of the ICC the power to conduct on-site investigations, during which vital evidence may be collected directly or, just as importantly, by contacting witnesses, is reserved to the prosecutor.[80] In the face of uncooperative states the pre-trial chamber is powerless to assist the defence; thus, an unacceptable procedural inequality affecting the evidentiary process is self-evident.[81]

(Decision on Brima-Kamara Defence Appeal Motion against Trial Chamber II Majority Decision on Extremely Urgent Confidential Joint Motion for the Re-appointment of Kevin Metzger and Wilbert Harris as Lead Counsel for Alex Tamba Brima and Brima Bazzy Kamara, *Prosecutor* v. *Brima et al.*, Case No. SCSL-2004-16-AR73, SCSL, A. Ch., 8 December 2005, para. 83). Note that in his Separate Opinion Judge Robertson argued in favour of 'operational independence of the Defence Office *vis-à-vis* the Registrar' (Separate and Concurring Opinion of Justice Robertson, para. 102(viii)).

[78] *Tadić* appeal judgment, para. 52.

[79] These admissibility criteria serve a twofold purpose. First, by requiring that in principle the parties should first themselves request assistance from states before turning to a judge or a chamber, one may prevent the judicial branch from being burdened with possibly unnecessary applications. Secondly, by demanding a certain degree of specificity and completeness with respect to the applications made, one may prevent states from receiving requests with which they cannot reasonably be expected to comply and one may protect the rights of third parties. The rights of third parties may, for example, be at stake when either party applies for the search of a number of not further defined premises for evidentiary items not specified. [80] Articles 54(2) and 99(4) of the ICC Statute.

[81] See G. Sluiter, *International Criminal Adjudication and the Collection of Evidence: Obligations of States*, at 321. See also Chapter 8, section 8.5 above.

10.5.2 The need for judicial intervention

An important issue in relation to the collection of evidence is what can lawfully be done by the parties themselves and for which activities judicial intervention is required. This issue arises particularly when the collection of evidence requires coercive measures infringing individual rights. It is especially important since the absence of judicial intervention, in cases where it would have been appropriate, may have serious consequences for the evidence's admissibility or weight.

Whereas the domestic law of criminal procedure generally contains detailed rules on methods of evidence-gathering infringing upon individual rights and liberties, extending to matters such as wiretaps, systematic observation, and infiltration, none of this is regulated in the legal framework of international criminal tribunals, with the exception of the questioning of persons or suspects.[82] The probable rationale for this lack of regulation is threefold. First, international criminal procedure is a skeleton legal framework to start with. Secondly, the compulsory collection of evidence is done mostly — if not entirely — by national authorities, which are bound by their own laws of criminal procedure. Thirdly, practice demonstrates that the prosecutors of the ad hoc tribunals have collected little evidence by compulsory process on their own initiative; rather, they have sought to rely on the results of compulsory process employed by national authorities for other purposes.[83]

Although the prosecutor has a broad power to collect evidence, specific coercive measures whether performed by the prosecutor directly or by national authorities, require a warrant.[84] The issuance of a warrant by a national court offers insufficient legal protection, as the latter lacks the overview of what is needed and justified in that particular investigation.[85] ICTY and ICTR practice on this point is rare, but the occasional decision mentions the issuance of a warrant for search and seizure operations.[86]

As judicial intervention serves an important protective function, the question arises whether this is always required from a human rights perspective. This question is not easy to answer. On the one hand, case law of human rights courts demonstrates that judicial permission is not an absolute condition for searches or the interception of

---

[82] Cf. Article 55 of the ICC Statute and Rule 42 of the ICTY, ICTR, and SCSL Rules.

[83] Note the interception of telecommunications in *Brđanin* and *Halilović*. Decision on the Defence 'Objection to Intercept Evidence', *Prosecutor* v. *Brdanin*, Case No. IT-99-36-T, ICTY, T. Ch. II, 3 October 2003; Decision on Motion for Exclusion of Statement of Accused, *Prosecutor* v. *Halilović*, Case No. IT-01-48-T, ICTY, T. Ch. I-A, 8 July 2005.

[84] It appears that May and Wierda adopt a different view, endowing the prosecutor with the power to conduct search and seizure operations on national territory (May and Wierda, *International Criminal Evidence*, at 62). In our view, this power is conditional upon a previously issued warrant.

[85] On this problem — the loss of protection when two jurisdictions are involved in a single criminal investigation — ICTY Judge Orie has written a landmark contribution: A. M. M. Orie, 'De verdachte tussen wal en schip of de systeem-breuk in de kleine rechtshulp', in E. André de la Porte et al. (eds), *Bij deze stand van zaken — bundel opstellen aangeboden aan A. L. Melai* (Arnhem: Gouda Quint, 1983), at 351–61.

[86] See Decision Stating Reasons for Trial Chamber's Ruling of 1 June 1999 Rejecting Defence Motion to Suppress Evidence, *Prosecutor* v. *Kordić*, Case No. IT-95-14/2, ICTY, T. Ch., 25 June 1999.

telecommunications.[87] On the other hand, the absence of judicial supervision should then be compensated for in the existence of written and unwritten rules 'indicat[ing] with reasonable clarity the scope and manner of exercise of the relevant discretion conferred on the public authorities'.[88] As such rules are totally absent in international criminal procedure, judicial intervention is in our opinion imperative when collection of evidence infringes upon individual rights, such as the inviolability of the home or the right to privacy.

10.5.3 Compelling the appearance of witnesses

Undeniably, witnesses are the most important evidentiary source in current international criminal proceedings and likely to be so in the future as well.[89] Thus, many of the parties' activities are carried out with the aim of obtaining the appearance of witnesses in court.[90] How is this achieved?

Every domestic system, both common-law and civil-law, provides for some means of compelling witnesses to testify in court.[91] Indeed, the criminal process would be seriously hampered if the giving of testimony in court were left to the discretion of the witness.

Amazingly, this is the case with the ICC where the 'principle of voluntary appearance' applies to witnesses before the Court.[92] The wording of the ICC Statute is in many respects problematic here. Not only does Article 93(1)(e) explicitly refer to 'voluntary appearance', Article 93(7) goes as far as attributing to the witness a right to 'informed consent'. If this applies to a witness who is detained by national authorities, should the Court then verify in respect of every witness before it whether he or she has travelled voluntarily to The Hague? Although the principle of 'voluntary appearance' appears ready for radical revision at the ICC's 2009 review conference, the question is what regime should be put in place and whether such a regime is likely to produce the desired results. This brings us to the law and practice of the ad hoc tribunals. The latter have installed in case law[93] and in their rules a regime of compellability of witnesses, albeit with important conditions and exceptions, and a corresponding regime of

---

[87] Cf. *Kruslin* v. *France*, 11801/85 [1990] ECtHR 10 (24 April 1990), *Funke* v. *France*, 10828/84 [1993] ECtHR 7 (25 February 1993), and *Camenzind* v. *Switzerland*, 21353/93 [1997] ECtHR 99 (16 December 1997).

[88] *Kruslin* v. *France*, para. 36.

[89] Meticulous documentation such as that kept by the Nazis is unlikely to be found elsewere.

[90] Although subpoenas have also been requested in relation to interviews out of court (pre-testimony interview) (Decision on Applications for Subpoenas, *Prosecutor* v. *Krstić*, Case No. IT-98-33-A, ICTY, A. Ch., 1 July 2003, para. 10).

[91] In common-law systems, like that of USA, this is done by the subpoena power and the corresponding contempt sanction. The Netherlands, on the other hand, allows for detention, not in the form of a criminal sanction, but as a (continuing) enforcement measure.

[92] For this and also a different, but incorrect, view, see C. Kress and B. Broomhall, 'Implementing Cooperation under the Rome Statute: A Comparative Synthesis', in C. Kress et al. (eds), *The Rome Statute and Domestic Legal Orders, Volume II: Constitutional Issues, Cooperation and Enforcement* (Baden-Baden: Editrice il Sirente Società Cooperativa a r.l., Fagnano Alto (AQ), 2005), at 529.

[93] In the *Blaškić* subpoena decision the Appeals Chamber referred to an inherent power to hold individuals in contempt when they fail to respond to a subpoena. See *Blaškić* subpoena appeal decision, paras 50, 59, and 60.

sanctions, in the form of contempt of court. Remarkably, until the twelfth revision of the rules (October/November 1997) the contempt power of the ICTY under Rule 77 was limited to witnesses refusing to answer questions, and Rule 91 provided for sanctions in respect of perjury. With this rule amended, the ICTY now has an expanded contempt power, which also applies to individuals who fail to comply with an order to appear.[94] In 1999 Rule 77 *bis* was added to the ICTY Rules dealing with the enforcement of penalties for contempt and perjury.[95]

While the law of contempt is intended to give teeth to the tribunals' competence to order the appearance of witnesses, its development and application have been problematic.[96] From a legal perspective there have been two problems. First, the judges have indulged in a penalizing exercise not specifically mandated by the statutes.[97] Second, contempt law is based on the common-law experience, where no precise definition of the charges is necessary; in the absence of a long history of contempt this leaves the defendant against contempt charges in international criminal proceedings in a difficult position. Besides these fundamental issues, two more practical problems have been very important. First, tribunals understandably cannot invest disproportionate time and energy in contempt charges. Secondly, especially in the case of witnesses, tribunals depend for the ultimate enforcement of a contempt sentence upon state cooperation, which may not be readily forthcoming in these particular instances.[98] In spite of a recent increase in contempt investigations and prosecutions,[99] the question of the deterrent effect of the law remains. It seems to us that any witness ordered by the ICTY or ICTR to appear has every ground not to be overly concerned about the possible consequences of refusal. It explains why parties and judges seek to avoid the subpoena route as far as possible. Furthermore, parties applying for subpoenas, especially the defence, face strict admissibility criteria, especially in respect of witnesses who enjoy possible testimonial privileges.[100]

---

[94] With some delay (on 27 May 2003), ICTR Rule 77 was amended to specify that the individual who fails to comply with a court order to attend is liable to contempt.   [95] There is no such rule in the ICTR RPE.

[96] For more detail, see G. Sluiter, 'The ICTY and the Offences against the Administration of Justice' (2004) 2 *JICJ*, at 631–41.

[97] In fact, from a very purist position, the tribunals' jurisdiction is confined to the crimes set out in the statute, not those contained in the rules.

[98] This may not only be because of a lack of political will, but also to do with the absence of adequate implementing legislation. Cooperation in relation to contempt charges was not what states had in mind when developing a cooperation relationship with international criminal tribunals. In the case of a contempt conviction of an ICTY counsel or a witness in an ICTY courtroom, for refusing to answer questions, execution of the sentence may be much easier. For example, an ICTY counsel may have considerable interest in paying a fine in order not to be refused audience before the ICTY.

[99] For example, Judgment on Contempt Allegations, *Prosecutor* v. *Beqaj*, Case No. IT-03-66-T, ICTY, T. Ch. I, 27 May 2005, and Decision on Contempt of the Tribunal, Contempt Proceedings against Kosta Bulatović, *Prosecutor* v. *Milošević*, Case No. IT-02-54/R-77.4, ICTY, T. Ch., 13 May 2005.

[100] See Decision on Assigned Counsel Application for Interview and Testimony of Tony Blair and Gerhard Schröder, *Prosecutor* v. *Milošević*, Case No. IT-02-54-T, ICTY, T. Ch., 9 December 2005. See also Decision on Interlocutory Appeals against Trial Chamber Decision refusing to Subpoena the President of Sierra Leone, *Prosecutor* v. *Norman et al.*, Case No. SCSL-2004-14-T, SCSL, A. Ch., 11 September 2006. In both decisions, however, applications were turned down not because of possible immunity obstacles, but because the defence failed to satisfy the chamber that testimony by the aforementioned head of state and government leader would be

The few disputes that have arisen in relation to the duty of witnesses to appear relate to questions of principle, such as evidentiary privileges. While evidentiary privileges are known in every criminal jurisdiction they generally concern the traditionally protected categories such as (close) family members of the accused, his or her counsel, doctors, etc. In this respect, international criminal justice faces additional challenges, related to the nature of the crimes and the circumstances under which they are committed. Thus, the ICTY, the ICTR, and the SCSL had to deal with the issue of the evidentiary privileges of a minister of defence,[101] a UN/SFOR general,[102] an ICRC employee,[103] a war correspondent,[104] and an employee of a human rights organization.[105] They all possessed specific knowledge on account of their official function or profession. The central question in respect of their testimony is whether competing rights and interests amount to a legitimate bar to disclosure.[106] The ICTY, the ICTR, and the SCSL have in their case law established a diverse picture. In respect of state organs, such as the minister of defence, the ICTY Appeals Chamber held that no subpoena could be issued to a state official as international law protects the internal organization of states and the acts of state officials should be attributed to the state.[107] Functional immunity for a witness is, however, confined to exactly that, namely knowledge connected to his or her official capacity. In that situation, the permission of the state concerned is required. Acting in a private capacity, for example having witnessed a crime while on holiday, state officials can be ordered to appear as witnesses. While this distinction may make sense as it has also been applied in respect of state immunities for perpetrators of international crimes,[108] its factual application is as problematic, since both perpetration and knowledge of war crimes is almost by definition in the realm of 'official capacity'.[109]

---

material to the defence. For a detailed analysis, see G. Sluiter, *International Criminal Adjudication and the Collection of Evidence: Obligations of States*, at 119–29.

[101] *Blaškić* subpoena appeal decision.

[102] Decision on Motion for Judicial Assistance to be Provided by SFOR and Others, *Prosecutor* v. *Simić et al.*, Case No. IT-95-9-PT, ICTY, T. Ch. III, 18 October 2000.

[103] Decision on the Prosecution Motion under Rule 73 for a Ruling Concerning the Testimony of a Witness, *Prosecutor* v. *Simić et al.*, Case No. IT-95–9-PT, ICTY, T. Ch. III, 27 July 1999.

[104] Decision on Interlocutory Appeal, *Prosecutor* v. *Brđanin and Talić*, Case No. IT-99–36-AR73.9, ICTY, A. Ch., 11 December 2002 (Randal decision).

[105] Decision on the prosecution's oral application for leave to be granted to Witness TF1-150 to testify without being compelled to answer any questions in cross-examination that the witness declines to answer on the grounds of confidentiality pursuant to Rule 70(B) and (D) of the Rules, *Prosecutor* v. *Brima et al.*, Case No. SCSL-04–16-T, SCSL, T. Ch. II, 16 September 2005 (Witness TF1-150 decision).

[106] Although formally one should distinguish between the duty to appear and the duty to answer questions and while strictly speaking evidentiary privileges only concern the latter duty, there is little sense in issuing a subpoena when no duty to answer questions can be established beforehand.

[107] *Blaškić* subpoena appeal decision, paras 42 and 43.

[108] 'Provided that it has jurisdiction under international law, a court of one State may try a former Minister for Foreign Affairs of another State in respect of acts committed prior or subsequent to his or her period of office, as well as in respect of acts committed during that period of office in a private capacity.' See *Case Concerning Arrest Warrant of 11 April 2000 (Democratic Republic of the Congo v. Belgium)*, No. 121, 14 February 2002, para. 61.

[109] Neither the interpretation of 'official capacity' offered by the Appeals Chamber, nor the examples mentioned there seem tenable:

> The same may hold true for the example propounded by the Prosecutor in her Brief: 'a government official who, while engaged on official business, witnesses a crime within the jurisdiction of the [International]

Another remarkable ruling in *Blaškić* is that members of peacekeeping forces should be regarded as acting in their private capacity for the purposes of issuing a subpoena. This ruling has been uncritically followed in subsequent case law. Notably, in *Todorović* SFOR was ordered to provide legal assistance to the accused, and Commanding General Tuzla Air Force base, General Shinseki, faced a threat of being served a subpoena.[110] In the view of the present authors, to regard the work of, for example, SFOR personnel as a 'private' affair is simply bizarre and does not correspond to the complex legal status of international peacekeepers, which to a considerable degree is governed by national (military) laws.[111] Another complication in respect of peacekeeping personnel lies in their mandate. In *Blaškič* the Appeals Chamber inferred from the fact that SFOR's mandate stems from the same source as the ICTY's, namely the Security Council, a duty to testify.[112] If both enterprises, the ICTY and SFOR, owe their mandate to the Security Council, which set them up in the interests of international peace and security, no hierarchy can be established; there is no ground in law that SFOR should jeopardize its mandate in the interest of the work of the ICTY.[113]

Besides questions of (state) immunity, the ICTY had to deal with the question of professional privileges. There is no doubt that the work of the ICRC, war correspondents, and human rights organizations is of great importance to the international community and public and that effective continuation of that work requires confidentiality. In dealing with these competing interests the ICTY has afforded special treatment to the ICRC; an ICTY Trial Chamber has accepted the ICRC's claim that it has

Tribunal being committed by a superior officer'. According to the Prosecutor: 'It cannot be argued that the official concerned is immune from orders to testify as to what was seen'. In this case, the individual was undoubtedly present at the event in his official capacity; however, arguably he saw the event *qua* a private individual. This can be illustrated by the example of a colonel who, in the course of a routine transfer to another combat zone, overhears a general issuing orders aimed at the shelling of civilians or civilian objects. In this case the individual must be deemed to have acted in a private capacity and may therefore be compelled by the International Tribunal to testify as to the events witnessed. By contrast, if the State official, when he witnessed the crime, was actually exercising his functions, i.e., the monitoring of the events was part of his official functions, then he was acting as a State organ and cannot be subpoenaed, as is illustrated by the case where the imaginary colonel overheard the order while on an official inspection mission concerning the behaviour of the belligerents on the battlefield (*Blaškić* subpoena appeal decision, para. 50).

[110] Decision on Motion for Judicial Assistance to be Provided by SFOR and Others, *Prosecutor* v. *Simić et al.*, Case No. IT-95–9-PT, ICTY, T. Ch. III, 18 October 2000, para. 62.

[111] The simplification by the Appeals Chamber that '[s]uch an officer is present in the former Yugoslavia as a member of an international armed force responsible for maintaining or enforcing peace and not *qua* a member of the military structure of his own country' is far from the reality of peacekeeping operations. See *Blaškić* subpoena appeal decision, para. 50.   [112] Ibid.

[113] See G. Sluiter, 'Commentary', in Klip and Sluiter, *Annotated Leading Cases, vol. V*, at 288–9:

I believe that no hierarchical relationship can be established between the ICTY and IFOR/SFOR. It is important to consider here that IFOR/SFOR was established more than two years after the ICTY and that no explicit duty to provide assistance to the ICTY has been imposed on IFOR/SFOR by the Security Council. One should also take into account some of the language in resolution 1031. Under operative paragraph 15, States participating in IFOR/SFOR have been authorised to take all necessary measures to maintain peace and security in Bosnia. This implies in my view that information need not be disclosed to the Tribunal if there are, as SFOR put it 'compelling requirements of operational security'. Security Council resolution 1031 (1995) offers a legal basis for such refusal to the Tribunal.

had a consistent practice as to the non-testimony of its delegates and employees before courts since the Second World War. The Trial Chamber decided that an absolute customary right existed which was also applicable to the ICTY.[114] Obviously, human rights organizations and war correspondents do not have the same international status as the ICRC, and in respect of that testimony a balancing exercise — between the interest of international prosecution to obtain evidence and the associated negative impact on these particular professions — may be called for.[115] The difficulty of this exercise lies in attributing weight to the cause of international criminal justice. Journalistic privileges, for example, are not new in criminal law and human rights law.[116] One may be tempted to dismiss the solutions found in the national context as inapplicable because they deal with less serious forms of criminality. On the other hand, war correspondents may also claim greater privileges for their particularly dangerous work than a local newspaper correspondent. From the point of view of consistency, one may take the absolute testimonial privilege attributed to the ICRC as a non-negotiable starting point and then ask to what degree the interests underlying the claimed privilege of another profession are less important than generally acknowledged ICRC interests. Another important factor is whether the testimony sought is expected to be incriminating or exculpatory. It would be particularly unfair to the accused if exculpatory evidence were withheld.[117]

10.6 PRESENTATION OF EVIDENCE

The pivotal phase between the collection of evidence and its admission is the presentation of evidence. In the adversarial system, where the principle of immediacy reigns, only information presented at trial in accordance with the rules can be adduced into evidence.[118] In contact to the civil-law trial, the presentation of evidence in the adversarial

---

[114] Decision on the Prosecution Motion under Rule 73 for a Ruling Concerning the Testimony of a Witness, *Prosecutor* v. *Simić et al.*, Case No. IT-95-9-PT, ICTY, T. Ch. III, 27 July 1999, paras 73 and 79. Note the Separate Opinion of Judge Hunt, who supported the decision in this particular case not to allow the testimony by the ICRC employee, but argued against an absolute testimonial immunity for the ICRC; rather, he argues, a balancing exercise should be conducted in each case individually. An interesting aspect of the decision on the ICRC is that the witness himself, a former employee, was prepared to testify, but the ICRC intervened, arguing that the knowledge held by this witness in fact belonged to the ICRC. Note should be taken of Rule 73(4) of the ICC Rules codifying the result of the ICTY decision.

[115] See Randal and Witness TF1-150 decisions (respectively ICTY and SCSL) referred to above (at footnotes 104 and 105 respectively). In these cases, the balancing exercise was not really necessary, as the journalist was asked to testify about information he had already made public and the human rights organization employee was not under a duty to appear; the prosecutor requested that he testify, but without having to answer certain sensitive questions.   [116] See *Goodwin* v. *UK*, 17488/90 [1996] ECtHR 16 (27 March 1996).

[117] This appears to be an important point in the approach taken by Judge Hunt in his argement against an absolute privilege for the ICRC, see Separate Opinion of Judge Hunt in *Todorović*; furthermore, the SCSL Trial Chamber ruled that the public interest in the work of human rights organizations should not outweigh the accused's right to a fair trial (Witness TF1-150 decision, para. 20).

[118] This is entirely different in civil-law systems where the 'dossier' is essentially assembled prior to trial. Nevertheless, the principle of immediacy is formally respected as the dossier is examined and discussed at trial. One

system is subjected to strict rules. This is partly to do with the fact that the jury needs to be shielded from irrelevant and unreliable information, but also has to do with the nature of the subjective truth-finding contest. The presentation of evidence is probably the aspect of the law of evidence in international criminal law where the absence of a jury is most keenly felt. Although they occur with some regularity — albeit far less frequently than in jury trials — typical jury-related objections such as those related to leading questions are thus out of place. Yet, the presentation of evidence in international criminal proceedings has retained the basic rules and notions of presentation of evidence that apply in adversarial proceedings.[119] We will explore these basic rules from two perspectives. First, which evidence may be presented? This question is intertwined with the issue of pre-trial disclosure, as it seems only fair in the adversarial procedure that only evidence is presented as announced prior to trial. Second, the question will be addressed to what extent evidence needs to be presented orally and the related right to and scope of cross-examination.

10.6.1 Pre-trial disclosure

There is in the adversarial system a direct connection between the evidence a party intends to present and the disclosure of material intended for use well ahead of the commencement of the trial. Unlike practice in the inquisitorial system, there is no dossier containing all the evidence, and one sees at trial only such evidence as the parties present. Pre-trial disclosure serves a twofold purpose. First, as a matter of fairness, it should prevent a trial by ambush; this applies especially to the prosecutor, as the accused has a right to adequate preparation of his or her defence and can only prepare with sufficient information as to the evidence the prosecutor intends to present at trial.[120] Conversely, the prosecutor need not be informed to the same degree about the defence's intentions, although the latter must not ambush the prosecutor with certain special defences, such as the defence of alibi.[121] Secondly, besides informing each other, parties to the proceedings must also notify the judge(s) of the number of witnesses they intend to call and other evidence they wish to present, with a view to effective trial management.[122]

A detailed account of the various disclosure obligations is beyond the scope of this book. The legal regimes speak for themselves, imposing far-reaching disclosure obligations on the prosecutor and disclosure obligations confined to special defences on the defendant.[123] While these disclosure rules originate in the common law, the specific

can imagine that the dossier is seldom fully read at trial. In the Netherlands, with a view to formally respecting the principle of immediacy, the judge — after having read out relevant parts of dossier — asks the parties if the dossier can be considered to have been presented in its entirety.

[119] For a better understanding of the basic adversarial rules pertaining to the presentation of evidence see A. Zuckerman, *The Principles of Criminal Evidence*, Chapter 7.

[120] On this fair-trial-related right, see Chapter 8, section 8.5.5.

[121] For critical observations in relation to the defence of alibi and related disclosure duties in international criminal law, see G. Sluiter, 'Commentary', in Klip and Sluiter, *Annotated Leading Cases, vol. X*, at 969–74.

[122] Effective trial management has received increasing attention under the pressure of the ad hoc tribunals' exit strategies and has resulted in the current elaborate versions of Rules 65 *ter*, 73 *bis*, and 73 *ter*.

[123] See Rules 66, 67, 68, 69, and 70 of the ICTY, ICTR, and SCSL Rules, Rule 79(1) of the ICC Rules.

demands of international criminal justice have resulted in important modifications. As an example we may mention the now accepted and legalized practice of 'rolling disclosure' in respect of protected witnesses.[124] This was created in response to lengthy trials, as a result of which a considerable period of time may lapse between disclosure of the protected witness's identity and the moment of giving testimony, with all the ensuing risks for the witness concerned. The solution was found in — exceptionally — disclosing the protected witness's identity after the commencement of the trial, but well ahead of the actual testimony.[125] One may, however, wonder to what extent the defence, once engaged in the trial, is still in a position to adequately prepare its defence in relation to that witness.[126] Furthermore, of significant importance, particularly in light of sensitive information which is intrinsically linked to war crimes, are the exceptions to the prosecutor's disclosure duty set out in Rule 70 of the ICTY and ICTR RPE. In essence they allow the prosecutor not to disclose information provided on a confidential basis, as long as that information is not presented as evidence at trial. The purpose of this rule is to reassure states and organizations, such as the ICRC, that sensitive information will not be used as evidence but will serve as a basis for the subsequent collection of evidence.

A pivotal element, in light of the accusatorial/inquisitorial dichotomy, is the prosecutor's disclosure obligation relating to exculpatory materials. Pursuant to Rule 68 of the ICTY and ICTR RPE, the prosecutor of the ad hoc tribunals and the SCSL must disclose to the defence exculpatory material or material that affects the credibility of prosecution evidence. For the ICC this obligation has achieved statutory status, in the form of a right of the accused.[127] At the heart of this duty lies not only fairness but the perceived role of an international prosecutor, being an organ of the court, as an 'impartial' party.[128] The ICC takes this a step further by imposing on its prosecutor, pursuant to Article 54(1) of the ICC Statute, a duty not only to disclose exculpatory information but to actively search for it. One should be realistic in respect of this perceived impartial role. If in practice in inquisitorial systems there is a strong investigative and prosecutorial focus on perceived guilt, how can one expect a truly impartial approach in an adversarial trial? Furthermore, the rule to disclose exculpatory evidence is extremely difficult to enforce. Not only may views differ as to whether a certain piece of evidence should be regarded as exculpatory,[129] an additional question that arises is to what extent the prosecutor's archives should be opened to the defence. The ICTY tries to steer a wise middle

---

[124] For more details see G. Sluiter, 'ICTR and the Protection of Witnesses' (2005) 3 *JICJ*, at 962–76.

[125] See the new Rule 69(A) and G. Sluiter, op. cit.

[126] Cf. Separate Dissenting Opinion of Judge Pavel Dolenc on the Decision and Scheduling Order on the Prosecution Motion for Harmonisation and Modification of Protective Measures for Witnesses, *Prosecutor v. Bagosora et al.*, Case No. ICTR-98-41-I, ICTR, T. Ch. III, 7 December 2001, para. 21.

[127] Article 67(2) of the ICC Statute.

[128] See S. Zappalà, 'The Prosecutor's Duty to Disclose Exculpatory Materials and the Recent Amendment to Rule 68 ICTY RPE' (2004) 2 *JICJ*, at 622.

[129] See on this matter May and Wierda, *International Criminal Evidence*, at 77–8. What is important is that exculpatory material is broader than evidence capable of being admitted in court. See Decision on Motion by Prosecution to Modify Order for Compliance with Rule 68, *Prosecutor v. Krnojelac*, Case No. IT-97-25-PT, ICTY, T. Ch. II, 1 November 1999, paras 2 and 11.

course, with disclosure requests having to be 'sufficiently clear', but without further specification as to what precisely this means.[130]

The application of the rule is furthermore entirely based on the expectation that the prosecution will fulfil its obligations in good faith.[131] However, there is no effective way of verifying that expectation in a timely fashion, and the abundance of defence motions related to Rule 68 appears to underline the need for such verification.[132] Finally, when a violation of the duty under Rule 68 has been established, the question is what sanctions should follow. We agree with Zappalà that the importance of Rule 68 for a fair trial and the high degree of confidence in the prosecutor call for heavy sanctions when a violation can be held to have occurred.[133] More generally, we wish to underline the difficulties inherent in Rule 68 in an adversarial procedure; hence the need to strengthen the position of the defence to collect exculpatory evidence independently.

10.6.2 The principle of orality and cross-examination

Rule 85 common to the RPE of the SCSL, the ICTY, and the ICTR governs the presentation of evidence.[134] It sets out the sequence to be followed in the presentation of evidence generally, starting with evidence for the prosecution, moving on to evidence for the defence, and followed by prosecution evidence in rebuttal and defence evidence in rejoinder. After the presentation of evidence by the parties related to the guilt or innocence of the accused, the trial chamber may order evidence *proprio motu*, and information may also be presented that assists the chamber in determining an appropriate sentence. This order is logical and also imperative from the perspective of the presumption of innocence and the burden of proof. In respect of the examination of witnesses, Rule 85 sets out the following sequence: examination-in-chief by the party calling the

---

[130] Decision on the Appellant's Motions for the Production of Material, Suspension or Extension of the Briefing Schedule, and Additional Filings, *Prosecutor* v. *Blaškić*, Case No. IT-95-14, ICTY, A. Ch., 26 September 2000, para. 40. [131] Ibid., para. 45.

[132] Only some examples thereof: Decision on 'Motion for Relief from Rule 68 Violations by the Prosecutor and for Sanctions to Be Imposed pursuant to Rule 68 *bis* and Motion for Adjournment while Matters Affecting Justice and a Fair Trial Can Be Resolved', *Prosecutor* v. *Brđanin*, Case No. IT-99-36-T, ICTY, T. Ch. II, 30 October 2002; Decision on the Defence Motion for Sanctions for the Prosecutors Continuing Violation of Rule 68, *Prosecutor* v. *Blaškić*, Case. No. IT-95–14, ICTY, T. Ch., 28 September 1998; Decision on the Defence Motion for 'Sanctions for Prosecutor's Repeated Violations of Rule 68 of the Rules of Procedure and Evidence', *Prosecutor* v. *Blaškić*, Case. No. IT-95-14, ICTY, T. Ch., 29 April 1998; Decision on the Defence Motion for Disclosure of Exculpatory Evidence, *Prosecutor* v. *Nzirorera et al.*, Case No. ICTR-98-44-I, ICTR, T. Ch. III, 7 October 2003; Decision on Joint Defence Motion on Disclosure of All Original Witness Statements, Interview Notes and Investigators Notes Pursuant to Rules 66 and/or 68, *Prosecutor* v. *Brima et al.*, Case No. SCSL-04-16-T, SCSL, T. Ch. II, 4 July 2005; Decision on motion to compel the production of exculpatory witness statement, witness summaries and materials pursuant to Rule 68, *Prosecutor* v. *Norman et al.*, Case No. SCSL-04-14-T, SCSL, T. Ch., 8 July 2004 (both SCSL decisions rejected the respective defence motions), and so on.

[133] S. Zappalà, 'The Prosecutor's Duty to Disclose Exculpatory Materials and the Recent Amendment to Rule 68 ICTY RPE', at 629.

[134] The ICC legal framework does not impose a similar rule, but leaves the presentation of evidence to the agreement of the parties or the directions of the Trial Chamber; see Article 64(8)(b) of the Rome Statute and Rule 140(1) of the ICC Rules.

witness, cross-examination by the opposing party, and re-examination by the calling party.[135]

In relation to testimonial evidence, the question arises to what extent the principle of orality applies in international criminal proceedings and how this affects the accused's right to cross-examination.

Reliance on oral evidence is one of the central features of adversarial jury trials.[136] While the absence of the jury in international criminal proceedings is an argument for downplaying the importance of the oral presentation of evidence, the very objective of transparent trials, with a view to reconciliation in the countries concerned, supports a strong reliance on oral evidence.

Furthermore, the oral presentation of evidence provides the best opportunity for the other party to challenge that evidence and allows the trier of fact to better assess the credibility of the evidence presented.[137] In this light, the international criminal tribunals initially strongly embraced the principle of orality; the first version of Rule 90, according to which witnesses shall be heard in principle directly by the chamber, and strong statements in jurisprudence, testify to this.[138] Nevertheless, the principle is under increasing attack as the judges have tried to establish mechanisms to introduce written witness statements, by amending Rule 90, taking out the principle of orality,[139] and by adopting first Rule 94 *ter* and then Rule 92 *bis*.[140] Since these changes, the principle of orality leads an obscure life in tribunal circles, as judges are divided over the admission of written witness statements.[141]

---

[135] Rule 85(B); note that a judge may at any stage put any question to the witness.

[136] Most of the evidence is adduced through the testimony of witnesses who appear before the court and either testify from their own recollection of events or produce documents (or other objects) to the authenticity of which they depose. See A. Zuckerman, *The Principles of Criminal Evidence*, at 86.

[137] See *Aleksovski* appeal judgment, paras 62–4. See also R. May and M. Wierda, 'Evidence before the ICTY', in May et al., *Essays on ICTY Procedure and Evidence*, at 254.

[138] For example, in the 'video-link' decision in the *Tadić* case, the Trial Chamber found that 'it is preferable for the Trial Chamber to have the benefit of the physical presence of the witnesses at trial' (Decision on the Defence Motions to Summon and Protect Defence Witnesses, and on the Giving of Evidence by Video-link, *Prosecutor* v. *Tadić*, Case No. IT-94-1-T, ICTY, T. Ch. II, 25 June 1996, para. 21). In a later decision the Appeals Chamber found it necessary 'to recall one of the fundamental principles governing the giving of evidence before the Trial Chambers, namely the principle that witnesses shall as a general rule be heard directly by the Judges of the Trial Chamber' (Decision on Appeal by Dragan Papić against Ruling to Proceed by Deposition, *Prosecutor* v. *Kupreškić et al.*, Case No., IT-95-16-AR73.3, ICTY, A. Ch., 15 July 1999, para. 18). In another decision, the ICTY Appeals Chamber ruled that 'it is acknowledged that the weight or probative value to be afforded to [hearsay] evidence will usually be less than that given to the testimony of a witness who has given it under a form of oath and who has been cross-examined' (Decision on Prosecutor's Appeal on Admissibility of Evidence, *Prosecutor* v. *Aleksovski*, Case No. IT-95-14/1-AR73, ICTY, A. Ch., 16 February 1999, para. 15). In the *Naletilić and Martinović* case Trial Chamber I of the ICTY confirmed the preference for live testimony (Decision on the Admission of Witness Statements into Evidence, *Prosecutor* v. *Naletilić and Martinović*, Case No. IT-98-34-T, ICTY, T. Ch. I Section A, 14 November 2001). Finally, on the question whether the statement of a deceased witness may be admitted into evidence see Decision on Appeal regarding Statement of a Deceased Witness, *Prosecutor* v. *Kordić and Čerkez*, Case No. IT-95-14/2-A, ICTY, A. Ch., 21 July 2000, para. 19.

[139] However, note that Rule 90 of the ICTR Rules still provides for the principle of orality.

[140] For a detailed critical account, see M. Fairlie, 'Due Process Erosion: The Diminution of Live Testimony at the ICTY', at 47.　　　　　　　　　　[141] See below the section on admission of written witness statements.

The method in which cross-examination is conducted may also give rise to problems in the particular context of international criminal proceedings. As Zuckerman put it:

The most effective method for testing a witness's evidence is cross-examination. The cross-examiner may use tactics designed to extract disclosures which the witness is reluctant to make, to prompt contradiction, to undermine confidence, to cast doubt on honesty and reliability, and generally to try and detract from the value of the testimony which the witness has given in-chief. While such impeachment methods are useful for ascertaining the truth, they may become oppressive and limits have to be placed on the cross-examiner's freedom.[142]

In the adversarial system the scope of cross-examination is the object of continuing dispute between litigants, particularly in relation to the presence of a jury.[143] This is not to the same degree the case in international criminal proceedings. In addition to the absence of a jury in the latter context, defence counsel, prosecutors, and judges with a civil-law background suffer from considerable unfamiliarity with cross-examination. A particular and recent problem is accused persons representing themselves, including conducting cross-examination of witnesses.[144] Lacking practical experience in this exercise, their cross-examination regularly exceeded the boundaries of 'relevance to issue and relevance to credibility'.[145]

The law of the ad hoc tribunals attempts to strike a fair balance between effective trial management and allowing for effective cross-examination, which is intertwined with the right to challenge incriminating testimony. Rule 90(H) of the ICTY Rules reads as follows:

(i) Cross-examination shall be limited to the subject-matter of the evidence-in-chief and matters affecting the credibility of the witness and, where the witness is able to give evidence relevant to the case for the cross-examining party, to the subject-matter of that case.

(ii) In the cross-examination of a witness who is able to give evidence relevant to the case for the cross-examining party, counsel shall put to that witness the nature of the case of the party for whom that counsel appears which is in contradiction of the evidence given by the witness.

(iii) The Trial Chamber may, in the exercise of its discretion, permit enquiry into additional matters.

In the practice of the ad hoc tribunals, judges may have a tendency to interfere with cross-examinations. In an adversarial system the conduct of cross-examinations is a highly delicate issue, as in that system 'a judge who actively injects himself into the examination of evidence places his neutrality at risk: he appears to be putting on the case for one of the parties'.[146] Furthermore, defendants have complained that restrictions on their cross-examination infringes upon their right to examine witnesses. The

---

[142] A. Zuckerman, *The Principles of Criminal Evidence*, at 93–4.

[143] One easily recalls all the objections called out by counsel in US courtroom dramas.

[144] On the issue of accused representing themselves, see Chapters 2, section 2.5 and 8, section 8.5.7.

[145] This was especially true of Milošević. See for example the transcripts of cross-examination by the accused of witnesses Elshani (21 February 2002, at 863–6) and Kadriu (8 March 2002, at 1741–56).

[146] M. Damaška, *Evidence Law Adrift*, at 89.

ICTR Appeals Chamber in *Akayesu* accepts restrictions on cross-examination, with a view to effective trial management:

It is clear to the Appeals Chamber that the Presiding Judge of the Trial Chamber had actually sought to underscore the vital distinction to be made, during cross-examination, between matters germane to the case and other extraneous comments of a general nature. In other words, when Judge Kama directed the parties to ask questions that are directly related to the facts as described in the Indictment, and not general questions, he was reminding them, properly so, that cross-examination should not be impeded by matters that were immaterial and/or not relevant to the case. Thus, Judge Kama's remarks were made squarely within his duty as the Presiding Judge of the Trial Chamber, to ensure that cross-examination not be impeded by useless and irrelevant questions. Such clarification was in no way intended to restrict or limit cross-examination. . . . It was solely meant to guide the proceedings to ensure that there were no undue departure from the case at bar. Accordingly, the Appeals Chamber finds that in so doing the Presiding Judge was merely performing his duty to exercise control over the process of examination and cross-examination of witnesses appearing before the Chamber as has since been enacted under the Rules. Consequently, the Appeals Chamber finds that Judge Kama's remarks imposed no undue limitation on the scope of cross-examination nor did they unfairly deprive Akayesu of his right to cross-examine Prosecution witnesses.[147]

In addition to such restrictions, the law of international criminal procedure also restricts cross-examination, as a result of the particular subject-matter jurisdiction. For example, the law of evidence of the ad hoc tribunals implicitly limits the cross-examination of victims of sexual assault, by not admitting in evidence information of previous sexual conduct and imposing limitations on the defence of consent. Consequently, the scope of cross-examination is more restricted than in domestic rape cases. While restrictions of this nature will generally meet with approval, and while the demands of the exit strategy may call for increased judicial intervention, cross-examination remains of vital importance for adversarial fact-finding in the context of international criminal proceedings.

10.7 ADMISSION OF EVIDENCE

Pivotal in the law of evidence is the admission of information into evidence.[148] Obviously — and this is the same in common-law and civil-law systems — only information that has been accepted as evidence by the trial chamber can constitute the basis for any decision.[149] It is therefore also self-evident that in criminal proceedings the question of admission has given rise to extensive and ferocious litigation.

If one takes as a starting point that information that has been presented in accordance with the applicable regulations is presumed to be admissible into evidence, the

---

[147] *Akayesu* appeal judgment, para. 318.

[148] Formally it is wrong to speak of 'evidence' prior to admission; before it is admitted one can only speak of 'information'.

[149] We leave aside here facts of common knowledge and adjudicated facts of which judicial notice is taken.

question arises as to what the rules pertaining to exclusion are. In the practice of the ad hoc tribunals one can distinguish three grounds of exclusion: mandatory exclusion, discretionary exclusion because of prejudice to the accused, and exclusion on account of lack of reliability. Before examining these three different regimes — and the special regime of written witness statements — we wish to make a few general remarks about exclusionary rules in international criminal proceedings.

10.7.1 Exclusionary rules in international criminal proceedings

The exclusion of relevant and probative evidence may seem a drastic measure in proceedings oriented towards establishing the truth. It comes as no surprise that although both adversarial and inquisitorial systems provide for exclusionary rules, they differ in scope and nature. Exclusion of evidence is more objectionable in a system focused on objective truth-finding than in a subjective truth-finding contest. Nevertheless, in the adversarial system the so-called exclusionary rule is under growing attack.[150] It is worthwhile to briefly introduce the three generally advanced rationales for the exclusion of evidence.

First, exclusion of evidence can be regarded as a remedy to which the accused is entitled in the face of violation of his or her fundamental rights.[151] Exclusion on this basis raises the questions of the extent to which the violated rule is meant to protect the accused's rights,[152] the extent to which the party introducing the evidence (the prosecutor) need be implicated in the collection of the evidence in dispute,[153] and whether exclusion of evidence is the only logical remedy.[154]

Secondly, exclusion of evidence can also be viewed as a sanction for police misconduct. This should then work as a deterrent for future misconduct and bolster enforcement of

---

[150] Cf. *Leon* v. *US*, US Supreme Court, 468 US 897 (1984).

[151] In this sense, generally see the ICTR Appeals Chamber's decision in *Barayagwiza*, when it is emphasized that every human rights violation requires a remedy: *Barayagwiza* I appeal decision.

[152] For example, to what extent can evidence obtained in violation of another state's sovereignty serve as the basis for a remedial right for the accused? This raises the question of the *Schutznorm* (the theory stating that one can only derive rights from a norm having this very purpose). The ICTY does not preclude an individual from raising the violation of state sovereignty (*Tadić* jurisdiction appeal decision, para. 55 and Decision on the Motion for Release by the Accused Slavko Dokmanović, *Prosecutor v. Dokmanović et al.*, Case No. IT-95-13a-PT, ICTY, T. Ch. II, 22 October 1997), but does not appear to attach a remedial right for the individual to it (and *Nikolić* jurisdiction trial decision, para. 141).

[153] In international criminal justice one of the problems is the relationship between the national authorities and the prosecutor in the arrest of persons and the collection of evidence. Although there are progressive—from the human rights viewpoint—approaches in *Barayagwiza*, *Mucić*, and *Halilović*, those decisions have not analysed the matter from the perspective of remedies for violations of individual rights, but the broader concept of 'the integrity of the court'.

[154] As will be further explored below, the law of evidence provides for the mandatory exclusion of evidence in Rule 95. In respect of violation of habeas corpus rights (unlawful and arbitrary arrest or detention), the ICTY has established in *Barayagwiza* and *Semanza* an alternative remedy in the form of reduction of the sentence. This has not been introduced as a remedy in respect of unlawfully obtained evidence. For an example of different practice see Article 359a of the Dutch Code of Criminal Procedure.

the law. This objective of the exclusionary rule is for obvious reasons particularly strong in adversarial systems.[155]

Thirdly, the exclusion of evidence serves the purpose of maintaining the integrity of the proceedings. The court and the trial proceedings should not be tainted by unlawfully obtained evidence. This purpose is different from the previous two in that the focus is not on either of the parties (remedy and sanction) but on the court, whose credibility is also at stake.

Looking at the relevant regulations (Rule 95 of the ICTR, the ICTY, and the SCSL and Article 69(7) of the ICC Statute), one notices that the exclusion of evidence in international criminal proceedings appears to be essentially based on the aforementioned third perspective. In light of the fact that international prosecutors do not have a police force at their disposal over which they have authority and for which they carry responsibility,[156] this is not surprising. In the particular context of international criminal proceedings an exclusionary rule based on its remedial and deterrent function makes little sense when the prosecutor him- or herself is generally not implicated in the collection of disputed evidence. On the other hand, there is also awareness that a complete disconnection between the activities of national authorities and international criminal tribunals dilutes the ultimate responsibility of the trial chamber to ensure the fairness of the trial.[157]

10.7.2 Mandatory exclusion

As has already been mentioned, the mandatory exclusion of evidence is provided for in Rule 95 of the ICTY and ICTR RPE and Article 69(7) of the ICC Statute.[158] The

---

[155] See *Leon* v. *US*, US Supreme Court, 468 US 897 (1984), where the 'benefits' of the exclusionary rule were analysed by the majority from the perspective of deterrence. In the situation under consideration, the Supreme Court's majority decided not to exclude the evidence as the police were acting on the basis of a search warrant, which later was declared unlawful. Since the police acted in good faith, excluding evidence serves no useful purpose, according to the majority. But note the vigorous dissent by Justice Brennan.

[156] For a different view, see *Simić*, where Judge Robinson compared in his Separate Opinion the role of SFOR to that of a police force in national systems (Separate Opinion of Judge Robinson, Decision on Motion for Judicial Assistance to Be Provided by SFOR and Others, *Prosecutor* v. *Simić et al.*, Case No. IT-95-9-PT, ICTY, T. Ch. III, 18 October 2000, para. 6).

[157] See *Barayagwiza* I appeal decision, paras 91 and 98; however, see also the disconcerting ICTR jurisprudence according to which the tribunal is not competent to supervise the legality of national arrests, searches, and seizures: Decision on the Defence Motion for Exclusion of Evidence and Restitution of Property Seized, *Prosecutor* v. *Nyiramasuhuko*, Case No. ICTR-97-21-T, ICTR, T. Ch. II, 12 October 2000, para. 26; Decision on the Defence Motion challenging the Lawfulness of the Arrest and Detention and seeking Return or Inspection of Seized Items, *Prosecutor* v. *Ngirumpatse*, Case No. ICTR-97-44-I, ICTR, T. Ch. II, 10 December 1999, para. 56; Decision on the Defence Motion concerning the Arbitrary Arrest and Illegal Detention of the Accused and on the Defence Notice of Urgent Motion to Expand and Supplement the Record of 8 December 1999 Hearing, *Prosecutor* v. *Kajelijeli*, Case No. ICTR-98-44-I, ICTR, T. Ch. II, 8 May 2000, para. 34; Decision on the Defence Motion for the Restitution of Documents and other Personal or Family Belongings Seized (Rule 40(C) of the Rules of Procedure and Evidence), and the Exclusion of such Evidence which may be used by the Prosecutor in preparing an Indictment against the Applicant, *Prosecutor* v. *Karemera*, Case No. ICTR-98-44-I, ICTR, T. Ch. II, 10 December 1999, para. 4.2; Decision on the Defence Motion challenging the Legality of the Arrest and Detention of the Accused and requesting the Return of Personal Items Seized, *Prosecutor* v. *Nzirorera*, Case No. ICTR-98-44-T, ICTR, T. Ch. II, 7 September 2000, para. 27.

[158] For a similar provision, with an interesting specification, see Section 34.2 of Regulation 2001/25 on the Amendment of UNTAET Regulation No. 2000/11 on the Organization of Courts in East Timor and UNTAET

content of Rule 95 has remained the same over the years: 'No evidence shall be admissible if obtained by methods which cast substantial doubt on its reliability or if its admission is antithetical to, and would seriously damage, the integrity of the proceedings.'[159] The title of the rule has, by contrast, been amended twice for the ICTY and once for the ICTR. Initially, the title referred to evidence obtained by means contrary to human rights. The reference to human rights was removed, but with the objective to expand the rule's scope of application.[160] Thus, not only human rights violations trigger mandatory exclusion, but also other violations that damage the integrity of the proceedings. Obviously, the safest way for a defendant would be to claim human rights violations first, as this certainly triggers Rule 95.[161] This is not always perceived in the same way in the tribunals' case law. In *Mucić* the ICTY Trial Chamber displayed no hesitation in excluding evidence obtained in what they believed to be a violation of human rights.[162] In *Brđanin*, by contrast, the Trial Chamber narrowed the scope of application of Rule 95.[163] Dealing with the results of allegedly unlawful wiretaps, the Trial Chamber found that Rule 95 applies only in case of serious human rights violations.[164] It drew an analogy with the ICTY's *Nikolić* case, where it was decided that in the case of unlawful arrest the ICTY should decline jurisdiction only when egregious human rights violations can be established.[165] The analogy is inappropriate, as the remedy that the defence demanded in *Nikolić* was the release of the accused and the end of the entire trial, whereas the exclusion of evidence is confined to one particular incident and piece of evidence. Furthermore, the Trial Chamber significantly departed from the rule's object and purpose, which was at the least to cover human rights violations, without there being any requirement as to the nature of these violations.

Brđanin followed suit to the extent that there is now a certain reluctance to resort to Rule 95 when the same result can be obtained via Rule 89(D), attributing a discretionary power to exclude evidence in the interests of a fair trial. For example, the non-application of Rule 43 led the Trial Chamber in *Halilović* to conclude that admission of

---

Regulation No. 2000/30 on the Transitional Rules of Criminal Procedure, UNTAET/REG/2001/25, 14 September 2001:

> The Court may exclude any evidence if its probative value is substantially outweighed by its prejudicial effect, or is unnecessarily cumulative with other evidence. No evidence shall be admitted if obtained by methods that cast substantial doubt on its reliability or if its admission is antithetical to, and would seriously damage, the integrity of the proceedings, including without limitation evidence obtained through torture, coercion or threats to moral or physical integrity.

[159] Note the different language of Rule 95 of the SCSL: 'No evidence shall be admitted if its admission would bring the administration of justice into serious disrepute.'

[160] Jones and Powles, *International Criminal Practice*, at 753.

[161] Here we witness a possible combination of two of the objectives of the exclusionary rule: a remedy for violation of the rights of the accused and protecting the integrity of the proceedings.

[162] Decision on Zdravko Mucić's Motion for the Exclusion of Evidence, *Prosecutor* v. *Delalić*, Case No. IT-96-21, ICTY, T. Ch., 2 September 1997. The Trial Chamber was wrong, however, in regarding the right to assistance from counsel during police interrogation as an internationally protected human right. See G. Sluiter's commentary in Klip and Sluiter, *Annotated Leading Cases, vol. I*, at 242–3.

[163] Decision on the Defence 'Objection to Intercept Evidence', *Prosecutor* v. *Brđanin*, Case No. IT-99-36-T, ICTY, T. Ch. II, 3 October 2003.   [164] Ibid., para. 61.

[165] *Nikolić* jurisdiction trial decision, para. 114.

the evidence thus obtained is outweighed by the accused's right to a fair trial.[166] Clearly, there is a fine line distinguishing Rule 95 from the fair trial imperatives of Rule 89(D). The test of Rule 95 should always come first, but judges may have a preference for keeping their options open and retain the opportunity to resort to the weighing exercise of Rule 89(D). What matters is that Rule 95 is confined to the methods by which the evidence was obtained; in our view, any clear human rights violation in that context triggers the application of Rule 95. Rule 89(D) is broader and also concerns the method in which evidence is presented, for example the late addition of witnesses.

The ICC Statute offered a different solution to the obscure text of Rule 95. Article 69(7) first requires a material violation of the Statute or human rights law; evidence obtained under these circumstances shall not be admissible if the violation substantially affects its reliability or if it seriously damages the integrity of the proceedings. There appears to be a circular relationship between the human rights violation set out in the *chapeau* of Article 69(7) and the integrity of the proceedings mentioned in Article 69(7)(b). Does admission of evidence obtained in violation of human rights not by definition damage the integrity of the proceedings? An interpretation of Article 69(7), according to which not every human rights violation damages the integrity of the proceedings, amounts to a departure from the original purpose of Rule 95 of ICTY and ICTR RPE, and also makes a mockery of human rights law as an indivisible set of minimum legal standards.

10.7.3 Discretionary exclusion to ensure a fair trial

We have already referred above to the residual and discretionary exclusion of evidence when admission would affect the fairness of the trial. Rule 89(D) of the ICTY reads in this respect as follows: 'A Chamber may exclude evidence if its probative value is substantially outweighed by the need to ensure a fair trial.'[167]

The ICC has no similar rule, but Article 69(4) allows the Court generally to rule on the relevance or admissibility of evidence taking into account — among other things — any prejudice that admission may cause to a fair trial. One may expect the ICC — in the face of such flexibility — to follow closely the law and practice of the ad hoc tribunals.

The purpose of Rule 89(D) is obvious: outside the realm of Rule 95 judges should be allowed to balance the importance of the evidence for effective prosecution against the degree of prejudice admission would cause the accused. This balancing exercise is not possible in relation to Rule 95, and explains the attraction of Rule 89(D) over any system of mandatory exclusion. Yet, Rule 89(D) has been drafted in a way that even when the evidence's probative value is substantially outweighed by the need to ensure a fair trial the chamber enjoys the discretion to admit the evidence. One wonders how a chamber could still admit evidence when its probative value is outweighed by the right

---

[166] Decision on Motion for Exclusion of Statement of Accused, *Prosecutor v. Halilović*, Case No. IT-01-48-T, ICTY, T. Ch. I, Section A, 8 July 2005, para. 26.

[167] Remarkably, this rule is not part of the ICTR's law of evidence. It remains to be seen, however, to what degree this has actually led to different results in ICTR case law. Even without Rule 89(D) the law of evidence is flexible enough to take into account prejudice to the accused when ruling on the admissibility of evidence.

to a fair trial, whereas such tainted evidence calls for mandatory exclusion as a matter of principle. The margin of appreciation for the chamber lies in the balancing exercise, but the latter should be more predictable. Moreover, in its current form the rule is subject to misinterpretation. For example, in *Kordić* the Chamber considered admission of certain transcripts into evidence as contrary to Rule 89(D).[168] However, as long as Rule 89(D) does not provide for mandatory exclusion, admission of evidence can logically not be contrary to that rule. In its current form Rule 89(D) appears at best to offer a rationale for exclusion based on common sense and fairness. Thus, when in *Halilović* evidence was excluded pursuant to Rule 89(D), it means that the ground for exclusion is the one set out in that rule.[169]

Looking at the material application of Rule 89(D), what matters is the manner in which chambers have balanced the evidence's probative value against the right to ensure a fair trial. The crucial line of distinction between this and Rule 95 is that the latter is confined to the method of collection, whereas Rule 89(D)'s scope of application is much broader and deals with the results of admission. Admission may not be considered fair, in the sense of Rule 89(D), for various reasons, including the method of collection. Again in *Halilović* the manner in which the statement of the accused was obtained was considered unfair, as the protection of Rule 43 was not ensured, but the Trial Chamber did not opt for Rule 95 and applied Rule 89(D) instead, concentrating on the effects of admission.[170] In *Kordić* Rule 89(D) was triggered because admission of transcripts was requested late in the trial and impeded the exercise of the right to cross-examination.[171]

Like Rule 95, Rule 89(D) has not been used very often. This is largely the result of the rather high threshold envisaged by the rule. What is needed for exclusion, which even then remains discretionary, is that the 'probative value' is substantially outweighed by fair-trial considerations. This is a high standard, especially when it concerns important evidence; and disputes over admission rarely concern unimportant evidence. Therefore, most admission disputes concern the evidence's relevance and probative value, which will be explored below.

10.7.4 Exclusion of evidence lacking relevance and probative value

Rule 89(C) of the ICTY, ICTR, and SCSL Rules reads as follows: 'A Chamber may admit any relevant evidence which it deems to have probative value.'

Article 69(4) of the ICC Statute seems to embody the same aspiration, though in more enigmatic terms, by referring to relevance and probative value.[172]

---

[168] Decision on Prosecutor's Submissions Concerning 'Zagreb Exhibits' and Presidential Transcripts, *Prosecutor v. Kordić*, Case No. IT-95-14/2, ICTY, T. Ch., 1 December 2000.

[169] Decision on Motion for Exclusion of Statement of Accused, *Prosecutor v. Halilović*, Case No. IT-01-48-T, ICTY, T. Ch. I, Section A, 8 July 2005.

[170] Ibid., admittedly, this is a fine line between Rule 95 and Rule 89(D), as Rule 95 is also concerned with the use of unlawfully collected evidence for trial.

[171] Decision on Prosecutor's Submissions Concerning 'Zagreb Exhibits' and Presidential Transcripts, *Prosecutor v. Kordić*, Case No. IT-95-14/2, ICTY, T. Ch., 1 December 2000.

[172] See also Rule 63(2) of the ICC Rules.

Rule 89(C) is clearly at the heart of the flexible law of evidence in international crim-inal proceedings. In *Blaškić* the ICTY Trial Chamber spoke of the principle of extensive admissibility of evidence,[173] and in *Musema* the ICTR Trial Chamber referred to free assessment of evidence.[174] We have already briefly explored above the perceived flexible law of evidence as a system of *liberté des preuves*. After an initial period of unrestricted admission of hearsay evidence, the ad hoc tribunals have developed important excep-tions and conditions, for at least two reasons. First, elements of fairness, such as the right to cross-examination, call especially in an adversarial setting for stricter scrutiny of admission than initially envisaged. Secondly, while in the domestic inquisitorial sys-tem there are no significant objections to putting 'everything' in the dossier, trial man-agement calls for caution in international criminal proceedings; overly generous admission may result in unworkable quantities of evidence to be scrutinized. The con-straints on easy admission may be found in specific provisions such as Rule 89(D), Rule 95, or Rule 92 *bis* and, essentially, in a stricter interpretation of Rule 89(C) itself. From contrary reasoning it follows that irrelevant evidence and evidence lacking probative value must be excluded. Challenges to relevance and probative value have resulted in interesting jurisprudence, displaying, on the one hand, a generally significant departure from 'free evidence' systems known to civil-law criminal jurisdictions. On the other hand, 'admit everything, determine weight later' is a maxim still frequently encountered in the ad hoc tribunals.

Starting off with the test of relevance,[175] it should be noted that the ad hoc tribunals have not excluded broad categories of evidence to the same extent as did the Nuremberg Tribunal, for example when the latter excluded evidence of crimes committed by the Allies as irrelevant.[176] Yet, the law of the ad hoc tribunals also allows us to identify the following categories of information as irrelevant for evidentiary purposes, albeit there is no truly consistent approach: prior sexual conduct in rape cases;[177] *tu quoque* defences, meaning adducing evidence that the 'other side' has committed similar or worse crimes than charged in the case at hand;[178] and character evidence.[179]

---

[173] *Blaškić* trial judgment, para. 34.   [174] *Musema* trial judgment, para. 75.

[175] Relevant evidence can be described as evidence that tends to prove or disprove a material issue; in other words, evidence is relevant 'if its effect is to make more or less probable the existence of any fact which is in issue, i.e. upon which guilt or innocence depends' (May and Wierda, *International Criminal Evidence*, at 102).

[176] Ibid., at 103. Note that at the IMTFE evidence showing that Japanese forces restored peace and tranquillity in China, evidence relating to the atomic bomb decision, and evidence related to crimes of the communist regime in China were excluded.

[177] See Rule 96(iv) of the ICTY, ICTR, and SCSL Rules, and Rule 72 of the ICC Rules. One may, however, question whether exclusion of this type of evidence is based on irrelevance or whether it serves to protect witnesses from harassment and humiliation, especially during cross-examination. In our opinion, the latter objective is the primary one, as evidence of prior sexual conduct could be relevant.

[178] See Decision on Evidence of the Good Character of the Accused and the Defence of *Tu Quoque*, *Prosecutor v. Kupreškić*, Case No. IT-95-16, ICTY, T. Ch. II, 17 February 1999, and Decision on Motion for Acquittal, *Prosecutor v. Kunarac et al.*, Case No. IT-96–23&23/1, ICTY, T. Ch. II, 3 July 2000. However, such evidence may be relevant for demonstrating selective and arbitrary prosecutorial policy; see Chapter 2, section 2.4. Furthermore, *tu quoque* evidence was accepted in the *Krajišnik* trial judgment.

[179] See Decision on Evidence of the Good Character of the Accused and the Defence of *Tu Quoque*, *Prosecutor v. Kupreškić*, Case No. IT-95-16, ICTY, T. Ch. II, 17 February 1999. Note, however, that character evidence was accepted in the *Ntakirutimana* trial judgment.

In addition to these categories, it is established in case law — and also in the context of international criminal proceedings — that only evidence within the scope of the indictment is relevant. When during trial evidence is given for acts not pleaded in the indictment, its exclusion is, however, not inevitable. The evidence of, for example, a rape not charged may serve to prove a consistent pattern of conduct relevant to serious violations of international humanitarian law in the sense of Rule 93, and is thus admissible pursuant to that rule.[180] Furthermore, charges of persecution as a crime against humanity may be so broad in scope that acts not pleaded in the indictment are nevertheless encompassed in the persecution charge; however, such an approach was overturned by the ICTY Appeals Chamber as unfair.[181]

An important bone of contention concerning the unique situation of the ICTR related to the admissibility of evidence about acts and conduct prior to 1 January 1994. Because all charges had to be within the period 1 January–31 December 1994, in order to be included in the ICTR's temporal jurisdiction, it appeared that evidence outside that period was irrelevant. This view has been rejected, since evidence related to acts and conduct prior to 1994 may assist the chamber in forming a better judgment of the accused's intentions during the year 1994.[182]

The central question is whether the reliability of evidence — for example concerning the credibility of a witness — is a matter for admissibility or concerns the weight of the evidence, to be determined at a later stage by the judges.[183] There are diverging views on this issue. On the one hand, there is a strong attachment to adversarial rules and principles: in any inquisitorial system the dossier will contain unreliable evidence, as professional judges will later determine its weight during the trial. In international criminal proceedings, however, reliability has developed as a test for admissibility in certain cases. On the other hand, in an extensive argument Judge Shahabuddeen made the case for taking unreliability as a bar to admitting evidence only in extreme situations, and argued that reliability and thus also admissibility should be taken as a starting point:

At the admissibility stage it is assumed, rather than found, that the evidence is credible. It is on the basis of that assumption that it is determined, at that stage, whether the evidence can advance the proof of the fact which has to be proved and is therefore probative. Evidence which cannot do that (even if it is assumed to be credible) is not probative; it is therefore not relevant and is not admissible. If, on the basis of an assumption that it is credible, it is determined that the evidence can establish the fact to be proved and is therefore admitted, the next question (to be answered at a later stage of the proceedings) is to what extent it does indeed establish the fact to be proved. It is this next question which raises the point whether the evidence is credible, including the issue

---

[180] See *Kvočka* trial judgment, para. 652. [181] *Kupreškić* appeal judgment, para. 92.

[182] See, for instance: *Nahimana et al.* trial judgment, para. 101, referring to a Separate Opinion of Judge Shahabuddeen: 'evidence dating to a time prior to 1 January 1994 can provide a basis from which to draw inferences, for example with regard to intent or other required elements of crimes committed within the limits of the temporal jurisdiction of the Tribunal'; Decision on the Defence Motions Objecting to a Lack of Jurisdiction and Seeking to Declare the Indictment Void *ab initio*, *Prosecutor* v. *Kabiligi and Ntabakuze*, Case No. ICTR-96-34-I, ICTR, T. Ch., 13 April 2000, para. 39: 'conspiracy is a continuing crime, the events that took place outside the period of the Statute can be taken into account if it can be shown that the conspiracy continued into the relevant period of the Statute'. [183] See May and Wierda, *International Criminal Evidence*, at 107–11.

whether, even if the witness is speaking truthfully, he is for one reason or another mistaken. And it is here that the presence or absence of reliability matters.

In general, then, a decision to admit assumes that the evidence is credible: it assumes matters, such as reliability, which go to credibility. The assumption that the evidence is credible is then verified after the making of a decision to admit it; this is part of the exercise concerned with the assessment of the weight to be assigned to the admitted evidence. If the evidence is then judged not credible, it is simply given no weight and eliminated from the proof, even though it was earlier admitted.[184]

Yet, it remains to be seen to what extent his views prevail in practice. One should at least consider the 'reliability standards' developed in *Kordić*.[185] The conclusion of the Appeals Chamber in that case is that evidence so lacking in reliability *must* be excluded.[186] Furthermore, the Appeals Chamber has offered indicia of reliability which must be considered prior to admission of disputed evidence, as follows:

(1) Has the statement been given under oath?

(2) Has the statement been subject to cross-examination?

(3) Is the statement first-hand or removed?

(4) Has the statement been made contemporaneously to the events?

(5) Has the statement been made through many levels of translation?

(6) Has the statement been given under formal circumstances, such as before a judge?[187]

As reasonable as these indicia may seem, the central question remains whether they justify exclusion. May and Wierda explain the crucial difference between exclusion and determining evidentiary weight.[188] The determination of evidentiary weight has the advantage that it can be done in light of all the evidence presented at trial, while a decision on admissibility is made on one piece of evidence treated in isolation.[189] According to some, the first is to be preferred — or is even necessary — in the difficult circumstances in which the tribunals operate.[190] Obviously, this fits perfectly in a free system of evidence, which the tribunals appear to have adopted. Although considerations of fairness may have played an important role in the choice of reliability as an admissibility criterion,[191] from a human rights perspective there appears to be room to admit evidence the defence could not challenge, so long as any finding of guilt is not solely or to a decisive extent based on this evidence.[192] Why has the ICTY not sought a solution

---

[184] *Musema* appeal judgment, Declaration of Judge Shahabuddeen, paras 8 and 9.

[185] Decision on Appeal Regarding Statement of a Deceased Witness, *Prosecutor v Kordić and Čerkez*, IT-95-14/2, ICTY, A. Ch., 21 July 2000. [186] Ibid., para. 28.

[187] Ibid., para. 27. [188] May and Wierda, *International Criminal Evidence*, at 109. [189] Ibid.

[190] A. Rodrigues and C. Tournaye, 'Hearsay Evidence', in May et al., *Essays on ICTY Procedure and Evidence*, at 291–305.

[191] Cross-examination which is prominently set out as the first indicium of reliability in *Kordić*. However, these considerations in and of themselves only fit within Rule 89(D). The view is in relation to Rule 89(C) that the absence of cross-examination affects the evidence's reliability.

[192] See *Van Mechelen et al.* v. *The Netherlands*, 21363/93; 21364/93; 21427/93 [1997] ECtHR 22 (23 April 1997), para. 55; *Doorson* v. *The Netherlands*, 20524/92 [1996] ECtHR 14 (26 March 1996), para. 76.

along these lines? The admission of evidence the reliability of which is challenged could be compensated for in rules requiring corroboration.[193]

10.7.5 Special regime: the admission of written statements

As most disputes concerning the admissibility of evidence have centred around written out-of-court statements (and still do so), the ad hoc tribunals have developed a special regime on that matter. It is a significant departure from the approaches adopted by the Nuremberg and Tokyo Tribunals. The latter provided for the simple admission of affidavits.[194] We have already said enough about the development of a stricter law of evidence by the ICTY and the ICTR, and the rationale underlying this development. In relation to the admission of written witness statements we should have regard to Rule 94 *ter* and its successor Rule 92 *bis*, and, importantly, their relationship to the general rules of evidence set out in Rule 89.

Rule 94 *ter* was adopted by a plenary meeting of ICTY judges in 1999, with the intention of enacting a system of presentation of evidence that could contribute to the shortening of the trials.[195] It reads as follows:

To prove a fact in dispute, a party may propose to call a witness and to submit in corroboration of his or her testimony on that fact affidavits signed by other witnesses in accordance with the law and procedure of the State in which such affidavits are signed. These affidavits are admissible if the other party does not object within five working days after the witness' testimony. If the party objects and the Trial Chamber so rules, or if the Trial Chamber so orders, the witnesses shall be called for cross-examination.

In practice, this rule proved to be unworkable as, among other things, it relied too heavily on state cooperation.[196] It was soon (December 2000) succeeded by Rule 92 *bis* and an addition to Rule 89, in the form of the following section (F): 'A Chamber may receive the evidence of a witness orally or, where the interests of justice allow, in written form.' This rule codified the departure from the principle of orality deleted from Rule 90(A) and provided a link to Rule 92 *bis*. The latter is supposed to embody a 'Solomon's judgement' in respect of the divergent tribunal jurisprudence concerning hearsay evidence. It

---

[193] In *Kordić* Trial Chamber III noted that it would not convict the accused on the basis of the statement of a deceased witness alone if it was not corroborated, see Decision on Appeal Regarding Statement of a Deceased Witness, *Prosecutor* v. *Kordić and Čerkez*, Case No. IT-95–14/2-A, ICTY, A. Ch., 21 July 2000, para. 6.

[194] See May and Wierda, *International Criminal Evidence*, at 210–17. The flexible admission of witness statements, and the lack of a requirement for the witness to appear for cross-examination, was in the case of the Nuremberg Tribunal based on Article 19 of the Charter, which states that the Tribunal shall not be bound by technical rules of evidence. In the case of the IMTFE a special provision was adopted to that end (Article 13(c)(3) of its Charter listing affidavits as admissible evidence).

[195] Sixth Annual Report of the International Tribunal for the Prosecution of Persons Responsible for Serious Violations of International Humanitarian Law Committed in the Territory of the Former Yugoslavia since 1991, 31 July 1999, para. 116.

[196] See, for further details, F. Guariglia, 'The Admission of Documentary Evidence and of Alternative Means to Witness Testimony in Proceedings Before the International Criminal Tribunal for the former Yugoslavia', in H. Fischer et al. (eds), *International and National Prosecution of Crimes Under International Law* (Berlin: Berlin Verlag, 2001), at 665–80.

embodies three main components. First, written statements instead of oral evidence *may* be admitted when they go to proof of a matter other than acts and conduct of the accused as charged in the indictment. Secondly, when the chamber makes the admission determination it shall take into account a list of factors in favour and against admission and shall ensure that the taking of the statement fulfils certain formal conditions. Thirdly, the formal conditions do not apply, under certain circumstances, to witnesses who have died or can no longer be traced, nor do they apply to transcripts from other tribunal proceedings.

Pivotal in this rule is the determination of 'acts and conduct of the accused as charged in the indictment'. When evidence relates to this it may not, according to Rule 92 *bis*, be admitted in written form. This is a significant departure from the initial flexible nature of the ICTY's law of evidence, installing a firm exclusionary rule, alien to any civil-law system. Judge O-Gon Kwon in the *Milošević* case rightly remarked in his declaration on the flexibility initially underlying Rule 89, and further emphasized the capability of professional judges to set aside irrelevant and unreliable statements.[197] In the application of Rule 92 *bis* the prosecutor has tried to save the flexibility of Rule 89 by arguing that Rule 92 *bis* does not prevent the (flexible) admission of a variety of evidentiary items pursuant to Rule 89(C).[198] As expected, the Appeals Chamber did not go along with this, as it would override the object and purpose of Rule 92 *bis* as *lex specialis*.[199] In *Galić* the Appeals Chamber obviously struggled with the relationship between Rule 89(C) and mandatory exclusion pursuant to Rule 92 *bis*. Interestingly, it considered one of the purposes of Rule 92 *bis* to be to restrict the admissibility of hearsay evidence to that which falls within its terms.[200] Apparently, there must be a reason for that restriction, which to a large degree lies in fairness and especially in the right to cross-examination. In this light, it is astonishing that the Chamber ruled that Rule 92 *bis* has no effect upon hearsay material which was not prepared for the purposes of legal proceedings. This produces the bizarre result that witness statements taken in accordance with all the safeguards of Rule 92 *bis* must be excluded when they concern acts and conduct of the accused, whereas the same evidence *may* be admitted if produced initially for other purposes than legal proceedings.

As already mentioned, the scope of 'acts and conduct of the accused' is of vital importance and raises difficult questions. Obviously, the purpose of specifying this class of acts was to exclude contextual elements and, in particular, many 'crime-based' witnesses in situations of command responsibility and joint criminal enterprise. However, in the case of command responsibility the question has also arisen whether acts and conduct of subordinates are so vital for determining the criminal responsibility of the accused as to exclude written statements dealing with that from the scope of Rule 92 *bis*. In *Milošević* Judge Robinson argued that acts and conduct of the accused should not be confined to

---

[197] Declaration of Judge O-Gon Kwon, appended to the Decision on Prosecution's Request to Have Written Statements Admitted under Rule 92 *bis*, *Prosecutor* v. *Milošević*, Case No. IT-02-54, ICTY, T. Ch., 21 March 2002, para. 3.

[198] Decision on Interlocutory Appeal concerning Rule 92 *bis* (C), *Prosecutor* v. *Galić*, Case No. IT-98-29-AR73.2, ICTY, A. Ch., 7 June 2002. [199] Ibid., para. 31.

[200] Ibid.

criminal responsibility pursuant to Article 7(1) of the Statute; rather, when a statement exposes the accused to criminal liability pursuant to Article 7(3) of the Statute — and we would mention liability under 'joint criminal enterprise' theory in this context — it implicates the accused in a critical way and should fall outside the scope of Rule 92 *bis*.[201] If 'acts and conduct of the accused' are narrowly interpreted as being confined to responsibility under Article 7(1), Judge Robinson is prepared to accept written statements into evidence, but only when the witness is available for cross-examination, which is in these circumstances not at the discretion of the chamber but a right of the accused.[202] In *Galić* the Appeals Chamber did not formally extend 'acts and conduct of the accused' to subordinates in respect of charges for command responsibility, but it did offer the following 'suggestion':

it may well be that the subordinates of the accused (or those alleged to be his subordinates) are so proximate to the accused that *either* (a) the evidence of their acts and conduct which the prosecution seeks to prove by a Rule 92 *bis* statement becomes sufficiently pivotal to the prosecution case that it would not be fair to the accused to permit the evidence to be given in written form, *or* (b) the absence of the opportunity to cross-examine the maker of the statement would in fairness preclude the use of the statement in any event. It must be emphasised, however, that the rejection of the written statement in any of these situations is not based upon any identification of that person's acts or conduct with the acts or conduct of the accused.[203]

What transpires from Rule 92 *bis* and its application is not a flexible regime for admission but the installation of a mandatory exclusionary rule — and an advisory exclusionary rule in the case of Article 7(3) responsibility — for testimonial evidence that the defendant could not challenge by means of cross-examination. It illustrates perfectly the tension between expediency and fairness which is in the context of international criminal proceedings further complicated by a derailed law of evidence. The latter suffers from its supposedly inquisitorial nature in a predominantly adversarial system. The ad hoc tribunals appear in the application of Rule 92 *bis* to stay largely on the safe side of the right set out in Article 21(4)(e) of the Statute, the right of the accused to confront witnesses against him. Robinson positions this as an absolute right in the abovementioned separate opinion in *Milošević*, but the jurisprudence of the European Court on Human Rights offers more possibilities than are at present used in the application of Rule 92 *bis*. The ICTY Appeals Chamber in *Galić* rightly mentions in footnote 34 that from a human rights perspective there is no absolute ban on the admission of statements of witnesses that the defendant could not challenge;[204] all that is required is that a conviction is *not solely or to a decisive extent* based on such evidence. In the light of this

---

[201] Separate Opinion of Judge Robinson, appended to the Decision on Prosecution's Request to Have Written Statements Admitted under Rule 92 *bis*, *Prosecutor v. Milošević*, Case No. IT-02-54, ICTY, T. Ch., 21 March 2002, paras 8 and 9.

[202] Ibid. Note the entirely opposite view of Judge O-Gon Kwon, already referred to above, which may not be ideal from the perspective of the defence, but corresponds far better to the ICTY's initial views on its law of evidence.

[203] Decision on Interlocutary Appeal concerning Rule 92 *bis* (C), *Prosecutor v. Galić*, Case No. IT-98-29-AR73.2, ICTY, A. Ch., 7 June 2002, para. 15.

[204] Decision on Interlocutary Appeal concerning Rule 92 *bis* (C), *Prosecutor v. Galić*, Case No. IT-98-29-AR73.2, ICTY, A. Ch., 7 June 2002.

finding, the application of Rule 92 *bis* by the ICTY appears unnecessarily cautious — at least from a human rights perspective.

It is not surprising in light of the difficulties surrounding Rule 92 *bis* that other international criminal tribunals have not regarded this rule as a role model. The judges of the SCSL at one of their first plenary meetings (March 2003) recognized the need to simplify Rule 92 *bis*.[205] This simplification, according to the SCSL Appeals Chamber in *Norman et al.*, was occasioned essentially by the need to facilitate the receipt into evidence of information collected by other organs, especially the Truth and Reconciliation Commission (TRC); this information may be admitted if the facts therein are relevant and their reliability is 'susceptible of confirmation'.[206] It also follows from this Appeals Chamber's 'explanatory memorandum' that the amended Rule 92 *bis* serves as a safety net for instances where judicial notice under Rule 94(A) is not feasible.[207] The amendment is undeniably confusing, as it deals with a different matter than Rule 92 *bis* was intended for in the first place. It follows from the Appeals Chamber's views that the simplified SCSL Rule 92 *bis* to a large degree deals with information that has not been collected for use in legal proceedings, like testimonies before the TRC. Conversely, the ICTY and ICTR's Rule 92 *bis* is solely concerned with statements taken for the purpose of legal proceedings. It follows from *Galić* that much of what the SCSL Appeals Chamber offers as explanation for the amended Rule 92 *bis* — namely simple admission of TRC testimonies — is already governed by the *lex generalis* of Rule 89(C). Hence, there appears little reason for the proposed SCSL amendment. Furthermore, it leaves a gap. What is the SCSL policy in respect of witness statements taken by OTP investigators? Given the purpose of the amended Rule 92 *bis*, these seem to be beyond its scope of application, but what does this mean for their admissibility and the right to cross-examination?

The uncertainties and difficulties surrounding the admission of written evidence in respect of fully functioning international criminal tribunals may in the (near) future also plague the ICC. Its Statute allows for the admission of documents and transcripts as long as this is not prejudicial to or inconsistent with the rights of the accused.[208] Rule 68, implementing Article 69(2) of the ICC Statute, offers a puzzling and extreme regulation of the admissibility of written statements, going well beyond Rule 92 *bis* of the ICTY and ICTR. Rule 68 allows for the admission of testimony previously recorded by video, audio, or in written form, provided that (1) both prosecutor and defence had the opportunity to examine the witness during the recording; or (2) the witness is present before the court, does not object to the submission of the previously recorded testimony, and all participants can examine the witness during the proceedings. This amounts to a full and absolute mandatory exclusionary rule when a party objects to admission and has not been in a position to examine the witness. This goes well beyond Rule 92 *bis*, as Rule 68 appears to cover every witness testimony — no matter for what purpose it has

---

[205] Note that rule 92 *bis* of the ICTR RPE was immediately effective for the SCSL, in the same way as all ICTR rules were, but with the possibility of amending the rules to suit the needs of the SCSL.

[206] Fofana — Decision on appeal against 'Decision on Prosecution's motion for judicial notice and admission of evidence', *Prosecutor* v. *Norman et al.*, Case No. SCSL-2004-14-AR73, SCSL, A. Ch., 16 May 2005, para. 26.

[207] Ibid., para. 27.   [208] Article 69(2) of the ICC Statute.

been collected — relating to every aspect of the indictment. Although this may appear to offer maximum protection to both parties in the sense of cross-examination, one may wonder whether the disadvantages of Rule 68 do not outweigh its perceived benefits. It is not difficult to envisage situations where potentially relevant and reliable evidence is withheld from the court, especially in view of the fact that witnesses cannot be compelled to appear before the ICC. Furthermore, as was already alluded to above, from a human rights perspective the sweeping language of Rule 68 is certainly not imperative.

10.8 STANDARD OF PROOF/EVALUATION OF EVIDENCE

The entire process of collecting, presenting, and admitting evidence reaches its climax in the evaluation of all accepted evidence against a certain standard of proof. The standard of proof and evaluation of evidence are always in the minds of both prosecutor and defence.

In this section three questions are addressed. First, what is the standard of proof and how does it function in the context of international criminal proceedings? Secondly, how should the judges reach this standard and, in particular, are they in the evaluation of evidence bound by certain minimum standards? Thirdly, how is weight accorded to evidence?

10.8.1 Proof beyond a reasonable doubt

The standard of proof for a conviction in international criminal proceedings is that of proof beyond a reasonable doubt, as articulated in Rule 87(A) of the ICTY, ICTR, and SCSL RPE and Article 66(3) of the ICC Statute. There is on this point very little difference between the common-law standard of 'beyond reasonable doubt' and the civil-law standard of '*conviction intime*'. What matters is that there should remain no doubt based on reason in relation to the guilt of the accused. There is, however, a vital procedural difference in that common-law jurisdictions have put considerable effort in defining 'reasonable doubt' with a view to instructing juries. This is because juries may be more inclined than professional judges to overlook the question of whether the 'beyond reasonable doubt' threshold is reached in any individual case.[209] Although there is no jury in international criminal proceedings, the transparency of the adversarial procedure and the application of Rule 98 *bis* ('no case to answer') has understandably resulted in judges elaborating on the standard of proof.[210]

---

[209] See A. Zuckerman, *The Principles of Criminal Evidence*, at 134–40.

[210] See *Jelisić* trial judgment, para. 108; Decision on Motion for Acquittal, *Prosecutor* v. *Kunarac*, Case No. IT-96-23&23/1, ICTY, T. Ch. II, 3 July 2000, para. 12; Decision on Motion for Acquittal Pursuant to Rule 98 *bis*, *Prosecutor* v. *Kvočka et al.*, Case No. IT-98-30/1, para. 12; *Delalić* appeal judgment, para. 434; *Jelisić* appeal judgment, paras 34–7.

10.8.2 Minimum standards of evidence

International criminal proceedings represent a free system of evidence. In reaching a finding of guilt the judges are not constrained by best rules on evidence or corroboration. This appears to fit within a flexible law of evidence, generally associated with civil-law systems. However, even in these one encounters more constraints when it comes to reaching a finding of guilt. In the Netherlands, for example, every evidentiary item needs corroboration to sustain a conviction, with the exception of the eyewitness testimony of law enforcement officials. There is also a special provision prohibiting the use of the evidence of co-accused in a joint indictment.[211] The law of the ad hoc tribunals contains no minimum rules on evidence, nor does it set out a list of permissible means of evidence. In case law the judges have been eager to underline the free system of evidence, by not adopting any rules of corroboration.[212] In *Akayesu* it was held that 'the Chamber can rule on the basis of a single testimony provided such testimony is, in its opinion, relevant and credible'.[213] Compared to national systems, the absence of corroboration rules is not troublesome. In the Netherlands, for example, the *unus testis nullus testis* rule is applicable, but this concerns the entire indictment. It is permissible to base a conviction on two witnesses who give evidence on different and unrelated parts of the accusation. Furthermore, an ICTY Trial Chamber has underlined that although corroboration is not required, where there is uncorroborated testimony on a material fact (and thus not the entire indictment!) a Trial Chamber will scrutinize the evidence with circumspection and may decide not to use it.[214]

One may be tempted to infer from Rule 96(i) of the ICTY and ICTR RPE that corroborative rules exist. As that provision stipulates that no corroboration is required in cases of testimony concerning sexual assault, defendants have argued that this should be seen as an exception to a general rule requiring corroboration. The argument was dismissed on the ground that Rule 96(i) purports to give these types of testimony the same reliability as that of ordinary witnesses.[215]

An interesting point already alluded to above is the interaction between admission and minimum evidentiary standards. When the admission of evidence is controversial, as is the case with hearsay evidence, the chamber has sought to reassure the objecting party that it will not prove a particular element of the indictment on the basis of that evidence alone.[216] This is a useful approach with benefits that might be worth incorporating in Rule 92 *bis*.[217]

---

[211] The testimony of a co-accused person cannot be used in evidence in a jointly tried case, as the Dutch legislators regarded such testimony as inherently unreliable; the co-accused person was considered to have a prejudicial interest in putting the blame on his co-accused. In practice, this matter has been solved by trying co-accused not jointly but simultaneously. In a simultaneous trial the testimony of a co-accused person is admissible.

[212] See *Tadić* trial judgment, paras 256 and 535–9; *Delalić* trial judgment, para. 594. But for a different perspective, see *Aleksovski* appeal judgment, paras 62–4.   [213] *Akayesu* trial judgment, paras 132–6.

[214] *Brđanin* trial judgment, para. 27.   [215] *Tadić* trial judgment, para. 536.

[216] See Decision on Appeal Regarding Statement of a Deceased Witness, *Prosecutor* v. *Kordić and Čerkez*, Case No. IT-95-14/2-A, ICTY, A. Ch., 21 July 2000, para. 6.

[217] One could imagine that evidence admitted pursuant to Rule 92 *bis* requires corroboration in other evidence. Support is found in the jurisprudence. In *Aleksovski* appeal judgment, paras 62–4, the ICTY Appeals

While one may be reluctant to introduce a category of 'second-rate' evidence in international criminal proceedings, it is equally hard to accept that proof of an important part of the indictment could now lawfully be sustained on a single statement introduced pursuant to Rule 92 *bis*.

The law of the ICC, like that of the ad hoc tribunals, does not provide for any minimum evidentiary requirements, except in proceedings based on an admission of guilt. In such situations the Trial Chamber must consider the admission together with any additional evidence presented.

10.8.3 Weight of evidence

One may be tempted to dismiss the questions raised above as lacking practical relevance, as tribunal judges tend to be careful in attributing weight to evidence and generally require large amounts of evidence to sustain a conviction. Indeed, in ICTY and ICTR case law disputes concern the reliability of evidence, especially testimonial evidence, rather than matters of corroboration. This brings us to the question of weight attributed to various types of evidence. As regards testimonial evidence, which is the most important source of evidence in present-day international criminal proceedings, the preference for live testimony, as being of the greatest weight, has been confirmed on several occasions.[218] Of less weight than live testimonial evidence is the taking of evidence by video-link, which provides a modern way for evidence to be obtained as nearly 'live' as possible.[219] The ICTY Trial Chamber also included the taking of testimony by means of video-link in the hierarchy of means of taking testimony, by holding that '[t]he evidentiary value of testimony provided by video-link, although weightier than that of testimony given by deposition, is not as weighty as testimony given in the courtroom'.[220]

These general preferences are of interest when it comes to attaching weight to evidence; but they do not amount to a best evidence rule. Cross-examination, giving evidence under oath, and the direct perception of the witness's demeanour are key factors in attaching weight to live testimony. In national criminal law jurisdictions, like the Netherlands, the reverse situation is often encountered, with more weight being attributed to written statements taken by the police. Such statements tend to be taken shortly after the fact, offering the best recollection of events, and minimize the risks of influencing the witness. As international criminal proceedings unfortunately tend to take place long after the commission of the crimes, written statements have few advantages over live testimony; in this light, the different weights generally given to live testimony and written statements is in the context of international criminal proceedings fully understandable.

Chamber ruled that direct testimonial evidence in court does not require corroboration; hence, written statements do require corroboration.

[218] See the case law mentioned in note 138 above.

[219] May and Wierda, 'Evidence before the ICTY', in May et al., *Essays on ICTY Procedure and Evidence*, at 255.

[220] Decision on the Defence Motions to Summon and Protect Defence Witnesses, and on the Giving of Evidence by Video-Link, *Prosecutor v. Tadić*, Case No. IT-94-1-T, ICTY, T. Ch. II, 25 June 1996, para. 21.

10.9 CONCLUSION

It follows from the above that one cannot but be highly critical in respect of the law of evidence in international criminal proceedings. The aspiration of combining civil-law and common-law elements in international criminal procedure has greatly affected the law of evidence. The drafters of the Rules can be reproached not only for combining elements that can hardly coexist in a coherent and effective system, but also for having offered insufficient guidance to the participants in the proceedings in the application of these elements. Subsequent amendments have resulted in a patchwork of norms striving to effect a compromise between flexibility and stricter rules. The result is an uncertain, obscure, and unworkable body of law that does not expedite proceedings, but offers numerous possibilities for parties to submit motions for the exclusion of evidence. What was and is needed is for a single system, coherent and logical, to be chosen and for detailed legislation on that system to be enacted. Indeed, more detailed legislation forces drafters to critically scrutinize and improve flaws in the system.

Remarkably, the ICC legal framework does not constitute an improvement; its law of evidence is possibly even more obscure than that of the ad hoc tribunals and contains some utterly contradictory elements. For example, how can one credibly combine the non-compellability of witnesses with a mandatory exclusionary rule for testimonial evidence not subject to cross-examination?

When assessing the law of evidence, the demands of expediency should be used with caution. In fact, the need for expeditious trials is often advanced as justification for many elements of the law of evidence (and amendments thereto) in international criminal proceedings. However, there are other demands on international criminal justice as well, and the law of evidence was not designed with a clear preconceived idea as to the essential features of international criminal trials. It is also a fallacy to expect miraculous 'solutions' for obscure rules, such as Rule 92 *bis*, which tend only to give rise to more (defence) motions, that further delay trials. Furthermore, the solutions advanced to expedite trials have to our knowledge far from produced that result.

The lessons to be learned from the law of evidence in international criminal proceedings are in our view quite simple. There are two mutually exclusive regimes — the strict and the flexible law of evidence — which can only function properly in their respective 'natural habitats', which is either the civil-law objective truth-finding contest or the common-law subjective truth-finding contest. Trying to install a flexible law of evidence in a predominantly adversarial trial under the current demands of international criminal justice is at the very least a highly dubious undertaking.

11

DEFENCE PRACTICE AT THE
INTERNATIONAL TRIBUNALS

SUMMARY

II.I INTRODUCTION

This chapter examines the prevalence, logic, and fortunes of defences used in cases before the tribunals. Much has been written about defences in international criminal law, but little about the *actual* defences crafted by tribunal defence teams. The focus has been on theoretically available defences, not on usage.[1] The practice of defence teams is thus virtually unknown outside the narrow circle of followers of tribunal proceedings. The ICTY Appeals Chamber has occasionally sought to shore up a 'true' sense of defence — as for example when it said that alibi is *not* a true defence[2] — but it has not explained why the distinction is useful or even interesting.[3] This chapter takes a fresh look at the subject. The common approach favouring theory is here replaced with a critical review of defence practice at the international tribunals.

Any submission seeking acquittal may be regarded as a kind of defence. Patterns of such submissions are classified under one of the headings in this chapter, unless the arguments are more appropriately dealt with in another part of this book (for example, under complaints about abuse of due-process rights, in Chapter 8, or under preliminary motions against jurisdiction, in Chapter 9).

One cannot emphasize enough the importance of the defence role at the international tribunals. The defence is one of the four pillars of each tribunal (standing alongside the judiciary, the prosecutor, and the registry), even though it has not always been so treated. Defence teams not only watch over the rights of the accused and ensure that an accused's case is presented in the most favourable way. The defence is, as well, the only constant force counteracting the prosecutor's expansionist tendencies in the international criminal jurisdiction. Whereas the prosecutor's de facto role is to maximize the range of conduct that is considered criminal in an international tribunal's jurisdiction, the defence's role is to guard the outer fringes of individual freedom from state — or, in this case, international — interference. A common misconception is that this latter role of the defence rests with tribunal judges. Several chapters of this book demonstrate that, in a sphere of law which has barely been codified, the judges'

---

[1] See, for example, Cassese, *International Criminal Law*, pp. 219–63; Y. Dinstein, 'Defences', in G. K. McDonald and O. Swaak-Goldman (eds), *Substantive and Procedural Aspects of International Criminal Law I* (Kluwer Law International, 2000), pp. 369–88; Y. Dinstein, *The Conduct of Hostilities Under the Law of International Armed Conflict* (Cambridge University Press, 2004), pp. 228–54; Dixon and Khan, *Archbold*, pp. 447–73; Schabas, *Genocide*, pp. 314–44; E. van Sliedregt, *The Criminal Responsibility of Individuals for Violations of International Humanitarian Law* (Cambridge University Press, 2004); and G. Werle, *Principles of International Criminal Law* (Asser Press, 2005), pp. 138–65. G.-J. Knoops's 'inductive method of inquiry' — see his *Defences in Contemporary International Criminal Law* (Transnational, 2001), p. 34 — is a kind of empiricism applied to the sphere of legal principle, not of practice. It is to be contrasted with the inductive method employed in this chapter.

[2] *Delalić et al.* appeal judgment, para. 581; see also ibid., para. 590, and *Kunarac et al.* trial judgment, para. 463.

[3] See also M. Scaliotti, 'Defences Before the International Criminal Court: Substantive Grounds for Excluding Criminal Responsibility — Part 1' (2001) 1 *Int'l Criminal Law Rev.* 111, 118, who asserts that the distinction between defences that operate as an excuse and defences that operate as a justification is fundamentally important from a theoretical viewpoint; but Scaliotti does not explain why.

tendency in this respect is unpredictable. Judges have sometimes been as expansionist as the prosecutor. Since there are no legislators in the tribunal system other than the judges, the defence is a particularly significant force to contain international criminal law and to uphold the principle of legality.[4]

II.2 *IN DUBIO MITIUS* AND *NULLUM CRIMEN SINE LEGE* DEFENCES

[The] pragmatical and flexible Anglo-Saxon system can operate well only in the countries with long traditions and developed court practice, and its advantages here appear as its disadvantages.[5]

Whole defences have been built on the argument that a given tribunal lacks jurisdiction over an offence. One could ask whether such attacks are best characterized as defences. They are found in many defence final trial briefs. As noted in earlier chapters, the subject-matter jurisdiction of the tribunals is in some respects well defined (for example, genocide) but in other respects strikingly ill-defined (for example, Article 3 of the ICTY Statute). Tribunal judges have been disinclined to practise *in dubio mitius* (a narrow reading of the statutes and other sources of international criminal law) and have tended to interpret the principle of *nullum crimen sine lege* leniently. Because the tribunals have experienced an expanding jurisdiction, it is no surprise that defence counsel have directed substantial resources to shield their clients from such expansion.

Only a few examples of this type of defence will be considered here. At the ICTY, the accused Hazim Delić argued that in adopting Article 3 of the ICTY Statute the Security Council never intended to permit prosecutions under this article for violations of Common Article 3 of the Geneva Conventions. Adherence to the principle of legality, he said, requires that the open-ended language of Article 3 be read down, at most to narrow analogies to what is already contained in that article.[6] Also to be read down, according to Delić, is the superior-responsibility provision in Article 7 of the ICTY Statute: it should be understood to apply only to commanders, or otherwise to civilians

---

[4] Defence attorneys working at the tribunals in many ways have had the cards stacked against them, especially at the ICTR, where the problems with conducting a defence are well documented. For defence complaints about anti-defence bias at the ICTR and obstruction by the Rwandan authorities see, for example, D. M. Paccioco, 'Defending Rwandans Before the ICTR: A Venture Full of Pitfalls and Lessons for International Criminal Law' (unpublished MS obtainable from Professor Paccioco, University of Ottawa); *Prosecutor v. Bagilishema*, Defence Closing Brief, 1 August 2000, paras 164–5; *Prosecutor v. E. Ntakirutimana and G. Ntakirutimana*, Defense Closing Brief, 22 July 2002, pp. 157, 179–80, 256–60; and *Prosecutor v. Nahimana*, Final Oral Submissions of the Accused, 20 August 2003, p. 9. The ICC and the SCSL are structured differently than the ICTY and the ICTR in this respect, institutionalizing the defence function to a much greater degree. See Regulation 77 of ICC Court Regulations, Regulations 150–3 of ICC Registry Regulations, and Rule 45 of the SCSL Rules.

[5] *Prosecutor v. Kvočka et al.*, Final Trial Brief [for Zoran Žigić], 29 June 2001, para. 250.

[6] *Prosecutor v. Delalić et al.*, Defendant Hazim Delić's Final Written Submission on the Issue of Guilt/Innocence, 28 August 1998, pp. 34–41. Though Delić did not succeed with this argument, he had a valid point: see further Chapter 4.

exercising the equivalent of military command authority; further, the commander's negligence must have *caused* the criminal conduct of the wayward subordinates.[7] Delić did not clearly explain his thesis that civilians having command responsibility are those, and only those, who exercise the equivalent of military command authority. Delić's thesis has not been properly considered by the tribunals even though there is a strong argument in favour of it. Indeed, the prosecutor and the judges have expanded the scope of command responsibility considerably, as argued in Chapter 7 of this book.[8]

Other ultimately unsuccessful defences in this category include that of Tihomir Blaškić, who argued that the Appeals Chamber had been wrong to read Article 4 of the fourth Geneva Convention broadly:

the Tadić Appeals Chamber said that in modern inter-ethnic wars, loyalty to a third state, based on ethnicity, is much more important than loyalty based on citizenship. However, with all due respect, it is our view that the decision of the Tadić Appeals Chamber is erroneous because Article IV of the Geneva Conventions explicitly and clearly requires the condition of different citizenship. The Court, in its decisions and its freedoms, has certain limits, and it is not possible to change a punitive provision at the expense of the accused.[9]

The argument was rejected by the Trial Chamber in its judgment.[10] In another case, Esad Landžo argued that in the international criminal jurisdiction murder is limited to 'killing with intent to kill' and anything less than that (for example, killing with intent to commit grievous bodily harm) should be excluded.[11] Thus he sought to avoid responsibility for beating prison-camp detainees to death. Hazim Delić, who was a defendant in the same case, made the same argument.[12] In the ICTR's *Rwamakuba* case, the defence argument, that joint criminal enterpise liability for genocide was not recognized at the relevant time by customary international law, failed.[13] The defence for Momcilo Krajišnik, at the ICTY, also attacked the JCE doctrine. It was meant for small-group criminality, the defence said (not unreasonably, as we explained in Chapter 7). But for a JCE to be situated 'over an entire country during a period of civil war, it is immensely difficult to posit what would have been natural and foreseeable on the basis of knowledge of the Defendant at the time, and without the benefit of hindsight'.[14] The Trial Chamber gave this argument limited attention.[15]

---

[7] *Prosecutor* v. *Delalić et al.*, Defendant Hazim Delić's Final Written Submission on the Issue of Guilt/Innocence, 28 August 1998, pp. 104–33.

[8] For an early critique of this tendency, see A. Zahar, 'Command Responsibility of Civilian Superiors for Genocide' (2001) 14 *Leiden J. Int'l Law* 591; for a full account of the problem, see Chapter 7.

[9] *Prosecutor* v. *Blaškić*, Final Oral Submissions on Behalf of Tihomir Blaškić, 28–30 July 1999, pp. 25268–71.

[10] *Blaškić* trial judgment, para. 146.

[11] *Prosecutor* v. *Delalić et al.*, Esad Landžo's Final Submission and Motion for Acquittal, 28 August 1998, pp. 78–88.

[12] *Prosecutor* v. *Delalić et al.*, Defendant Hazim Delić's Final Written Submission on the Issue of Guilt/Innocence, 28 August 1998, pp. 152–63.

[13] *Prosecutor* v. *Rwamakuba*, Decision on Interlocutory Appeal Regarding Application of Joint Criminal Enterprise to the Crime of Genocide, 22 October 2004.

[14] *Prosecutor* v. *Krajišnik*, Defence Final Brief Pursuant to Rule 86(B), 18 August 2006, para. 118.

[15] *Krajišnik* trial judgment, paras 876–7.

II.3 *IN DUBIO PRO REO* AND NON-PROOF OF ELEMENTS OF CRIMES

While the argument from non-proof of elements is not a defence in the sense of being an excuse or a justification,[16] it is an argument extensively used by defence counsel. Some defences, for example that of Tihomir Blaškić, have consisted of little else. In terms of word-count, it is the leading defence.[17]

The prosecution of crimes in the tribunals' jurisdiction leaves itself wide open to arguments from non-proof of elements. One reason is that crimes in this jurisdiction are composed of multiple contextual elements in addition to the actus reus and mens rea of each crime. If one or more of these general elements can be defeated, the defendant's conduct will not have been shown to be a crime in the relevant sense. The aim is to assert, 'My conduct is not what it seems, for the context is different', or 'You have no jurisdiction over these acts occurring in this different context'. This line of defence is related to defensive efforts to question or narrow the tribunals' jurisdiction, the definition of its substantive law, and its application to the facts (matters dealt with elsewhere in this book, as well as immediately above), but for all practical purposes the arguments are deployed also in the manner of a defence to factual allegations.

At the ICTY, Anto Furundžija's lawyers launched his defence with an argument of precisely this kind:

But first let me address the assertion that the Prosecution has proved armed conflict in this case.... I submit to you, Your Honours, that I have spent a lot of time poring over the transcripts, and you will not find one bit of evidence that the army of Bosnia-Herzegovina and the HVO clashed during the relevant period. What they have shown is an attack on civilians by the HVO. They didn't tell you when that conflict between the armies began. The best they could do was tell you that there were trenches dug about May 22nd [1993], and that that is an indication that there must have been a conflict.[18]

---

[16] See P. H. Robinson, 'Criminal Law Defences: A Systematic Analysis' (1982) 82 *Colum. L. Rev.* 199, 213 ff.

[17] See the defence submissions in *Prosecutor* v. *Kupreškić et al.*, and especially: Defence's Closing Brief [for Dragan Papić], 5 November 1999 (leading to Papić's acquittal); The Defence's Closing Brief [for Mirjan Kupreškić], 5 November 1999 (leading to partial acquittal in the first instance and full acquittal on appeal); Closing Argument of the Counsel of the Accused Zoran Kupreškić, 5 November 1999 (same result as for Mirjan Kupreškić); Closing Argument of the Counsel of the Accused Drago Josipović, 5 November 1999 (largely unsuccessful). Other defences in this category include: *Prosecutor* v. *Bagilishema*, Defence Closing Brief, 1 August 2000; *Prosecutor* v. *Kunarac et al.*, Final Trial Brief Submissions by the Defence, 10 November 2000; *Prosecutor* v. *Kvočka et al.*, Final Trial Brief Submissions by the Defence of the Accused Mlado Radić, 29 June 2001; *Prosecutor* v. *Kvočka et al.*, Final Trial Brief [for Zoran Žigić], 29 June 2001, paras 42–234; *Prosecutor* v. *Vasiljević*, Defence Final Trial Brief, 28 February 2002; *Prosecutor* v. *Naletilić and Martinović*, Final Brief of the Accused Mladen Naletilić aka Tuta, 23 October 2002; *Prosecutor* v. *Galić*, Defence's Final Trial Brief, 22 April 2003; *Prosecutor* v. *Stakić*, Defendant Milomir Stakić's Final Brief, 5 May 2003; *Prosecutor* v. *Blagojević and Jokić*, Final Brief of Vidoje Blagojević, 27 September 2004; and *Prosecutor* v. *Blagojević and Jokić*, Defendant Dragan Jokić's Final Trial Brief, 27 September 2004.

[18] *Prosecutor* v. *Furundžija*, Final Oral Submissions on Behalf of Anto Furundžija, 22 June 1998, p. 675. For similar arguments see *Prosecutor* v. *Delalić et al.*, Esad Landžo's Final Submission and Motion for Acquittal,

The first success of this approach came in the *Tadić* case, where it was found, in the trial court, that an international armed conflict had not been proven to exist at the relevant time.[19] The success was short-lived. The Appeals Chamber changed the test, ruled against the majority in the lower court, and added grave breaches to the list of Tadić's convictions.[20] But the question of whether an international armed conflict can be satisfactorily proven — and, if so, for which time period — has haunted the ICTY ever since. Mario Čerkez and other defendants since Tadić have spent considerable resources attacking arguments for the existence of an international conflict, primarily by distinguishing the findings in *Tadić* on the facts, and by arguing in favour of an internal conflict occurring at a different time or place than in the *Tadić* case.[21] Aware of the burdens that the international-conflict argument entails, the prosecutor has avoided grave-breach charges whenever in doubt, preferring the more nebulous provision of violations of the laws or customs of war, where in most cases it is sufficient to prove that an armed conflict existed, without further qualification.

Another general element that has come under frequent attack is the precondition of the crime of persecution that a widespread or systematic attack targeting civilians on discriminatory (national, political, ethnic, or religious) grounds is under way. This line of defence has been helped by a conceptual problem. The case of one state conquering another and then persecuting members of a religious or cultural minority in the subjugated state — the Nazi model — is importantly different from the case of two ethnic or national groups taking up arms against each other for the purpose of controlling territory within the borders of a collapsing state. In the latter case the armed conflict is by its very nature ethnically 'discriminatory', and in that context any attack on civilians of the other side will tend to fall under the definition of persecution, even if it is not intended as such, as one defendant complained:

[The] conflict [was] between two recognizable forces of similar characteristics . . . The aim of the conflict between the two forces [was] the preservation of parts of the territory, which both sides claim to be their own. So, the main motive of both sides is not based on national, political, ethnic or religious grounds, but rather it is the preservation or conquering of the disputable parts of the territory. . . . The Prosecutor has shown no evidence which proves that the crime against the

28 August 1998, pp. 183–7; *Prosecutor v. Delalić et al.*, Defendant Hazim Delić's Final Written Submission on the Issue of Guilt/Innocence, 28 August 1998, pp. 94–103; *Prosecutor v. Aleksovski*, Final Trial Brief Submissions by the Defence, 9 November 1998, pp. 6–13; and *Prosecutor v. Blaškić*, Final Oral Submissions on Behalf of Tihomir Blaškić, 28–30 July 1999, pp. 25249–68, 25277–82.

19 *Tadić* trial judgment, para. 607. See also *Prosecutor v. Aleksovski*, Final Trial Brief Submissions by the Defence, 9 November 1998, pp. 29–41 (citing the *Tadić* first-instance judgment in support).

20 *Tadić* appeal judgment, paras 80–171.

21 *Prosecutor v. Čerkez and Kordić*, Defendant Mario Čerkez's Final Trial Brief, 13 December 2000, pp. 57–80 (esp. p. 76, where the facts in *Tadić* are distinguished in fine detail). The defence drew the following response from the Trial Chamber: 'it would be wrong to construe the Appeals Chamber's decision as meaning that evidence as to whether a conflict in a particular locality has been internationalised must necessarily come from activities confined to the specific geographical area where the crimes were committed, and that evidence of activities outside that area is necessarily precluded in determining that question' (*Kordić and Čerkez* trial judgment, para. 70). The Trial Chamber's grounds for finding that the armed conflict was international were revised and improved on appeal: *Kordić and Čerkez* appeal judgment, paras 350–74.

Muslims during the military conflict came about because of the implementation of a discriminatory policy by the [Croatian side].[22]

Other defences in this category, all of them ultimately unsuccessful, include that of Radomir Kovač, who argued that because the conflict in Foča municipality, in Bosnia-Herzegovina, was initiated by the Muslim side, and because the Serb reaction was only in self-defence and was not planned, the prosecutor had failed to prove that there existed in Foča a widespread or systematic attack against a Muslim civilian population, a precondition for a crime against humanity.[23] Esad Landžo argued that on the facts of his case the victims were not 'protected persons' in the sense of the Geneva Conventions, because both victims and perpetrators were residents of Bosnia-Herzegovina, and so the victims were not in the hands of 'a Party to the conflict or Occupying Power of which they are not nationals', as required by the Conventions.[24] This, he suggested, was enough to have the grave-breach charges against him dismissed. Hazim Delić argued that Article 2 of the ICTY Statute was inapplicable to him for any act committed prior to 31 December 1992 because at that time Bosnia-Herzegovina was not a party to the Geneva Conventions.[25] He also developed Landžo's argument, that even if the Geneva Conventions were in force, they did not apply to the Čelebići detainees, for they, like their captors, were nationals of Bosnia-Herzegovina.[26] Zoran Vuković argued that even if the prosecutor were able to prove that he had raped a Muslim girl, his crime was not part of a widespread or systematic attack on a civilian population, and thus not a crime against humanity, as it had been 'undertake[n] exclusively to satisfy his sexual drive'.[27] (This argument targets the nexus requirement of crimes against humanity. See Chapter 6. The Trial Chamber answered that all that mattered in such a context was the accused's awareness of an attack against the Muslim civilian population and that his victim was a member of that population.)[28]

Defence teams seek weaknesses also in the proof of specific elements of crimes or modes of responsibility. Here again they are well served by the unusual range of elements, many of them vaguely defined, constituting the crimes and modes of responsibility that have been incorporated into the tribunals' jurisdiction. A notable success was in the defence of Hazim Delić. The defence argued that the prosecutor had failed to prove that Delić had command authority at the Čelebići prison-camp, and specifically that he had the authority to issue binding orders or punish violations of such orders.[29]

---

[22] *Prosecutor* v. *Čerkez and Kordić*, Defendant Mario Čerkez's Final Trial Brief, 13 December 2000, pp. 94–5.

[23] *Prosecutor* v. *Kunarac et al.*, Final Trial Brief Submissions by the Defence, 10 November 2000, pp. 197–8.

[24] *Prosecutor* v. *Delalić et al.*, Esad Landžo's Final Submission and Motion for Acquittal, 28 August 1998, pp. 177–8.

[25] *Prosecutor* v. *Delalić et al.*, Defendant Hazim Delić's Final Written Submission on the Issue of Guilt/Innocence, 28 August 1998, p. 13.

[26] Ibid. pp. 65–81. For the same argument, see *Prosecutor* v. *Čerkez and Kordić*, Defendant Mario Čerkez's Final Trial Brief, 13 December 2000, pp. 60–1. The argument was answered in the *Delalić et al.* appeal judgment, para. 81, and the answer was reiterated in the *Kordić and Čerkez* appeal judgment, para. 330.

[27] *Prosecutor* v. *Kunarac et al.*, Final Trial Brief Submissions by the Defence, 10 November 2000, p. 289.

[28] *Kunarac et al.* trial judgment, para. 816.

[29] *Prosecutor* v. *Delalić et al.*, Defendant Hazim Delić's Final Written Submission on the Issue of Guilt/Innocence, 28 August 1998, pp. 134–51.

The Trial Chamber, agreeing, found that the evidence was indicative of a degree of *influence* which Delić had on some occasions in the mistreatment of detainees:

> However, this influence could be attributable to the guards' fear of an intimidating and morally delinquent individual who was the instigator of and a participant in the mistreatment of detainees, and is not, on the facts before this Trial Chamber, of itself indicative of the superior authority of Mr. Delić sufficient to attribute superior responsibility to him.[30]

This became a common defence in prison-camp settings.[31] In one unusual case, the self-confessed former warden of the KP Dom prison-camp in Foča staked his whole defence on the argument that the camp in reality was two institutions, one of which — the one he was in charge of — was crime-free. Unlikely as this partition might sound, the accused Milorad Krnojelac probably had no other defence option open to him:[32] once a position of superiority is proven, especially in a prison-camp setting, crimes against inmates systematically committed by subordinates will inevitably be brought home to the warden; so Krnojelac invented two camps, one run by him for the civilian authority, providing normal prison services for convicted persons, and the other run independently by the army, for prisoners of war and Muslim civilian detainees.[33] The army had a warden for its part of the operation, and thus Krnojelac could maintain that the witnesses who identified him as the warden were right as to his title, but misguided as to his sphere of influence. He was not successful.[34]

The popularity of this kind of defence has to do with the fact that, in prosecuting persons from conflict zones such as Rwanda or the former Yugoslavia, the prosecutor must prove that the defendant had control over one or more of the several armed groups hastily formed to fill the vacuum left behind by a collapsing state. The notion of lawful authority can vanish along with the state. The ad hoc armed groups either fall outside any stopgap constitutional order, or, if recognized within it, may not in reality operate in the manner officially ordained. In either case, one is obliged to look at the facts to reconstruct chains of authority. Where the accused person was a member of the uppermost leadership, this can be an extremely confusing task. It is for this reason that prosecutions of senior figures at the ICTY, in particular, have relied so heavily on the intellectually woolly doctrine of joint criminal enterprise:[35] proof of a group objective and criminal intent is

---

[30] *Delalić et al.* trial judgment, para. 806.

[31] The defence for Zlatko Aleksovski argued that the prosecutor had not proven that the defendant was a member of a military unit having control over the guards at the Kaonik prison-camp, who were members of the Bosnian-Croat military police or army reserve. It was said on behalf of the defendant that he was a warden charged with administrative tasks: *Prosecutor* v. *Aleksovski*, Final Trial Brief Submissions by the Defence, 9 November 1998, pp. 14–15, 18–19, 42–7. See also *Prosecutor* v. *Kvočka et al.*, Final Trial Brief Submissions by the Defence of the Accused Mlado Radić, 29 June 2001, pp. 45–84, 187 (Radić had no control over other guards on his shift who were committing the crimes).

[32] It should be noted that even in Krnojelac's strategically desparate situation he did not attempt to argue the defence of superior orders. As explained below, superior orders is an unworkable defence at the tribunals (unless transformed into the defence of duress), not simply because it is purportedly excluded by the tribunal Statutes (although not at the ICC), but because the violations of the laws of war prosecuted at the tribunals are so blatant.

[33] *Prosecutor* v. *Krnojelac*, Final Written Submissions of Milorad Krnojelac, 13 July 2001, paras 43–193.

[34] The Trial Chamber accepted that the military had leased part of the camp from the civilian authority, but did not accept that Krnojelac, as warden, was not responsible for all personnel and detainees throughout the camp: *Krnojelac* trial judgment, paras 102–7.

[35] See Chapter 7.

considered easier than proof of multilayered relationships of 'effective control' leading from the accused down to the perpetrator on the ground.[36]

In the *Blaškić* case, where joint criminal enterprise was not charged, much of the defence was directed at showing that Blaškić did not control, or only half-controlled, various armed forces. For example:

The special-purpose unit Vitezovi were not within the chain of command of General Blaškić. They were occasionally attached ... And to be attached means that that unit may be used in a particular battle, but no disciplinary measures can be taken against members, the commander cannot be dismissed, it is outside the plan of logistic supply, so it simply means the right to deploy it. ... So that the commander of the Vitezovi unit or the military police allows Blaškić to use that unit, but the main chain of command always remains the same.[37]

This prepared the ground for a concluding defensive manoeuvre: 'When you have multiple lines of command, you cannot accept the thesis of the Prosecutor ... that if apparent organised violative acts occur on the ground, they must have been ordered, and because they occurred in the Operative Zone of Colonel Blaškić, he must have ordered them.'[38]

The Trial Chamber found that Blaškić did control the military police, so this defence failed at first.[39] However, on appeal the defence succeeded.[40]

There have been cases where a former low-ranking member of the armed forces does not dispute his control over a well-defined (and small) fighting unit, but develops his

---

[36] A typical formulation of the JCE doctrine in ICTY indictments of former leaders aims to link up, with one simple stroke, the activities of tens of thousands of persons by way of their intentional states (the illustration is from the indictment of Momčilo Krajišnik, 7 March 2002, para. 7):

> Numerous individuals participated in this joint criminal enterprise. Each participant, by acts or omissions, contributed to achieving the objective of the enterprise. Momčilo Krajišnik and Biljana Plavšić worked in concert with other members of the joint criminal enterprise, including Radovan Karadžić and Nikola Koljević. Other members of the joint criminal enterprise included: Slobodan Milošević, Zeljko Raznatović (aka 'Arkan'), General Ratko Mladić, General Momir Talić, Radoslav Brđanin, and other members of the Bosnian Serb leadership at the Republic, regional and municipal levels; members of the SDS leadership at the Republic, regional and municipal levels; members of the Yugoslav People's Army, the Yugoslav Army, the army of the Serbian Republic of Bosnia and Herzegovina, later the army of the Republika Srpska, the Bosnian Serb Territorial Defence, the Bosnian Serb police, and members of Serbian and Bosnian Serb paramilitary forces and volunteer units and military and political figures from the (Socialist) Federal Republic of Yugoslavia, the Republic of Serbia and the Republic of Montenegro.

ICTY case law does not require proof of effective control in the case of a JCE.

[37] *Prosecutor* v. *Blaškić*, Final Oral Submissions on Behalf of Tihomir Blaškić, 28–30 July 1999, pp. 25003–4 and passim. Blaškić argued, on a different tack, that the prosecutor had misconstrued the defendant's powers to punish his actual subordinates for crimes:

> Blaškić did not have any powers in criminal procedure whatsoever, except for one, to detain temporarily the known perpetrator of a crime and then hand him over to the prosecutor and the police. He could not interfere in any stage of the criminal procedure, and he did not have legal authority to do so ... courts and offices of the prosecutor are linked to the justice ministry and civilian structures, and they are not within the Operative Zone of Central Bosnia [i.e. Blaškić's military command].

For similar reasons, Blaškić claimed to have had no powers over civilian or military prisons; ibid., pp. 24970–91.

[38] *Prosecutor* v. *Blaškić*, Final Oral Submissions on Behalf of Tihomir Blaškić, 28–30 July 1999, p. 25049.

[39] *Blaškić* trial judgment, paras 722–5.

[40] *Blaškić* appeal judgment, paras 340–3, 382–421 (among others).

defence by attributing the alleged crimes to other units operating in the area.[41] In the case of Mario Čerkez, this tactic was to a large extent successful.[42]

There are other variants to avoiding responsibility within command structures. In *Krstić* the defendant argued that the Muslim men fleeing Srebrenica — who were ultimately executed in large numbers — were not captured by forces subordinated to the Drina Corps, in which the defendant was a senior commander. Moreover, according to Krstić, while the executions themselves were carried out by a unit of the Drina Corps, the order to execute the prisoners was external to the Corps and was not passed down the Corps command in a regular fashion. Krstić at any rate had been sent off to oversee an operation in Žepa, and so had no responsibility for the incident in Srebrenica.[43]

A defence can be very strong where a legal element is being applied by the prosecutor in a novel context, in such a way as to amount to an invitation to the Trial Chamber to expand its jurisdiction. The resulting defence could take the form of a *nullum crimen sine lege* defence, or simply emphasize non-proof of the specific element. In the ICTR's *Bagilishema* case, the accused, who was a civilian, was charged with command responsibility. Civilian command responsibility was at the time (and still is) a poorly analysed doctrine and a source of enormous confusion in the jurisprudence of the tribunals. There is no dispute that a military commander is duty-bound to prevent illegal activity by his or her subordinates, and may be held responsible for their crimes. This duty was customary by the end of the nineteenth century.[44] As discussed in Chapter 7, it is much less clear whether persons who are not military commanders are also in certain circumstances affected by the legal duty which is a precondition for command responsibility — and, if so, by what rationale. The tribunals have assumed that it follows from proof of the existence of a 'superior–subordinate relationship' that the superior in question had the relevant duty to prevent or punish unlawful conduct of subordinates.[45] However, there exist superior–subordinate relationships where no such duty is present, and, indeed, where such a duty cannot conceivably operate (for example, in the context of organized crime families). For the reasons given in Chapter 7, proof of a duty to control subordinates in the case of non-military superiors is likely to be difficult, unless the defendant was part of a prima facie legitimate military or quasi-martial organization, such as a prison-camp, or in control of a military or militia-like unit with a prima facie legitimate role, such as a police force.

By the time of the *Bagilishema* case, the ICTR had convicted two civilians in managerial or administrative roles, Musema and Kayishema, of command responsibility.

---

[41] See, for example, *Prosecutor* v. *Čerkez and Kordić*, Defendant Mario Čerkez's Final Trial Brief, 13 December 2000, pp. 26–57, 83–9, 100–4.   [42] See *Kordić and Čerkez* appeal judgment, paras 849, 898, 913, 924.

[43] *Prosecutor* v. *Krstić*, Final Submissions of the Accused, 21 June 2001, pp. 89–99, 105–18 ('he did not see that he was responsible for or empowered to deal with other problems').

[44] See Article 1 of the Regulations to the (Hague) Convention (II) with Respect to the Laws and Customs of War on Land, 29 July 1899. In *United States* v. *Wilhelm von Leeb et al.*, XI Trials of War Criminals 462, at 512, the Tribunal declared that: 'Under basic principles of command authority and responsibility, an officer who merely stands by while his subordinates execute a criminal order of his superiors which he knows is criminal *violates a moral obligation* under international law. By doing nothing he cannot wash his hands of international responsibility.' (Emphasis added.)   [45] E.g. *Delalić et al.* trial judgment, para. 377.

The prosecutor's case was that the two men had headed bands, consisting of their employees, formed to murder Tutsi civilians. The Trial Chambers deciding the two cases were content to use a loose notion of 'influence' or 'control' to find command responsibility, failing to explain by what legal reasoning Musema and Kayishema had been saddled with a legal duty to prevent or punish crimes committed by their employees — a necessary condition for vicarious responsibility. Bagilishema's defence recognized the flaw in the jurisprudence and emphasized that the accused's relationship with his staff was merely 'managerial', the sole exception being the communal police, over whom he did have effective control (inclusive of a duty to control).[46] The Trial Chamber accepted these submissions, and thus the question of the defendant's vicarious liability was significantly narrowed.[47]

Rape-related charges have raised defences whose main target is the element of lack of consent to sexual relations.[48] Radomir Kovač relied entirely on this strategy for his defence. He argued that the transfer of women and children to a 'collection centre' in Foča was not a case of 'arrest of civilians, but only [of] their relocation because of danger for their lives due to combat actions'.[49] In the defendant's explanation, the transfer of four women from the 'collection centre' to his own apartment was also with the aim of ensuring their safety.[50] From this it followed, according to Kovač, that the women were not regarded by the defendant as 'exchange commodities', an aspect of the mens rea which according to him was needed for the crime of sexual enslavement. More specifically on the question of consent, Kovač said:

> During the stay... [the women] had complete freedom of movement, the house being situated outside of a populated area, with broad fields surrounding it, they were not locked in and could at any time leave the said house and escape if they were not themselves consenting to the stay in that house, and thus, consenting to all the other things that had occurred in that house.[51]

'All the other things' is a reference to what the defence saw as an assortment of household chores, including sexual relations:

> It is clear that the relationship between the accused Kovač and witness FWS-87 was very close and according to the observations of [defence] witnesses, it was an intimate relationship, so that it was not noticed that witness FWS-87 was under any fear or some other pressure.[52]

Having paused to remark on the 'great and significant difference between a slap on the face and "beating"'[53] — a distinction which of course borders on the absurd — Kovač's defence concluded that 'witness FWS-87 is not claiming that the accused

---

[46] *Prosecutor v. Bagilishema*, Defence Closing Brief, 1 August 2000, paras 43–89, 186–243 (in the separately numbered legal part).   [47] *Bagilishema* trial judgment, paras 163–5.

[48] The ICTY judges anticipated the defence, and included it within Rule 96 of the ICTY Rules: 'In cases of sexual assault: . . . (ii) consent shall not be allowed as a defence if the victim (a) has been subjected to or threatened with or has had reason to fear violence, duress, detention or psychological oppression, or (b) reasonably believed that if the victim did not submit, another might be so subjected, threatened or put in fear.' Thus the defence must attempt to undermine the prosecutor's proof of points (a) and (b).

[49] *Prosecutor v. Kunarac et al.*, Final Trial Brief Submissions by the Defence, 10 November 2000, pp. 195–6.

[50] Ibid., pp. 204–11.   [51] Ibid., p. 213 (further developed ibid., pp. 233–4).   [52] Ibid., p. 235.

[53] Ibid., p. 228.

Kovač had ever threatened her, beat her or in any other way implied some action which would jeopardize her physical or psychological integrity'. The victim's 'resistance' was not 'real and continuous' or 'clearly expressed'.[54] Thus, according to Kovač, the prosecutor failed to prove lack of consent, and therefore also failed to prove rape.[55] Essentially the same approach was taken by Zoran Vuković, whose legal test was that lack of consent 'must be constant and permanent' if it is to change the nature of the sexual act into an act of rape.[56]

The court gave short shrift to the arguments of both accused.[57] It said that consent must be given voluntarily, as a result of the victim's free will assessed in the circumstances. Where a person was subjected to, or threatened with, or had reason to fear violence, detention, or psychological oppression, or reasonably believed that if she did not submit, another person might be so subjected, threatened, or put in fear, any apparent consent expressed by that person was not freely given.[58]

Other examples of non-proof of specific elements follow.

(1) Dragoljub Kunarac's defence argued that the defendant was for the entire period of the indictment a 'simple soldier' with no effective control over others, and so could not have had command responsibility for the rapes carried out by fellow soldiers.[59] While the Trial Chamber did not agree that Kunarac was a simple soldier, for he was periodically given command of soldiers seconded to him, it did agree that the prosecutor had failed to show that the soldiers were under the defendant's effective control at the time they committed the offences.[60]

(2) Zlatko Aleksovski's defence argued that the detainees taken handcuffed from the Kaonik prison-camp to join operations of the Bosnian-Croat army were not used as human shields, since they were never physically located in such a way as to shield the soldiers. If there was intent to use them as shields, such use was never realized.[61] As for those detainees who were taken from the camp to dig trenches at the front lines, they were not, in effect, treated differently from the local civilian population, who were also obliged to contribute to the war effort by digging trenches, etc.[62]

(3) Radislav Krstić denied that genocidal intent characterized his conduct during the Srebrenica massacres. The killings of Muslim males who were actual or potential military combatants were carried out not with the intent to destroy the Muslims as a group, but with the intent to eliminate those who would take up arms against the Serb side. It was, in any case, an operation led by Krstić's superior, Ratko Mladić. In the

---

[54] Ibid., pp. 296–8. [55] Ibid., pp. 235, 248–59. [56] Ibid., pp. 276–7, 288–9.

[57] *Kunarac et al.* trial judgment, paras 748–81, 811–17. [58] Ibid., paras 460, 464.

[59] *Prosecutor v. Kunarac et al.*, Final Trial Brief Submissions by the Defence, 10 November 2000, pp. 173–84. Co-defendant Radomir Kovač also argued that he was a 'simple soldier'; ibid., pp. 189–91.

[60] *Kunarac et al.* trial judgment, para. 628.

[61] *Prosecutor v. Aleksovski*, Final Trial Brief Submissions by the Defence, 9 November 1998, pp. 25–27, 60–1.

[62] Ibid., pp. 53–6. Similarly, see *Prosecutor v. Blaškić*, Final Oral Submissions on Behalf of Tihomir Blaškić, 28–30 July 1999, pp. 25303–12; *Prosecutor v. Čerkez and Kordić*, Defendant Mario Čerkez's Final Trial Brief, 13 December 2000, pp. 111–16 (citing Yugoslav legislation authorizing compulsory work units in time of war).

immediately following attack on the 'safe area' of Žepa, commanded by Krstić himself, most men of military age were allowed to leave the area.[63] The ICTY Appeals Chamber agreed with Krstić (although for different reasons) that the evidence did not sufficiently support the allegation that he himself intended genocide.[64]

(4) Ferdinand Nahimana denied any association with RTLM radio as of 6 April 1994, arguing that therefore he could not be held responsible for any incitement to genocide broadcast over the radio after that date.[65]

In the area of non-proof of elements of crimes, three specialized types of argument are deployed with some frequency: paucity of the evidence, attributable to witness unreliability; paucity of the evidence arising from non-production of physical or documentary evidence; and invalid inferences. These defence types are examined below.

II.4 UNCORROBORATED, UNRELIABLE, OR INCREDIBLE WITNESS TESTIMONY

Anto Furundžija's defence attempted to shake the judges' confidence in the prosecutor's case by emphasizing that the case was founded on one main witness:

The Prosecution's entire case is based on one witness, and that's Witness A. And it's not just based on her, but, specifically, it is based on her ability to recollect events, her ability to recall times, to recall dates, to recall places, sequences, people. You would have to believe in her abilities beyond a reasonable doubt if you were to convict Anto Furundžija based on her current reconstruction of events. Because, unlike most cases that you will try, there is no corroborating evidence for Witness A.[66]

This becomes a line of defence when conjoined with submissions on the supposed unreliability of the sole prosecution witness to the acts in question, which for the reasons discussed below is a readily available ingredient in the context of the tribunals.[67]

The circumstances of the tribunals have fostered a peculiar narrative and counternarrative on the credibility of witnesses, and in particular of victim-witnesses, which turns on the lapse of years since the occurrence of the events and on the extreme physical or mental violence suffered by the victims. To these plain facts are brought to bear ideas of ongoing conspiracies as well as conflicting precepts of 'pop

---

[63] *Prosecutor* v. *Krstić*, Final Submissions of the Accused, 21 June 2001, pp. 29–41, 69–82.

[64] *Krstić* appeal judgment, para. 137.

[65] *Prosecutor* v. *Nahimana*, Final Oral Submissions of the Accused, 20 August 2003, pp. 73–9.

[66] *Prosecutor* v. *Furundžija*, Final Oral Submissions on Behalf of Anto Furundžija, 22 June 1998, pp. 676–7.

[67] For an example of how the two components come together, see ibid., p. 702. Tribunal judges normally do not hesitate to accept the evidence of a sole prosecution witness, no matter what the witness's relationship with the victim. For example, 'The Trial Chamber again notes that there are countless crimes in which the only witness to the event is a relative, and this relationship should not automatically undermine the credibility of the witness' (*Kvočka et al.* trial judgment, para. 662).

psychology' on such matters as memory retention, recollection veracity, witness suggestivity, and the impact of 'culture' on the formation of beliefs.[68] All sides to tribunal proceedings indulge in this kind of speculation. The *Akayesu* Trial Chamber, for example, speculated that 'The recounting [by a witness] of this traumatic experience is likely to evoke memories of the fear and the pain once inflicted on the witness and thereby affect his or her ability fully or adequately to recount the sequence of events in a judicial context'.[69] The *Kunarac* court took exactly the opposite approach: 'The Trial Chamber attaches much weight to the identification of [the accused] Vuković by FWS-75 because of the traumatic context during which the witness was confronted with Vuković in Buk Bijela as well as in Radomir Kovač's apartment'.[70] The psychologizing of human behaviour is a den of contradiction.

However, here we shall concentrate not on the judges but on the defence. In a submission made on behalf of Furundžija about Witness A, the defence attempted to combine the vulgar idea that a female victim of armed conflict is necessarily made vulnerable and impressionable, with the immanent suspicion that the former Yugoslavia is awash with interest groups whose aim is to rewrite history by any means, or simply to settle old scores:

You can see the situation now. A woman [Witness A] who is at her low point psychologically and psychiatrically is being asked by a man who has facts, who has a purpose and a motive... So what happens? A statement is written. Not by Witness A. Witness A doesn't recall ever giving a statement. She says it was a conversation. And you can imagine how that conversation went. 'Neighbour, I've heard stories about you. Tell me what happened.' And she can't string two sentences together. 'Well, let me write it for you.' She says one name, Accused B. He says, 'Wasn't his boss [Furundžija] there? It could be his boss was there, somewhere in there.' And the name gets written in.[71]

Another example, from the *Čelebići* case:

This Court does not need any of the psychiatrists who participated in this trial to explain the power of suggestion.... These witnesses watched the news, saw the arrest of Esad Landžo, read about the charges against him, met the Association of Detainees in Belgrade, had a seminar in which the Prosecutor participated... to discuss the story that they would tell. A composite story emerged. Rumor becomes truth. These people convinced themselves with ease that they had seen and heard things which they did not and could not have seen or heard. What they now remembered was what others had told them.... [Landžo] is the token guard, and each Serb witness has tailored his tale to fit the revenge that he sought.[72]

Zlatko Aleksovski's defence took the same approach:

Most of [the prosecution witnesses] who were staying in the facility Kaonik talked about having heard screams, crying for help, curses, threats, but did not see in person who was crying for help,

---

[68] On the last point, counsel for the Ntakirutimanas theorized that Rwanda's 'oral' culture led ordinary people — later, 'witnesses' — to believe that they knew first-hand what they had merely heard others say had happened: *Prosecutor v. E. Ntakirutimana and G. Ntakirutimana*, Defense Closing Brief, 22 July 2002, p. 30.

[69] *Akayesu* trial judgment, para. 142.   [70] *Kunarac et al.* trial judgment, para. 789.

[71] *Prosecutor v. Furundžija*, Final Oral Submissions on Behalf of Anto Furundžija, 22 June 1998, p. 680.

[72] *Prosecutor v. Delalić et al.*, Esad Landžo's Final Submission and Motion for Acquittal, 28 August 1998, pp. 139–40.

cursing or threatening. The witnesses interrogated by the Prosecutor could not name specific persons who had committed a punishable act.... Analysing the witnesses' testimonies of the disputable facts, the unquestionable impression is that the witnesses have been instructed and manipulated by the secret police controlled by the Bosnian Muslims as indicated by the fact their depositions were taken in the premises of the police in Zenica in a pre-trial proceeding.[73]

It has even been alleged that witnesses have been tortured by local authorities to obtain their initial statements.[74]

At the ICTR, where the exclusive prosecution of Hutu persons against a backdrop of totalitarian government in Rwanda has facilitated an atmosphere of paranoia in the ranks of the defence, the foundations of the defence of collusion were laid in the *Akayesu* case (albeit haphazardly),[75] reworked in subsequent cases,[76] and used to found a whole defence strategy in *Ntakirutimana*.

The Ntakirutimanas (father and son) combined a four-month-long alibi with the argument that the evidence against them was concocted by political operators who controlled the prosecutor's witnesses. The reason was that the RPF rebels who installed themselves as the government of Rwanda 'needed to eliminate all Church leadership from 1994' (Ntakirutimana senior was a pastor) to maintain their control of the country.[77] More importantly, the RPF, for the sake of its own legitimacy as the overthrower of an internationally recognized government, needed to establish that Rwanda had experienced not just crimes against humanity, not just ad hoc genocidal acts, but a full-blown, one-sided, centrally planned genocide perpetrated by the elite of the *ancien régime*. Only this 'fact', followed by accusations of inaction levelled against the international community (meant to elicit white guilt), could guarantee the survival of a political minority in a position of absolutist control, already more than a decade old.[78] The defence argued — in 150 extremely readable pages — that there was only one explanation for the string of inaccuracies, inconsistencies, and sudden in-court recollections in the body of incriminatory evidence:

All of the Prosecutor's fact witnesses came from Rwanda. They were in some degree chosen, screened, approved, or all three by the RPF [government]. At the very best they were somehow found in Rwanda by the ICTR, more than a year for the first witness and up to six years for the

[73] *Prosecutor* v. *Aleksovski*, Final Trial Brief Submissions by the Defence, 9 November 1998, pp. 17–18.

[74] *Prosecutor* v. *Kvočka et al.*, Final Trial Brief [for Zoran Žigić], 29 June 2001, paras 50.4–50.5.

[75] *Akayesu* trial judgment, paras 44–7. Not until its closing arguments did the Akayesu defence suggest that the witnesses who had testified against the accused were colluding in a 'syndicate of informers', which denounced people for political reasons or in order to acquire their property. In the course of the trial the defence had filed only one motion for perjury and not otherwise confronted a witness with an accusation of false testimony. In dismissing the defence submissions, the Trial Chamber said that 'it is only fair to a witness, whom the Defence wishes to accuse of lying, to give him or her an opportunity to hear that allegation and to respond to it'.

[76] See, for example, *Prosecutor* v. *Rutaganda*, Final Oral Submissions of the Accused, 17 June 1999, p. 38; *Prosecutor* v. *Bagilishema*, Defence Closing Brief, 1 August 2000, conclusion following para. 620 ('The role allegedly played by Bagilishema and the witnesses' general description of the events themselves are so different [from each other] that the only reasonable conclusion to be drawn is that all the witnesses concocted some or all of their testimonies regarding these events'); *Kajelijeli* trial judgment, paras 84–98 (the witness was targeted by the RPF rebels, who concocted evidence against him when they came to power).

[77] *Prosecutor* v. *E. Ntakirutimana and G. Ntakirutimana*, Defense Closing Brief, 22 July 2002, p. 19.

[78] Ibid., pp. 172–4.

last after the events to be investigated. They were interviewed by investigators working on a temporary basis who did not know the language, the region, the people, or much of its history through translators who were overwhelmingly Rwandan and subject to selection, or rejection, directly, or indirectly by the RPF.[79]

This did not work for the Ntakirutimanas, but André Rwamakuba was acquitted by an ICTR Trial Chamber because there was suspicion of fabrication by some witnesses:

> Several Defence witnesses also gave testimony to Witness GIN's personality.... During the genocide, the witness lost her mother and one of her siblings. According to Defence Witness 3/22 who has known GIN since she was very young, and Defence Witness 5/15, who also has a close relationship to GIN, she has been greatly affected by her experience in 1994 and had changed since then. Witness 3/22 described GIN as someone who is highly emotional, dishonest, and not trustworthy. Witness 7/14 submitted that GIN was plotting with other people to fabricate evidence against key figures of Gikomero. Witness GIN's criminal record indicating a conviction in Rwanda for the murder of a colleague, was also raised by the Defence to undermine her credibility.[80]

Defendants have thus sought to dismiss the evidence against them en masse as 'recitations presented by ventriloquist dummies'.[81] The downside of this approach is that judges may perceive it as a slight upon victim-witnesses, more likely to harm the cause of the defence than to assist it. Conspiracy theories, always in the form of carefully chosen facts arranged in one inflexible way, are fragile structures, easily collapsed with a bit of prodding by the court.[82] In general, this line of defence is very weak, and at times simply ridiculous, so it understandably has had little success.

Defences proceeding from the unreliability of a witness draw extensively on differences between written statements made by the witness and his or her eventual testimony in court (often years later). This line is perhaps better conceptualized as a cross-examination technique whose proceeds, pieced together at the end of the case, become a ramrod against the prosecutor's case. For example:

> [Witness] DD testified at trial that he saw Dr. Gérard shoot Pastor Munyandinda and his daughter Erina at Gitwe Primary school, which was mentioned for the first and only time in his July 28, 2001 statement. This statement also included the first false claims that the accused shot his wife, children, uncle and a child at Mubuga primary school which were, in turn, changed immediately before trial, then dropped. Despite the fact that DD testified about the alleged killings of Pastor

---

[79] Ibid., p. 163.   [80] *Rwamakuba* trial judgment, para. 133.

[81] *Prosecutor* v. *Delalić et al.*, Esad Landžo's Final Submission and Motion for Acquittal, 28 August 1998, p. 11; see also *Prosecutor* v. *Vasiljević*, Defence Final Trial Brief, 28 February 2002, pp. 15–85, 104–11.

[82] The *Ntakirutimana* Trial Chamber collapsed the defence argument like a house of cards (*Ntakirutimana* trial judgment, paras 766, 768):

> Witness 9 asserted that the objective of the four meetings attended by Kabera and Witnesses FF and GG was to plan 'the arrest of people they did not like, people the[y] were not happy with within that region.' Yet, this alleged purpose of the meeting would seem to exclude the two Accused, who had left the country in July 1994.... [In any case,] the Chamber sees nothing remarkable in the suggestion that, shortly after the events of 1994, meetings were convened by authorities at which lists of suspects were drawn up with the help of ordinary citizens. Assuming Witness 9's evidence is true, the Chamber is not inclined to find, on this basis, that there may have been a campaign of deceit against the two Accused which influenced the Prosecution's case.

Munyandinda and his daughter, the Prosecutor did not refer to this allegation in his brief. It is human to hide things you are ashamed of.[83]

Entire defences are based on this approach.[84] The weakness they exploit is the passage of a decade, more or less, between incident and testimony, during which the peculiarities of the international criminal context bear fruit. It is not unusual for a witness to arrive in court with a statement given to the local authorities soon after the events (and prior to the establishment of the international tribunals), a statement given through an interpreter to investigators of the (international) prosecutor's office, a follow-up statement given a year or more later, and a supplementary statement (with assorted corrigenda and last-minute recollections) prepared in anticipation of the court appearance. The loss or non-production of a statement can become a major issue.[85] Considering the degradation of evidence in the process of translation and the differing or changing interests of local and international prosecutors, it is no surprise that defence teams seize on these differences and have a field day in cross-examination.[86] As one defence attorney exclaimed in mock frustration: 'Memory, the fragility of memory!'[87] Another said: 'Such allegations which significantly differ at the time of giving different statements, illustrate that the witness has shown that her testimony is not credible and that her credibility as a witness is brought in doubt to such an extent that no decision of the tribunal can be based on any of her testimonies.'[88] What these attorneys do not notice, or are content to keep concealed, is that the narrative of unreliable witness memory has its roots less in a corresponding reality, than in the systemic features of a drawn-out and many-sided international criminal process, summarized above.

This of course is not to say that memory does not fade or change over time, or that witnesses do not occasionally go overboard, or lie,[89] to help the prosecutor, exposing

---

[83] *Prosecutor v. E. Ntakirutimana and G. Ntakirutimana*, Defense Closing Brief, 22 July 2002, p. 137; this same technique is utilized throughout pp. 45–170.

[84] In addition to the Ntakirutimana brief, see, for example, *Prosecutor v. Furundžija*, Final Oral Submissions on Behalf of Anto Furundžija, 22 June 1998, pp. 681–96; *Prosecutor v. Kunarac et al.*, Final Trial Brief Submissions by the Defence, 10 November 2000, pp. 162–6, 202–49, 275–82 (in this last instance, which concerned the accused Vuković, the defence was partially successful); *Prosecutor v. Kvočka et al.*, Final Trial Brief Submissions by the Defence of the Accused Mlado Radić, 29 June 2001, pp. 119–56; *Prosecutor v. Kvočka et al.*, Final Trial Brief [for Zoran Žigić], 29 June 2001, paras 42–234; *Prosecutor v. Nahimana*, Final Oral Submissions of the Accused, 20 August 2003, passim.

[85] *Prosecutor v. Nahimana*, Final Oral Submissions of the Accused, 20 August 2003, pp. 20–4. For example:

> We had the rather fascinating situation with her where she had apparently given a statement, apparently it had been taped, some excerpts had been used in the course of the support for the brief presented by the Prosecutor; but when it came to providing statements, apparently the statements had gone missing from the Office of the Prosecutor. Not only that, the tapes had gone missing from the Office of the Prosecutor. The best they could do was to provide us with some . . . partial notes from the investigator, but it was not a complete picture and not a satisfactory manner. And as I've indicated, she said in evidence for the first time some things which were not said in any of those extracts as well.

[86] See, for example, Josipović's submissions (ultimately unsuccessful) on the key witness EE: *Prosecutor v. Kupreškić et al.*, Closing Argument of the Counsel of the Accused Drago Josipović, 5 November 1999, pp. 20–8.

[87] *Prosecutor v. Furundžija*, Final Oral Submissions on Behalf of Anto Furundžija, 22 June 1998, p. 694.

[88] *Prosecutor v. Kunarac et al.*, Final Trial Brief Submissions by the Defence, 10 November 2000, p. 227.

[89] A news report by the Hirondelle Press Agency, dated 18 May 2005, on two dramatic recantations by ICTR witnesses, goes some way to explain the cynicism and even paranoia among Arusha defence teams: 'Witnesses who had accused the former minister of higher education of Rwanda, Jean de Dieu Kamuhanda, Wednesday turned round and recanted their allegations at the Appeals Chamber of the International Criminal Tribunal for

themselves to attack by making observational or factual claims that seem unlikely in themselves, are contradicted by other evidence, are coloured by information received in the years after the incident, are proffered for the first time in the courtroom without prior warning, are based on rumour or hearsay, or are otherwise easily made to seem doubtful.[90] Some defences have drawn almost exclusively on highly detailed technical attacks on the credibility of evidence which do not necessarily question the motives of the witness but look to the coherence of the evidence taken as a whole.[91] The ICTY Appeals Chamber has said that a Trial Chamber must always proceed with extreme caution when assessing evidence given by a single identification witness under difficult circumstances.[92] The acquittal of Ignace Bagilishema by an ICTR Trial Chamber came down to the rejection of an observational claim by an otherwise reliable witness:

In looking towards Gatwaro Hill and the alleged location of the Accused and Kayishema, Witness G's line of sight would have had to travel at a gentle upward angle through the low-roofed and presumably crowded porch and its supporting columns, out over a 50-metre stretch of equally crowded field, before it reached the steep verdant backdrop of Gatwaro, 55 to 65 metres away, where hundreds of attackers are said to have assembled. Although under favourable conditions of observation, a familiar face may be easily recognisable [over that distance] the Chamber is concerned as to how the witness was able to specifically identify the Accused and Kayishema amongst the attackers.[93]

In another case, the brothers Zoran and Mirjan Kupreškić, who finally had all charges against them dismissed on appeal, were acquitted of one count by the Trial Chamber on the ground that the key witness to the incident, KL, had been embellishing his testimony over time:

The difficulty concerning the credibility of this witness's evidence is that it was not until ten months after the incident that he firmly identified Zoran and Mirjan Kupreškić as the perpetrators of the massacre of his family. Despite the horror of what had happened and his supposed knowledge of those responsible, he did not divulge the fact when interviewed on 18 and 19 April for a local television station or (more significantly) when interviewed by investigators on 22 April 1993, when he said that he did not recognise the perpetrators. On 1 October 1998, when interviewed by an investigating judge, the witness said only that the figures resembled Zoran and Mirjan Kupreškić.[94]

The Trial Chamber here did no more than restate the core of the defence's arguments for rejecting KL's identification evidence. The defence's full analysis[95] is devastating for

Rwanda. . . . "I never saw him simply because I was not there. I had already fled. . . . I ask for forgiveness, I lied," [said one of the witnesses] explaining that he had been blinded by the pain of losing his loved ones.'

[90] For a useful analysis of factors contributing to inaccurate recollection ('innocent deficiencies'), see *Prosecutor v. Bagilishema*, Defence Closing Brief, 1 August 2000, paras 137–57. The reliance of witnesses (and of the prosecutor) on hearsay came under especially fierce attack in *Prosecutor v. Nahimana*, Final Oral Submissions of the Accused, 20 August 2003, pp. 6–7, 13, 22–3, one of the more memorable submissions being that 'None of these documents, these magazine articles, are signed, save one from Adrien Rangira in *Kanguka*, which simply says that Ferdinand Nahimana was reported to say the southerners were like the Tutsis. These are documents which are of the very sort which should not be admitted in evidence. This is not a trial by the media merely because it is labelled the "media trial." This is a trial according to rules of evidence.'

[91] A good example is the Bagilishema defence, where a multitude of observational snippets were shown not to add up to an internally consistent story: *Prosecutor v. Bagilishema*, Defence Closing Brief, 1 August 2000, passim.

[92] *Kupreškić et al.* appeal judgment, para. 134.   [93] *Bagilishema* trial judgment, para. 649.

[94] *Kupreškić et al.* trial judgment, para. 397.

[95] *Prosecutor v. Kupreškić et al.*, The Defence's Closing Brief [for Mirjan Kupreškić], 5 November 1999, pp. 34–54; *Prosecutor v. Kupreškić et al.*, Closing Argument of the Counsel of the Accused Zoran Kupreškić, 5 November 1999, pp. 81–6, 93–102. Zlatko Kupreškić's brief is of lesser quality.

the witness's credibility, yet far from unsympathetic to the witness-victim himself, whose family was killed before his eyes. Steering clear of conspiracy theories and other distractions, it amounts to a model example of this kind of defence.

Zoran and Mirjan Kupreškić were convicted by the Trial Chamber in relation to another incident involving an uncorroborated witness, dubbed H, only to have that conviction reversed on appeal. As the defence put it, this was another case 'of a subsequent identification of the perpetrators as against an original assertion that it was impossible to identify anyone because the assailants were disguised'.[96]

The lone witnesses to the various incidents in this case — KL, H, and others — seem to have formed their memories of the identities of the perpetrators in conversations with each other, without necessarily being aware of the unfolding of this cognitive process. The Appeals Chamber accepted the essence of the two brothers' submissions to the Trial Chamber,[97] noting, for example, that the lower court had failed to consider material discrepancies going directly to H's credibility and identification of the defendants. A memorable moment in the Appeals Chamber's 18,000-word analysis of the Trial Chamber's errors on this point comes with the observation that H's fervour in affirming her identification of Zoran and Mirjan Kupreškić matched her fervour in denying the making of a statement which the Trial Chamber itself finally accepted she had made:

> The Trial Chamber accepted Witness H's evidence based, in large part upon her confident demeanour, notwithstanding her adamant and yet, mistaken, denial that the [December 1993] statement was hers. . . . the trial record reveals that Witness H gave no explanation about why she may have been confused about whether or not she made the December 1993 Statement. Moreover, the significance of the December 1993 Statement, for the present purposes, lies not in the contents of the document, but in the fact that Witness H denied she made it at all. Given that the Trial Chamber's assessment of Witness H hinged so dramatically upon its assessment that her confident in-court testimony was an indicator of reliability, her mistake as to the December 1993 Statement took on increased significance.[98]

Occasionally the argument from witness unreliability has been taken to extremes, as in the case of *Kunarac* where the testimony of rape victims was analysed by the defence against standards of logical consistency and narrative completeness and coherence that were unrealistic, in the sense that no judge would entertain them.[99] The defendant Kovač said, for example: 'If witness FWS-87 remembers this event, [which was] only an attempt by an unknown soldier to enter the apartment, then it is completely certain that she would have remembered if some other soldier had actually come to the apartment at a given time, especially if that soldier was raping FWS-75 or taking her away.'[100] This is just more pop psychology.[101] But the defence's recurrent error in

---

[96] *Prosecutor* v. *Kupreškić et al.*, The Defence's Closing Brief [for Mirjan Kupreškić], 5 November 1999, p. 61.

[97] Ibid., pp. 54–77; *Prosecutor* v. *Kupreškić et al.*, Closing Argument of the Counsel of the Accused Zoran Kupreškić, 5 November 1999, pp. 86–92.   [98] *Kupreškić et al.* appeal judgment, para. 145.

[99] See *Prosecutor* v. *Kunarac et al.*, Final Trial Brief Submissions by the Defence, 10 November 2000, pp. 108–62.

[100] Ibid., p. 228. Cf. *Prosecutor* v. *Kvočka et al.*, Final Trial Brief Submissions by the Defence of the Accused Mlado Radić, 29 June 2001, pp. 85–119 (a witness making rape allegations cannot be credited if she has a criminal record).

[101] A typical judicial response is: 'The Trial Chamber considers that these "discrepancies" alleged by the Defense are minor and understandable when several witnesses testify to the same incident and do not affect the overall

Kunarac was also to imagine that tribunal judges assemble the evidence into a kind of documentary film, whose frames tell a complete and logical story ('[As] she is unable to describe either the house or the layout of the rooms, or the place where she was raped, it is obvious that this witness can not be believed'[102]). In the large cases before the tribunals, which are not amenable to that degree of reconstruction, what happens in fact is that the judges apply their minds like a strobe light to the evidence, selecting the salient features corresponding to the legal elements of the crimes, and — upon finding those features believable — drawing conclusions directly from them.[103] Against this judicial psychology, a nit-picking defence, whose only point is that the evidence of prosecution witnesses leaves questions unanswered and just might support an interpretation other than the most natural interpretation of the evidence, is sure to fail.

Witnesses purporting to be 'experts' are also regularly attacked as unreliable by the defence, especially at the ICTR, where several candidates have in fact been dismissed by the Trial Chambers as lacking expertise.[104]

II.5 NON-PRODUCTION OF PHYSICAL OR DOCUMENTARY EVIDENCE

Non-production of physical evidence or of forensic reports analysing physical evidence (and in particular concerning the cause of death of the victim, the victim's identity, and the murder weapon) is among the factors that make tribunal practice unusual. The paucity of documentary evidence to substantiate matters that in domestic courts would normally require substantiation through forensic analysis or through production of, say, hospital records, was first raised by Aleksovski's defence:

None of the heard witnesses submitted any medical documentation supporting their alleged injuries they received at Kaonik, nor has the Prosecutor entered as evidence the documents on these injuries. Medical documentation about injuries is an objective fact subject to professional verification of forensic medicine experts in order to evaluate the seriousness and health risk of an

---

credibility of the witnesses' (*Kvočka et al.* trial judgment, para. 596); or, 'His confusion is understandable considering the content of his testimony and the amount of time that had passed since the event' (ibid., para. 608).

[102] *Prosecutor* v. *Kunarac et al.*, Final Trial Brief Submissions by the Defence, 10 November 2000, p. 126.

[103] This robust approach to witness testimony has been fully supported by the Appeals Chamber of the ad hoc tribunals, as the following example demonstrates (*Semanza* appeal judgment, para. 221):

> Nevertheless, even if there were some contradictory evidence on this subject, the Appellant has failed to demonstrate that the Trial Chamber was unreasonable in convicting the Appellant without being absolutely sure about the vehicle in which he arrived at the crime scene. In the view of the Appeals Chamber, even if there was uncertainty about the vehicle in which the Appellant arrived at Musha church (and the Trial Chamber did not decide this question), this matter was secondary, as the Trial Chamber had sufficient and credible evidence going to the Appellant's presence at and participation in the massacre at Musha church.

[104] *Prosecutor* v. *Nahimana*, Final Oral Submissions of the Accused, 20 August 2003, pp. 25–9 (use of 'expert' testimony at the ICTR should be dismissed as unreliable because it is mostly unrelated to the field of the witness's purported expertise).

injury and to explain the reasons and means of causing it. . . . The witnesses' subjective judgement is not a credible basis for the evaluation of the existence of a physical or psychic injury.[105]

However, that is precisely the basis on which the tribunals have rested their findings in an overwhelming number of cases. An early attempt, in the *Rutaganda* case, to support a murder allegation with a series of expert reports concerning a burial site located near the defendant's former business premises was criticized by the defence as inconclusive, since, among other problems, fewer bodies were exhumed from that site than were alleged to have been buried.[106] The Trial Chamber agreed with the defence that the reports were worthless and that no physical evidence corroborated the murder allegation, but nevertheless did not hesitate to find the allegation proven on the basis of the eyewitness testimony of one witness:

> The Prosecutor failed to show a direct link between the findings of Professor Haglund and Dr. Peerwani and the specific allegations in the Indictment. . . . the Chamber is not satisfied that the grave site referred to by Witness Q and the one exhumed by Professor Haglund are one and the same. . . . Based on the testimony of Witness Q, the Chamber is satisfied beyond any reasonable doubt that the Accused ordered men under his control to take fourteen detainees, including at least four Tutsis, to a deep hole located near Amgar garage and that on the orders of Georges Rutaganda and in his presence, his men killed ten of the said detainees with machetes. The bodies of the victims were thrown into the hole.[107]

The prosecutor got into worse trouble in the *Ntakirutimana* case, where physical evidence of mass killings at the Mugonero Complex in Rwanda was led through a lay person who had happened to be present at the exhumations. The defence characterized his evidence as incredible and absurd,[108] and the Trial Chamber appeared to agree.[109]

For Zoran Žigić, who was charged at the ICTY with several murders, the failure of the prosecutor to locate the bodies and establish the cause of death of the allegedly murdered persons meant that normal criminal procedure at the tribunals had been 'reduced to talk'.[110] Yet, he insisted, the requirement of 'substantial causal relation between the conduct of the accused and the death of a victim' placed a burden on the prosecutor to produce at least some evidence, at a physical level of description, of physical objects and causal links.[111] According to Žigić, in the case of one purported victim, there was even evidence that no such person existed (the only family in the region with a closely similar surname was not missing any of its members), let alone was killed.[112] The problem of de-personalization of victims in the context of large-scale crimes must place some limits, Žigić hinted, on the prosecution of persons where victim-specific evidence is lacking.[113]

---

[105] *Prosecutor* v. *Aleksovski*, Final Trial Brief Submissions by the Defence, 9 November 1998, p. 23.

[106] *Prosecutor* v. *Rutaganda*, Final Oral Submissions of the Accused, 17 June 1999, pp. 36–9, 73–7.

[107] *Rutaganda* trial judgment, paras 258–61.

[108] *Prosecutor* v. *E. Ntakirutimana and G. Ntakirutimana*, Defense Closing Brief, 22 July 2002, pp. 100–2.

[109] *Ntakirutimana* trial judgment, fn. 477 ('His estimates appear to be based on the number of coffins used and, more critically, on the number of people required to lift a coffin after it had been filled').

[110] *Prosecutor* v. *Kvočka et al.*, Final Trial Brief [for Zoran Žigić], 29 June 2001, para. 30.1.

[111] Ibid., paras 34, 75.2.   [112] Ibid., paras 77–86.2.

[113] Ibid., para. 87.2 (where frustration is tinged with sarcasm: 'Perhaps it would have been less unacceptable had Žigić been charged with the murder of NN (John Doe) right from the beginning').

An overdependence on circumstantial evidence was portrayed by the defendant as leading to a relaxation of the standard for making safe inferences.[114]

A peculiarity of the tribunal system is the great difficulty associated with producing witnesses in court. Unlike the average municipal criminal process, where every significant witness is located by the police and made to give at least a statement, in the international system most of the witnesses to an incident are never finally identified. When a witness is located, he or she may not wish to give a statement, let alone travel to a court in another country to testify. There is very little the investigator or the court can do in such situations. Subpoenas have been issued by the tribunals to some witnesses, usually on the understanding that the witness is willing to cooperate, but prefers to do so under the 'compulsion' of a subpoena to avoid being branded a 'collaborator' with international justice. The tribunals are otherwise very reluctant to use the formal powers they possess to compel witness testimony, not simply because they wish to avoid complications in their relations with states, but because they do not wish to endanger witnesses, many of whom have objective reasons to fear for their safety or for that of their families should it become known — as it very well might, during any attempt to enforce a subpoena — that they are cooperating with the tribunal. Within this distinctive mix one finds as well the social imperative that a member of an ethnic group must not testify against another member of the same group, even if that would involve speaking the truth. For these reasons and many more, the international criminal process is unique.

The above digression into the politics of witness availability frames Zoran Žigić's next argument. The defendant had attempted to contact former cell mates of one of the murder victims, whom the prosecutor had not called. Predictably, they refused to testify for the defence.[115] In the end, a total of four persons called by the prosecutor testified in relation to the murder. Žigić's response, while rhetorical, effectively draws attention to a complacent tribunal mindset:

The Defence asks … what would have happened if [two of the four witnesses] called by the Prosecution had not appeared at the trial, the way the others [approached by the defence] refused to. In that case, only two of the Prosecution's witnesses would have been left, the ones who accuse Žigić, and the Trial Chamber would have never been able to hear from those who actually were in the White House [detention centre] about other versions of the incident, in fact, much more reliable ones. This calls for the Defence to argue with even more conviction that no one should be convicted of murder based on what a couple of witnesses say, without any material traces and other evidence.[116]

---

[114] Ibid., para. 38. Other examples of non-production of forensic evidence of death or injury: *Akayesu* trial judgment, para. 41 ('no medical examination had been conducted on the alleged victims to verify that the injuries which they claimed were sustained as a result of the accused's actions'); *Prosecutor* v. *Kunarac et al.*, Final Trial Brief Submissions by the Defence, 10 November 2000, pp. 36–41, 114–15, 275 (absence of medical documentation proving permanent physical ('gynaecological') damage or associated psychological injuries caused to female detainees in the course of sexual assaults); *Prosecutor* v. *Bagilishema*, Defence Closing Brief, 1 August 2000, para. 288 (no evidence of ultimate fate of a person allegedly killed).

[115] *Prosecutor* v. *Kvočka et al.*, Final Trial Brief [for Zoran Žigić], 29 June 2001, para. 116.3. Žigić observed that 'The Prosecution decided to go with a 'one-nation' and 'one-religion' composition of its witnesses' (ibid., para. 223.1). This swipe aside, it is true that there is no obligation on tribunal prosecutors to call every significant witness to an incident. The prosecutor is in practice free to take the most favourable selection.

[116] Ibid., para. 116.7.

At the ICTR, not only is documentation scarce, it is carefully controlled by the Rwandan government, which has done everything within its powers to avoid prosecution of its own (RPF) members, past and present. In the *Nahimana* case, the most document-intensive of the ICTR cases, the defence complained that it did not get to see a single document from the RPF archives in its original state:

> What you know from the evidence, and this is a general comment that applies to all the documents, is that you have not received in this Trial Chamber one single original document from the Prosecutor. You have not received any statements from those who have been the original providers of the documents to certify as to the authenticity of the copy, to confirm that the copy accurately and completely represents the original document held by the organisation or individual. . . . We, of course, accept that in the jurisprudence of these Chambers and of the ICTY, documents are admissible, but that doesn't deny the need to ensure that they are authentic, that they are not tampered with. We have seen many of the documents are incomplete, some aren't legible; copies of documents cannot be, by the Defence, certified as to their reliability in the way that tests can be carried out on original documents.[117]

The same was true, more critically, of the recordings of the radio broadcasts, on which rested the case against two of the accused in the *Nahimana* case.[118]

11.6 INVALID INFERENCES FROM CIRCUMSTANTIAL EVIDENCE

The official tribunal standard for making inferences from circumstantial evidence is that the inference must be the only reasonable inference on the evidence. Defence teams have directed considerable resources to the enforcement of this standard,[119] with varying degrees of success.

Tihomir Blaškić argued before the ICTY Trial Chamber:

> You cannot infer as a matter of logic, from an event on the ground, that it was ordered by a super-commander. It could have been wilful. It could have been committed contrary to the orders of the superior command, if that actual ability to control did not exist or did not exist in a uniform and consistent manner across time and the relevant space.[120]

He was unsuccessful. But when he repeated the argument on appeal he got better results:

> The Appeals Chamber considers that the Trial Chamber drew an adverse inference from the number and sequence of orders in evidence, and indeed, from the absence of orders . . . However, when it did so, the Trial Chamber failed to explain or to provide a basis for its inference.

---

[117] *Prosecutor* v. *Nahimana*, Final Oral Submissions of the Accused, 20 August 2003, p. 10.

[118] Ibid., p. 11.

[119] One defendant announced that he was staking his whole defence on pre-emptively refuting possible incriminating inferences from circumstantial evidence: *Prosecutor* v. *Kvočka et al.*, Final Trial Brief [for Zoran Žigić], 29 June 2001.

[120] *Prosecutor* v. *Blaškić*, Final Oral Submissions on Behalf of Tihomir Blaškić, 28–30 July 1999, p. 25050.

Moreover, it is difficult to conceive of a situation in which the absence of evidence that an individual gave an order could reasonably give rise to an inference that he did do so, and this case does not present such a situation. The Appeals Chamber finds that this inference is not reasonable.[121]

Surely it is easy enough to conceive of situations where an action must have been undertaken pursuant to an order, which allows an inference to that end, even if there is no direct evidence of such an order. But in this case the Appeals Chamber's narrow approach worked well for Blaškić.

The aforementioned complications in command and control of armed units caused by the emergence of fledgling substitutes for state authority and roving paramilitaries have been exploited by defence teams to undermine inferences from 'patterns' of events. Blaškić again:

The Prosecution wants you to draw an inference that what happened in Ahmići and all these other places, the common thread is Blaškić because he's the commander of the territory. But if you look at what happened in these different places, you see that the common theme is local variation, local factors, local influences, events of retaliation, events of revenge, looting for personal gain. . . . You have to ask yourself whether the patterns of violence support the kind of grandiose, criminal, master scheme planned and implemented by Colonel Blaškić that the Prosecutor urges or whether the world is more complex and less black and white, and if you look at the details, you see other common themes and threads that do not run to our client.[122]

The defence in *Kunarac* argued at length that the prosecutor had mischaracterized 'temporary collection shelters' as civilian detention centres, and cautioned the ICTY Trial Chamber against preferring one description when the other was equally plausible. Far from detaining ordinary civilians, said the defence, the Serb authorities in Foča, faced with a flood of persons of every ethnicity displaced by the armed conflict, accommodated them temporarily in whatever facilities were available and treated them in the manner of 'refugees'. The conditions were harsh, but 'better living conditions and food could neither be found with the inhabitants [of the municipality] who were also without water, without electricity'.[123] Displaced persons were free to come and go, but most remained put because they had no better place to go to. The fact that some witnesses experienced the 'collection' centres as prisons was an illusion, according to the defence, created by the harshness of the general circumstances.[124]

Another defence team preferred to view alleged civilian detention centres as security screening centres, and compared the situation in Bosnia-Herzegovina with that in the

---

[121] *Blaškić* appeal judgment, para. 519.

[122] *Prosecutor* v. *Blaškić*, Final Oral Submissions on Behalf of Tihomir Blaškić, 28–30 July 1999, pp. 25200, 25202.

[123] *Prosecutor* v. *Kunarac et al.*, Final Trial Brief Submissions by the Defence, 10 November 2000, pp. 54, 195–6, 267. This argument is often present in defence submissions. See, for example, *Prosecutor* v. *Čerkez and Kordić*, Defendant Mario Čerkez's Final Trial Brief, 13 December 2000, pp. 50–2 ('There is no evidence that would show that the reason for internment was other than safety of the internees and safety of own troops'); *Prosecutor* v. *Krnojelac*, Final Written Submissions of Milorad Krnojelac, 13 July 2001, para. 195; and *Prosecutor* v. *Simić et al.*, Defendant Miroslav Tadić's Final Brief, 7 July 2003, paras 214–73 (labour was not forced, but rather a work obligation incumbent upon all), and 484–556 (transfer of detainees was voluntary and effected for reasons of family reunification).

[124] Cf. *Prosecutor* v. *Krnojelac*, Final Written Submissions of Milorad Krnojelac, 13 July 2001, para. 132 (in order to prevent 'simulation of ethnic cleansing' purportedly staged by the Muslim political party to attract international sympathy, 'Muslims were for some time forbidden to leave Foča'; to this end many were held by the Serb authorities in detention centres).

United States in the 1940s, when citizens of Japanese origin were interned for security reasons.[125]

In the *Krstić* case, the defence cautioned the court against concluding from the fact of mass civilian movement that that movement was a planned act of expulsion by the attacking side. In a civil war, 'the need of the civilian population, feeling jeopardized by the war operations, to seek refuge in areas controlled by the military forces of their ethnic community . . . is only natural'. Like 'collateral damage', displacement is often foreseeable, but also often unintended. Intent cannot be inferred from the mere fact of displacement.[126]

Zoran Žigić admitted that while he was occasionally 'excessive' in his treatment of Muslims, he (a Serb) was also excessive in his treatment of Serbs, so much so that he was sentenced to prison for mistreating a Serb.[127] Thus the mens rea of persecution was not provable against him, and the fact that he was known to use the derogatory term 'balija' to refer to Muslims was nothing but a 'vulgar joke . . . frequently found in taxi drivers, bohemians and people under the influence of alcohol', all of which Žigić readily admitted that he was.[128]

A defence which was conducted almost entirely on the basis of refuting inferences — in this case inferences about the meaning of words — was that of Ferdinand Nahimana, the alleged director of RTLM radio in Rwanda (Nahimana denied that he held this position). The failings of this case are examined in detail in Chapter 5. It suffices to outline here the prosecutor's case, which was that the meaning of two Kinyarwanda words, *'inyenzi'* and *'inkotanyi'*, had by April 1994 changed to denote any Tutsi civilian, not just any member of the (largely Tutsi) RPF rebel force. The defence tried to show that, on the contrary, the radio's verbal attacks against the *inyenzi/inkotanyi* followed closely upon RPF military advances, and therefore that the correct semantic inference was that the meaning of these key words had not shifted.[129]

II.7 RELATIVIZING CONDUCT TO EXTREME CIRCUMSTANCES AND THE DEFENCE OF GOOD CHARACTER

That a defence of good character is available at the ad hoc tribunals is not evident from the ICTY's case law, which at first glance might even suggest the opposite. In an often-cited decision in the *Kupreškić et al.* case, the Trial Chamber played down the significance of

---

[125] *Prosecutor* v. *Čerkez and Kordić*, Defendant Mario Čerkez's Final Trial Brief, 13 December 2000, pp. 105–8, citing *Hirabayashi* v. *United States*, 320 US 81 (1943) and *Korematsu* v. *United States*, 323 US 214 (1944) for the proposition that in such cases temporary internment is not prohibited.

[126] *Prosecutor* v. *Krstić*, Final Submissions of the Accused, 21 June 2001, pp. 79–80, 120–122.

[127] *Prosecutor* v. *Kvočka et al.*, Final Trial Brief [for Zoran Žigić], 29 June 2001, paras 213–213.1, 216.

[128] Ibid., para. 209.2.

[129] *Prosecutor* v. *Nahimana*, Final Oral Submissions of the Accused, 20 August 2003, pp. 70–4, 79.

character evidence:

> Generally speaking, evidence of the accused's character prior to the events for which he is indicted before the International Tribunal is not a relevant issue inasmuch as (a) by their nature as crimes committed in the context of widespread violence and during a national or international emergency, war crimes and crimes against humanity may be committed by persons with no prior convictions or history of violence, and that consequently evidence of prior good, or bad, conduct on the part of the accused before the armed conflict began is rarely of any probative value before the International Tribunal, and (b) as a general principle of criminal law, evidence as to the character of an accused is generally inadmissible to show the accused's propensity to act in conformity therewith.[130]

This statement of principle — the origin of which is in the realm of theory, not practice — leaves the door open a fraction, without indicating, however, the circumstances under which evidence of prior good character would be relevant or admissible. The same result is apparent in the *Kajelijeli* case, where the ICTR Appeals Chamber found that the good-character defence was not effective on the facts of that case, implying, nevertheless, that the desired impact might have been achieved with better facts.[131]

If there is a tendency at the ICTY, it is to slot good-character evidence with the factors going to mitigation of sentence, and otherwise to follow the *Kupreškić* decision.[132] But as is so often the case, defence theory differs from defence practice. In this instance we need to turn to the case law of the ICTR. The defence of good character was first used in the *Bagilishema* case, with stunning success.

The acquittal of Ignace Bagilishema was achieved by convincing the majority of the Trial Chamber that he was a person of good — resiliently good — character. This is not to say that Bagilishema succeeded by a non-proof-of-elements strategy. In other words, it would not be accurate to say that the majority were left with the impression that the defendant was not, after all, a bad man because the prosecutor had failed to prove criminal conduct. On the contrary: non-proof-of-elements in Bagilishema's case succeeded as thoroughly as it did because the defence managed to convince the majority that Bagilishema was a fundamentally decent man[133] — not quite the Rwandan Schindler, as his lawyer argued, but something along those lines. Evidence that did not fit this view of the defendant (such as witness G's identification of him on Gatwaro Hill, mentioned above) was rationalized away.

---

[130] *Prosecutor* v. *Kupreškić et al.*, Decision on Evidence of the Good Character of the Accused and the Defence of Tu Quoque, 17 February 1999.

[131] *Kajelijeli* appeal judgment, para. 311 ('This evidence can in no way, even when taken together with the testimony of other witnesses as to the Appellant's alleged good conduct towards Tutsis before and during 1994, diminish the weight of the evidence going to the Appellant's culpability for intent to commit genocide and acts of genocide against Tutsis . . . Such selective assistance to Tutsis who are known by the Appellant and had previously been assisted by the Appellant . . . is not decisive').

[132] See, for example, *Blagojević and Jokić* trial judgment, para. 854 ('Dragan Jokić ensured the safe passage through a minefield of a group of Bosnian Muslim boys. The Trial Chamber has assessed this evidence in light of the fact that Dragan Jokić has been convicted for the crime of persecutions, which requires discriminatory intent. The Trial Chamber considers that this act, in the midst of ongoing fighting, merits consideration when arriving at the appropriate sentence. The Trial Chamber will consider it as a mitigating circumstance').

[133] See *Prosecutor* v. *Bagilishema*, Defence Closing Brief, 1 August 2000, paras 47–112.

The exact logic of the defence of good character has never been openly articulated. The court in *Bagilishema* said that 'where such evidence is shown to be particularly probative to the charges at hand, then the burden will be upon the Prosecutor to dispel any resulting doubts there may be regarding its case'.[134] Judge Gunawardana, in his Separate Opinion in support of the majority view, elaborated this idea somewhat:

The evidence shows more than mere prior good character or lack of previous disposition by the Accused to commit such crimes. It indicates that, prior to the events in 1994, the Accused had consistently conducted himself in a manner that is completely at odds with the conduct alleged by the Prosecution during the events in 1994.... Thus it becomes all the more important, for the Prosecution to prove that the Accused formed or manifested the requisite mens rea.[135]

The logic seems to be that a strong defence of prior good character — meaning, in particular, evidence from the period just prior to the alleged crimes of an intent inconsistent with the mens rea element required for the crimes — severely weakens the prosecutor's chances of proving the mens rea, but only in those cases in which: first, the mens rea is the gist of the case (for example, in a case alleging conspiracy, or alternatively joint criminal enterprise, where distant principal perpetrators perform the actus reus); and, secondly, there is no direct evidence of the mens rea, meaning, therefore, that an inference from circumstantial evidence is the only available mechanism of proof. Thus the weight of a virtuous past will bear fully on a questionable present. The basis for what is, in effect, an effort by the defence to construct in the minds of the judges a presumption against mens rea,[136] is nothing more than the intuition that while good people can change for the worse in changed circumstances, there are limits to how much moral change is possible from one moment to the next.

Bagilishema created expectations that the defence of good character would bear fruit in other cases, but so far this has not happened. Ramsey Clark elaborated the defence with style and passion throughout his representation of Pastor Ntakirutimana. The prognosis was good: a mass of evidence by eminent and impartial witnesses attested to the pastor's popularity and flawless prior character. Not only did the pastor not discriminate against the Tutsi, he was actively opposed to such conduct.[137] This was acknowledged by the Trial Chamber.[138] Moreover, the elderly and ailing pastor's alleged role in the crimes was peripheral — complicity and encouragement — and therefore heavily reliant on proof of mens rea. As in the case of Bagilishema, there was no credible evidence in the pastor's case directly establishing the mens rea.

When comparing the two cases, there is no obvious reason why Ntakirutimana's defence of good character failed while Bagilishema's succeeded.[139] A differently

---

[134] *Bagilishema* trial judgment, para. 116; cited with approval in *Ntakirutimana* trial judgment, para. 731.

[135] *Bagilishema* trial judgment, paras 32–3 of Judge Gunawardana's Separate Opinion.

[136] See *Prosecutor* v. *Bagilishema*, Defence Closing Brief, 1 August 2000, para. 108: 'The Defence submits that where the good character of an accused has been established, the Chamber must admit that he is less likely to have committed the crimes charged.'

[137] *Prosecutor* v. *E. Ntakirutimana and G. Ntakirutimana*, Defense Closing Brief, 22 July 2002, pp. 1–6, 174–8.

[138] *Ntakirutimana* trial judgment, paras 733–46.

[139] Bagilishema's pre-conflict character was not as sterling as that of pastor Ntakirutimana; see *Bagilishema* trial judgment, para. 128.

composed Trial Chamber, with only slightly higher expectations of what it takes to prove mens rea circumstantially, could have acquitted the pastor.[140]

A variety of the defence of good character is that the accused's conduct in the circumstances alleged is to be excused by the very extremeness or chaos of those circumstances. The ICTY Appeals Chamber would have such a defence dismissed:

A finding that a 'chaotic' context might be considered as a mitigating factor in circumstances of combat operations risks mitigating the criminal conduct of all personnel in a war zone. Conflict is by its nature chaotic, and it is incumbent on the participants to reduce that chaos and to respect international humanitarian law. While the circumstances in Central Bosnia in 1993 were chaotic, the Appeals Chamber sees neither merit nor logic in recognising the mere context of war itself as a factor to be considered in the mitigation of the criminal conduct of its participants.[141]

This comment is at best harmless, but it does contain one weakness: it is not 'incumbent' on a 'participant' to reduce chaos where the chaos is caused by forces outside the participant's control. The armed forces in civil wars are generally less coordinated and disciplined than in cross-border wars between regular armies, and, as we have seen earlier, defence teams devote a significant portion of their strategy to undermining alleged command-and-control relationships between the defendant and the perpetrators of crimes. Even the day-to-day operation of detention centres is said to have been essentially 'anarchic'.[142]

In the *Bagilishema* case the defence went one step further, conjuring up, almost, an armed group of thugs and murderers it called the Abakiga. The Abakiga, who hardly rate a mention in any other ICTR case before or since, supposedly 'invaded' Mabanza commune where Bagilishema was mayor, committed crimes against the Tutsi civilians, and then promptly returned to the unspecified place whence they came.[143] The Trial Chamber accepted that the mayor's authority had been weakened by the chaos of war,

---

[140] Compare the *Bagilishema* defence with the following attempts (all unsuccessful) to use good character to displace mens rea: *Erdemović* trial judgment, para. 105 ('According to his own testimony, he grew up in multi-ethnic surroundings in a non-nationalistic environment. Before the war, he had friends from all the groups — Serbs, Croats, Muslims — with whom he maintained cordial relations'); *Prosecutor* v. *Krnojelac*, Final Written Submissions of Milorad Krnojelac, 13 July 2001, para. 112 ('a few days after the outbreak of the war in Foča, where divisions on ethnic grounds had already largely taken place, he did not change his Muslim doctor [but] continued to have his check-ups with him on the basis of full confidence and trust in him'); *Prosecutor* v. *Blaškić*, Final Oral Submissions on Behalf of Tihomir Blaškić, 28–30 July 1999, pp. 25176, 25184, 25197 (Colonel Stewart, of UNPROFOR, went to Ahmići on 22 April 1993, six days after the attack on the village, 'and after a careful inspection, he found eight bodies, two outside of a structure and six more in a cellar of a burned and collapsed house. . . . He sent a letter on that same day to Colonel Blaškić. . . . Blaškić himself toured Ahmići on the 27th of April, and after his inspection, he attended a press conference in Busovaca and made a clear statement denouncing the crime and calling for public support for an investigation. His exact words were recorded in contemporaneous notes. . . . The Prosecutor is confusing motive with intent. Why Blaškić wanted to investigate Ahmići is legally irrelevant. The fact that he did, the fact that he wanted to and the fact that he took steps, reasonable steps, under what were very difficult circumstances to do so means that he lacked the mens rea necessary to commit the crime alleged of failure to punish'); *Kajelijeli* trial judgment, paras 99–115 (four Tutsi witnesses testified that they owed their lives to the accused; it was illogical to say that the accused hated Tutsi, when he had intervened to save them); and *Prosecutor* v. *Simić et al.*, Dr. Blagoje Simić's Public (Redacted and Corrected) Final Trial Brief, 7 July 2003, paras 370–85 ('Bagilishema, like Dr. Simić, had not personally participated in any murders, violence, or other unlawful conduct, and in fact had tried to aid victims of the violence').   [141] *Blaškić* appeal judgment, para. 711.

[142] See, for example, *Prosecutor* v. *Kvočka et al.*, Final Trial Brief Submissions by the Defence of the Accused Mlado Radić, 29 June 2001, p. 84.

[143] *Prosecutor* v. *Bagilishema*, Defence Closing Brief, 1 August 2000, paras 245–9 and (in the separately numbered legal section) 100–30, 160–85.

and absolved him of all killings in the commune.[144] Of the Abakiga it said: 'an impression remains of the Abakiga as roaming opportunistic bands, generally unknown to their victims, with diverse but uncertain origins, lacking in hierarchy or organization, roused rather than led, thriving in the relative anarchy of the times, with essentially two aims: the elimination of Tutsi, and general looting'.[145] The artifice of the Abakiga — a defendant's *deus ex machina* — is not merely an example of defence ingenuity, it is indicative of what is possible in the international criminal process, where judges with no local knowledge of history, culture, language, or topography are given snippets of information, as seen fit by the parties in an adversarial system, from which to construct a 'reality' against which to assess the truthfulness of indictment allegations.[146]

11.8 ALIBI, IMPOSSIBILITY, AND MISTAKEN IDENTITY

The defence of alibi was first raised as a core defence in the *Tadić* case. Tadić's alibi failed, as will be explained below, and the defence failed again when it was raised by Dragoljub Kunarac. It has never again been raised as a main defence at the ICTY.[147] On the other hand, at the ICTR, alibi has been the main defence of no fewer than 14 defendants since 1998 (more than half the number of accused who went to trial),[148] despite the fact that there, too, it has failed each time, except on the last occasion, in the *Rwamakuba* case. The reasons for this almost universal lack of success of the alibi defence are explored below.

Rule 67 of the ICTY RPE provides that:

As early as reasonably practicable and in any event prior to the commencement of the trial: . . . (ii) the defence shall notify the Prosecutor of its intent to offer: (a) the defence of alibi; in which case the notification shall specify the place or places at which the accused claims to have been present at the time of the alleged crime and the names and addresses of witnesses and any other evidence upon which the accused intends to rely to establish the alibi.

Tadić's defence was that he had never been in the Omarska or Keraterm camps. In particular, on 18 June 1992, when three incidents allegedly involving him occurred at Omarska, he was living in Prijedor and working as a traffic policeman. The evidence on this point turned out to be of no help to the accused, since on that day his shift at the police checkpoint did not begin until 9 p.m., whereas the incidents were timed to an earlier part of the day. However, in the opinion of the Trial Chamber, the problems with

---

[144] *Bagilishema* trial judgment, paras 326–8.   [145] Ibid., para. 221.

[146] Note that this defence (substituting 'Interahamwe' for 'Abakiga') had no success in the *Akayesu* case: *Akayesu* trial judgment, paras 30–1.

[147] The defence was invoked as a secondary line of defence, with limited application, by Zoran Žigić and Mitar Vasiljević.

[148] Namely, Clément Kayishema, Obed Ruzindana, Georges Rutaganda, Alfred Musema, Elizaphan Ntakirutimana, Gérard Ntakirutimana, Laurent Semanza, Eliézer Niyitegeka, Juvénal Kajelijeli, Jean de Dieu Kamuhanda, Emmanuel Ndindabahizi, Mikaeli Muhimana, Aloys Simba, and André Rwamakuba.

Tadić's chosen defence ran deeper. For example, in relation to a beating timed to the night of 9 July 1992, the records of the police checkpoint revealed that Tadić was assigned to the checkpoint from 7 p.m. until 7 a.m. the following morning. The Trial Chamber's response was that even if the records were accepted as accurately reflecting the shifts to which the accused was assigned, they only established the hours during which he was *meant* to be on duty at the checkpoint, not that he was actually present there during those hours.[149] The 'entirely general evidence' of Tadić's former fellow traffic policeman regarding the accused's constant presence at the checkpoint during duty hours was of no assistance to the accused, when weighed against the 'specific and precise evidence' detailing Tadić's words and actions, as recounted by witnesses to the beating incidents.[150] The Trial Chamber concluded:

The accused's general denial of ever having been at the Omarska camp is rejected in view of the overwhelming credible testimony to the contrary. His assignment at the Orlovici checkpoint provides no conclusive alibi; rather it merely reflects his assignment there. The Defence evidence as to off-duty hours while living in Banja Luka and Prijedor is wholly unspecific as to dates and times and only establishes that he was generally resident there.[151]

The result in *Tadić* illustrates the difficulty of establishing an alibi defence in a multi-incident case covering a long period of time and a geographic area encompassing the defendant's place of residence. Critically, the *Tadić* alibi was levied not against a circumstantial case but against the identification evidence of several prosecution witnesses. The *Tadić* Trial Chamber accurately diagnosed the causes of this losing defence position, the very position in which many ICTR defendants were soon to place themselves:

A major cause of difficulty for the Defence lies in the [assertion] that the accused, although present within the region, was not involved in any of the activities alleged in the Indictment, but was instead leading his own quite innocent life and living with his family. Such a defence does not readily afford a complete answer to charges in the Indictment, since it cannot be expected, even in the most favourable circumstances, to provide anything like a 24-hour, day-by-day and week-by-week account of the accused's whereabouts.[152]

This remark suggests that alibi is the wrong *kind* of core defence for most cases before the tribunals. For alibi to be sustained as a core defence it would have to be conjoined with a comprehensive attack on witness credibility, amounting to a conspiracy theory, as is often the practice at the ICTR. Short of that, an alibi's only chance of success is in piecemeal usage in instances where the identification evidence is weak, as was the case in *Rwamakuba*.[153]

Kunarac's alibi for several dates in July and August 1992 was that he was engaged in war operations away from the locations where the crimes allegedly involving him were committed.[154] Kunarac complained about the indictment's casual approach to the timing of many of those crimes, making a defence of alibi extremely difficult.[155] He was nevertheless able to produce one or more witnesses for nearly every alibi date to testify

---

[149] *Tadić* trial judgment, para. 277.   [150] Ibid., para. 278.   [151] Ibid., para. 434.
[152] Ibid., para. 533.   [153] *Rwamakuba* trial judgment, paras 70–84, 195–200.
[154] *Prosecutor v. Kunarac et al.*, Final Trial Brief Submissions by the Defence, 10 November 2000, p. 88.
[155] Ibid., p. 89.

that he had been with that witness 'all the time' at locations other than the crime sites.[156] He also argued mistaken identity in relation to all rape victims.[157] The Trial Chamber acknowledged the difficulty for the defence of putting forward an alibi for a month-long period. It then focused in on the gaps in the alibi, finding that at best the evidence provided by most of the alibi witnesses covered short periods: hours, sometimes even a few minutes. Only one witness claimed to know where Kunarac was during the night hours. The court took into account the accused's ability (due to his authority) to move about easily, and his access to transport most of the time.[158] Even within the framework of his alibi, Kunarac never slept at a location more than 20 kilometres from the crime sites. Kunarac was also not helped by the fact that the contours of his alibi did not appear in a statement he gave to the prosecutor when the indictment was served on him.[159] The fact that Kunarac embellished the alibi with several inherently implausible elements indicates that this choice of defence was an act of desperation, a measure of last resort. While better constructed alibis may be found in tribunal cases, an air of resignation and fatality is evident in almost all of them.[160]

II.9 SUPERIOR ORDERS

Despite significant academic discussion on the defence of superior orders,[161] it is almost by definition not a live defence at the tribunals. Persons accused before the tribunals are senior military or civilian leaders, or, if low-ranking, they are accused of very serious crimes. In neither case can they have been unaware of the illegal nature of the orders resulting in the alleged crimes. If they did perform the acts they are accused of pursuant to orders, then they (or any reasonable person in their position) would have realized that the orders were illegal. The ICTY Statute, Article 7(4) provides:

The fact that an accused person acted pursuant to an order of a Government or of a superior shall not relieve him of criminal responsibility, but may be considered in mitigation of punishment if the International Tribunal determines that justice so requires.[162]

---

[156] Ibid., pp. 89–108.   [157] Ibid., pp. 110, 118, 130.

[158] *Kunarac et al.* trial judgment, paras 594–9.   [159] Ibid., paras 600–25.

[160] In one case, Zoran Vuković presented evidence concerning an injury he claimed to have sustained to his testicles some weeks prior to the date of commission of a rape he was charged with. He asserted that the injury caused ongoing pain and 'excluded [the] possibility of erection in the period of at least three weeks'. (*Prosecutor* v. *Kunarac et al.*, Final Trial Brief Submissions by the Defence, 10 November 2000, p. 284.) The Trial Chamber dismissed the argument as insufficiently supported by evidence, meaning that Vuković had failed to demonstrate even a reasonable possibility that that was so. (*Kunarac et al.* trial judgment, paras 800–5.)

[161] See, e.g., Green, *Essays*, pp. 245–82; also: J. L. Bakker, 'The Defence of Obedience to Superior Orders: The Mens Rea Requirement' (1989) 17 *Am. J. Crim. L.* 55; A. D'Amato, 'Superior Orders vs. Command Responsibility' (1986) 80 *Am. J. Int'l L.* 604; G. Dufour, 'La défense d'ordres supérieurs existe-t-elle vraiment?' (2000) 840 *Revue internationale de la Croix-Rouge* 969; P. Gaeta, 'The Defence of Superior Orders: The Statute of the International Criminal Court versus Customary International Law' (1999) 10 *Eur. J. Int'l L.* 172; and M. J. Osiel, 'Obeying Orders: Atrocity, Military Discipline, and the Law of War' (1998) 86 *Calif. L. Rev.* 939.

[162] Taken essentially word for word from the IMT Charter, Article 8: 'The fact that the Defendant acted pursuant to order of his Government or of a superior shall not free him from responsibility, but may be considered in mitigation of punishment if the Tribunal determines that justice so requires.'

The ICC also provides for the defence in Article 33 of its Statute:

The fact that a crime within the jurisdiction of the Court has been committed by a person pursuant to an order of a Government or of a superior, whether military or civilian, shall not relieve that person of criminal responsibility unless: (a) The person was under a legal obligation to obey orders of the Government or the superior in question;[163] (b) The person did not know that the order was unlawful; and (c) The order was not manifestly unlawful. . . . For the purposes of this article, orders to commit genocide or crimes against humanity are manifestly unlawful.

Where the order is coupled with an immediate threat to the defendant, then, even if the order is illegal on its face, the defendant may be able to pursue the defence of duress. This is examined in the next section.

II.IO DURESS AND FORCE OF CIRCUMSTANCES (NECESSITY)

The defence of duress was examined at length by the ICTY Appeals Chamber in *Erdemović*, the Appeals Chamber's first judgment. The majority (Judges McDonald and Vohra, joined by Li in a short Separate Opinion) held that duress does not afford a complete defence in international law to a soldier charged with a crime against humanity or a war crime that involves the killing of an innocent person. Strong Dissenting Opinions were issued by Cassese and Stephen.[164]

At neither tribunal has the defence of duress in fact been pleaded against a charge that involves the direct taking of innocent life. The question of the validity of the defence arose for consideration in *Erdemović* only because certain statements made by the accused in the course of the hearing before the Trial Chamber would have rendered his guilty plea 'equivocal', had the defence been available to him as a matter of law.

It should be emphasized at the outset that it almost certainly follows from *Erdemović*, even though the majority opinion does not say so explicitly, that the defence of duress *is* available in international law to an accused who is charged with a lesser crime than the killing of an innocent person. It was the killing of innocents in Erdemović's case that led to the split decision. But for which lesser crimes is the defence available? As explained further below, the logic of the majority raises the possibility that duress will not excuse a class of acts which, falling short of killing, are nonetheless considered heinous and indefensible as a matter of international legal policy. There is virtually no tribunal case law on these two points, hence the uncertainty.

[163] The ICC's threefold test includes the condition of a legal obligation subsisting in the subordinate to obey the superior's orders. The tribunals have neglected this element of a legal obligation, even though it is essential not only for the operation of the defence of superior orders, but also for the notions of 'ordering' and command responsibility as forms of personal liability. See further Chapter 7.

[164] The rule was cited in *Delalić et al.* trial judgment, para. 1229, citing the *Erdemović* sentencing judgment (no. 2); *Todorović* trial judgment, para. 111; and *Krstić* trial judgment, para. 714 (the latter two both citing the *Erdemović* appeal judgment); and see further below.

Where the defence is available, the accused must satisfy four elements: (1) the act charged was done under an immediate threat of severe harm to life or limb; (2) there was no adequate means of averting such harm; (3) the crime committed must be the lesser of two evils, that is, not disproportionate to the harm threatened; and (4) the situation leading to duress must not have been voluntarily brought about by the person coerced.[165]

Kvočka et al. is the only[166] tribunal case where duress was raised as a defence (and not merely in favour of mitigation). The Trial Chamber very briefly considered Dragoljub Prcac's submission that he was forced to work at the Omarska camp 'under duress', dismissing the plea for lack of evidence.[167] Prcac, a person of 'some' influence at the camp (but certainly not a high-ranking authority),[168] was not found to be directly involved in committing crimes against Omarska detainees. He was convicted, rather, for continuing to work at the camp, aware of its abusive conditions of detention.[169] It seems that under these circumstances, which involve a person of lesser authority not directly committing acts of violence against innocents, the defence of duress was straightforwardly available to the accused, even though he was charged with war crimes and crimes against humanity. The Trial Chamber had, at this point in its judgment, no in-principle objection.[170]

However, in another section of the same judgment, an inconsistent statement by the Trial Chamber is found:

Even if a knowing participant in a criminal enterprise was unwilling to resign because it would prejudice his career, or he feared he would be sent to the front lines, imprisoned, or punished, the Trial Chamber emphasizes that this is not an excuse or a defense to liability for participating in war crimes or crimes against humanity. It is well established in the jurisprudence of this Tribunal that duress is not a defense to committing war crimes or crimes against humanity.[171]

The first part of this observation is directed against the defendant Miroslav Kvočka, who, as the Trial Chamber noted, did not claim duress (not even in mitigation). Kvočka's position at Omarska was 'duty officer' and direct subordinate of the camp commander.[172] He had more authority than Prcac, but like Prcac he did not commit (in person) any crimes against detainees at the camp.[173] It would seem that the Trial Chamber was inconsistent in allowing the defence in principle for one accused, but ruling it out for the other (albeit in a dictum). In any case, the Trial Chamber in the

---

[165] These elements are variously formulated; see *Erdemović* trial judgment (no. 1), para. 17; and *Erdemović* appeal judgment, paras 42 and 68 of the McDonald/Vohra opinion; para. 5 of Li's opinion; paras 16, 41, and 50 of Cassese's opinion; and paras 14 and 67 of Stephen's opinion.

[166] In *Prosecutor* v. *Delalić et al.*, Esad Landžo's Final Submission and Motion for Acquittal, 28 August 1998, pp. 69–78, Landžo's submissions on duress were so weak and incoherent that the Trial Chamber did not even acknowledge them. [167] *Kvočka et al.* trial judgment, para. 427.

[168] Ibid., para. 438. [169] Ibid., paras 456–7.

[170] Cf. the affirmation of the defence of duress in the *Blaškić* trial judgment, para. 769, which however is not referenced to any authority: 'Duress, where established, does mitigate the criminal responsibility of the accused when he had no choice or moral freedom in committing the crime. This must consequently entail the passing of a lighter sentence if he cannot be completely exonerated of responsibility.'

[171] Citing the *Erdemović* appeal judgment. The quoted text is from para. 403 of the *Kvočka et al.* trial judgment.

[172] *Kvočka et al.* trial judgment, para. 361. [173] Ibid., para. 397.

quoted excerpt misstated the ICTY's jurisprudence concerning duress, broadening the rule well beyond the *Erdemović* majority's narrow ruling (killing of innocents), to which the excerpt professes to be referenced.

The Statutes and Rules of the ad hoc tribunals say nothing about the defence of duress. On the other hand the ICC Statute allows the defence without explicitly fore-closing it to any class of acts, even to the killing of innocents. The standard elements are present, except that proportionality is subjectified:

A person shall not be criminally responsible if, at the time of that person's conduct: . . . (d) The conduct which is alleged to constitute a crime within the jurisdiction of the Court has been caused by duress resulting from a threat of imminent death or of continuing or imminent serious bodily harm against that person or another person, and the person acts necessarily and reasonably to avoid this threat, provided that the person does not intend to cause a greater harm than the one sought to be avoided. Such a threat may either be: (i) Made by other persons; or (ii) Constituted by other circumstances beyond that person's control.[174]

The last clause alludes to the defence of necessity, or duress of circumstances, to which we shall return below.

The inclusion of this provision in the ICC Statute vindicates the minority opinions in *Erdemović*. However, even without this additional argument, *Erdemović* at a three–two split is so finely balanced that a Trial Chamber could well loyally follow the majority by making the defence unavailable in a case of killing of innocents, yet register objections which would force a reconsideration, or at least clarification, of the received position by the Appeals Chamber. It should also be noted that the majority's ruling was limited in its final formulation to *soldiers* (raising the prospect of a distinction where the defend-ant is a civilian).[175]

Two central arguments of the *Erdemović* majority[176] are perhaps the weakest links in its reasoning. In the first place, the majority acknowledged that the penal codes of civil-law systems with few exceptions recognize duress as a complete defence to all crimes. In some other jurisdictions (including common-law systems with the exception of United States jurisdictions which have adopted section 2.09 of the American Legal Institute's Model Penal Code),[177] murder and, less consistently, other serious offences have been specifically excepted from the operation of the defence of duress. For example, Canada, with an unusually long list of exceptions in addition to murder, does not recognize the defence in cases of attempted murder, treason, sexual assault, forcible abduction, hostage taking, robbery, and aggravated assault, to name the main categories.[178]

The *Erdemović* majority reasoned that the differing positions of the legal systems of the world mean that there is no consistent rule which answers the question whether duress is a defence to the killing of an innocent person.[179] Because the majority could

---

[174] Article 31 of the ICC Statute.

[175] *Erdemović* appeal judgment, para. 19 (and the McDonald/Vohra opinion para. 32 and especially para. 84).

[176] Hereafter meaning the McDonald/Vohra opinion.

[177] See *R. v. Howe* [1987] AC 417; *R. v. Gotts* [1992] 2 AC 412; and *United States v. Rockwood*, US Court of Appeals for the Armed Forces, 30 September 1999.

[178] Criminal Code of Canada, s. 17. See also *Perka v. R.* (1984) 13 DLR (4th) 1.

[179] *Erdemović* appeal judgment, para. 72 (McDonald/Vohra opinion).

not see how to reconcile the positions, it felt it was appropriate to decide the matter on policy grounds (see below). However, as Judge Cassese observed, it was also open to the majority to conclude that since no consistent exception can be found to the general rule that an act committed under duress is not a criminal offence, the general rule should have been allowed to prevail.[180]

Secondly, on the question of policy, the *Erdemović* majority considered that if national law denies duress as a defence even in a case in which a single innocent life is taken due to action under duress, international law cannot admit duress in cases which involve the killing of innocents on a large scale (Erdemović executed dozens of persons). Citing 'countless examples' of threats brought to bear upon combatants by their superiors when the superiors are confronted with any show of reluctance on the part of the combatants to carry out orders to perform acts in clear breach of international humanitarian law, the majority wrote: 'Thus, our rejection of duress as a defence to the killing of innocent human beings does not depend upon what the reasonable person is expected to do. We would assert *an absolute moral postulate* which is clear and unmistakable for the implementation of international humanitarian law.'[181]

The majority's willingness to assert an absolute rule contrasts with its praise for the flexibility of the other arm of its solution, namely that in cases of loss of innocent life, the circumstances which compelled the convicted person to commit the act would mitigate his or her punishment. That this combination of absolutist inflexibility and pragmatist flexibility might lead to an unjust result is suggested by an example supplied by Cassese: The defendant, a concentration-camp inmate, is starved and beaten for months. She is told after a savage beating that if she does not kill another inmate, who has already been beaten with metal bars and will certainly be beaten to death before long, her eyes will be gouged out there and then. She proceeds to kill the other inmate. Cassese's comment, self-evidently accurate, puts in question the majority's moral absolute: 'it would require an extraordinary — and perhaps impossible — act of courage to accept [having] one's eyes being plucked out'.[182] The defendant here had been reduced to an instrument by means of which another person committed murder.

The above case is of course one in which the accused takes the life of a person who is about to be killed anyway. Erdemović, a Croat in a Bosnian-Serb unit, executed his victims knowing that they would in any case be killed by his fellow soldiers and that if he resisted, he too would be lined up, with the civilians, and shot. The minority was of the view that while cases of killing to save one's life, where it is not a foregone conclusion that the victim will be killed, should anyway fail the proportionality test (see the third element of the defence of duress, above), *Erdemović*-type cases raise the possibility that it is unjust and illogical for the law absolutely to expect an accused to sacrifice his or her life where the victim's fate is sealed. The result of the act is abhorrent, but the act itself

---

[180] Ibid., para. 11 (Cassese opinion).   [181] Ibid., para. 83 (McDonald/Vohra opinion), emphasis added.

[182] Ibid., para. 47 (Cassese opinion). Cf. *I. G. Farben trial*: 'an order emanating from a superior . . . is a complete defence where it is given under such circumstances as to afford the one receiving it of no other moral choice than to comply therewith' (*Trial of Carl Krauch et al.*, 10 LRTWC 1, 54). See also K. J. M. Smith, 'Duress and Steadfastness: In Pursuit of the Unintelligible' (1999) *Crim. L. Rev.* 363.

is forced and is not accompanied by mens rea. Therefore, a judge is entitled to consider the circumstances as part of a defence. The *Erdemović* majority's response to this argument is weak,[183] and this weakness subsists in the jurisprudence after all these years.

In conclusion, it cannot be emphatically stated that the availability of duress as a defence before the ad hoc tribunals is limited by preconditions (such as non-killing of innocents) additional to the four standard elements of the defence, listed above.

II.II MILITARY NECESSITY

That military necessity was originally a limit on state action, and should still function as a limit, seems to have been forgotten. The modern denigration of military necessity goes back at least to the Nuremberg trials after World War II, where some defendants argued that military necessity justified their atrocities against civilian populations ... military necessity is widely regarded today as an insidious doctrine invoked to justify almost any outrage.[184]

Military necessity and related defensive arguments of military advantage are controversial because of their potential to subvert the legal regulation of armed conflict.

The laws governing armed conflict were developed with military practicalities at the forefront, by balancing the requirements of humanity with military necessity. Some positive prohibitions are expressly qualified by a military necessity exception; others contain no such exception. Compare the following provisions, taken from the fourth Geneva Convention (GC) of 1949 and from the ICC Statute:

Detention

GC Art. 42: The internment or placing in assigned residence of protected persons may be ordered only if the security of the Detaining Power makes it absolutely necessary ...

GC Art. 49: ... The Occupying Power shall not detain protected persons in an area particularly exposed to the dangers of war unless the security of the population or imperative military reasons so demand ...

GC Art. 78: If the Occupying Power considers it necessary, for imperative reasons of security, to take safety measures concerning protected persons, it may, at the most, subject them to assigned residence or to internment ...

ICC: no equivalent exceptions.

Displacement

GC Art. 49: ... Nevertheless, the Occupying Power may undertake total or partial evacuation of a given area if the security of the population or imperative military reasons so demand. Such evacuations may not involve the displacement of protected persons outside the bounds of the

---

[183] See *Erdemović* appeal judgment, paras 79–81 (McDonald/Vohra opinion).

[184] B. M. Carnahan, 'Lincoln, Lieber and the Laws of War: the Origins and Limits of the Principle of Military Necessity' (1998) 92 *Am. J. Int'l L.* 213, 230.

occupied territory except when for material reasons it is impossible to avoid such displacement. Persons thus evacuated shall be transferred back to their homes as soon as hostilities in the area in question have ceased . . .

ICC Art. 8(2)(e): Other serious violations of the laws and customs applicable in armed conflicts not of an international character, within the established framework of international law, namely, any of the following acts: . . . (viii) Ordering the displacement of the civilian population for reasons related to the conflict, unless the security of the civilians involved or imperative military reasons so demand; . . .

Property damage

GC Art. 53: Any destruction by the Occupying Power of real or personal property belonging individually or collectively to private persons, or to the State, or to other public authorities, or to social or cooperative organizations, is prohibited, except where such destruction is rendered absolutely necessary by military operations.

GC Art. 147: Grave breaches to which the preceding Article relates shall be those involving any of the following acts, if committed against persons or property protected by the present Convention: . . . extensive destruction and appropriation of property, not justified by military necessity and carried out unlawfully and wantonly.

ICC Art. 8(2)(a): Grave breaches of the Geneva Conventions of 12 August 1949, namely, any of the following acts against persons or property protected under the provisions of the relevant Geneva Convention: . . . (iv) Extensive destruction and appropriation of property, not justified by military necessity and carried out unlawfully and wantonly; . . .

ICC Art. 8(2)(b): Other serious violations of the laws and customs applicable in international armed conflict, within the established framework of international law, namely, any of the following acts: . . . (xiii) Destroying or seizing the enemy's property unless such destruction or seizure be imperatively demanded by the necessities of war; . . .

ICC Art. 8(2)(e): Other serious violations of the laws and customs applicable in armed conflicts not of an international character, within the established framework of international law, namely, any of the following acts: . . . (xii) Destroying or seizing the property of an adversary unless such destruction or seizure be imperatively demanded by the necessities of the conflict.

Thus it may be seen that military necessity is available as a defence only in relation to certain acts of detention, displacement, or destruction of property.

In the *Hostages* case, a US military tribunal acquitted the accused Lothar Rendulic of charges of destruction of property on the following reasoning:

We are not called upon to determine whether urgent military necessity for the devastation and destruction in the province of Finnmark actually existed. We are concerned with the question whether the defendant at the time of its occurrence acted within the limits of honest judgment on the basis of the conditions prevailing at the time. The course of a military operation by the enemy is loaded with uncertainties, such as the numerical strength of the enemy, the quality of his equipment, his fighting spirit, the efficiency and daring of his commanders, and the uncertainty of his intentions. These things when considered with his own military situation provided the facts or want thereof which furnished the basis for the defendant's decision to carry out the 'scorched earth' policy in Finnmark as a precautionary measure against an attack by superior forces. It is our considered opinion that the conditions as they appeared to the defendant at the time were sufficient, upon which he could honestly conclude that urgent military necessity warranted the decision made. This being true, the defendant may have erred in the exercise of his judgment but he was guilty of no criminal act.[185]

This is a subjective approach, which attempts to assess the situation in light of military realities by recognizing that armed conflict requires split-second decision-making often without the benefit of all the relevant information.

In the *Peleus* case, a British military court rejected a plea of military necessity by the accused, Heinz Eck, who was a commander of a German U-boat submarine that sank a Greek merchant ship. The U-boat then opened fire and launched grenades at the lifeboats and survivors. The defence argued that this was operational necessity, since the debris from the sunken ship would mark the spot of the incident, alerting aircraft to the location of the U-boat. The tribunal accepted that there was a military need to conceal the location of the U-boat. However, it found that the action taken was not objectively necessary since the accused could have best protected his boat and crew by removing himself from the area at high speed. Thus the operational necessity could have been complied with more efficiently without cruelty.[186]

Military necessity requires more than mere military advantage, but falls short of requiring absolute necessity. It requires that rational and reasonable military reasons are articulated to demonstrate why the impugned act or course of conduct was required to achieve a particular military goal. Some references to military necessity in the various conventions are further qualified by adjectives such as 'imperative' or 'urgent' military necessity.

The principle of proportionality and the prohibition of unnecessary suffering both contain a balance between the military necessity to be gained and the harm to be done. Where the military advantage is high, courts may tolerate a level of incidental (collateral) civilian casualties and suffering.

The modern international criminal tribunals have not considered the defence of military necessity in any detail. In *Krstić* the Trial Chamber briefly considered the question of military necessity in relation to transfers of the civilian population. The court observed that Article 49 of the fourth Geneva Convention (quoted above) and Article 17 of Additional Protocol II allow total or partial evacuation of civilians if 'imperative military reasons so demand'. Finding that there was no military threat after the taking of Srebrenica, the court rejected the accused's arguments of military necessity. It concluded that the transfer of civilians was part of a 'well organised policy whose purpose was to expel the Bosnian Muslim population from the enclave. The evacuation was itself the goal and neither the protection of the civilians nor imperative military necessity justified the action.'[187]

The defendants in the *Kordić and Čerkez* case were both charged with the crime of extensive destruction of property not justified by military necessity, under Article 2 (d) of the ICTY Statute, and with wanton destruction not justified by military necessity, under Article 3(b). Since the absence of military necessity is formulated as an element of the crime, the burden of proving that the destruction was not justified by military necessity

---

[185] 8 LRTWC 34, 69.   [186] 1 LRTWC 1, 15–16.   [187] *Krstić* trial judgment, para. 527.

was on the prosecutor, who called witnesses to testify that the military objectives were secured by excessive force beyond military necessity. The court found that there was a pattern of destruction not justified by military necessity and convicted both accused for the Article 3 offences.[188]

In *Blaškić* the Trial Chamber stated that 'targeting civilians or civilian property is an offence when not justified by military necessity'.[189] This was an error, since at least since the time of the *Hostages* case it has been recognized that the targeting of civilians, as such, is without exception unlawful.[190]

II.12 SELF-DEFENCE, PROVOCATION, REPRISALS, AND THE DEFENCE OF RECIPROCITY OR *TU QUOQUE*

The defences under this heading overlap. They explore the limits of permissible action in response to an illegal act, normally by a member of the enemy forces.

Dario Kordić and Mario Čerkez were the first ad hoc tribunal defendants to raise the defence of self-defence. 'The Bosnian Croat community in the Lasva Valley', said Čerkez, far from being the aggressor, 'was surrounded, outnumbered, and very nearly wiped out by the larger Bosnian Muslim community'.[191] The conflict, in his view, was about 'the survival of the Croats'.[192] The Trial Chamber replied that self-defence is a defence open to a person who acts to defend another person (including the actor himself or herself) or property from attack, provided that the acts constitute a 'reasonable, necessary, and proportionate' reaction to the attack.[193] Having offered this exploratory and — in the context of armed conflict — entirely inadequate formulation, the *Kordić and Čerkez* court, noting that the ICTY Statute is silent on this form of defence, then fell back on Article 31 of the ICC Statute, which states:[194]

A person shall not be criminally responsible if, at the time of that person's conduct: . . . (c) The person acts reasonably to defend himself or herself or another person or, in the case of war crimes, property which is essential for the survival of the person or another person or property which is essential for accomplishing a military mission, against an imminent and unlawful use of force in a manner proportionate to the degree of danger to the person or the other person or property protected. The fact that the person was involved in a defensive operation conducted by forces shall not in itself constitute a ground for excluding criminal responsibility under this subparagraph.

This definition maintains the criteria of 'reasonable' and 'proportionate' (but not the *Kordić and Čerkez* Trial Chamber's criterion of 'necessity', which is superfluous) while making explicit the requirement that the attack causing the defensive reaction is both

---

[188] *Kordić and Čerkez* trial judgment, para. 808.   [189] *Blaškić* trial judgment, para. 180.
[190] 8 LRTWC 34, 66. See also Chapter 4.
[191] *Prosecutor* v. *Čerkez and Kordić*, Defendant Mario Čerkez's Final Trial Brief, 13 December 2000, p. 20.
[192] Ibid., p. 95.   [193] *Kordić and Čerkez* trial judgment, para. 449.   [194] Ibid., para. 450.

imminent and, most importantly, unlawful. It is the very unlawfulness of the attack which excuses a response which would otherwise be unlawful. Thus a non-combatant cannot legally harm an enemy combatant, except in self-defence against the use of (or threat of) force that is prohibited by the laws or customs of war. This, perhaps, is the only straightforward application of the defence of self-defence. Other examples lead us into provocation, or the legal quagmire of reprisals, which are dealt with separately below.

The last sentence in the ICC's provision is merely didactic, not part of the definition of the defence of self-defence. It is meant as a reminder of the difference between the relevant dire situation of defending oneself against an unlawful attack and the irrelevant dire situation of being on the losing side of a regular fight. The latter situation does not excuse, for example, use of prohibited weapons or methods of warfare. (While it is tempting to say that imminent loss on the battlefield does not, in any circumstances, excuse unlawful action, several states have made reservations — or can be expected to espouse views — which entail the contrary. The commander-in-chief whose country is about to be overrun by enemy forces might order the use of nuclear weapons, obviating one disaster by creating another.)[195]

The Trial Chamber in *Kordić and Čerkez* was of the view that the dire situations alluded to by the defendants were of the irrelevant kind:

> The defence case that these events amounted to a civil war in which the Bosnian Croats were on the defensive, and themselves subject to persecution, is rejected. For these purposes . . . the fact that individual atrocities were committed against Bosnian Croats is irrelevant although they may be the subject of other criminal proceedings.[196]

The appeal on this point was summarily rejected.[197]

Just as the laws of physics as we experience them hold good until we arrive in the neighbourhood of a black hole, so the laws of warfare govern the conduct of armed forces until the field of battle is warped to such a degree that the ordinary laws cease to be mutually advantageous and lose their moral force; this marks a return to lawlessness, until a victor emerges by brute force and the laws of ordinary circumstances are restored. The closing stages of the Second World War, both in Europe and Japan, might

---

[195] See, for example, France's second reservation to Additional Protocol I of 1977:

> Se référant au projet de protocole rédigé par le Comité International de la Croix Rouge qui a constitué la base des travaux de la conférence diplomatique de 1974–1977, le gouvernement de la République Française continue de considérer que les dispositions du protocole concernent exclusivement les armes classiques, et qu'elles ne sauraient ni réglementer ni interdire le recours a l'arme nucléaire, ni porter préjudice aux autres règles du droit international applicables a d'autres activités, nécessaires a l'exercice par la France de son droit naturel de légitime défense (www.icrc.org/ihl.nsf).

[196] *Kordić and Čerkez* trial judgment, para. 827; cf. para. 642 ('The Trial Chamber finds that the overwhelming evidence points to a well-organised and planned HVO attack upon Ahmići with the aim of killing or driving out the Muslim population, resulting in a massacre. The assertion that this attack was justified strategically, defensively, or in any other way, is wholly without foundation').

[197] *Kordić and Čerkez* appeal judgment, paras 812, 838. On self-defence, see also *Prosecutor* v. *Slobodan Milošević*, Amici Curiae Submissions on the Law of Self-Defence as Stipulated in Parts (B) and (C) of the Order of the Chamber to the Amicus of 11 December 2002, 14 July 2003.

stand as an example of this, if indeed there was a stretch of that war fought in compliance with the then laws or customs of war.

The black-hole equivalent in the field of international criminal law makes its presence felt when a party to a conflict conducts itself — or is construed by the other side as conducting itself — unlawfully. Such provocation may draw an unlawful response from the aggrieved party which does not violate the laws of war, as such, but which is the first step to ever greater lawlessness. The UK made the following reservation to Additional Protocol I:

The obligations of Articles 51 and 55 are accepted on the basis that any adverse party against which the United Kingdom might be engaged will itself scrupulously observe those obligations. If an adverse party makes serious and deliberate attacks, in violation of Article 51 or Article 52 against the civilian population or civilians or against civilian objects, or, in violation of Articles 53, 54 and 55, on objects or items protected by those Articles, the United Kingdom will regard itself as entitled to take measures otherwise prohibited by the Articles in question to the extent that it considers such measures necessary for the sole purpose of compelling the adverse party to cease committing violations under those Articles, but only after formal warning to the adverse party requiring cessation of the violations has been disregarded and then only after a decision taken at the highest level of government. Any measures thus taken by the United Kingdom will not be disproportionate to the violations giving rise thereto and will not involve any action prohibited by the Geneva Conventions of 1949 nor will such measures be continued after the violations have ceased.[198]

In the defence of Radislav Krstić, who at the relevant time was chief-of-staff of the Drina Corps, his counsel, having reviewed numerous violations of UN Security Council resolutions by the Bosnian-Muslim side in early 1995, asked rhetorically:

What was the Drina Corps command supposed to do? To watch the Muslims arming themselves, carrying out various sabotage and terrorist actions, killing civilians and fighters? Should the Drina Corps command believe that they would still respect both the UN and the safe zone regime? Do the actions, mentioned in the documents above, not provide legitimacy enough for the Drina Corps command to engage in combat activities intended to prevent the above-mentioned illegal actions on the part of the Muslim armed forces? And even more so given that either oral or written protests addressed to UN representatives in Srebrenica and Sarajevo did not bring any results.[199]

The Serb hand was forced, 'provoked by diverse forms of violations of the safe zone'. The 'climax', according to the defence, came on 26 June 1995, when nine Muslim 'sabotage-terrorist' groups penetrated Serb-held territory, killed soldiers and civilians, and set a Serb village on fire.[200] Krstić's forces reacted with a 'legitimate' operation of 'limited scope and proportions' — consistent, as the defence wished to emphasize, with Article 60 of Additional Protocol I to the Geneva Conventions — an operation whose purpose was not, at that moment, to take over Srebrenica, but merely to sever supply lines to Muslim forces operating inside the protected zone.[201]

---

[198] See www.icrc.org/ihl.nsf.
[199] *Prosecutor* v. *Krstić*, Final Submissions of the Accused, 21 June 2001, pp. 53–4.
[200] Ibid., pp. 58, 63–4.   [201] Ibid., pp. 61–3.

This is certainly a plausible line of defence, although strictly in terms of the Additional Protocol it excuses no more than the Serbs' decision to treat the zone's protected status as having fallen into abeyance.[202]

Krstić felt, however, that the provocation engendered by the illicit actions of the enemy forces — hostile preparations, strikes against civilian targets, etc. — excused a prima facie illicit Serb reaction going well beyond non-recognition of a UN safe zone. In Chapter 4 we examine the thorny issue of proportionality in attacks. The fact that this area of the law is unsettled and, moreover, not easily amenable to definition, leaves room for mounting a defence which effectively relies on provocation to excuse *reprisals* dressed in the garb of 'proportional' retaliation with 'collateral damage', as in the following example:

> According to some information (UN observers), there were [Serb] artillery actions [in Srebrenica] which exceeded the level of operative requirements for an efficient realization of military aims ... [However,] if the information on the number of artillery, tank and mortar shells was correct, those actions were aimed at primarily military targets, and the damage of the civilian facilities which ensued was exclusively collateral or a consequence of the transfer of military targets and facilities of the Muslim army to the civilian facilities (post office, town hall, hotels, restaurants, etc.).[203]

According to this conception of events, one unlawful decision provoked another, and so began, tit for tat, the steady approach towards the black hole of international humanitarian law, with members of the Muslim army taking cover in civilian facilities (thus rendering civilian objects indistinguishable from enemy targets), and, when the Drina Corps finally entered Srebrenica, removing their uniforms and mixing in with the civilian population.[204]

How effective this strategy is as a defence is another question. It is true that in combat situations for which no rules have been developed, where it is generally not possible to tell the lawful from the unlawful, the defence could be expected in principle to have the upper hand. At the same time, the judges are likely to avoid an assessment of the overall situation, focusing instead on isolated incidents (the mass execution of male captives in *Krstić*, the killing by sniper fire of a woman collecting water from a stream in the *Galić* case), where an assessment using the ordinary rules is still feasible.

Self-defence overlaps with the defences of *tu quoque* and reprisals, as the following defence submissions illustrate:

(1) The illegal actions of the Muslim armed forces in the area of Srebrenica 'provided full rights and legitimacy to the Drina Corps command to take necessary combat activities aimed at protecting their people and the army being threatened'.[205]

---

[202] Article 60 of Additional Protocol I provides, in subparagraph 7, that 'If one of the Parties to the conflict commits a material breach of the provisions of [the article], the other Party shall be released from its obligations under the agreement conferring upon the zone the status of demilitarized zone. In such an eventuality, the zone loses its status but shall continue to enjoy the protection provided by the other provisions of this Protocol and the other rules of international law applicable in armed conflict.'

[203] *Prosecutor* v. *Krstić*, Final Submissions of the Accused, 21 June 2001, pp. 64–5. See also *Prosecutor* v. *Slobodan Milošević*, Amici Curiae Brief on Issues of Cross-Examination by the Accused in Person Including the 'Tu Quoque' Principle, 5 March 2002; and S. Yee, 'The Tu Quoque Argument as a Defence to International Crimes, Prosecution or Punishment' (2004) 3 *Chinese J. Int'l L.* 87.

[204] *Prosecutor* v. *Krstić*, Final Submissions of the Accused, 21 June 2001, p. 83.   [205] Ibid., p. 55.

(2) According to the *Kunarac* defence, the hostilities in Foča were initiated by the Muslims. Conditions of life in the 'collection' (detention) centres were no worse than the conditions in the centres run by the Muslim side, where Serb displaced persons were held.[206]

(3) 'The Prosecutor claims that persecution of the Muslims started in spring 1992...[but] there were not the Muslims who were unprotected and unarmed, exposed to self-will, provocation, maltreatment and attack of the Croats, but both sides took roughly equal part in incidents.'[207]

II.I3 DIMINISHED MENTAL RESPONSIBILITY

Rule 67 of the ICTY RPE (on reciprocal disclosure) provides that:

As early as reasonably practicable and in any event prior to the commencement of the trial:...(ii) the defence shall notify the Prosecutor of its intent to offer:...(b) any special defence, including that of diminished or lack of mental responsibility; in which case the notification shall specify the names and addresses of witnesses and any other evidence upon which the accused intends to rely to establish the special defence.

Esad Landžo, the Čelebići prison-camp guard, was the first to argue the defence of diminished mental responsibility. He was at pains to distinguish it from that of insanity. (On the latter plea, see below.) Diminished mental responsibility is a defence that has enjoyed little or no traction at the tribunals despite repeated defence efforts. The problem with the defence stems from the assumption of some defence lawyers that the moral and psychological landscape of armed conflict can be presumed to be alien to the average person, including the tribunal judge, thus opening the door to a new discourse on the human psyche and on moral responsibility. In this discourse chains of causality which are normally considered fictional are rendered real.

Alas, this new discourse tends to dissolve into a patchwork of non sequiturs:

[Landžo] was sickly, asocial and dependent. Overlap this basic personality disorder with Post Traumatic Stress Disorder and what is created is a state of mind that results in diminished mental capacity. The triggering trauma was Esad Landžo being forced to view and participate in brutal murders and tortures as a part of military training in...1991. Anyone, much less an eighteen year old boy, who is forced to watch a demonstration of how to successfully slit a human being's throat actuated on a live civilian woman would have suffered a severe trauma. The mental health experts demonstrated how Esad Landžo was unable to exercise his own free will in the Čelebići Barracks in 1992.[208]

---

[206] *Prosecutor* v. *Kunarac et al.*, Final Trial Brief Submissions by the Defence, 10 November 2000, pp. 17 ff., 267.
[207] *Prosecutor* v. *Čerkez and Kordić*, Defendant Mario Čerkez's Final Trial Brief, 13 December 2000, p. 18.
[208] *Prosecutor* v. *Delalić et al.*, Esad Landžo's Final Submission and Motion for Acquittal, 28 August 1998, p. 10. A supposed 'distinction between wartime and peacetime morality' is developed ibid., pp. 76–7.

Milorad Krnojelac, the prison-camp warden, used the argument from diminished mental responsibility in an attempt to defeat the element of intent needed by the prosecutor to trap him in the web of a joint criminal enterprise. Because such intent can be derived from knowledge of the purposes of the enterprise (for example, torture of detainees), Krnojelac denied having knowledge of crimes systematically perpetrated in the camp:

The expert witnesses for psychology and psychiatry [found that] Krnojelac is presented as a personality with anxiety, which under newly created circumstances previously unknown to him [reacts] by showing a reduced ability for global assessment of the situation at hand, by slowing down his motoric capabilities, by weakening of the already reduced intellectual efficiency... Under such circumstances, the accused was unsure of himself, insecure and anxious for proper execution of his tasks. For these reasons he was completely focused on hyperactivity in his work and in such a situation remained unable to assess the circumstances.[209]

We are back in the realm of pop psychology. It is not only the absence of a credible scientific basis that weakens these lines of defence, it is the ambiguity verging on meaninglessness of such phrases as 'unable to exercise his own free will'. If Landžo had no 'free will' and Krnojelac was unable to 'assess the circumstances', then why should any of their contemporaries have been any different? And if few others were any different, does it follow that personal responsibility must be qualified — or as Landžo would have it, nullified — in contexts in which it would seem most advisable, from a judicial perspective, to maintain full personal responsibility for criminal acts? Radomir Kovač said in his defence that 'Psychological tension was certainly raised in those persons who had taken part in the armed combat and had certainly brought about a weakening of the control mechanisms in social behaviour'.[210] Yet, unless the defence of diminished mental responsibility is used to protect the special class of persons mentioned further below, or is transformed into a defence of duress, the defence is doomed because it negates responsibility to an extent which no judge is prepared to accept.[211]

There is at least in theory a viable way to make a limited defence of diminished mental responsibility. The Trial Chamber in *Delalić et al.* adopted the position as it was in the UK. It held that the defendant has to show on the balance of probabilities an 'abnormality of mind' arising from a condition of arrested or retarded mental development, or from causes induced by disease or injury. This mental disability must have substantially impaired the defendant's responsibility for the acts in question.[212] Although the Trial Chamber did not elaborate, what this must mean is that the defendant's ability to

---

[209] *Prosecutor* v. *Krnojelac*, Final Written Submissions of Milorad Krnojelac, 13 July 2001, para. 115.
[210] *Prosecutor* v. *Kunarac et al.*, Final Trial Brief Submissions by the Defence, 10 November 2000, p. 261.
[211] Cf. *Jelisić* appeal judgment, para. 70:

It is sufficient for our purposes here to point out that there is no per se inconsistency between a diagnosis of the kind of immature, narcissistic, disturbed personality on which the Trial Chamber relied and the ability to form an intent to destroy a particular protected group. Indeed, as the prosecution points out, it is the borderline unbalanced personality who is more likely to be drawn to extreme racial and ethnical hatred than the more balanced modulated individual without personality defects. The Rules visualise, as a defence, a certain degree of mental incapacity and in any event, no such imbalance was found in this case.

[212] *Delalić et al.* trial judgment, paras 1166, 1172.

act rationally must have been irregular or easily overpowered, and that this cognitive weakness is attributable to physical causes, for example, brain damage or very low IQ, and not — as almost every defendant would have preferred — to contextual elements of the armed conflict.

The defence, thus understood, cannot be strong enough to excuse the defendant — as it is only 'diminished' rational capacity which is pleaded, not the defence of insanity — but it may result in a lesser sentence.[213] By making the defence's success dependent upon medical evidence of a condition with a physical component, the *Delalić* Trial Chamber closed the door on psychological speculation of the kind cited earlier.

Landžo did produce assessments of his health. They portrayed him as lacking in self-esteem, feeling 'empty' and dependent, having disorders of 'adjustment', 'anxiety', and 'personality', 'changing colour like a chameleon', and being narcissistic, impulsive, and anti-social. These assessments were based on interviews with Landžo starting in 1996. His 'condition' was purportedly caused by 'brainwashing' by Croatia's military and by the impact of the atrocities he had witnessed.[214] The court had little difficulty concluding that, even allowing for a personality disorder, Landžo was quite capable of controlling his actions in 1992.[215] He was found guilty of grave breaches of the Geneva Conventions and violations of the laws or customs of war by reason of his murder of three detainees at the Čelebići camp and his sadistic treatment and torture of others. He was sentenced to 15 years' imprisonment, without mitigation for his mental state at the time.

Several psychiatric assessments were produced on behalf of another defendant, Mitar Vasiljević. His defence cited a family history of mental illness, stress, and alcoholism, combining at the relevant place and time — Višegrad, Bosnia-Herzegovina, 1992 — to distort the defendant's mind, so that 'his accountability was substantially reduced'.[216] In making this argument Vasiljević sought to dismiss available psychiatric evidence that he was insane, preferring (for reasons that are not clear) the label of diminished mental responsibility, even though he recognized that this would 'not exclude the criminal responsibility of the accused, if he would be found guilty under any counts', but would be important instead for sentencing.[217]

The *Vasiljević* court in its judgment considered these matters under the heading of mitigation of punishment, while describing diminished mental responsibility as a 'partial defence'.[218] The court gave a new definition — different from the *Čelebići* definition — of the burden of proof that this defence presupposes: 'an accused suffers from a diminished mental responsibility where there is an impairment to his capacity to appreciate the unlawfulness of or the nature of his conduct or to control his conduct so

---

[213] The ICTY Appeals Chamber objected to the form, although not to the substance, of the Trial Chamber's decision. It accepted 'that the relevant general principle of law upon which, in effect, both the common law and the civil law systems have acted is that the defendant's diminished mental responsibility is relevant to the sentence to be imposed and is not a defence leading to an acquittal in the true sense' (*Delalić et al.* appeal judgment, para. 590). This is another example of the Appeals Chamber's occasional theoretical project of distinguishing proper defences from other arguments supposedly improperly categorized as defences.

[214] *Prosecutor* v. *Delalić et al.*, Esad Landžo's Final Submission and Motion for Acquittal, 28 August 1998, pp. 34–51, 70–1.   [215] *Delalić et al.* trial judgment, para. 1186. Cf. *Delalić et al.* appeal judgment, para. 593.

[216] *Prosecutor* v. *Vasiljević*, Defence Final Trial Brief, 28 February 2002, pp. 78–81.   [217] Ibid., p. 81.

[218] *Vasiljević* trial judgment, para. 282 and fn. 677.

as to conform to the requirements of the law'.[219] This pronouncement was based on a short survey, in a footnote, of a handful of penal codes, ending in the disclaimer that 'The specific extent of the impairment required before mitigation becomes available in some countries in both systems (for example, "substantial") has been ignored for the sake of identifying the relevant general principles, as has the requirement in some common law countries that the impairment result from an abnormality of mind'.[220] The result of this dubious quest for generality is a definition so watered down that the defence of diminished responsibility is thrown open to anyone who can show 'impairment', whether with a physiological basis or not. It seems, however, that the court finally rejected Vasiljević's partial defence as 'highly speculative' precisely because there was no demonstration of a mental condition with a physiological basis.[221]

There is no express provision in the ICC Statute concerned with the consequences of a cognitive impairment amounting to only 'diminished' mental responsibility. There is, however, Article 31 of the ICC Statute, which provides in relevant part:

A person shall not be criminally responsible if, at the time of that person's conduct: ... (b) The person is in a state of intoxication that destroys that person's capacity to appreciate the unlawfulness or nature of his or her conduct, or capacity to control his or her conduct to conform to the requirements of law, unless the person has become voluntarily intoxicated under such circumstances that the person knew, or disregarded the risk, that, as a result of the intoxication, he or she was likely to engage in conduct constituting a crime within the jurisdiction of the Court.[222]

II.14 PLEA OF INSANITY

Insanity at the time of commission of the acts in question is a complete defence to a charge, leading to acquittal. A challenge to the presumption of sanity by a plea of insanity before the tribunals would be dealt with in accordance with the English M'Naghten Rules. This at least is what we must conclude from the Appeals Chamber's remark that in the case of such a plea the defendant bears the onus of establishing on the balance of probabilities that at the time of the offence the defendant was labouring under such a defect of reason, from disease of the mind, as not to know the nature and quality of his act, or, if he did know, that he did not know that what he was doing was wrong.[223]

---

[219] Ibid., para. 283.   [220] Ibid., fn. 677.

[221] Ibid., paras 284–95. See also *Todorović* sentencing judgment, paras 93–5, and P. Krug, 'The Emerging Mental Incapacity Defense in International Criminal Law: Some Initial Questions of Implementation' (2000) 94 *Am. J. Int'l L.* 317.

[222] At the ICTY, Mitar Vasiljević was presented by his defence as being an alcoholic during the relevant period, relying on the supposition that he was often drunk to account for actions that Vasiljević 'could not remember' performing, such as writing out and signing 'security guarantees' for selected persons (*Prosecutor* v. *Vasiljević*, Defence Final Trial Brief, 28 February 2002, pp. 35–6). The Trial Chamber rejected this defence as unsubstantiated (*Vasiljević* trial judgment, para. 294).   [223] *Delalić et al.* appeal judgment, para. 582.

Article 31(1) of the ICC Statute incorporates the plea of insanity under very similar terms:

A person shall not be criminally responsible if, at the time of that person's conduct: (a) The person suffers from a mental disease or defect that destroys that person's capacity to appreciate the unlawfulness or nature of his or her conduct, or capacity to control his or her conduct to conform to the requirements of law.

At the ad hoc tribunals, Vladimir Kovačević is the only person so far found not to have the capacity to enter a plea or to stand trial. He is confined at a psychiatric institute in Serbia, to which he was transferred from the ICTY.[224]

II.15 POLITICALLY MOTIVATED, OSTENTATIOUS, OR INJUDICIOUS PROSECUTION

The early ICTY cases were of minor figures: Tadić, Erdemović, Furundžija, and others. This was not a matter of prosecutorial choice, but of poor state cooperation. Yet it became a sore point for some of the accused. Esad Landžo, the guard at the Čelebići prison-camp, was the first to argue that the tribunal had no business going after minor figures like himself.[225] This idea can be played out as an argument against jurisdiction, but it is also plausibly cast as a defence — akin to that of superior orders — when it takes the form: 'I was swept up by the events like a leaf in a storm'. This picture is meant to assimilate the minor perpetrator to the category of victim. As Landžo — who indeed proclaimed himself to be a victim — put it, there was a risk that the ICTY's moral authority would 'be squandered in the pursuit of common soldiers and prison guards'. On that basis, he called upon the court to dismiss the charges against him. The humble role he played was itself his shield.[226]

Landžo speculated that the reason why the prosecutor picked on him, despite his lowly status ('small fry', in Landžo's description of himself), was that the institution needed a token Bosnian-Muslim defendant to offset the institution's apparent emphasis, at the time, on proof of Bosnian-Serb responsibility.[227] He argued that the decision to prosecute ought not to be based on any improperly discriminatory factor, such as race or religion.[228] The threshold showing he sought to make was that the

---

[224] See *Prosecutor* v. *Vladimir Kovačević*, Public Version of the Decision on Accused's Fitness to Enter a Plea and Stand Trial, 12 April 2006.

[225] *Prosecutor* v. *Delalić et al.*, Esad Landžo's Final Submission and Motion for Acquittal, 28 August 1998, pp. 7–10, 19–21, 147–51.　　　　　　　　　　　　　　　　　　　　[226] Ibid., pp. 10, 21.

[227] Ibid., pp. 9, 16.

[228] Ibid., p. 16, citing in his support a US Supreme Court ruling that the administration of criminal law may not be 'directed so exclusively against a particular class of persons... with a mind so unequal and oppressive as to amount to a practical denial by the state of that equal protection of the laws' which is the constitutional right of all persons: *Yick Wo* v. *Hopkins*, 118 US 356 (1886), 373.

prosecutor had declined to prosecute similarly situated suspects of other 'races or religions'; and that he himself was singled out for prosecution on the basis of his race or religion. The situation at the time, as Landžo saw it, was that the three Bosnian Muslims in the *Delalić* case, including himself, were the only Muslims to have been brought before the tribunal. At around that time, moreover, the indictments against several minor figures of Serbian etnicity had been withdrawn due to lack of institutional resources. Given the prosecutor's avowed new policy (of May 1998) of concentrating resources on the cases of persons who had held higher office, it followed in Landžo's reasoning that the decision to maintain the indictment against him was improperly selective.[229]

Landžo's defence was barely considered by the *Delalić* Trial Chamber, which seems to have thought it not worth engaging with.[230] The Appeals Chamber, on the other hand, dealt with the defence at some length. It recognized, in the first place, that Article 21 of the ICTY Statute prohibits discrimination in the application of the law on grounds such as religion, opinion, or national or ethnic origin. It said that the prosecutor is subject to this requirement of non-discrimination, and more generally to the principle of equality before the law, from which the requirement is derived.[231] For Landžo to succeed he would have had to produce clear evidence that the prosecutor's intent was to discriminate against him on improper grounds. The Appeals Chamber found, however, that the decision to continue the trial against Landžo was 'consistent' with the prosecutor's stated policy of focusing not only on persons holding higher levels of responsibility but also on those who, like Landžo, were responsible for 'exceptionally brutal or otherwise extremely serious offences'. The persons against whom charges had been withdrawn were not facing trial at the time, and therefore their cases could be distinguished.[232]

At the ICTR, there is a prevailing sense among defence teams that the prosecutions are politically motivated. The prosecutions are, without doubt, one-sided: those (Hutu) associated with the government are prosecuted, but those (Tutsi) who took part in the rebellion are not. The *Ntakirutimana* defence expressed the problem in this way:

Events have shown that the ICTR cannot function independently of its political mandate, the RPF, the government of Rwanda, or its agents including IBUKA [a victim-support group] and African Rights. The demeaning submission of the ICTR to pressure by the government of Rwanda in the reversal of its decisions dismissing the indictment against Jean-Bosco Barayagwiza, the repeated conflicts between Rwanda and its agents with the ICTR which have resulted in ICTR deference to the demands of the government of Rwanda and IBUKA; . . . the acceptance of patently false information from the Justice Minister of Rwanda concerning the teaching record of Judge Gasasira at the National University and Judges college [whom the Ntakirutimanas had

---

[229] *Prosecutor* v. *Delalić et al.*, Esad Landžo's Final Submission and Motion for Acquittal, 28 August 1998, pp. 16–19, 21–2. [230] *Delalić et al.* trial judgment, para. 1281 (cf. para. 176).
[231] *Delalić et al.* appeal judgment, para. 605. [232] Ibid., paras 614–17.

wanted to recruit to their defence team]; the inability of the ICTR to proceed with trials as the government of Rwanda and IBUKA withhold witnesses in Rwanda are but a few of the illustrations of the crippling dependence on and deference of the ICTR to Rwanda.[233]

11.16 CONCLUSION

This survey shows that the defences provided for in the constitutive documents of the tribunals are largely irrelevant in practice. The workhorse defences are those which target jurisdiction and proof of legal elements, the latter focusing on witness credibility and the moral disintegration and chaos caused by civil wars. The student is encouraged to take the empirical study of defences to the next level of development, using this chapter as a guide.

---

[233] *Prosecutor v. E. Ntakirutimana and G. Ntakirutimana*, Defense Closing Brief, 22 July 2002, p. 261.

PART IV

TRIBUNAL—STATE INTERACTIONS: COORDINATION AND IMPACT

12

RELATIONS WITH NATIONAL JURISDICTIONS

SUMMARY

12.1 INTRODUCTION

An important aspect of the functioning of international criminal tribunals is their relationship with national jurisdictions. A distinction should be made between the substantive (criminal law) aspects of this relationship and the procedural aspects. The former concerns the effect and implementation of substantive international criminal law in the domestic legal order. In concrete terms, it raises, for example, the question of the effect of ICTY jurisprudence on command responsibility for national prosecutions of international crimes. This and other matters are discussed in Chapter 13. The present chapter examines the procedural aspects of the relationship between international and national criminal jurisdictions. Those issues fall into one of three central areas.

First, the starting point in any discussion of the relationship between national and international courts is the division of tasks, or, as it were, the workload. The jurisdiction of all international criminal tribunals is concurrent with that of national courts. However, different mechanisms have been developed for assigning priority to, or preference for, the national or the international criminal jurisdiction. Understanding those mechanisms is of obvious importance, as misinterpretation may affect the legality and legitimacy of certain prosecutions.

Secondly, there is the question of legal assistance, or cooperation in criminal matters. This is a vital element of effective investigations and prosecutions, as it is indeed between domestic criminal justice systems. However, the dependence of the international criminal justice systems on state cooperation is unparalleled, as international criminal tribunals and courts have only limited investigatory and prosecutorial powers of their own. The present chapter makes some general observations on the cooperation regimes of international criminal tribunals.

Finally, this chapter addresses the question of the authority and effect of decisions of international criminal tribunals in the domestic legal order, and, conversely, the consequences of domestic decisions at the national level. This question is essentially about the authority of final judgments and *ne bis in idem*, or double jeopardy. As to other decisions of international criminal tribunals, their effect at the national level is generally only relevant in the sphere of legal assistance and has been dealt with under that heading elsewhere in this book.

12.2 CONCURRENT JURISDICTION: PRIMACY AND COMPLEMENTARITY

12.2.1 General remarks

Since the crimes within the jurisdiction of international criminal tribunals — the so-called core crimes of genocide, crimes against humanity, and war crimes — generally give rise to universal jurisdiction,[1] the concurrence of their jurisdiction with that of every state is inevitable. At no time has it been envisaged that an international criminal tribunal would exercise exclusive jurisdiction.[2] An important negative consequence of exclusive jurisdiction would be that other fora are prevented from exercising jurisdiction.

---

[1] This generalization does not do justice to the complicated questions related to the exercise of universal jurisdiction. Since this is outside the scope of the present book, we refer to the existing literature on this matter. In particular, we recommend L. Reydams, *Universal Jurisdiction: International and Municipal Legal Perspectives* (Oxford: Oxford University Press, 2003), K. Randall, 'Universal Jurisdiction under International Law' (1988) 66 *Texas L. Rev.*, at 786–91, and M. Henzelin, *Le principe de l'universalité en droit pénal international* (Basle, Geneva, Munich: Helbing and Lictenhahn, 2000).

[2] In respect of the ICTY, see Morris and Scharf, *Insider's Guide*, at 124. See also the Report of the Secretary-General, para. 64: 'it was not the intention of the Security Council to preclude or prevent the exercise of jurisdiction by national courts'.

If not all crimes can be investigated — which is the case with international criminal tribunals whose resources are very limited — a number of the most serious crimes may go unpunished.[3] However, it should be noted that internationalized courts operating within a domestic context may for good reasons, namely to centralize expertise within one particular national court, be given exclusive jurisdiction over certain crimes; this jurisdiction is then exclusive in respect of other national courts, but not in respect of foreign courts.[4]

Although situations of concurrent jurisdiction are not uncommon — for example both the state of nationality of the suspect and the state where the crime was committed may lawfully exercise jurisdiction — there are compelling reasons to regulate the exercise of jurisdiction in respect of international crimes. The first important reason relates to the duty incumbent upon states to investigate and prosecute certain international crimes. This means that a significant number of states may exercise jurisdiction over such offences, as a result of which the positive jurisdictional conflict will potentially be of greater scope and involve more parties than is normally the case in inter-state relations. Another reason concerns the specific nature and mandate of each international criminal tribunal, which calls for specific regulation that does justice to the tribunal's intended object and purpose. For example, an ad hoc tribunal established by the Security Council with a view to restoring and maintaining peace and security understandably plays a prominent role in relation to national courts. Such a tribunal should in the interests of peace have priority over concurrent national jurisdictions, in the sense that national courts should not be allowed to frustrate that objective. On the other hand, the ICC is intended to serve a more limited purpose, essentially that of reviewing national court practice, which has priority. This different focus has to do with the Court's permanent nature and universal aspirations that make the fulfilment of its mandate on the basis of primacy practically impossible. Finally, there are the efforts by the international community to reinforce the national court structure by means of internationalized criminal tribunals. Those bodies may be part of or closely affiliated with the national court structure. In this context regulation of jurisdictional conflicts with other states may not be easy due to the principle of sovereign equality, as a result of which no priority can be established in the (conflicting) exercise of national criminal jurisdiction.[5]

---

[3] In this respect it should be noted that the Secretary-General in his report on the ICTY mentions that 'national courts should be encouraged to exercise their jurisdiction in accordance with their relevant national laws and procedures' (ibid.).

[4] This is the case with the East Timor panels and also with the Extraordinary Chambers for Cambodia. See Section 2.3 of UNTAET Regulation No. 2000/15 of 6 June 2000 on the Establishment of Panels with Exclusive Jurisdiction over Serious Criminal Offences (prescribing exclusive jurisdiction of the panels over serious offences committed between 1 January 1999 and 25 October 1999). In the case of the Cambodian Extraordinary Chambers, the legal framework does not explicitly provide for exclusive jurisdiction in respect of other courts, but this appears unnecessary in light of the place of the Chambers within the existing Cambodian court structure (cf. Article 2 of the Cambodian law on the Establishment of the Extraordinary Chambers).

[5] See P. Gaeta, 'Les règles internationales sur les critères de compétence des juges nationaux', in A. Cassese and M. Delmas-Marty (eds), *Crimes internationaux et juridictions internationales* (Paris: Presses Universitaires de France, 2002), at 209–11. In our view, even when a conventional rule or a rule of customary international law obliges a state to exercise jurisdiction, it cannot be concluded that this rule gives the jurisdictional basis of the state concerned

12.2.2 Primacy: the ICTR, the ICTY, and the SCSL[6]

The Statutes of the ICTY, the ICTR, and the SCSL contain almost identical provisions on concurrent jurisdiction and primacy.[7] The only important difference is that whereas the primacy of the ICTR and the ICTY extends to every national court,[8] the primacy of the SCSL only concerns the national courts of Sierra Leone. This is because the Court's method of establishment prevents the imposition of cooperation obligations on other states, which are a precondition of effective primacy.[9] Consequently, there is, in relation to other national courts, an unregulated situation of concurrent jurisdiction.

The practical application of primacy is governed by Rules 9, 10, and 11 of the ICTR, ICTY, and SCSL Rules of Evidence and Procedure (RPE). The substantive grounds for deferral are set out in Rule 9. There is a remarkable difference in approach between the ICTY, on the one hand, and the ICTR and SCSL on the other. Rule 9 of the ICTY RPE mirrors in the first two grounds for deferral Article 10 of its Statute on *ne bis in idem*. This means that a deferral order may be issued when a case is not diligently investigated or prosecuted at the national level and when an investigation or prosecution is based on an ordinary crime. The third and final ground — which is most used in practice — enables deferral when 'what is in issue is closely related to, or otherwise involves, significant factual or legal questions which may have implications for investigations or prosecutions before the Tribunal'. Initially, Rule 9 of the ICTR RPE was identical, but it was later amended.[10] The current text of this rule — also reproduced in Rule 9 of the SCSL RPE — is exclusively oriented to the wishes of the Tribunal and offers practically unfettered discretion as regards deferral. Thus, deferral may be ordered when the crimes in question are the subject of an investigation by the prosecutor or should be so — taking into account, inter alia, the seriousness of the offences, the status of the accused at the time of the alleged offences, the general importance of the legal questions involved in the case — or are the subject of an indictment confirmed by the Tribunal. The amendment may be explained by the Tribunal's wish to strengthen its position in relation to Rwanda's expanding investigation of crimes and prosecution of persons in which the ICTR prosecutor is also interested.

In the exercise of deferral the ICTY was immediately confronted with a challenge in the *Tadić* case.[11] As investigations in Germany clearly did not fall within the ambit of

---

priority over the jurisdictional bases of other states. This certainly underlines the necessity of coordination between states in situations of (positive) jurisdictional conflicts.

[6] For an extensive study of the primacy of the ICTY and the ICTR and the ICC's principle of complementarity, see B. S. Brown, 'Primacy or Complementarity: Reconciling the Jurisdiction of National Courts and International Criminal Tribunals' (1998) 23 *Yale J. Int'l Law*, at 383, and J. K. Kleffner, 'Complementarity in the Rome Statute and National Jurisdictions', unpublished PhD thesis, University of Amsterdam, 2007.

[7] Article 9 of the ICTY Statute, Article 8 of the ICTR Statute, and Article 8 of the SCSL Statute.

[8] More precisely, to the national courts of UN members; only the latter are bound to give effect to requests for deferral. See Decision on Defence Motion to Obtain Cooperation from the Vatican Pursuant to Article 28, *Prosecutor v. Bagosora et al.*, Case No. ICTR-98-41-T, ICTR, T. Ch. I, 13 May 2004.

[9] See section 12.3 below.

[10] Rule 9 of the ICTR RPE was amended at the ICTR Fourth Plenary Session (1–5 June 1997).

[11] *Tadić* jurisdiction appeal decision.

Rule 9(i) or (ii), the question arose as to how the Tribunal would interpret Rule 9(iii). In *Tadić*, the Appeals Chamber refused to review the Trial Chamber's application of Rule 9(iii), affording the Chamber a very wide margin of appreciation.[12] The defence team in *Tadić* furthermore sought to narrow the grounds of deferral by connecting Rule 9 to Article 10(2) of the Statute. The defence argued that only the *ne bis in idem* grounds set out in Article 10(2) may serve as grounds for deferral.[13] The Trial Chamber simply denied that argument.[14]

In subsequent jurisprudence a number of elements became relevant for the applicability of Rule 9(iii). In the *Musema*, *Radio Mille Collines*, and *Bagosora* deferrals, it was a matter of concern for the ICTR — then still applying the same Rule 9(iii) as the ICTY — that the competent national courts could only prosecute for war crimes, as neither Swiss nor Belgian criminal legislation at that time contained provisions on crimes against humanity and genocide.[15] Subsequent prosecution by the ICTR for crimes against humanity or genocide would then have been barred by *the ne bis in idem* provision of Article 9 of the ICTR Statute.[16] The position of witnesses seems also to be a crucial factor in the application of Rule 9(iii). In this respect, the Trial Chambers adopted the position that the burden on witnesses of testifying twice should be avoided.[17] It is remarkable that the safety of witnesses also plays a role in the deferral decisions.[18] One may wonder whether the safety of witnesses is not better served with trials only in Belgium or Switzerland, which result in less exposure and may offer better mechanisms for protection.

Rule 9(iii) of the ICTY RPE undoubtedly offers the most neutral ground for deferral, bearing no prejudice to the state concerned. However, in one deferral procedure the ICTY prosecutor argued that a refusal to cooperate indicated that proceedings in the state concerned, the Federal Republic of Yugoslavia, were not independent and impartial and were designed to shield the accused from criminal responsibility.[19] The Trial Chamber did not venture into a review of the quality of proceedings in the FRY and stuck to the 'diplomatic' Rule 9(iii) ground.[20] This illustrates the inherent sensitivity of

---

[12] Ibid., para. 52.

[13] See Decision on the Defence motion on the principle of Non-bis-in-idem, *Prosecutor* v. *Tadić*, Case No. IT-94-1-T, ICTY, T. Ch., 14 November 1995, especially para. 31 where the defence refers to statements made by France, the UK, the USA, and Russia in the Security Council as confining the grounds for deferral to those set out in Article 10(2) of the Statute.   [14] Ibid., paras 30 and 33.

[15] Decision on the Formal Request for Deferral Presented by the Prosecutor, *Prosecutor* v. *Musema*, Case No. ICTR-96-5-D, ICTR, T. Ch. I, 12 March 1996, para. 12; Decision on the Formal Request for Deferral Presented by the Prosecutor, *Prosecutor* v. *Radio Television Libre des Mille Collines SARL*, Case No. ICTR-96-6-D, ICTR, T. Ch. I, 12 March 1996, para. 11; Decision on the Application by the Prosecutor for a Formal Request for Deferral, *Prosecutor* v. *Bagosora*, Case No. ICTR-96-7-D, ICTR, T. Ch. I, 17 May 1996, para. 13.

[16] In this respect it is noteworthy that the exceptional grounds of Article 9(2) do not come into play, as national authorities could charge the accused with war crimes; see further below, section 12.4.

[17] Decision on the Formal Request for Deferral Presented by the Prosecutor, *Prosecutor* v. *Musema*, para. 13; Decision on the Formal Request for Deferral Presented by the Prosecutor, *Prosecutor* v. *Radio Television Libre des Mille Collines SARL*, para. 12; Decision on the Application by the Prosecutor for a Formal Request for Deferral, *Prosecutor* v. *Bagosora*, para. 12.   [18] Ibid.

[19] Decision on the Proposal of the Prosecutor for a Request to the Federal Republic of Yugoslavia (Serbia and Montenegro) to Defer the Pending Investigations and Criminal Proceedings to the Tribunal, *Prosecutor* v. *Mrkšić et al.*, Case No. IT-95-13-R61, ICTY, T. Ch. II, 10 December 1998, at 3.   [20] Ibid., at 4–5.

Rule 9(ii), which plays a far more prominent role in the ICC context, as will be demonstrated below.

There have been some remarkable developments in the ad hoc tribunals' practice concerning their primacy in concurrent jurisdiction.[21] Since the early years, no deferral decisions have been issued. The main reason probably lies in an ever improving coordination between states and the ad hoc tribunals, given that states may consult with them before starting investigations. It has also helped that a more transparent prosecutorial policy of the ad hoc tribunals has emerged, even though there has been a significant shift in the ICTY prosecutorial targets from the low-level to the mid-level and finally to the high-level perpetrators, combined with a Chamber-led initiative to refer low-to-mid-level indictees back to national jurisdictions.

The ad hoc tribunals have over the years taken upon themselves a coordinating and supervising role in the national prosecution of international crimes. The first step was the role of the ICTY in the Rules of the Road project. In February 1996, the parties to the General Framework Agreement for Peace in Bosnia and Herzegovina (the Dayton Agreement) agreed that 'persons other than those already indicted by the International Tribunal may be arrested and detained for serious violations of international humanitarian law only pursuant to a previously issued order, warrant or indictment that has been reviewed and deemed consistent with international legal standards by the International Tribunal'.[22] Within the ICTY the prosecutor manages the Rules of the Road project and thus exercises significant powers in respect of national prosecutions.[23] One may wonder whether this is in conformity with the ICTY's mandate and its Statute, which provides for unconditional concurrent jurisdiction in Article 9(1), unless a formal request for deferral has been issued.

The latest development in the exercise of concurrent jurisdiction is the transfer of cases or proceedings to national courts in the context of the ad hoc tribunals' exit strategy.[24] It is a better solution than the mere withdrawal of indictments, as occurred in the past with lower-level perpetrators.[25] The implementation of this part of the exit strategy is governed by Rule 11 *bis* of the ICTY and ICTR RPE.[26] The rule has been amended and currently allows for transfer to any state. As a result, the state which arrests and transfers an accused may be able to do so not only with a view to prosecution by the

---

[21] The SCSL has not had any practice in respect of deferral requests. This is because there have been no prosecutions of crimes within the jurisdiction of the SCSL by the Sierra Leone courts.

[22] The imminent ground for this agreement was the arrest of eight Bosnian Serbs by the Bosnian government, which caused tensions in the region.

[23] For more information, see ICTY Ninth Annual Report (2004), paras 286–90.

[24] The UN Security Council imposed on both the ICTY and the ICTR an exit strategy, which aimed to finalize investigations and prosecutions on specific dates. For more details, see D. A. Mundis, 'Completing the Mandates of the Ad Hoc International Criminal Tribunals: Lessons from the Nuremberg Process?' (2005) 28 *Fordham Int'l Law J.*, at 591–615.

[25] On 5 May and 8 May 1998 respectively, Judge Vohrah and Judge Riad granted the leave requested by the OTP to withdraw the charges against 14 accused in the Omarska and Keraterm indictments. The charges against the following 11 accused in the Omarska indictment have been withdrawn: Zdravko Govedarica, Gruban, Predrag Kostić, Nedeljko Paspalj, Milan Pavlić, Milutin Popović, Drazenko Predojević, Zeljko Savić, Mirko Babić, Nikica Janjić and Dragomir Saponja. See press release CC/PIU/314-E, The Hague, 8 May 1998.

[26] For an extensive overview and analysis of Rule 11 *bis* and its application in practice, see S. Williams, 'ICTY Referrals to National Jurisdictions: Fair Trial or a Fair Price?' (2006) 17 *CLF*, at 177–222.

ICTY or the ICTR, but also on the understanding that the accused might be prosecuted by a third state, which may be at odds with the rule of speciality.[27] Rule 11 *bis* (F) provides for the interesting, but in light of the exit strategy perhaps only theoretical, possibility of exercising primacy by requesting deferral back to the tribunal of a case previously transferred to national courts.

At the time of writing, November 2006, a significant Rule 11 *bis* practice has already developed. At the ICTY 11 accused were referred to the Bosnian War Crimes Chamber for prosecution.[28] One should, however, also mention that the ICTY refused referral in one instance. The case of Dragomir Milošević was not referred to the War Crimes Chamber because it was 'too serious':

> The campaign alleged in the Indictment and the crimes with which Dragomir Milosevic has been charged stand out when compared with other cases before the Tribunal, especially in terms of alleged duration, number of civilians affected, extent of property damage, and number of military personnel involved. It is also evident that the Prosecution's case imputes significant authority to Dragomir Milosevic. The Referral Bench therefore concludes that the gravity of the crimes charged and the level of responsibility of the accused, particularly when they are considered in combination, requires that the present case be tried at the Tribunal. Therefore, there is no need to consider other factors.[29]

The ICTR has not yet transferred a single indicted person to national jurisdictions, in spite of clear intentions to do so.[30] Compared to the ICTY, the ICTR faces two major problems in respect of the use of Rule 11 *bis*. First, the most appropriate trial forum, Rwanda, is problematic in the sense that it allows for the death penalty and that a fair and expeditious trial may be difficult to realize bearing in mind the current state of the Rwandan judicial infrastructure.[31] Secondly, other states may lack an appropriate jurisdictional basis to prosecute genocide. In *Bagaragaza* the competent ICTR Trial Chamber refused referral to Norway because that state could not prosecute for genocide:

> In this case, it is apparent that the Kingdom of Norway does not have jurisdiction (*ratione materiae*) over the crimes as charged in the confirmed Indictment. In addition, the Chamber recalls that the crimes alleged — genocide, conspiracy to commit genocide and complicity in

---

[27] The purpose of the speciality rule is to ensure that transfer of an accused is only for a specific purpose, namely prosecution by the ICTY or ICTR and not by a third state. In the *Ntuyahaga* case ICTR judges considered this rule a crucial obstacle in the transfer of an accused-after withdrawal of the indictment — to Belgium; see Declaration on a point of law by Judge Laïty Kama, President of the Tribunal, Judge Lennart Aspegren and Judge Navanethem Pillay, 22 April 1999. For a critical view on the Rule 11 *bis* procedure from the perspective of extradition law, see M. Bohlander, 'Referring an Indictment from the ICTY and ICTR to Another Court — Rule 11bis and the Consequences for the Law of Extradition' (2006) 55(1) *Int'l & Comparative Law Q.*, at 219–26.

[28] Rahim Ademi, Dušan Fuštar, Momčilo Gruban, Gojko Janković, Dušan Knežević, Paško Ljubičić, Željko Mejakić, Mirko Norac, Mitar Rašević, Radovan Stanković, and Savo Todović.

[29] Decision on Referral of a Case pursuant to Rule 11 bis, *Prosecutor* v. *Dragomir Milošević*, Case No. IT-98-29/1-PT, ICTY, Referral Bench, 8 July 2005.

[30] Letter dated 29 May 2006 from the President of the International Criminal Tribunal for the Prosecution of Persons Responsible for Genocide and Other Serious Violations of International Humanitarian Law Committed in the Territory of Rwanda and Rwandan Citizens Responsible for Genocide and Other Such Violations Committed in the Territory of Neighbouring States between 1 January and 31 December 1994 addressed to the President of the Security Council (UN Doc. S/2006/358), paras 39–42.

[31] In this sense, although using more cautious language, ibid.

genocide — are significantly different in term of their elements and their gravity from the crime of homicide, the basis upon which the Kingdom of Norway states that charges may be laid against the Accused under its domestic law. The Chamber notes that the crime of genocide is distinct in that it requires the 'intent to destroy, in whole or in part, a national, ethnical, racial or religious group, as such'. This specific intent is not required for the crime of homicide under Norwegian criminal law. Therefore, in the Chamber's view, the *ratione materiae* jurisdiction, or subject matter jurisdiction, for the acts alleged in the confirmed Indictment does not exist under Norwegian law. Consequently, Michel Bagaragaza's alleged criminal acts cannot be given their full legal qualification under Norwegian criminal law, and the request for the referral to the Kingdom of Norway falls to be dismissed.[32]

The ICTY is in a better position. The challenges by the defence concentrate essentially on the quality of the trial, especially fair trial rights, and detention in Bosnia. With the improved legal framework governing the activities of the War Crimes Chamber in combination with a monitoring role for the ICTY there are indeed no major obstacles to referral.[33]

It is interesting to reflect on the 'schizophrenic' elements of the Rule 11 *bis* procedure. Defendants who object to referral generally do so out of fear of worse treatment in Bosnia and higher sentences.[34] But one of the vital factors in allowing the referral of an accused is his or her level of responsibility. In other words, in order to argue against referral the defence may have to adopt the awkward position of claiming that the defendant qualifies as the 'most responsible person'.[35] Referral proceedings have compelled the Referral Bench to be critical of ICTY proceedings. With a view to 'convincing' the accused that he will not be worse off with the War Crimes Chamber it has, for example, emphasized that the accused's right to an expeditious trial is probably better ensured outside the ICTY.[36] It thereby appears to confirm that this right is not protected in the ad hoc tribunals.[37]

---

[32] Decision on the Prosecution Motion for Referral to the Kingdom of Norway, *Prosecutor v. Bagaragaza*, Case No. ICTR-2005-86-R11bis, ICTR, T. Ch. III, 19 May 2006, para. 16. We welcome this decision with approval and note with surprise that the ICTR prosecutor called for this referral, whereas the idea underlying the ICTR is to prosecute for international crimes and that deferral from national jurisdiction to the ICTR is pursuant to Rule 9 fully appropriate when the conduct concerned is prosecuted as an 'ordinary' crime at the national level.

[33] For the most recent restatement of the Rule 11 *bis* standards, see Decision on Savo Todović's Appeals against Decisions on Referral under Rule 11bis, *Prosecutor v. Rašević and Todović*, Cases No. IT-97-25/1-AR11bis.1 & 2, ICTY, A. Ch., 4 September 2006. For a critical analysis, see S. Williams, 'ICTY Referrals to National Jurisdictions: Fair Trial or a Fair Price?' (2006) 17 *CLF*, at 177–222.

[34] The converse situation is also possible: Bagaragaza was very much in favour of his referral to Norway, possibly in expectation of that country's high standards of imprisonment conditions and in light of the fact that he could 'only' be tried for murder in Norway and not for genocide; see Decision on the Prosecution Motion for Referral to the Kingdom of Norway, *Prosecutor v. Bagaragaza*, Case No. ICTR-2005-86-R11bis, ICTR, T. Ch. III, 19 May 2006.

[35] On how defendants have tried to get around this dilemma, see para. 17 of Decision on Savo Todović's Appeals against Decisions on Referral under Rule 11bis, *Prosecutor v. Rašević and Todović*, Cases No. IT-97-25/1-AR11bis.1 & 2, ICTY, A. Ch., 4 September 2006, where the appellant argued that he should not be regarded as one of the 'most senior leaders suspected of being most responsible', but that this category was not confined to the 'architects' and that he could be considered part of this group in the sense of being an 'intermediary actor'.

[36] See Decision on Referral of Case under Rule 11 bis, *Prosecutor v. Stanković*, Case No. IT-96-23/2-PT, Referral Bench, 17 May 2005, para. 77: 'Indeed, referral may well result in the case being brought to trial sooner than would have been possible if the case were to remain with the Tribunal.'

[37] For more detail, see Chapter 8, section 8.5.3.

12.2.3 Complementarity: the ICC[38]

The principle of complementarity lies at the heart of the functioning of the ICC. It is diametrically opposite to the primacy of the ad hoc tribunals; pursuant to the principle of complementarity, the ICC monitors the primary jurisdiction of national courts. The standards of review and the practical application of the principle of complementarity are the object of Article 17 of the ICC Statute. The gist of that provision is that a case is admissible to the ICC only when national courts are or have been *unable* or *unwilling* to genuinely prosecute that case. Although Article 17 offers certain guidelines as to what is to be understood by 'unwillingness' and 'inability', the Court's jurisprudence has yet to formulate precisely the standards of review. Two elements in the definition of unwillingness are similar to the ground of primacy in Rule 9(ii) of the ICTY RPE, namely that proceedings are conducted independently and impartially (Article 17(2)(c)) and are not designed to shield the accused from criminal responsibility (Article 17(2)(a)). We have seen above that the ICTY has been very reluctant to use this ground to assert primacy, which may foreshadow the political sensitivities that will also confront the ICC. Indeed, it is a major step to determine that national proceedings do not live up to their obligations for the prosecution of the most serious international crimes. Furthermore, the state being criticized may very well be the one whose cooperation will be most required should the ICC take over the case.

A group of experts has offered the ICC prosecutor helpful advice in the formulation of a 'complementarity policy'.[39] Among other things, the experts have developed a set of criteria for determining inability or unwillingness and for dealing with the burden and standard of proof regarding these standards. The informal paper tackles such sensitive issues as the effect of national amnesties, within and outside the context of truth and reconciliation commissions.[40] It is beyond the scope and objective of this book to elaborate on these important issues.

The first experiences of the ICC in respect of the principle of complementarity immediately give rise to serious questions. The first three investigations of the ICC prosecutor — the Democratic Republic of the Congo, the Central African Republic, and Uganda — have been triggered by referrals made by those states pursuant to Article 14 of the ICC Statute.[41]

Interestingly, these so-called self-referrals seem to have been solicited by the ICC prosecutor, when he proclaimed in respect of the Congo that 'a referral and active support

---

[38] See J. T. Holmes, 'The Principle of Complementarity', in Lee, *Making of the Rome Statute*, at 41–78; see also M. M. El Zeidy, 'The Principle of Complementarity: A New Machinery to Implement International Criminal Law' (2002) 23 *Michigan J. Int'l Law*, at 869–975.

[39] Expert consultation process on complementarity in practice; informal paper at www.icc-cpi.int/library/organs/otp/complementarity.pdf (last visited 9 November 2006). [40] Ibid.

[41] Decision Assigning the Situation in Uganda to Pre-Trial Chamber II, Case No. ICC-02/04, ICC, Presidency, 5 July 2004; Decision Assigning the Situation in the Democratic Republic of Congo to Pre-Trial Chamber I, Case No. ICC-01/04, ICC, Presidency, 5 July 2004; Decision assigning the situation in the Central African Republic to Pre-Trial Chamber III, Case No. ICC-01/05, ICC, Presidency, 19 January 2005.

from the DRC would assist his work'.[42] A negotiated division of cases between national courts and the ICC, which seems to be the prosecutor's approach, raises pointed questions in respect of the practical application of the principle of complementarity. It should be emphasized that negotiated self-referrals — also referred to as waiver of complementarity[43] — are not *contra legem*, as nothing in the Statute prohibits this. Furthermore, there are several arguments of legal policy that support self-referral, especially that the state concerned will normally be more cooperative in the case of a self-referral and that concerns about any imbalance in the exercise of prosecutorial powers — *proprio motu* powers — are to a certain extent accommodated.[44] However, there are risks involved. First of all, negotiated self-referrals while not against the letter of the Statute, may be against the spirit of the principle of complementarity, the basis of which is the primary duty of states to investigate and prosecute international crimes. They also open the door to states to take it as a starting point in legal policy that cases may be allocated to the ICC. In the long run this may create an unbearable burden for the Court. One may also wonder whether negotiated self-referrals fit into a long-term vision of prosecutorial strategy, or instead reflect a wish to turn the ICC into an active institution as soon as possible.[45] Finally, one must mention the risk of 'selective or asymmetrical self-referrals'.[46] Cassese in this regard emphasized that the three self-referrals were all directed at crimes committed by rebels in a civil war situation.[47] He pointed out the risk that this first practice might lead to 'states using the Court as a means of exposing dangerous rebels internationally, so as to dispose of them through the judicial process of the ICC'.[48]

12.3 COOPERATION WITH INTERNATIONAL CRIMINAL TRIBUNALS

12.3.1 Introductory remarks

Once an international criminal tribunal has determined that it has jurisdiction or a case is admissible before it, the question of cooperation with national jurisdictions arises.

---

[42] Press release of 23 June 2004, available at www.icc-cpi.int/press/pressreleases/26.html (last visited 9 November 2006).

[43] See C. Kress, ' "Self-Referrals" and "Waivers of Complementarity" — Some Considerations in Law and Policy' (2004) 2 *JICJ*, at 944–8.

[44] See P. Gaeta, 'Is the Practice of "Self-Referrals" a Sound Start for the ICC?' (2004) 2 *JICJ*, at 950.

[45] Understandable as this wish may be, the ICTY experience demonstrates that this may result in a somewhat inconsistent and non-uniform prosecutorial policy. Admittedly, when the Tribunal started functioning, there were few accused in the dock and, with a view to getting its first cases, it casts its net over relatively insignificant and low-ranking figures, notably, D. Tadić. Subsequently, with more indictees in the Tribunal's custody, the focus of the prosecutorial policy shifted to the leaders bearing the most responsibility and persons alleged to have committed exceptionally brutal and otherwise serious crimes (confirmed in *Delalić et al.* appeal judgment, para. 614).

[46] C. Kress, ' "Self-Referrals" and "Waivers of Complementarity" — Some Considerations in Law and Policy', at 946.

[47] A. Cassese, 'Is the ICC Still Having Teething Problems' (2006) 4 *JICJ*, at 436.   [48] Ibid.

For the international criminal tribunals, effective cooperation is indispensable.[49] Their statutes and jurisprudence embody aspirations to this end. As they cannot be subjected to a thorough analysis in this book,[50] we confine ourselves here to some general observations on the cooperation regimes and their main features, focusing on the ICTY, the ICTR, and the ICC because the cooperation of the internationalized institutions for Sierra Leone, East Timor, and Cambodia is generally confined to those states. Furthermore, because the internationalized courts for East Timor and Cambodia may be understood as part of the domestic judiciary, the normal means of obtaining legal assistance is via extradition and legal assistance treaties to which East Timor and Cambodia are parties.[51]

When examining legal assistance to international criminal tribunals, a distinction can be made between four main categories of cooperation: cooperation by transferring national prosecutions to the international court or tribunal; transfer of the accused; cooperation related to investigations and the production of evidence; and cooperation with respect to the enforcement of sentences. In essence, these forms of cooperation are identical to the forms of inter-state legal assistance, the only difference being that the terminology used may vary with a view to emphasizing the different nature of the cooperation relationship between international criminal tribunals and national jurisdictions.

The general observations below focus on transfer of accused persons and cooperation in investigations and the production of evidence. The transfer of proceedings is the result of the exercise of primacy or the principle of complementarity and has been examined above. Cooperation in the enforcement of sentences is to a large extent based on voluntary assistance from states and is therefore not discussed below. Finally, we examine legal

---

[49] There are two striking differences between national criminal jurisdictions and international criminal tribunals that necessitate cooperation. First, international criminal tribunals do not have at their disposal law-enforcement officials to carry out various acts of criminal procedure for them. Secondly, even if this were the case, these officials would not have powers to carry out (certain) acts within the jurisdiction of a sovereign state.

The image of entirely helpless courts and tribunals without cooperation requires, however, some modification. The recent and current practice of the ICTY and ICTR in fact demonstrates a high degree of 'self-help'; representatives of the prosecutor in particular undertake numerous on-site investigations, such as exhumation of mass graves. Arguably, with the expansion of the tribunals, at present they do have available to them certain law-enforcement officials, who may carry out some investigatory acts in the territory of states. Yet, it should not be forgotten that even 'self-help' requires a degree of (passive) assistance and not everything can be done through 'self-help'. Furthermore, the ICC and the internationalized criminal tribunals may not enjoy the same legal and practical benefits as the ad hoc tribunals in autonomous investigations.

[50] For more detail on cooperation with international and internationalized criminal tribunals, see, for example, G. Sluiter, *International Criminal Adjudication and the Collection of Evidence: Obligations of States* (Antwerp: Intersentia, 2002); B. Swart and G. Sluiter, 'The International Criminal Court and International Criminal Cooperation', in H. A. M. von Hebel et al. (eds), *Reflections on the International Criminal Court — Essays in Honour of Adriaan Bos* (The Hague: Asser, 1999), at 91–128; B. Swart, 'International Cooperation and Judicial Assistance — General Problems', in Cassese et al., *Rome Statute Commentary*, at 1561–79; J. Meissner, *Die Zusammenarbeit mit dem Internationalen Strafgerichtshof nach dem Römischen Statut* (Munich: Verlag C. H. Beck, 2003); and P. Mochochoko, 'International Cooperation and Judicial Assistance', in Lee, *Making of the Rome Statute*, at 305–17.

[51] For a more detailed analysis of legal assistance to internationalized criminal tribunals, see G. Sluiter, 'Legal Assistance to Internationalized Criminal Courts and Tribunals', in C. P. R. Romano et al. (eds), *Internationalized Criminal Courts — Sierra Leone, East Timor, Kosovo, and Cambodia* (Oxford: Oxford University Press, 2004), at 379–406.

assistance from states to international criminal tribunals, and not the converse, since there is no duty on international criminal tribunals to offer assistance to national courts.

12.3.2 Jurisprudential developments

The Statutes of both the ICTR and the ICTY contain just a few words on the organization of legal assistance in only one provision (Article 28 of the ICTR Statute and Article 29 of the ICTY Statute). Although this is remarkable in view of the importance of this matter for the operation of the tribunals, it gave the judges the opportunity to shape the cooperation regime in the rules and, especially, in the case law. The judges seized that opportunity in the *Blaškić* case and have developed a most effective cooperation regime from the perspective of the ICTY and the ICTR.[52] The case concerned the refusal of Croatia, via its minister of defence, to comply with a request to hand over certain documents as evidence to the ICTY. Croatia justified its refusal to cooperate by, among other things, referring to the negative consequences for its national security, as the documents requested contained sensitive military information. In order to establish the hierarchy between the jurisdiction of the ad hoc tribunals and that of states, and the consequences thereof for the legal assistance concept, the ICTY introduced in the *Blaškić* decision the so-called 'horizontal' and 'vertical' relationships.[53] It referred to inter-state cooperation in criminal matters as 'horizontal' in nature.[54] A horizontal relationship is based on the sovereign equality of states, resulting in the adage *par in parem non habet imperium*.[55] The nature of the relationship is such that a state has no jurisdiction over another sovereign and thus may not order another state to perform certain acts. The ICTY Appeals Chamber found that its primacy over national courts and its power to address binding orders to states concerning a broad variety of judicial matters clearly established a 'vertical' relationship with states.[56] The Appeals Chamber limited the scope of the vertical relationship to the judicial and injunctory powers of the Tribunal, acknowledging that in the area of enforcement 'the International Tribunal is still dependent upon States and the Security Council'.[57]

The objective of what one might call the *Blaškić* coup is obvious: appropriating for the ICTY the most effective cooperation model. All subsequent case law is directed to the consolidation and also the expansion of that effective cooperation model. In a number of decisions the submission of states to the ICTY's superior position is confirmed, as is the duty to cooperate.[58] Simultaneously with the developments in the case law, the judges adjusted certain rules in order to reflect the vertical cooperation model.[59] Finally, the cooperation model has been expanded towards imposing obligations also on non-state

---

[52] See *Blaškić* subpoena trial decision and *Blaškić* subpoena appeal decision.

[53] *Blaškić* subpoena appeal decision, para. 47.   [54] Ibid.   [55] Ibid., para. 41.

[56] Ibid.

[57] Undoubtedly, the Appeals Chamber alluded to the enforcement of the orders for legal assistance; it failed to mention that enforcement of sentences equally depends on a state's volition and that the Tribunal cannot order a state to enforce sentences.

[58] Two examples: Order, *Prosecutor* v. *Blaškić*, Case No. IT-95-14-T, ICTY, T. Ch. I, 21 July 1998; Request to the Government of Bosnia and Herzegovina, *Prosecutor* v. *Delalić and others*, Case No. IT-96-21-T, ICTY, T. Ch. II *quater*, 16 October 1997.   [59] See Rules 54 *bis*, 70, and 108 *bis*.

entities, such as the Republika Srpska,[60] international organizations, such as the European Union,[61] and organs of international organizations, such as SFOR.[62]

Having consolidated and clarified the cooperation model, ICTY and ICTR practice is increasingly geared towards the enforcement of cooperation duties, which will be examined in section 12.3.5.

12.3.3 Distinctive features of the vertical cooperation model

As explained above, the ICTY jurisprudence has aimed in particular at establishing a vertical cooperation model. This has not only shaped the content of the cooperation relationship between this tribunal and states, but also served as an important precedent for shaping the cooperation regime of the ICC. But what does the vertical cooperation regime mean in practical terms? We examine this question in the following paragraphs.

Grounds for refusal

The traditional treaties regulating cooperation between states in criminal matters generally contain a variety of grounds on the basis of which the requested state may — or sometimes even must — refuse the requested assistance.[63] As a result, the extent of the obligation to provide assistance to another state is quite limited.

In a cooperation relationship of a more vertical nature the grounds for refusal set out in the inter-state legal assistance treaties are not applicable, or at least not to the same degree. The cooperation law of the ICTY and the ICTR — and also of the SCSL in respect of Sierra Leone only — is most vertical in this respect. In *Blaškić* the Appeals Chamber explicitly ruled that one may not read into Article 29 of the ICTY Statute grounds for refusal.[64] The ICC Statute, on the other hand, contains a number of grounds for refusal. Although they are not as numerous and extensive as those contained in extradition and mutual legal assistance treaties, the extent of the duty to assist the ICC is not as far-reaching as the duties vis-à-vis the ad hoc tribunals. On this point, therefore, the ICC cooperation regime should be positioned between the traditional inter-state cooperation regime and that of the ad hoc tribunals.

Reciprocity

States are generally only prepared to provide legal assistance to another state if there is an expectation of reciprocity.[65] The principle of reciprocity is laid down in, or follows

---

[60] Binding Order to the Republika Srpska for the Production of Documents, *Prosecutor* v. *Krstić*, Case No. IT-98-33-PT, ICTY, T. Ch. I, 12 March 1999.

[61] Order for the Production of Documents by the European Community Monitoring Mission and its Member States, *Prosecutor* v. *Kordić and Čerkez*, Case No. IT-95-14/2-T, ICTY, T. Ch. III, 4 August 2000.

[62] Decision on Motion for Judicial Assistance to be Provided by SFOR and Others, *Prosecutor* v. *Simić et al.*, Case No. IT-95-9-T, ICTY, T. Ch. III, 18 October 2000.

[63] For instance, Articles 2–11 of the European Convention on Extradition, 13 December 1957, ETS 24; Article 2 of the European Convention on Mutual Assistance in Criminal Matters, 20 April 1959, ETS 30.

[64] *Blaškić* subpoena appeal decision, para. 63.

[65] This is not to say that the 'lack of reciprocity' is always a material ground for refusing the requested assistance. See H. Grützner, 'International Judicial Assistance and Cooperation in Criminal Matters', in M. Cherif Bassiouni

from, the various legal assistance treaties.[66] International criminal tribunals have been created to prosecute only a limited number of crimes. Therefore, assistance is in principle meant to be given exclusively by states to the tribunals. This is not to say that in certain situations assistance from international criminal tribunals to states may not be welcome. Here we have to bear in mind that a situation of concurrent jurisdiction implies that these institutions cannot prosecute all perpetrators.

Rule 11 *bis* of the ICTY and the ICTR provides for a formal mechanism of legal assistance to national courts.[67] However, in contrast with the inter-state context, this is only a very limited form of assistance and, very importantly, is by no means an obligation on the part of the ICTY or the ICTR.

Those who drafted the Rome Statute acknowledged that assistance by the ICC to a state may advance the prosecution of war criminals in general, and provided within the Statute for the *possibility* of offering assistance to states. Article 93(10) of the ICC Statute authorizes the Court to cooperate with, and to provide assistance to, a state party, in respect of crimes within the Court's jurisdiction or of a serious crime under the national law of the requesting state. But because it imposes no duty upon the Court to provide any assistance,[68] it is difficult to speak of a reciprocal and equal cooperation relationship. This lack of reciprocity in the *duty* to provide assistance is another distinctive feature of the ICTY, ICTR, and ICC cooperation models.

Dispute settlement

If a dispute regarding the extent of the duty to cooperate occurs in the horizontal legal assistance relationship, the states settle it on a consensual basis by resort to a third impartial party. In the horizontal model, it is unthinkable for either the requesting or requested side to decide such a dispute itself.

In a vertical cooperation relationship, involving assistance to a hierarchically superior international criminal tribunal, a *compulsory* dispute settlement mechanism exists, namely, the tribunal making the request. The attribution to the requesting party of the task of settling disputes is undoubtedly the most fundamental deviation from the horizontal legal assistance model and most indicative of a legal assistance relationship based on a hierarchy paradigm.

In *Blaškić*, the ICTY claimed this as part of its inherent jurisdiction.[69] It then institutionalized it in Rule 7 *bis*. Unlike the statutes of the ad hoc tribunals, the ICC Statute explicitly regulates the settlement of disputes between states and the Court. Article 119(1) of the ICC Statute provides that '[a]ny dispute concerning the judicial functions of the Court shall be settled by the decision of the Court'.

and V. Nanda, *A Treatise on International Criminal Law. Volume II: Jurisdiction and Cooperation* (Springfield, Illinois: Thomas, 1973), at 230.

[66] For instance, Article 2(7) of the European Convention on Extradition, 13 December 1957, ETS 24; Article 5(2) of the European Convention on Mutual Assistance in Criminal Matters, 20 April 1959, ETS 30.

[67] See especially Rule 11 *bis* (D), providing for the transfer of the accused to national jurisdictions and the transfer of evidence in possession of the prosecutor.

[68] See K. Prost and A. Schlunck, 'Article 93', in Triffterer, *Commentary on the Rome Statute*, at 1117.

[69] *Blaškić* subpoena appeal decision, para. 68.

Questions concerning cooperation with, and legal assistance to, the Court may be considered part of the 'judicial functions of the Court'.[70] Therefore, by ratifying the Statute, in particular by accepting Article 119 of the ICC Statute, states parties have conceded the ultimate interpretation of the extent of the duty to cooperate to the requesting side, namely the ICC.

Evaluation

With respect to two important elements of a vertical cooperation regime, lack of reciprocity and the requesting court or tribunal being the final arbiter in cooperation disputes, there is practically no difference between the ad hoc tribunals and the ICC. The only distinction is that the extent of the obligations is slightly less in the case of the ICC, as a result of the presence of a number of grounds for refusal in the Statute. It is thus fair to characterize the ICTY and ICTR cooperation model as vertical and the ICC model as predominantly vertical. Does this mean that in practice the ad hoc tribunals and the ICC may count on a similar volume of assistance? Probably not. The problem is not so much the cooperation model itself as the model's limited scope of application in the case of the ICC, namely, only to the ICC states parties — which are still far fewer in number than UN members — and the lack of potentially strong enforcement support in the form of the UN Security Council.

Another question is how the internationalized criminal tribunals fit into the vertical cooperation model. One view is that the internationalized institutions for Sierra Leone and Cambodia also enjoy the benefit of vertical legal assistance regimes, albeit of limited application. On the basis of the bilateral agreements establishing these courts or tribunals the states concerned, Cambodia and Sierra Leone, have taken upon themselves full and unconditional cooperation obligations.[71] Other states, however, do not have any cooperation obligations towards those courts as such.[72] The situation of the East Timor and Kosovo courts is more complex, as they are part of temporary UN administrations. Certainly, one may discern obligations towards those administrations in general, for example obligations on the part of Yugoslavia towards UNMIK,[73] but it is far more difficult to pinpoint concrete cooperation duties in respect of the prosecution of international crimes. One may explain in this light the conclusion of a memorandum of understanding between UNTAET (East Timor) and Indonesia governing, among other things, the provision of legal assistance to the special panels.[74] The sensitivity inherent in the issue of the crimes committed in East Timor for Indonesia ensured that this legal assistance treaty does not represent a vertical cooperation relationship in the sense described above.[75]

---

[70] In this sense, R. Clark, 'Article 119', in Triffterer, *Commentary on the Rome Statute*, at 1245.

[71] Article 16 of the UN/Sierra Leone Agreement; Article 25 of the UN/Cambodia Agreement.

[72] Exception may be made for Liberia, which was specifically mentioned by the UN Security Council and called upon to cooperate fully with the SCSL (UNSC Res. 1478 (2003)). On this issue, see G. Sluiter, 'Legal Assistance to Internationalized Criminal Courts and Tribunals', at 402.   [73] See UNSC Res. 1244 (1999), para. 18.

[74] Memorandum of Understanding between the Republic of Indonesia and the United Nations Transitional Administration in East Timor Regarding Cooperation in Legal, Judicial and Human Rights Related Matters, Jakarta, 5 April 2000.

[75] For more details, see G. Sluiter, 'Legal Assistance to Internationalized Criminal Courts and Tribunals', at 391–3.

A common problem for all internationalized criminal tribunals is that they do not have a unilateral power to settle cooperation disputes, which is probably the most vital element of a vertical cooperation regime. The legal frameworks dealing with cooperation provide for the traditional horizontal approach of settling disputes on a footing of equality, by means of negotiation.[76]

It is thus safe to conclude that internationalized criminal tribunals do not enjoy the benefit of a vertical cooperation relationship with a plurality of states. The practical difficulties that this may entail are illustrated by, for example, the prosecution of Charles Taylor by the SCSL. Taylor relatively easily succeeded in staying out of the reach of the SCSL till late March 2006, that is, more than three years after being indicted by the SCSL.[77] This could have been anticipated, but the international community — especially the UN Security Council — did not consider it necessary to install a vertical cooperation regime.[78]

12.3.4 Duty to cooperate under international law

We now turn to the content and scope of the duty to cooperate under international law. For both states and international criminal tribunals, this is a matter of vital importance.

Legal basis

Before elaborating on the extent of the duty to cooperate, it is necessary to identify the legal basis of this duty. A distinction will be made between the ad hoc tribunals and the ICC.

For the ICTY and the ICTR, the first and most important legal basis of the duty to cooperate consists of the statutes, the Security Council resolutions establishing the tribunals, and ultimately the UN Charter.

In operative paragraph 4 of Resolution 827 (1993) the Security Council, acting under Chapter VII, deems that all states shall cooperate fully with the ICTY and its organs in accordance with the resolution and the tribunal's statute.[79] There can be no doubt from the wording of this resolution that it is intended to impose a duty to cooperate upon states. Security Council Resolutions 827 and 955, regarding the duty to cooperate, refer to all states and not only to UN members.[80] As far as non-member states are concerned, they are in principle not bound by the Charter and Security Council resolutions.[81] The practice of the ad hoc tribunals with respect to UN non-members is

---

[76] Article 15.2 of the MOU between Indonesia and UNTAET; Article 19 of the UN/Sierra Leone Agreement; and Article 29 of the UN/Cambodia Agreement.

[77] The indictment dated 7 March 2003 featured 17 counts of crimes against humanity, war crimes, and other serious violations of international humanitarian law (amended shortly before his arrest in Nigeria on 29 March 2006 and reducing the number of counts to 11).

[78] G. Sluiter, 'Legal Assistance to Internationalized Criminal Courts and Tribunals', at 382–8.

[79] See also the Security Council Resolution 955 (1994), containing identical language with respect to the ICTR.

[80] This is why V. Morris and M. P. Scharf assume that states that are not members of the UN are also obliged to cooperate, see Morris and Scharf, *Insider's Guide*, at 311; and Morris and Scharf, *International Criminal Tribunal for Rwanda*, at 638. As will be demonstrated, this position is shared in neither ICTY nor ICTR case law.

[81] Based on the adage *pacta tertiis nec nocent nec prosunt*, a general rule of international law, codified in Article 34 of the Vienna Convention on the Law of Treaties.

varied. The FRY has always been considered to be under a duty to cooperate, although there are doubts about its UN membership during a certain period of time.[82] Switzerland, on the other hand, was not regarded as being under a duty to cooperate with the tribunals, when it was not a UN member. For example, Judge Hunt, in confirming the indictment against Slobodan Milošević and others, also considered the issuing of certain orders requested by the prosecutor under Article 19(2) of the ICTY Statute.[83] One of the prosecutor's applications related to the issuing of arrest orders or warrants to all UN member states and Switzerland. In considering this request, Judge Hunt held:

States Members of the United Nations are bound to comply without undue delay with any order of the Tribunal for the arrest or detention of any person, but it is not suggested that the Confederation of Switzerland is similarly bound. The transmission of the certified copy of the

[82] For example, see Order to the Federal Republic of Yugoslavia for service of documents, *Prosecutor* v. *Mrksić et al.*, Case No. IT-95-13a, ICTY, T. Ch., 19 December 1997. The doubts as to the membership of the FRY of the UN are based on the following. In 1992, on the recommendation of the Security Council (Resolution 777 (1992), 19 September 1992), the General Assembly considered that the FRY could not continue automatically the membership of the former Socialist Federal Republic of Yugoslavia in the United Nations and should therefore apply for membership (see General Assembly Resolution 47/1, UN Doc. A/RES/47/1, 22 September 1992).

Nevertheless, the FRY always regarded itself as the legitimate successor of the Socialist Federal Republic of Yugoslavia (SFRY) and never evaded obligations vis-à-vis the ICTY on the basis of the argument that it was not a member of the UN. After Milošević was succeeded by Vojislav Koštunica, the FRY was readily admitted as a UN member (see Security Council Resolution 1326 (2000), recommending to the General Assembly to that effect). The Federal Republic of Yugoslavia was admitted as a member of the United Nations by General Assembly Resolution 55/12, UN Doc. A/RES/55/12, 1 November 2000. Consequently, one might argue that during the period from 22 September 1992 until 1 November 2000 the FRY was not a member of the United Nations. This is what the Netherlands, Belgium, Canada, the UK, and Germany argued before the ICJ in the case concerning the legality of the use of force against the FRY. These states argued that the ICJ did not have jurisdiction; the FRY was clearly not a member of the UN, because it had not reapplied for membership. Consequently, it was argued, the FRY could not be considered to be *ipso facto* a party to the ICJ Statute by virtue of Article 93, para. 1, of the UN Charter. See Legality of Use of Force, *Serbia and Montenegro* v. *Belgium*, ICJ, verbatim record of public sitting of 11 May 1999.

Matters are not so simple, however. The UN Secretariat permitted the permanent mission of the SFRY to the UN to continue to operate and accredited officials of the FRY as representatives of the SFRY mission. In that capacity, these representatives have circulated documents, participated in the work of various UN committees, and attended Security Council meetings as observers. What is more, the UN continued to collect the contribution of the FRY during this period. For further details, see N. Schrijver, 'Kroniek van het Internationaal Publiekrecht' (2001) 9 *Nederlands Juristenblad*, at 499–500; and S. Murphy, 'Barring of FRY representative at UN Security Council' (2000) 94 *AJIL*, at 677–8. Thus, in response to the arguments of some states in the ICJ case referred to above, the FRY referred to a letter it had received dated 29 September 1992 from the Legal Counsel of the UN Secretariat (UN Doc. A/47/485), which contends for its part that General Assembly Resolution 47/1 '[neither] terminate[d] nor suspend[ed] Yugoslavia's membership in the Organization', and that that resolution did not take away from Yugoslavia '[its] right to participate in the work of organs other than Assembly bodies' (Legality of Use of Force, *Serbia and Montenegro* v. *Belgium*, Order of 2 June 1999, *ICJ Reports*, especially at 124, 135–6 (para. 32 of the Order)). The ICJ refrained from giving its views on the UN membership ('Whereas, in view of its finding in paragraph 30 above, the Court need not consider this question for the purpose of deciding whether or not it can indicate provisional measures in the present case' (ibid., at 136)).

Finally, it should also be mentioned that the Security Council never considered the 'non-membership' to result in an absence of a duty on the FRY to cooperate. During the period from 1992 to 2000 the Council confirmed the FRY's duty to assist the ICTY and condemned it for non-compliance with this duty (see Security Council Resolution 1207 (1998)).

[83] Decision on Review of Indictment and Application for Consequential Orders, *Prosecutor* v. *Milošević et al.*, ICTY, T. Ch., 24 May 1999.

warrants to be sent to the Confederation of Switzerland should therefore *be expressed in terms of a request for assistance rather than an order*[84] (emphasis added).

Likewise, in a more recent decision in *Bagosora et al.* the ICTR Trial Chamber refused to order the Vatican to provide legal assistance:

The Chamber is not satisfied that the Defence has adequately demonstrated that the Tribunal has the authority to compel a non-member state of the United Nations to cooperate with it. The enforcement of any order issued pursuant to Article 28 is ultimately the responsibility of the Security Council acting under Chapter VII of the United Nations Charter. The Tribunal's coercive authority cannot exceed Chapter VII, which by its plain language imposes obligations on member states of the United Nations only.[85]

In addition to the UN Charter, an important basis for the duty to cooperate is the Dayton Peace Agreement, concluded between the states and one entity constituting the former Yugoslavia.[86] Although the essential purpose of this agreement is to restore and to maintain peace in the former Yugoslavia, assistance to the work of the ICTY is considered an important aspect of this purpose. According to the 1996 Annual Report of the ICTY, by signing the Dayton Accords the parties thereto have formally recognized the Tribunal and undertaken to cooperate with it.[87] The Agreement is particularly important as a legal basis for the duty of the FRY and the Republika Srpska to cooperate with the ICTY, in light of the doubts discussed above about the applicability of the UN Charter.

The ICTY has referred in its case law to the Dayton Agreement as an (additional) basis for the duty to cooperate. In the *Blaškić* case the Appeals Chamber held that the states and entities of the former Yugoslavia are obliged to cooperate with the Tribunal.[88] It also noted that this obligation was restated in the Dayton Agreement.[89] In the *Krstić* case Judge Jorda issued a binding order for the production of documents to Republika Srpska on 12 March 1999.[90] He based the order on Article 29 of the Statute and Rule 54 of the ICTY RPE, and had regard to the obligations of Republika Srpska under the Dayton Agreement.[91] Finally, in the *Karadžić and Mladić* case, reference was made to the Dayton Agreement, especially Republika Srpska's obligation under that treaty to cooperate with the Tribunal.[92]

---

[84] Ibid., para. 23.

[85] Decision on Defence Motion to Obtain Cooperation from the Vatican Pursuant to Article 28, *Prosecutor* v. *Bagosora et al.*, Case No. ICTR-98-41-T, ICTR, T. Ch., 13 May 2004, para. 3.

[86] General Framework Agreement for Peace in Bosnia and Herzegovina and the Annexes thereto, initialled in Dayton, Ohio on November 21, 1995, signed in Paris on 14 December 1995. The Dayton Agreement comprises the General Framework Agreement and 11 Annexes. For a discussion of the agreement, see J. Jones, 'The Implications of the Peace Agreement for the International Criminal Tribunal for the former Yugoslavia' (1996) 7 *European J. Int'l Law*, at 226–44 ; P. Akhavan, 'The Yugoslav Tribunal at a Crossroads: The Dayton Peace Agreement and Beyond' (1996) 18 *Human Rights Quarterly*, at 259–85, P. Gaeta, 'The Dayton Agreements and International Law' (1996) 7 *European J. Int'l Law*, at 147–63 ; F. Aolain, 'The Fractured Soul of the Dayton Peace Agreement: A Legal Analysis' (1998) 19 *Michigan J. Int'l Law*, at 957–1004.

[87] A/51/292, S/1996/665, para. 166, at 39.   [88] *Blaškić* subpoena appeal decision, para. 53.

[89] Ibid.

[90] Binding order to the Republika Srpska for the production of documents, *Prosecutor* v. *Krstić*, Case No. IT-98-33-PT, ICTY, T. Ch. I, 12 March 1999.   [91] Ibid.

[92] Review of the Indictments pursuant to Rule 61 of the Rules of Procedure and Evidence, *Prosecutor* v. *Karadžić and Mladić*, Case Nos IT-95-5-R61 and IT-95-18-R61, ICTY, T. Ch. I, 11 July 1996, para. 100.

In addition to the general duty to cooperate with the ad hoc tribunals under the UN Charter and, as far as the ICTY is concerned, also under the Dayton Agreement, some bilateral agreements have been concluded between the ad hoc tribunals, sometimes represented by the UN, and states, serving as a legal basis for specific forms of cooperation. These agreements include the headquarters agreements with the host states[93] and the surrender agreements concluded between the United States and the two tribunals.[94]

We turn now to the ICC. The picture here seems less complicated, although there are still some intriguing issues in determing the legal basis underlying the duty to provide legal assistance.

The first and obvious legal basis for the duty to cooperate is the Treaty of Rome, containing the ICC Statute. The question arises whether a possible legal basis for the duty of non-party states to cooperate may be identified. Compared to the ad hoc tribunals, the ICC will be confronted by a much larger number of non-party states, which are not bound by the Statute to cooperate with the Court. Nonetheless, these states' assistance may in certain investigations and prosecutions be crucial to the effective functioning of the Court. The drafters of the ICC have tried to come up with devices regulating the cooperation of a non-party state.

First of all, a non-party state may pursuant to Article 12(3) of the Statute accept the Court's jurisdiction on an ad hoc basis.[95] This entails the duty to cooperate with respect to a particular case, in accordance with Part 9 of the ICC Statute. As a result, with respect to a particular case the state will have accepted the same duties as a state party.

As far as states are concerned that are not (yet) parties and that have not accepted the Court's jurisdiction on an ad hoc basis, Article 87(5) of the Statute enables the Court to conclude ad hoc cooperation agreements with such states. The existence and extent of a duty to cooperate on the basis of an ad hoc arrangement depend entirely on its content. It could vary from assistance at the discretion of the non-party state with respect to a particular case, or even a particular act of assistance, to full cooperation by a state in accordance with the Statute.[96] One must bear in mind that a non-party state is in this respect in rather a strong negotiating position and can easily impose its own conditions of assistance.

---

[93] Agreement between the United Nations and the Kingdom of the Netherlands Concerning the Headquarters of the International Tribunal for the Prosecution of Persons Responsible for Serious Violations of International Humanitarian Law Committed in the Territory of the Former Yugoslavia Since 1991, S/1994/848, 19 July 1994 and Corrigendum, S/1994/848/Corr. 1, 25 August 1994 and Agreement between the United Nations and the United Republic of Tanzania Concerning the Headquarters of the International Tribunal for Rwanda, 3 August 1995, reprinted in the Appendix to the First Annual Report of the ICTR, UN Doc. A/51/399-S/1996/778. For a discussion, see Julian J. E. Schutte, 'Legal and Practical Implications, from the Perspective of the Host Country, Relating to the Establishment of the International Tribunal for the Former Yugoslavia' (1994) 5 *CLF*, at 423–50.

[94] Agreement on Surrender of Persons between the United States of America and the ICTY, 5 October 1994; Agreement on Surrender of Persons between the United States of America and the ICTR, 24 January 1995; for more details on those special agreements, see K. J. Harris and R. Kushen, 'Surrender of Fugitives to the War Crimes Tribunals for Yugoslavia and Rwanda: Squaring International Legal Obligations with the US Constitution' (1996) 7 *CLF*, at 561–604.

[95] An example here is Côte d'Ivoire, which has as a signatory state accepted the exercise of jurisdiction by the Court with respect to crimes committed in its territory since 19 September 2002 (press release of 15 February 2005, ICC Registry).

[96] An example of the latter is a signatory state which is expected to ratify the Statute in the near future, but whose cooperation is required urgently.

When we consider the legal basis of the duty to cooperate with the ICC, it is imperative to take into account the special role of the Security Council. According to Article 13 of the ICC Statute, the Security Council, when acting under Chapter VII of the UN Charter, may 'trigger' the jurisdiction of the Court by referring to the prosecutor a situation in which one or more of the crimes mentioned in Article 5 appear to have been committed.[97] The Statute is silent on what this means for the duty of states to cooperate. One may indeed envisage that — in the interests of international peace and security — the duty to assist the ICC in the case of a Security Council referral is extended to all UN members. The referral of the situation in Darfur (Sudan) to the ICC by Resolution 1593 (2005) reflects, however, a more minimalistic approach. Operative paragraph 2 of that Resolution provides as follows:

Decides that the Government of Sudan and all other parties to the conflict in Darfur, shall cooperate fully with and provide any necessary assistance to the Court and the Prosecutor pursuant to this resolution and, while recognizing that States not party to the Rome Statute have no obligation under the Statute, urges all States and concerned regional and other international organizations to cooperate fully.

The fact that duties are not imposed on non-party states other than Sudan can be explained in light of the still strong opposition to the ICC of the USA and other members of the Security Council.[98] The duty imposed upon Sudan raises a number of questions. First, what is meant by 'cooperate fully'? As no reference to the Statute is made this leaves us very much in the dark. The implications are far from clear; one may be tempted to infer from 'full cooperation' a limited or no role for the principle of complementarity, in deviation from the Statute. The argument would then be that the principle of complementarity may hinder full cooperation and, as a result, is not envisaged by the Council to apply.[99] Operating on the assumption that the Council intends Sudan to cooperate in accordance with the obligations set out in the Statute for states parties, one can identify a number of problems. For example, to what extent can Article 88 be applicable to Sudan? This provision obliges states parties to have procedures available under national law for all forms of cooperation set out in Part 9 of the Statute.

---

[97] The possibility of the Security Council referring 'cases' to the Court had already been recognized in Article 23(1) of the 1994 ILC Draft Statute for an International Criminal Court (Report of the International Law Commission, 46th session, 2 May–22 July 1994, UNGAOR A/49/10, at 84). However, within the compilation of proposals forming the basis for the negotiations in Rome, the possibility of the Security Council submitting cases to the ICC was only mentioned as an option in square brackets (see UN Doc. A/CONF.183/2/Add.1, at 34).

On the relationship between the ICC and the Security Council, see L. Yee, 'The International Criminal Court and The Security Council: Articles 13 (b) and 16', in Lee, *Making of the Rome Statute*, at 143–52.

[98] In this respect, see operative paragraph 6 of Resolution 1593, building upon SC Resolutions 1422, 1487, and 1497:

Decides that nationals, current or former officials or personnel from a contributing State outside Sudan which is not a party to the Rome Statute of the International Criminal Court shall be subject to the exclusive jurisdiction of that contributing State for all alleged acts or omissions arising out of or related to operations in Sudan established or authorized by the Council or the African Union, unless such exclusive jurisdiction has been expressly waived by that contributing State.

[99] In support of the view that the principle of complementarity does not apply to Security Council referrals see G. P. Fletcher and J. D. Ohlin, 'The ICC — Two Courts in One?' (2006) 4 *JICJ*, at 428–33.

While its validity is justified for states which have ample opportunity to prepare ratification, its application to Sudan appears unreasonable. But does this then mean, for example, that Sudan can pursuant to Article 89(1) of the Statute use national procedural law as an obstacle to surrender of persons to the Court? This is highly uncertain, absent more detailed clarification from the Security Council of what it means by full cooperation. Secondly, there is a problem in respect of the addressees of the duty to cooperate. As Sudan is not addressed as a state, but as a 'government' and 'other parties to the conflict', the question arises whether the national courts are in fact envisaged. In other words, does a refusal to cooperate by Sudanese courts fall outside the scope of application of Resolution 1593, bearing in mind the separation of powers between the executive and judicial branches?

In light of the problems indicated one can but conclude that the first Security Council referral is highly problematic from the perspective of state cooperation. Not only is the ICC Statute, which contains hardly any separate rules pertaining to Security Council referrals, deficient but the Council has also failed to provide for an adequate legal framework in the referring resolution.

Besides the above-mentioned legal bases for a 'general' duty to provide legal assistance mention should also be made of future agreements that will regulate specific aspects of the functioning of the Court, and may thereby serve as the legal basis for particular obligations. Examples are the Agreement on the Privileges and Immunities of the Court, the Headquarters Agreement with the Netherlands, and agreements regulating the enforcement of sentences imposed by the Court.[100]

It follows from the above that for the ICC also there are many legal bases for the duty to cooperate. The applicable legal basis will depend on the nature of the assistance sought, and from which state it is sought. When we examine below the content of the duty to cooperate, the focus will for the sake of simplicity be on the duty to cooperate as governed by the UN Charter (ICTY and ICTR) and the ICC Statute.

Content of the duty to cooperate

In respect of the ICTY and ICTR it has been said that the duty to cooperate is absolute and unconditional. However, this is too broad a generalization. It is true that the Appeals Chamber emphasized in *Blaškić* that no state can unilaterally invoke a ground of refusal and deny a request or order on that ground.[101] However, this is merely to say that the Tribunal, given the vertical relationship with states, is the ultimate judge of the legitimacy and applicability of a ground of refusal. The Tribunal may adopt the same view as a state and rule that there is indeed a legitimate ground to deny a request. The Appeals Chamber, to that effect, explicitly held that the Tribunal should not be insensitive to 'legitimate state concerns'.[102]

It is thus not correct to say that there are no grounds to refuse or postpone cooperation. States should be aware that there is room for review of a request or order; this

---

[100] The first such agreement is the Agreement between the ICC and the Federal Government of Austria on the Enforcement of Sentences of the ICC, signed 27 October 2005, ICC-PRES-A103-AT-05.
[101] *Blaškić* subpoena appeal decision, para. 65.   [102] Ibid., para. 67.

may even be desirable.[103] The difficulty in identifying possible grounds for refusal is to ascertain what the 'legitimate state concerns' are to which the tribunals must give consideration. On the basis of the unique relationship between states and the tribunals and on the basis of case law, it is possible to indicate grounds of refusal which, in all likelihood, the tribunals may also recognize as valid reasons to withhold cooperation. Probably the easiest way to identify these grounds is to look at inter-state practice and examine whether grounds of refusal in that context have any relevance or validity in the relationship with the ad hoc tribunals. Some examples are considered below.

In the inter-state context it is still quite common for certain states to refuse to extradite their own nationals.[104] There is, however, no reason to apply this ground of refusal to the transfer of accused persons to the ad hoc tribunals.[105] Nevertheless, the non-extradition of nationals, especially when it has constitutional status, tends to be advanced as one of the major obstacles in the ICC ratification process.[106] Other typical grounds for refusing assistance in the inter-state context are the political offence exception, the double criminality requirement, and the *ne bis in idem* condition. The political offence exception is based on a number of grounds, including non-intervention in the internal matters of other states.[107] For crimes within the tribunals' jurisdiction this ground cannot be considered applicable. Even in traditional extradition law, crimes within the jurisdiction of the tribunals are generally acknowledged to be excluded from the political offence exception.[108]

The double criminality requirement means that the act for which extradition or transfer has been requested constitutes an offence according to the laws of both the requesting and the requested party. The requirement is based on the position that a state should not assist in the prosecution of conduct which it deems itself not to constitute 'criminal behaviour'. This ground for refusal may seem appropriate for

---

[103] In particular in the case of requests from the prosecutor. However, the judges also may err. In the case of the return of Dragan Opačić, a witness in *Tadić*, to Bosnia, it could be argued that the Tribunal failed to ascertain that he would not be mistreated while in detention there. The major difficulty in that case was of course that the Tribunal had given its word to the government of Bosnia and Herzegovina to return Opačić after testimony, pursuant to Rule 90 *bis*. See Order for the return of a detained witness, *Prosecutor* v. *Tadić*, Case No. IT-94-1-T, ICTY, T. Ch., 27 May 1997.

[104] The FRY has to date invoked this ground as a justification for refusing to transfer indicted war crimes suspects of Yugoslav nationality. It may also be a problem for other civil-law European states. See for further details S. O'Shea, 'Interaction Between International Criminal Tribunals and National Legal Systems' (1995–6) 28 *New York University J. Int'l Law and Politics*, at 389–92.

[105] It should be noted that the term 'extradition' has been deliberately avoided in the legal frameworks of the ad hoc tribunals. The objective clearly is to prevent the application of 'extradition-related' obstacles to transfer. See also Rule 58 which declares inapplicable domestic impediments to transfer.

[106] See Second Report of the International Law Association's Committee on the ICC, submitted to the Toronto Conference, June 2006, available at www.ila-hq.org/html/layout_committee.htm (last visited 9 November 2006), at 3.

[107] See C. Van den Wyngaert, *The Political Offence Exception to Extradition: The Delicate Problem of Balancing the Rights of the Individual and the International Public Order* (Deventer/Boston: Kluwer, 1980), at 2–4.

Note also how the Netherlands justified — in part — the refusal to extradite the German Emperor to a 'special tribunal', as envisaged by the Versailles Treaty (1919): 'ni une respectable tradition séculaire qui a fait de ce pays de tout temps une terre de refuge pour les vaincus des conflits internationaux, ne permettent au Gouvernement des Pays-Bas de déférer au désir des Puissances en retirant à l'ex-empereur le bénéfice de . . . cette tradition' (Dutch diplomatic note of 21 January 1920 to the Allies, as cited in Cassese, *International Criminal Law*, at 328).

[108] See Article 7 of the Genocide Convention and the 1975 Additional Protocol to the European Convention on Extradition; for a more detailed analysis, see C. Van den Wyngaert, *The Political Offence Exception to Extradition: The Delicate Problem of Balancing the Rights of the Individual and the International Public Order*, at 139–47.

certain offences, but not in the case of the most serious international crimes.[109] It should be emphasized that a duty exists under international law to make most of the crimes set out in the Statutes punishable offences under domestic law.[110]

Another common ground of refusal in inter-state cooperation in criminal matters is *ne bis in idem*. According to this ground, a state may refuse to comply with a request for assistance if this request concerns prosecution for an offence for which the accused has already been tried. The Statutes of the ad hoc tribunals contain a specific *ne bis in idem* regulation, according to which, with two exceptions, a person who has been tried by a national court may not be tried again by the tribunal. This provision could serve, under certain circumstances, as a ground of refusal, but its scope of application is of course determined by the tribunal.[111]

Finally, there are in legal assistance treaties between states provisions which authorize the requested state to deny a request if this is likely to prejudice the sovereignty, security, *ordre public*, or other essential interests of its country.[112] 'Sovereignty', 'security', and possibly also 'other essential interests' are closely related grounds for refusal and can be treated together as 'sovereignty-related' grounds of refusal. With respect to these grounds, it is important to note that the very establishment of the ad hoc tribunals and their primacy over national courts already constitute an infringement of national sovereignty. The ICTY Appeals Chamber held in the *Tadić* case that such infringement was fully justified on the basis of the UN Charter, in particular the restriction of national sovereignty in favour of the mandate of the UN Security Council.[113] Consequently, where the duty to cooperate would infringe upon a state's sovereignty, the justification ultimately lies in Article 2(7) of the UN Charter.[114] The Appeals Chamber of the ICTY emphasized in the *Blaškić* subpoena decision that 'sovereignty-related' interests cannot unilaterally be invoked as grounds for withholding assistance. In addition to the general argument that these grounds are not applicable to the special relationship with the ad hoc tribunals, the Appeals Chamber also correctly referred to their subject-matter jurisdiction, which of necessity often deals

---

[109] Yet, Switzerland has incorporated the double criminality requirement in its implementing law regulating cooperation with the ad hoc tribunals (see English translation printed in 1995 ICTY Yearbook, at 325 *et seq.*). Article 10(1) of that law setting out the conditions for transfer provides as follows:

> Any person may be transferred for criminal prosecution to the international tribunal concerned if the request and the attached documents show that the offence:
>
> a. falls within the jurisdiction of the international tribunal, and
> b. it is punishable under Swiss law.

[110] This is certainly the case when a treaty imposes this obligation upon a state party. If the crime is not the object of a treaty, such as crimes against humanity, the duty to penalize this offence under domestic law might be found in customary international law. As to whether customary international law obliges states to prosecute international crimes, see Cassese, *International Criminal Law*, at 301–3.

[111] For the scope of this provision see below, section 12.4.

[112] See, as an example, Article 2(b) of the European Convention on Mutual Assistance in Criminal Matters (1959). In extradition treaties, these grounds for refusal do not play a prominent role, with the exception of the *ordre public* clause.

[113] See *Tadić* jurisdiction appeal decision, paras 55–60; see also the Separate Opinion of Judge Sidhwa to this decision, in particular para. 86 and the commentary of H. Fischer in Klip and Sluiter, *Annotated Leading Cases, vol. I*, at 140–2.   [114] Confirmed in the *Blaškić* subpoena appeal decision, para. 65.

with military issues.[115] There appears thus to be a general inclination at the tribunals not to honour sovereignty-related grounds of refusal.[116] However, legitimate state concerns could very well include essential national interests, including national security interests. Although the tribunal will always try to reconcile the (legitimate) interests of a requested state with those of the tribunal,[117] possibly by amending the request, in certain circumstances the interests of the requested state may prevail.

A situation in which the ICTY and the ICTR clearly are to be expected to take a refusal seriously is when the refusal is occasioned by reasons which are central to the functioning of the tribunals. As examples one may mention violation of internationally protected human rights arising from the execution of a request for assistance, or determination that a request for assistance is in (clear) violation of the tribunal's own rules and procedures.[118] These are legitimate state concerns, but they also affect the tribunal's own *ordre public*. It is on this last basis that those grounds of refusal, when validly raised, are most likely to be accepted.

Compared to the statutes of the ad hoc tribunals, the ICC Statute spells out in far more detail the content of cooperation obligations incumbent upon states parties. A central provision is Article 86, which imposes upon states parties a general duty to provide legal assistance to the Court. This general duty is divided into more specific duties, namely:

(1) the duty to comply with requests for surrender (Article 89);

(2) the duty to comply with requests for other forms of cooperation (Article 93);

(3) the duty to comply with requests for assistance, including on-site investigations (Article 99);

(4) the duty for the host state to execute sentences of imprisonment (Article 103(4)); and

(5) the duty to comply with requests for the execution of fines and forfeiture and reparation orders (Article 109, see also Article 75).

However, the Statute contains certain grounds of refusal, which makes for a reduced cooperation duty compared to the ICTY and the ICTR. The insertion in the ICC Statute of certain grounds for refusing and postponing legal assistance is the result of protracted and sometimes painful negotiations between those for and against imposing far-reaching obligations on states towards the Court.[119] In view of these long and complex negotiations, one may argue that states may advance no other grounds for refusing or postponing assistance. However, this view does not conform with a systematic

---

[115] Ibid.

[116] This was also emphasized by criticizing domestic laws which made cooperation with the tribunals conditional upon the absence of prejudice to sovereignty, security, or national interests: ibid., para. 66.

[117] In the *Blaškić* subpoena appeal decision a number of possible practical steps were proposed with the aim of making allowance for legitimate national security concerns, see paras 67–9.

[118] For more detail, see G. Sluiter, *International Criminal Adjudication and the Collection of Evidence: Obligations of States*, at 199–202.

[119] For an account of this aspect of the drafting history, see P. Mochochoko, 'International Cooperation and Judicial Assistance', in Lee, *Making of the Rome Statute*, at 310–14.

interpretation of the Statute. The duty to consult, as set out in Article 97 of the ICC Statute, is not necessarily confined to problems regarding the implementation of the request related to one of the grounds of refusal set out in the Statute. It is then, of course, for the Court to decide whether grounds for refusal not mentioned in the Statute carry sufficient weight to justify refusal of the request.

The grounds for refusal in the Statute are the result of a compromise. Some of them are understandable or even inevitable, taking account of the fact that the ICC is a new international organization established by sovereign states. The refusal of assistance if this would prejudice a state's national security (Articles 93(4) and 72 of the ICC Statute) or if there is a conflicting request for assistance (Article 90 of the Statute) are examples of this type. Other grounds for refusal that are specified in the Statute can be regarded as less fortunate in the framework of an international criminal court with jurisdiction over the most serious crimes and to which states adhere voluntarily. An example is Article 93(3) of the ICC Statute which allows states to refuse assistance 'on the basis of an existing fundamental legal principle of general application'. The Statute of the ICC, in particular the priority accorded to human rights pursuant to Article 21(3), offers sufficient safeguards to make such a ground for refusal unnecessary.

One must also look with some suspicion at the grounds for postponing the execution of requests for assistance in Articles 94 and 95 of the ICC Statute. Their application may be especially harmful for urgent requests. Furthermore, it remains to be seen how states interpret the various references to domestic procedural law with respect to the implementation of requests for assistance.[120] States may even use procedural law as an impediment or excuse for delay in the implementation of cooperation requests. The practice of the so-called bilateral immunity agreements between the USA and a number of ICC states parties, pursuant to Article 98(2), offers a dangerous precedent as to the good-faith interpretation of cooperation duties.[121]

The question arises whether the presence of a number of grounds for refusal in the ICC Statute may prevent it from fulfilling its mandate. It is true that the Court faces greater difficulties in the field of legal assistance than the ad hoc tribunals. The latter not only benefit from more extensive obligations for states to cooperate, but also can rely, at least on paper, on the assistance of practically every state in the world.

---

[120] See Articles 89(1), 93(1), and 99(1).

[121] The central provision of the so-called BIAs (bilateral immunity agreements) is the following:

> Persons of one Party present in the territory of the other shall not, absent the expressed consent of the first Party, (a) be surrendered or transferred by any means to the International Criminal Court for any purpose, or (b) be surrendered or transferred by any means to any other entity or third country, or expelled to a third country, for the purpose of surrender to or transfer to the International Criminal Court.

The position of the USA is that such agreements are 'expressly contemplated' by Article 98(2) of the ICC Statute (Statement of Ambassador Negroponte, United States Permanent Representative to the UN, 12 July 2002). Commentators are highly critical as to whether (1) the conclusion of a BIA is compatible with being a loyal state party to the ICC ('Organisationstreue'), and (2) the envisaged scope of application of the BIA falls within the ambit of Article 98(2). See Joint Opinion by J. Crawford, P. Sands, and R. Wilde (at the request of Lawyers' Committee on Human Rights, available at www.iccnow.org/documents/SandsCrawfordBIA14June03.pdf (last visited 9 November 2006) and S. Zappalà, 'The Reaction of the US to the Entry into Force of the ICC Statute: Comments on UN SC Resolution 1422 (2002) and Article 98 Agreements' (2003) 1 *JICJ*, at 114–34.

Nevertheless, it is not the presence of certain grounds for refusal in the Statute that constitute the greatest threat to the functioning of the ICC. It is rather the defective regulation of certain important forms of assistance that raises most concerns. Two examples may be considered. The experiences of the ad hoc tribunals illustrate the importance of live testimony in the courtroom and the conduct of on-site investigations. One would expect the ICC Statute to contain strong obligations for states to provide these forms of assistance. Surprisingly, this is not the case. Under the ICC Statute witnesses cannot be compelled to testify (Article 93(1)(e) and 93(7)).[122] This implies that witnesses may frequently have to be heard outside the courtroom, which will undoubtedly have an impact on the probative value of the testimony. As to the conduct of on-site investigations, there was strong opposition in Rome from certain delegations which felt that investigations on their territory were too great an intrusion on their sovereignty. The final compromise is that there is only a very limited duty for states parties to allow on-site investigations on their territory, and then only to be conducted by the prosecutor (Article 99(4)).[123] One may indeed wonder how investigations and prosecutions can be completed successfully if all actors involved in the proceedings, namely the prosecutor, the defendant, and the judges, cannot familiarize themselves with the scene of the crime and conduct investigations there, or can do so only with great difficulty.[124]

12.3.5 Enforcement of the duty to cooperate

The credibility and force of a legal duty depend on the possibilities of enforcement of this duty. Although the enforcement of obligations under international law is a highly politicized matter, the presence of adequate legal procedures remains of great importance. Therefore, a brief inquiry will be made into the legal remedies available to international criminal tribunals to enforce compliance.

It is important to note that enforcement of cooperation by states does not fall within the mandates of the ad hoc tribunals, but rather it is to be left to others who are better equipped to actually enforce cooperation. This becomes apparent when one reads the statutes and the RPE. Furthermore, it has been firmly established by the Appeals Chamber in the *Blaškić* case that the ICTY 'is not vested with any enforcement or sanctionary power vis-à-vis States'.[125] The question then arises as to the means that are available to the tribunals to make others enforce cooperation. There are essentially two options. First, the judges of the tribunals may make a judicial finding of non-compliance and, secondly, they may report it to the Security Council.

---

[122] See Chapter 10, section 10.5.3.

[123] For the consequences for the equality of arms of the limitation of the scope of this provision to the prosecutor, see Chapter 8, section 8.5.1.

[124] In this respect it must be noted that the unfortunate regulation of on-site investigations in the ICC Statute already seems to have had an impact on the practical application of the principle of complementarity. The negotiated self-referrals concerning the Congo, Uganda, and the Central African Republic seem to be in part the result of the fact that an uncooperative state may easily frustrate on-site investigations (P. Gaeta, 'Is the Practice of "Self-Referrals" a Sound Start for the ICC?', at 951: 'If the territorial State is uncooperative then the investigations *in situ* will be practically impossible'). [125] *Blaškić* subpoena appeal decision, para. 33.

As far as a finding of non-compliance is concerned, the Trial Chamber in the *Blaškić* case considered this to be in itself a sanctionary power vis-à-vis the non-complying state. On the question of what the 'penalty' could be in the case of a subpoena issued to a state, the Trial Chamber considered that '[t]he "penalty" may be no more than a finding that a State has failed in its duty to comply with an order, which itself is a censure and form of penalty'.[126] The Appeals Chamber did not consider such a finding to be penal in nature, and to pave the way for the issue of a subpoena, but it may have accepted that such a finding was a means of enforcing cooperation. It is also possible that it merely regarded the making of a finding of non-compliance as an indispensable step to real enforcement measures, to be taken by the Security Council or states. In any case, risk of a judicial finding of non-compliance may already be an important tool in enforcing cooperation.

The power to report to the Security Council judicial findings of non-compliance is not based on the Statute. The Appeals Chamber derives this power from the relationship between the two tribunals and the Council.[127] In other words, this power is neither an explicit power set out in the Statute, nor an inherent power, but it is a corollary of the fact that the Tribunal is a subsidiary organ of the Security Council.

The power to report to the Security Council instances of non-compliance with tribunal requests or orders has been implemented in the Rules of Evidence and Procedure. Initially, until July 1997, the possibility to report non-compliance was the object of Rules 11, 13, 59, and 61. Rule 11 deals with non-compliance with a request for deferral, which may result in the Trial Chamber requesting the president of the Tribunal to report the matter to the Security Council. Rule 13 is concerned with discontinuance of proceedings for a crime for which a person has already been tried by the Tribunal. If a national court fails to give effect to a Trial Chamber request to discontinue the proceedings, the president may report the matter to the Security Council. Rule 59 focuses on the failure of a state to execute an arrest warrant or transfer order. In such a situation the Tribunal may, through the president, notify the Security Council. Finally, the Rule 61 procedure, which consists of a review of the indictment in case of non-execution of an arrest warrant and transfer order, provides for notification to the Security Council by the Tribunal's president (see Rule 61(E)). In addition to these rules, a new Rule 7 *bis* was adopted at the 13th plenary session of the judges, held on 24 and 25 July 1999.[128] This rule is a kind of residual clause, for when the Tribunal wishes to notify the Security Council of situations of non-compliance which are not covered by the other rules.[129] According to Rule 7 *bis* (A), a situation of non-compliance not covered by Article 29 may be reported by the president to the Security Council, on the advice of a judge or Trial Chamber. This provision is mainly intended to cover orders issued under Rule 54, such as the production of evidence. Rule 7 *bis* (B) allows the prosecutor to report non-cooperation by a state to the president of the Tribunal, who shall then submit the matter to the Security Council. Expanding Rule 7 *bis* to other instances of

---

[126] *Blaškić* subpoena trial decision, para. 62.   [127] *Blaškić* subpoena appeal decision, para. 33.

[128] See Fourth Annual Report of the ICTY, UN Doc. A/52/375, S/1997/729, para. 56.

[129] For more detail, see Daryl A. Mundis, 'Reporting Non-Compliance: Rule 7bis', in May et al., *Essays on ICTY Procedure and Evidence*, at 421–38.

non-compliance and opening up the procedure to the prosecutor seems to meet the practical needs of the tribunals.

The rules all speak of 'notifying the Security Council' or 'submitting the matter to the Security Council'. What is to be understood by these general terms? Should the Tribunal merely report the facts to the Council? Or may it also make suggestions as to appropriate enforcement measures to be taken?

In the *Blaškić* subpoena decision, the Appeals Chamber clearly indicated that the Tribunal should simply report the judicial finding of non-compliance to the Council. It held that '[t]he finding by the International Tribunal must not include any recommendations or suggestions as to the course of action the Security Council may wish to take as a consequence of that finding'.[130]

The ICTY president, in particular, has reported a number of instances of non-compliance to the Security Council, all involving states of the former Yugoslavia.[131] The outcome of those reports is difficult to measure. Although the reports may not always produce the desired resulted — full compliance with cooperation requests — they undoubtedly have a political impact, including isolation of the state concerned. A further important element of those reports is that they have never been substantively challenged by the Security Council; as a result, the Council has effectively acceded to the claim of the ICTY to a vertical cooperation regime.

In the case of the ICC the mechanisms of enforcement differ depending on the legal basis underlying the duty to provide assistance.

We shall first examine the enforcement of the duties of the contracting parties under the ICC Statute. Pursuant to Article 87(7) of the Statute, there is a clear chronological order in the steps to be taken to induce compliance with a request for assistance. The Court first makes a judicial finding of non-compliance where a state party fails to comply with a request to cooperate with the Court, in contravention of the provisions of the Statute. After a *judicial* finding of non-compliance, the Court may refer the matter to the Assembly of States Parties. The possibility for the prosecutor directly to submit a report of non-compliance to the Assembly is thus excluded. Although the Assembly was established by the ICC Statute, it is difficult to see it as part of the 'Court'. Article 1 of the ICC Statute establishes the Court and Article 112(1) establishes the Assembly of States Parties. Their separate character is confirmed by Article 34 of the Statute, which does not include the Assembly as an organ of the Court. The Assembly has, pursuant to Article 112, a number of tasks, including to 'consider pursuant to article 87, paragraphs 5 and 7, any question relating to non-cooperation' (Article 112(2)(f) of the ICC Statute). The fact that the Statute is silent on measures to be adopted vis-à-vis a

---

[130] *Blaškić* subpoena appeal decision, para. 36.

[131] For instance, on the continued non-cooperation by the FRY with the Tribunal see the letter sent from the President of the Tribunal, Judge Gabrielle Kirk McDonald, to the President of the Security Council on 16 March 1999, press release of 18 March 1999, JL/PIU/386-E and the letter from President Jorda dated 23 October 2002, press release of 23 October 2003, JDH/PIS/706-e; on the non-cooperation by Croatia, President McDonald's letter to the Security Council dated 25 August 1999, press release of 25 August 1999, CC/PIS/433-E. Several cases of non-compliance on behalf of the FRY, Croatia, and Bosnia and Herzegovina were reported in the final letter of President McDonald to the Security Council on the outstanding issues of state non-compliance dated 2 November 1999, press release of 2 November 1999, JL/PIS/444-E.

state in breach of its obligation to cooperate is surprising and makes one wonder how effective the responses by the Assembly to violations of the duty to cooperate will be. There is also some inconsistency in relation to a state's other duties under the Statute. If a state party fails to meet its obligations regarding the financing of the Court, the Statute provides for a specific sanction: the state shall, depending on the extent of the breach, have no vote in the Assembly and in the Bureau.[132] It is probable that similar measures could also be taken in relation to a state that is in breach of its duty to provide legal assistance to the Court.

Article 87(5)(b) of the ICC Statute provides for the possibility for the Court to submit to the Assembly a report on a violation of the duty to cooperate pursuant to an ad hoc agreement concluded between the Court and a non-party state. It is implied that the non-party state, by virtue of the above agreement, has agreed to the possibility of such a submission. However, it should be borne in mind that a non-party state whose cooperation is required is in a strong negotiating position and may wish to provide ad hoc assistance subject to a number of conditions, which may in principle exclude the involvement of the Assembly. Even if a non-party state accepts the role of the Assembly in enforcing the duty to cooperate, one may seriously question the effectiveness of the Assembly in this respect. What actions could it possibly take to convince a non-party state to comply with the terms of the ad hoc cooperation agreement? There is no vote in the Assembly to take away, and no financial contribution to increase.

Finally, one has to consider the situation in which the Court exercises jurisdiction following the referral of a case to it by the Security Council. When a state party fails to cooperate under the Statute with respect to an investigation or prosecution triggered by a Security Council deferral, Article 87(7) of the ICC Statute is applicable and the Court may make a judicial finding of non-cooperation. However, the next step is different. Instead of the Court referring the finding of non-compliance to the Assembly, it must submit the finding to the Security Council. This difference can be explained in part by the fact that the Council, in referring a case to the prosecutor, is acting under Chapter VII of the UN Charter. This means that the interests of international peace and security demand effective prosecution. Should effective prosecution be impossible, the same interests of international peace and security require that the Council be informed. The drafters of the Statute seem to have considered the Council to be the appropriate sole exclusive enforcement mechanism in these circumstances. This view may be based on the absence of any relationship between non-party states and the Assembly of States Parties, as well as on the logic of preventing possible overlaps between the Security Council and Assembly enforcement mechanisms. This goes a long way towards explaining why Article 87(7) of the Statute does not attribute any enforcement role to the Assembly in the case of a prosecution triggered by the Security Council. One may, however, wonder whether giving the Security Council sole competence is a wise choice. For various reasons, the Council may not wish to respond, or is not in a legal position to respond, to breaches of the duty to provide assistance under the Statute. Should the Council not respond, it is desirable that the Assembly remain in a position to deal with

---

[132] See Article 112(8) of the ICC Statute.

violations of the duty to cooperate by contracting parties, as the latter violate obligations not only under the UN Charter, but also under the ICC Statute.

As to the internationalized courts, they enjoy limited enforcement mechanisms. The first problem is that — in respect of states whose assistance is most needed — three internationalized courts, East Timor, Cambodia, and Sierra Leone, seem to lack a formal and direct enforcement mechanism. The relevant agreements stipulate that (cooperation) disputes need to be settled through negotiation.[133] Yet, those internationalized courts remain free to state that in their opinion cooperation duties have been breached. The Rules of the SCSL provide for an alternative to Rule 7 *bis* of the ICTY and ICTR; Rule 8 of the SCSL allows a trial chamber, when failure to cooperate on the part of Sierra Leone has been established, to 'refer the matter to the President to take appropriate action'. What is to be understood by appropriate action is uncertain, but one can imagine that in the absence of an institutionalized enforcement mechanism it includes raising political support for the Court's position and, as a result, increasing the pressure on the Sierra Leone authorities to effect compliance. One may also imagine reporting non-compliance to the Security Council, but the latter may only employ enforcement measures if the failure to cooperate raises concerns about international peace and security. The Security Council might be more inclined to respond to the Kosovo and East Timor courts, which are — albeit indirectly — the result of the Security Council's initiative to set up temporary administrations for those regions. The Cambodian Extraordinary Chambers and the SCSL do not have similar ties to the Council, even though the SCSL was set up at the request of the Council.[134]

12.4 AUTHORITY OF FINAL JUDGMENTS:
NE BIS IN IDEM[135]

The authority and effect of judgments in a transjurisdictional context is a matter that marks the end of proceedings in jurisdiction A and the beginning of proceedings in jurisdiction B. In the relationship between international criminal tribunals and national jurisdictions there are essentially two questions regarding the authority of final judgments. The first concerns the effect of final judgments of international criminal tribunals for national proceedings, the second, conversely, arises in respect of the effect of national judgments for the proceedings of international criminal tribunals. In this section we explore those questions in the light of the principle of *ne bis in idem*, according to which an individual should not be tried twice for the same conduct.

---

[133] Article 15.2 of the MOU between Indonesia and UNTAET; Article 19 of the UN/Sierra Leone Agreement; and Article 29 of the UN/Cambodia Agreement.   [134] See Chapter 1, section 1.2.4.

[135] For a thorough analysis, see C. Van den Wyngaert and T. Ongena, '*Ne bis in idem* Principle, Including the Issue of Amnesty', in Cassese et al., *Rome Statute Commentary*, at 705–29, and I. Tallgren, 'Article 20', in Triffterer, *Commentary on the Rome Statute*, at 419–34.

The starting point for all international and internationalized criminal courts is the human rights context. Among other instruments, Article 14(7) ICCPR and Article 4 of the Seventh Protocol to the ECHR protect an individual from being tried again for conduct for which he or she has already been convicted or acquitted. Obviously, this right should also be protected by international criminal tribunals. All accused persons tried in international and internationalized criminal proceedings enjoy *ne bis in idem* protection.[136] In two instances, Kosovo and Cambodia, this protection follows from the direct applicability of international human rights instruments, especially the ICCPR. This raises, of course, the question of the scope of application of Article 14(7) ICCPR. The most problematic issue is that this provision is said not to guarantee *ne bis in idem* with respect to the national jurisdictions of two or more states, but only to prohibit double jeopardy with regard to an offence adjudicated in a given state.[137] It is to be expected that the internationalized courts for Kosovo and Cambodia offer a broader interpretation, which is also more in line with other internationalized and international criminal tribunals, and do not prosecute an individual again for conduct for which he or she has already been convicted or acquitted, unless the exceptions discussed below apply.

The most complete *ne bis in idem* protection is offered by the ICC Statute. Article 20 takes all possible *ne bis in idem* situations into account: first, internal (the right not to be tried twice by the ICC, Article 20(1)); secondly, external, from the state perspective, also referred to as 'downward *ne bis in idem*' (the right not to be tried again by another court after ICC acquittal or conviction (Article 20(2)); and thirdly, external, from the ICC perspective, also referred to as 'upward *ne bis in idem*' (the right not to be tried again by the ICC after acquittal or conviction by another court). Remarkably, other international and internationalized criminal tribunals, with the exception of the East Timor special panels,[138] overlook internal *ne bis in idem* protection and deal only with the upward and downward situations.[139]

There are common elements in how the international and internationalized criminal tribunals have regulated upward and downward *ne bis in idem* protection. These common elements embody national courts' aspirations for a vertical relationship. In the downward *ne bis in idem* situation this is reflected in the unconditional duty of states to respect the final international judgment; the upward *ne bis in idem* situation, however, contains important exceptions. For the ICTR, the ICTY, and the SCSL these exceptions are that the act for which the accused was tried was characterized as an ordinary crime; or that the national court proceedings and were not impartial or independent,

---

[136] Article 9 of the ICTR Statute, Article 10 of the ICTY Statute, Article 20 of the ICC Statute, UNMIK Regulation 1999/24 on applicable law (declaring, among other things, the ECHR and ICCPR applicable to all criminal proceedings in Kosovo), Section 4 of UNTAET Regulation No. 2000/30 on Transitional Rules of Criminal Procedure (as amended by Regulation 2001/25 of 14 September 2001), Article 13 of the UN/Cambodia Agreement (declaring Article 14 of the ICCPR applicable), and Article 9 of the SCSL Statute.

[137] See *A.P.* v. *Italy*, Communication 204/1986, Human Rights Committee, decision of 2 November 1987, paras 7.3 and 8, and *A.R.J.*v. *Australia*, Communication 692/1996, Human Rights Committee, views adopted 28 July 1997, para. 6.4.

[138] Section 4 of UNTAET Regulation No. 2000/30 on Transitional Rules of Criminal Procedure (as amended by Regulation 2001/25 of 14 September 2001).

[139] See Article 9 of the ICTR Statute, Article 10 of the ICTY Statute, and Article 9 of the SCSL Statute.

or were designed to shield the accused from international criminal responsibility; or that the case was not diligently prosecuted. The legal framework of the ICC and the East Timor special panels contain only the second ground, in a more elaborate form. There is apparently no need to refer to 'ordinary crime characterization' as an exception to *ne bis in idem* protection. When a state prosecutes for ordinary crimes, one may argue that subsequent prosecution for war crimes, for example, is always possible as this cannot be seen as the same offence, at least not in the legal sense.[140]

The exceptions referred to above amount to important review standards for national courts. Their unilateral nature — in that national courts are prevented from adopting similar standards in respect of international criminal tribunals — is another illustration of the vertical relationship to national courts.

For the ICTY and the ICTR this is an understandable position, given that they enjoy primacy over all the courts of UN members. The approach of the ICC Statute is more problematic. Article 20(2) appears to impose obligations on all other courts, in that they may not try persons for a crime within the ICC Statute for which that person has already been convicted or acquitted by the ICC. In respect of the courts of non-party states this goes too far and is not in keeping with the fundamental *pacta tertiis nec nocent nec prosunt* rule.[141] It can also not be said that the provision codifies an existing rule of customary international law, as we have seen above that the *ne bis in idem* principle has no transjurisdictional effect in the human rights context. The special panels for East Timor and the SCSL have adopted a more modest approach. Pursuant to their applicable laws and regulations the downward *ne bis in idem* effect is confined to the national courts of East Timor and Sierra Leone respectively.[142] This better suits the scope of cooperation obligations.

The upward effect of *ne bis in idem* protection mirrors the discussion of the division of cases between international criminal tribunals and national courts, in respect of the exercise of primacy or complementarity. Indeed, the element of review of national proceedings plays a role both before and after a final judgment. Undeniably, the existence of a final judgment does not always mean that a state has prosecuted international crimes 'in good faith'. Thus, the same questions may arise that have been addressed in respect of the exercise of primacy and complementarity, even though the inability standard (Article 17(3) of the ICC Statute) appears no longer relevant. The outcome of a final judgment is in this regard apparently seen as proof of the state's ability to prosecute international crimes.[143] The gist of the exceptions to the upward effect of *ne bis in*

---

[140] See for a different view, C. Van den Wyngaert and T. Ongena, '*Ne bis in idem* Principle, Including the Issue of Amnesty', in Cassese et al., *Rome Statute Commentary*, at 725–6. They submit that the 'ordinary crime' concern is accommodated by the reference in Article 20(3) of the ICC Statute to conduct proscribed by Articles 6, 7, or 8 of the Statute. [141] See Article 34 of the VCLT.

[142] See Section 4.1 of UNTAET Regulation No. 2000/30 on Transitional Rules of Criminal Procedure (as amended by Regulation 2001/25 of 14 September 2001) and Article 9(1) of the SCSL Statute.

[143] The situation of an acquittal being the result not of bad intentions on the part of the state, but of a serious lack of (investigative) resources (inability) is thus not addressed by the *ne bis in idem* provisions. This not being one of the exceptions, the conclusion should be that such a judgment bars subsequent prosecution by an international criminal tribunal.

idem protection is that the results of 'sham trials', which have as their sole or essential objective the shielding of the accused from criminal responsibility or disproportionately mitigating the sentence, are unacceptable.[144] This raises again the question of the interpretation of such a standard. Obviously, this question must be connected to the review standards in the context of primacy and complementarity. However, the primacy and complementarity standards are wider and offer more possibilities for reviewing national investigative and prosecutorial activities in respect of international crimes.[145] This is entirely justified given the interest, and right, of the individual concerned in the finality of his or her case. Therefore, the standards of review should in the context of a *ne bis in idem* situation be more narrowly construed than the similar verbatim standards in the context of primacy or complementarity.

A final practical element of the *ne bis in idem* principle concerns the question of the deduction of time spent in detention where an international criminal tribunal makes use of one of the *ne bis in idem* exceptions. The ICTR, ICTY, and SCSL Statutes contain a special provision regulating this matter, aiming at deduction. Given the restricted (temporal) jurisdiction and the crimes concerned there appears to be no practical need for the statutes to contain regulations to deal with the situation where a national penalty exceeds (an expected) ICTY, ICTR, or SCSL penalty. The ICC Statute does not contain a similar provision, but contains a general deduction provision in Article 78(2).[146]

It is not surprising that there is hardly any practice in respect of the *ne bis in idem* principle. States and international criminal tribunals may be expected to monitor their respective activities. It is in everybody's interest to settle jurisdiction conflicts prior to a trial, and certainly prior to a final judgment. Just a few ICTY and ICTR decisions therefore touch upon *ne bis in idem* issues.

Reference has already been made to the *Tadić ne bis in idem* decision in the context of primacy.[147] Although the title mentions *ne bis in idem*, the defence motion was in fact concerned with the alleged unjustified exercise of primacy by the ICTY in respect of German investigations regarding Tadić. It was also recognized by the defence that the accused was not tried in the sense of Article 10 of the ICTY Statute and, as a result, no *ne bis in idem* violation could be established.[148]

Ne bis in idem considerations played a role, albeit merely serving as a background, in two ICTR decisions. The *Bagosora* deferral decision mentioned a possible later *ne bis in idem* obstacle as one of the reasons for requesting Belgium to defer investigations

[144] The characterization of the conduct as an 'ordinary crime' may fit within those bad faith intentions, but not always. This is a vital difference between the ICTY, ICTR, and SCSL Statutes, on the one hand, and the ICC Statute and the East Timor legal framework on the other. The former contain the 'ordinary crime' exception as an objective standard; the latter, however, do not contain it and appear to be exclusively oriented towards bad faith conduct.

[145] They also include the objective standard of Rule 9(iii) of the ICTY, ICTR, and SCSL Rules and the ICC inability standard; see above, section 12.2.2.

[146] See also Section 10(3) of UNTAET Regulation No. 2000/15 of 6 June 2000 on the establishment of panels with exclusive jurisdiction over serious criminal offences, containing identical language.

[147] Decision on the Defence Motion on the Principle of Non-bis-in-idem, *Prosecutor* v. *Tadić*, Case No. IT-94-1-T, ICTY, T. Ch., 14 November 1995.   [148] Ibid.

against the accused to the ICTR.[149] The Chamber observed that prosecution of Bagosora for war crimes, the only possibility under Belgian law at the time, would bar subsequent prosecution by the ICTR for crimes against humanity or genocide.[150] In the *Ntuyahaga* case the ICTR prosecutor asked permission to withdraw the indictment, with a view to allowing prosecution at the national level, especially in Belgium.[151] The defence, however, asked for an acquittal, certainly with a view to triggering the far-reaching effects of a downward *ne bis in idem* situation. The Chamber ruled that at this stage, without presentation of the evidence, this was not legally possible.[152]

12.5 CONCLUSION

The relationship of international criminal tribunals with national jurisdictions contains three major elements: allocation of cases, cooperation, and recognition of judgments. There is a strong link between the allocation of cases and the recognition of judgments. The central and most sensitive point in this link is the degree of supervision to be exercised by international criminal tribunals over national efforts to bring to justice persons suspected of international crimes. The vital difference between the ad hoc tribunals and the ICC regarding this supervision is that the former enjoy in the interests of international peace and security primacy over domestic investigations and prosecutions. While their legal frameworks contain criteria for primacy related to the quality of national investigations and prosecutions, the ICTY and ICTR have exclusively resorted to the 'neutral' ground that the case is of interest to the tribunal. This illustrates the difficulties inherent in 'disqualifying' national justice systems. It serves as a useful background against which to assess the ICC practice of self-referrals, which obviates the need for a 'quality assessment' of national activities and is also likely to produce more effective state cooperation. Yet, self-referrals also carry risks, and it seems to us that the Court can no longer step away from one of its vital tasks, namely supervising national investigations and prosecutions.

The degree of supervision in respect of national investigations and prosecutions is also reflected in the respective cooperation regimes. It is self-evident that the primacy of the ad hoc tribunals has resulted in a cooperation regime that infringes more on state sovereignty than the ICC's complementary mandate. However, the differences essentially lie in the scope of the duty to cooperate and are by all means acceptable, if one bears in mind the widely diverging circumstances under which the ad hoc tribunals and the ICC were set up. What is far more problematic in terms of ICC cooperation

---

[149] Decision on the Application by the Prosecutor for a Formal Request for Deferral, *Prosecutor* v. *Bagosora*, Case No. ICTR-96-7-D, ICTR, T. Ch. II, 17 May 1996, para. 13. [150] Ibid.

[151] Decision on the Prosecutor's Motion to Withdraw the Indictment, *Prosecutor* v. *Ntuyahaga*, Case No. ICTR-98-40-T, ICTR, T. Ch. I, 18 March 1999. [152] Ibid., at 7.

practice is that (1) a significant number of states are not parties and thus have no obligations towards the Court, and (2) vital forms of cooperation — assisting the Court in compelling witnesses to give testimony and allowing on-site investigations — are not provided for in the Statute at all or are the result of a very meagre and highly unsatisfactory compromise. These issues present a grand challenge for the conference to be held in 2009 to review the ICC Statute.

13

INTERNATIONAL CRIMINAL LAW AND THE DOMESTIC LEGAL ORDER: THE NATIONAL APPLICATION OF INTERNATIONAL CRIMINAL LAW

SUMMARY

13.1 INTRODUCTION

The advent and proliferation of various forms of international criminal adjudication should not make us lose sight of the role of national courts in the implementation of international criminal law. Just as the courts of member states of the European Union are 'outposts' in the application of EU law, the national courts of every state have an all-important role in the enforcement of international criminal law. The extent to which national courts do in fact apply international criminal law depends on a number of factors. Both domestic legislative and prosecutorial activity in this field, which precondition any judicial process, generally depend on a combination of factors, including, but not limited to, the state's international obligations under various treaties criminalizing certain conduct and commitment to implement them, participation in international criminal judicial bodies, and the state's involvement or interest in armed conflicts. The result is a highly diversified picture, in which no two identical ways of implementing international criminal law in the domestic legal order can be identified. This fragmented national practice may also be the consequence of the absence of an (international) supervisory body ensuring a certain degree of uniformity in the national application of international criminal law. Admittedly, the establishment and work of the ad hoc tribunals and of the ICC have clarified the content and scope of rules and principles of international criminal law. It must also be acknowledged that those tribunals and courts have had and will continue to have a certain harmonizing effect. However, their legal frameworks contain neither obligations nor even guidance for states as to the implementation of international criminal law. Such obligations may be contained in the other sources of international law, such as custom and treaties, pre-existing statutes, and the rules of international criminal courts and tribunals. However, one can discern at least three problems in this respect. First, treaties containing obligations in the field of international criminal law are generally concerned with penalizing and prosecuting certain conduct — for example, genocide — and tend not to contain rules on modes of criminal responsibility, defences, and other important elements of substantive criminal law. Secondly, treaty obligations by definition raise the problem of non-ratifying states as an obstacle to a universally shared international criminal justice system and legal environment.[1] Thirdly, while in this light one may be tempted to resort to international customary law as binding upon all states, it is generally vague and especially in the field of international criminal law lacks convincing practice and *opinio juris*.[2]

---

[1] See Report of the Secretary-General on ICTY, para. 34:

> In the view of the Secretary-General, the application of the principle nullum crimen sine lege requires that the international tribunal should apply rules of international humanitarian law which are beyond any doubt part of customary law so that the problem of adherence of some but not all States to specific conventions does not arise. This would appear to be particularly important in the context of an international tribunal prosecuting persons responsible for serious violations of international humanitarian law.

[2] On the problematic role of customary international law in the field of international criminal law, see Chapter 3, section 3.2. See also Fletcher and Ohlin, who reached a highly critical conclusion:

> To sum up, customary international law has no role in international criminal law, except perhaps to increase the options for the defence. To use custom to enhance the prospects of conviction is to violate the fundamental assumptions of modern criminal law. 'Customary law' is anathema in the criminal courts of every civilized society. The reason for legislation is to drive custom from the system and to create a regime based on rules and standards declared publicly, in advance, by a competent authority. The Rome Statute represents public standards of that sort but the rules of customary international law — whether real or imagined — do not (G. P. Fletcher and J. D. Ohlin, 'Reclaiming Fundamental Principles of Criminal Law in the Darfur Case' (2005) 3 *JICJ*, at 559).

A fascinating tension overshadows the entry of international criminal law into the 'receiving' domestic legal order.

On the one hand, to ensure the uniformity and integrity of their legal system, states in enforcing criminal law are inclined not to make a distinction between national and international crimes. On the other hand, a number of unique features of international criminal law have been firmly established as intrinsic to the legal principle of individual responsibility for international crimes. The main challenge for a viable international criminal justice system, with domestic criminal courts as vital outposts, lies in striking an appropriate balance between the familiarity to national judges of domestic criminal law and the imperative and particular demands of international criminal law.

The present chapter offers a selective introduction into those matters, which does not do justice to the fascinating but also complicated legal issues involved.[3] It furthermore presents a limited overview of national implementation practices in respect of a number of essential elements of international criminal law, such as universal jurisdiction, the irrelevance of official capacities, the doctrine of command responsibility, the reduced applicability of the defence of superior orders, and the non-applicability of statutes of limitations. The fundamental question that runs through this discussion is whether the considered manifestations of national practice amount to a faithful implementation of international criminal law.

13.2 NATIONAL PRACTICES: AN OVERVIEW

Domestic enforcement of international criminal law takes a variety of forms. One can discern the following historical milestones in the development of the approach of states to sanctioning international crimes.

After the Second World War numerous countries proceeded with the criminal prosecution of international crimes. It has to be admitted that those prosecutions were not exclusively concerned with war crimes or crimes against humanity, but also with such crimes as treason and assisting the enemy in wartime.[4] What is more, the prosecutions were primarily based on the jurisdictional principles of (active and passive) nationality and territoriality. Enforcement of international criminal law was thus not the central focus, but rather a corollary of the breach by the culprit of the state's own legal order. However, it may be said that the post-Second World War prosecutions nevertheless marked a sincere effort to apply in a significant number of states rules of international criminal law which had previously been established by the Nuremberg and Tokyo trials.

---

[3] For a recent and excellent study dealing with this matter in detail, we recommend W. N. Ferdinandusse, *Direct Application of International Criminal Law in National Courts* (The Hague: T. M. C. Asser Press, 2006).

[4] For example, in *R. Wagner and six others* (Case No. 13, 1946), the Permanent Military Tribunal at Strasbourg and Court of Appeal found the accused, Gauleiter and head of the Civil Government of Alsace during the occupation, on the basis of Article 75(4) of the French *Code Pénal* on treason guilty of 'having during the years 1940 to 1942 incited French nationals to bear arms against France, by addressing to them appeals to join the Wehrmacht at a time when France was at war with Germany', UNWCC, III LRTWC, at 40.

While most of the post-Second World War trials were frequently the result of the passing of national ad hoc legislation, the adoption of the four Geneva Conventions in 1949, the affirmation of the principles underlying the Charter of the Nuremberg Tribunal by the UN General Assembly in 1946,[5] and the subsequent adoption of the Nuremberg principles by the ILC in 1950,[6] as well as the conclusion of the Genocide Convention, triggered legislative reforms of a fundamental nature in a considerable number of countries. These reforms transposed the 'grave breaches regime' and the notion of genocide into the domestic legal order, as well as certain key principles of international criminal law, such as the limited applicability of the defence of superior orders. In some states the laws adopted then are still in force. Decades after the Second World War, these laws were applied almost exclusively in respect of crimes committed during the war, and the most notable examples are the trials of *Eichmann* in Israel[7] and of *Barbie* and *Touvier* in France.[8] The problem of the aforementioned laws is that they implement current international criminal law only partially.

Important developments in this field, exemplified by the adoption by the UN of the conventions establishing certain international crimes (such as torture and apartheid), the expansion of the category of war crimes to serious violations of laws and customs governing the conduct of internal armed conflicts in the ICTY jurisprudence,[9] and the growing importance of the obligatory exercise of universal jurisdiction based on the *aut dedere aut iudicare* rule, were often ignored at the national level.

The establishment of the ad hoc tribunals for the former Yugoslavia and for Rwanda gave an important impetus to the national enforcement of international criminal law. The Statutes of the ICTR and the ICTY neither contain new norms of international criminal law, nor impose additional obligations on states to implement and apply this body of law in their domestic legal orders. The importance of the ICTY and the ICTR

---

[5] Affirmation of the Principles of International Law Recognized by the Charter of the Nürnberg Tribunal, GA Res. 95(I), UN GAOR, 1st session, part 2, at 1144, UN Doc. A/236 (1946).

[6] Principles of International Law Recognized in the Charter of the Nuremberg Tribunal and in the Judgment of the Tribunal, adopted by the International Law Commission of the United Nations in 1950, *Report of the International Law Commission Covering its Second Session, 5 June–29 July 1950*, Doc. A/1316, at 11–14.

[7] Judgment, *Attorney-General of the Government of Israel* v. *Adolf Eichmann*, Case No. 40/61, District Court of Jerusalem, 11 December 1961, reprinted in (1968) 36 *ILR*, at 18–276, affirmed by the Judgment of the Israel Supreme Court, 29 May 1962, reprinted in (1968) 36 *ILR*, at 277–342. On this trial, see L. C. Green, 'The Eichmann Case' (1960) 23 *Modern Law Rev.*, at 507–15; H. Silving, 'In re Eichmann: A Dilemma of Law and Morality' (1961) 55 *AJIL*, at 307–58; C. Olivier, 'The Attorney-General of the Government of Israel v. Eichmann' (1962) 56 *AJIL*, at 805–45; H. Arendt, *Eichmann in Jerusalem: A Report on the Banality of Evil* (New York: Penguin Books, 1964).

[8] Judgments, *Fédération Nationale des Déportés et Internés Résistants et Patriotes et al.* v. *Klaus Barbie*, Cour de Cassation, Chambre Criminelle, 6 October 1983, 26 January 1984, 20 December 1985, and 3 June 1998, reprinted in (1988) 78 *ILR*, at 125–48, and (1995) 100 *ILR*, at 332–7. See also A. Cassese, 'Klaus Barbie: An Exemplary Life of an Executioner', in A. Cassese, *Violence and Law in the Modern Age* (Princeton: Princeton University Press, 1988), at 97–118; Judgment, *Fédération Nationale des Déportes et Internés Résistants et Patriotes et al.* v. *Touvier*, Cour de Cassation, Chambre Criminelle, 27 November 1992, reprinted in (1995) 100 ILR, at 358–64.

[9] *Tadić* jurisdiction appeal decision, para. 137. Generally on rules applicable in internal armed conflicts and the diminution of the value of traditional distinction between international and internal armed conflicts for the purpose of legal regulation, see R. Müllerson, 'International Humanitarian Law in Internal Conflicts' (1997) 2 *J. of Conflict and Security Law*, at 109–33.

lies rather in reminding states of their obligations under existing international law and of their important role in the enforcement of international criminal law. Furthermore, the ICTY and the ICTR assisted states considerably by clarifying the scope and content of certain key aspects of international criminal law, including the definitions and elements of international crimes, as well as the fundamental rules pertaining to individual criminal responsibility (command responsibility, defences, and other matters). Finally, the conflicts in the former Yugoslavia and Rwanda resulted in the arrival of a large number of refugees in other states, including European countries, which became increasingly interested in prosecuting refugees involved in international crimes.

What activities have the establishment and work of the ICTY and the ICTR provoked at the national level? There has been no frenetic legislative reform, except in Belgium, which adopted the Act to Implement the 1949 Geneva Conventions and Additional Protocols in 1993.[10] But there has been at the national level increased prosecutorial activity based on the post-Second World War legislation. As mentioned, a number of European states initiated and finalized prosecutions against the citizens of Rwanda and of the former Yugoslavia, who were residing in those states, often as refugees.[11] The legal context of those proceedings was sometimes obscure and inadequate. This can be illustrated by proceedings in the Netherlands concerning Dutch jurisdiction over war crimes committed abroad by non-nationals. In connection with the investigation of war crimes allegedly committed by a Bosnian Serb in Bosnia, the question arose whether the Dutch War Crimes Act of 1952 was applicable only to armed conflict taking place in the Netherlands or to which the Netherlands is a party or whether it also applied to armed conflict outside the Netherlands in which the Netherlands took no part at all.[12] After protracted proceedings, the Dutch Supreme Court ultimately determined that a reasonable interpretation of the Act demanded its applicability to conflicts outside the Netherlands, hence providing for universal jurisdiction.[13] In other countries courts also faced difficulties when establishing competence over war crimes committed in the former Yugoslavia and in Rwanda. With regard to the former Yugoslavia, the issue of the nature of the conflict arose in Germany. In

---

[10] Loi du 16 juin 1993 relative à la répression des infractions graves aux Conventions internationales de Genève du 12 août 1949 et aux Protocols I et II du 8 juin 1977, additionnels à ces Conventions, *Moniteur Belge*, 5 August 1993. The Act was abrogated by Article 27 of Law of 5 August 2003 on serious violations of international humanitarian law.

[11] The first ICTY/ICTR-related trial took place in Denmark in 1994, concerning a Croat refugee convicted for grave breaches (*Prosecution* v. *Sarić*, Eastern Division of High Court (Third Chamber), 25 November 1994). Trials followed in Germany (Bavarian Higher Regional Court (Munich), 23 May 1997, convicting a Bosnian Serb; the *Jorgić* case, Higher Regional Court at Dusseldorf, 26 September 1997, sentencing a Bosnian Serb to life imprisonment for genocide); in Belgium (Court of Cassation (Second French Chamber), 31 May 1995, convicting a Rwandan national for war crimes; *Prosecutor* v. *Ntezimana, Higaniro, Mukangango, and Mukabutero (the 'Butare Four')*, Assize Court of Brussels, 8 June 2001, affirmed in Court of Cassation, 9 January 2002; for a commentary, see L. Reydams, 'Belgium's First Application of Universal Jurisdiction: the *Butare Four* Case' (2003) 1 *JICJ*, at 428–36); and Switzerland (Military Tribunal, Division 1, 18 April 1997, Bosnian Serb acquitted of war crimes for lack of evidence; Military Court of Cassation, 27 April 2001, convicting a Rwandan burgomaster to 14 years' imprisonment for war crimes committed in an internal armed conflict).

[12] Article 1 of the Dutch War Crimes Act confined the law's applicability to crimes committed during armed conflict.

[13] *Re Knezević*, Dutch Supreme Court, 11 November 1997, NJ (Dutch Law Reports) 1998/463.

order to be able to apply the grave breaches regime, a German court ruled that the conflict in the former Yugoslavia should be seen as international.[14] As to the Rwandan conflict, the Swiss Court of Appeal partially reversed the finding of a lower court that the grave breaches regime applied to that particular conflict.[15]

The creation and functioning of the ICTY and the ICTR have revealed the major shortcomings of the legislative framework implementing international criminal law, namely, the lack of universal jurisdiction and absence of certain international crimes from national criminal codes, for instance, violations of international humanitarian law in internal armed conflicts. The creation of the ICC prompted necessary legislative reforms to remedy those defects.

We have alluded above to the most natural form of national application of international criminal law, by means of national criminal prosecutions. However, there is also an increasing application of international criminal law in both civil and administrative proceedings.

The resort to international criminal law in national civil proceedings essentially takes place in the United States, where two laws, the Alien Tort Claims Act (1789) and the Torture Victim Protection Act (1991),[16] are increasingly used as tools to hold individuals liable *in civilibus* for (serious) violations of human rights and humanitarian law. The Alien Tort Claims Act provides US courts with jurisdiction over any civil action by an alien for a tort committed in violation of the law of nations or a treaty of the USA; the Torture Victim Protection Act provides for a federal cause of action for torture committed anywhere in the world.[17] The potentially broad application of both Acts combined with a certain judicial activism has resulted in rather voluminous and interesting case law, where victims of international crimes or other (serious) violations of international law seek civil damages.[18] International criminal law plays a prominent role in this civil litigation. For example, in the cases against *Lumintang*[19] and *Garcia and Vides Casanova*[20] the courts resorted to the international law of command responsibility to determine individuals' (civil) liability for international crimes. Furthermore, in the

---

[14] *Jorgić* case, Higher Regional Court, Dusseldorf, 26 September 1997. The appeal against that decision was dismissed in higher instances (Case No. 3 StR 215/98, Federal Court of Justice, 30 April 1999 and Case No. 2 BvR 1290/99, Federal Constitutional Court, 12 December 2000).

[15] Military Court of Appeal 1A, 26 May 2000. [16] 28 USC §1350.

[17] For a discussion of both acts, see, among many others, J. A. Menon, 'The Alien Tort Statute' (2006) 4 *JICJ*, at 372–86; N. Norberg, 'The US Supreme Court Affirms the Filartiga Paradigm' (2005) 4 *JICJ*, at 387–400; I. Poullaos, 'The Nature of the Beast: Using the Alien Tort Claims Act to Combat International Human Rights Violations' (2002) 80 *Washington University Law Quarterly*, at 327–58; J.-M. Simon, 'The Alien Tort Claims Act: Justice or Show Trials?' (1993) 11 *Boston University Int'l Law J.*, at 1–78.

[18] The landmark and first decision in an impressive Catalogue of cases was the *Filartiga* case of 30 June 1980 in which an alien residing in the USA issued a complaint alleging torture of his brother by a former official of Paraguay (*Filartiga* v. *Peña-Irala*, Court of Appeals (2nd Circuit), 30 June 1980, 630 F.2d 876; 1980 US App. LEXIS 16111). For a commentary, see, among many others, M. Danaher, 'Torture as a Tort in Violation of International Law: Filartiga v. Pena-Irala' (1981) 33 *Stanford Law Rev.*, at 353–69.

[19] *Jane Doe* v. *Major General Johny Lumintang*, Case No. 00-674, US District Court for the District of Columbia, 10 September 2001.

[20] *Ford* v. *Garcia and Vides-Casanova*, 289 F.3d 1283, US Court of Appeals, 11th Circuit, 30 April 2002; *Romagoza Arce et al.* v. *Garcia and Vides Casanova*, 400 F.3d 1340, US Court of Appeals, 11th Circuit, 4 January 2006.

application of this and other parts of international criminal law the courts paid ample consideration to the ICTY and ICTR case law.

International criminal law also plays an increasingly important role in administrative cases concerning the position of refugees. According to Article 1F of the Convention relating to the Status of Refugees,[21] refugee status shall not be given to any person with respect to whom there are serious reasons for considering that he or she has committed a crime against peace, a war crime, or a crime against humanity.[22] In determining whether or not a person has committed one of these crimes, rules of international criminal law should be and are taken into account. In this category of cases, the focus is not only on whether the conduct concerned amounts to, for example, a crime against humanity. To determine the person's responsibility for the criminal conduct it may also be necessary to apply important international criminal law concepts, such as command responsibility, or to deal with defences in the light of international criminal law. In the Canadian *Moreno* case the interesting question arose as to the limits of criminal liability for torture: can a soldier who observed acts of torture but failed to intervene because he thought he would be killed if he did, be considered as having 'committed crimes against humanity' in the sense of Article 1F of the Convention relating to the Status of Refugees?[23] Although in this case the Canadian court dealt with the matter mainly on the basis of Canadian law, one may expect a more prominent role for international criminal law on those matters in comparable cases.[24]

13.3 THE PRESENT STAGE: THE EFFECT OF THE ICC'S PRINCIPLE OF COMPLEMENTARITY

The establishment of the ICC has important consequences for the implementation of international criminal law. For the correct application of this body of law at the national level the ICC Statute and the Elements of Crimes embody a further development and clarification of its norms. This may be of great use to the courts of both states parties and non-party states in criminal, civil, and administrative proceedings.[25]

It transpires from recent state practice that the effect of the principle of complementarity is of greater importance. According to this principle, which can be found in the

---

[21] Adopted on 28 July 1951 by the United Nations Conference of Plenipotentiaries on the Status of Refugees and Stateless Persons convened under General Assembly Resolution 429(V) of 14 December 1950.

[22] For a discussion, see, among many others, A. Rasulov, 'Criminals as Refugees: The "Balancing Exercise" and Art. 1F (B) of the Refugee Convention' (2002) 16 *Georgetown Immigration L. J.*, at 815–34.

[23] *Moreno* v. *Canada (Minister of Employment and Immigration)*, [1994] 1 F.C. 298 (CA), 14 September 1993.

[24] It is to be noted that the *Moreno* case precedes important case law of the ICTY and the ICTR. Concerning the matter of accomplice versus innocent bystander, a useful ICTY precedent is *Furundžija*, in which the 'observation' by a commander of torture and sexual assault committed by his subordinates is qualified as aiding and abetting in that crime (*Furundžija* trial judgment, especially paras 232–5).

[25] An intriguing question which national courts may have to face when applying provisions of the ICC Statute is the extent to which those norms reflect customary international law. This is controversial in respect of a number of elements of criminal responsibility under the ICC Statute, such as, for example, the issue of a mistake of fact.

Preamble, paragraph 10, as well as in Articles 1, 17, and 20(3) of the ICC Statute, cases are only admissible before the ICC when states are unable or unwilling to carry out prosecutions.[26] In other words, states parties to the ICC have the primary responsibility for enforcing international criminal law. Although the ICC Statute contains no obligations concerning the implementation of international criminal law in the domestic legal order, a number of states parties have faithfully translated its provisions regarding crimes into national law as the rationale underlying the complementarity principle prescribes. Indeed, one can conceive of a number of strong arguments as to why states should implement the substantive international criminal law provisions of the ICC Statute. The most convincing of them is that in order for the ICC to perform its complementarity function effectively, comprehensive and good faith implementation is indispensable.[27]

Thus there are statements in several explanatory memoranda to and comments on ICC implementing legislation that the principle of complementarity triggered or was an important factor in serious legislative reforms.[28]

In light of the aforementioned 'effective' application of the principle of complementarity, the importance of the ICC rulings on admissibility, especially the determinations on 'inability' and 'unwillingness', is difficult to overestimate. States thus have to decide which parts of international criminal law set out in the ICC Statute need to be implemented in the domestic legal order in order to anticipate an 'inability or unwillingness' condemnation by the Court. Commentators have indicated some elements that will be of considerable importance for the Court in determining inability or unwillingness.[29] They concern first of all the crimes set out in the Statute, which must be implemented in domestic law as international crimes; as a result, prosecution as ordinary crimes will in all likelihood result in an inability determination.[30] Secondly, the scope of criminal responsibility, including grounds excluding criminal responsibility, should be in keeping with international criminal law. This means, for example, that the absence of command responsibility in domestic criminal law or the acceptance of a defence of superior orders in respect of crimes against humanity will probably be seen as inability or unwillingness. Finally, it is to be expected that the Court will look critically at the scope of application of domestic law in relation to international crimes. One may expect that failure to exercise universal jurisdiction over crimes within the jurisdiction of the ICC when possible or even imperative under international law is the reason for a determination of unwillingness or inability.[31] Furthermore, restrictions on the exercise of

[26] The principle of complementarity has been examined from a procedural perspective, namely regarding the allocation of cases, in Chapter 12, section 12.2.3.

[27] J. Kleffner, 'The Impact of Complementarity on National Implementation of Substantive International Criminal Law' (2003) 1 *JICJ*, at 94. Kleffner also offers several other arguments in favour of faithful implementation; ibid., at 90–4.

[28] On the legislative experiences in Australia, Belgium, and the Netherlands, ibid., at 88.   [29] Ibid.

[30] Ibid., at 95. In this respect it should be noted that, mirroring the principle of complementarity, the *ne bis in idem* protection of the ad hoc tribunals and the ICC does not extend to national convictions and acquittals for 'ordinary crimes'. See Chapter 12, section 12.4.

[31] For a more prudent and different view, ibid., at 109, where the author makes the exercise of universal jurisdiction in the complementarity relationship with the Court dependent upon (1) the absence of exercise of jurisdiction by states with a stronger title, or (2) the absence of exercise of jurisdiction by the ICC (i.e. reverse complementarity).

jurisdiction, such as immunities under international law, must be confined to those situations that are required under international law.[32]

In light of the uncertainties surrounding the principle of complementarity, particularly with regard to the precise standards of review and the margin of appreciation allocated to national prosecuting authorities, it is interesting that a number of states parties have taken this opportunity to make far-reaching legislative reforms implementing international criminal law. The result is a number of new 'international crimes acts', which either replace or supplement the older post-Second World War legislation.[33] The impetus for these may therefore be not only the effect of the principle of complementarity but also the late reparation of a deficient legislative scheme under the sources of international law other than the Rome Statute.

The practical application of the products of the legislative reforms will probably take some time to become apparent. These laws have no retroactive effect. Conduct previous to their entry into force is still covered by the legislation that existed at the time of the conduct, with all its shortcomings.

13.4 INTERNATIONAL NORMS AS DOMESTIC CRIMES: SOME OBSERVATIONS ON DIRECT EFFECT, OVER-INCLUSION, AND UNDER-INCLUSION

One of the most important questions in respect of international norms concerns their effect in the domestic legal order. When it comes to implementing international norms, the general rule is that states enjoy freedom in means and methods of implementation.[34] The other side of this coin, however, is that states cannot invoke the provisions of their internal law as justification for their failure to perform international obligations.[35] Regarding these means and methods, two distinguished approaches can

---

[32] Ibid., at 102–6.

[33] Examples of states that have adopted legislation implementing the substantive criminal law set out in the ICC Statute, or are in the process of doing so, are: Uruguay, Trinidad and Tobago, Argentina, Australia, Germany, the UK, Canada, the Netherlands, and Italy. Legislation can be found at www.iccnow.org/?mod=romeimplementation (last visited 10 November 2006).

[34] See, among others, E. Denza, 'The Relationship between International and National Law', in M. D. Evans (ed.), *International Law* (Oxford: Oxford University Press, 2003), at 419; W. N. Ferdinandusse, *Direct Application of International Criminal Law in Domestic Courts*, at 132-6. The ICJ has confirmed significant leeway for states to choose the means of implementation of their international obligations (see *Germany* v. *United States (LaGrand Case)*, 27 June 2001, *ICJ Reports* 2001, para. 125). But note that important exceptions exist, such as the law of the European Union, where the ECJ asserted primacy and direct effect for EU law (*Van Gend en Loos* v. *Nederlandse Administratie der Belastingen* [1963] *ECR* 1; [1963] *CMLR* 105 and *Costa* v. *E.N.E.L.* [1964] *ECR* 585; [1964] *CMLR* 425).

[35] Cf. the *Free Zones* case ((1932), PCIJ, Ser. A/B, no. 46, at 167); Advisory Opinion in the *Greco-Bulgarian Communities* case ((1930), PCIJ, Ser. B, no. 17, at 32); the *Polish Nationals in Danzig* case ((1931), PCIJ, Ser. A/B, no. 44, at 24). Article 27 of the VCLT codifies this rule for treaty obligations.

be discerned: monism and dualism.[36] The dualist approach starts from the assumption of the separation between the national and international legal order. As a result, the effect of international law within the legal order of dualist states requires legislation, in addition to the ratification legislation. The purest form of monism consists of the direct effect of a treaty within the domestic legal order as of its entry into force for the state concerned. 'Direct effect' implies that the entire treaty becomes part of the domestic legal order, and no domestic legislation — apart from the act of ratification — is required to entail that result.[37]

The question arises of the extent to which treaties containing international criminal law, or perhaps even international criminal law that is part of customary international law, can have direct effect in the domestic legal order without transformation into domestic law. Were such direct effect possible, there would probably be a more immediate and therefore more faithful application of international criminal law.[38] One may, however, wonder whether there is an important difference between the effect of norms containing individual rights and the effect of those containing obligations. In monist states the direct effect is confined to parts of treaties which are self-executing, in the sense that they directly attribute clear rights to individuals.[39] The direct effect of obligations may be seen as unfair: the individual may benefit but should not suffer from a state's negligence in adequately implementing international obligations in the domestic legal order. This is illustrated by a decision of the Court of Justice of the European Communities regarding the Netherlands using a non-implemented EC directive as the basis for criminal responsibility.[40] The Court ruled that a member state which had not adopted the implementing measures required by the directive within the prescribed period may not plead, as against individuals, its own failure to perform the obligations which the directive entails.[41]

In the field of international criminal law there is the important difference that international crimes concern individuals directly, whereas EU directives are addressed to states. From the perspective of international law, there is no clear impediment to the direct effect of international criminal law at the national level. Both the ICCPR and the ECHR contain provisions protecting the individual's right not to be subjected to retroactive criminalization of conduct, but those provisions make it perfectly clear that this is not confined to the domestic legal order.[42] In other words, the conduct prosecuted

---

[36] For more detailed studies on the complicated issues involved, we refer to H. Kelsen, *Das Problem der Souveranität und die Theorie des Völkerrechts — Beitrag zu einer reinen Rechtslehre* (Tübingen: J. C. Mohr, 1920); B. Conforti, *International Law and the Role of Domestic Legal Systems* (The Hague: Nijhoff/Kluwer, 1993); F. Jacobs and S. Roberts, *The Effect of Treaties in Domestic Law* (London: Sweet & Maxwell, 1987).

[37] Only the publication of the treaty is required to produce this direct effect. See J. A. Frowein and K. Oellers-Frahm, 'L'application des traités dans l'ordre juridique interne', in P. M. Eisemann, *L'intégration du droit international et communautaire dans l'ordre juridique national — étude de la pratique en Europe* (The Hague/London/Boston: Kluwer Law International 1996), at 11–12.

[38] This is one of the arguments used in the human rights debate in favour of monism: an enhanced protection of human rights.

[39] On the requirement of self-executing treaty provisions, see W. N. Ferdinandusse, *Direct Application of International Criminal Law in National Courts*, at 136–40.

[40] Case 80/86, *Kolpinghuis Nijmegen BV* [1987] *ECR* 3969.   [41] Ibid., para. 8

[42] Cf. Article 7 of the ECHR and Article 15 of the ICCPR. For more detail on this question, see M. Boot, *Nullum Crimen Sine Lege and the Subject Matter Jurisdiction of the International Criminal Court* (Antwerp/Oxford/

has to be a crime in either the domestic or the international legal order. What then is the problem of the direct effect of international criminal law before national courts, especially in states that have adopted a monist approach to international law in general? While this cannot be fully addressed here, we offer an introduction to this problem by examining some prominent case law.

The question of direct effect arose and was addressed in the *Bouterse* case in the Netherlands.[43] The issue was whether a former military commander and head of the state of Surinam, Desi Bouterse, could be tried in the Netherlands for acts of torture allegedly committed in 1982. From the perspective of the principle of *nullum crimen sine lege*, this proved to be highly problematic. The Torture Convention (CAT) dates from 1984, and the Dutch Torture Convention Implementation Act was enacted in 1988. The Court of Appeals of Amsterdam circumvented the language of the principle of legality set out in Article 1 of the Dutch Penal Code and Article 16 of the Dutch Constitution by distinguishing between retrospective and retroactive law.[44] Unlike retroactive law, prohibited by the legality principle, retrospective law is seen to be merely declaratory of existing customary law.[45] The argument then is that both the CAT and the Dutch Implementation Act can be applied retrospectively to cover conduct that had already been criminalized under Dutch law, but not in the form of torture (for example, serious mistreatment). The Supreme Court rejected this approach for the reason that only a clear retrospective application set out in either the CAT or the Dutch Implementation Act may serve as an exception to the principle of legality. The Supreme Court furthermore interpreted 'statutory criminal provision' as referring to written law only. As a result, only cases concerning conduct which was at the time of commission criminalized by either domestic law or a treaty are admissible before Dutch courts. Although the insertion of treaty provisions within the scope of the *nullum crimen* principle set out in Article 1 of the Dutch Penal Code and Article 16 of the Dutch Constitution demonstrated a progressive approach, the inclusion of customary international law appears also to be a permissible approach, consistent with international human rights law. In this respect the European Court of Human Rights' case of *Streletz, Kesstler, and Krenz* v. *Germany* ('the *German Border Guards* case') is instructive.[46] The applicants were accused of and convicted by the courts of reunified Germany for having incited or participated in the homicide of a number of citizens of East Germany attempting to flee to West Germany. The applicants submitted to the European Court that the acts on account of which they had been prosecuted did not constitute offences at the time when they were committed, according to the law of East

---

New York: Intersentia, 2002), at 127–78, and W. N. Ferdinandusse, *Direct Application of International Criminal Law in National Courts*, at 230–48.

[43] *In re Bouterse*, Dutch Supreme Court, 18 September 2001, NJ (Dutch Law Reports) 2002/559, English translation in (2001) 32 *Netherlands Y'book Int'l Law*, at 282–96.

[44] *In re Bouterse*, Amsterdam Court of Appeals, 20 November 2000, LJN no.: AA8395.

[45] L. Zegveld, 'The Bouterse Case' (2001) 32 *Netherlands Y'book of Int'l Law*, at 101.

[46] *Streletz, Kesstler, and Krenz* v. *Germany*, 34044/96; 35532/97; 44801/98 [2001] ECtHR 230 (22 March 2001). On this case, see J. Arnold et al., 'The German Border Guard Cases before the European Court of Human Rights' (2003) 11(1) *European J. of Crime, Criminal Law and Criminal Justice* (2003), at 67–92; R. Geiger, 'The German Border Guard Cases and International Human Rights' (1998) 9 *European J. of Int'l Law*, at 540–9.

Germany and international law, and that their conviction by the German courts had therefore breached Article 7(1) of the Convention. In an interesting decision the Court ruled that *nullum crimen sine lege* does not refer to a basis in the written international law only. It considered that the offences charged need to be defined with sufficient accessibility and foreseeability by the rules of international law on the protection of human rights, and made in this respect an explicit reference to crimes against humanity, even if at the time of the judgment those crimes were not codified in any treaty in force.[47] Other decisions and doctrine also indicate that unwritten international law qualifies as law and meets the demands of the international *nullum crimen* rule.[48] What matters is that these sources are sufficiently accessible and foreseeable.[49] This standard is generally easily met in respect of international and other serious crimes. Thus, in the *German Border Guards* case the European Court of Human Rights cited with approval the German *Bundesverfassungsgericht* which held that:

> The decisive factor is that the killing of an unarmed fugitive by sustained fire was, in the circumstances of the case, such a dreadful act, not justifiable by any defence whatsoever, that it must have been immediately apparent and obvious even to an indoctrinated person that it breached the proportionality principle and the elementary prohibition on the taking of human life.[50]

While there is in the background strong reliance on natural-law concepts, the question arises whether the interpretation of accessibility and foreseeability is at all times reasonable in respect of international crimes. This matter came to the fore in the SCSL Appeals Chamber decision dealing with child recruitment as a crime under international law at the time of the commission.[51] The defence argued in a jurisdictional motion that child recruitment was no crime under international law at the time indicated in the indictment, and therefore the exercise of jurisdiction violated the principle of *nullum crimen sine lege*. While the majority considered the crime to be part of customary international law at the alleged time of commission, Justice Robertson's dissenting opinion contained some forceful points. In favour of a strict legality rule, he submitted:

> Here, the Prosecution asserts with some insouciance that 'the principle of *nullum crimen sine lege* is not in any case applied rigidly, particularly where the acts in question are universally regarded as abhorrent and deeply shock the conscience of humanity.' On the contrary, it is precisely when the acts are abhorrent and deeply shocking that the principle of legality must be most stringently applied, to ensure that a defendant is not convicted out of disgust rather than evidence, or of a non-existent crime. *Nullum crimen* may not be a household phrase, but it serves as some protection against the lynch mob.[52]

---

[47] *Streletz et al.* v. *Germany* [2001] ECtHR, paras 105 and 106.

[48] Cf. *Furundžija* trial judgment, para. 177. For more detail, including an overview of literature and case law, see W. N. Ferdinandusse, *Direct Application of International Criminal Law in National Courts*, at 235–6.

[49] Ibid., at 236–48.

[50] *K.-H.W.* v. *Germany*, 37201/97 [2001] ECtHR 229 (22 March 2001).

[51] Decision on Preliminary Motion based on Lack of Jurisdiction (Child Recruitment), *Prosecutor* v. *Norman*, Case No. SCSL-2004-14-AR72(E), SCSL, A. Ch., 31 May 2004.

[52] Dissenting Opinion of Justice Robertson, Decision on Preliminary Motion based on Lack of Jurisdiction (Child Recruitment), *Prosecutor* v. *Norman*, Case No. SCSL-2004-14-AR72(E), A. Ch., 31 May 2004, para. 12. In support of this strict approach, see M. Shahabuddeen, 'Does the Principle of Legality Stand in the Way of Progressive Development of Law?' (2004) 2 *JICJ*, at 1009–10.

Closely connected to the legality question is the extent to which national criminal law systems should faithfully implement international criminal law, or whether they are allowed to be under- or over-inclusive. More concretely, what are the arguments pertaining to lesser or greater criminal responsibility than is envisaged under international law?

At the national level there are many examples of both under- and over-inclusive implementation of international criminal law. For example, clearly *international* crimes are prosecuted as ordinary crimes (under-inclusion),[53] or in the implementation of genocide a category of protected groups is added, such as political groups or social groups (over-inclusion).[54]

The desirability or undesirability of either approach was adequately addressed by The Hague District Court in the *Van Anraat* case.[55] One of the vital issues in that case was whether the aiding and abetting of genocide — by providing the Hussein regime with the chemical components used for the production of the chemical weapon that was subsequently employed against the Kurdish population — should be governed by international criminal law or by Dutch criminal law. The problem lay in the apparent discrepancy between the mens rea for aiding and abetting under international criminal law (actual knowledge) and that under Dutch criminal law (allowing for a 'should have known' standard). The court decided in favour of applying international criminal law, on the following grounds, which are worth quoting in full:

A proper application of important rules of international criminal law by the national criminal court judge serves two purposes. In the first place he has to meet with the requirements and expectations of international criminal law regarding the penalization and prosecution of international crimes, which entails that liability under Dutch law should not fall short as opposed to liability under international law. Apart from that however, the Dutch judge must also respect the limits of liability according to international law. The court considers both elements to be of importance.

With respect to the second element the public prosecution service holds the view that conventional-law obligations to penalization represent minimum obligations and therefore the Netherlands are always allowed to go beyond those limits and exceed the bounds of international liability. In the opinion of the court the prosecution service does not acknowledge the place of these conventions and crimes within an international system of standards of criminal law. By assuming a larger liability under national law than customary under international law, in some cases based on national law a crime could be considered as an offense pertaining to international law, whereas the international community does not consider it as such. In this respect an important argument for the court concerning international crimes to give preference to the bounds of international liability instead of national liability, refers to universal jurisdiction connected with international crimes.

---

[53] Note however that this situation may also amount to over-inclusion. This may be the case when somebody is prosecuted for murder whereas the taking of life was justified under the laws of war; see W. N. Ferdinandusse, *Direct Application of International Criminal Law in National Courts*, at 118.

[54] For an overview of states that have been over-inclusive in this respect, see ibid., at 24.

[55] The Hague District Court, Judgment of 23 December 2005, case no. LJN: AU8685; for the English translation use LJN: AX6406. For a commentary, see H. G. van der Wilt, 'Genocide, Complicity in Genocide and International v. Domestic Jurisdiction — Reflections on the *Van Anraat* Case' (2006) 4 *JICJ*, at 239–57.

Exceeding the liability limits of international criminal law, when a case is brought to trial under national law, could cancel the international basis for universal jurisdiction, while the latter can only be applied to practices that are indictable as criminal offenses under international law. In relation to this subject the prosecution argued that in the present proceedings there is no question of excessive jurisdiction from an international law point of view, [seeing] that the accused is prosecuted based on the active nationality principle. The necessary consequence resulting from these considerations that, within the framework of starting proceedings against international crimes committed abroad, different standards of liability can be applied to Dutch nationals and foreign nationals, is considered by the court to be unacceptable, in any event when it concerns the crime of committing genocide.[56]

The Hague District Court thus rejected as a matter of principle both over- and under-inclusion in the national application of international criminal law. A vital question was whether this concerned all rules of international criminal law. The court, basing itself on parts in the explanatory memorandum to the Dutch International Crimes Act, limited direct applicability to 'international rules on liability under criminal law concerning international crimes essentially deviat[ing] from national criminal law'.[57]

The position of the court fits within a progressive Dutch approach on the effect of international law within the domestic legal order and it also passes the test of legality under Dutch law, as set out in the *Bouterse* case, as (1) the scope of criminal responsibility was less under international law than under Dutch law, and (2) the ultimate basis for criminal responsibility can, in contrast to the Bouterse situation, be found in written international law, namely the Genocide Convention, which explicitly covers complicity. The approach has attracted criticism by Harmen van der Wilt who argues that the international criminal law system still displays ambiguity on many points of law and should not always be taken as offering proper guidance; instead, domestic courts would do better to resort to the familiar domestic criminal law notions.[58] The District Court, however, '[c]ontrary to the prosecution, ... holds that the case law was sufficiently crystallized out regarding this subject, [seeing] that this matter was regularly discussed and the appeal chamber of the ICTY and the ICTR repeatedly explained and confirmed the state of the law'.[59] Furthermore, it should be noted that domestic law may also be far from clear in respect of genocide and other international crimes.

The *Van Anraat* case displays some of the complicated legal issues involved in the application of international criminal law in national criminal practice. While the aim of rejecting over- and under-inclusion may be difficult to achieve in practice, in the prosecution of international crimes national courts may be expected to act as outposts of the international community, requiring the application of the essentials of the criminal law of that community. To do less amounts to a failure to meet international obligations, to do more to a distortion of the fragile system of international criminal law, especially if conduct at the national level is wrongly labelled as giving rise to international criminal responsibility. Thus, the *Van Anraat* approach appears to fit very well into the

---

[56] Judgment of 23 December 2005, The Hague District Court, para. 6.3. [57] Ibid., para. 6.2.

[58] H. G. Van der Wilt, 'Genocide, Complicity in Genocide and International v. Domestic Jurisdiction — Reflections on the *Van Anraat* Case', at 254.

[59] Judgment of 23 December 2005, The Hague District Court, para. 6.5.1.

implementation of the ICC Statute's substantive criminal law in the national legal order, based on the principle of complementarity. The Dutch explanatory memorandum on the international crimes act can be cited as embodying faithful implementation:

The point of departure is that the general rules of national criminal law are applicable, except when national criminal law does not provide for certain rules, or in case of rules that clearly deviate from those that apply under the Statute of the ICC.[60]

13.5 THE QUESTION OF UNIVERSAL JURISDICTION

The notion of international crimes is immediately associated with universal jurisdiction. The universality principle can be defined as providing every state with jurisdiction over a limited category of offences generally recognized as of universal concern, regardless of the location of the offence and the nationalities of the offender and the victim.[61] It is thus a permissive rule under international law, the exercise of which has gradually developed in respect of certain internationally criminalized conduct into a mandatory rule on the basis of *aut dedere aut iudicare* obligations.[62]

The notion of universal jurisdiction has attracted much scholarly comment, especially in recent years.[63] The increased attention to universal jurisdiction emphasizes the prominence of this concept as a general principle of international criminal law. It is undisputed that universal jurisdiction is an important tool in effectively implementing the substantive norms of international criminal law. Yet, states were initially reluctant to provide for or apply it, out of concern for (jurisdictional) conflicts with other states or for the undeniably inherent difficulty in successfully prosecuting a case from 'abroad'.

Since universal jurisdiction goes hand in hand with international crimes, one must trace the development of the latter concept to find references to universality. The first references to the universality principle in the crimes within the ICC's jurisdiction[64] are

---

[60] Explanatory Memorandum, II *Parliamentary Documents* (2001–2), 28 337, no. 3, at 29.

[61] K. C. Randall, 'Universal Jurisdiction under International Law' (1988) 66 *Texas Law Rev.*, at 788. For a definition of the concept of universal jurisdiction, see also R. O'Keeffe, 'Universal Jurisdiction — Clarifying the Basic Concept' (2004) 2 *JICJ*, at 744–7.

[62] This means that the suspect has either to be tried or to be extradited; if extradition is not possible the exercise of universal jurisdiction may thus be mandatory. For the underlying rationale of the *aut dedere aut iudicare* rule see E. M. Wise, 'Extradition: The Hypothesis of a Civitas Maxima and the Maxim Aut Dedere Aut Iudicare' (1991) 62 *Int'l Review of Penal Law*, at 109–34. For the *aut dedere aut iudicare* rule in connection with universal jurisdiction, see also R. van Elst, 'Implementing Universal Jurisdiction over Grave Breaches of the Geneva Conventions' (2000) 11 *LJIL*, at 815–54.

[63] See among others L. Reydams, *Universal Jurisdiction: International and Municipal Legal Perspectives* (Oxford: OUP, 2003), K. Randall, 'Universal Jurisdiction under International Law', at 786–91, R. O'Keeffe, 'Universal Jurisdiction — Clarifying the Basic Concept', at 735–60, and M. Henzelin, *Le principe de l'universalité en droit pénal international* (Basle, Geneva, Munich: Helbing and Lictenhahn, 2000).

[64] Generally piracy and slave-trading are identified as the first international crimes giving rise to universal jurisdiction under customary law; see for an analysis K. C. Randall, 'Universal Jurisdiction under International Law', at 791–900.

in the post-Second World War jurisprudence. For example, in the *Hostages* case the US court in Nuremberg considered that '[a]n international crime is ... an act universally recognized as criminal, which is considered a grave matter of international concern and for some valid reason cannot be left within the exclusive jurisdiction of the state that would have control over it under ordinary circumstances'.[65] Also of importance in the development of the universality principle is its use in the *Eichmann* case. Israel relied on a combination of the passive nationality and protective principles (the crimes in question having been intended to exterminate the Jewish people), but the reliance on universality was essential, since Israel was not a state at the time of the commission of the crimes. The Jerusalem Supreme Court concluded on this matter that:

> Not only do all the crimes attributed to the appellant bear an international character, but their harmful and murderous effects were so embracing and widespread as to shake the international community to its very foundations. The State of Israel therefore was entitled, pursuant to the principle of universal jurisdiction and in the capacity of a guardian of international law and an agent for its enforcement, to try the appellant. That being the case, no importance attaches to the fact that the State of Israel did not exist when the offences were committed.[66]

The Supreme Court's findings illustrate one approach of universal jurisdiction: prosecuting as the guardian of international law, thus acting on behalf of the international community. This approach reflects the naturalist *civitas maxima* view, according to which there is an international constitutional order and international crimes which offend this international order may as such be prosecuted by every member of the international community.[67] This is in contrast with the view of universal jurisdiction as a matter of delegation. In this positivist tradition, based on the maxim *nemo plus iuris transferre potest quam ipse habet*, an explicit delegation by the international community, viz. other states holding more generally accepted titles of jurisdiction, such as the territoriality or nationality principles, is required.[68] As will be explored further below, these different views on universal jurisdiction came visibly to the fore in the *Arrest Warrant* case, in which the Democratic Republic of the Congo challenged before the ICJ Belgium's exercise of universal jurisdiction over a Congolese national.[69]

---

[65] *List and others* (*Hostages* case), US Military Tribunal sitting at Nuremberg, Judgment of 19 February 1948, *TWC* XI, 1230–1319.

[66] *Attorney General of Israel* v. *Eichmann*, 36 ILR 2777, at 304 (Israel Supreme Court 1962).

[67] Henzelin refers to this approach as absolute universal jurisdiction and places it in the naturalist international law tradition: 'Selon la théorie de l'universalité dite "absolue", un Etat peut exercer une compétence pénale en exécution d'un devoir transcendant, de droit divin ou de droit naturel, voire d'un besoin de "justice humaine". L'Etat agit en quelque sorte en tant que bras armé d'un entité supérieure aux Etats, d'une "civitas maxima"' (M. Henzelin, 'La Compétence Pénale Universelle. Une question Non Résolue par l'Arrêt Yerodia', (2002) 4 *Revue Générale de Droit International Public*, at 821). In this respect Bassiouni mentions an 'idealistic universalistic position [that] recognizes certain core values and the existence of overriding international interests as being commonly shared and accepted by the international community' (M. C. Bassiouni, 'Universal Jurisdiction for International Crimes: Historical Perspectives and Contemporary Practice' (2002) 42 *Virginia J. Int'l Law*, at 96).

[68] M. Henzelin, 'La Compétence Pénale Universelle', at 836. Bassiouni takes a more cautious approach to universal jurisdiction as the pragmatic policy-oriented one that recognizes that occasionally certain commonly shared interests of the international community require an enforcement mechanism that transcends the interests of singular sovereignty (M. C. Bassiouni, 'Universal Jurisdiction for International Crimes', at 97).

[69] *Case concerning the Arrest Warrant of 11 April 2000 (Democratic Republic of the Congo* v. *Belgium)*, No. 121, ICJ, Judgement, 14 February 2002, *ICJ Reports* 2002.

An increasing number of treaties provide for universal jurisdiction, often of a mandatory nature. The Geneva Conventions contain no direct reference to universal jurisdiction. However, they provide that:

Each High Contracting Party shall be under the obligation to search for persons alleged to have committed, or to have ordered to be committed, such grave breaches, and shall bring such persons, regardless of their nationality, before its own courts. It may also, if it prefers, and in accordance with the provisions of its own legislation, hand such persons over for trial to another High Contracting party concerned, provided such High Contracting Party has made out a prima facie case.[70]

Nevertheless, the Conventions' drafting history provides evidence that this obligation is implied in the *aut dedere aut iudicare* obligation.[71] With regard to war crimes that are not part of the 'grave breaches' regime, one has to resort to customary international law. The statutes and jurisprudence of international criminal tribunals constitute ground-breaking work in developing the notion of war crimes as international crimes. For the protagonists of universal jurisdiction in the *civitas maxima* tradition this may in itself be sufficient to attract universal jurisdiction. A more positivist approach may also require an explicit delegation, which may not be discerned on the basis of customary international law.

The language of the Genocide Convention is more ambiguous. Article 6 provides that:

Persons charged with genocide or any of the other acts enumerated in Article 3 shall be tried by a competent tribunal of the State in the territory of which the act was committed, or by such international penal tribunal as may have jurisdiction with respect to those Contracting Parties which shall have accepted its jurisdiction.

From this provision and the drafting history, universal jurisdiction cannot be inferred. However, it is contended that developments subsequent to the adoption of the Convention, including decisions of international and national courts, provide convincing proof of the existence of universal jurisdiction over genocide under customary international law.[72]

Crimes against humanity and the crime of aggression are not the object of a specific treaty; the attachment of universal jurisdiction to those crimes is therefore a matter of customary international law. Whether this is the case has been the object of much academic debate. Evidence of custom is available, albeit in small quantities, for crimes against humanity.[73] The case of crimes of aggression is more difficult. Although crimes against peace were raised to the level of international crimes by the Nuremberg Tribunal, there is simply no state practice on universal jurisdiction.[74] An additional

---

[70] Article 49 of Geneva Convention I, Article 50 of Geneva Convention II, Article 129 of Geneva Convention III, and Article 146 of Geneva Convention IV.

[71] See for further details R. van Elst, 'Implementing Universal Jurisdiction over Grave Breaches of the Geneva Conventions', at 815–54. See also M. C. Bassiouni, 'Universal Jurisdiction for International Crimes', at 117.

[72] For an overview, see Schabas, *Genocide*, at 360–8.

[73] M. C. Bassiouni, 'Universal Jurisdiction for International Crimes', at 119; and see also A. Cassese, *International Criminal Law*, at 293–5.

[74] A commentator has referred to 'lessons of a failure': A. L. Paulus, 'Peace Through Justice? The Future of the Crime of Aggression in a Time of Crisis' (2004) 50 *Wayne Law Rev.*, at 25–32.

complicating element is that the content of the crime of aggression has still not been authoritatively established, as states parties to the ICC treaty are still struggling to find a definition.

Since states have for long been reluctant to prosecute international crimes on the basis of universal jurisdiction, the content and scope of the universality principle under international law remains unclear. The progressive use of the principle by Belgium triggered disputes with other states, which — understandably — objected to the indictment of their prominent state officials.[75] One of those disputes concerned the issuing of a warrant for the arrest of the then Minister of Foreign Affairs of the Democratic Republic of the Congo in respect of crimes against humanity. The dispute reached the ICJ which was expected to provide a certain degree of clarity as to the limits of universal jurisdiction and the scope of state immunities in relation to international crimes.[76] Although the Court's decision fails to address the question of universal jurisdiction, which was not considered necessary since the dispute could be settled on the basis of the analysis of state immunities,[77] the individual opinions of a number of judges and

---

[75] Belgium's implementation of the universality principle combined universal jurisdiction with the particularities of its criminal justice system, namely the possibility of trials *in absentia* and an important role for private parties in criminal proceedings. As a result, Belgium became a forum where victims and human rights groups could have high-ranking foreign state officials publicly indicted, without there necessarily being any link between the offense or a victim and Belgium. As a result of growing criticism, a law was adopted in April 2003 installing mechanisms to curtail the exercise of universal jurisdiction. On Belgium's application of universal jurisdiction, including an overview of many prominent foreigners who have been the object of criminal investigation, see D. Vandermeersch, 'Prosecuting International Crimes in Belgium' (2005) 3 *JICJ*, at 400–21.

[76] *Case Concerning the Arrest Warrant of 11 April 2000*. For a discussion, see, inter alia, M. Henzelin, 'La compétence pénale universelle. Une question non resolue par l'arrêt Yerodia' (2002) 4 *Revue Générale de Droit International Public*, at 819–54; A. Orakhelashvili, 'Arrest Warrant of 11 April 2000' (2002) 96 *AJIL*, at 677–84; N. Schultz, 'Ist *Lotus* verblüht? Anmerkung zum Urteil des IGH vom 14. Februar 2002 im Fall betreffend den Haftbefehl vom 11. April 2000' (2002) *Zeitschrift für ausländisches öffentliches Recht und Völkerrecht*, at 703–55; M. Sassoli, 'L'arrêt Yerodia: Quelques remarques sur une affaire au point de collision entre les deux couches de droit international' (2002) 4 *Revue Générale de Droit International Public*, at 791–817; S. Wirth, 'Immunity for Core Crimes? The ICJ's Judgmentin the *Congo* v. *Belgium* Case' (2002) 13 *European J. Int'l Law*, at 877–93; A. Cassese, 'When May Senior State Officials Be Tried for International Crimes? Some Comments on the *Congo* v. *Belgium* Case' (2002) 13 *European J. Int'l Law*, at 853–75.

[77] See paragraph 46 of the Judgment in *Case Concerning the Arrest Warrant of 11 April 2000*:

> As a matter of logic, the second ground should be addressed only once there has been a determination in respect of the first, since it is only where a State has jurisdiction under international law in relation to a particular matter that there can be any question of immunities in regard to the exercise of that jurisdiction. However, in the present case, and in view of the final form of the Congo's submissions, the Court will address first the question whether, assuming that it had jurisdiction under international law to issue and circulate the arrest warrant of 11 April 2000, Belgium in so doing violated the immunities of the then Minister for Foreign Affairs of the Congo.

For critical comment on the ICJ's dodging of the universality question, see Joint Separate Opinion of Judges Higgins, Kooijmans, and Buergenthal, para. 16:

> [t]he Court should have 'found it appropriate' to deal with the question of whether the issue and international circulation of a warrant based on universal jurisdiction in the absence of Mr. Yerodia's presence on Belgian territory was unlawful. This should have been done before making a finding on immunity from jurisdiction, and the Court should indeed have 'examined in some detail various problems raised' by the request as formulated by the Congo in its final submissions.

the ensuing scholarly comment on the decision give insight into two diverging approaches. The approach adopted by Belgium comes down to the above-mentioned *civitas maxima* perspective on universal jurisdiction: any member of the international community is entitled to prosecute in order to protect universally recognized important values and therefore no link with the trial forum is required.[78] In this doctrine of absolute universal jurisdiction, there is thus no requirement of *forum deprehensionis*. Opposed to this is the more positivist and pragmatic approach. Cassese provides six grounds against absolute universal jurisdiction.[79] Probably the most important reason for objecting to absolute universal jurisdiction is the expectation that it may easily lead to international disputes.[80] Therefore, it is argued that universal jurisdiction under international law should be confined to those situations where the suspect is present on the territory of the investigating or prosecuting state. An important argument against this so-called conditional universal jurisdiction is that it seriously restricts a state's investigative powers; in the absence of any other jurisdictional basis, the latter may even be prevented from undertaking investigations in anticipation of the arrival of an individual suspected of international crimes.[81] Furthermore, absolute universal jurisdiction corresponds to the need for a wide net of available jurisdictions to combat impunity for international crimes.[82]

Against the above background the question arises as to the direction in which the universality principle will develop. Undeniably the new national 'international crimes acts', triggered by the ICC's principle of complementarity and resulting in state practice, play a vital role in this respect. Those acts, with the exception of those of Belgium,

---

[78] See A. Cassese, 'When May Senior State Officials Be Tried for International Crimes? Some Comments on the *Congo v. Belgium* Case', at 859.

[79] A. Cassese, *International Criminal Law*, at 289–90.

[80] Ibid., at 290 and see also the strong views expressed by Judge Guillaume in his Separate Opinion to the *Arrest Warrant* case, para. 15:

> But at no time has it been envisaged that jurisdiction should be conferred upon the courts of every State in the world to prosecute such crimes, whoever their authors and victims and irrespective of the place where the offender is to be found. To do this would, moreover, risk creating total judicial chaos. It would also be to encourage the arbitrary for the benefit of the powerful, purportedly acting as agent for an ill-defined 'international community'. Contrary to what is advocated by certain publicists, such a development would represent not an advance in the law but a step backward.

[81] Note in this respect the objections of Henzelin:

> on ne voit également pas très bien ce qui empêcherait un Etat de procéder à certaines investigations ou recherches préliminaires pour recueillir des preuves, y compris si l'auteur présumé ne se trouve pas sur son territoire — at a fortiori si les autorités de cet Etat ne savent pas s'il est présent, ne serait-ce que pour vérifier s'il est présent. Il serait nottament aberrant que des victimes ne puissent même pas déposer plainte ou faire enregistrer leur déposition (M. Henzelin, 'La compétence pénale universelle. Une question non resolue par l'arrêt Yerodia', at 843).

[82] Cf. the Joint Separate Opinion of Judges Higgins, Kooijmans, and Buergenthal to the *Arrest Warrant* case, para. 58: 'If the underlying purpose of designating certain acts as international crimes is to authorize a wide jurisdiction to be asserted over persons committing them, there is no rule of international law (and certainly not the *aut dedere* principle) which makes illegal co-operative overt acts designed to secure their presence within a State wishing to exercise jurisdiction.'

Germany,[83] and the Congo,[84] appear to adopt conditional universal jurisdiction, in the sense that for the application of those laws the presence of the suspect on national territory is required.[85] The explanatory memorandum to the Dutch International Crimes Act provides us with the rationale for this choice, which may apply to other countries as well. It is acknowledged that international law is probably still 'neutral' concerning the permissibility of absolute universal jurisdiction; yet, since there is no duty to establish absolute universal jurisdiction and since exercise thereof is associated with a number of problems, including an increased risk of international disputes, the choice of conditional universal jurisdiction is justified.[86]

The question arises whether this is a regrettable development. In a number of countries the legislature has undeniably been influenced by the Belgian example and to a certain degree by the Spanish example,[87] where complaints procedures and overzealous investigating magistrates have endangered friendly relations with other states. The problem is, however, that the desirability of either the absolute or the conditional universal jurisdiction approach cannot be dissociated from national criminal justice systems. In the case of Belgium it is not so much the establishment of absolute universal jurisdiction as the organization of its criminal procedure that has resulted in serious

[83] Absolute universal jurisdiction for Belgian courts is based on Article 7 of the Act Concerning the Punishment of Grave Breaches of Humanitarian Law (Act of 16 June 1993 (*Official Journal*, 5 August 1993, at 17751–5), as modified by the Act of 10 February 1999 (*Official Journal*, 23 March 1999, at 9286–7), 38 ILM 918 (1999)); Germany also seems to allow for absolute universal jurisdiction. However, the prosecuting authorities have considerable discretion not to prosecute when the accused is not present on German territory (Article 3(5) of the Act to Introduce the Code of Crimes against International Law of 26 June 2002).

[84] See Article 18 Projet de Loi portant Mise en Oeuvre du Statut de la Cour Pénale Internationale, available at www.iccnow.org/documents/DRCDraftLegFren.pdf (last visited 13 November 2006): 'Les infractions prévues par la présente loi sont punissables même quand elles ont été commises à l'étranger ou quand elles ne présentent pas de lien avec le territoire congolais.' This is, in light of the Congo's position in the *Arrest Warrant* case, remarkable language.

[85] The United Kingdom does not establish universal jurisdiction, but only jurisdiction on the basis of the territoriality and active nationality principles. See sections 51 and 58 of the International Criminal Court Act 2001, available at www.nottingham.ac.uk/shared/shared_hrlcicju/United_Kingdom/International_ Criminal_Court_Act_ 2001_English_.doc (last visited 15 November 2006). Conditional universal jurisdiction has been or will be established by, inter alia, the Netherlands (Article 2 of the International Crimes Act, available at www.iccnow.org/ documents/NL.IntCrAct.pdf (last visited 15 November 2006), South Africa (Article 4.2 of the International Criminal Court Bill, available at www.iccnow.org/documents/SouthAfricaLegEng.pdf (last visited 15 November 2006)), Uruguay (Article 4, Proyecto de Ley sustitutivo de la Comisión, available at www.iccnow.org/documents/ProyectoSustitutivoComisionCPI1July05.pdf (last visited 15 November 2006)), Ecuador (Articles 1 and 2, Proyecto de Ley sobre Delitos conte la Humanidad, available at www.iccnow.org/documents/EcuadorDraft LegSpa.pdf (last visited 15 November 2006)), Argentina (Articles 3 and 4, Proyecto de Ley de implementación del estatuto de Roma de la Corte Penal Internacional, available at www.iccnow.org/documents/S-2078-06_ Estatuto_Roma1Jul05.pdf (last visited 15 November 2006)), and Canada (Article 8(b) of the Crimes Against Humanity and War Crimes Act, 2000, available at www.iccnow.org/documents/Canada.CrAgH.WcrEng.pdf (last visited 15 November 2006)).

[86] Explanatory Memorandum, *Parliamentary Documents* II, 2001–2, 28 337, no. 3, at 18.

[87] In Spain there is also an active and progressive approach to the prosecution of international crimes, which is evidenced by its request to the UK to extradite General Pinochet. From a recent case it follows that the progressive approach extends to the application of universal jurisdiction. See H. Ascensio, 'The Spanish Constitutional Tribunal's Decision in *Guatemalan Generals* — Unconditional Universality is Back' (2006) 4 *JICJ*, at 586–94.

frictions with other states and in what appears a prosecutorial overreach.[88] In criminal justice systems with a certain degree of prosecutorial discretion, a prosecutor enjoys the necessary margin of appreciation to balance the interest of prosecution with other serious competing interests. Thus, one may in this light completely understand the decision of the German prosecution service not to indict Rumsfeld, then a US defence minister, for war crimes.[89] In the exercise of prosecutorial discretion, the principle of subsidiarity was applied, in the sense that US courts are the primary forum for such cases and it was not proven that jurisdiction was unavailable there.[90] By this exercise of prosecutorial discretion, introducing a principle of subsidiarity which is neither very suitable for application at the investigative stage[91] nor very realistic in light of the jurisdictional possibilities available in the USA, one removes the rough edges from absolute universal jurisdiction. As a result, one may wonder why absolute universal jurisdiction is problematic in states with a tradition of prosecutorial discretion, especially if one bears in mind that absolute universal jurisdiction may be indispensable in the investigation of crimes alleged to have been committed by suspects who are not present on national territory.[92]

As to the conditional universal jurisdiction incorporated in recent 'international crimes acts', questions of interpretation will certainly arise, with potentially serious consequences for the exercise of jurisdiction. A central matter will be the determination of presence on national territory, which many states specify as a precondition for universal jurisdiction. Is continuing presence required, presence at the commencement of any act of investigation, or may a (prolonged) presence in the past be sufficient? Since there is as yet no rule of international law against absolute universal jurisdiction, a teleological interpretation seems justified. In this respect, we stress that the underlying

---

[88] In Belgium, '[a]ny person who claims to have been the victim of a crime or délit is allowed to report it and become the partie civile (a private party who either institutes a prosecution independently or joins himself to the public prosecution) in proceedings before a judge' (B. Pesquié and Y. Cartuijvels, 'The Belgian System', in M. Delmas-Marty and J. R. Spencer (eds), *European Criminal Procedure* (Cambridge: Cambridge University Press, 2002), at 94).

[89] See Decision of German general prosecuting attorney of the federal court on the complaint against Rumsfeld et al., 10 February 2005; original German decision and English translation available at www.ccr-ny.org/v2/legal/september_11th/sept11Article.asp?ObjID=1xiADJOOQx&Content=472 (last visited 14 November 2006). The prosecution's decision was upheld in the Higher Regional Court (Oberlandesgericht) Stuttgart, 5th Senate for Criminal Matters, Decision (Beschluss) of 13 September 2005 (available ibid.).

[90] See Decision of German general prosecuting attorney of the federal court on the complaint against Rumsfeld et al., 10 February 2005:

> Only if criminal prosecution by primarily competent states, or an international court, is not ensured or cannot be ensured, for instance if the perpetrator has removed himself from criminal prosecution by fleeing abroad, is the interception-jurisdiction of German prosecutorial authorities activated. This hierarchy is justified by the special interests of the home country of the perpetrator and victim in criminal prosecutions, as well as by the usually greater proximity of these first-to-be-called-upon jurisdictions to the evidence.

[91] In this sense, see C. Kress, 'Universal Jurisdiction over International Crimes and the *Institut de Droit International*' (2006) 4 *JICJ*, at 580.

[92] Support for absolute universal jurisdiction in the Netherlands at least in order to allow investigative activities to move forward is provided by A. Klip, 'Komt er een eind aan de nationale strafvervolging van internationale misdrijven?', in P. M. Russen Groen et al. (eds), *Iets bijzonders — Liber amicorum prof. Jhr. Mr. M. Wladimiroff* (The Hague: SDU Uitgevers, 2002), at 268.

purpose of designating certain acts as international crimes is to authorize the assertion of wide jurisdiction over persons committing them.[93]

13.6 IMMUNITIES UNDER INTERNATIONAL LAW AS A BAR TO THE APPLICATION OF INTERNATIONAL CRIMINAL LAW

Although it is generally agreed — and regarded as a principle of international criminal law — that international immunities from prosecution do not apply to international crimes, it is a highly complicated matter. Both the different classes of immunities and the content and scope of immunities under international law have given and still give rise to confusion. This of course has to do with the recent spectacular but not very coherent developments in this field.[94]

It is beyond the scope of this chapter to provide a detailed analysis of international law on immunities in respect of international crimes; yet some introductory remarks are necessary. Immunities are closely related to the notion of jurisdiction; because of this, they do not affect an individual's international criminal responsibility, but concern only the enforcement of such responsibility via the legal process.[95] Whether this legal process is lawful under the international law of immunities will depend on three factors: the nature of the trial forum, the status of the accused at the time of commission of the crime and the time of arrest, and the criminal conduct which is object of the trial.

The extent to which national courts may exercise jurisdiction over their own state officials, such as the president or members of parliament, is in the first instance governed not by international, but by domestic law. However, if a state neither tries nor extradites a national accused of international crimes, it may incur state responsibility on the basis of *aut dedere aut iudicare* obligations.[96]

Of more interest is the position of non-national courts. In inter-state relations the sovereign equality of states plays a prominent role, preventing a court of state A sitting in judgment of the *iure imperii* acts of state B (state immunity). Furthermore, immunities are based also on functional considerations.[97] Thus, foreign courts respect functional

---

[93] Joint Separate Opinion of Judges Higgins, Kooijmans, and Buergenthal to the *Arrest Warrant* case, para. 58.

[94] For a thorough and recent study on immunities in relation to international crimes, we recommend R. van Alebeek, 'The Immunity of States and their Officials in the Light of International Criminal Law and International Human Rights Law', unpublished PhD thesis, University of Leiden, 2006.

[95] In this respect we take a slightly different approach from Cassese, who distinguishes between functional immunities as relating to the individual criminal responsibility and personal immunities as relating to the exercise of jurisdiction (A. Cassese, *International Criminal Law*, at 265–73). See also the ICJ Judgment in the *Arrest Warrant* case, para. 60: 'Immunity from criminal jurisdiction and individual criminal responsibility are quite separate concepts. While jurisdictional immunity is procedural in nature, criminal responsibility is a question of substantive law.'

[96] See above, section 13.5.

[97] For far more detail on the twin pillars of immunities and their complicated relationship *inter se*, see R. van Alebeek, 'The Immunity of States and their Officials in the Light of International Criminal Law and International Human Rights Law', at 75–212.

inter-state exchanges or communications, as well as allowing the unimpeded operation of the other state's organs in conducting its public functions. As a result, diplomats and government members on official missions enjoy functional protection from foreign courts (state immunity and diplomatic immunity). This has given rise to two classes of immunities, the first concerning official acts and the second concerning *official persons* performing state functions, both of which fall outside the reach of any foreign jurisdiction.

International immunities do not play a similarly important role in international courts. As these courts receive the support of a large number of states, they operate in a vertical relationship with states, and the sovereign equality of states is no longer at issue.[98] This is also why the ICJ ruled that international immunities do not apply to international criminal courts and specifically mentioned the ICTY and the ICC.[99] The reference to the ICC appears to imply that the existence of a large number of states parties may be sufficient to justify the non-application of immunities, and that this is also the case in relation to non-party states.

In the jurisprudence a distinction tends to be made between persons claiming immunities, depending on their status. High-ranking state officials and diplomats in office are said to enjoy absolute immunity for every act while they occupy their posts.[100] Former heads of state or former diplomats no longer enjoy absolute personal immunities, but only immunities in respect of official acts; private acts fall outside the scope of international immunities.[101]

This last point brings us to the nature of the act. The distinction between official and private acts was strongly confirmed in the *Arrest Warrant* case, where the ICJ stated:

after a person ceases to hold the office of Minister for Foreign Affairs, he or she will no longer enjoy all of the immunities accorded by international law in other States. Provided that it has jurisdiction under international law, a court of one State may try a former Minister for Foreign Affairs of another State in respect of acts committed prior or subsequent to his or her period of office, as well as in respect of acts committed during that period of office in a private capacity.[102]

---

[98] The 'vertical relationship' was introduced by the ICTY in the *Blaškić* case in respect of the cooperation relationship with states; see Chapter 12, section 12.3.4. Also see Decision on Immunity from Jurisdiction, *Prosecutor v. Taylor*, Case No. SCSL-2003-01-I, SCSL, A. Ch., 31 May 2004, para. 51: 'The principle of state immunity derives from the equality of sovereign states and therefore has no relevance to international criminal tribunals which are not organs of a state but derive their mandate from the international community.'

[99] *Arrest Warrant* case, para. 61. Note that the SCSL was not mentioned, but the latter made it clear in *Taylor* that it in fact belongs to the same category (Decision on Immunity from Jurisdiction, *Prosecutor v. Taylor*, Case No. SCSL-2003-01-I, SCSL, A. Ch., 31 May 2004).

[100] Ibid., *Arrest Warrant* case, para. 54: 'the functions of a Minister for Foreign Affairs are such that, throughout the duration of his or her office, he or she when abroad enjoys full immunity from criminal jurisdiction and inviolability.' Paragraph 58 states that there is no exception to this rule. See also Joint Separate Opinion of judges Higgins, Kooijmans, and Buergenthal, para. 83:

We agree, therefore, with the Court that the purpose of the immunities attaching to Ministers for Foreign Affairs under customary international law is to ensure the free performance of their functions on behalf of their respective States (Judgement, para. 53). During their term of office, they must therefore be able to travel freely whenever the need to do so arises. There is broad agreement in the literature that a Minister for Foreign Affairs is entitled to full immunity during official visits in the exercise of his function.

[101] Ibid., para. 61.   [102] Ibid.

This obiter dictum raises the question of whether international crimes may be included in the 'private acts' referred to by the ICJ. Given the nature of most international crimes, they fall within the sphere of official acts. As has been observed, they are very seldom committed in a private capacity.[103] Were this the case, former diplomats and state officials would continue to enjoy immunity for international crimes. Such a position seems difficult to reconcile with the growing importance of international crimes within international law. How can the international law on immunities be balanced against the duty to prosecute and try (certain) international crimes? One possible solution is to class international crimes by definition as private acts for which no immunity exists.[104] However, this does not accord with reality.[105] A better view is that international crimes have developed as an exception to immunities for official acts.[106]

In light of the above, the question arises how states have dealt — and will deal — with the tension between international immunities and the prosecution of international crimes. Jurisprudence prior to *Pinochet*[107] is scarce. On the rare occasion that states have prosecuted foreign heads of state or other high officials the immunity claim itself was considered inapplicable. Thus, in the *Noriega* case a US court ruled that Noriega was not entitled to head of state immunity, since he was not Panama's legitimate leader.[108] It needs to be borne in mind, however, that Noriega was not charged with international crimes. Such crimes did — and still do — play a role in various civil suits in the USA on the basis of the Alien Tort Claims Act.[109] In the cases against

[103] A. Cassese, 'When May Senior State Officials Be Tried for International Crimes? Some Comments on the *Congo* v. *Belgium* Case', at 868.

[104] See *Arrest Warrant* case, Joint Separate Opinion of Judges Higgins, Kooijmans, and Buergenthal, para. 83:

> It is now increasingly claimed in the literature (see e.g., Andrea Bianchi 'Denying State Immunity to Violators of Human Rights', 46 *Austrian Journal of Public and International Law* (1994), pp. 227–228) that serious international crimes cannot be regarded as official acts because they are neither normal State functions nor functions that a State alone (in contrast to an individual) can perform: (Goff, J. (as he then was) and Lord Wilberforce articulated this test in the case of *1º Congreso del Partido* (1978) QB 500 at 528 and (1983) AC 244 at 268, respectively). This view is underscored by the increasing realization that State-related motives are not the proper test for determining what constitutes public State acts. The same view is gradually also finding expression in State practice, as evidenced in judicial decisions and opinions. (For an early example, see the judgement of the Israel Supreme Court in the *Eichmann* case; Supreme Court, 29 May 1962, 36 *International Law Reports*, p. 312.) See also the speeches of Lords Hutton and Phillips of Worth Matravers in *R* v. *Bartle and the Commissioner of Police for the Metropolis and Others*, ex parte Pinochet ('Pinochet III'); and of Lords Steyn and Nicholls of Birkenhead in 'Pinochet I', as well as the judgement of the Court of Appeal of Amsterdam in the *Bouterse* case (*Gerechtshof Amsterdam*, 20 November 2000, para. 4.2).

See also M. Sassoli, 'L'arrêt Yerodia: Quelques remarques sur une affaire au point de collision entre les deux couches de droit international', at 802.

[105] Cf. M. Sassoli, 'L'arrêt Yerodia: Quelques remarques sur une affaire au point de collision entre les deux couches de droit international', at 802, where this reasoning is labelled absurd.

[106] Cf. A. Cassese, 'When May Senior State Officials Be Tried for International Crimes? Some Comments on the *Congo* v. *Belgium* Case', at 870. Cassese establishes this exception on the basis of the irrelevance of official capacity for international criminal responsibility.

[107] *R.* v. *Bow Street Metropolitan Stipendiary Magistrate and others, ex parte Pinochet Ugarte*, three decisions by the House of Lords: House of Lords 1998 [1998] 4 All ER 897 ([1998] 3 WLR 1456 HL); House of Lords 1999 [1999] 1 All ER 577 ([1999] 2 WLR 272); House of Lords 1999 [1999] 2 All ER 97.

[108] *United States* v. *Noriega*, District Court for the Southern District of Florida, 746 F. Supp. 1510 (S.D. Fla. 1990).

[109] See above, section 13.2.

Karadžić and Marcos immunity was not granted, but for different reasons. In *Karadžić* the court easily adopted the 'Noriega' approach in that Karadžić was leading an entity not recognized as a state, namely Republika Srpska.[110] In *Marcos*, however, the court offered an interesting conclusion in the light of the official/private acts dichotomy. It ruled that massive cases of torture could not be considered legitimate official acts, and therefore the court had no problem holding Marcos accountable for them as private offences.[111]

Generally US courts honour State Department requests for immunity for a head of state.[112] In the *Mugabe* case the New York District Court therefore dismissed on jurisdictional grounds victims' claims naming as defendants the Zimbabwe President Robert Mugabe and other Zimbabwe government officials entitled to invoke sovereign or diplomatic immunity.[113] This decision was issued post-*Pinochet* and the court acknowledged important developments in the field of state immunities in relation to international crimes. As a result, the court found a sufficient basis to exercise jurisdiction over the claims asserted against the Zimbabwe African National Union-Patriotic Front 'ZANU-PF', the country's ruling party.[114]

Since *Pinochet* there have been few prosecutions of acting or former heads of state for international crimes. Obviously, states are reluctant to proceed with such prosecutions because of the foreign policy implications. The Belgian legislative reforms have already been mentioned as an exception. The special circumstances of that state resulted in complaints being lodged against prominent foreign government leaders and/or officials.[115] The ICJ's *Arrest Warrant* case and tensions with the United States in particular prompted a more cautious position.[116] In France a complaint was filed against the Libyan head of state Muammar Ghaddafi concerning acts of terrorism in respect of a French aircraft. The French *Cour de Cassation* declined to exercise jurisdiction on account of immunities accruing to Ghaddafi as acting head of state.[117]

The new national 'international crimes acts', triggered by the establishment of the ICC, may shed some light on the future direction of international immunities in

---

[110] *Kadić* v. *Karadžić*, Court of Appeals, 2nd Circuit, 70 F.3d 232 (1995), at 244 (34 ILM 1995 1595). The court held that the defendant had been head of an entity not recognized as a state by the USA and therefore was not protected by the Foreign Sovereign Immunity Act.

[111] *Republic of the Philippines* v. *Marcos*, 862 F.2d 1355, 1361 (9th Cir. 1988).

[112] M. A. Tunks, 'Diplomats or Defendants?: Defining the Future of Head-of-State Immunity' (2002) 52 *Duke L. J.*, at 674.

[113] *Tachiona* v. *Mugabe*, 169 F. Supp. 2d 259, 278–81 (SDNY 2001).

[114] Ibid., and *Tachiona* v. *Mugabe*, 2002 WL 31799018 (SDNY). For a commentary on both decisions, see N. M. Walsh, 'Tachiona v. Mugabe' (2002) 15 *New York Int'l Law Rev.*, at 91–9.

[115] See D. Vandermeersch, 'Prosecuting International Crimes in Belgium', at 408, where many examples are given, including the following: 'Belgian courts were tasked with several new investigations initiated by civil petitioners under the provisions of the law adopted on 16 June 1993, concerning incumbent heads of state or of government, such as Saddam Hussein, Fidel Castro, Paul Kagame, Yasser Arafat, Ariel Sharon and George Bush Senior.'

[116] In Belgium this has resulted in corrective legislation according to which either one of the civil petitioners must be a Belgian national at the time the proceedings were initiated, or one of the alleged perpetrators must have been residing in Belgium at the date of entry into force of the law (5 August 2003). See ibid.

[117] *Arrêt* of 13 March 2001, No. 1414. For a critical commentary see S. Zappalà, 'Do Heads of State in Office Enjoy Immunity from Jurisdiction for International Crimes? The Ghaddafi Case before the French *Cour de Cassation*' (2001) 12 *EJIL*, at 595–612.

relation to the core crimes. Some states clearly had the benefit of being able to take the *Arrest Warrant* case into account. For example, Article 16 of the Dutch International Crimes Act seeks to codify the ICJ's ruling in the *Arrest Warrant* case, but also anticipates future developments in the field of international immunities:

Criminal prosecution for one of the crimes referred to in this Act is excluded with respect to:

(a) foreign heads of state, heads of government and ministers of foreign affairs, as long as they are in office, and other persons in so far as their immunity is recognised under customary international law;

(b) persons who have immunity under any Convention to which the Netherlands is a party.

This provision is flexible, which is illustrated by the reference to customary international law, and saves the Netherlands from having to adopt at this time a certain stance on the scope of immunities of former heads of state and other former officials. From the explanatory memorandum one senses the difficulty of interpreting the ICJ's obiter dictum in the *Arrest Warrant* case that former heads of state enjoy immunity for official but not for private acts. The Dutch government adopted the defendable position that a broad interpretation should be given to acts committed in a private capacity.[118] Although it is not stated in so many words, this category should then cover international crimes.

Other 'international crimes acts' tend to neglect the question of immunities, with the exception of the (draft) laws of the Congo and Ecuador.

The Congolese draft act implementing the ICC Statute contains a far-reaching immunity clause:

La présente loi s'applique à tous de manière égale, sans aucune distinction fondée sur la qualité officielle.

Les immunités ou règles de procédures spéciales qui peuvent s'attacher à la qualité officielle d'une personne, en vertu du droit interne ou du droit international, n'empêchent pas le juge d'exercer sa compétence à l'égard de cette personne.[119]

This seems inconsistent with the absolute immunity for (certain) acting state officials, as confirmed in the *Arrest Warrant* case. Remarkably, this provision is also inconsistent with the Congo's pleading position before the ICJ in its immunity dispute with Belgium.

The Ecuadorian draft act on crimes against humanity stipulates that the act applies to every individual irrespective of the individual's official capacity whether as a member of the Ecuadorian government, or of a foreign government.[120] Again, this seems to allow for the prosecution of foreign state officials.

While the above provisions allow for the prosecution of foreign state officials — as it is possible that other legislative frameworks also allow — the extent to which states will

---

[118] Explanatory Memorandum, *Parliamentary Documents* II, 2001–2, 28 337, no. 3, at 20.

[119] Article 9 of the Projet de Loi portant Mise en Oeuvre du Statut de la Cour Pénale Internationale, available at www.iccnow.org/documents/DRCDraftLegFren.pdf (last visited 13 November 2006).

[120] Article 4 of the Proyecto de Ley Sobre Delitos Contra La Humanidad, available at www.iccnow.org/documents/EcuadorDraftLegSpa.pdf (last visited 13 November 2006), translated by the authors.

make use of that possibility remains to be seen. In light of the *Arrest Warrant* case a more cautious approach may be expected. Without future state practice, the international law on immunities in relation to international crimes will probably remain unclear.

13.7 THE NATIONAL APPLICATION OF SOME GENERAL PRINCIPLES OF INTERNATIONAL CRIMINAL LAW

13.7.1 Command responsibility

The application of command responsibility by international criminal tribunals has been analysed in Chapter 7, section 7.3. While the content of this doctrine under international law thus needs no further discussion, in the context of this chapter it is worth sketching developments in the national context. As with other principles of international criminal law, a distinction can be made between the pre- and the post-ICC Statute period.

One of the most important cases concerning the doctrine of command responsibility was that of the Japanese general Yamashita. He was tried by a US Military Commission and charged with 'command responsibility' for war crimes in the Philippines.[121] The Commission apparently proposed a strict liability for commanders. The defence offered by Yamashita, that the lines of communication with his troops were severed and that it was not possible for him to ensure their compliance with the laws of war, was rejected. Instead, the Commission ruled that there was '[e]vidence to show that the crimes were so extensive and widespread, both as to time and area, that they must have been wilfully permitted by the accused, or secretly ordered by the accused'.[122]

The impact of *Yamashita*, a difficult case, on the development of the doctrine of command responsibility is significant. It has frequently been used in the ICTY and ICTR jurisprudence. Yet, there is not a great deal of post-Second World War national practice. Interesting cases that can be mentioned concern decisions by US courts *in poenalibus* and *in civilibus*.

The first such case concerns the My Lai massacre in the Vietnam War. Captain Medina was charged at a court martial with the premeditated murder of an unknown number of Vietnamese nationals murdered by his men.[123] The prosecution in his case

---

[121] Trial of General Tomoyuki Yamashita (US Military Commission, Manila (8 October–7 December 1945)), *LRTWC*, vol. IV (UN War Crimes Commission, London, 1949, reprinted Buffalo, NY), p.1. For a detailed analysis of the trial, see R. R. Lael, *The Yamashita Precedent: War Crimes and Command Responsibility* (Wilmington, Delaware: Scholarly Resources, 1982).

[122] *Yamashita*, para. 12 (verdict and sentence).

[123] *United States* v. *Medina*, CM 427162 (1971). For a commentary on *Yamashita* and *Medina*, see M. L. Smidt, 'Yamashita, Medina and Beyond: Command Responsibility in Contemporary Military Operations' (2000) 164 *Military Law Review*, at 155–234.

argued that Medina knew exactly what was going on and that he had the power to stop the killing simply by making a radio call. Regarding the issue of knowledge, the court elected to apply a narrower standard than in *Yamashita*: what was required in the court's view is the actual knowledge and not the 'should have known' standard.[124] The reason for the deviation from *Yamashita* may lie in the fact that the prosecution was for national crimes only (Medina was not charged with war crimes). Had Medina been charged with war crimes, the result might have been a different command responsibility test.

US cases based solely on international crimes include the more recent civil suits pursuant to the Alien Torts Claims Act and the Torture Victim Protection Act. The cases against Garcia (2002) and Lumintang (2001) dealt with the doctrine of command responsibility in light of the ICTY case law. *Garcia* concerned the abduction, torture, and murder of US nationals by members of the Salvadorian National Guard. Garcia was at that time El Salvador's Minister of Defence and the plaintiffs held him accountable as a commander for the (war) crimes of his subordinates.[125] A vital issue in the litigation was the degree of control the defendant had over his subordinates and what test was appropriate under the doctrine of command responsibility. Tracing the development of the concept back to *Yamashita*, the court embarked on a rather elaborate analysis of the *Delalić* judgment to establish the appropriate test and to apply it to the case at issue. Remarkably, the court also used Article 28 of the ICC Statute to determine the content and scope of the command responsibility doctrine, although the USA is not a party to this treaty.[126] There is a more internationally oriented approach in *Garcia* than in *Medina* and a return to the stricter *Yamashita* test.

Lumintang was as army deputy chief of staff of Indonesia held accountable by plaintiffs for the war crimes committed by his subordinates in East Timor in 1999. The doctrine of command responsibility was applied to his case on the basis of both international and US law.[127] However, the decision offers no thorough analysis, nor does it allude to the relevant ICTY case law. The court, taking into account previous US case law, simply concludes that Lumintang served as commander of subordinate members of the TNI (Indonesia's military) in East Timor who perpetrated the acts of violence which injured the plaintiffs; he knew or should have known that the subordinates in East Timor were committing, were about to commit, or had committed widespread and systematic human rights violations, and failed to act to prevent or punish the violations.[128] The recent US case law thus offers an example of the application of the doctrine of command responsibility that is largely consistent with international case law.

Following the Yugoslav and Rwanda conflicts, national prosecutions were not primarily concerned with command responsibility (since the bigger fish were primarily the focus of the ICTR and the ICTY). Arguably, an essential factor might have been the

---

[124] *United States* v. *Medina*, CM 427162 (1971).

[125] *Ford* v. *Garcia*, US Courts of Appeals, 11th Circuit, 30 April 2002. For a commentary, see S. D. Murphy, 'Doctrine of Command Responsibility in US Human Rights Cases' (2002) 96 *AJIL*, at 719–23.

[126] Ibid., para. 1.

[127] *Doe* v. *Lumintang*, US District Court for the District of Columbia, 10 September 2001.

[128] Ibid., para. IIA.

absence of command responsibility as a mode of liability in domestic penal codes. Until recently 'command responsibility' seems to have been reserved for military legal manuals and codes of military justice.[129] If the concept of command responsibility is included in any of the post-Second World War war crimes acts, its content and scope is often vague. One example is Article 9 of the Dutch War Crimes Act (1952): 'Equally punishable is the superior who knowingly tolerates that his subordinate commits such an offence.'

The Belgian Act of 1993 — thus prior to the ICTY jurisprudence clarifying command responsibility — contains an obscure mode of liability, only vaguely resembling command responsibility:

Equally punishable is . . . a person who is aware of an order which is aimed at the commission of such crimes, or who is aware of attempts to commit such crimes, and is able to interfere, but fails to do so.[130]

The codification of command responsibility in Article 28 of the ICC Statute was thus most welcome as a guide for national legislators and courts. Not only does Article 28 provide for a mode of liability for military commanders, but it also lays down the principles of the criminal responsibility of civilian superiors, a matter which until then had been addressed only marginally in national laws.

The new generation of international crimes acts implement Article 28 of the ICC Statute quite faithfully, sometimes even reproducing that provision verbatim (see the Congo or the UK) or by making a direct reference to it (see New Zealand and Uruguay).[131] States that have incorporated command responsibility, either directly or indirectly, into their domestic law following the adoption of the Rome Statute, or are in the process of doing so, are: Canada,[132] Germany,[133] New Zealand,[134] the United Kingdom,[135] the Democratic Republic of the

---

[129] See e.g. Article 77 of the US Uniform Code of Military Justice; Australian Defence Force Publication 37; and UK Manual of Military Law, at 178.   [130] Article 4 of the Law of 16 June 1993.

[131] See for the provisions of these laws notes 136, 135, 134, and 137 respectively, below.

[132] Section 5, Crimes against Humanity and War Crimes Act (2000), available at www.iccnow.org/documents/Canada.CrAgH.WcrEng.pdf (last visited 15 November 2006): military and civilian commanders; the provision sets out in detail the content and scope of command responsibility.

[133] Section 4 of the Act to Introduce the Code of Crimes against International Law of 26 June 2002, available at www.iccnow.org/documents/GermanCodeOfInternation4C1.pdf (last visited 15 November 2006): military commanders and other superiors; the provision does not set out in detail the content and scope of command responsibility.

[134] Section 12 (General Principles of criminal law), International Crimes and International Criminal Court Act 2000, available at http://rangi.knowledge-basket.co.nz/gpacts/public/text/2000/an/026.html (last visited 15 November 2006). This section states that Article 28 of the Rome Statute is applicable to proceedings for offences set out in the Act; its applicability is, however, subject to 'any necessary modifications'.

[135] Section 65, International Criminal Court Act 2001, available at www.nottingham.ac.uk/shared/shared_hrlcicju/United_Kingdom/International_Criminal_Court_Act_2001__English_.doc (last visited 15 November 2006); the provision applies to military and civilian commanders; the wording of subsections 2 and 3 is identical to that of Article 28 of the ICC Statute.

Congo,[136] Uruguay,[137] Ecuador,[138] Argentina,[139] Malta,[140] Australia,[141] and the Netherlands.[142]

Analysis of the above acts reveals some remarkable divergence with regard to command responsibility. For example, in the United Kingdom liability on the basis of command responsibility is regarded as aiding, abetting, counselling, or procuring the commission of the offences;[143] neither the ICC Statute nor the legislation of other states implementing Article 28 of that Statute makes this association but rather treats command responsibility as a *sui generis* form of liability specific to international crimes. Likewise, the Dutch International Criminal Court Act makes a distinction between intentional and culpable command responsibility that cannot be found in the Statute.[144] The 'reduced liability' forms of command responsibility such as aiding or abetting (UK), accomplice liability (Malta), or culpable command responsibility, are unknown to international criminal law in general and the ICC Statute in particular. One may therefore wonder whether these forms of 'reduced' command responsibility amount to an adequate implementation of the ICC's substantive criminal law in light of the complementarity principle.

While the above examples are illustrative of some continuing diverging treatments of command responsibility in national criminal justice systems, the recent international crimes acts certainly offer a more uniform picture of the doctrine's scope and content than in the past. Furthermore, in their application of national command responsibility

---

[136] Article 16 of the Projet de Loi portant Mise en Oeuvre du Statut de la Cour Pénale Internationale, available at www.iccnow.org/documents/DRCDraftLegFren.pdf (last visited 13 November 2006); this provision reproduces the wording of Article 28 of the ICC Statute.

[137] Article 10, Anteproyecto de Ley — Genocidio, Crimenes de lesa Humanidad, Crimenes de Guerra y Cooperación con la Corte Penal Internacional and Article 10, Proyecto de Ley sustitutivo de la Comisión (avilable at www.iccnow.org/documents/Uruguay_LopezGoldaracena_Aug2005.pdf and www.iccnow.org/documents/ProyectoSustitutivoComisionCPI1July05.pdf (last visited 15 November 2006); this is a short provision dealing with superiors in general; it does not distinguish between military and civilian 'commanders'.

[138] Article 17 of the Proyecto de Ley sobre Delitos conte la Humanidad, available at www.iccnow.org/documents/EcuadorDraftLegSpa.pdf (last visited 15 November 2006); the provision copies the wording of Article 28 of the ICC Statute.

[139] Article 6 of the Proyecto de Ley de implementación del estatuto de Roma de la Corte Penal Internacional, available at www.iccnow.org/documents/S-2078–06_Estatuto_Roma1Jul05.pdf (last visited 15 November 2006); this provision declares the rules and principles of international criminal law to have supplementary application thus it includes command responsibility.

[140] Section 54E of the International Criminal Court Act, Act XXIV of 2002, available at www.iccnow.org/documents/MaltaDraftICCImpLeg.pdf (last visited 15 November 2006); the provision reproduces the wording of Article 28 of the ICC Statute.

[141] Subdivision K 268.115 of the International Criminal Court (Consequential Amendments) Act 2002, available at www.iccnow.org/documents/AustraliaICCActNo42.2002.pdf (last visited 15 November 2006); the provision adds command responsibility as a form of liability, copying the language of Article 28 of the ICC Statute.

[142] Article 9 of the International Crimes Act, available at www.iccnow.org/documents/NL.IntCrAct.pdf (last visited 15 November 2006). This provision is entitled 'extension of criminal responsibility' and makes no distinction between military and civilian superiors. The provision makes an interesting distinction between 'intentional' and 'culpable' command responsibility. Intentional negligence of duties amounts to 'full responsibility', whereas culpable negligence can only result in a liability to two-thirds of the maximum sentence.

[143] Section 65(4) of the International Criminal Court Act 2001. Section 54E(4) of the Maltese International Criminal Court Act regards an individual held liable under command responsibility as an accomplice in the commission of the offence.   [144] See Article 9 of the International Crimes Act.

provisions, national courts will undoubtedly (continue to) take into account relevant jurisprudence of international criminal courts. The British and Maltese acts even explicitly stipulate that in interpreting and applying the domestic command responsibility provision courts shall take into account any relevant judgment or decision of the ICC.[145]

13.7.2 Defences: the extent of availability of superior orders

Like any criminal justice system, international criminal law includes a number of defences which may excuse either the act committed or the perpetrator. The scope and content of those defences have been treated in Chapter 11, section 11.9, and again we confine ourselves here to issues concerning national application. If we take the ICC Statute as a recent codification of defences in international criminal law, it is clear that a number of the defences are similar to those that are generally available in domestic criminal justice systems for ordinary crimes. Examples of such defences are mental incapacity, involuntary intoxication, self-defence, and duress (Article 31 of the ICC Statute). These defences are the result of deriving common general principles of criminal law from the various legal families. However, one important defence which is applicable and valid in respect of ordinary crimes generally does not apply to international crimes: superior orders and prescription of law (see Article 33 of the ICC Statute). Since Nuremberg it has been generally accepted that 'Befehl ist Befehl' does not apply to international crimes.[146] However, rejection of the defence of superior orders may vary from absolute (strict liability theory) to conditional (liability in the case of manifestly unlawful orders). The matter is further complicated by the relationship to other defences. It has been submitted that 'superior orders' cannot constitute a defence per se but may be a factual element in assessing whether the required mens rea can be established or whether the defences of duress (the moral choice test) or mistake of fact are applicable.[147] However, as is now evidenced by Article 33 of the ICC Statute, the view on superior orders as an autonomous defence has — in the case of not manifestly illegal orders — prevailed.[148]

Given the diverging views on superior orders, there has been considerable variety in the ways in which this defence has been applied at national level, at least prior to the implementation of the ICC Statute.

---

[145] Section 65(5) of the International Criminal Court Act 2001. This directive to national courts may have been considered appropriate because of the dualist system in the UK, where the national legal order is strictly separated from the international legal order. See also Section 54E(5) of the Maltese International Criminal Court Act, which not only mentions jurisprudence of the ICC, but also 'any other relevant international jurisprudence'.

[146] See Principle IV of the Principles of the Nuremberg Tribunal, adopted by the UN General Assembly (Affirmation of the Principles of International Law Recognized by the Charter of the Nürnberg Tribunal, GA Res. 95 (I), UN GAOR, 1st Sess., pt. 2, at 1144, UN Doc. A/236 (1946)): 'The fact that a person acted pursuant to order of his Government or of a superior does not relieve him from responsibility under international law, provided a moral choice was in fact possible to him.'

[147] This is the view of Dinstein: Y. Dinstein, *The Defense of 'Obedience to Superior Orders' in International Law* (Leyden: A.W. Sijthoff, 1965). In the *Erdemović* appeal judgment this was also the position of Judges McDonald and Vohrah (Joint Separate Opinion of Judge McDonald and Judge Vohrah, para. 34).

[148] This is also the position of Judge Cassese in the *Erdemović* appeal judgment (Separate and Dissenting Opinion of Judge Cassese, para. 15).

In the aftermath of the Second World War the American Court in Nuremberg, acting pursuant to Control Council Law No. 10, issued some interesting rulings concerning superior orders. In the *Hostages* case the position of a conditional defence of superior orders was adopted:

If the illegality of the order was not known to the inferior, and he could not reasonably have been expected to know of its illegality, no wrongful intent necessary to the commission of a crime exists and the inferior will be protected. But the general rule is that members of the armed forces are bound to obey only the lawful orders of their commanding officers and they cannot escape criminal liability by obeying a command which violates international law and outrages fundamental concepts of justice.[149]

In the same vein, the Tribunal offered similar rulings in respect of superior orders in the *Einsatzgruppen* case[150] and the *High Command* case,[151] although some important differences need to be mentioned. In the *Einsatzgruppen* case the defence of superior orders was dealt with in relation to the defences of duress and mistake of law, in respect of both of which the Tribunal applied a stringent test. In the *High Command* case the Tribunal seemed to move to a presumption in favour of the legality of superior orders:

Military commanders in the field with far reaching military responsibilities cannot be charged under international law with criminal participation in issuing orders which are not obviously criminal or which they are not shown to have known to be criminal under international law. Such a commander cannot be expected to draw fine distinctions and conclusions as to legality in connection with orders issued by his superiors. He has the right to presume, in absence of specific knowledge to the contrary, that the legality of such orders has been properly determined before their issuance. He cannot be held criminally responsible for a mere error in judgement as to [a] disputable legal question.[152]

Remarkably, the acceptance of a limited defence of superior orders, associated with other defences or not, seems contrary to Article II(4)(b) of Control Council Law No. 10, which completely ruled out superior orders as a defence. The categorization of superior orders under another defence, such as the defence of necessity, as the Tribunal did in the cases *Flick*, *Farben*, and *Krupp*,[153] seems a somewhat artificial method for getting around the aforementioned provision.

Other post-Second World War jurisprudence confirms the above decisions. An interesting case — bringing in the new question of what constitutes an 'order' — is the South African *Werner* case.[154] The facts are that a German POW detained in South Africa was convicted of murdering another POW suspected of spying. Since the homicide had apparently been ordered by a German officer hiding in the camp, the defence of superior orders was invoked. The defence was primarily rejected on account of its manifest illegality. However, even if this was not the case, the appeal court ruled that

---

[149] *Hostages* case (*US* v. *Wilhelm List et al.*), Judgment, NMT, Vol. II, at 1236.

[150] *Einsatzgruppen* case (*US* v. *Otto Ohlendort et al.*), Judgment, NMT, Vol. IV, at 471.

[151] *High Command* case (*US* v. *Wilhelm von Leeb et al.*), Judgment, NMT, Vol. II, at 534.   [152] Ibid.

[153] *Farben* case, Judgment, NMT, Vol. VIII, at 1174–9; *Flick* case, Judgment, NMT, Vol. VI, at 1200–1; *Krupp* case, Judgment, NMT, Vol. IX, at 1435–9.

[154] *R.* v. *Werner and another*, Appellate Division 20 May 1947, 1947 (2) *South African Law Reports* 828(A).

the defence would not have been available because the accused was not legally bound to obey the orders of the German officer, since the officer had no authority in the POW camp on South African territory.[155] Below we will encounter another case in which the authority to issue an order is challenged. In the present case the South African court apparently adopted the view that no order in the sense of the defence of superior orders had been issued. To treat the matter from the perspective of formal 'authority' does not do justice to the defence of superior orders. One may imagine a number of situations where orders may lack legal authority. Rather, on the basis of the facts the court should examine the superior/subordinate relationship, and determine whether it still exists and is of such a nature that one could not expect the subordinate to disobey.

In subsequent national jurisprudence the issue of 'manifest illegality' played an increasingly important role. National courts seemed prepared to accept that in the case of orders which were not manifestly unlawful no liability incurs; this is done either in the form of an accepted superior orders defence or via another defence, often duress. One notices, however, that courts take different views on the determination of 'manifestly illegal' orders.

In *Eichmann* the Israeli district court and Supreme Court found that superior orders issued to Eichmann were manifestly illegal and contrary to the basic ideas of law and justice.[156] It was necessary for the manifest illegality in the eyes of the Jerusalem district court to be determined on the basis of an objective test.[157]

In the US cases *US* v. *Kinder* and *Calley* the 'objective test' is further developed. In *US* v. *Kinder* manifestly illegal is that order 'as to admit of no doubt of its unlawfulness to a man of ordinary sense and understanding'.[158]

Likewise, the instructions by the judge to the members of the court martial in the *Calley* case concerning the My Lai massacre read as follows:

The acts of a subordinate done in compliance with an unlawful order given him by his superior are excused and impose no criminal liability upon himself unless the superior's order is one which a man of ordinary sense and understanding would, under the circumstances, know to be unlawful, or if the order in question is actually known to be unlawful.[159]

In these cases there is no ruling that — as embodied in Article 33 of the ICC Statute — orders to commit crimes against humanity or genocide are by definition manifestly illegal. However, in a Nigerian case some interesting observations were made in

---

155 Ibid.

156 Judgment, *Attorney-General of the Government of Israel* v. *Adolf Eichmann*, Case No. 40/61, District Court of Jerusalem, 11 December 1961, reprinted in (1968) 36 ILR, paras 216–21, and Judgment of the Israel Supreme Court, 29 May 1962, reprinted in (1968) 36 ILR, at 277–342.

157 Ibid., para. 218:

In this respect our Law follows Article 8 of the London Charter under which the International Military Tribunal at Nuremberg was set up, and Article II4(b) of Law No. 10 of the Allied Control Council for Germany, under which courts were set up to try subsequent cases against war criminals. They also refuse to accept a plea of 'superior orders' as exempting from responsibility, but permit the court to consider the existence of such an order as grounds for mitigation of the penalty.

158 *US* v. *Kinder* (1954) 14 *CMR* 742.

159 *United States* v. *Calley*, Instructions from the Military Judge to the Court Martial Members, March 1971, in Friedman, II, 1703–27.

connection with the 'manifestly illegal' determination, including the court's final conclusion that crimes against humanity must be punished. The case of *Pius Nwaoga* v. *Nigeria* concerns the murder of civilians by three officers of the Rebel Biafran army, disguised in civilian clothes, all taking place in a town under the control of federal troops.[160] One of the officers invoked the defence of superior orders. The trial judge addressed the 'manifest illegality' issue and observed that since the order to eliminate the deceased was given by an officer of an illegal regime, his orders are necessarily unlawful and obedience to them involves a violation of the law and the defence of superior orders is untenable.[161] Such a formal approach to the defence of superior orders, by inquiring into the (lawful) origin of the order, is inappropriate and entails the risk of making the defence inapplicable in internal armed conflicts. The Nigerian Supreme Court did not explicitly endorse this part of the ruling, but focused on the nature of the operation, which was conducted by saboteurs, disguised in civilian clothes. Although it did not explicity say so, the Court seemed to have difficulty giving saboteurs, who were violating the laws of war themselves, the protection of the defence of superior orders. In addition, as already mentioned, the Court found the criminal conduct to amount to crimes against humanity and on that basis apparently refused the defence of superior orders.

In the Canadian *Finta* case there is a clear rejection of an autonomous defence of superior orders; it is dealt with under the defence of duress and here the central question is whether a moral choice was possible.[162]

The Italian *Hass and Priebke* case brings us back to the manifest illegality issue. An interesting aspect of that decision is that it brings in a subjective element, which serves, however, only to limit the availability of the defence of superior orders. Even if the objective test were to apply, it would be of no avail if two elements of a subjective test are not met:

1. the accused is not aware of the illegality of the order;
2. the accused is not indifferent to the question of legality of the order. In other words, if it is apparent that the illegality of the order would not influence the accused's decision whether or not to give effect to it, the defence of superior orders cannot be invoked.[163]

The above subjective test is a useful contribution to the development of 'superior orders'. Indeed, a preliminary question for every court should be whether the illegality of an order would in fact influence the accused's conduct if he or she had knowledge thereof. The problem is, as with practically any subjective test, that this will be extremely difficult to determine.

---

[160] *Pius Nwaoga v. Nigeria*, Supreme Court, 3 March 1972, *All Nigeria Law Reports*, Part 1, Vol. 1, at 149 (also reproduced in (1979) 52 ILR, at 494).   [161] Ibid.

[162] *R.* v. *Finta*, Supreme Court of Canada, 24 March 1994 (*R.* v. *Finta* [1994] 1 *SCR* 701), para. 3.74: 'Essentially obedience to a superior order would appear to provide a valid defence unless the act is so outrageous as to be manifestly unlawful. Further, in any case, an accused will not be convicted of an act committed pursuant to an order wherein he or she had no moral choice but to obey.'

[163] *Hass and Priebke*, Military Court of Appeal of Rome/Supreme Court of Cassation, 7 March 1998/16 November 1998. Summary in English is available at www.icrc.org/ihl-nat.nsf/46707c419d6bdfa24125673e00508145/ 0370fc27370b3776c1256c8c0055e44d!OpenDocument (last visited 20 November 2006).

Although national case law seems to be moving in one direction, with the manifest illegality concept as common ground, the above-mentioned cases illustrate some of the difficulties inherent in the defence of superior orders. Again, one may expect the ICC Statute to offer some welcome guidance. Indeed, 'manifestly unlawful' is specified to a certain degree in Article 33(2) of the ICC Statute and the defence of superior orders appears now to have been clearly accepted as an autonomous defence in respect of orders which are not manifestly unlawful. In light of the complexity of the defence, continued guidance by international case law remains indispensable.

Several recently adopted or proposed international crimes acts have implemented Article 33 of the Rome Statute, albeit in different ways and to different degrees. Since in most national systems prescription of law and superior orders amount to a valid and complete defence, some states have tried to combine this defence with some of the particularities of Article 33 of the ICC Statute. This is the case with the Netherlands. Article 11 of the Dutch International Crimes Act implements the gist of Article 33 by using the terminology of Article 43 of the Dutch Penal Code. The latter provision allows for a complete defence in the case of superior orders. The slight difference in terminology is not likely to result in a distorted application of the defence of superior orders.[164] A number of other states have also enacted provisions which differ slightly in terminology from the standard of Article 33 of the ICC Statute. Section 14 of the Canadian Crimes Against Humanity and War Crimes Act in its first two subsections reproduces almost verbatim Article 33 of the ICC Statute. An interesting addition is the mens rea qualification in subsection 3, according to which a belief that the order was lawful cannot be based on information encouraging or justifying the commission of inhumane acts against a civilian population or an identifiable group. Practically verbatim copies of Article 33 can also be found in the draft act of the Congo.[165] Even if there are some deviations from the language used in Article 33, domestic laws tend to contain the vital elements of no knowledge of illegality, manifest illegality, and exclusion of crimes against humanity and genocide.[166] The most direct and therefore probably the most faithful implementation of Article 33 can again be found in the legislation of those states that declare this and other provisions directly applicable, as is the case with New Zealand.[167]

The above laws are thus moving towards uniformity, and it may be expected that other states will follow, thereby making laudable efforts faithfully to implement substantive norms of international criminal law as set out in the ICC Statute.

13.7.3 The non-applicability of statutes of limitations

In many states the elapse of a certain period of time constitutes a bar to the prosecution of criminal conduct or the enforcement of a sentence imposed. This is referred to as a statute of limitations and essentially applies to the criminal justice systems of civil-law

---

[164] It may be expected that in the application of Article 11 of the Dutch International Crimes Act the courts will be guided by international law and international jurisprudence.

[165] Articles 14 and 15 of the Projet de Loi portant Mise en Oeuvre du Statut de la Cour Pénale Internationale.

[166] Article 3 of the German Act; Section 268.116 of the Australian Act.

[167] Section 12(1)(a)(xi) of the International Crimes and International Criminal Court Act 2000.

states and far less so to common-law traditions. The underlying rationale of a statute of limitations is twofold. First, the passage of time affects the quality of justice, namely the probative value of evidence; evidence gets lost and witnesses' memories may fail them. Secondly, the interest of society in prosecution decreases with the passage of time. These grounds are certainly not uncontested. With new forensic techniques, such as DNA, it is now possible to obtain highly reliable evidence concerning crimes that were committed long ago. Furthermore, and more fundamentally, the more serious the criminal conduct the longer (international) society wishes to maintain its interest in prosecution. Of course, this applies especially to international crimes, which means that in relation to those crimes only the first element of the underlying rationale of statutes of limitations remains applicable.[168]

The question arises to what extent the non-applicability of a statute of limitations to international crimes is part of general international law and has as such been faithfully implemented in the domestic legal order. Two treaties specifically oblige states parties not to apply statutory limitations to war crimes and crimes against humanity. The first is the Convention on the Non-applicability of Statutory Limitations to War Crimes and Crimes Against Humanity and is open to all states.[169] The second is confined to members of the Council of Europe and is the European Convention on the Non Applicability of Statutory Limitations to Crimes Against Humanity and War Crimes.[170] Neither convention has, however, been widely ratified.[171] The question of whether a rule of customary international law exists is, as always, extremely difficult to answer. An additional complicating factor is that the idea of statutory limitations is less familiar to common-law countries. Furthermore, state practice, in the form of national statutes of limitations, has not been uniform and unambiguous. There is certainly no uniform practice of non-applicability in respect of every international crime.[172] This has led Cassese to conclude that no broad customary rule has yet evolved on this matter.[173]

Although no uniform practice can be discerned, one can identify a number of national decisions that, first of all, illustrate the problems pertaining to statutes of limitations and, secondly, have contributed to the development of the law on this matter.

The Hungarian constitutional court was called upon in 1993 to review the constitutionality and the compatibility with international law of a law enacted by the parliament in order to extend the non-applicability of statutory limitations to offences committed

---

[168] The *Demjanjuk* proceedings painfully illustrated how witnesses' memories may result in miscarriages of justice; this is what the Israel Supreme Court had to say about it (Judgment, 29 July 1993):

> The main issue of the indictment sheet filed against the appellant was his identification as Ivan the Terrible, an operator of the gas chambers in the extermination camp at Treblinka ... By virtue of this gnawing [new evidence indicating mistaken identity] ... we restrained ourselves from convicting the appellant of the horrors of Treblinka. Ivan Demjanjuk has been acquitted by us, because of doubt, of the terrible charges attributed to Ivan the Terrible of Treblinka. This was the proper course for judges who cannot examine the heart and mind, but have only what their eyes see and read.

[169] UN General Assembly Resolution 3068 (XXVIII), 26 November 1968, 754 *UNTS* 73.

[170] 25 January 1974, ETS No. 82.

[171] The UN Convention entered into force on 11 November 1970 and has been ratified by 48 states; the European Convention has obtained only three ratifications and entered into force on 27 June 2003.

[172] Cf. Cassese, *International Criminal Law*, at 317.   [173] Ibid., at 319.

during the events of 1956. The court offered some interesting observations as to the status of the non-applicability of statutory limitations under international law. It stated that in respect of war crimes and crimes against humanity:

> those states which prosecute these crimes on the basis of international law may apply their own domestic penal laws concerning the statute of limitation and are not compelled to declare that their statutory limitations may never expire. The 1968 New York Convention on the non-applicability of statutory limitations for the punishment of war crimes and crimes against humanity, as well as the 1974 European Convention addressing a similar subject matter, may not be regarded as part of customary international law or a generally recognized principle of international law. But those states which ratified either one of the two conventions assumed the international obligation to declare, even with retroactive force, that the statutes of limitation may never expire with respect to the war crimes and crimes against humanity enumerated in the conventions.[174]

In contrast with the above views are the decisions in the cases of *Barbie* and *Hass and Priebke*. As early as 1984 the French *Cour de Cassation* mentioned explicitly in *Barbie* that the prohibition on statutory limitations has become part of customary international law.[175] The Italian courts in *Hass and Priebke* went a step further by describing the rule on the non-applicability of statutory limitations as having attained the status of *jus cogens*.[176] However, a recent Mexican judgment did not hesitate to apply statutory limitations in respect of torture, dealing with a request for extradition from Spain for genocide, torture, and terrorism.[177]

From the above it is clear that national jurisprudence is diverse. The codification of the non-applicability of statutory limitations in Article 29 of the ICC Statute may be expected to result in a more uniform national practice. Article 29 stipulates that the crimes within the jurisdiction of the Court shall not be subject to any statute of limitation. The scope of application of Article 29 undeniably concerns states parties, since the ICC legal framework does not contain any such rules; hence, there is no internal relevance for Article 29. The objective of Article 29 is twofold. First, in the area of state cooperation Article 29 implies that states cannot plead statutes of limitations in the context of the absence of double criminality. In other words, a situation at the national level that statutes of limitations apply and that therefore no double criminality has been attained cannot be a legitimate excuse for failure to comply with surrender requests or other requests for cooperation.[178] Secondly — and more importantly for the purposes of the present discussion — Article 29 may be expected to play an important role in the

---

[174] Decision of the Constitutional Court No. 53/1993. (X.13.) AB, available in an unofficial English translation at www.icrc.org/ihl-nat.nsf/46707c419d6bdfa24125673e00508145/e781668ba0b17804c1256b220039e303!OpenDocument (last visited 15 November 2006).

[175] *Fédération nationale des déportés et internés et al.* v. *Barbie* (1984) 78 ILR 125, 135.

[176] *Hass and Priebke*, Military Court of Appeal of Rome/Supreme Court of Cassation, 7 March 1998/16 November 1998.

[177] *Cavallo* case, 11 January 2001, Juez Sexto de Distrito de Procesos Penales Federales en el Distrito Federal, Extradición de Miguel Angel Cavallo/Expediente de extradición 5/2000, summary available at www.icrc.org/ihl-nat.nsf/46707c419d6bdfa24125673e00508145/b0f85099943c7a24c1256d0900560d21!OpenDocument (last visited 15 November 2006). It is noteworthy that the Minister of Foreign Affairs 'corrected' the judge by arguing that the crime of torture cannot be subject to statutory limitations because of its legal nature and implication.

[178] For more detail, see G. Sluiter, *International Criminal Adjudication and the Collection of Evidence: Obligations of States* (Antwerp: Intersentia, 2002), at 189. See also Chapter 12, section 12.3.3 above.

application of the principle of complementarity, more specifically in determining a state's unwillingness or inability to prosecute international crimes. A state which fails to prosecute because statutes of limitations apply is not likely to meet the required standards of 'ability' and 'willingness'.

A review of the various international crimes acts indicates that the non-applicability of a statute of limitations is not an element of a number of national laws. Given the prominent place and unequivocal language of Article 29, this is unlikely to be the result of an oversight by national legislative authorities. Two obvious reasons for this omission may be advanced. First, as has already been mentioned, the concept of a statute of limitations is unfamiliar to common-law jurisdictions; and if it applies, there are far-reaching exceptions which include serious criminal conduct. Secondly, even states that do apply statutes of limitations in general may already have made an exception for very serious crimes, in particular the crimes set out in the ICC Statute.

Nevertheless, the following states have implemented Article 29 of the ICC Statute in their new 'international crimes act': the Netherlands (excluding the applicability of statutory limitations in the penal code),[179] Germany (further specifying Article 29 of the ICC Statute by referring to prosecution and the execution of sentences),[180] New Zealand (direct reference to and direct application of Article 29 of the ICC Statute),[181] the Democratic Republic of the Congo,[182] Ecuador (also referring to non-applicability in respect of both prosecution and the enforcement of sentences),[183] and Italy.[184]

An interesting additional element of the implementation of Article 29 of the ICC Statute in the Congo and Ecuador is that international crimes cannot be the object of an amnesty or a pardon.[185] This goes beyond the requirements of Article 29. However, in the context of the debate on the permissibility of amnesties in respect of crimes set out in the ICC Statute, those laws may constitute, along with subsequent practice, an important interpretative tool of the Statute favouring the prohibition of amnesties.[186]

13.8 CONCLUSION

The above overview reveals a progressive development in the application of international criminal law in the domestic legal order. State practice is moving towards uniformity, with states attempting faithfully to apply the key concepts of international

---

[179] Article 13 of the International Crimes Act.

[180] Article 5 of the Act to Introduce the Code of Crimes against International Law.

[181] Section 12(1)(a)(vii) of the International Crimes and International Criminal Court Act.

[182] Article 17 of the Projet de Loi portant Mise en Oeuvre du Statut de la Cour Pénale Internationale.

[183] Article 6 of the Proyecto de Ley sobre Delitos conte la Humanidad.

[184] Article 7 of the Progetto di Legge, No. 2724, available at www.iccnow.org/documents/ItalyProposed ICCLegItalian.pdf (last visited 15 November 2006).

[185] Article 17 of the Projet de Loi portant Mise en Oeuvre du Statut de la Cour Pénale Internationale and Article 6 of the Proyecto de Ley sobre Delitos conte la Humanidad.

[186] On amnesties in the context of the ICC, see, among many others, C. Stahn, 'Complementarity, Amnesties and Alternative Forms of Justice: Some Interpretative Guidelines for the International Criminal Court' (2005) 3 *JICJ*, at 695–720.

criminal law. States are increasingly assisted in their endeavours by a growing and more coherent body of international criminal law. The climax in that development to date has been the codification of the central elements of international criminal law in the ICC Statute. The latter represents a sincere attempt to infer from both international and national practice the core of contemporary international criminal law, the rules that really matter, and to distinguish international criminal law from domestic criminal law. Of course, being the product of a compromise, the ICC Statute may not faithfully codify international criminal law in all respects, but it nevertheless presents a solid basis for further development.

For the uniform application of international criminal law, which will permit that body of law to develop as a viable and coherent set of rules, it is of a vital significance that most states parties to the ICC Statute have accepted the underlying assumptions and objectives of the complementarity principle, even when there is no concrete obligation to do so.

While this has resulted in impressive legislative developments, all of which owe much to the codification of the substantive international criminal law in the ICC Statute, there is no guarantee that the application of this body of law by national courts will be unproblematic. The Dutch *Van Anraat* case has adequately illustrated the complicated legal matters ensuing from the *cohabitation* of national and international criminal justice systems. The major challenge for future practice lies in connecting these two systems, by striking an appropriate balance between the *essentials* of international criminal law and the *familiarity* to national judges of the national criminal justice system. In our opinion, significant deviation from the central rules of international criminal law may not necessarily violate a state's international obligations, as may be the case when national implementation is over-inclusive, but may damage the international criminal justice system. It must be borne in mind that the latter is still very fragile and is in most respects dependent upon national criminal justice systems.

INDEX